THE YALE EDITION OF THE
WORKS OF SAMUEL JOHNSON
VOLUME X

Political Writings

PREVIOUSLY PUBLISHED

SAMUEL JOHNSON

Political Writings

EDITED BY DONALD J. GREENE

LIBERTY FUND   INDIANAPOLIS

Originally published in 1977 by Yale University Press as volume 10 of *The Yale Edition of the Works of Samuel Johnson.* Paperbound edition published 2000 by Liberty Fund, Inc.

04   03   02   01   00   P   5   4   3   2   1

Library of Congress Cataloging-in-Publication Data

Johnson, Samuel, 1709–1784.
    Political writings/Samuel Johnson; Donald J. Greene, editor.
        p.   cm.
    Originally published as vol. 10 of the Yale edition of the works of Samuel Johnson. New Haven: Yale University Press, 1977.
    Includes bibliographical references and index.
    ISBN 0-86597-275-3 (pbk.: alk. paper)
    1. Great Britain—Politics and government—18th century.
    2. Political science. I. Greene, Donald Johnson. II. Title.
PR3522.G72   2000
320.91′09′033—dc21   99-16127

Liberty Fund, Inc.
8335 Allison Pointe Trail, Suite 300
Indianapolis, IN 46250-1684

EDITORIAL COMMITTEE

PREFACE

The plan of this collection of political writings by Johnson is explained at the end of the second section of the "Introduction," and there is no need to repeat it here. What should be added, however, is that the fairly detailed historical commentary I have provided was written a considerable time ago, and unforeseen circumstances (chiefly economic) have delayed its appearance in print. In the interim, much good work has been done on the political history of Great Britain during Johnson's lifetime. Had they been available, I should have been happy to make use of such works as (among others) John Brooke's *King George III* (1972) and Reed Browning's *The Duke of Newcastle* (1975) to support some of the generalizations about the political events of the time that I permit myself. Since, ironically, the delay has resulted in the appearance of the volume during the celebration of the bicentennial of the Declaration of Independence of the United States of America, it would have been tempting to discuss *Taxation No Tyranny* in the light of Brooke's contention that the "American Revolution" was not a revolution in the sense that the French and Russian revolutions were, but a rebellion, like that of the Dutch against the King of Spain in the sixteenth century; that it was "the first great nationalist rising of modern times. . . . The Declaration of Independence marks the emergence of nationalism as a force in modern history"; that "the fathers of the American republic were the heirs of the Tory tradition in British politics, and perhaps the only true Tories in the world today are to be found in the United States." So far as I can tell, however, valuable as this recent historical writing has been in filling in gaps in detail, there has been little modification of the basic outline of the political scene in the reigns of George II and George III that I have relied on—that sketched by Sir Lewis Namier,

vii

John B. Owen, and others listed in the first footnote to the "Introduction"—and no serious distortion of Johnson's political pronouncements will occur, I believe, by continuing to view them in that framework.

I acknowledge my gratitude to those who read the work before publication and offered valuable suggestions: James L. Clifford, Robert Halsband, Allen T. Hazen, the late Frederick W. Hilles, Matthew Hodgart, Gwin J. Kolb, Herman W. Liebert, and John H. Middendorf, the general editor of the series, and to Professor Middendorf's editorial assistants, Barbara Jetton and Marjorie David. A good deal of the editorial work was done during my tenure of a senior fellowship of the Canada Council, and I wish to express my gratitude to that body.

D. J. G.

The following organizations and individuals have generously contributed to the publication of the present volume: The American Society for Eighteenth-Century Studies, the Edwin J. Beinecke Trust, John M. Bullitt, Terence Carmody, Chester F. Chapin, James L. Clifford, Paul Fussell, Jr., Robert Halsband, Raymond E. Hartz, Miss Joyce Hemlow, Frederick W. Hilles, C. Beecher Hogan, Mrs. Donald F. Hyde, Gwin J. Kolb, Louis A. Landa, Wilmarth S. Lewis, Herman W. Liebert, N. Floyd McGowin, Dr. Lawrence McHenry, John H. Middendorf, Arthur G. Rippey, Roland Sawyer, William K. Wimsatt.

A number of changes have occurred in the Editorial Committee since the publication of the previous volume. We record with sorrow the deaths of the following members, whom we hold in affectionate memory: Frederick W. Hilles, Robert F. Metzdorf, L. F. Powell, and William K. Wimsatt. We regret the resignation of M. J. C. Hodgart. It is a pleasure to report the appointment to the Editorial Committee of James Gray, Arthur G. Rippey, Gwin J. Kolb, and Albrecht B. Strauss, who was elected Secretary of the Committee. In the final stages of the preparation of this volume, the General Editor was assisted by a grant from the National Endowment for the Humanities. For this support the Editorial Committee is sincerely grateful.

CONTENTS

ILLUSTRATIONS

INTRODUCTION

I

The historical scholarship of the past four decades, beginning with the work of Sir Lewis Namier,[1] has destroyed beyond any likelihood of repair the Victorian myth of the political structure of England during the eighteenth century, and with it the Victorian picture of the political position of various eighteenth-century figures, including Samuel Johnson. That myth, popular because it was easy to grasp and because it could readily be used by propagandists to serve partisan interests, dominated British historiography for about a century, from the time of Lord Macaulay in the 1830's and 40's down to that of his grand-nephew, George Macaulay Trevelyan, in the 1920's and 30's. Though it seems unlikely that it can subsist much longer in the face of its unanimous abandonment by serious historical scholars, it is dying with great reluctance. Since it still interferes with the twentieth century's attitude

1. A decade or so ago, a reasonably complete bibliography of post-"Whig interpretation" historiography of eighteenth-century Britain could be comprehended in around a dozen titles (cf. D. J. Greene, *The Politics of Samuel Johnson*, 1960, p. 288, n. 7). It is now far beyond the scope of a footnote. An excellent guide to recent work on the century will be found in the bibliographical essays by William A. Bultmann, "Early Hanoverian England," and J. Jean Hecht, "The Reign of George III," in Elizabeth C. Furber, ed., *Changing Views on British History: Essays on Historical Writing Since 1939* (1966). A few titles of particular use to the student of Johnson's political background are Sir Lewis Namier, "Monarchy and the Party System" and "Country Gentlemen in Parliament," in his *Personalities and Powers* (1955); Robert Walcott, *English Politics in the Early Eighteenth Century* (1956); John B. Owen, *The Rise of the Pelhams* (1957); J. H. Plumb, *Sir Robert Walpole* (1956-   ) (2 vols. published of a projected 3-vol. study); Richard Pares, *King George III and the Politicians* (1953); *Letters from George III to Lord Bute, 1756–1766*, ed. Romney Sedgwick (1939) (Sedgwick's introduction is important); Archibald S. Foord, *His Majesty's Opposition, 1714–1830* (1964).

toward Johnson, we should do well to spend some time examining it.

The Victorian or "Whig"[2] interpretation of eighteenth-century British history itself originated in eighteenth-century British politics. Popularized in the nineteenth century by Macaulay, J. R. Green, Lecky, and others, it took its inspiration from hints found in Burke's writings in support of the Rockingham Whig faction in the 1760's and 70's and other political propaganda of the time. The Rockingham group, the successors of the Whigs who followed the leadership of Sir Robert Walpole and the Pelhams (Henry Pelham and his brother, the Duke of Newcastle) in the earlier eighteenth century and the predecessors of those who followed Charles James Fox and Earl Grey in the early nineteenth, after enjoying many years of power in the reigns of George I and II, found themselves out of office on the accession of George III in 1760. Since the young George had made no secret of his loyalty to the politics of his father, Frederick, Prince of Wales, one of the most persistent leaders of opposition to Walpole, the Rockinghamites could not have been too much surprised when the new monarch, determined to preserve the traditional right of independence of the executive, sought his ministers among Whigs outside the Walpole-Pelham-Rockingham succession—his boyhood tutor and Prince Frederick's political adviser, the Scottish Earl of Bute; William Pitt, later Earl of Chatham, who had begun his career in the 1730's as one of the most vociferous anti-Walpolian "Patriot" Whigs; George Grenville, Pitt's brother-in-law, though now politically at odds with him. Nor should it have astonished the Rockinghamites when politically ambitious young men like Lord North, Lord Shelburne, and the Duke of Grafton gravitated away from them and accepted office under other auspices.

2. The phrase "the Whig interpretation of history" comes from Herbert Butterfield's important monograph bearing that title (1931). It must not be taken to mean simply that Macaulay and the rest favoured the Whigs; it means, according to Butterfield, the method of historical interpretation which views as laudable anything that contributed to bringing about the state of things which in fact came to pass, and as deplorable anything which militated against that outcome—the "ratification of the present," as he calls it.

During the rest of the century, indeed, the Marquess of Rockingham and his successor, Charles James Fox, headed ministries only during two short periods, in 1765 and again in 1782–83—at the end, in a coalition with their old enemy, Lord North, which disgusted the electorate with its bold cynicism.

These developments were natural enough in a political context where few important ideological divisions existed, as was normally the situation in eighteenth-century Britain (and as it has been throughout a great deal of the history of the United States); where political contests were largely jockey-ings for power in a setting of constantly shifting alliances and groupings. But they caused intense resentment among the Rockinghamites, displaced after so many decades in power; and their theoretician and propagandist, Edmund Burke,[3] in his *Thoughts on the Cause of the Present Discontents*, 1770, worked out an elaborate "line" to justify that resentment. With that touch of the paranoid which characterizes a good deal of Burke's political writing, the work hinted at con-spiratorial activities by George III and an "Inner Cabinet" of "the King's Friends" to subvert the constitution and re-store royal absolutism. A corollary was that the Rocking-hamites were the only vehicles of "Whiggism" pure and undefiled, the preservers of the authentic tradition of the Glorious Revolution of 1688, whereas the other Whig politi-cians, who collaborated with George III, were self-seeking betrayers of that tradition, and therefore no more than

---

3. The notion that Burke and Johnson, because they have both been described as "conservatives," were politically sympathetic, cannot be seriously entertained. The evidence usually cited in support of this thesis consists of praise bestowed by Johnson on Burke's intellectual powers and eloquence. For Burke as politician, however, Johnson had nothing but the harshest condemnation; e.g., "In private life he is a very honest gentleman; but I will not allow him to be so in public life. People *may* be honest, though they are doing wrong: that is between their Maker and them. But *we*, who are suffering by their pernicious conduct, are to destroy them. We are sure that ———— acts from interest. We know what his genuine principles were. They who allow their passions to confound the distinc-tions between right and wrong are criminal. They may be convinced; but they have not come honestly by their conviction" (*Life*, III. 45 f.; see also II. 222 f., 348).

"Tories" in disguise.[4] Nineteenth-century historians followed their lead and with a straight face labelled Bute, Grafton, North, and the younger Pitt Tories, a designation that would have astonished them and many of their contemporaries.

Tories in the eighteenth century were for the most part the "country gentlemen," the "squirearchy," the "gentry,"[5] hereditary possessors of relatively small manorial estates in the English countryside. They contributed from a fourth to a fifth of the membership of the House of Commons (they were underrepresented in the House of Lords, peerages then as later being awarded to loyal supporters of the current ministry). In the Commons, they remained mostly inarticulate back-benchers, sporadically giving their votes to some minister —Harley or North or the younger Pitt—who pleased them. But basically they were not much interested in playing an active role on the national political scene, though they were very active in local politics; concerned that agriculture be supported and land taxation be kept down, and that the central government should interfere with them as little as possible. They were generally "isolationists," "little Englanders," suspicious of foreign involvements that might lead to wars and higher taxes. They prided themselves on their political independence, frequently dividing their votes equally on both sides of a controversial measure—indeed, they were sometimes referred to as "the independent members." Henry Fielding's Squire Western is a caricature of the type by an urban, "Patriot" Whig, no doubt libellous as regards the education, speech, and manners of the average Tory squire,

4. The Tories maintained, with considerable justification, that this was also a slander against *them*: "In 1688, the Tories concurred in the bringing about the Revolution, eminently concurred, and therefore they have as just a right to the fruits of it as any other set of men in Britain, whatever some may pretend to the contrary" (*The Sentiments of a Tory in Respect to a Late Important Transaction*, 1741, quoted in Greene, *Politics*, p. 275).

5. The political position of "the gentry" in the seventeenth century has recently been the subject of much investigation and debate. H. R. Trevor-Roper has maintained, "It [the Great Rebellion of the 1640's] was the blind revolt of the gentry against the Court, of the provinces against the capital" ("The Country-House Radicals," in his *Men and Events*, 1958, p. 179). The subsequent history of the Tories in the eighteenth century suggests a continuation of provincial "grass-roots" resistance to the Establishment in Westminster.

but reasonably accurate as regards his political attitudes.
After 1714, they never had the parliamentary strength or the
cohesiveness to form anything that could possibly be called a
"Tory" administration, though their votes, holding the balance of power between conflicting Whig factions, could affect
the existence of ministries—it was their defection which
brought about the downfall of the North ministry in 1782.

A Whig, *per contra*, was an activist in national politics,
someone anxious that the central administration push the
country's future in a direction congenial to the interests of
his own economic group. "Big business" in the City of
London and Bristol tended to be Whig; so did the upper
strata of the peerage, with their huge holdings of land (often
discovered, in the later part of the century, to be profitably
underlaid with coal)—the dukes and marquesses whom Burke
admired and served so faithfully, on the ground that what
was good for the Rockinghams and Richmonds was good for
Britain. Naturally, not all Whigs wanted to push the country
in precisely the same direction or to secure governmental
power for the same collection of individuals: the great political
contests of the century were all between warring groups of
Whigs, with occasional Tories as fitful and tepid allies on one
side or the other.

To identify all these fluctuating Whig groupings and sort
out their aims would require a volume in itself, though very
often their aims can be summed up as merely the acquisition
of office and patronage. One highly important opposition in
matters of large national policy can, however, be discerned.
The Pittites were distinctly the spokesmen for the business
community, and the tendency of the policies they advocated
was always in the direction of aggressive commercial and
imperial expansion, so as to provide an ever broader base for
British trading and industrial enterprise. The Walpole-
Pelham-Rockingham group, on the other hand, representing
the more diversified and secure interests of the great ter-
ritorial magnates—"old money," by contrast with the "new
money" of business—tended to be more cautious and conservative. In 1739, Pitt and his allies manoeuvred Walpole
into war with Spain, in order to force an opening for Britain
in the Spanish monopoly of South American and Pacific

trade, and presently brought about his downfall. This victory proved only temporary; Walpole's political heirs, Henry Pelham and Newcastle, kept their grip on the helm during the 1740's and 50's. But in 1756, with the commencement of the Seven Years' War—the Great War for the Empire, as Lawrence Gipson calls it[6]—Pitt won the game. Britain emerged from the war with a huge overseas empire, and her future as the great commercial world-power of the nineteenth century was assured. It should be noted that the role of the modern Conservative Party in Great Britain as the party of that country's industrial, trading, and financial interests is an inheritance from the younger Pitt and his successors—not from the eighteenth-century Tories. They, as might be expected, generally preferred the lesser evil of the Walpolians to the Pittites; when Walpole was fighting for his political life, in 1741, they supported him rather than the Whig opposition with their votes in the Commons.[7] Johnson, after violently attacking Walpole for a short time in the late 1730's, came around to defending him; his detestation of the Pitts and what they stood for never wavered throughout his later life.

Burke, Junius, and other anti-ministerial propagandists in the 1760's and 70's, however, succeeded in altering the nomenclature of party, for the nineteenth century if not for their own; though the beginnings of the change can be detected in the later part of the eighteenth century, when we find Boswell, Mrs. Thrale, and other younger contemporaries of Johnson using "Tory" somewhat as it came to be used in the Victorian histories—that is, to designate someone who supported the Grenville, Grafton, and North administrations, the designation "Whig" now being monopolized by the Rockinghamites, in almost permanent opposition. (That this is *not* how Johnson and his generation used the terms is clear

6. In his multivolumed history, *The British Empire Before the American Revolution* (1936–70). In an essay, "Samuel Johnson and the Great War for Empire," in *English Writers of the Eighteenth Century*, ed. John H. Middendorf (1971), I attempt to bring together the evidence for SJ's attitude toward the war, its origins, and its aftermath.

7. In the vote in the House of Commons on 13 Feb 1741, on Sandys's motion to remove Walpole from office, 20 Tories voted against the motion and another 35 abstained. Johnson (presumably) defends their action in a note appended to the *Gentleman's Magazine*'s report of the division (*GM*, XIII [Apr 1743], 181).

when we find Johnson, in *The False Alarm*, 1770, warmly
defending the actions of the Grafton-North ministry in the
Wilkes affair, and at the same time condemning the "frigid
neutrality" of "*the Tories*" on the subject.[8]) Macaulay later
developed this terminological innovation into a grandiose yet
marvellously simple philosophy of history and political science.
History is the record of the inevitable "progress" of the
British people down the centuries; throughout this time all
politically minded individuals can be divided into two classes:
those who seek to assist that advance (the Whigs), and are
therefore to be approved of, and those who seek to halt it or
turn it backward (the Tories), and are therefore to be condemned. In Macaulay's own words,

> The History of England is emphatically the history of
> progress. It is the history of a constant movement of the
> public mind, of a constant change in the institutions of
> a great society. . . . We have often thought that the
> motion of the public mind in our country resembles that
> of the sea when the tide is rising. Each successive wave
> rushes forward, breaks, and rolls back; but the great
> flood is steadily coming in.[9]

> Throughout the whole of that great movement [from
> Magna Carta, 1215, to the Reform Act, 1832] there have
> been, under some name or other, two sets of men, those
> who were before their age, and those who were behind
> it. . . . Though a Tory may now be very like what a Whig
> was a hundred and twenty years ago, the Whig is as
> much in advance of the Tory as ever.[1]

It is hard to know whether the audacity or the naïveté of
these postulates is the more breathtaking (though it must be
pointed out, in defence of Macaulay's acumen, that in all this
he is constructing a basis for the glorification of his own party,
Lord Grey's Whigs, the successors of Burke's and Rockingham's, and for the support of the fiercely contested Reform
Bill, which they passed in 1832; for doing so, he was richly

8. P. 344 below.
9. Review of Sir James Mackintosh, *History of the Revolution*, in F. C. Montague,
ed., *Critical and Historical Essays* (1903), II. 72–74.
1. Review of Lord Mahon, *War of the Spanish Succession, ibid.*, I. 531.

rewarded by party patronage, his five-year appointment as
Member of the Council for India making him independently
wealthy for the rest of his life). Yet the notion that all political
history since the beginning of time can be explained in terms
of such a dichotomy—Whig versus Tory, or progressive versus
reactionary, or "left wing" versus "right wing"[2]—seems to
exercise an almost irresistible attraction on the modern
mind. When it is pointed out that Johnson's Toryism was
not very much like what the twentieth century calls "Toryism," one of the most frequent responses is "Oh, you mean
he was more of a Whig than we had thought?" The answer, of course, is that he was not at all a Whig; he was
completely a Tory; but that an eighteenth-century Tory
was as different from what is called a Tory in the twentieth century as a "liberal" of Queen Victoria's reign (who
believed that the freedom of individual enterprise to accumulate wealth should be unhampered by any interference from governments) is from a mid-twentieth-century
American "liberal" (who believes precisely the opposite); in
short, that the Macaulayan dichotomy is a fallacy, and to try
to interpret such subtle and complex political thinking as
Johnson's in terms of it will inevitably result in gross distortion.

II

To understand Johnson's political views, then, we must
firmly resist the temptation to impose on the political events,
attitudes, and vocabulary of eighteenth-century Britain any
such "left-versus-right" pattern as that contrived by Macaulay
and later theorizers: it simply does not apply. We must also,

2. The history of this metaphor, supposed to derive from the semicircular
seating of the revolutionary French National Assembly, would make an interesting study. How arbitrary the terms are may be seen in an early use of them by
Sir Adolphus Ward, *The Electress Sophia and the Hanoverian Succession*, 2nd ed.
(1909), p. 550. Ward is speaking of dissident Episcopal clergymen in Scotland
after the Revolution of 1688: "The tendency was for such men to conform to
Presbytery, but they formed a distinct 'left wing.'" Nowadays students would
instinctively term the Scottish Episcopalians, many of them Jacobites, "right
wing" and the Presbyterians, sturdy supporters of the Revolution, "left wing,"
even though (and this is presumably Ward's point) in Scotland at the time
Presbyterianism was orthodox, official, "the Establishment," and Episcopalians
were a dissenting minority.

of course, rid our minds of the various legends about Johnson himself that literary historians have assiduously constructed and propagated during the past two centuries, and be willing to look at the evidence of his own political writings with clear eyes and see what they actually say.

One of the most persistent of these legends has been that which maintains that Johnson was not really politically minded at all, and that his scanty and trivial writings on political matters may be safely neglected. The beginnings of this legend can be traced in the pages of Boswell, who did not meet Johnson until after the first two of Johnson's three major periods of close political involvement, those concerned with the attack on Walpole in the late 1730's and early 1740's, and with the Seven Years' War, two decades later. Boswell indeed had little opportunity, during Johnson's lifetime at least, to acquaint himself thoroughly with the writings of Johnson which resulted from those involvements, for many of them remained obscurely known until considerably later. The third period, that of Johnson's defence of certain actions of the administrations of the Duke of Grafton and Lord North in the early 1770's, did coincide with the time of Boswell's acquaintance with him. Boswell makes a show of doing his duty by Johnson's four pamphlets of this period, but clearly he is not as much interested in them as in something like the *Journey to the Western Islands of Scotland*, which displays more fully what Boswell probably thought of as the "real" Johnson—the "personality," rather than the thinker and writer—and deals with matters more familiar to Boswell than the complexities of the English political scene. Moreover, on the subjects of two of those works, *The False Alarm* and *Taxation No Tyranny*, Boswell's opinions are the reverse of Johnson's: he sympathizes with his friend Wilkes and the rebellious American colonists, and in his account of the pamphlets in the *Life*, he does not hesitate to impugn their competence most vigorously. Basically, though, Boswell is not much interested in exploring political questions in depth.[3]

3. Frank Brady, *Boswell's Political Career* (1965), shows that Boswell was willing to devote much attention to certain political matters—in particular, that of trying to get a seat in Parliament for himself—but the book confirms the statement above. "He made no pretense to political theory, or even to a large view of affairs, like Burke," Brady says (p. 2).

Although he does not suppress the political side of Johnson, it is accurate to say that he gives it little more than a perfunctory and superficial treatment; and something of this impression of superficiality tends—like so many things in the *Life*—to be transferred by the reader from Boswell to the image of Johnson himself.

Boswell, if not sympathetic to Johnson's politics, at least generally goes through the motions of taking them seriously. Macaulay, whose influence in shaping and perpetuating the Johnson myth of the nineteenth century and later was enormous—and still remains so—does not; or rather, it is constitutionally impossible for Macaulay, his political views rigidly set in the pattern of the nineteenth-century "Whig interpretation," to furnish any objective treatment of one who so obstinately refuses to conform to that pattern; and so he adopts the simple expedient of denying that Johnson's political thinking can be called thinking at all—his political attitudes are merely the unreasoned, blindly instinctive responses of a bigoted "Tory" reactionary. Macaulay had only a slight acquaintance with Johnson's political writings, having laid his eyes on no more than the pamphlets of the 1770's—which, being direct onslaughts against positions that Macaulay's own party, the Rockingham-Fox-Grey Whig succession, had taken up, were anathema[4]—and the parliamentary debates, of which he apparently made no more careful study than did Boswell. Had Macaulay really tried to come to grips with Johnson's political ideas, he might have found them extremely disturbing to his own rigid preconceptions; perhaps it is because he is vaguely aware of this that he dismisses that whole side of Johnson from serious consideration. Macaulay, as a practising politician with important axes of his own to grind, can perhaps be forgiven for these tactics. It is more distressing to find them continuing to be used by successive generations of literary scholars who presumably have no such excuse as Macaulay's. A representative, if awkwardly phrased, statement may be found in a highly respected and in-

4. How violently they were resented may be judged by Burke's reaction, reported by Boswell, to *Thoughts on Falkland's Islands* (1771). See n. 7, p. 348 below.

fluential recent monograph on Johnson: "He never turned much thought to the subject of politics, at least in written form."

The present volume, it is expected, will show how drastically mistaken such a judgement is. And, knowing Johnson's values, interests, and modes of thought generally, we should find it *a priori* most remarkable if it were true. "Of political evil," Johnson once wrote, "if we suppose the origin of moral evil discovered, the account is by no means difficult, polity being only the conduct of immoral men in public affairs."[5] Given Johnson's intense concern throughout his life with problems of human morality, and his commitment as a writer to expounding them for the benefit of his readers, it would be astonishing to find him arbitrarily relinquishing this task at the nebulous boundary between private and public morality. In fact, he did nothing of the kind. He was as political as any dedicated moral writer can and should be: "political" in the sense that George Orwell insists all his own writing essentially is, motivated by a "desire to push the world in a certain direction, to alter other people's ideas of the kind of society they should strive for. . . . My starting point is always a feeling of partisanship, a sense of injustice. . . . I write . . . because there is some lie that I want to expose, some fact to which I want to draw attention."[6] There were few political and social lies in the eighteenth century that we cannot find Johnson somewhere in his writings or his recorded conversation strenuously trying to expose.

Even in the narrowest sense of the word "politics," there were few periods in Johnson's life when he was not close to the political life of the day.[7] Staffordshire, during his youth, was a hotbed of sometimes violent political activity. Oxford, both during his time of residence as an undergraduate and later in the century, when he revisited it frequently and

5. Review of Soame Jenyns, *A Free Enquiry into the Nature and Origin of Evil*, *Literary Magazine* (1757).

6. "Why I Write," in his *Collected Essays, Journalism, and Letters*, ed. Sonia Orwell and Ian Angus (1968), I. 4, 6.

7. For a fuller account of what is summarized in the four following paragraphs, see Greene, *Politics*.

maintained many close friendships there, was extremely active politically.[8] London, when he arrived there at the age of twenty-seven, was in the midst of some of the most intense political turmoil in its history, enduring for several years until Walpole's downfall in 1742. The young hack at once plunged into the thick of it, not merely turning out a series of bitterly satirical political diatribes, but occupying himself for some years as the semi-official reporter of the parliamentary proceedings that led up to Walpole's overthrow. Violence is the keynote of these early writings—even in the parliamentary reporting, the campaign against Walpole gave him many opportunities to practise the rhetoric of invective; and given the circumstances of his youth—a poverty-stricken intellectual watching the rewards of privilege being bestowed on contemporaries with less brains and learning than his but with friends in the right places (i.e., Whig places)—it is not hard to understand why this violence should have been present.

But it cannot be said that age, fame, and financial security notably mellowed his political idiom: he was quite an old man when he shocked a company of sedate Oxford dons by toasting the next insurrection of the Negroes in the West Indies. True, for a decade or so after the fall of Walpole, the political scene was relatively quiescent—as was the political side of Johnson, occupied with the *Dictionary* and *The Rambler* (in both of which, however, political allusions are by no means absent).[9] But with the coming of the great struggle for overseas empire between France and Britain, which culminated in the Seven Years' War of 1756 to 1763, we find Johnson again eagerly plunging into political controversy, this time as an editor and journalist fiercely opposing the national policy of aggressive war-making, expansionism, Francophobia, and "patriotism"; and apparently getting himself dismissed from at least two such posts for the intransigence of his opposition to these popular measures.

8. See W. R. Ward, *Georgian Oxford: University Politics in the Eighteenth Century* (1958).

9. As well as the notorious *Dictionary* definitions of *excise* and *pension*, publicized by Boswell (both represent familiar opposition attitudes) and of "*Renegado.* . . . Sometimes we say a *Gower*," suppressed at the printer's, there is the lesser-known "*Irony.* A mode of speech in which the meaning is contrary to the words: as, *Bolingbroke was a holy man.*"

The early 1760's were also the time of the "revolution" in the structure of political power in Britain marked by the accession to the throne of the young George III, who had inherited the tradition of his father, Frederick, Prince of Wales, of hostility to the seemingly entrenched authority of Walpole and his successors, the Pelhams and Rockinghamites. Johnson, like other oppositionists of the previous reign, at first hoped for something like a "New Deal" at the hands of this young and "uncorrupted" monarch; his hope was, however, expressed cautiously ("He has long been in the hands of the Scots") and quickly faded. This is a most obscure period in Johnsonian biography, but fascinating hints emerge from it of his close connexion with active politicians of the time: Gerard Hamilton, for whom (apparently) he wrote his *Considerations on Corn*; Robert Chambers, the Vansittarts, George Dempster, Lord Elibank, some of whom were involved in the defence of the East India Company against attacks by the Chatham administration (Johnson seems to have undertaken some piece of writing in connexion with this affair);[1] Bute and his allies, Wedderburn and Charles Jenkinson. There is still much that is not clear, and perhaps never will be, about the circumstances of the award of Johnson's pension by the Bute administration—Jenkinson, at least, seems to have thought that its terms laid Johnson under some obligation to help him compose a pamphlet defending the Peace of Paris.[2]

1. See *Letters* 187.2 (11 Dec 1766): "If you [Chambers] could get me any information about the East Indian affairs, you may promise that if it is used at all, it shall be used in favour of the Company," and *Letters* 187.3 (22 Jan 1767), asking for the papers tabled in the House of Commons: "We will pay for transcribing if that be of any difficulty. What other papers shall be put into our hands, shall be used if they are used at all, in defence of the Company." Who "we" are is not known, nor whether any writing by Johnson actually resulted. Of an earlier, obscure project, Johnson did write five sheets—80 octavo pages—for which he demanded payment from Cave. This was a substantial "Historical design," which was to be "the most complete account of Parliamentary proceedings that [can] be contrived," was to run to 35 sheets (560 octavo or 280 quarto pages), and was apparently to deal with (at least) the reign of George I (see *Letters* 15, 16, 17). It has not yet been identified or recovered.

2. See D. J. Greene, "Johnson, Jenkinson, and the Peace of Paris," *Johnsonian News Letter*, XI (Sept 1951), 8–11. In a government list of pensioners of the 1780's (Public Record Office 30/8/229, f. 77), Johnson is included in a category headed "Writers Political," which also contains Shebbeare, Cawthorne ("a prolific author in the news-papers"), the widow of Hugh Kelly, and the sisters and daughters of "Mr. Lind, author of several political works," rather than in

Later Johnson was intimate for many years with Henry Thrale, M.P. for Southwark, for whom he wrote a good deal of election publicity,[3] and with William Strahan, M.P., the printer, who went so far as to recommend Johnson to the attention of the ministry as a potentially valuable member of the House of Commons. (Would he have been any more out of place, one wonders, than Burke, whose abilities, everyone agreed, were literary, or perhaps theatrical, rather than parliamentary?) That an active public life did not lack attraction for Johnson is clear, as we recall his display of emotion when a friend suggested to him that had he been able to enter the legal profession as a youth, he might have become Lord Chancellor, with the title of Lord Lichfield. Although his restrained enthusiasm for what George III might accomplish did not last long, and although in private he expressed himself vigorously about the incompetence of Lord North, he seems to have felt an obligation to support the Grafton and North ministries—perhaps as the least of a number of evils—and in his four pamphlets of the 1770's he exposed himself to an incredible amount of opposition invective (much of it directed at his pension) by vigorously defending ministerial policies which he approved. But his gloomy private remarks, during the last decade of his life, about the course of disaster on which Britain seemed to be heading indicate that he was no more a complacent admirer of the political *status quo* at the end of his political life than he had been at the beginning of it.

As for Johnson's political writings, a really comprehensive listing would include much more than what appears in the present volume. It would include *London,* a stridently political versification of the polemic stock-in-trade of the "patriot" opposition to Walpole; the "State of Affairs in Lilliput," an exuberant Swiftian satire on the current political situation, printed as the introduction to the *Gentleman's Magazine's* series of reports of the parliamentary debates from 1739 to 1744,

---

the next classification, headed merely "Literary," and including "Dr. Kennicott: the King's subscription to his translation of the Bible," the daughter-in-law of "the famous Dr. Bentley," Mrs. Lloyd, "widow of the late master of Westm^r School," and, interestingly, Baretti.

3. See J. D. Fleeman, "Dr. Johnson and Henry Thrale, M.P.," in *Johnson, Boswell, and Their Circle: Essays Presented to L. F. Powell* (1965).

and in this edition included with them; his massive contributions to the debates themselves; essays in *The Idler* (e.g., Nos.
10 and 20) and *The Weekly Correspondent*; important reviews—
for instance, those of the political memoirs of Sarah, Duchess
of Marlborough, of Tytler's book on Mary, Queen of Scots,
and the Casket Letters; the life of Frederick the Great, and
important parts of the lives of Blake, Drake, and Milton;
numerous editorial contributions to periodicals—prefaces to
the annual volumes of the *Gentleman's Magazine*,[4] substantial
portions of regular features such as the *Literary Magazine*'s
"Historical Memoirs" and the *Gentleman's Magazine*'s "Foreign
History," monthly synopses of current events at home and
abroad. Highly important statements concerning the theoretical foundations of Johnson's political views are to be found in
some of the "dissertations" that he dictated at Boswell's
request, his contributions to the Vinerian law lectures of
Robert Chambers, and—perhaps the most important of all
his political pronouncements—the two sermons usually numbered 23 and 24.

All these, however, will have to be consulted in the volumes
of this edition which print Johnson's sermons, his reviews, and
so on. The rationale of the present volume has been merely to
include writings with a political emphasis which do not
readily fall into one or another of these other *genres*. They
include (a) the publications which in eighteenth- and nineteenth-century editions of Johnson's *Works* were printed under
the heading of "Political Tracts"—the four pamphlets of the
1770's, which Johnson reprinted together under that title in
1776, and to which later editors of the *Works* added *Marmor
Norfolciense* and some of the political essays from the *Literary
Magazine* of 1756; (b) other political articles from the *Literary
Magazine*, not hitherto reprinted; (c) *A Compleat Vindication of
the Licensers of the Stage*, which early editors seem not to have
recognized as a "political tract" as violent as *Marmor Norfolciense*, published only two weeks earlier; (d) small miscellaneous pieces first appearing in the *Gentleman's Magazine*,
Universal Visiter, and *British Magazine*, or as separate publica-

4. E. L. McAdam, Jr., "Johnson, Walpole, and Public Order," in *Johnson,
Boswell, and Their Circle*, calls attention to the political content of the preface
written by Johnson for the first Index of the *Gentleman's Magazine* (1753).

tions (*Thoughts on the Coronation*, the introduction to the *Proceedings of the Committee for Clothing French Prisoners of War*); and one ("Considerations on Corn") not published in Johnson's lifetime, and here edited from the manuscript. In a handful of these—notably, in *Thoughts on the Coronation*—the political content may seem slight; still, it is interesting to note how readily Johnson could find political implications in matters so seemingly unpolitical as the route of a coronation procession.

I have provided fairly heavy explanatory annotation for these pieces, on the assumption that fully to understand Johnson's text in most of them, the reader needs to be thoroughly familiar with the background of political history of the time. Moreover, I have taken advantage of the fact that the items in the volume are fairly evenly spaced throughout Johnson's lifetime to try to provide in the introductory notes to the individual pieces successive instalments, so to speak, of Johnson's "political life." The reader may find this arrangement, in which the narrative is interspersed with specimens of Johnson's own political writing in each phase of his political activities, somewhat less dry than would be a long, detailed account isolated in the Introduction to the volume.

III

On two questions concerning Johnson's politics, there can no longer be any doubt: he did write a great deal about political matters, and he did think a great deal about them. The third question, or set of questions, may prove more controversial: what is the nature and quality of his political thinking? how searching, how competent is it? how rewarding is it for the modern reader? on what basic principles of political and social theory does it rest? For my own part, from the time I first encountered Johnson's approach to political questions, I have found it immensely refreshing, stimulating, thought-provoking, most valuable in the way it cuts through the received cant, the vague unexamined clichés of most political discussion, to get down to the fundamental question: what forms of political action (if any) are likely to make the life of the individual on this earth more one to be enjoyed and less one to be endured? Johnson's pragmatic, even "existential," methods of political analysis seem to me as "modern," as incisive, as sound, as many students now find his not dissimilar approach to literary criticism—"alive and life-giving," as F. R. Leavis calls it.[5]

One hesitates to pin a neat label on any aspect of Johnson's diverse and complex intellectual life. It is easier to say what he is not, politically, than what he is. He is not a Lockean Whig—nor, what perhaps amount to much the same thing, a "prescriptive right" Burkean, a Victorian *laissez-faire* liberal, a twentieth-century neoconservative: he attributes no mystic sanctity to the possession of property, or to the notion that the main function of government is to guarantee to "haves" the uninterrupted enjoyment of it and uncontrolled liberty to use it to exploit "have-nots" (though he certainly agrees with Locke on the desirability of "the rule of law" and government by consent as against any form of despotism). He is not a modern "idealistic liberal," who believes that by the use of some magic formula—universal suffrage, the organization of a League of Nations, equal division of wealth, "desegregation" —Utopia can be achieved within a generation or so:

> BOSWELL: So, Sir, you laugh at schemes of political improvement?
> JOHNSON: Why, Sir, most schemes of political improvement are very laughable things.[6]

(Though it should be noted that Johnson says "most," not "all.") Nor is he an "idealistic" or "romantic" conservative, like Sir Walter Scott or the Vicomte de Bonald or Disraeli or Carlyle (in *Past and Present*), weaving fantasies of a return to a mythical Middle Age where, under a benevolent authoritarianism, the rich loved the poor and the poor loved the rich. I have elsewhere suggested[7] that it may help to understand his political thinking if we view it in the tradition of what might be called "skeptical" (or "radical" or "empirical") conservatism, the essential feature of which is distrust of grandiose *a priori* theory and dogma as the basis for political action, though it by no means denies that appropriate political action should be taken to rectify abuses and injustices, and to improve the human condition in so far as political action can improve it.

5. "Johnson as Critic," *Scrutiny*, XII (Summer 1944), 187.
6. *Life*, II.102.
7. *Politics*, pp. 252–58.

Some have been disturbed by this characterization: their reasoning seems to be that since we *know* Johnson to have been a "High Church" Anglican and a "Tory," his political thinking must have essentially followed the line attributed to the stereotype of the "High Church" or ultramontane Roman Catholic conservative of the twentieth century—veneration for prescriptive authority, dogmatic adherence to the *status quo*, distrust of change of any kind—and any account of his political position which fails to emphasize these matters must be perverse. It is true that Johnson believed, with Hooker, that "All change is of itself an evil, which ought not to be hazarded but for evident advantage,"[8] and because of that belief, he cannot be denied the designation "conservative." But the last four words of the dictum must not be ignored: when advantage is evident, change is justified. It may be useful here to recapitulate some of the more significant positions Johnson takes in his political writings, and consider what they add up to. He attacks censorship of the stage and governmental efforts to stifle the intellectual life of a country (*Vindication of the Licensers*). His "monarchism" he maintains concurrently with a striking lack of reverence for monarchs, and with the opinion that the theory of "divine right" is "all stuff";[9] his boasted belief in "subordination" does not

8. *Works* (1787), IX.173 ("Plan of a Dictionary").

9. See the references indexed under "Monarchs and monarchy: SJ and" in *Politics*. G. B. Hill (*Miscellanies*, II.466) notes a report by Robert Forbes, Bishop of Ross and Caithness, that at a dinner in Edinburgh in 1773, Johnson remarked, "George the First was a robber, George the Second a fool, and George the Third is an idiot." Hill is dubious, because Boswell says of the evening, "I must lament that I was so indolent as to let almost all that passed evaporate into oblivion," and if Johnson had made such a remark about George III, Boswell would surely have remembered it. This is a shaky argument: Boswell's oblivion may, as on other occasions, have been alcoholic. Thomas Cooper's report is significant: "In a political conversation which I had with Dr. Johnson he said, 'I believe in no such thing as the *jure divino* of kings. I have no such belief; but I believe that monarchy is the most conducive to the happiness and safety of the people of every nation, and therefore I am a monarchist, but as to its divine right, that is all stuff. I think every people have the right to establish such government as they may think most conducive to their interest and happiness' " (E. A. and G. L. Duyckinck, *Cyclopaedia of American Literature*, 1855, II.333). Cooper, a British radical who migrated to America, became President of the University of South Carolina.

preclude a readiness to administer ferocious insults to a Lord
Chesterfield, Lord Bolingbroke, or Lord Lyttelton. He favors
strict governmental regulation of the agricultural economy
by means of export controls and subsidies to producers
("Further Thoughts on Agriculture," "Considerations on
Corn"). He deplores the colonizing and missionary activities
of Europeans, including the British, in America and Africa
(preface to *Lobo*, life of Drake, preface to *The World Displayed*).
He inveighs against Negro slavery, especially as practised by
the British sugar planters in the West Indies—"a race of men
whom, I suppose, no other man wishes to resemble"—and
has scathing contempt for those American patriots who emit
"loud yelps" for liberty while denying it to their Negro slaves
(*Taxation No Tyranny*). He charges the English-descended settlers in America with having robbed and cheated the Indians of their land, so that they are in no position to take a
high moral stand about their own property "rights"; he sees
the dispute between them and the French over American
territory—the dispute which was to become the Great War
for the Empire—as no more than "the quarrel of two robbers
for the spoils of a passenger," and on the whole thinks the
French are on the stronger moral ground, since they have
treated the Indians somewhat more decently than the English
have ("An Introduction to the Political State of Great-
Britain," "Observations on the Present State of Affairs"). In
the Wilkes affair, he defends the right of the House of Commons to exclude from membership individuals they consider
undesirable, without interference from any other body (*The
False Alarm*)—a right that both British and American representative bodies have continued to insist on. He attacks the
interested chauvinism that would plunge England into war
with Spain over a piece of barren territory in the name of
"national honour" and for the political and monetary capital
that might accrue to the warmongers (*Thoughts on Falkland's
Islands*). Though he laments the depopulation of the High-
lands of Scotland through emigration, and at times can feel
the romantic appeal of the tightly knit feudal life of the clan
system, in the end his verdict on that life is "The system of
insular subordination . . . cannot afford much delight in the
view. . . . The inhabitants were for a long time perhaps not

unhappy; but their content was a muddy mixture of pride and ignorance, an indifference for pleasures which they did not know, . . . and a strong conviction of their own importance" (*Journey to the Western Islands*). On the question of whether the American colonies shall be allowed to establish their independence of the central government in London, he thinks that the "secessionist" arguments are fallacious and that the political unity of the Empire and the sovereignty of the central government should be maintained, by force if necessary (*Taxation No Tyranny*). Clearly such a set of positions is not very compatible with the modern stereotype of a Tory.

Much controversy has been stirred up by the assertion that Johnson resolutely refused to base his thinking about political matters on any such metaphysical or supernatural concepts as Locke's "original compact" or Burke's "sacred prescription" or the "natural law" of mediaeval and Renaissance theorists.[1] Nevertheless, the evidence from Johnson's writings is unequivocal. Government is for him a purely pragmatic and utilitarian affair: human beings are happier in an organized society than in a state of anarchy; for law and order to be maintained, the power to use force must be placed in the hands of someone, and no other divine or metaphysical sanction is required to justify that power than the mere fact of that necessity. The key statements in Johnson's political "theory" are "All government is ultimately and essentially absolute" and "The first laws had no law to enforce them, the first authority was constituted by itself."[2] One might think that these assertions—made, not in casual conversation, or in youth, but in print, in highly serious dissertations on politics written for public consumption at the height of Johnson's mature powers—would be conclusive: "All government is ultimately and essentially absolute" seems impossible to reconcile with "All government finds its sanction in natural law, or prescriptive right, or the original compact." Yet many readers, now as in Johnson's own time, are made very uneasy

---

1. See D. J. Greene, "Samuel Johnson and 'Natural Law'," *Journal of British Studies*, II (May 1963), 59–75, and the exchanges with Peter J. Stanlis in subsequent numbers of that journal.

2. See below, pp. 422 and 322.

by it and feel that somehow or other it must be explained away. There is no need to do so. Students have been troubled by the resemblance the resolute empiricism and pragmatism of this position bears to those of such highly secular philosophers as Hobbes and Bentham.[3] It is nevertheless a position that has been held by a great many devout and well-instructed Christians over the centuries, though not, it must be admitted, by those brought up in the ultramontane and theocratic doctrines which dominated Roman Catholic teaching between the French Revolution and the Second Vatican Council. To try here even to begin to sum up the immense amount of discussion that has taken place, from the time of Augustine down to that of Karl Barth and beyond, of the complex question of the relation between the Kingdom of God and the kingdom of this world would be impossible. But it can at least be stated that a large body of Christian opinion has held that "Polity being only the conduct of immoral men in public affairs," an artifact of sinful human beings in a fallen world, it is wrong to regard the activities of political man as somehow a vehicle of divine revelation. A succinct statement of this position can be found in Charles Davis's F. D. Maurice Lectures of 1966:

3. To assert this resemblance is not, as some have thought, the same thing as saying that Johnson was "a disciple of Hobbes" (see Robert Shackleton, "Johnson and the Enlightenment," in *Johnson, Boswell, and Their Circle*, p. 82); apparently it needs to be pointed out that ideas can be transmitted by collateral channels as well as direct ones. Not that all sincere Christians necessarily abhorred the notion that it might be possible to learn something from Hobbes. The similarities, and even direct indebtedness, of Pascal to Hobbes have been a commonplace of Pascal criticism, from Fontenelle down to Sainte-Beuve and beyond. Gilbert Chinard (*En lisant Pascal*, Lille-Genève, 1948, p. 36) speaks of "les affinités intellectuelles, le parallélisme des vues scientifiques et les ressemblances des vues politiques que l'on peut constater entre l'auteur du *De Cive* et l'auteur des *Pensées*. . . . En plusieurs circonstances et sur des points fort différents, Hobbes a fortement influencé la pensée pascalienne et lui a servi de point de départ." Moreover, the simple-minded old attitude that anything "Mr. Hobbs the Atheist" wrote must necessarily be wrong and wicked is being drastically modified by recent careful studies of his thought.

On affinities between Johnson and "utilitarianism," see Robert Voitle, *Samuel Johnson the Moralist* (1961). For an interpretation of Johnson's thought radically different from that which modern advocates of "natural law" attribute to him, see Paul K. Alkon, *Samuel Johnson and Moral Discipline* (1967).

The implication of the new stance of the Roman Catholic Church [since the Declaration on Religious Freedom of the Second Vatican Council] is that the State is a secular reality. . . . The State, then, for Christians is not sacred. Political authority comes from God only in the sense in which the entire world, including man as a social being, comes from God. But no State has an immediate divine mandate. All political systems are relative and changing. They come within the sphere of man's developing understanding, and are subject to his intelligent modification and control.[4]

Pascal, whom Johnson read and admired, had said much the same thing more forcefully three centuries earlier:

Men maintain that justice does not consist in . . . customs, but that it resides in natural laws, common to every country. . . . The joke is that the caprice of man has so many vagaries that there is no such law. . . . The only universal rules are the laws of the country. . . . Whence comes this? From the force which is in them. . . . Force is the sovereign of the world, and not opinion. . . . Custom alone makes equity, for this sole reason, that it is received: that is the mystical foundation of its authority.[5]

Clearly it is possible for devout Christian belief to subsist along with a rigorously secular approach to political theory.

The theological basis of Johnson's sympathy with a "secularist" view of political theory rather than with the position that by an inspection of human history we can detect universal "natural laws," sanctioned by God, on which we should base political action, is implicit in his review of Soame Jenyns's *Free Enquiry into the Nature and Origin of Evil,* 1757: to attempt to find moral norms in the behaviour of corrupted sublapsarian man, and then to imagine that what one has found somehow defines the Divine Will, amounts, Johnson says, to "dogmatic limitations of Omnipotence." The pragmatic basis

4. Charles Davis, *God's Grace in History* (1966), pp. 29 f.
5. Blaise Pascal, *Oeuvres complètes* (1954), ed. Jacques Chevalier, Sects. 230, 238, 242. In older editions, these are found in what is usually marked "Chapter v" of the *Pensées.* My translation.

of his position is the observed fact that throughout history "interested faction" has seldom had difficulty finding ways of appealing to "the laws of nature" in justification of its own self-seeking actions.[6]

This last very serious consideration—not "blind prejudice" —lies at the heart of Johnson's longest and most elaborately argued piece of political writing, *Taxation No Tyranny:* the hypocrisy with which the propagandists of the American Revolution appeal to "universal law," divine and natural, in support of their demand for "freedom" for themselves, while they deny it to their Negro slaves, and in support of their contention that "their" property should be immune from alienation by means of governmental taxation, property which they stole from its Indian owners without any qualms of conscience, seems to him disgusting, and, if unchallenged, extremely dangerous in its implications for the future. Few students have agreed with me[7] in regarding *Taxation No Tyranny* as a successful, indeed masterly, answer to what Johnson says it is an answer to, the resolutions of the Continental Congress of 1774 and the political thinking incorporated or implied in them (though not necessarily the final answer to the practical question of what to do about the rebellious colonies, which it nowhere purports to be). Discussion of this work is still obscured by the mists of received Whig and American school-book history; in time, when the work of the present generation of scholarly historians of the eighteenth century has become better known, it may be possible to approach Johnson's argument with a more objective eye. But the problem of how to assess the nature and quality of Johnson's political thought is one that can continue to be fruitfully debated for a long time; and this volume attempts to provide, what has hitherto been wanting, a convenient place in which to consult a good deal, if far from all, of Johnson's written expression of that thought.

6. "The laws of Nature, the rights of humanity, the faith of charters, the danger of [i.e., to] liberty, the encroachments of usurpation, have been thundered in our ears, sometimes by interested faction, and sometimes by honest stupidity" *Taxation No Tyranny* (p. 418 below).

7. Though one admirer of the work—perhaps surprisingly, considering his generally low opinion of Johnson—was Coleridge. See below, p. 409.

NOTE ON THE TEXT

The headnote to each item in the volume discusses any special textual problems of that item. One piece (*Considerations on Corn*, p. 301) is edited from the holograph manuscript, the rest from early printed editions, occasionally with assistance in the form of corrections in Johnson's hand on proof sheets (*Taxation No Tyranny*) or a published copy of the work (*Marmor Norfolciense*). In editing from print, the copy-text has been that of the earliest known authorized edition, with Johnson's substantive changes in later editions incorporated into the text and earlier readings included in the notes. For the majority of pieces in the volume, there is only one edition, the first, of any authority. The last four, however, *The False Alarm*, *Thoughts on . . . Falkland's Islands*, *The Patriot*, and *Taxation No Tyranny*, received considerable revision by Johnson. The aim of the edition has been to reproduce Johnson's final intentions, as well as they can be ascertained. All variants of any substantive interest are recorded in the notes.

In keeping with the general textual practice of the edition, the spelling and hyphenation of the copy-texts have been retained, even though there may be inconsistencies within the text. Capitalization has been cautiously modernized; i.e., if some significant shade of meaning might be obscured by reducing a capital letter to lower case, the capital has been retained. Punctuation follows that of the copy-text, unless some compositorial error, or important discrepancy between eighteenth-century and modern usage, might endanger the modern reader's grasp of Johnson's meaning; in such cases, the punctuation has been adjusted and the change noted. One principle adhered to in earlier volumes of the Yale Edition has been applied here with great caution, that of changing italic type, used for dialogue, emphasis, or quotation

in the early editions, to roman type surrounded by quotation
marks. There is very little in these political pieces that can
be strictly classified as dialogue. But there is a good deal of
quotation—passages taken verbatim from a pamphlet Johnson is examining and criticizing; words attributed to an
opponent; real or imaginary remarks by earlier authors;
passages of poetry, maxims, proverbs, and so on. It is sometimes uncertain whether italics are being used to indicate
quotation or merely to emphasize; hence it has seemed wiser
not to prejudice the reader's interpretation by interfering
with the italicization. Indeed, it could be argued that Johnson's (or his printers') practice of using italics in a piece of
controversial prose serves both functions, emphasis and the
indication of quotation, at the same time, and that to reduce
such passages to roman type, while it might minimally facilitate the speed of reading by the modern student, would
do so at the cost of significant loss of meaning.

CHRONOLOGICAL TABLE

FLT = First Lord [Commissioner] of the Treasury (after 1714 usually, though not always, the king's chief minister). Ch. Ex. = Chancellor of the Exchequer (second-ranking member of the Treasury commission).

BRITISH HISTORY		SAMUEL JOHNSON
George I dies; George II king.	1727	
	1728	To Pembroke College, Oxford (Oct.).
Frederick Lewis created Prince of Wales.	1729	Returns to Lichfield (Dec.).
Townshend quarrels with Walpole and resigns.	1730	
	1731	Michael Johnson (father) dies.
	1732	Usher at Market Bosworth school. Quarrels with Sir Wolstan Dixie.
Walpole forced to withdraw Excise Bill. Chesterfield dismissed as Lord Steward for opposing it.	1733	At Birmingham. Translates *A Voyage to Abyssinia*.
Sir William Yonge, Sec. at War (till 1746).	1735	Marries Elizabeth (Jervis) Porter.
	1736	At Edial school. Begins *Irene*.
Stage Licensing Act passed. Queen Caroline dies (Nov.).	1737	Nathaniel Johnson (brother) dies. To London (Mar.). Begins work for Cave.
Inquiry into Spanish treatment of British seamen. Birth and christening of Prince George of Wales (later George III) (June).	1738	*London; Life of Sarpi; State of Affairs in Lilliput* (intro. to *Debates*); Eubulus and Pamphilus letters.
War declared on Spain (Oct.).	1739	*Marmor Norfolciense; Vindication of the Licensers;* tr. of Crousaz' *Commentary* on Pope. Extended visit to Midlands.

BRITISH HISTORY		SAMUEL JOHNSON
Sir William Wyndham dies. Anson begins voyage around the world.	1740	Lives of Blake, Drake, Barretier. Probably assisting Guthrie with *Debates*.
Motion in Parliament to remove Walpole (Feb.). War of Austrian Succession begins. General election; Walpole's support diminished.	1741	Sole writer of *Debates*. Abridgment of *Monarchy Asserted*. Probably contributes to "Foreign History" and discussion of wool exports in *Gentleman's Magazine*.
Walpole resigns; created Earl of Orford (Feb.). Carteret, Newcastle, Secs. State; Sandys, Ch. Ex.; Gower, Lord Privy Seal. Pulteney created Earl of Bath.	1742	Continues with *Debates* and "Foreign History." Review of *Conduct of Duchess of Marlborough*.
Battle of Dettingen. Controversy over use of Hanoverian troops in British army.	1743	Savage dies. Continues with *Debates*. Work on Harleian library. "Historical Account of Parliament" (lost).
Carteret (Granville) forced to resign over war and foreign policy. Henry Pelham, FLT; Newcastle, Sec. State; Hardwicke, Lord Chancellor; Lyttelton, George Grenville, junior ministers.	1744	*Life of Savage; Harleian Miscellany;* "Essay on Small Tracts and Fugitive Pieces"; (perhaps) report of debate on Hanoverian troops.
Invasion by Charles Edward (the Young Pretender).	1745	*Observations on Macbeth;* sermon for Henry Hervey Aston.
Granville, Bath, ministers for two days. Pelhams resume office. Chesterfield, Sec. State (till 1748); Pitt, Paymaster General.	1746	Signs contract for *Dictionary*.
General election; Gower-Anson group win Lichfield seats.	1747	*Plan* of *Dictionary* (dedicated to Chesterfield).
Peace of Aix-la-Chapelle.	1748	Preface to *Preceptor*.
	1749	Letter on fireworks; *Vanity of Human Wishes. Irene* produced (epilogue by Sir William Yonge).

BRITISH HISTORY		SAMUEL JOHNSON
	1750	Begins *Rambler* (to 1752).
Frederick, Prince of Wales, dies.	1751	*Life of Cheynel.*
	1752	Elizabeth Johnson (wife) dies.
Hostilities between French and British in India and America; French advance toward Ohio valley.	1753	Takes Frank Barber under his care. Contributes to *Adventurer* (to 1754).
Henry Pelham dies. Newcastle, FLT; Henry Fox, Sec. at War, then Sec. State; Anson, First Lord of Admiralty. French take Fort Duquesne.	1754	*Life of Cave.*
Braddock defeated by French. Russian and Hessian subsidy treaties attacked by Pitt. Pitt and Grenville dismissed. Lyttelton, Ch. Ex.	1755	Letter to Chesterfield. Hon. M.A., Oxford. *Dictionary* published.
Treaty of Westminster (Jan.), allying Britain and Prussia against France. War declared on France (May) (Seven Years' War). G. Townshend's first Militia Bill defeated in Lords. Admiral Byng fails to prevent French taking Minorca; courtmartialed (Dec.) and executed. Newcastle resigns (Nov.). Pitt, Sec. State.	1756	Preface to Rolt's *Dictionary of Commerce;* "Further Thoughts on Agriculture." Edits *Literary Magazine* (Apr.): "Political State of Great Britain"; "Observations" on Present State of Affairs, Militia Bill, Russian and Hessian treaties, letter from Gallo-Anglus; reviews of Evans' *Middle Colonies,* pamphlets on Byng, *History of Minorca.* Life of Frederick the Great.
Pitt dismissed (Apr.). Coalition ministry (June): Newcastle, FLT; Pitt, Sec. State; Anson, Admiralty; Halifax, Board of Trade and Plantations. Clive wins Battle of Plassey (June). Unsuccessful expedition to Rochefort (Sept.).	1757	Review of Soame Jenyns's *Origin of Evil;* intro. to *London Chronicle;* "speech" on Rochefort expedition.

BRITISH HISTORY		SAMUEL JOHNSON
Louisbourg taken (July). Fort Duquesne taken (renamed Fort Pitt, now Pittsburgh).	1758	Begins *Idler* (to 1760). Observations on the war in *Universal Chronicle;* "Of the Duty of a Journalist" (*Univ. Chron.*).
Battle of Minden (Aug.). Quebec taken (Sept.). French navy defeated at Quiberon (Nov.).	1759	Sarah Johnson (mother) dies. *Rasselas;* intro. to *The World Displayed.*
Montreal taken. George II dies (aged 77) (Oct.); George III (aged 22) king. Bute in cabinet.	1760	"Bravery of English Common Soldiers"; intro. to *Proceedings of Committee for Clothing French Prisoners;* review of Tytler's *Inquiry* into Mary, Queen of Scots.
Pondicherry (India) taken. French begin peace negotiations. Bute, Sec. State (Mar.). Pitt resigns (Oct.) over question of war with Spain.	1761	Assists with Gwynn's *Thoughts on the Coronation.*
Newcastle resigns (May). Bute, FLT; Grenville, Egremont, Secs. State; Dashwood, Ch. Ex. Charles Jenkinson, Bute's private secretary.	1762	Awarded pension of £300 (July).
Peace of Paris (Feb.). Bute resigns (May). Grenville, FLT; initiates policy of economy to pay war costs. Egremont, Halifax, Secs. State.	1763	Meets Boswell. Jenkinson sends papers on Peace of Paris (returned 1765).
Wilkes arrested on general warrant, over *North Briton* No. 45; freed by Chief Justice Pratt (Camden); expelled from House of Commons.	1764	Lines in Goldsmith's *The Traveller.*
Stamp Act passed (Mar.). Grenville dismissed (July). Rockingham, FLT; Grafton, Sec. State; Newcastle, Privy Seal (dies 1768). Burke, Rockingham's private secretary.	1765	Meets Thrales. Prayer on "Engaging in politicks with Hamilton." Writes election publicity for Thrale. Shakespeare edition published. LL.D., Dublin.

BRITISH HISTORY		SAMUEL JOHNSON
Stamp Act repealed (Mar.); declaratory act affirming right to tax colonies passed. Rockingham dismissed (July). Pitt (Chatham), Privy Seal; Shelburne, Sec. State; Grafton, FLT; Camden, Lord Chancellor; Charles Townshend, Ch. Ex. Riots over price of bread; embargo on export of wheat.	1766	Contributes to Chambers' Vinerian lectures. "Considerations on Corn"(?)
Inquiry into East India Company. Chatham incapacitated (resigns 1768). Townshend sponsors duties on tea, etc., in America. Grafton, FLT; North, Ch. Ex.; Shelburne (resigned 1768), Sec. State.	1767	Correspondence with Chambers over defense of East India Company.
General election. Wilkes defeated in London, elected in Middlesex. Junius letters begin.	1768	Election publicity for Thrale.
Wilkes expelled by House of commons; re-elected twice by Middlesex; House declares his opponent elected. Junius' Letter to the King (Dec.).	1769	Paragraph in *Gentleman's Magazine* concerning Sir Joseph Mawbey, Thrale's colleague as MP for Southwark.
Grafton resigns (Jan.). North, FLT. Grenville's Contested Elections Act passed. Spanish occupy Falkland Islands.	1770	*The False Alarm* (Jan.); concluding lines of *The Deserted Village*.
After diplomatic negotiations, Spanish agreed to evacuate Falkland Islands.	1771	*Thoughts on Falkland's Islands* (Mar.). Recommended to Government by Strahan as Parliamentary candidate.
	1772	Preface to Hoole's *Present State of East India Conpany's Affairs*(?).
Act authorizing export of tea to America by East India Company. "Boston tea party" (Dec.).	1773	Tour of Scotland with Boswell.

BRITISH HISTORY		SAMUEL JOHNSON
Port of Boston closed. Quebec Act passed. First Continental Congress, Philadelphia. General election (Nov.). C. J. Fox dismissed as junior minister.	1774	*The Patriot* (Nov.). Election publicity for Thrale.
Burke's speech on conciliation (Mar.). Actions at Lexington and Concord (Apr.). Battle of Bunker Hill (June).	1775	*Journey to Western Islands of Scotland* (Jan.); *Taxation No Tyranny* (Mar.). Visit to France with Thrales (autumn). D.C.L., Oxford.
British evacuate Boston (Mar.). American Declaration of Independence (July).	1776	

SHORT TITLES

Chapman-Hazen—R. W. Chapman and Allen T. Hazen, *Johnsonian Bibliography: A Supplement to Courtney*, 1939 (Oxford Bibliographical Society Proceedings and Papers, v).

Dictionary—Johnson's *Dictionary of the English Language*, 4th ed., 1773.

GM—*Gentleman's Magazine*

Letters—*The Letters of Samuel Johnson*, ed. R. W. Chapman, 3 vols. 1952; referred to by number.

Life—Boswell's *Life of Johnson*, ed. G. B. Hill, revised and enlarged by L. F. Powell, 6 vols. 1934–50; Vols. v and vi (2d ed.), 1964.

Lives—*Lives of the English Poets*, ed. G. B. Hill, 3 vols. 1905.

LM—*Literary Magazine: or Universal Review*, 1756–58.

Miscellanies—*Johnsonian Miscellanies*, ed. G. B. Hill, 2 vols. 1897.

Politics—Donald J. Greene, *The Politics of Samuel Johnson*, 1960 (reissued 1973).

POLITICAL WRITINGS

"PAMPHILUS" ON CONDOLENCE. 1738.

Although Boswell and other biographers indulged in much speculation about the early development of Johnson's Toryism, in fact little is known of any strong political proclivities on Johnson's part before his arrival in London in 1737. To be sure, one of his earliest extant pieces of prose, written in his sixteenth year, has a decided political slant—a Latin school-exercise, based on Horace, *Odes*, I. 2, inveighing against modern commercially inspired imperialist expansion: *"Avaritia adeo est insatiabilis, ut quasi pars mundi jam nata vix satis auri gemmarumque contineret . . . amor auri nostras naves inpulit qua nunquam Romani sig-"*[1]—here the published fragment breaks off. It is a theme that remains central in Johnson's political thinking throughout his life, recurring in works as early as the "State of Affairs in Lilliput" (1738) and as late as *A Journey to the Western Islands of Scotland* (1775), and accounting for, among other things, his aversion to William Pitt and to the American colonists. It cannot be too much emphasized that Johnson's primary complaint against the Americans was precisely that "imperialism" with which later Americans were fond of charging Europeans: that, impelled by the desire for gain, *"novae regiones atavis incognitae quaeruntur illarumque incolae"*—in this case, the Indians and Negroes—*"subjuguntur."* Johnson sees little morally to choose between the activities of the Spanish colonizers in South and Central America and of the English colonizers in the West Indies and the Thirteen Colonies; he feels that the whole sordid business of European expansion in the sixteenth and seventeenth centuries is a blot on the record of modern civilization.

But apart from this significant little piece of juvenilia, perhaps the only real evidence of Johnson's interest in politics before 1738 is his remark late in life that "difference of opinion" between him and Gilbert Walmesley, a stout Walpolian Whig, did not keep them apart,[2] and some passages in *Irene*, probably thought out as early as 1736, which deal rather with general political theory than specific events of the time.[3]

When Johnson arrived in London, however, he found himself caught up in the feverish political activity that surrounded the final years of Sir Robert Walpole's administration, and during 1738 and 1739 no more vitriolic pen than his was found writing in the service of the opposition to Walpole. That opposition consisted of many diverse elements, temporarily united in their determination to oust the Minister, but otherwise poles apart in their political aspirations. In order to understand Johnson's writings of the time, an attempt must be made to distinguish some of the

1. *Letters*, Vol. I, frontispiece. See *Politics*, p. 259.
2. "Smith," *Lives*, II. 21 (par. 73).
3. See *Politics*, Ch. III.

3

more important political groupings of the late thirties and early forties.[4] First, of course, there were Walpole himself, since 1721 First Lord of the Treasury, and his allies, notably his brother, "Old Horace" Walpole; Henry Pelham and his brother the Duke of Newcastle; Philip Yorke, Earl of Hardwicke, the Lord Chancellor; John, Lord Hervey, Queen Caroline's confidant and, after 1740, Lord Privy Seal; and most important of all, George II and, till her death in 1737, the brilliant Queen Caroline. Walpole had attained his position after years of internecine struggle among the Whigs who took office after the accession of George I in 1714, triumphing over politicians so powerful as Sunderland and Stanhope: it is well to remember that Walpole was never the leader of "*the* Whig party" of the early eighteenth century, but the leader of one fluctuating group—on the whole, the more cautious and conservative, the less doctrinaire wing—of those who called themselves by that name.

Of the opposition, the most powerful, determined, and articulate group consisted of those dissident Whigs to whom Walpole had denied what they thought their rightful share of power; they were led, in the late 1730's, by William Pulteney and John, Lord Carteret, astute men and dangerous opponents. On their fringe were to be found other important Whig magnates alienated from Walpole—his brother-in-law Lord Townshend (who died in 1738); the prestigious Lord Chesterfield; the Duke of Bedford and his "Bloomsbury gang," generally conceded to be less concerned over principles than spoils. A younger group of Whigs, the "boy Patriots" or "the cousin-hood," made up of William Pitt and his relations Lord Temple, George Grenville, and George Lyttelton (supported by old Lord Cobham), clamored for more enterprising foreign and commercial policies than Walpole sponsored. And then there were the Parliamentary Tories—the "country gentlemen," proprietors of smaller landed estates than those of the great Whig aristocrats like Newcastle, not eager for executive office nor very active in national politics, jealous of any increase of power on the part of the central government, sulkily opposed to foreign entanglements and the taxes for military establishments that stemmed from them, permanently in opposition to almost every administration in the eighteenth century; but when it came to a showdown, generally supporting Walpole against his Whig opponents. Outside Parliament there were Frederick, Prince of Wales, and Henry St. John, Viscount Bolingbroke, once leader of a Tory administration under Queen Anne, then attainted, exiled, for a time chief minister to the Stuart Pretender, later permitted to return to England, though not to

4. John B. Owen, *The Rise of the Pelhams* (1957), has a good treatment of the period 1741–44. J. H. Plumb's biography of Sir Robert Walpole, when completed, should be invaluable to students of the period. For the Tories, see Owen, pp. 66–75, and Sir Lewis Namier, "Country Gentlemen in Parliament," in *Personalities and Powers* (1955), pp. 59–77. What is referred to as Toryism in the standard nineteenth-century and early twentieth-century accounts of the time is for the most part myth. For the Opposition, C. B. Realey, *The Early Opposition to Sir Robert Walpole, 1720–1727* (1931) and A. S. Foord, *His Majesty's Opposition, 1714–1830* (1964) are helpful.

resume his seat in the House of Lords, now loftily professing a philosophical superiority to all party. Both men were the centers of small coteries, containing a high percentage of "intellectuals." The shifting alliances among all these opposition groups and individuals were most complex and still need to be carefully worked out.

In the twelve months between May 1738 and May 1739, Johnson contributed four substantial pieces of writing to the flood of opposition propaganda—the poem *London*, the "State of Affairs in Lilliput" (the introduction to the *Debates in the Senate of Lilliput* and, in this edition, printed with them), *Marmor Norfolciense*, and *A Compleat Vindication of the Licensers of the Stage*, as well as some smaller pieces such as the two letters printed immediately below. In these we find Johnson involved in some odd activities and associations—indulging in jingoism against Spain, praising Lyttelton and Pitt, lending his pen to the praise of Prince Fred, vindicating the right of that professional liberal Henry Brooke to harangue against the *status quo* in church and state. But political opposition makes strange, if temporary, bedfellows, and it is reasonable to suppose that Johnson remained basically a Tory throughout this period. When Walpole's position became seriously endangered in February 1741, Johnson defended the action of the Parliamentary Tories in coming to his rescue and keeping Pulteney and Pitt out of office.[5] He seems to have written nothing against Walpole after 1739, and in later life spoke in his praise. Little as Johnson liked Walpolianism, when it came to the point he liked the alternatives to Walpole—Pulteney, Pitt, Bolingbroke[6]—even less. In this he agreed with the Parliamentary Tories.

Apart from the competence of the writing—and as bitter, tumultuous, slashing satire it is very competent—there is not a great deal to distinguish these early political pieces of Johnson's from the rest of the torrent of anti-Walpole invective that was pouring forth at the time. The charges of dictatorship and corruption, of political, moral, and intellectual degeneracy that Johnson hurls against the regime are not very different from those made in the *Craftsman* and *Common Sense* by Pulteney, Bolingbroke, and Chesterfield, or by Pope, Swift, Fielding, and innumerable lesser writers in the verse and prose satires of the day. Perhaps one generalization may be permitted: Johnson's writings distinguish themselves from most of the others by a tendency to venture beyond Walpole and indulge in outrageous personal innuendo against the King himself. To be sure, George's domestic life was conspicuously vulnerable to such attacks. Even during Caroline's lifetime, his annual visits to his mistress in Hanover, Amalie von Wallmoden, had caused scandal ("Lest ropes be wanting in the tempting spring / To rig another convoy for the k——g" [*London*, ll. 246–47]; this is one of

5. See the editorial note appended to Johnson's report of the House of Commons debate of 13 Feb 1741 (reprinted in *Politics*, p. 130).
6. Bolingbroke is sometimes wrongly thought to represent Toryism at this time. For Johnson's detestation of him, see his definition of *irony* in the *Dictionary*, and Boswell's *Life, passim*. For other Tories' dislike, see the pamphlet *The Sentiments of a Tory* (1741), quoted at length in *Politics*, pp. 272–79.

a number of Johnson's allusions to George's sex-life, others being the conclusion of the "Pamphilus" letter below and a stanza in "*Post-Genitis*" in *Marmor Norfolciense*, "*Jam feret ignavus, / Vetitâque libidine pravus*," which Johnson then translates as "While he lies melting in a lewd embrace").

Caroline died in November 1737. In January 1738, both Houses of Parliament tendered George addresses of extravagant condolence. In June 1738, George brought Wallmoden to England, installed her as *maîtresse en titre*, and later made her Countess of Yarmouth. The wonderfully human "inside story" of these transactions Johnson and the rest of the general public had no means of knowing: it was not until the nineteenth century that Hervey's *Memoirs* (1733–37) were published, with their classic story of the exchange between the sobbing George and the dying Caroline, who was urging him to remarry—"Non, j'aurai des maîtresses!" "Mon Dieu, cela n'empêche pas."[7] As it was, Johnson was provided with the occasion for one of his most effective short pieces of writing of the period.

This is one of two letters signed "Pamphilus" that appeared in the *Gentleman's Magazine* in 1738. The second, in the October number, is a protest against the impropriety of allowing the lines "Life is a jest, and all things show it; / I thought so once, but now I know it" to appear on Gay's monument in Westminster Abbey. As it has no political reference (though, since it too deals with memorials to the dead, it has some relation to the previous letter), it is printed in another volume of this edition of Johnson's works. The second letter was attributed to Johnson on internal evidence by A. A. McLeod in *Notes and Queries* (20 Jan 1951, p. 32). In 1957, Jacob Leed (*Modern Philology*, LIV [May], 221–29) attributed both the "Pamphilus" letters, noting the connexion of the earlier one with two passages in one of Johnson's letters of 1738 to Cave (*Letters* 9), "An answer to another Query I am very willing to write," and "[I] desire you to propose the Question to which you wish for an answer." Further arguments for the attribution of both letters were adduced by D. J. Greene (*PMLA*, LXXIV [Mar 1959], 75–84) and F. V. Bernard (*Modern Philology*, LXII [Aug 1964], 42–44).

The "Query" referred to in Johnson's letter is one of sixteen "Political Questions" printed in the June 1738 number of the *Gentleman's Magazine* (pp. 310–11), which readers are invited to discuss. They are shrewdly and amusingly framed so as to incorporate many of the issues which were at the moment the subject of debate between the Walpolites and the opposition. As they are so cleverly done, and as Johnson's reply to Question 1 was so promptly forthcoming in the next issue of the magazine, it is tempting to speculate that Johnson himself, so closely involved with Cave at the time in the editing of the magazine, had a hand in drawing them up. At any rate, they provide background for an understanding of the first "Pamphilus" letter and of the general political atmosphere of the time, and it may be useful to reprint them here.

> Being desired to publish some *political questions* for the consideration of our readers and correspondents, we have taken the liberty to enlarge

7. J. H. Plumb, *The First Four Georges* (1956), also gives a sympathetic and perceptive account of the relationship between George and Caroline.

the catalogue; and if the ingenious please to favour us with any pertinent argument, remark, letter, dialogue, conversation or speech, within doors, or without, on these subjects, 'twill be gratefully acknowledged, and inserted with the author's name, or without, as desired.

QUESTION I.

Whether his Majesty's most gracious speech at the opening the last session of Parliament, was treated with proper delicacy in the addresses from both Houses? which see p. 50.

QUESTION II.

Whether the Parliament's continuing the land forces from year to year is not the same thing as keeping up a standing army?

QUESTION III.

Whether the voters for 12,000, or the voters for 18,000 to be kept up this year were most on the side of liberty? or the best patriots?

QUESTION IV.

Whether the House of Commons could not form a true judgment, what countenance the court of Spain gives their Guarda Costas, who plunder our merchants, or whether proper application was made in their behalf, by the ministers; without having every individual paper thereto relating laid before them?

QUESTION V.

If only 10,000 seamen appear'd on Feb. 2 to be the necessary number for the year 1738, what occasion'd the voting double that number on April 10?

QUESTION VI.

Whether the tedious forms in national assemblies be not a great remora to heroic or successful exploits?

QUESTION VII.

Whether it be true policy in the Parliament of Britain, to support the colony of Georgia?

QUESTION VIII.

Whether that colony is preserved by any measures taken there?

QUESTION IX.

Whether the new bridge ought to be built at the Horse-Ferry, or at Palace-yard?

QUESTION X.

Whether the working buttons in a loom, ought to be suppressed by act of Parliament, since an equal quantity of mohair is thereby consum'd as when wrought by the needle?

QUESTION XI.

Whether the people ought to know the reasons, that determine their representatives to vote for or against any bill?[8]

QUESTION XII.

Whether the commissioners for Greenwich Hospital, ought to be impower'd to sell any part of the Derwentwater estate?

QUESTION XIII.

How far the importation of iron from America ought to be prohibited?

QUESTION XIV.

Whether the money raised by a general tax on the whole nation, ought to be apply'd to repairing or beautifying St Peters and St Margarets, Westminster?

QUESTION XV.

Where there was any combination to enhance the price of Newcastle coals? and what were the proper means to prevent the bad effects of it?

QUESTION XVI.

Whether it be for the advantage of trade in general, to take of[f] the drawback of linnens imported from foreign countries?

The "addresses of condolence" so caustically treated by "Pamphilus" were the addresses of thanks to the King by both Houses of Parliament, always tendered for the speech from the throne at the opening of Parliament, which in 1738 had taken place on 24 January. Since Queen Caroline had died only two months before, they contained much elaborately phrased "condolence." For instance, from that of the House of Lords:

> It is with the greatest humility we take this first opportunity of approaching your Royal Person, to lament the irreparable loss sustained by your Majesty and these Kingdoms, in the death of that excellent Princess, our late most gracious Queen; and with hearts overwhelmed with grief, to condole with your Majesty, on this melancholy and solemn occasion,

and from that of the Commons:

> To speak our utmost sense of the great loss your Majesty and these Kingdoms have sustained, would be to revive and aggravate what we wish to alleviate and dispel; but we hope your Majesty will pardon the intrusion of our sincere condolence, when you reflect on the double duty, by which we are bound, as affectionate subjects to your Majesty,

8. A significant question when the *Gentleman's Magazine*, in the same number, began to print (illegally) accounts of the Parliamentary debates.

and as representatives of the people of Great Britain, not to pass over in silence this object of your distress and their universal mourning.[9]

The Commons address then continues with two paragraphs of extravagant eulogy of Caroline's virtues, and concludes with the wish "that your Majesty's known resolution may aid time, in alleviating your sorrow for that loss which nothing can repair, and in restoring to your Majesty . . . tranquillity of mind." The Lords' address was equally laudatory. It is true, the courtliness of idiom that so distresses Johnson is even yet retained in parliamentary addresses to the Sovereign, and is no more than a historical tradition. Still, Johnson makes good use of the opportunity to deliver some well-thought-out morality on a subject that touched him deeply —the proper attitude of the living toward death—and, as well, to make some political capital for the opposition to Walpole and the Court.

The text that follows is that of the *Gentleman's Magazine*, VIII (July 1738), 347-49, the only one known.

9. The addresses are given in the *Gentleman's Magazine*, VIII (1738), 50-51.

Examination of a Question Proposed in the Magazine of June, p. 310

MR. URBAN,

Those criticks who would persuade us that they have made deep searches into the mind of man, and have founded their precepts, not upon caprice but nature, have laid it down as an uncontroverted rule, that a writer, whose intention is to delight, ought never to exhaust the subject he treats of, by shewing it in all its light, or expanding it in all its branches, but should give the reader the satisfaction of adding something that he may call his own, and thus engage his attention by flattering his vanity.

Tho' I am no bigot to the science of criticism, nor much an advocate for the authority claimed by its professors, of ascertaining taste, and setting bounds to fancy, I shall let this rule pass unexamined, both because few authors are capable of transgressing it, and because I believe it founded on a true principle, that our natural self-love makes us receive greater pleasure from a just thought struck out by ourselves, than from one communicated by an author.

It is perhaps for this reason that I was better entertained with the queries in your last magazine, than with any other part of the book; for by turning my thoughts upon a great variety of subjects, they gave me an opportunity of enjoying the proper pleasure of a reasonable being, of conversing with my own mind, and summoning by turns its different faculties of memory, judgment, and imagination.

Of these questions none employed me longer, or led me through a wider range of ideas than the first, perhaps for no other reason than that it had the advantage of making the first impression, for it is of much less importance to the publick than many of the rest, and I believe not very closely connected with any private interest. Perhaps likewise my attention might be awaken'd by the pompous assemblage of such awful sounds as are crouded together in that short interrogatory. A faithful subject and true Briton feels a kind of reverential horrour, a mixture of zeal, admiration and submission, that takes hold of his whole soul, at the mention of *King* and *Houses of Parliament*.

The latter he cannot reflect on without awakening the sublime conceptions of our liberties, our constitution, our virtue, our independence, our laws, and our commerce; nor hear the name of the former without annexing to it the ideas of majesty, generosity, magnanimity, vigilance, conservation of our religious and civil rights, and protection from slavery and arbitrary power, and all other virtues and glories which are inseparably united to the crown of Great Britain.

Whatever was the cause, I could not easily forbear considering this question, and indulging such thoughts as arose upon it, which were perhaps sometimes too ludicrous for the subject, and sometimes too serious for most of your readers.

Condolence, as it imports, in its original signification, a sympathy in grief, or fellowship in mourning, is a most amiable exertion of a mild and benevolent temper, and has been always observed to be an essential part of the character of a good man; ἀγαθοὶ ἀριδάκρυες ἄνδρες,[1] say the Greeks; and *Lachrymae nostri pars optima sensus*,[2] is the celebrated sentiment of a Latin poet. But condolence has degenerated from its first

---

1. "Good men are given to tears": quoted as a proverb in a note by Eustathius to *Iliad*, i. 349. The note is given in Pope's version of Homer, where SJ probably encountered it. The *GM* does not print breathings and accents.

2. Juvenal, xv. 133–34: "[*Natura*] *lacrimas dedit;* / *Haec nostri pars optima sensus*."

intention, and, like honesty, friendship, publick spirit and a thousand other pleasing sounds, retains only the shadow of its primitive meaning;[a] it implies now, not any virtue, but an empty ceremony, a resemblance of virtue, and is no more than one of the numerous appellations that hypocrisy has assumed to commend herself to mankind.

Condolence is now only part of the farce which the great act for the wise to laugh at, a sort of burthen upon affluence and high station, to extenuate the envy which the glare of their fortune might excite in those below them, who would be tempted to repine at their own condition, did they not see that happiness is more equally distributed than wealth, and that tho' they are sometimes exposed to the insolence or malice of their enemies, they have however this consolation, that they are not obliged to congratulate their advancement, or condole their losses.

If we regard *Condolence*, not as a mere form, but as an expression of real pity, and generous concern, it requires, like every other act of virtue, some degree of prudence to direct the practice of it, lest the good intention be defeated for want of a due regard to particular circumstances, and grief be heightned rather than abated by ill-tim'd and injudicious kindness.

I am now considering *Condolence* as one of the duties of life, in which view it must necessarily imply some degree of consolation, for that can never be a social duty which is of no benefit to society; and what is the advantage of such benevolence as tends only to emasculate and depress the soul by encreasing its emotions, or to impress more strongly the sense of a misfortune, by recounting the advantages and pleasures it has taken away? That only is the condolence of a friend which encourages and animates, which dispels the gloom, and clears up the soul, that shows a misfortune in its best light, and makes a calamity sit less heavy.

To attain this end, it is necessary that we administer our counsels at a proper time; not too soon, while the mind is smarting with a fresh wound, and can dwell upon nothing but its own pains; in those moments of impatience and emo-

a. meaning; *emend.*] meaning, *GM*

tion, the wisest exhortations will avail but little. Much less ought it to be too long delay'd, till the soul has wearied itself to rest, or apply'd for relief to business or diversions. Consolation then is at least an impertinent assistance where the danger is over, and may have still a worse effect, it may recall too strongly to the mind those ideas which it had so long been striving to banish.

But above all, to make our advice effectual, we ought to convince the afflicted person, that our concern is real; for we are to remember that at these hours passion reigns absolute in the breast, and that our persuasions are not attended to as the dictates of reason but affection. To raise and cultivate this opinion of our sincerity, we ought cautiously to avoid all affectation of language or address, we are not then to wanton in luxuriance of diction, to point our sentences, or polish our periods; grief is an enemy to metaphor and allusion, and pity does not naturally play the rhetorician.[3] No man out of a romance was ever comforted by hearing of the "never-to-be-forgotten virtues" of a dead friend, or much affected with the tenderness of an acquaintance, who expresses his apprehension lest "he should make those wounds bleed afresh, which it is his interest, and shall be his endeavour to heal."[4] If such consolations afford any remedy in grief, it must be by converting it into anger.

Such is the intention, and such are the rules of private and friendly condolence; as for publick addresses of this kind, as I know not from what motives they proceed, or with what intention they are presented, I pretend not to judge of their propriety. The stile of some of them has been very extraordinary; but as the Houses are on some occasions above forms of law, they may well be above those of ceremony. In an address to Queen Anne on the death of Prince George of Denmark, one of the Houses declared their hopes that "her grief would not hinder her from thinking of another husband,"[5]

3. Leed, Greene, and Bernard (see headnote) all note the resemblance of this passage to SJ's comments on *Lycidas*.

4. Both quotations in this sentence are from the House of Lords' address to the King (*Gentleman's Magazine*, VIII [1738], 50).

5. See [Cobbett's] *Parliamentary History*, VI. 777 (28 Jan 1709). The address of both Houses reads, "We most humbly beseech . . . that your Ma-

which however decent to the Queen, must be own'd *no improper* advice to the widow; yet it receiv'd, to use Queen Elizabeth's phrase on a like occasion, an "answer answerless."[6] The addresses now under our consideration seem, in my poor opinion, drawn up in direct opposition to the maxims which have been laid down by the best authorities. For what could be the effect of those long panegyrics, which certainly were not intended to inform the King of any thing he knew not before, but a *revival of that grief which his majesty had so far subdued as to assure them it should not interrupt or delay publick business? What need was there to enumerate the excellencies that he was best acquainted with, or to press him to exert his fortitude when he was giving eminent proofs of it? Here is abundance of grief, but no consolation; the Commons indeed promise money,[7] which must be allow'd a comfortable cordial, yet perhaps that might have wanted power to dispel so deep a melancholy, had not his majesty in his princely prudence, out of his tender affection to his people, and paternal regard to their civil and religious rights, timely discovered a more effectual remedy.[8]

Yours, PAMPHILUS.

*That such was the effect of the address appears from his majesty's most gracious answer, not yet in your *Magazine:*[9]—Gentlemen, I return you my thanks for this dutiful and very affectionate address. I am so sensibly touched by this convincing proof of your particular regard to me, that I am not *able*, in this distress, to command myself sufficiently to express the just sense, I have, of your affection and concern for me upon this occasion.

jesty would not so far indulge your just grief, as to decline the thoughts of a second marriage." The address originated in the House of Commons, and the first version was expressed more strongly. Anne's curt reply concludes, "The subject of this address is of such a nature, that I am persuaded you do not expect a particular answer."

6. This phrase, often used to describe Elizabeth's replies to representations from Parliament urging her to marry, is found, according to the *OED* (s.v. "answerless"), in a letter

from Elizabeth to Leicester, 1586.

7. SJ unfairly distorts the fact that a normal part of the speech from the throne at the opening of a Parliamentary session is a notice from the Crown that supplies will be asked for; and in the House of Commons' reply, an assurance is normally given that supplies will be granted.

8. Madame von Wallmoden.

9. The King's reply to the Lords' address had been printed in the *Gentleman's Magazine*, Jan 1738, p. 50, but not his reply to that of the Commons.

"EUBULUS" ON CHINESE AND
ENGLISH MANNERS. 1738.

In the same number of the *Gentleman's Magazine* as "Pamphilus" on condolence is another letter signed with a Greek pseudonym, "Eubulus" (prudent, well advised),[1] which also contains a personal attack on George II. This was first attributed (unreservedly) to Johnson by John Nichols in the *Gentleman's Magazine* for January 1785 (p. 6); the attribution was repeated in "The Autobiography of Sylvanus Urban," *Gentleman's Magazine*, 1856 (p. 272). The letter was first reprinted in Johnson's collected works in 1788 (xiv.552), and continued to be reprinted in subsequent editions. L. F. Powell (*Life*, ii.483) is undoubtedly right in his judgement that it "may have been touched by Johnson, but is not, I think, wholly his." The second to fifth paragraphs sound very much like Johnson; the opening paragraph could conceivably be his; but the last long paragraph is almost certainly by another hand. Possibly this last paragraph was contributed by some hanger-on of the Prince of Wales, and Johnson in his capacity of sub-editor of the *Gentleman's Magazine* ingeniously expanded this fatuous little piece of propaganda on behalf of Frederick into an advertisement for the translation of Du Halde's *History of China* (then being published by Cave) and, as well, another series of insults to George II.

The occasion referred to in the last paragraph of the letter was the public baptism[2] of the infant Prince George of Wales (later King George III) on 21 June (O.S.) 1738. The sensitive marquess of Frederick's household was Henry Brydges, Marquess of Carnarvon, later second Duke of Chandos. I do not know who his ducal competitor for the post of proxy was. The somewhat misleading title "Letter on Du Halde's *History of China*" was given to the piece by the editor of *Works* (1788), Vol. xiv, and repeated in subsequent collections. There is no title in the *Gentleman's Magazine;* there

1. SJ also uses "Eubulus" as the name of the writer of *Ramblers* 26 and 27.

2. A somewhat uncanonical proceeding, since the baby prince had already been baptized privately on the day of his birth, 24 May (O.S.), there being some doubt of his survival. Perhaps Bishop Secker, who officiated on both occasions, used for the second one the form of service in the Prayer Book entitled "The publick receiving of such as have been privately baptized." But Lord Egmont reports, "The King was desired to name [i.e., to stand as godfather], but he said since the Prince had privately caused the child to be baptized (though it was on account that the doctors thought he would die that day) he would have nothing to do about the affair" (Hist. MSS Comm., *Diary of the Earl of Egmont*, 1923, ii.496). There had been an even worse squabble between the Prince of Wales and his parents over the birth of his first child, Princess Augusta, the year before (Hervey, *Memoirs, sub anno* 1737).

14

it bears, however, the page headline "Remarkable example in a prince and subject"—an inept abbreviation of the expression in the text "so remarkable an example of spirit and firmness in a subject, and of conviction and compliance in a prince."

The only authoritative text is that of the *Gentleman's Magazine*, VIII (July 1738), 365–66, which is followed here.

["Eubulus" on Chinese and English Manners]

MR. URBAN,

There are few nations in the world, more talk'd of, or less known, than the Chinese.[1] The confus'd and imperfect accounts[a] which travellers have given of their grandeur, their sciences and their policy, have hitherto excited admiration, but have not been sufficient to satisfy even a superficial curiosity. I therefore return you my thanks for having undertaken, at so great an expence, to convey to English readers the most copious and accurate account,[2] yet published, of that remote and celebrated people, whose antiquity, magnificence, power, wisdom, peculiar customs, and excellent constitution, undoubtedly deserve the attention of the publick.

As the satisfaction found in reading descriptions of distant countries arises from a comparison which every reader naturally makes, between the ideas which he receives from the relation, and those which were familiar to him before; or, in other words, between the countries with which he is acquainted, and that which the author displays to his imagination; so it varies according to the likeness or dissimilitude of the manners of the two nations. Any custom or law unheard and unthought of before, strikes us with that *surprize* which is the effect of novelty; but a practice conformable to our own

a. accounts *emend.*] account *1738*

---

1. A good account of the attitude of eighteenth-century Englishmen in general, and SJ in particular, toward China is found in William W. Appleton, *A Cycle of Cathay* (1951). Earlier, in his preface to *A Voyage to Abyssinia* (1735), SJ had expressed more skepticism of glowing accounts of Chinese "politeness."

2. The translation of J. B. Du Halde, *Description . . . de la Chine* (Paris, 1735) made by SJ's colleague on the *Gentleman's Magazine*, William Guthrie, and one Green, and published by Edward Cave, 1738–41 (*Life*, II.483).

pleases us, because it flatters our self-love, by showing us that our opinions are approved by the general concurrence of mankind. Of these two pleasures, the first is more violent, the other more lasting; the first seems to partake more of instinct than reason, and is not easily to be explain'd, or defin'd; the latter has its foundation in good sense and re-flection, and evidently depends on the same principles with most human passions.

An attentive reader will frequently feel each of these agree-able emotions in the perusal of Du Halde. He will find a calm, peaceful satisfaction, when he reads the moral precepts, and wise instructions of the Chinese sages; he will find that virtue is in every place the same, and will look with new contempt on those wild reasoners,[3] who affirm that morality is merely ideal, and that the distinctions between good and ill are wholly chimerical.

But he will enjoy all the pleasure that novelty can afford, when he becomes acquainted with the Chinese government and constitution; he will be amazed to find that there is a country where nobility and knowledge are the same, where men advance in rank as they advance in learning, and promotion is the effect of virtuous industry,[4] where no man thinks ignorance a mark of greatness, or laziness the privilege of high birth.

His surprise will be still heightned by the relations he will there meet with of honest ministers, who, however in-credible it may seem, have been seen more than once in that monarchy, and have adventured to admonish the emperors of any deviation from the laws of their country, or any error in their conduct, that has endanger'd either their own safety, or the happiness of their people. He will read of emperors, who, when they have been address'd in this manner, have neither storm'd, nor threaten'd, nor kick'd their ministers, nor thought it majestick to be obstinate in the wrong;[5] but have, with a greatness of mind worthy of a Chinese monarch,

---

3. Perhaps Shaftesbury and his fol-lowers.

4. This refers to the elaborate Chi-nese system of examinations for public office.

5. George II's irascibility and stub-bornness were notorious; see Hervey, *Memoirs, passim.*

brought their actions willingly to the test of reason, law, and morality, and scorn'd to exert their power in defence of that which they could not support by argument.

I must confess my wonder at these relations was very great, and had been much greater, had I not often entertained my imagination with an instance of the like conduct in a prince of England, on an occasion that happened not quite a century ago, and which I shall relate, that so remarkable an example of spirit and firmness in a subject, and of conviction and compliance in a prince, may not be forgotten. And I hope you will look upon this letter as intended to do honour to my country, and not to serve your interest by promoting your undertaking.

The prince, at the christening of his first son, had appointed a noble duke to stand as proxy for the father of the princess,[6] without regard to the claim of a marquis, (heir apparent to a higher title) to whom, as lord of the bed-chamber then in waiting, that honour properly belong'd.—— The marquis was wholly unacquainted with the affair, till he heard at dinner the duke's health drank by the name of the prince he was that evening to represent. This he took an opportunity after dinner of enquiring the reason of, and was informed by the prince's treasurer[7] of his highness's intention. The marquis immediately declar'd, that he thought his right invaded, and his honour injur'd, which he could not bear without requiring satisfaction from the usurper of his privileges; nor would he longer serve a prince who paid no regard to his lawful pretensions. The treasurer could not deny that the marquis's claim was incontestable, and by his permission acquainted the prince with his resolution. The prince thereupon sending for the marquis demanded, with a resentful and imperious air, how he could dispute his commands, and by what authority he presumed to control him in the management of his own family, and the christening

---

6. Actually for Friedrich III, Duke of Saxe-Gotha-Altenburg, the brother of Augusta, Princess of Wales. Her father, Friedrich II, had died in 1732. Many of the London newspapers and magazines made this mistake in reporting the ceremony; the *Daily Advertiser* (23 June 1738), however, gives the relationship correctly.

7. Henry Arthur Herbert, later Earl of Powis.

of his own son. The marquis answered, that he did not
encroach upon the prince's right, but only defended his own:
that he thought his honour concern'd, and as he was a young
man, would not enter the world with the loss of his reputation.
The prince, exasperated to a very high degree, repeated his
commands; but the marquis, with a spirit and firmness not
to be depress'd or shaken, persisted in his determination to
assert his claim, and concluded with declaring that he would
do himself the justice that was denied him, and that not
the prince himself should trample on his character. He was
then order'd to withdraw, and the duke coming to him,
assured him, that the honour was offer'd him unask'd; that
when he accepted it, he was not informed of his lordship's
claim, and that now he very willingly resign'd it. The marquis
very gracefully acknowledg'd the civility of the duke's expressions, and declar'd himself satisfied with his grace's conduct; but thought it inconsistent with his honour to accept
the representation as a cession of the duke, or on any other
terms than as his own acknowledged right. The prince, being
inform'd of the whole conversation, and having upon enquiry
found all the precedents on the marquis's side, thought it
below his dignity to persist in an error, and restoring the
marquis to his right upon his own conditions, continued
him in his favour, believing that he might safely trust his
affairs in the hands of a man, who had so nice a sense of
honour, and so much spirit to assert it.

EUBULUS.

MARMOR NORFOLCIENSE. 1739.

Johnson's authorship of this piece was known to initiates soon after its publication: we find Pope writing to Jonathan Richardson, "Mr. Johnson published afterwards [i.e., after *London*] another poem in Latin with Notes the whole very Humerous call'd the Norfolk Prophecy." The English version of the poem seems to have led an underground existence for some decades. An adaptation of it printed in the *London Evening Post*, June 29–July 1, 1762, was said by its contributor to be "a prophecy found on a stone in Ridley-Poole, Cheshire, foretold by NIXON, who wrote the Cheshire prophecy . . . given to me in the year 1747 by a Friend." Like Johnson's it laments the enfeebled condition of Britain, and was no doubt intended as Pittite propaganda directed against Bute's peace negotiations with France and Spain. A different adaptation appeared in *The New Foundling Hospital for Wit* (1769), III, 29, entitled "Inscription found upon a stone ploughed up in a field in Devonshire, that was formerly a lake," and is likewise an attack on Bute: "A Scottish thane shall triumph in this land, / And English subjects die at his command."[1]

But it was not until 1775 that *Marmor Norfolciense* was publicly attributed to Johnson. In that year, as a riposte to Johnson's pamphleteering of the time, a political opponent who called himself "Tribunus"[2] reprinted it with a sarcastic dedication to Johnson, expressing wonder how that stalwart, pensioned supporter of the *status quo* could have been thought the writer of so inflammatory a "Republican" or "bloody Jacobite" tract (the adjectives are quoted from *Marmor* itself, p. oo below). It was included in the supplementary Volume XIV (1788) of Johnson's collected works (reprinted

1. I am indebted to Professor Helen Louise McGuffie for calling attention to the 1762 version. Although it appeared shortly before Johnson's pension was announced, it seems to contain no specific gibe against him. Indeed, one couplet, "On Belgia's shores shall British Hosts bestrewn, / Slain in her Feuds and Quarrels, not her own," makes it seem probable that it really was a production of 1747, when the British and allied forces were disastrously defeated at the Battle of Laffeldt in Belgium (as two years earlier at Fontenoy). No British troops were engaged in military operations in the Netherlands in 1762, or indeed at any time in the Seven Years' War. Robert Nixon, fl. 1620?, "the Cheshire prophet," was, as the *Concise DNB* puts it, "an idiot inspired at intervals to deliver oracular prophecies," which were published by John Oldmixon in 1714. The 1769 version seems anachronistic, for Bute had left office in 1763, never to return, though it was frequently insinuated that he still remained the power behind the throne. Of course, this version may have been reprinted in the *Foundling Hospital* from some earlier newspaper appearance.

2. Francis Webb (*DNB*).

from the 1775 version), and continued to appear in succeeding editions of the *Works*, with the usual accretion of textual error.

The pamphlet was first advertised for sale on 11 May 1739 (*Daily Advertiser*). Nothing is known of how Johnson came to write it, or the circumstances of its composition. Although some thrusts in it seem outdated for the spring of 1739—Italian opera (p. 31) had finally collapsed in London in the early months of 1738, and Queen Caroline (p. 31) had died in November 1737—references to the naval force under Haddock in the Mediterranean (p. 41) and to the convention of the Pardo, hotly debated in Parliament in March 1739 (p. 31), point to its having been written, or at least revised, not long before the date of publication. The famous story about the enraged government's issuing a warrant for Johnson's arrest and his having to "go underground" in Lambeth for a time is told by Hawkins (*Life*, p. 72), unfortunately with no indication of its source. In spite of a good deal of research, nothing has yet been uncovered to verify or support it. As J. L. Clifford points out (*Young Sam Johnson*, 1955, pp. 215–16), Brett, the printer of *Marmor*, was also the printer of the Opposition paper, *Common Sense*, and was taken into custody because of a passage in it two months before the appearance of Johnson's pamphlet.

The political prophecy, serious and satiric, has a long history in England, going back to the Middle Ages (see Rupert Taylor, *The Political Prophecy in England*, 1911). The same device as Johnson's, that of an old and cryptic rhyming inscription newly brought to light, was used by Swift in *The Windsor Prophecy* (1711) to chastise some of his political antagonists of the time. Both Swift and Johnson may well have owed some of their inspiration to Wharton's familiar song, the *Marseillaise* of the Revolution of 1688:

> There was a prophecy found in a bog,
> Lilliburlero, bullen a la!
> That we should be ruled by an ass and a hog,
> Lilliburlero, bullen a la!

Johnson adds to the fun by having a bumbling pedant of an antiquarian, an orthodox Walpolite, try to explicate the prophetic verses—this is essentially a Swiftian technique, the assumption of the mask of the seemingly well-intentioned but not very bright defender of what the author wishes to attack. Satire of antiquaries and classical scholars was a popular sport of the time—see *The Dunciad, passim*, and Johnson's own *Rambler* 82. The serious study of epigraphy had recently begun to flourish: the Royal Society's *Philosophical Transactions* and even the *Gentleman's Magazine* were carrying many reports of discoveries and interpretations of ancient inscriptions on stones, and publications like Selden's classic *Marmora Arundelliana* (1628), *Marmor Maffeianum* (1715), and *Marmora Pisaurensia* (1738) gave Johnson the title of his essay.

Opinions have varied about the effectiveness of the piece. Pope, we saw, found it "very humerous"; Hawkins, Hill, and others found it less so. Certainly when compared with Swift's great satirical essays (and Johnson's obvious aping of Swift—the dead pan, the mock logic, the long catalogues—makes it inevitable that it should be so compared), *Marmor* is not the same kind of thing at all: where Swift takes a comparatively small area of disease, and expertly and relentlessly probes every crevice of it with his scarifying needle, Johnson lustily lays about him with a bludgeon at everything in sight. Politically, *Marmor* is not very interesting; its targets are the commonplaces of opposition propaganda of the time (except that Johnson goes further than most of his contemporaries in insulting the King, and indeed kings in general). What holds the piece together and gives it genuine satiric merit is the wonderful psychological portrait of the commentator, a type of the closed mind, the smug, self-deceived scholarly hypocrite, the pseudo-intellectual who is really anti-intellectual, the apologist and beneficiary of authoritarianism. It suited Johnson, as well as Pope and Swift, to equate him with the Walpolite, but he is the universal and timeless enemy of truth and virtue. There is nothing superficial or unsubtle in the irony of such remarks (of the commentator's) as "that sobriety and modesty with which it becomes every learned man to treat a subject of such importance," "with what laborious struggles against prejudice and inclination, with what efforts of reasoning, and pertinacity of self-denial, I have prevailed upon myself to sacrifice the honour of this monument to the love of truth," "that great undertakings can only be executed by a great number of hands is too evident to require any proof." Johnson, in his dry Johnsonian way, can do as well as can Pope and Swift in theirs with this solemn and judicious ass, the eternal hierophant of the great goddess Dullness.

The prime authority for the text is the 1739 edition, which is followed here, except for the silent correction of a number of obvious misprints. The compositorial style of 1739 is somewhat old-fashioned: many spellings (e.g., "meer," "lyed," "remembred," "wast" for *waste*, "born" for *borne*) smack more of the seventeenth century than the eighteenth, as does frequent inconsistency in such matters as the use of *-ed* or *-'d* in the past tense of verbs, and of *-ic* or *-ick*. In keeping with the general editorial policy of this edition, such variations of spelling have been preserved.

Some years ago Dr. J. D. Fleeman discovered, in the Manchester Central Library, a copy of the 1739 edition with some marginal corrections in Johnson's (early) hand. The title page is inscribed, in another hand, "The Present of the Author, Mr S. J^n." According to the records of the Manchester Public Library, the copy was bought in 1864 or 1865 at the sale of the library of Charles Bradbury, who lived in The Crescent, Salford, and was described as "the eminent collector of antiquities and works of art." The work is not listed separately in the Bradbury sale catalogue, and no earlier owner has yet been traced. Most of the half-dozen marginal corrections are of obvious printer's errors, some of which were corrected in eighteenth- and nineteenth-century editions of the piece. One correction, however ("interpretation" for "inscription," p. 39), obvious though it seems when attention is called to it, escaped the earlier editors; and one ("calcatos" for "calceatos," pp. 24, 40) may, since "calceatos" appears twice in the text, be Johnson's error rather than the printer's, perhaps pointed out to Johnson after publication by some friend who was a better classicist. Johnson's marginal corrections have been incorporated in the text and signalled in the textual notes.

Marmor Norfolciense: Or an Essay on an Ancient
Prophetical Inscription, in Monkish Rhyme, Lately
Discover'd near Lynn in Norfolk. By Probus Britanicus

In Norfolk near the town of Lynn,[1] in a field which an
ancient tradition of the country affirms to have been once a
deep lake or meer, and which appears from authentick records
to have been call'd, about two hundred years ago, *Palus*, or
the Marsh, was discover'd not long since a large square stone,
which is found upon an exact inspection to be a kind of coarse
marble, of a substance not firm enough to admit of being
polish'd, yet harder than our common quarries afford, and
not easily susceptible of injuries from weather or outward
accidents.

It was brought to light by a farmer, who observing his
plough obstructed by something, through which the share
could not make its way, order'd his servants to remove it.
This was not effected without some difficulty, the stone being
three feet four inches deep, and four feet square in the super-
ficies, and consequently of a weight not easily manageable.
However, by the application of levers, it was at length raised,
and convey'd to a corner of the field, where it lay for some
months entirely unregarded: nor perhaps had we ever been
made acquainted with this venerable relique of antiquity, had
not our good fortune been greater than our curiosity.

A gentleman,[2] well known to the learned world, and distinguish'd by the patronage of the Maecenas of Norfolk,[3]
whose name, was I permitted to mention it, would excite the
attention of my reader, and add no small authority to my
conjectures, observing, as he was walking that way, that the

---

1. Except for a brief interval after
his expulsion from the House of Commons in 1712, Robert Walpole sat
as M.P. for Lynn Regis (King's Lynn)
from 1702 to 1742, virtually the whole
of his long political life. East Anglia
generally had a long-standing "Whig"
parliamentary tradition, and Norfolk
was the special preserve of the Wal-
poles and Townshends.

2. Perhaps the great Richard Bentley is glanced at—a good Whig, and
master of the most important college
in nearby, Whiggish Cambridge.

3. Walpole's alleged failure to encourage learning and the arts was a
charge frequently laid by his critics.
"Whose name" goes with "gentleman," not "Maecenas"—the latter
word being a satiric thrust at Walpole.

clouds began to gather and threaten him with a shower, had recourse for shelter to the trees under which this stone happen'd to lie, and sat down upon it in expectation of fair weather. At length he began to amuse himself in his confinement, by clearing the earth from his seat with the point of his cane; and had continued this employment some time, when he observed several traces of letters antique and irregular, which by being very deeply engraven were still easily distinguishable.

This discovery so far raised his curiosity, that going home immediately, he procured an instrument proper for cutting out the clay, that fill'd up the spaces of the letters, and with very little labour made the inscription legible, which is here exhibited to the public:

Post-Genitis.

Cum lapidem hunc, magni
Qui nunc jacet incola stagni,

Vel pede equus tanget,
Vel arator vomere franget,

Sentiet aegra metus,
Effundet patria fletus,

Littoraque ut fluctu,
Resonabunt oppida luctu:

Nam foecunda rubri
Serpent per prata colubri,

Gramina vastantes,
Flores fructusque vorantes,

Omnia foedantes,
Vitiantes, et spoliantes;

Quanquam haud pugnaces,
Ibunt per cuncta minaces,

Fures absque timore,
Et pingues absque labore.

Horrida dementes
Rapiet discordia gentes,

Plurima tunc leges
Mutabit, plurima reges

Natio, conversâ
In rabiem tunc contremet ursâ

Cynthia, tunic latis
Florebunt lilia pratis,

Nec fremere audebit
Leo, sed violare timebit,

Omnia consuetus
Populari pascua laetus.

Ante oculos natos
Calcatos⁴ et cruciatos

Jam feret ignavus,
Vetitâque libidine pravus.

En quoque quod mirum,
Quod dicas denique dirum,

Sanguinem equus sugit,
Neque bellua victa remugit.

These lines he carefully copy'd, accompanied in his letter
of July 19, with the following translation:

To Posterity.

Whene'er this stone, now hid beneath the lake,
The horse shall trample, or the plough shall break,

---

4. Printed *calceatos* in 1739; in the Manchester copy *cea* is underlined and *ca* is written in the margin in SJ's hand. Nichol Smith and McAdam (*Poems of Samuel Johnson*, 1941, p. 110) emended *"calceatos"* to *"calcatos"* on conjecture. In classical Latin, *calceatos* can only mean "shod," not "trampled." This, however, is "monkish" Latin, and perhaps some show of argument can be made for mediaeval contamina-

tion of *calco* by *calceo*. Gildas, *De Excidio Britanniae*, which SJ might have read, seems to use *calciant* in the meaning of classical *calcant* (Migne, *Patrologia Latina*, LXXIX.363). The editors of Vol. VI in the Yale Edition of Johnson's *Works* were persuaded (ironically, by the present editor) to restore *calceatos*. However, it now appears that SJ was persuaded to change *his* mind. See also headnote, p. 21, and p. 40, note h.

Then, O my country! shalt thou groan distrest,
Grief swell thine eyes, and terror chill thy breast.
Thy streets with violence of woe shall sound,
Loud as the billows bursting on the ground.
Then thro' thy fields shall scarlet reptiles stray,
And rapine and pollution mark their way.
Their hungry swarms the peaceful vale shall fright
Still fierce to threaten, still afraid to fight;
The teeming year's whole product shall devour,
Insatiate pluck the fruit, and crop the flow'r:
Shall glutton on the industrious peasants[5] spoil,
Rob without fear, and fatten without toil.
Then o'er the world shall Discord stretch her wings,
Kings change their laws, and kingdoms change their kings.
The bear enrag'd th' affrighted moon shall dread;
The lilies o'er the vales triumphant spread;
Nor shall the lyon, wont of old to reign
Despotic o'er the desolated plain,
Henceforth th' inviolable bloom invade,
Or dare to murmur in the flow'ry glade;
His tortur'd sons shall die before his face,
While he lies melting in a lewd embrace;
And, yet more strange! his veins a horse shall drain,
Nor shall the passive coward once complain.

I make not the least doubt, but that this learned person has
given us, as an antiquary, a true and uncontrovertible representation of the writer's meaning, and am sure he can confirm it by innumerable quotations from the authors of the
middle age, should he be publickly call'd upon by any man
of eminent rank in the republic of letters; nor will he deny the
world that satisfaction, provided the animadverter proceeds
with that sobriety and modesty, with which it becomes every
learned man to treat a subject of such importance.

---

5. When this line is repeated on p.
35 below, the reading is "peasant's."
But "peasants" (without an apos-
trophe) is SJ's normal, perhaps in-
variable, form of the possessive plural,
and it is difficult to say which of the
two variant readings he intended. Reprints of the verses in the *Gentleman's
Magazine*, IX (May 1739), 269, and
June, p. 324, and in the *London Magazine*, IX (1739), 244, read "peasant's."

Yet with all proper deference to a name so justly celebrated, I will take the freedom of observing that he has succeeded better as a scholar than a poet; having fallen below the strength, the conciseness, and at the same time below the perspicuity of his author. I shall not point out the particular passages in which this disparity is remarkable, but content myself with saying in general, that the criticisms, which there is room for on this translation, may be almost an incitement to some lawyer, studious of antiquity, to learn Latin.

The inscription which I now proceed to consider, wants no arguments to prove its antiquity to those among the learned, who are versed in the writers of the darker ages, and know that the Latin poetry of those times was of a peculiar cast and air, not easy to be understood, and very difficult to be imitated, nor can it be conceived that any man would lay out his abilities on a way of writing, which though attain'd with much study could gain him no reputation, and engrave his chimaeras on a stone to astonish posterity.

Its antiquity therefore is out of dispute, but how high a degree of antiquity is to be assign'd it, there is more ground for enquiry than determination. How early Latin rhymes made their appearance in the world is yet undecided by the critics. Verses of this kind were call'd Leonine; but whence they derived that appellation the learned Camden confesses himself ignorant,[6] so that the stile carries no certain marks of its age. I shall only observe farther on this head, that the characters are nearly of the same form with those on King Arthur's coffin,[7] but whether from their similitude we may venture to pronounce them of the same date, I must refer to the decision of better judges.

Our inability to fix the age of this inscription necessarily infers our ignorance of its author, with relation to whom many controversies may be started worthy of the most profound learning, and most indefatigable diligence.

The first question that naturally arises is, Whether he was

---

6. *1788* refers to *Remains* (1614), p. 337.

7. Camden, *Remains* (1674, p. 479, section on "Epitaphs"), tells the story of the accidental unearthing, at Glastonbury during the Middle Ages, of the coffin, which bore a Latin inscription.

a Briton or a Saxon. I had at first conceived some hope, that in this question, in which not only the idle curiosity of virtuosos, but the honour of two mighty nations is concerned, some information might be drawn from the word *patria*, (my country) in the third line; England being not in propriety of speech the country of the Saxons; at least not at their first arrival. But upon farther reflection this argument appear'd not conclusive, since we find that in all ages, foreigners have affected to call England their country, even when like the Saxons of old they came only to plunder it.

An argument in favour of the Britons, may indeed be drawn from the tenderness, with which the author seems to lament his country, and the compassion he shows for its approaching calamities. I, who am a descendant from the Saxons, and therefore unwilling to say any thing derogatory from the reputation of my forefathers, must yet allow this argument its full force: for it has been rarely, very rarely, known that foreigners however well treated, caressed, enriched, flatter'd or exalted, have regarded this country with the least gratitude or affection,[8] till the race has by long continuance, after many generations, been naturaliz'd and assimilated.

They have been ready upon all occasions to prefer the petty interests of their own country, though perhaps only some desolate and worthless corner of the world.[9] They have employ'd the wealth of England, in paying troops to defend mud-wall towns, and uninhabitable rocks, and in purchasing barriers[1] for territories of which the natural sterility secured them from invasion.

This argument, which wants no particular instances to

---

8. A traditional Opposition complaint. See Macaulay, *History of England*, Ch. XI and elsewhere, for the outcries against William III as a Dutchman. The first two Georges were often similarly regarded as outsiders.

9. The Opposition's stock description of Hanover.

1. In 1715, George I, as Elector of Hanover, purchased from Denmark the duchies of Bremen and Verden, in order to bolster the defences of the electorate. The maintenance of Hanover's possession of these territories was an element in his and his son's diplomacy, and British arms were used to enforce it. See W. Michael, *Englische Geschichte im achtzehnten Jahrhundert* (5 vols., 1896–1955), Vol. I, Ch. XI, and John J. Murray, *George I, the Baltic, and the Whig Split of 1717* (1969).

confirm it, is, I confess, of the greatest weight in this question, and inclines me strongly to believe that the benevolent author of this prediction must have been *born a Briton*.[2]

The learned discoverer of the inscription was pleased to insist with great warmth upon the etymology of the word *patria*, which signifying, says he, "the land of my father," could be made use of by none, but such whose ancestors had resided here: but in answer to this demonstration, as he call'd it, I only desired him to take notice, how common it is for intruders of yesterday, to pretend the same title with the ancient proprietors, and having just received an estate by voluntary grant, to erect a claim of "hereditary right."[3]

Nor is it less difficult to form any satisfactory conjecture, concerning the rank or condition of the writer, who contented with a consciousness of having done his duty, in leaving this solemn warning to his country, seems studiously to have avoided that veneration, to which his knowledge of futurity undoubtedly entitled him, and those honours which his memory might justly claim from the gratitude of posterity, and has therefore left no trace, by which the most sagacious and diligent enquirer can hope to discover him.

This conduct alone ought to convince us, that the prediction is of no small importance to mankind, since the author of it appears not to have been influenced by any other motive, than that noble and exalted philanthropy, which is above the narrow views of recompense or applause.

That interest had no share in this inscription, is evident beyond dispute, since the age in which he lived received neither pleasure nor instruction from it. Nor is it less apparent

---

2. A polemic word, part of the "patriot" vocabulary. Cf. Thomson's "Britons never will be slaves" (1740) and George III's accession speech, "Born and educated in this country, I glory in the name of Britain [?Briton]." SJ's pseudonym "Probus Britannicus" is politically significant.

3. The "hereditary right" of the Hanoverian dynasty was defective, in that not only the descendants of James II but also those of Charles I (through his daughter Henrietta, Duchesse d'Orléans) and of the older brothers and sisters of the Electress Sophia had been passed over, on account of their Roman Catholicism. When George I ascended the throne in 1714, "it was to the exclusion of some fifty-seven relatives with better hereditary titles" (Michael, I. 1). The Hanoverians thus owed their possession of the throne, strictly speaking, to the "voluntary grant" of the Act of Settlement, 1701.

from the suppression of his name, that he was equally a stranger to that wild desire of fame, which has sometimes infatuated the noblest minds.

His modesty, however, has not been able wholly to extinguish that curiosity, which so naturally leads us, when we admire a performance, to enquire after the author. Those whom I have consulted on this occasion, and my zeal for the honour of this benefactor of my country has not suffer'd me to forget a single antiquary of reputation, have almost unanimously determined, that it was written by a king. For where else, said they, are we to expect that greatness of mind, and that dignity of expression, so eminently conspicuous in this inscription.

It is with a proper sense of the weakness of my own abilities, that I venture to lay before the public, the reasons which hinder me from concurring with this opinion, which I am not only inclined to favour by my respect for the authors of it, but by a natural affection to monarchy, and a prevailing inclination to believe that every excellence is inherent in a king.

To condemn an opinion so agreeable to the reverence due to the regal dignity, and countenanced by so great authorities, without a long and accurate discussion, would be a temerity justly liable to the severest censures. A supercilious and arrogant determination of a controversy of such importance, would doubtless be treated by the impartial and candid with the utmost indignation.

But as I have too high an idea of the learning of my contemporaries, to obtrude any crude hasty or indigested notions on the public, I have proceeded with the utmost degree of diffidence and caution, I have frequently review'd all my arguments, traced them backwards to their first principles, and used every method of examination to discover whether all the deductions were natural and just, and whether I was not imposed on by some specious fallacy; but the farther I carried my enquiries, and the longer I dwelt upon this great point, the more was I convinced, in spite of all my prejudices, that this wonderful prediction was not written by a king.

For after a laborious and attentive perusal of histories, memoirs, chronicles, lives, characters, vindications, pane-

gyricks and epitaphs, I could find no sufficient authority for
ascribing to any of our English monarchs, however gracious
or glorious,[4] any prophetical knowledge or prescience of
futurity. Which, when we consider how rarely regal virtues
are forgotten, how soon they are discover'd, and how loudly
they are celebrated, affords a probable argument at least,
that none of them have laid any claim to this character. For
why should historians have omitted to embellish their accounts
with such a striking circumstance, or if the histories of that
age are lost by length of time, why was not so uncommon an
excellence transmitted to posterity in the more lasting colours
of poetry. Was that unhappy age without a Laureat? Was
there then no Young or Philips? no Ward or Mitchel[5] to
snatch such wonders from oblivion, and immortalize a prince
of such capacities? If this was really the case, let us congratulate
ourselves upon being reserved for better days, days so fruitful
of happy writers, that no princely virtue can shine in vain.
Our monarchs are surrounded with refined spirits, so penetrating that they frequently discover in their masters great
qualities invisible to vulgar eyes, and which, did not they
publish them to mankind, would be unobserved for ever.

   Nor is it easy to find in the lives of our monarchs many
instances of that regard for posterity, which seems to have
been[a] the prevailing temper of this venerable man. I have

a. *om.* 1739

4. It is probably only an amusing
coincidence that the phraseology of
this sneer echoes that of the modern
text of the National Anthem: both
adjectives were used over and over
again in royal panegyrics—e.g., in
Cibber's official odes. Still, the early
history of "God Save the King" is
obscure, and the latest editor of Henry
Carey's poems (Frederick T. Wood,
1930, p. 253) ventures to suggest that
"it was composed by Carey in the
heat of an anti-Spanish fervour in
1739." Early printed versions give the
first line as "God save great George,
our King": the provenance of the
variant "our gracious King" seems to
be unknown, but it could conceivably

be early. During the early decades of
its life, the song was regarded as
government propaganda. Thomson's
"Rule, Britannia" (1740) was the opposing, "patriot" song.

   5. *1788* identifies Edward Young,
Ambrose Philips, Edward Ward, and
Joseph Mitchell. Perhaps only Mitchell, known as "Sir Robert Walpole's
poet," is a really happy choice. Young
and Philips, whose lives SJ later included in his collection, were by no
means contemptible, for all their
staunch support of Walpole; and
"Ned Ward of Grub Street" was, in
his early career at least, violently
anti-Whig.

seldom in any of the gracious speeches delivered from the throne, and received with the highest gratitude and satisfaction by both Houses of Parliament, discover'd any other concern than for the current year, for which supplies are generally demanded in very pressing terms, and sometimes such as imply no remarkable solicitude for posterity.[6]

Nothing indeed can be more unreasonable and absurd, than to require that a monarch, distracted with cares and surrounded with enemies, should involve himself in superfluous anxieties by an unnecessary concern about future generations. Are not pretenders, mock-patriots, masquerades, operas, birth-nights, treaties, conventions, reviews, drawing-rooms, the births of heirs, and the deaths of queens,[7] sufficient to overwhelm any capacity but that of a king? Surely he that acquits himself successfully of such affairs, may content himself with the glory he acquires, and leave posterity to his successors.

That this has been the conduct of most princes, is evident

---

6. The annual Speech from the Throne, in which the government announces its legislative plans for the session of Parliament just beginning, continues to be composed in a style of dry, formal understatement. It is perhaps a sign of SJ's political inexperience that he should make such a point of its traditional limitations. The fulsome language of the formal Addresses of Thanks for the speech is equally conventional.

7. Public masquerade balls, a current fad, were much denounced as contributing to immorality (see *London*, l. 29). Opera was involved in politics, with the King supporting Handel's company and the Prince of Wales supporting Porpora's (later Hasse's), but SJ's quip is outdated, both projects having collapsed a year or two earlier; most Englishmen, like SJ himself, still regarded it as "exotick" (i.e., foreign) and "irrational." Birth-nights (on the evening of the King's birthday) and drawing-rooms

were formal royal receptions. The Convention of the Pardo, signed 14 Jan 1739, between Britain and Spain, was the subject of much debate in and out of Parliament. Great scandal was caused when, on 31 July 1737, the Prince of Wales bundled his pregnant wife into a coach and fled from his father's supervision at Hampton Court to St. James's Palace, where the Princess was hurriedly delivered of their first child. Lord Hervey, *Memoirs*, gives all the political and obstetrical detail. The reference to the death of Queen Caroline (20 Nov 1737) seems callous; but it may well be directed at George's crudity in bringing his Hanoverian mistress, Amalie Wallmoden, to England in June 1738 (see pp. 5f. above). Perhaps the inclusion of pretenders and mock-patriots in this list of "trivia" may indicate that SJ considered neither the Jacobites nor the Pittites as worthy of serious consideration.

from the accounts of all ages and nations,[8] and therefore I hope it will not be thought that I have, without just reasons, deprived this inscription of the veneration it might demand as the work of a king.

With what laborious struggles against prejudice and inclination, with what[b] efforts of reasoning, and pertinacity of self-denial, I have prevailed upon myself to sacrifice the honour of this monument to the love of truth, none who are unacquainted with the fondness of a commentator will be able to conceive. But this instance will be, I hope, sufficient to convince the public that I write with sincerity, and that whatever my success may be, my intentions are good.

Where we are to look for our author it still remains to be considered, whether in the high road of public employments, or the by-paths of private life.

It has always been observed of those that frequent a court, that they soon, by a kind of contagion, catch the regal spirit of neglecting futurity. The minister forms an expedient to suspend or perplex an enquiry into his measures for a few months,[9] and applauds and triumphs in his own dexterity. The peer puts off his creditor for the present day, and forgets that he is ever to see him more. The frown of a prince, and the loss of a pension have indeed been found of wonderful efficacy, to abstract men's thoughts from the present time, and fill them with zeal for the liberty and welfare of ages to come.[1] But I am inclined to think more favourably of the author of

b. what emend.] that 1739

---

8. This comprehensive sarcasm, coupled with other remarks in his later writings, could be cited to show that SJ was by no means the devotee of monarchism that legend makes him out to be. See, e.g., the "Memoirs of the King of Prussia" (1756–57) and the entry "Kings" in Life, index.

9. The most notorious example was in connexion with Lord Bathurst's motion (Feb 1733) for an inquiry into the affairs of the South Sea Company. It was actually passed by the House of Lords, against the government's

wishes; but Walpole and Newcastle deftly manoeuvred so as to stifle any real investigation. A more recent incident was Samuel Sandys's motion, in 1738, for the production to the House of Commons of the government's secret instructions to governors, military commanders, and diplomatic agents relating to the alleged Spanish depredations. It was defeated.

1. Most of the leaders of the opposition to Walpole had formerly held some public office or sinecure and been dismissed: e.g., Pulteney's name

this prediction, than that he was made a patriot by disappointment or disgust. If he ever saw a court, I would willingly believe, that he did not owe his concern for posterity to his ill reception there, but his ill reception there to his concern for posterity.

However, since truth is the same in the mouth of a hermit, or a prince, since it is not reason but weakness, that makes us rate counsel by our esteem for the counsellor, let us at length desist from this enquiry, so useless in itself, in which we have room to hope for so little satisfaction. Let us show our gratitude to the author, by answering his intentions, by considering minutely the lines which he has left us, and examining their import without heat, precipitancy, or party-prejudices, let us endeavour to keep the just mean, between searching ambitiously for far-fetched interpretations, and admitting such low meaning, and obvious sense,ᶜ as is inconsistent with those great and extensive views, which it is reasonable to ascribe to this excellent man.

It may be yet farther asked, whether this inscription, which appears in the stone be an original, and not rather a version of a traditional prediction in the old British tongue, which the zeal of some learned man prompted him to translate and engrave in a more known language for the instruction of future ages, but as the lines carry at the first view a reference both to the stone itself, and very remarkably to the place where it was found, I cannot see any foundation for such a suspicion.

It remains now that we examine the sense and import of the inscription, which, after having long dwelt upon it with the closest and most laborious attention, I must confess myself not yet able fully to comprehend. The following explications therefore are by no means lay'd down as certain and indubitable truths, but as conjectures not always wholly satisfactory even to myself, and which I had not dar'd to

---

c. obvious sense] obvious and low sense *1739;* and low *deleted Manchester copy*

---

was struck from the list of Privy Councillors in 1731, Chesterfield was dismissed as Lord Steward in 1733, Pitt was deprived of his army commission in 1736. This sarcasm against the Whig "mock-patriots" should be noted: SJ is opposing Walpole, not as a disaffected Whig, but as a Tory.

propose to so enlightned an age, an age which abounds with
those great ornaments of human nature, sceptics, anti-
moralists and infidels, but with hopes that they would excite
some person of greater abilities, to penetrate farther into the
oraculous obscurity of this wonderful prediction.

Not even the four first lines are without their difficulties, in
which the time of the discovery of the stone seems to be the
time assigned for the events foretold by it.

> *Cum lapidem hunc, magni*
> *Qui nunc jacet incola stagni,*
>
> *Vel pede equus tanget,*
> *Vel arator vomere franget,*
>
> *Sentiet aegra metus,*
> *Effundet patria fletus,*
>
> *Littoraque ut fluctu,*
> *Resonabunt oppida luctu.*

> Whene'er this stone, now hid beneath the lake,
> The horse shall trample, or the plough shall break,
> Then, O my country! shalt thou groan distrest,
> Grief in thine eyes, and terror in thy breast.
> Thy streets with violence of woe shall sound,
> Loud as the billows bursting on the ground.

"When this stone," says he, "which now lyes hid beneath
the waters of a deep lake, shall be struck upon by the horse, or
broken by the plough, then shalt thou, my country, be astonish'd with terrors, and drown'd in tears, then shall thy
towns sound with lamentations, as thy shores with the roarings
of the waves." These are the words literally render'd, but how
are they verified? The lake is dry, the stone is turned up, but
there is no appearance of this dismal scene. Is not all at home
satisfaction and tranquillity? all abroad submission and compliance? Is it the interest or inclination of any prince or state
to draw a sword against us? and are we not nevertheless
secured by a numerous standing army, and a king who is
himself an army? Have our troops any other employment than

to march to a review? Have our fleets encounter'd any thing
but winds and worms? To me the present state of the nation
seems so far from any resemblance to the noise and agitation of
a tempestuous sea, that it may be much more properly compared to the dead stillness of the waves before a storm.

> *Nam foecunda rubri*
> *Serpent per prata colubri,*
>
> *Gramina vastantes,*
> *Flores fructusque vorantes,*
>
> *Omnia foedantes,*
> *Vitiantes, et spoliantes;*
>
> *Quanquam haud pugnaces,*
> *Ibunt per cuncta minaces,*
>
> *Fures absque timore,*
> *Et pingues absque labore.*

Then thro' thy fields shall scarlet reptiles stray,
And rapine and pollution mark their way.
Their hungry swarms the peaceful vale shall fright,
Still fierce to threaten, still afraid to fight;
The teeming year's whole product shall devour,
Insatiate pluck the fruit, and crop the flow'r:
Shall glutton on the industrious peasant's spoil,
Rob without fear, and fatten without toil.

He seems, in these verses to descend to a particular account
of this dreadful calamity; but his description is capable of
very different senses with almost equal probability.

"Red serpents," says he, (*rubri colubri* are the Latin words,
which the poetical translator has render'd "scarlet reptiles,"
using a general term for a particular, in my opinion too
licentiously.) "Red serpents shall wander o'er her meadows,
and pillage and pollute," &c. The particular mention of the
colour of this destructive viper may be some guide to us in this
labyrinth, through which, I must acknowledge, I cannot yet
have any certain path. I confess that when a few days after
my perusal of this passage, I heard of the multitude of lady-

birds[2] seen in Kent, I began to imagine that these were the fatal insects, by which the island was to be laid wast, and therefore look'd over all accounts of them with uncommon concern. But when my first terrors began to subside, I soon recollected that these creatures, having both wings and feet, would scarcely have been called serpents; and was quickly convinced, by their leaving the country without doing any hurt, that they had no quality, but the colour, in common with the ravagers here described.

As I am not able to determine any thing on this question, I shall content myself with collecting, into one view, the several properties of this pestiferous brood,[3] with which we are threatened, as hints to more sagacious and fortunate readers. Who when they shall find any "red animal" that ranges uncontrouled over the country and devours the labours of the trader, and the husbandman; that carries with it corruption, rapine, pollution and devastation; that threatens without courage, robs without fear, and is pamper'd without labour, they[4] may know that the prediction is compleated. Let me only remark farther, that if the stile of this as of all other predictions is figurative, the serpent, a wretched animal that crawls upon the earth, is a proper emblem of low views, self-interest, and base submission,[5] as well as of cruelty, mischief, and malevolence.

I cannot forbear to observe in this place, that as it is of no advantage to mankind to be forewarned of inevitable and insurmountable misfortunes, the author probably intended to hint to his countrymen the proper remedies for the evils he describes. In this calamity on which he dwells longest,

---

2. Or (American) lady-bugs, i.e., red-coated insects. I have not found any other reference to this phenomenon.

3. The red-coated soldiers of the regular ("standing") army—an object of the Tories' detestation since the days of Cromwell. In Feb 1738 William Shippen had moved, and Pulteney supported, the reduction of the number of troops authorized from 17,400 to 12,000 (*Parliamentary History,* IX.375-467).

4. Grammar would require the deletion of this pronoun.

5. In *1739* the sentence reads "low views and self-interest base submission"; this is corrected in SJ's hand in the Manchester copy; the correction was also made by the editor of *1788.*

and which he seems to deplore with the deepest sorrow, he points out one circumstance, which may be of great use to disperse our apprehensions, and awaken us from that panick which the reader must necessarily feel, at the first transient view of this dreadful description. These serpents, says the original, are *haud pugnaces*, "of no fighting race": they will threaten, indeed, and hiss, and terrify the weak, and timorous, and thoughtless, but have no real courage or strength. So that the mischief done by them, their ravages, devastations and robberies, must be only the consequences of cowardice in the sufferers, who are harrassed and oppressed only because they suffer it without resistance. We are therefore to remember whenever the pest here threatned shall invade us, that submission and tameness will be certain ruin, and that nothing but spirit, vigilance, activity, and opposition can preserve us from the most hateful and reproachful misery, that of being plundered, starved, and devoured by vermin and by reptiles.

> *Horrida dementes*
> *Rapiet discordia gentes,*
>
> *Plurima tunc leges*
> *Mutabit, plurima reges*
>
> *Natio,*

Then o'er the world shall discord stretch her wings
Kings change their laws, and kingdoms change their kings

Here the author takes a general survey of the state of the world, and the changes that were to happen about the time of the discovery of this monument in many nations. As it is not likely that he intended to touch upon the affairs of other countries any farther than the advantage of his own made it necessary, we may reasonably conjecture, that he had a full and distinct view of all the negotiations, treaties, confederacies, of all the triple and quadruple alliances,[6] and

---

6. The Triple Alliance, 1717, of Britain, France, and Holland (enlarged by the addition of Austria in 1718) was the foundation of British foreign policy in the early part of the eighteenth century.

all the leagues offensive and defensive, in which we were to be engaged, either as principals, accessaries, or guarrantes,[7] whether by policy, or hope, or fear, or our concern for preserving the *Ballance of Power*,[8] or our tenderness for the liberties of Europe. He knew that our negotiators would interest us in the affairs of the whole earth, and that no state could either rise or decline in power, either extend or lose its dominions, without affecting our[d] politics and influencing our councels.

This passage will bear an easy and natural application to the present time, in which so many revolutions have happened, so many nations have changed their masters,[9] and so many disputes and commotions are embroiling almost every[e] part of the world.

That almost every state in Europe and Asia, that is, almost every country then known is comprehended in this prediction may be easily conceived, but whether it extends to regions at that[f] time undiscovered, and portends any alteration of government in Carolina and Georgia,[1] let more able or more daring expositors determine.

———*Conversâ*
In rabiem tunc contremet ursâ

Cynthia,

d. *om. 1739; inserted in SJ's hand Manchester copy*   e. almost every] almost in every *1739; corrected Manchester copy*   f. *om. 1739; inserted in SJ's hand Manchester copy*

---

7. *1775* and *1788* emend to "guarantees." But this is an older spelling of the word: see *OED* ("guarantee," sb. 1).

8. I retain *1739*'s sarcastic italics. The expression was comparatively new and Whiggish. Smollett says (*History of England*, 1757-58, Book II, Ch. 3) that "old Horace" Walpole, Sir Robert's ambassador to Paris and The Hague, was "termed, in derision, 'the balance master'."

9. Within a space of fifty years, Europe was embroiled in the Wars of the Successions to the Spanish, Polish, and Austrian thrones. Also involved in the diplomacy of the time were changes in the dynasties ruling Lorraine, Tuscany, Parma, and the Two Sicilies, as well as the deposition of James II and his heirs from the English throne.

1. The seditious innuendo in the choice of these two names is easily discovered. Its cleverness is somewhat diminished by the fact that Queen Caroline had died a year and a half before. The status of the colonies of Georgia and Carolina was, however, being discussed early in 1739, since it was affected by the Convention of the Pardo (see Lord Egmont, *Diary*, Feb and Mar 1739).

Apprehenfions raifed in the *Turkifh* Empire, of which a Crefcent or new Moon is the imperial Standard, by the increafing Power of the Emprefs of *Ruffia*, whofe Dominions lie under the Northern Conftellation called the *Bear*.

—— *Tunc latis*
Florebunt Lilia Pratis,

The Lilies o'er the Vales triumphant fpread;

The Lillies borne by the Kings of *France* are an apt Reprefentation of that Country; and their flourifhing over wide extended Valleys, feems to regard the new Increafe of the *French* Power, Wealth and Dominions, by the Advancement of their Trade, and the Acceffion of *Lorain*. This is at the firft View an obvious, but perhaps for that very Reafon not the true Infcription. How can we reconcile it with the following Paffage.

Nec fremere audebit
Leo, fed violare timebit,
Omnia confuetus
Populari Pafcua lætus.   Nor

A page from *Marmor Norfolciense,* with a correction in Johnson's hand. Courtesy of The Manchester Public Libraries.

The bear enrag'd, th' affrighted moon shall dread;

The terror created to the moon by the anger of the bear, is a strange expression, but may perhaps relate to the apprehensions raised in the Turkish empire, of which a crescent or new moon is the imperial standard, by the increasing power of the Empress of Russia,[2] whose dominions lie under the northern constellation called the Bear.

——*Tunc latis*
Florebunt lilia pratis,

The lilies o'er the vales triumphant spread;

The lillies borne by the kings of France are an apt representation of that country; and their flourishing over wide extended valleys, seems to regard the new increase of the French power, wealth and dominions, by the advancement of their trade, and the accession of Lorain.[3] This is at the first view an obvious, but perhaps for that very reason not the true interpretation.[g] How can we reconcile it with the following passage.

Nec fremere audebit
Leo, sed violare timebit,

Omnia consuetus
Populari pascua laetus.

Nor shall the lyon, wont of old to reign
Despotic o'er the desolated plain,
Henceforth th' inviolable bloom invade,
Or dare to murmur in the flow'ry glade;

g. inscription *1739;* corrected in *SJ's* hand *Manchester copy*

---

2. Anna Ivanovna (reigned 1730–40), niece of Peter the Great. In June 1737, the Russians inflicted a serious defeat on the Turks at Ochakov, and peace was being negotiated. SJ probably brings this in merely to satirize the extent (and, in his opinion, unimportance) of Britain's far-flung "entangling alliances." He later made fun of Mrs. Salusbury's concern over Polish, Russian, and Turkish affairs (*Miscellanies*, I.235; II.391–2).

3. Ceded to France in 1735, in exchange for Tuscany, by Francis, Duke of Lorraine, later Emperor Francis I, husband of Maria Theresa.

In which the lyon that used at pleasure to lay the pastures waste, is represented as not daring to touch the lillies, or murmur at their growth: the lyon, 'tis true, is one of the supporters of the arms of England, and may therefore figure our countrymen, who have in ancient times made France a desert. But can it be said, that the lyon dares not murmur or rage (for *fremere* may import both) when it is evident, that for many years this whole kingdom has murmur'd! however, it may be at present calm and secure, by its confidence in the wisdom of our politicians and the address of our negotiators.

Ante oculos natos
Calcatos[h] *et cruciatos*

Jam feret ignavus,
Vetitâque libidine pravus.

His tortur'd sons shall die before his face,
While he lies melting in a lewd embrace;

Here are other things mentioned of the lyon equally unintelligible, if we suppose them to be spoken of our nation, as that he[i] lies sluggish, and depraved with unlawful lusts,[4] while his off-spring is trampled and tortur'd before his eyes.[5] But in what[j] place can the English be said to be trampled or tortur'd? Where are they treated with injustice or contempt? What nation is there from pole to pole that does not reverence the nod of the British king? Is not our commerce

h. calcatos] calceatos *1739;* cea *underlined and* ca *written in margin in SJ's hand Manchester copy* (see p. 24, n. 4)   i. he *emend.*] she *1739*   j. what *emend.*] that *1739*

---

4. George II's liaison with Amalie von Wallmoden, later created Countess of Yarmouth, caused much scandal (see pp. 5f. above).

5. Captain Robert Jenkins of the brig *Rebecca* testified before a House of Commons investigating committee in Mar 1738 that his ship had been boarded and his ear cut off by a Spanish *guarda costa* in 1731. There were numerous other such atrocity stories, much publicized by the opposition.

unrestrained? Are not the riches of the world our own? Do not our ships sail unmolested, and our merchants traffick in perfect security? Is not the very name of England treated by foreigners in a manner never known before? Or if some slight injuries have been offered, if some of our petty traders have been stopped, our possessions threaten'd, our effects confiscated, our flag insulted, or our ears crop'd, have we lain sluggish and unactive? have not our fleets been seen in triumph at Spithead? Did not Hosier visit the Bastimentos, and is not Haddock now stationed at Port Mahon?[6]

> *En quoque quod mirum,*
> *Quod dicas denique dirum,*
>
> *Sanguinem equus sugit,*
> *Neque bellua victa remugit.*

And, yet more strange! his veins a horse shall drain,
Nor shall the passive coward once complain.

It is farther asserted in the concluding lines, that the horse shall suck the lyon's blood. This is still more obscure than any of the rest, and indeed the difficulties I have met with ever since the first mention of the lyon are so many and great, that I had, in utter despair of surmounting them, once desisted from my design of publishing any thing upon this subject; but was prevailed upon by the importunity of some friends, to whom I can deny nothing, to resume my design; and I must own that nothing animated me so much as the hope they

---

6. Spithead, off Portsmouth, is the usual scene of naval displays and reviews. In Mar 1726, Vice-Admiral Francis Hosier led a naval expedition to the Caribbean, to blockade the Spanish stronghold of Portobello in Panama. In two years, some 4,000 British sailors, including Hosier himself, fell victim to disease. Richard ("Leonidas") Glover, a stalwart "patriot" poet, lamented the disaster and deplored the government's maladministration in the popular ballad "Hosier's Ghost." Admiral Nicholas Haddock was sent, in May 1738, to patrol the coast of Spain with a naval squadron—an ineffective move, in the Opposition's opinion. The island of Bastimentos is off Panama. Port Mahon, in Minorca, then a British possession, was the chief British naval base in the Mediterranean.

flatter'd me with, that my essay might be inserted in the
Gazetteer,[7] and so become of service to my country.

That a weaker animal should suck the blood of a stronger
without resistance is wholly improbable and inconsistent with
the regard for self-preservation, so observable in every order
and species of beings. We must therefore necessarily endeavour
after some figurative sense not liable to so insuperable an
objection.

Were I to proceed in the same tenour of interpretation, by
which I explained the moon and the lilies, I might observe
that a horse is born in the arms of H——.[8] But how then does
the horse suck the lyon's blood? Money is the blood of the
body politic. —— But my zeal for the present happy establishment will not suffer me to pursue a train of thought that
leads to such shocking conclusions. The idea is detestable,
and such as, it ought to be hoped, can enter into the mind of
none but a virulent Republican, or bloody Jacobite. There is
not one honest man in the nation unconvinced how weak an
attempt it would be to endeavour to confute this insinuation.
An insinuation which no party will dare to abet, and of so
fatal and destructive a tendency, that it may prove equally
dangerous to the author whether true or false.

As therefore I can form no hypothesis on which a consistent
interpretation may be built, I must leave these loose and
unconnected hints entirely to the candour of the reader, and
confess that I do not think my scheme of explication just,
since I cannot apply it throughout the whole, without involving myself in difficulties, from which the ablest interpreter
would find it no easy matter to get free.

Being therefore convinc'd upon an attentive and deliberate
review of these observations, and a consultation with my

---

7. The *Daily Gazetteer*, which commenced publication in 1735, followed
a strict pro-government line. The
Opposition maintained that it was
distributed free of charge, at public
expense, to disseminate government
propaganda. See *London*, l. 72, and
the *Compleat Vindication of the Licensers*,
p. 71 below.

8. The white horse, the badge of the
great Guelph house of Saxony, from
whom the Hanoverian electors descended, was prominent on the arms of
Hanover, and hence appeared in the
British royal arms between the accession of George I and that of Victoria,
when Hanover was separated from
Britain.

friends, of whose abilities I have the highest esteem, and whose impartiality, sincerity, and probity I have long known and frequently experienc'd, that my conjectures are in general very uncertain, often improbable, and sometimes little less than apparently false, I was long in doubt whether I ought not entirely to suppress them, and content myself with publishing in the *Gazetteer*, the inscription, as it stands engraven on the stone, without translation or commentary, unless that ingenious and learned society, should favour the world with their own remarks.

To this scheme, which I thought extremely well calculated for the public good, and therefore very eagerly communicated to my acquaintance and fellow students, some objections were started, which as I had not foreseen, I was unable to answer.

It was observed first, That the *Daily Dissertations* publish'd by that fraternity, are written with such profundity of sentiment, and fill'd with such uncommon modes of expression, as to be themselves sufficiently unintelligible to vulgar readers, and that therefore the venerable obscurity of this prediction, would much less excite the curiosity and awaken the attention of mankind, than if it were exhibited in any other paper, and plac'd in opposition to the clear and easy stile of an author generally understood.

To this argument, formidable as it was, I answer'd, after a short pause, that, with all proper deference to the great sagacity and advanc'd age of the objector, I could not but conceive that his position confuted itself, and that a reader of the *Gazetteer*, being by his own confession accustom'd to encounter difficulties, and search for meaning where it was not easily to be found, must be better prepar'd than any other man for the perusal of these ambiguous expressions. And that, besides, the explication of this stone, being a task, which nothing could surmount but the most acute penetration join'd with indefatigable patience, seem'd in reality reserv'd for those who have given proofs of both in the highest degree by reading and understanding the *Gazetteer*.

This answer satisfied every one but the objector, who with an obstinacy, not very uncommon, adher'd to his own opinion, tho' he could not defend it; and not being able to make any reply, attempted to laugh away my argument, but found

the rest of my friends so little dispos'd to jest upon this important question, that he was forced to restrain his mirth,
and content himself with a sullen and contemptuous silence.

Another of my friends, whom I had assembled on this
occasion, having owned the solidity of my answer to the first
objection, offer'd a second, which in his opinion could not be
so easily defeated.

"I have observ'd," says he, "that the essays in the *Gazetteer*,
tho' written on very important subjects by the ablest hands
which ambition can incite, friendship engage, or money
procure, have never, tho' circulated through the kingdom with
the utmost application, had any remarkable influence upon
the people. I know many persons of no common capacity,
that hold it sufficient to peruse these papers four times a
year;[9] and others who receive them regularly, and without
looking upon them, treasure them under ground[1] for the
benefit of posterity. So that the inscription may, by being
inserted there, sink once more into darkness and oblivion,
instead of informing the age, and assisting our present ministry
in the regulation of their measures."

Another observ'd that nothing was more unreasonable
than my hope that any remarks or elucidations would be
drawn up by that fraternity, since their own employments
do not allow them any leisure for such attempts. Every one
knows that panegyric is in its own nature no easy task, and
that to defend is much more difficult than to attack; consider
then, says he, what industry, what assiduity it must require,
to praise and vindicate a ministry like ours.

It was hinted by another, that an inscription which had no
relation to any particular set of men amongst us, but was
compos'd many ages before the parties, which now divide
the nation,[2] had a being, could not be so properly convey'd

---

9. Presumably in gratitude for the
quarterly payment of their stipends
from the government.

1. The familiar allusion to what
Pope called "the martyrdom of jakes."
Is this SJ's sole excursion into scato-
logy?

2. The Opposition, following the

lead of Bolingbroke in his *Dissertation
on Parties*, 1733, found it useful to
deplore "the spirit of party" in politics. (As did the government; the
classic theoretical reply to Bolingbroke, Burke's *Thoughts on the Present
Discontents*, did not appear until 1770.)

to the world by means of a paper, dedicated to political debates.

Another to whom I had communicated my own observations in a more private manner, and who had inserted some of his own arguments, declar'd it, as his opinion, that they were, tho' very controvertible and unsatisfactory, yet too valuable to be lost; and that tho' to insert the inscription in a paper of which such numbers are daily distributed at the expence of the public, would doubtless be very agreeable to the generous design of the author, yet he hop'd that as all the students, either of politics or antiquities, would receive both pleasure and improvement from the dissertation, with which it is accompanied, none of them would regret to pay for so agreeable an entertainment.

It cannot be wonder'd that I have yielded at last to such weighty reasons, and such insinuating compliments, and chosen to gratify at once the inclination of friends, and the vanity of an author. Yet I should think I had very imperfectly discharg'd my duty to my country, did I not warn all whom either interest or curiosity shall incite to the perusal of this treatise, not to lay any stress upon my explications.

How a more compleat and indisputable interpretation may be obtain'd, it is not easy to say. This will, I suppose, be readily granted, that it is not to be expected from any single hand, but from the joint enquiries and united labours of a numerous society of able men, instituted by authority, selected with great discernment and impartiality, and supported at the charge of the nation.

I am very far from apprehending that any proposal for the attainment of so desirable an end, will be rejected by this inquisitive and enlightned age, and shall therefore lay before the public the project which I have form'd and matur'd by long consideration, for the institution of a society of commentators upon this inscription.

I humbly propose, that thirty of the most distinguish'd genius be chosen for this employment, half from the Inns of Court, and half from the army, and be incorporated into a society for five years, under the name of the *Society of Commentators*.

That great undertakings can only be executed by a great

number of hands, is too evident to require any proof; and I
am afraid all that read this scheme will think that it is chiefly
defective in this respect, and that when they reflect how many
commissaries were thought necessary at Seville,[3] and that
even their negotiations entirely miscarried, probably for want
of more associates, they will conclude that I have propos'd
impossibilities, and that the ends of the institution will be
defeated by an injudicious and ill-tim'd frugality.

But if it be consider'd, how well the persons I recommend
must have been qualify'd by their education and profession
for the provinces assign'd them, the objection will grow less
weighty than it appears. It is well known to be the constant
study of the lawyers to discover in acts of parliament, mean-
ings which escap'd the committees that drew them up, and
the senates that pass'd them into laws, and to explain wills
into a sense wholly contrary to the intention of the testator.
How easily may an adept in these admirable and useful arts,
penetrate into the most hidden import of this prediction? A
man accustom'd to satisfy himself with the obvious and
natural meaning of a sentence, does not easily shake off his
habit, but a true-bred[k] lawyer never contents himself with one
sense when there is another to be found.

Nor will the beneficial consequences of this scheme terminate in the explication of this monument; they will extend
much farther: for the commentators having sharpen'd and
improv'd their sagacity by this long and difficult course of
study, will, when they return into public life, be of wonderful
service to the government, in examining pamphlets, songs,
and journals, and in drawing up informations, indictments,
and instructions for special juries.[4] They will be wonderfully

k. rue-bred *1739*

---

3. Perhaps SJ's mistake for "Sois-
sons," where a numerous "congress"
of representatives of European powers
assembled in 1728, and dispersed two
years later without having achieved
any concrete result. The British-
Spanish negotiations at Seville resulted in the Treaty of Seville, signed
9 Nov 1729, and were conducted by

only two British plenipotentiaries, William Stanhope (later Lord Harring-
ton) and Benjamin Keene.

4. A special jury is drawn from a
panel restricted to persons of substantially higher financial and social
qualifications than those of an ordinary jury. In *Rex vs. Francklin*, 1731,
the printer of the *Craftsman* was tried

fitted for the posts of Attorney and Solicitor General,[5] but will excell above all, as licensers for the stage.

The gentlemen of the army[6] will equally adorn the province to which I have assign'd them, of setting the discoveries and sentiments of their associates, in a clear and agreeable light. The lawyers are well known not to be very happy in expressing their ideas, being for the most part able to make themselves understood by none but their own fraternity. But the geniusses of the army have sufficient opportunities by their free access to the levee and the toilet,[7] their constant attendance on balls and assemblies, and that abundant leisure which they enjoy beyond any other body of men, to acquaint themselves with every new word and prevailing mode of expression, and to attain the utmost nicety and most polish'd prettiness of language.

It will be necessary, that during their attendance upon the society, they be exempt from any obligation to appear on Hyde-Park; and that upon no emergency, however pressing, they be call'd away from their studies, unless the nation be in immediate danger by an insurrection of weavers, colliers, or smugglers.[8]

(for seditious libel) by a special rather than a common jury, at the request of the prosecution, and Walpole's law officers were accused of making the special jury a tool to help them get convictions in such cases (see *London*, l. 252). The political implications of the use of the special jury—it is alleged to be necessarily more friendly to the *status quo* than the ordinary jury—were emphasized as recently as 1947, in the widely publicized case of *Laski vs. the Newark Advertiser* (see Kingsley Martin, *Harold Laski, 1893–1950*, 1953).

5. The chief law officers of the Crown, responsible for public prosecutions. In 1739 they were Dudley Ryder and John Strange.

6. For later lampoons by SJ on the character of the professional soldier,

see *Idler* 5, 21 ("The most contemptible of human stations, that of a soldier in time of peace"), and 30. It is clear (e.g., in "Remarks on the Militia Bill," 1756) that SJ shared the traditional Tory distrust of a permanent, professional army (under the control of the Crown), preferring the idea of a national militia of part-time soldiers (under the control of Parliament). When SJ's name was drawn to serve with the trainbands (the militia of London), he responded with alacrity, even furnishing himself with a sword and musket (*Life*, IV, 319).

7. Occasions for formal reception of visitors by the King.

8. The Speech from the Throne at the opening of Parliament in 1737 deplored numerous such riots which had recently taken place, particularly

There may not perhaps be found in the army such a number of men, who have ever condescended to pass through the labours and irksome forms of education in use among the lower classes of people, or submitted to learn the mercantile and plebeian arts of writing and reading; I must own, that tho' I entirely agree with the notions of the uselessness of any such trivial accomplishments in the military profession, and of their inconsistency with more valuable attainments, tho' I am convinc'd that a man who can read and write becomes, at least, a very disagreeable companion to his brother soldiers, if he does not absolutely shun their acquaintance, that he is apt to imbibe from his books odd notions of liberty and independency, and even sometimes of morality and virtue, utterly inconsistent with the desirable character of a pretty gentleman: tho' writing frequently stains the whitest finger, and reading has a natural tendency to cloud the aspect, and depress that airy and thoughtless vivacity, which is the distinguishing characteristic of a modern warrior, yet on this single occasion I cannot but heartily wish that by a strict search, there may be discover'd in the army fifteen men who can write and read.

I know that the knowledge of the alphabet is so disreputable among these gentlemen, that those who have by ill fortune formerly been taught it, have partly forgot it by disuse, and partly conceal'd it from the world, to avoid the railleries and insults to which their education might make them liable:[1] I propose therefore, that all the officers of the army may be examin'd upon oath[9] one by one, and that if fifteen cannot be selected who are at present so qualify'd, the deficiency may be supply'd out of those who having once learned to read, may

1. liable: *1788*] liable, *1739*

the notorious Porteous affair in Edinburgh. The Opposition seized the opportunity to accuse the government of maladministration, Carteret moving for a Parliamentary inquiry (*Parliamentary History*, IX. 1274–1311).

9. Part of the satire. For SJ on the folly and immorality of numerous administrative oaths, see "Remarks on the Militia Bill" and *Life, passim*. The attitude was a Tory one, stemming from the multiplicity of "loyalty oaths" of one kind or another required by the regimes of William III and George I.

perhaps, with the assistance of a master, in a short time refresh their memories.

It may be thought, at the first sight of this proposal, that it might not be improper to assign to every commentator a reader and secretary; but it may be easily conceiv'd, that not only the public might murmur at such an addition of expence, but that by the unfaithfulness or negligence of their servants, the discoveries of the society may be carry'd to foreign courts, and made use of to the disadvantage of our own country.

For the residence of this society, I cannot think any place more proper than Greenwich-Hospital,[1] in which they may have thirty apartments fitted up for them, that they may make their observations in private, and meet once a day in the painted hall to compare them.

If the establishment of this society be thought a matter of too much importance to be defer'd till the new buildings are finish'd, it will be necessary to make room for their reception, by the expulsion of such of the seamen as have no pretensions to the settlement there, but fractur'd limbs, loss of eyes, or decay'd constitutions, who have lately been admitted in such numbers, that it is now scarce possible to accommodate a nobleman's groom, footman, or postilion, in a manner suitable to the dignity of his profession, and the original design of the foundation.

The situation of Greenwich will naturally dispose them to reflection and study; and particular caution ought to be us'd, lest any interruption be suffer'd to dissipate their attention, or distract their meditations: for this reason, all visits and letters from ladies are strictly to be prohibited; and if any of the members shall be detected with a lap-dog, pack of cards, box of dice, draught-table, snuff-box, or looking glass, he shall for the first offence be confin'd for three months to water-gruel, and for the second be expell'd the society.

Nothing now remains, but that an estimate be made of the expences necessary for carrying on this noble and gen-

---

1. Founded in 1694 by William and Mary as an asylum for disabled naval veterans. I know nothing of the occasion for SJ's insinuations that the sailors were being victimized in order to provide for noblemen's dependants. SJ lived in Greenwich after he first came to London in 1737.

erous design. The salary to be allow'd each professor cannot be less than 2000*l.* a year, which is indeed more than the regular stipend of a commissioner of excise;[2] but it must be remembred, that the commentators have a much more difficult and important employment, and can expect their salaries but for the short space of five years; whereas a commissioner (unless he imprudently suffers himself to be carry'd away by a whimsical tenderness for his country) has an establishment for life.

It will be necessary to allow the society in general, 30000*l.* yearly for the support of the public table, and 40000*l.* for secret service.[3]

Thus will the ministry have a fair prospect of obtaining the full sense and import of the prediction, without burthening the public with more than 65000*l.* which may be paid out of the sinking fund;[4] or if it be not thought proper to violate that sacred treasure by converting any part of it to uses not primarily intended, may be easily rais'd by a general poll-tax, or excise upon bread.

---

2. For an earlier caustic reference to excise, see *London*, l. 29; there are numerous later ones. Excise, from the time of its introduction in England in 1643, seems to have been more generally associated with Whig than Tory administrations, although it was a statute introduced by the Tory Harley (9 Anne, c.11) that Michael Johnson's leather-making fell foul of in 1725. SJ's notorious definition in the *Dictionary* need not be referred to personal animus: what Tory polemicists chiefly criticized about the excise laws was the giving of quasi-judicial powers to excise commissioners appointed and removable by the executive—the extension of *droit administratif*. Cf. Blackstone, *Commentaries*, 2nd ed., (1769), 1.318 ("The rigour and arbitrary proceedings of excise-laws seem hardly compatible with the temper of a free nation"); IV.278.

3. Walpole's "corruption" was supposed to be carried on by means of the "secret service money"—a portion of the King's civil list revenues for which no public accounting was made. Much was said about it by the Opposition during the debate, in 1736, on Pulteney's motion that the King be asked to settle £100,000 *per annum* on the Prince of Wales, out of the civil list. "Support of the public table" may perhaps be interpreted as aimed at that perennial target of English oppositionists, the expense of the Royal Household.

4. In 1717, Walpole had been instrumental in establishing the "inviolable" Sinking Fund, through which the national debt was to be steadily retired. Later, however, he used it to make up deficits in current revenue.

Having now compleated my scheme, a scheme calculated for the public benefit, without regard to any party, I intreat all sects, factions, and distinctions of men among us, to lay aside for a time their[m] party-feuds and petty animosities, and by a warm concurrence on this urgent occasion, teach posterity to sacrifice every private interest to the advantage of their country.

FINIS.[n]

m. that *in some copies of 1739*, their *in others; corrected in Manchester copy in a hand other than SJ's*   n. om. *in some copies of 1739*

A COMPLEAT VINDICATION OF THE
LICENSERS OF THE STAGE. 1739.

Henry Brooke is a figure of some importance in the history of eighteenth-century English literature and political thought. He is usually connected with the later rather than the earlier part of the century—his most famous book, *The Fool of Quality*, was published 1766–70 and won new fame when reprinted by John Wesley in 1781 as *The History of Henry Earl of Morland*. He links up with the French Revolution and the Romantic movement: C. E. Vaughan, in the *Cambridge History of English Literature* (Vol. x, Ch. 3), says of him, "Brooke had grasped far more of what Rousseau came to teach the world, and had felt it more intensely, than [Henry] Mackenzie. Before we can find anything approaching to this keenness of feeling, this revolt against the wrongs of the social system, we have to go forward to the years immediately succeeding the outbreak of the French revolution: in particular to the years from 1790 to 1797—the years of Paine and Godwin, of Coleridge's 'penny trumpet of sedition' . . . ." Caroline Spurgeon, in another chapter of the same *History* (Vol. ix, Ch. 12), remarks on Brooke's indebtedness to William Law and Jakob Böhme, and the appreciation of his work by the Methodists. "It [*Henry Earl of Morland*] became," she says, "favourite reading with generations of devout Wesleyans, and, in this form, passed through many editions." The first instinct of the Johnsonian student, when he finds the "arch-Tory" Johnson allied with Brooke at the outset of their careers, may be to laugh and pass the conjunction off as one of the quaint ironies of history. Yet Johnson, too, like Brooke and Wesley, was profoundly influenced by Law; Johnson, too, keenly felt the wrongs of the social system, not only in the 1730's but throughout his life. Just how the "Toryism" of Johnson is to be defined, what the basic ideology of Toryism generally in eighteenth-century England really consisted in—these are questions that still await competent investigation by serious historians.

At any rate, Walpole's government in 1739 had no doubts that Brooke's play *Gustavus Vasa* was a penny trumpet of sedition—and if sedition means incitement to rebellion, the modern reader who makes his way through this pointed allegory of the downfall of a corrupt Prime Minister (and the expulsion of the foreign king who supported him) may be inclined to agree with the government, Brooke's protestations to the contrary notwithstanding. In that the hero Gustavus has a better hereditary right to the Swedish throne than the Danish usurper, it might also be regarded as Jacobite propaganda. Had the play been quietly suppressed under the old, vaguely defined powers of the Lord Chamberlain (successor to the Master of the Revels), as was done with Gay's *Polly* ten years before, the public reaction might not have been so vigorous. Unfortunately, in 1737, the government, exasperated by some theatrical squibs of the time, had taken the trouble to codify these powers of suppression in a statute, 10 Geo. II, c.28. (The act was repealed in 1843, but the licensing provisions were repeated in the Theatres Act, 6 & 7 Vict., c.68) The act passed through Parliament quickly, with no opposition, it is said, except from Lord Chesterfield; it was argued that it did no more than put on the statute books powers long exercised by prescription. But by doing so, it publicized them and made them subject to the scrutiny of such keen critics as Samuel Johnson and, later, Bernard Shaw. Astonishingly, the licensing of plays by the Lord Chamberlain was not abolished until 1968.

To assist him in the work of censorship, the Lord Chamberlain was empowered to appoint an examiner and deputy-examiner of plays, with stipends of £400 and £200 annually. All three offices were political; in 1739 they were held, respectively, by the Duke of Grafton, Walter Chetwynd, and Edward Capell. Grafton (the second duke), an old, inoffensive wheel-horse of the regime, and Capell, a minor writer, later Johnson's rival as an editor of Shakespeare, were probably of less importance in the *Gustavus Vasa* case—the first suppression of a play under the act of 1737—than Chetwynd, who likely acted for Walpole in the matter. It may be of signi-ficance in examining Johnson's part in the affair that the Chetwynds were one of the most active and influential political families of Staffordshire. They had once been Tories; they became Walpolites; now, in 1739, the two leading members of the family, John, Viscount Chetwynd, and William Richard Chetwynd, both M.P.'s for Stafford, were in opposition again. William Chetwynd of Brocton, the examiner of plays, was still, however, a supporter of Walpole, and no doubt owed his appointment to Walpole's wish to keep or regain what he could of the family's influence. Johnson certainly knew about the Chetwynds: another Walter Chetwynd, of Gren-don, had been Whig M.P. for Lichfield from 1715 to 1731, and the exam-iner's mother was one of the Sneyds of Keele, an old Lichfield Tory family with whom Johnson was acquainted (see H. E. Chetwynd-Stapylton, *The Chetwynds of Ingestre*, 1892). The self-seeking politics of the Chetwynds in the early eighteenth century resembles that of their neighbours and political associates, the Leveson Gowers of Trentham: we know what Johnson thought of *them* (*"renegado . . .* sometimes we say, a *Gower"*). It is not inconceivable that resentment at the Chetwynds' disloyalty to the Staffordshire Tories accounted for some of the virulence of Johnson's pamphlet, and perhaps even was the principal cause of his undertaking it in the first place.

In an advertisement on 17 March 1739 (*Daily Advertiser*) Brooke gave the story to the public:

> Whereas on the 24th of last February, the copy of a play entitled Gustavus Vasa, the Deliverer of his Country, (then in Rehearsal at Drury-Lane Theatre) was deliver'd to Mr. Chetwin, the Deputy-Licenser, agreeable to a statute in such case made and provided; and whereas the author of the said play has from time to time, and

as often as a violent indisposition, under which he still labours, would permit, waited on, and earnestly sollicited the said Mr. Chetwin to license the acting of the said play: But farther, whereas the said Mr. Chetwin, by various delays, and under various pretences has deferr'd licensing the said play for one-and-twenty days, being seven days beyond the express time limited and appointed by the statute, and hath without excepting to any single line or sentiment in the said play, or assigning any publick or apparent cause, or reason, for refusing to license or procure a license for the same, tho' often urged by the author to shew or assign such cause, or reason; this author apprehending that he is greatly aggriev'd, in order to repair the damages he hath thereby sustain'd, proposes to print the said play by subscription on royal paper at five shillings each copy, and humbly hopes the encouragement of every impartial lover of virtue and liberty.

Henry Brooke

Further details are given in the Prefatory Dedication to the Subscribers in the printed version of the play: "This piece was about five weeks in rehearsal, the day was appointed for acting, I had disposed of many hundred tickets, and imagined I had nothing to fear but from the weakness of the performance." The subscriptions were enthusiastically taken up; among the subscribers' names (nearly a thousand) appear those of Johnson, Chesterfield, and Swift (ten copies). The play was finally published 5 May 1739, after a delay due to Brooke's illness.

A Compleat Vindication of the Licensers was first advertised for sale 25 May. If Johnson did not begin writing it until he had seen Brooke's play in print, this is another testimonial to his rapidity of composition. There is no evidence that Johnson was known during his lifetime to be the author of the *Vindication*. The sole authority for his composition of it seems to be the statement in "An Account of the Writings of Dr. Samuel Johnson" in the *European Magazine*, Jan 1785, p. 9, "This pamphlet is ascribed to Dr. Johnson, on the authority of an old bookseller, who remembered the publication of it." But the attribution has never been questioned, and is not likely to be.

The *Vindication* is to be read with *Marmor Norfolciense*, which preceded it into print by only a fortnight. The charges against the Walpolians are the same; the technique, that of the ironic mask of the vindicator of what the author wishes condemned, is the same. The sensitive reader may, however, detect a sharpening of tone in the portrait of the "vindicator" by comparison with that of the "commentator" of *Marmor*. The party-liner in *Marmor* is such a bumbling idiot that one cannot take him very seriously; the speaker in the *Vindication* is more intensely dedicated to the bad cause of authoritarian obscurantism, more vicious, more dangerous. The argument against censorship by executive decree, against the abuse of executive power generally, is cogently, even brilliantly, put: in such comments as "What is power but the liberty of acting without being accountable?" and "Our intention was ... to empower him [the Lord Chamberlain] to do that *without* reason, which *with* reason he could do before," Johnson goes to the heart of important questions of political theory. Throughout the piece one feels something of the libertarian passion of a Swift or an Orwell. As a manifesto of the freedom of the stage and the press, as an action in the endless defence of the human mind against the forces of thought-control, Johnson's *Vindication* is not unworthy to be mentioned in the same breath as its archetype, Milton's *Areopagitica*.

The text here follows that of 1739, the only authoritative edition. The pamphlet was reprinted in *Works* (1788), Vol. xiv, and subsequent collections.

A Compleat Vindication of the Licensers of the Stage, from the Malicious and Scandalous Aspersions of Mr. Brooke, Author of Gustavus Vasa. With a Proposal for Making the Office of Licenser More Extensive and Effectual. By an Impartial Hand

It is generally agreed by the writers of all parties, that few crimes are equal, in their degree of guilt, to that of calumniating a good and gentle, or defending a wicked and oppressive administration.[1]

It is therefore with the utmost satisfaction of mind, that I reflect how often I have employ'd my pen in vindication of the present ministry, and their dependents and adherents, how often I have detected the specious fallacies of the advocates for independence, how often I have softened the obstinacy of patriotism, and how often triumphed over the clamour of opposition.

I have, indeed, observed but one set of men upon whom all my arguments have been thrown away, which neither flattery can draw to compliance, nor[a] threats reduce to sub-

a. nor *1788*] not *1739*

---

1. Cf. "To Mr. Urban," *Gentleman's Magazine*, Jan 1739, pp. 3–4: "To clear the character of a good king from the aspersions of faction, or misrepresentations of jealousy, is the duty of every man who has an opportunity of undeceiving the deluded; but it is much more his duty to warn a people against any intended encroachments upon their rights or liberties, as the happiness of twenty thousand is of twenty thousand times more value than the happiness of one." This piece was attributed to SJ (no doubt correctly) by Hill, *Life*, 1.139, n. 2.

mission, and who have, notwithstanding all expedients that
either invention or experience could suggest, continued to
exert their abilities in a vigorous and constant opposition of
all our measures.

The unaccountable behaviour of these men, the enthusiastick resolution with which, after a hundred successive
defeats, they still renewed their attacks, the spirit with which
they continued to repeat their arguments in the senate,
though they found a majority determined to condemn them,
and the inflexibility with which they rejected all offers of
places and preferments[2] at last excited my curiosity so far,
that I applied myself to enquire with great diligence into the
real motives of their conduct, and to discover what principle
it was that had force to inspire such unextinguishable zeal,
and to animate such unwearied efforts.

For this reason I attempted to cultivate a nearer acquaintance with some of the chiefs of that party, and imagined that
it would be necessary for some time to dissemble my sentiments that I might learn theirs.

Dissimulation to a true politician is not difficult, and therefore I readily assumed the character of a proselyte, but found
that their principle of action was no other, than that which
they make no scruple of avowing in the most publick manner,
notwithstanding the contempt and ridicule to which it every
day exposes them, and the loss of[b] those honours and profits
from which it excludes them.

This wild passion, or principle, is a kind of fanaticism by
which they distinguish those of their own party, and which
they look upon as a certain indication of a great mind. *We*
have no name for it *at court*,[3] but among themselves, they term
it by a kind of cant-phrase, *a regard for posterity.*

This passion seems to predominate in all their conduct, to
regulate every action of their lives, and sentiment of their

b. *om. 1739*

2. Like many others, SJ was to be disillusioned when, after the fall of Walpole in 1742, Carteret, Sandys, and other Whig "patriots" accepted "places" (and Pulteney an earldom) with unseemly alacrity. Lyttelton and

Pitt had to wait a few years longer for the tangible rewards of their patriotism.

3. "At court" means roughly "in the administration."

minds; I have heard L—— and P——,[4] when they have made a vigorous opposition, or blasted the blossom of some ministerial scheme, cry out, in the height of their exultations, "This will deserve the thanks of posterity!" And when their adversaries, as it much more frequently falls out, have outnumber'd and over-thrown them, they will say with an air of revenge, and a kind of gloomy triumph, "Posterity will curse you for this."[5]

It is common among men under the influence of any kind of frenzy, to believe that all the world has the same odd notions that disorder their own imaginations. Did these unhappy men, these deluded patriots, know how little we are concerned about posterity, they would never attempt to fright us with their curses, or tempt us to a neglect of our own interest by a prospect of their gratitude.

But so strong is their infatuation, that they seem to have forgotten even the primary law of self-preservation, for they sacrifice without scruple every flattering hope, every darling enjoyment, and every satisfaction of life to this "ruling passion," and appear in every step to consult not so much their own advantage as that of *posterity*.

Strange delusion! that can confine all their thoughts to a race of men whom they neither know, nor can know; from whom nothing is to be feared, nor any thing expected; who cannot even bribe a special jury,[6] nor have so much as a single riband[7] to bestow.

---

4. *1788* supplies a footnote, "Lyttelton and Pitt." Bishop Percy recounts SJ's boyhood acquaintance with George Lyttelton, "with whom, having some colloquial disputes, he is supposed to have conceived that prejudice which so improperly influenced him in the life of that worthy nobleman" (*Miscellanies*, ii. 208). In view of SJ's praise of Lyttelton here, some doubt may linger about the accuracy of Percy's psychologizing.

5. The most notable occasion for charges against Walpole of disregard for posterity was in 1736, when he budgeted an expenditure of £600,000 for current uses out of the Sinking Fund.

6. See n. 4, p. 46 above.

7. The broad ribbons of the orders of knighthood, the Garter, the Thistle, and the Bath—the blue, green, and red silken threads of *Gulliver's Travels*, Book i. Walpole was distinguished during his term of office by being awarded the Garter, one of the exceedingly few commoners (like Sir Winston Churchill) to be so honoured. The Order of the Bath had been "revived" by Walpole and George I in 1725, chiefly to reward political supporters; the action was much satirized at the time.

This fondness for posterity is a kind of madness which at Rome was once almost epidemical, and infected even the women and the children. It reigned there till the entire destruction of Carthage, after which it began to be less general, and in a few years afterwards a remedy was discovered, by which it was almost entirely extinguished.[8]

In England it never prevailed in any such degree, some few of the ancient barons[9] seem indeed to have been disorder'd by it, but the contagion has been for the most part timely checked, and our ladies have been generally free.

But there has been in every age a set of men much admired and reverenced, who have affected to be always talking of posterity, and have laid out their lives upon the composition of poems for the sake of being applauded by this imaginary generation.

---

8. That Rome's success over its rival Carthage marked the beginning of the decline of "primitive Roman virtue" was a commonplace frequently repeated. It is found in the Roman historians themselves, e.g., Sallust, *De Bello Catilinario* (which SJ translated— see *Life*, IV. 383, n. and Yale *Works*, I.367): "*Carthago aemula imperi Romani ab stirpe interiit, cuncta maria terraeque patebant: saevire fortuna ac miscere omnia coepit. . . . Igitur primo pecuniae, deinde imperi cupido crevit; ea quasi materies omnium malorum fuere*" (Ch. x). Sallust goes on to expound this thesis at some length. Among Roman "patriotic" women, one thinks particularly of Cornelia, the mother of the Gracchi, whose activities were regarded as marking the last struggles of primitive Roman patriotism. The "remedy" SJ refers to may be the rise of dictators like Sulla (the modern analogy being Walpole).

Very likely SJ had also been reading Montesquieu, *Considérations sur les causes de la grandeur des Romains et de leur décadence* (1734): "Rome was no more a city whose people possessed the same spirit, the same love of liberty, and the same hatred of tyranny; in which jealousy of the power of the senate and the prerogatives of the great—mixed always with respect —was in reality nothing other than a love of equality" (trans. J. Baker, 1882, Ch. IX). Montesquieu's interesting view of what makes a healthy national constitution is not unlike that found in *The Sentiments of a Tory* (1741); see n. 4, p. xvi above.

By 1756, SJ had mitigated his admiration for the early Romans—"a people who, while they were poor, robbed mankind, and as soon as they became rich, robbed one another" (review of Thomas Blackwell's *Memoirs of the Court of Augustus*).

9. E.g., the barons of the time of Magna Carta. It is as surprising to find SJ propagating the Whig legend (to which Burke gave a fresh impetus) of the English aristocracy as the founders and protectors of the country's freedom as it is to find him extolling the primitive virtues of the Roman republic. Nothing of the kind is to be found in the later Johnson.

The present poets I reckon amongst the most inexorable enemies of our most excellent ministry, and much doubt whether any method will effect the cure of a distemper which in this class of men may be termed not an accidental disease, but a defect in their original frame and constitution.

Mr. Brooke, a name I mention with all the detestation suitable to my character,[1] could not forbear discovering this depravity of his mind in his very prologue, which is filled with sentiments so wild, and so much unheard of among those who frequent levees and courts, that I much doubt, whether the zealous licenser proceeded any further in his examination of his performance.

He might easily perceive that a man,

Who bade his moral beam through every age,[2]

was too much a bigot to exploded notions, to compose a play which he could license without manifest hazard of his office, a hazard which no man would incur untainted with the love of posterity.

We cannot therefore wonder that an author, wholly possessed by this passion, should vent his resentment for the licenser's just refusal, in virulent advertisements, insolent complaints, and scurrilous assertions of his rights and privileges, and proceed in defiance of authority to solicite a subscription.

This temper which I have been describing is almost always complicated with ideas of the high prerogatives of human nature, of a sacred unalienable birthright, which no man has conferr'd upon us, and which neither kings can take, nor senates give away,[3] which we may justly assert whenever and

---

1. That of "an impartial hand," presumably.

2. *Gustavus Vasa*, prologue, ll. 29–30: "He ['our bard'] to no state, no climate, bounds his page / But bids his moral beam thro' every age."

3. The doctrine of the inalienability of the individual's right to life, liberty, and property Locke had made the fundamental axiom of his political theory, and it was much insisted on in the eighteenth century, e.g., in the American Declaration of Independence. By 1775, SJ was in a position to deal it a shrewd blow: "If they [the American colonists] had a right to English privileges, they were accountable to English laws, and what must grieve the lover of liberty to discover, had ceded to the king and

by whomsoever it is attacked, and which, if ever it should
happen to be lost, we may take the first opportunity to
recover.

The natural consequence of these chimeras is contempt of
authority, and an irreverence for any superiority but what
is founded upon merit, and their notions of merit are very
peculiar, for it is among them no great proof of merit to be
wealthy and powerful, to wear a garter or a star, to command
a regiment or a senate, to have the ear of the minister or of the
king, or to possess any of those virtues and excellencies which
among us intitle a man to little less than worship and prostra-
tion.

We may therefore easily conceive that Mr. Brooke thought
himself intitled to be importunate for a license, because, in
his own opinion, he deserved one, and to complain thus loudly
at the repulse he met with.

His complaints will have, I hope, but little weight with the
publick, since the opinions of the sect in which he is inlisted
are exposed and shewn to be evidently and demonstrably
opposite to that system of subordination and dependence to
which we are indebted for the present tranquillity of the
nation, and that chearfulness and readiness with which the
two Houses concur in all our designs.

I shall however, to silence him intirely, or at least to shew
those of our party, that he ought to be silent, consider singly
every instance of hardship and oppression which he has dared
to publish in the papers, and to publish in such a manner
that I hope no man will condemn me for want of candour
in becoming an advocate for the ministry, if I can consider
his advertisements as nothing less than *an appeal to his country*.

Let me be forgiven if I cannot speak with temper of such
insolence as this: Is a man without title, pension, or place, to
suspect the impartiality or the judgment of those who are
intrusted with the administration of publick affairs? Is he,
when the law is not strictly observed in regard to him, to
think himself "aggrieved,"[4] to tell his sentiments in print,

parliament, whether the right or not,
at least the power of disposing, *without
their consent, of their lives, liberties, and
properties* [SJ's italics]" (*Taxation No*

Tyranny, p. 429 below).

4. Quoted from Brooke's advertisement of 17 Mar 1739, p. 54 above.

assert his claim to better usage, and fly for redress to another tribunal?

If such practices are permitted, I will not venture to foretell the effects of them, the ministry may soon be convinced that such sufferers will find compassion, and that it is safer not to bear hard upon them than to allow them to complain.

The power of licensing in general, being firmly established by an Act of Parliament, our poet has not attempted to call in question, but contents himself with censuring the manner in which it has been executed, so that I am not now engaged to assert the licenser's authority, but to defend his conduct.

The poet seems to think himself aggrieved, because the licenser kept his tragedy in his hands one and twenty days, whereas the law allows him to detain it only fourteen.

Where will the insolence of the malecontents end? Or how are such unreasonable expectations possibly to be satisfied? Was it ever known that a man exalted into a high station dismissed a suppliant in the time limited by law? Ought not Mr. Brooke to think himself happy that his play was not detained longer? If he had been kept a year in suspense, what redress could he have obtained? Let the poets remember when they appear before the licenser, or his deputy, that they stand at the tribunal from which there is no appeal permitted,[5] and where nothing will so well become them as reverence and submission.

Mr. Brooke mentions in his preface his knowledge of the laws of his own country,[6] had he extended his enquiries to the civil law, he could have found a full justification of the licenser's conduct, *Boni judicis est ampliare suam auctoritatem.*[7]

---

5. SJ's objection to the Licensing Act, like his objection to the excise regulations, is not a trivial one, and is heard even more frequently in the twentieth than the eighteenth century. It is the perennial objection to *droit administratif*, the conferring of judicial powers on executive departments, without preserving the safeguards provided in the regular process of the law courts—the right of confronting one's accusers, the right of being heard in one's defence, the right of appeal, and so on.

6. "When I wrote the following sheets I had studied the ancient laws of my country": *Gustavus Vasa*, A Prefatory Dedication to the Subscribers.

7. A version of an old legal maxim. "Sir Joseph Jekyll said, it was a saying of a very great man, *boni judicis est ampliare jurisdictionem*" (*Precedents in Chancery*, 1771, p. 329). "Lord Mans-

If then it be "the business of a good judge to enlarge his authority," was it not in the licenser the utmost clemency and forbearance, to extend fourteen days only to twenty one.

I suppose this great man's inclination to perform at least this duty of a good judge, is not questioned by any, either of his friends or enemies, I may therefore venture to hope that he will extend his power by proper degrees, and that I shall live to see a malecontent writer earnestly soliciting for the copy of a play, which he had delivered to the licenser twenty years before.

"I waited," says he, "often on the licenser, and with the utmost importunity entreated an answer."[8] Let Mr. Brooke consider, whether that importunity was not a sufficient reason for the disappointment. Let him reflect how much more decent it had been to have waited the leisure of a great man,[9] than to have pressed upon him with repeated petitions, and to have intruded upon those precious moments which he has dedicated to the service of his country.

Mr. Brooke was doubtless led into this improper manner of acting, by an erroneous notion that the grant of a license was not an act of favour but of justice, a mistake into which he could not have fallen, but from a supine inattention to the design of the statute, which was only to bring poets into subjection and dependence, not to encourage good writers, but to discourage all.

There lies no obligation upon the licenser to grant his sanction to a play, however excellent, nor can Mr. Brooke demand any reparation, whatever applause his performance may meet with.

Another grievance is, that the licenser assigned no reason for his refusal. This is a higher strain of insolence than any of the former. Is it for a poet to demand a licenser's reason for his proceedings? Is he not rather to acquiesce in the decision of

---

field said, 'The true maxim is "*Boni judicis ampliare justitiam*," not "*ampliare jurisdictionem*." ' " (Lord Campbell, *Lives of the Chief Justices of England*, 1858, Ch. xxxiv).

8. Presumably paraphrased from

Brooke's advertisement (pp. 53f. above).

9. A popular satiric phrase for Walpole; on its implications, see Fielding, *Jonathan Wild*. As applied here to the obscure William Chetwynd, it is telling.

authority, and conclude that there are reasons which he cannot comprehend?

Unhappy would it be for men in power, were they always obliged to publish the motives of their conduct. What is power but the liberty of acting without being accountable? The advocates for the licensing act have alledged, that the Lord Chamberlain has always had authority to prohibit the representation of a play for just reasons. Why then did we call in all our force to procure an Act of Parliament? Was it to enable him to do what he has always done, to confirm an authority which no man attempted to impair, or pretended to dispute; no certainly: Our intention was to invest him with new privileges, and to empower him to do that *without* reason, which *with* reason he could do before.

We have found by long experience, that to lie under a necessity of assigning reasons, is very troublesome, and that many an excellent design has miscarried by the loss of time spent unnecessarily in examining reasons.

Always to call for reasons, and always to reject them, shews a strange degree of perverseness, yet such is the daily behaviour of our adversaries, who have never yet been satisfied with any reasons that have been offered by us.

They have made it their practice to demand once a year the reasons for which we maintain a standing army.[1]

One year we told them that it was necessary, because all the nations round us were involved in war; this had no effect upon them, and therefore resolving to do our utmost for their satisfaction, we told them the next year that it was necessary because all the nations round us were at peace.

This reason finding no better reception than the other, we had recourse to our apprehensions of an invasion from the Pretender, of an insurrection in favour of *gin*, and of a general disaffection among the people.[2]

---

1. The authority of the Crown (the executive) for maintaining a regular army had to be renewed annually by Parliament in the Mutiny Act. In the 1730's the passage of the act was often made the occasion for opposition orators (frequently Tories) to question the whole principle of standing armies, a sore point with Tories since the days of Cromwell.

2. See, e.g., the Speech from the Throne at the opening of Parliament, 1 Feb 1739 (*Parliamentary History*, x. 874) and a royal proclamation (*Lon-*

But as they continue still impenetrable, and oblige us still to assign our annual reasons, we shall spare no endeavours to procure such as may be more satisfactory than any of the former.

The reason we once gave for building barracks[3] was for fear of the plague, and we intend next year to propose the augmentation of our troops for fear of a famine.

The committee, by which the act for licensing the stage was drawn up,[4] had too long known the inconvenience of giving reasons, and were too well acquainted with the characters of great men, to lay the Lord Chamberlain, or his deputy, under any such tormenting obligation.

Yet lest Mr. Brooke should imagine that a license was refused him without just reasons, I shall condescend to treat him with more regard than he can reasonably expect, and point out such sentiments as not only justly exposed him to that refusal, but would have provoked any ministry less merciful than the present to have inflicted some heavier penalties upon him.

His prologue is filled with such insinuations as no friend of our excellent government can read without indignation and abhorrence, and cannot but be owned to be a proper introduction to such scenes as seem designed to kindle in the audience a flame of opposition, patriotism, publick spirit, and independency, that spirit which we have so long endeavoured to suppress, and which cannot be revived without the entire subversion of all our schemes.

---

don *Gazette*, No. 7683, 11–14 Mar 1737/8): "Wicked and ill-designing persons . . . have, of late, excited and encouraged divers riots and tumults on the occasion of the arresting and prosecuting offenders against the said act [the 'Gin Act' of 1736, a highly unsuccessful attempt to enforce virtual prohibition of spirits]."

3. There was great opposition in eighteenth-century England to the idea of housing troops in permanent barracks (see Sir John Fortescue in *Johnson's England*, 1933, I. 66, and at greater length in his *History of the British Army*, 1899–1930). They were regarded as a symbol of military domination of the populace by a "standing army" subservient to the will of a Cromwell-like dictator. See p. 36 n. 3, p. 282 n. 5.

4. It consisted of Henry Pelham (chairman), Bubb Dodington, Sir Joseph Jekyll (Master of the Rolls), Dudley Ryder (Attorney-General), and John Strange (Solicitor-General) (*Commons Journals*, 20 May 1737).

This seditious poet not content with making an open attack upon us, by declaring in plain terms, that he looks upon freedom as the only source of publick happiness and national security, has endeavoured with subtlety, equal to his malice, to make us suspicious of our firmest friends, to infect our consultations with distrust, and to ruin us by disuniting us.[5]

This indeed will not be easily effected, an union founded upon interest and cemented by dependance is naturally lasting: But confederacies which owe their rise to virtue or mere conformity of sentiments are quickly dissolved, since no individual has any thing either to hope or fear for himself, and publick spirit is generally too weak to combat with private passions.

The poet has, however, attempted to weaken our combination by an artful and sly assertion, which, if suffered to remain unconfuted, may operate by degrees upon our minds in the days of leisure and retirement which are now approaching, and perhaps fill us with such surmises as may at least very much embarrass our affairs.

The law by which the Swedes justified their opposition to the incroachments of the King of Denmark he not only calls

Great Nature's law, the law within the breast

but proceeds to tell us that it is

——Stamp'd by Heav'n upon th' unletter'd mind.[6]

By which he evidently intends to insinuate a maxim which is, I hope, as false as it is pernicious, that men are naturally fond of liberty till those unborn ideas and desires are effaced by literature.

The author, if he be not a man mew'd up in his solitary study and entirely unacquainted with the conduct of the present ministry, must know that we have hitherto acted upon different principles. We have always regarded *letters* as great obstructions to our scheme of subordination, and have[c] there-

c. have *1788*] are *1739*

5. To appreciate SJ's remarks in these paragraphs, Brooke's Prologue   to *Gustavus Vasa* should be consulted.

6. *Gustavus Vasa*, Prologue, ll. 18, 20.

fore, when we have heard of any man remarkably *unletter'd*, carefully noted him down as the most proper person for any employments of trust or honour, and considered him as a man in whom we could safely repose our most important secrets.

From among the uneducated and *unletter'd* we have chosen not only our embassadors[7] and other negotiators, but even our journalists and pamphleteers, nor have we had any reason to change our measures or to repent of the confidence which we have placed in ignorance.

Are we now therefore to be told that this law is

Stamp'd upon th' unletter'd mind?

Are we to suspect our place-men, our pensioners,[d] our generals, our lawyers, our best friends in both Houses, all our adherents among the atheists and infidels, and our very gazetteers, clarks, and court-pages, as friends to independency? Doubtless this is the tendency of his assertion, but we have known them too long to be thus imposed upon, the *unletter'd* have been our warmest and most constant defenders, nor have we omitted any thing to deserve their favour, but have always endeavoured to raise their reputation, extend their influence, and encrease their number.[8]

In his first act he abounds with sentiments very inconsistent with the ends for which the power of licensing was granted; to enumerate them all would be to transcribe a great part of his play, a task which I shall very willingly leave to others, who, tho' true friends to the government, are not inflamed with zeal so fiery and impatient as mine, and therefore do not

d. pensioners *1788*] pensions *1739*

7. The alleged illiteracy and vulgarity of "old Horace" Walpole, Ambassador to France and to Holland, were frequently satirized. J. H. Plumb (*Sir Robert Walpole: The Making of a Statesman*, 1956, pp. 122–23) cites the charges against him and undertakes his defence.

8. This paragraph is a neat piece of sophistry by SJ. Brooke is obviously extolling illiteracy and ignorance as bulwarks of libertarian feeling. SJ, who would never have supported such a Rousseauist position, ingeniously twists it to make the Walpolian vindicator complain, "This is unfair— the illiterate are on *our* side."

feel the same emotions of rage and resentment at the sight of those infamous passages, in which venality and dependance are represented as mean in themselves, and productive of remorse and infelicity.

One line which ought, in my opinion, to be erased from every copy by a special Act of Parliament, is mentioned by Anderson,[9] as pronounced by the hero in his sleep,

O Sweden, O my country, yet I'll save thee.[1]

This line I have reason to believe thrown out as a kind of[e] watch-word for the opposing faction, who, when they meet in their seditious assemblies, have been observed to lay their hands upon their breasts, and cry out with great vehemence of accent,

O B——,[2] O my country, yet I'll save thee.

In the second scene he endeavours to fix epithets of contempt upon those passions and desires which have been always found most useful to the ministry, and most opposite to the spirit of independency.

Base fear, the laziness of lust, gross appetites,
These are the ladders and the grov'ling foot-stool
From whence the tyrant rises——
Secure and scepter'd in the soul's servility[3]
He has debauched the genius of our country
And rides triumphant, while her captive sons

e. of *emend.*] of a *1739*

---

9. Described in the list of characters as "chief lord of Dalecarlia," in western Sweden, and Gustavus's supporter. When the play opens, Gustavus is working obscurely in the Dalecarlian mines. With the assistance of Anderson, he organizes a rebellion among the Dalecarlian miners and peasants that eventually overthrows the regime of the Danish usurper, Cristiern.

1. *Gustavus Vasa*, Act i, Scene i.
2. I.e., "Britain." To "glory in the name of Britain" was part of the "patriot" idiom (see n. 2, p. 28 above).
3. *Gustavus Vasa* (Act i, Scene 2) has a full stop after "servility." The change in punctuation makes little difference to the sense.

Await his nod, the silken slaves of pleasure,
Or fetter'd in their fears.—

Thus is that decent submission to our superiors, and that proper awe of authority which we are taught in courts, termed "base fear" and the "servility of the soul." Thus are those gayeties and enjoyments, those elegant amusements, and lulling pleasures which the followers of a court are blessed with, as the just rewards of their attendance and submission, degraded to "lust," "grossness," and "debauchery." The author ought to be told, that courts are not to be mentioned with so little ceremony, and that though gallantries and amours are admitted there,[4] it is almost treason to suppose them infected with debauchery or lust.

It is observable that when this hateful writer has conceived any thought of an uncommon malignity, a thought which tends in a more particular manner to excite the love of liberty, animate the heat of patriotism, or degrade the majesty of kings, he takes care to put it in the mouth of his hero, that it may be more forcibly impressed upon his reader. Thus Gustavus, speaking of his tatters, cries out,

——Yes, my Arvida,
Beyond the sweeping of the proudest train
That shades a monarch's heel, I prize these weeds,
For they are sacred to my country's freedom.[5]

Here this abandoned son of liberty makes a full discovery of his execrable principles, the tatters of Gustavus, the usual dress of the assertors of these doctrines, are of more divinity, because they are sacred to freedom than the sumptuous and magnificent robes of regality itself. Such sentiments are truly detestable, nor could any thing be an aggravation of the author's guilt, except his ludicrous manner of mentioning a monarch.

The "heel of a monarch," or even the print of his "heel" is

---

4. On some of George II's "gallantries and amours," see pp. 5f. above.

5. Act I, Scene 3. Arvida is "of the royal blood of Sweden, friend and cousin to Gustavus."

a thing too venerable and sacred to be treated with such levity, and placed in contrast with rags and poverty. He, that will speak contemptuously of the *heel* of a *monarch*, will, whenever he can with security, speak contemptuously of his head.[6]

These are the most glaring passages which have occurr'd, in the perusal of the first pages; my indignation will not suffer me to proceed farther, and I think much better of the licenser, than to believe he went so far.[7]

In the few remarks which I have set down, the reader will easily observe that I have strained no expression beyond its natural import, and have divested myself of all heat, partiality, and prejudice.

So far therefore is Mr. Brooke from having received any hard or unwarrantable treatment, that the licenser has only acted in pursuance of that law to which he owes his power, a law which every admirer of the administration must own to be very necessary, and to have produced very salutary effects.

I am indeed surprised that this great office is not drawn out into a longer series of deputations, since it might afford a gainful and reputable employment to a great number of the friends of the government; and I should think instead of having immediate recourse to the deputy-licenser himself, it might be sufficient honour for any poet, except the Laureat,[8] to stand bare-headed in the presence of the deputy of the deputy's deputy in the nineteenth subordination.[9]

Such a number cannot but be thought necessary if we take into consideration the great work of drawing up an *Index Expurgatorius* to all the old plays; which is, I hope, already undertaken, or if it has been hitherto unhappily neglected, I take this opportunity to recommend.

---

6. E.g., Charles I's? It is clear that, whatever the nature of SJ's Toryism, it included little idolatry of King Charles the Martyr.

7. And so SJ too is spared the labour of perusing any more of Brooke's dull dramaturgy.

8. Colley Cibber. Ironically, in the cast prefaced to *Gustavus Vasa* (presumably that which rehearsed it at Drury-Lane), the villainous Prime Minister Trollio, representing Walpole, is played by "Mr. Cibber." But this was more probably Theophilus, Colley's son. The part of Gustavus was given to Quin.

9. Capell's appointment as deputy to Chetwynd, himself deputy to Grafton, occasioned some satire.

The productions of our old poets are crouded with passages very unfit for the ears of an English audience, and which cannot be pronounced without irritating the minds of the people.

This censure I do not confine to those lines in which liberty, natural equality, wicked ministers, deluded kings, mean arts of negotiation, venal senates, mercenary troops, oppressive officers, servile and exorbitant taxes, universal corruption, the luxuries of a court, the miseries of the people, the decline of trade, or the happiness of independency are directly mentioned. These are such glaring passages as cannot be suffered to pass without the most supine and criminal negligence. I hope the vigilance of the licensers will extend to all such speeches and soliloquies as tend to recommend the pleasures of virtue, the tranquillity of an uncorrupted head,[1] and the satisfactions of conscious innocence; for though such strokes as these do not appear to a common eye to threaten any danger to the government, yet it is well known to more penetrating observers that they have such consequences as cannot be too diligently obviated, or too cautiously avoided.

A man, who becomes once enamour'd of the charms of virtue, is apt to be very little concerned about the acquisition of wealth or titles, and is therefore not easily induced to act in a manner contrary to his real sentiments, or to vote at the word of command; by contracting his desires, and regulating his appetites, he wants much less than other men, and every one versed in the arts of government can tell[f] that men are more easily influenced in proportion as they are more necessitous.

This is not the only reason why virtue should not receive too much countenance from a licensed stage,[2] her admirers and followers are not only naturally independent, but learn

f. tell *1788*] tell; *1739*

---

1. Did SJ write "heart"? There is nothing especially admirable about a tranquil head. Nine paragraphs below, SJ has the writer praise the "tranquillity of ignorance."

2. Cf. *London*, l. 59: "And warbling eunuchs fill a licens'd stage" (later editions). This may well have been SJ's original version: the other reading is "silenc'd stage," but a stage on which eunuchs are warbling can hardly be called silenced.

such an uniform and consistent manner of speaking and acting, that they frequently by the mere force of artless honesty surmount all the obstacles which subtlety and politicks can throw in their way, and obtain their ends in spite of the most profound and sagacious ministry.

Such then are the passages to be expunged by the licensers: In many parts indeed the speeches will be imperfect, and the action appear not regularly conducted, but the Poet Laureat may easily supply these vacuities by inserting some of his own verses in praise of wealth, luxury, and venality.

But alas! all those pernicious sentiments which we shall banish from the stage, will be vented from the press, and more studiously read because they are prohibited.[g]

I cannot but earnestly implore the friends of the government to leave no art untry'd by which we may hope to succeed in our design of extending the power of the licenser to the press, and of making it criminal to publish any thing without an *imprimatur*.

How much would this single law lighten the mighty burden of state affairs? With how much security might our ministers enjoy their honours, their places, their reputations, and their admirers, could they once suppress those malicious invectives which are at present so industriously propagated, and so eagerly read, could they hinder any arguments but their own from coming to the ears of the people, and stop effectually the voice of cavil and enquiry.

I cannot but indulge myself a little while by dwelling on this pleasing scene, and imagining those "halcyon-days" in which no politicks shall be read but those of the *Gazetteer*, nor any poetry but that of the Laureat; when we shall hear of nothing but the successful negotiations of our ministers, and the great actions of ————.[3]

How much happier would this state be, than those perpetual jealousies and contentions which are inseparable from knowl-

g. prohibited. *emend.*] prohibited? *1739*

---

3. Supply "the king." George's competence as a soldier was never despicable, though his great moment of triumph was still to come, when he personally led his army to what was called a victory in the Battle of Dettingen, 1743. See n. 7, p. 42 above.

edge and liberty, and which have for many years kept this nation in perpetual commotions.

But these are times rather to be wished for than expected, for such is the nature of our unquiet countrymen, that if they are not admitted to the knowledge of affairs, they are always suspecting their governors of designs prejudicial to their interest, they have not the least notion of the pleasing tranquillity of ignorance, nor can be brought to imagine that they are kept in the dark, lest too much light should hurt their eyes. They have long claimed a right of directing their superiors, and are exasperated at the least mention of secrets of state.[4]

This temper makes them very readily encourage any writer or printer, who, at the hazard of his life or fortune, will give them any information; and while this humour prevails there never will be wanting some daring adventurer who will write in defence of liberty, and some zealous or avaricious printer who will disperse his papers.

It has never yet been found that any power, however vigilant or despotick, has been able to prevent the publication of seditious journals, ballads, essays and dissertations, *Considerations on the present State of Affairs*, and *Enquiries into the Conduct of the Administration.*[5]

---

4. Cf. SJ's "Essay on the Origin and Importance of Small Tracts and Fugitive Pieces" (the introduction to the *Harleian Miscellany*), 1744: "The form of our government which gives every man that has leisure or curiosity or vanity the right of inquiring into the propriety of public measures and by consequence obliges those who are intrusted with the administration of national affairs to give an account of their conduct to almost every man who demands it, may be reasonably imagined to have occasioned innumerable pamphlets, which would never have appeared under arbitrary governments, where every man lulls himself in indolence under calamities of which he cannot promote the re-

dress, or thinks it prudent to conceal the uneasiness of which he cannot complain without danger." Equally forthright affirmations by SJ of the Englishman's right to know what his government is doing and to make his opinion of it freely known can be found in his preface to the *Gentleman's Magazine*, 1743, the preface to *The Preceptor*, 1748, and elsewhere.

5. Cf. *Considerations upon the Present State of Our Affairs, at Home and Abroad* (T. Cooper, [Jan] 1739), attributed by *1788* to George Lyttelton, and *An Enquiry into the Conduct of Our Domestick Affairs, from the Year 1721 to the Present Time* (1734), by William Pulteney. There were many other pamphlets with similar titles.

Yet I must confess, that considering the success with which the present ministry has hitherto proceeded in their attempts to drive out of the world the old prejudices of patriotism and publick spirit, I cannot but entertain some hopes that what has been so often attempted by their predecessors, is reserved to be accomplished by their superior abilities.

If I might presume to advise them upon this great affair, I should dissuade them from any direct attempt upon the liberty of the press, which is the darling of the common people, and therefore cannot be attacked without immediate danger. They may proceed by a more sure and silent way, and attain the desired end without noise, detraction, or opposition.

There are scatter'd over this kingdom several little seminaries in which the lower ranks of people, and the younger sons of our nobility and gentry are taught,[6] from their earliest infancy, the pernicious arts of spelling and reading, which they afterwards continue to practise very much to the disturbance of their own quiet, and the interruption of ministerial measures.

These seminaries may, by an Act of Parliament, be at once suppressed, and that our posterity be deprived of all means of reviving this corrupt method of education, it may be made felony to teach to read, without a license from the Lord Chamberlain.

This expedient, which I hope will be carefully concealed from the vulgar, must infallibly answer the great end proposed by it, and set the power of the court not only above the insults of the poets, but in a short time above the necessity of providing against them. The licenser having his authority thus extended will in time enjoy the title and the salary without the trouble of exercising his power, and the nation will rest at length in ignorance and peace.

FINIS.

---

6. Grammar schools, like that of Lichfield? Or even more elementary institutions, like those of Dame Oliver and Tom Browne, which SJ attended? The specifying of *younger* sons of the nobility is interesting; presumably the eldest sons attended Eton or Westminster.

A DEBATE BETWEEN THE COMMITTEE OF THE HOUSE OF COMMONS AND OLIVER CROMWELL. 1741.

The source of this piece was a 112-page octavo pamphlet published in 1660 ("Printed by John Redmayne for Philip Chetwind") and entitled *Monarchy Asserted, To be the best, most Ancient and legall form of Government, in a conference had at Whitehall, with OLIVER late Lord Protector & a Committee of Parliament: Made good by the Arguments of* [ten names] *Members of that Committee*.[1] By the use of this title, as well as in a short preface ("By a Lover of his King and Countrey"), the sponsors of the 1660 edition made it clear that it was published at this time as a piece of royalist propaganda, intended to support the cause of the restoration of Charles II. "When once the sword had subdued the scepter," the preface begins, "and policy (though covered with the vail of piety) had advanced the military above the civil power: thou canst not (if a native) be ignorant, what were the sad effects of our Civil War. Magistracy and ministry despised, law and gospel slighted, propriety [i.e., property] invaded, parliaments garbled, and made subservient to ambitious greatness," and so on. Then the point is made that even the Parliament of the 1650's came to realize that the traditional institution of English monarchy was a salutary check on the despotism of a Cromwell, and that the "learned speeches" of the leading Parliamentarians printed in the work are to this effect.

The pamphlet was reprinted in 1679, with no substantial alterations, perhaps in connexion with the controversies that arose over the Exclusion Bill. Why Cave decided to reprint it in 1742 and to publish the following "abridgement" of it in the *Gentleman's Magazine* in 1741 can only be a matter for speculation. Perhaps the inference its readers were expected to draw was that there was a distinct parallel between the "tyranny" of Cromwell and that of Walpole: certainly such charges are forcibly made in the parliamentary debates on Carteret's and Sandys's motions to dismiss Walpole which took place in February 1741, the same month the "abridgement" appeared in the *Gentleman's Magazine*, debates brilliantly "reported" by Johnson.

Cave's reprint of *Monarchy Asserted* was not published until more than

1. Wood, *Athenae Oxonienses* (1691–92), lists it among the works of Nathaniel Fiennes, who was one of the leading participants in the discussion. But if Johnson's theory is right that it is merely a shorthand transcription, virtually unedited, it can hardly be said to have had an author. The violent partisanship of the preface hardly suits Fiennes, who held high office during the time of "the sad effects of our Civil War."

74

a year later, in May 1742. By that time Walpole had resigned, a fact which perhaps accounts for the scarcity of copies of it: the political excitement having died down, Cave may have decided that it was unlikely to have much of a sale and placed only a small printing order. Allen Hazen has suggested (*Johnson's Prefaces and Dedications*, 1937, p. 249) that Johnson edited the 1742 reprint: this seems plausible enough, if he had already undertaken the onerous task of condensing it for the *Gentleman's Magazine* in 1741.[2] The 1742 pamphlet is a full reprint of the 1660 text, but a comparison of the two does reveal a certain amount of intelligent editing: as Johnson says in the introduction to the "abridgement" in the *Gentleman's Magazine*, the 1660 text is abominably "ungrammatical, intricate, and obscure," whether this is the fault of the printer, the shorthand-writer whom Johnson postulates, or the incoherence of some of the speakers themselves, in particular Cromwell. It may be of interest, especially to students of Johnson's work as a textual editor of Shakespeare, to note some of the editorial work, which is clearly designed to try to make sense for the modern reader out of passages that in *1660* are obscure or contain obsolete phraseology. For instance, the title of *1660* reads "a conference had . . ."; *1742* makes it "a conference *held*." The preface "To the Reader" in *1660* reads "Though our grand politicians . . . framed for us many models of government . . . yet none did *Quadrare*" [italics in the original]; *1742* changes "*Quadrare*" to "quadrate" (i.e., "suit"). Cromwell's speeches in *1660* ramble on in a most baffling manner. The editor of *1742* struggles gallantly to repunctuate them, often by means of a plentiful use of dashes, so as to make them more readable; for instance, "To proceed that way, it will be a favour to me, otherwise I shall deal plainly with you: it doth put me out of the method of my own conceptions" (*1660*, pp. 5–6) becomes in *1742* "To proceed that way, it will be a favour to me. Otherwise—I shall deal plainly with you—it doth put me out of the method of my own conceptions." Cromwell's first speech begins, in *1660*, "Sir, I think that neither you nor I but meet with a very good heart, to come to some issue of this great businesse; and truly that is, that I cannot assure you." *1742* enables us to follow the train of thought better by changing "and truly that is" to "*but* truly that is" and then annotating the next "that" in a footnote "For *what*, as in other places." Page 13 of *1660* ends with the statement "It's better and more safe for the chief magistrate, to keep that which hath no doubt then." Page 14 continues with "The Parliament laying their interest and their regard to you together, and giving you this advice, this is *vox populi*." The *1742* editor reorders it thus: " . . . to keep that which hath no doubt. Then [i.e., "in addition"] the Parliament laying their interest. . . . " To the long list of names of members of the committee, *1742* adds a good deal of useful historical annotation: "Lord Chief Justice" of *1660* is expanded—accurately, since both took part in the discussions—to "Oliver St. John, Lord Chief Justice," and "Lord Chief Justice Glynn,

2. Hazen had never seen a copy of the advertised octavo edition, and noted only one listing of it, in an 1822 sale catalogue. As he points out, the Yale copy of the folio is inscribed on the title page, "The editor, Doctor Samuel Johnson."

Chief justice of the upper bench"; "Lord Howard" becomes "Charles, Lord Viscount Howard," and so on. This is conscientious editing, whoever did it.[3]

The other editorial task, that of condensing the sprawling report into about one-third of its original length so as to fit it into two numbers of the *Gentleman's Magazine* in 1741, was a much more difficult one than that of merely polishing and annotating the 1660 text for the reprint of 1742. Boswell, who first attributed the magazine version to Johnson (on "internal evidence"), referred to it in his *Life* (i.150) as a "Debate on the Proposal of Parliament to Cromwell, to assume the Title of King, abridged, methodised [in later editions of the *Life*, "modified"], and digested." It is all these, and

---

3. Since the 1742 edition of *Monarchy Asserted* is scarce, and since there is a chance that the footnotes are by SJ, it may be useful to reprint them here (the "Advertisement" is given in Allen T. Hazen, *Johnson's Prefaces and Dedications*, 1937, p. 150, and will be reprinted in another volume of this edition):

Text, 1742	*Footnote*
p. [1] Your highness is pleased to *mention the government	*It appears from this reference to what Cromwell had said, that part of this conference is omitted; or it may refer to his speech April 8.
truly, that is, †that I cannot assure you	†For *what*, as in other places.
I have made this ‖ motion of it to myself	‖Perhaps *notion*.
p. 2 I confess I did not so strictly examine that order of *reference	*Perhaps *Conference*.
p. 3 *For that particular which your Highnesse did formerly intimate	*i.e., with regard to, as for.
p. 4 The chief magistrate, if he should prove *otherwise	*That is, otherwise *than Good*.
p. 8 A law made long before any of our late differences had a being, in the 11* Henry VII	*See Supplement to Gent. Mag. for 1741, x. 702
p. 11 it is in your power to dispose and settle, and before,† we can have confidence that what you doe settle, will be as authentick as those things that were before, (especially as to the individual thing, the name or title) upon parliamentary account	†That is, before the Settlement.

more. Confronted with the confusion of the original, Johnson seems, understandably enough, to have decided that it was hopeless to try to follow the 1660 text in detail, and, noting the most important ideas expressed in the speeches of Cromwell and the parliamentary delegates, worked them up in his own words, thus composing what was virtually a new and original work. To eliminate the vast amount of repetition and irrelevance in the individual speeches of the delegates, he combines them into one continuous and reasonably lucid argument, merely printing in the margins the names of the speakers who from time to time had made the particular points found at this place in his text.

As Hill remarked (*Life*, 1.150, n. 2), the work is interesting as "showing the method which [Johnson] often followed in writing the Parliamentary Debates" of the 1740's. Hill gives a brief example of how Johnson puts together a number of disjointed remarks by Cromwell into one concise and polished sentence. Here is another example: the following, in *1660*,

It was said, that kingship is not a title but an office, so interwoven with the fundamental laws of this nation, as if they could not, or well could not be executed, and exercised without, partly (if I may say so) upon a supposed ignorance of the law that it hath of any other title, it knows

---

p. 14 The alteration destroyes the foundation, which is prescription, and annexes *it to a name that the law of the land hath no acquaintance with.	*That is, the office.
p. 15	In the margin of this speech were the following inconnected sentences; whether they were heads that had been spoken to, and not fully taken down by the short-hand writer, or hints in Mr. Lenthall's own writing, which he intended to enlarge upon, does not appear.
p. 26 You may well remember what the issue was of the last conference I had with you, and what the *stick was then	*Difficulty *or* Stop.
things revealed to us, (and such things are the subject matter of this *instrument* of yours) are, as farre as they may have relation to me, †that you and I may consider, what may be for publick good, that so they may receive such an impression as can humanely be given to them	†What *or* such as.

no other, neither doth any other know of it, the reciprocation of is
said this [*sic*] title, or name, or office, as you please to say is understood in the dementions of it, in the power and prerogatives of it, which
are by the law made certain, and the law can tell when it keeps within
compass, and when it exceeds its limits, and the law knowing this, the
people can know it also, and people do love what they know, and it
will neither be *pro salute populi*, nor for our safety to obtrude upon them
names, that they do not, nor cannot understand

becomes, in the *Gentleman's Magazine* version,

It has been urged, with great appearance of strength, that the title of
King is the only title by which the laws acknowledge the chief magistrate of this nation, that the title cannot be changed without supposing
a change in the office, and that a change in the office would be a
dangerous innovation, productive of debate, jealousy, and suspicion;
that the limits of this new-erected authority would be unknown to the
people, as being unsettled by the law; that the people are best pleased
with institutions which they have long known, and that therefore it
would neither contribute to the public happiness, nor to our own
security, to obtrude upon the nation titles and offices either new in
reality or in appearance.

There are also many passages in the "Debate" to which nothing at all in the
original corresponds—passages intended to make a rough transition smooth,
to emphasize a conclusion, to make explicit a crucial point in the argument
that was only obscurely implied in the original. Yet, as far as one can tell
without making an exhaustively minute comparative study of the two pieces,
Johnson seems to be trying to represent fairly the gist of the original work,
without intruding his own views and prejudices (it is noteworthy that he
completely omits the tendentious preface of *1660*, although it presumably
expresses much of his own attitude toward the Civil War). This "Debate,"
then, will be of interest to the student of Johnson in much the same way as
the contemporary parliamentary debates which he was reporting at the
same time as he wrote this, and which appear in other volumes of the present
edition.[4]
    The only text of the Cromwell "Debate"—it seems hitherto not to have
been reprinted—is that of the *Gentleman's Magazine* for February and March
1741 (XI. 93–100, 148–154). The text of the February instalment exists in
two states, one (found in the copies of the *Gentleman's Magazine* in the
University of Toronto central library, the Griffith collection at the University
of Texas, and the Henry E. Huntington Library, San Marino) much more
corrupt than the other, commoner one. Probably the corrupt state is the
later one, the result of a hasty, unsupervised resetting because of some
accident to the type while stored and awaiting a reimpression of this number

4. I am indebted to Professor Arthur Sherbo for allowing me to use a comparative analysis he has made of the content of *Monarchy Asserted* and the "Debate"
in the *Gentleman's Magazine*.

of the magazine (this later setting will be designated *1741a* in the textual notes below, and the earlier setting *1741*).[5] Even the earlier setting, however (as well as the March instalment, which seems to exist in only one state), contains a considerable number of printer's errors. Most of these are recorded below, though some minor ones have been silently corrected.

In the original the names of speakers are printed in the margin; in the present edition these are printed in footnotes keyed to the first word of the line in the original next to which the name appears.

5. I am grateful to Professor William B. Todd, of the University of Texas, for the results of a careful study of the variant states of the February instalment of the "Debate." In support of the hypothesis that the more corrupt setting is the later rather than the earlier state, Professor Todd points out that gathering N, as well as M (which contains the "Debate"), is reset in the Toronto and Griffith copies, and that the numbering of the first page of M as 93 (it is preceded by page 88), which might be thought to indicate that the pages were set hastily in the first place, is in fact a *correction* of a misnumbering of pages that had begun in the January issue of the magazine.

A Debate Between the Committee of the House of Commons in 1657, and O. Cromwell, upon the Humble Petition and Advice of the Parliament, by Which He Was Desired to Assume the Title of King

The following debate will, doubtless, engage the attention of our readers, not only by the importance of the question, but by the reputation of those who were deputed to discuss it, and the strength of the arguments employed by them, which, we hope, is not impaired by our method of[a] expression.

The difficulty of procuring this debate, which was published in 1660, and we believe never afterwards re-printed,[1] inclined us to insert it in our magazine without alteration; but we found it, upon a closer examination, by no means adapted to the taste of those who expect entertainment and instruction at the same time; or require, at least, to be improved without unnecessary labour; for the speeches being taken, probably in short-hand, with[b] omissions of passages less important, and of such words as the writer imagined him-

a. of *1741a*] or *1741*   b. without *1741a*

1. It was reprinted London, 1679.

self able to supply from the general contexture of the sentence
and drift of the discourse, which is frequently practised by
short-hand writers, are either for want of memory, or care in[c]
the copier, so ungrammatical, intricate and obscure, so full
of broken hints, imperfect sentences, and uncouth expressions,
that very few would have resolution, or curiosity sufficient to
labour in search of knowledge through so many obstructions.
Nor should we have attempted it, had we not been encouraged
by the hopes of preserving others from so disgusting a task.

The various arguments made use of by the several members
of the Committee, we have reduced, to avoid repetition, into
one series or discourse, and annexed to each argument, in the
margin, the names of those by whom it was produced.

On April the 11th, [according to Whitlocke, on the 4th,][2]
the Protector was attended by the Committee, appointed by
the Parliament, to receive and answer his doubts and scruples
relating to their request and advice, that he would assume the
title of King, but the Protector being unwilling to disclose
his own sentiments, till he was informed of the reasons by
which the Parliament had been determined, the following
arguments were offered by the Committee, which consisted
of 100 members, those who were deputed to treat on this subject, being

> Oliver St. John, Lord Chief Justice
> Lord Chief Justice Glynne
> Mr. Whitlocke, one of the Commissioners of the Treasury
> Mr. Lisle ⎫ Commissioners of the Great Seal
> Mr. Fines ⎭
> My[d] Lord Broghill
> Mr. Lenthall, Master of the Rolls
> Sir Charles Wolseley
> Sir Richard Onslow
> Colonel Jones

c. of *1741a*   d. My *emend.*] Mr. *1741, 1741a*

---

2. Here and later SJ refers to the   *the English Affairs* (1682, reprinted
account of the conference given in   1732).
Bulstrode Whitelocke, *Memorials of*

May it please your Highness,

It is with great satisfaction, that we see ourselves deputed by the Parliament to confer with your Highness, upon the settlement of the publick tranquillity, and the establishment of such a form of government as may best promote the great ends for which government was instituted, for which we have been so long labouring, and for which we have hazarded our fortunes and our lives. We doubt not of finding your Highness ready to concur in any lawful measures, that can contribute to the happiness of the public, to the pacification of those differences that have so divided them, and to the perpetuity of that freedom which has been so dearly purchased, and so successfully defended. And we cannot forbear to inform you that, in our opinion, in the opinion of the Parliament, and of the people who are represented by it, these purposes cannot be effectually prosecuted by your Highness without assuming not the office only, but the title likewise of King.

Your Highness may demand why, having[3] already made you Protector, invested you with the office of chief magistrate, and intrusted you with the care of our liberties, our commerce, and our honour, we are now grown weary of our institution, and desire to restore a title, which a long series of wicked administration has made it proper to abrogate? To this we can easily answer, that our request is the request of the people, the people whose interest is chiefly to be considered, and to whom it is[4] your highest honour to be a faithful servant. That they have a right to judge for themselves, to promote their own happiness by their own measures, and to distinguish their servants by what name or titles they shall judge most proper, cannot be denied. Monarchy has always been thought by this nation, the most eligible form of government, and the title of King has been always considered by them as essential to it. The office[5] has never been complained of, nor the title changed, even by those parliaments that have made the strictest enquiries into the defects of our constitution, and have had power to reform whatever they disliked. The office in general was always regarded as useful and necessary, and

---

3. *Margin:* Chief Justice Glynne
4. *Margin:* Sir Charles Wolseley

5. *Margin:* Sir Charles Wolseley, Ch. Justice Glynne

the title was reverenced, when the conduct of him that held it was condemned. It is never prudent to make needless alterations, because we are already acquainted with all the consequences of known establishments and antient forms; but new methods of administration may produce evils which the[6] most prudent cannot foresce, nor the most diligent rectify. But least of all are such changes to be made as draw after them the necessity of endless alterations, and extend their effects thro' the whole frame of government.

That the change of the title of King to that of Protector, or any other, would affect the remotest links of subordination, and alter the whole constitution, is evident, at the most superficial and transient view of the laws and customs of the nation. Every officer of justice[7] acts in the King's name, and by the King's authority, an authority that gives life and efficacy to law, and makes every sentence valid and binding. In all criminal cases the law knows not any prosecutor but the King, nor can inflict any punishment but in his name.

If it be urged, the judges have already taken[8] their commissions in the name of the Lord Protector, and supposed his authority and that of the King to be the same, let it be remembered that the judges themselves were far from concurring in their opinions, they whose province it is to justify the proceedings of the government to the people, were not satisfied themselves, and even those that complied[e] with least reluctance pleaded rather the resistless force of necessity, than the authority of law or the evidence of reason; and let us not reduce our judges to say, when either the captious or the conscientious enquirer shall demand the reasons of their conduct, that they act not as they *ought* but as they *must*.

In desiring you to assume this title, the Parliament has regard not only to conscience but prudence, not only to the people's happiness but to your safety. The office of Protector is new and unheard of till now, and by consequence unknown[9] to the law, nor understood with regard to its relation to other

e. compiled *1741a*

---

6. *Margin:* Whitlocke
7. *Margin:* Whitlocke Lenthal Glynne Fines Broghill
8. *Margin:* Glynne
9. *Margin:* Whitlocke Glynne Lisle Broghill

parts of the constitution; so that neither the duties of Protector are known by the people, nor those of the people by the Protector; such ignorance and uncertainty can produce nothing but disputes, murmurs and confusion.

The knowledge of our duty is necessarily previous to the practice of it, and how can any man know his duty to a magistrate to whose authority he is a stranger?[1] The limits of obedience to a Protector are settled by no law, nor is there any statute in being that condemns any attempt to shake off his authority. For this reason it is not without long hesitation and importunate persuasion, that juries are prevailed upon to assign the name, and fix the guilt of treason to any[2] conspiracies against your life or government. The King's authority is supported by the law, and his person is exempt from violation; but the Protector's office has no such sanction, and his power may therefore be, if not justly, yet legally resisted; nor is his person secured any otherwise than that of the meanest subject.

The Protector is, indeed, in a state of greater difficulty and embarrassment than any other member of the community; he is obliged to obey the laws, but with regard to his office is not protected[3] by them; he is restrained by the law from any exorbitant exertions of power, but not supported by it in the due exercise of his authority. This defect in the supreme magistracy must affect all subordinate authority; those who act by the Protector's commission, can receive from him no other power than such as he is invested with, a power which the laws of the nation, those laws to which on all occasions every man must appeal, disavow, and reject. So that no man can be obliged by law to admit the determinations of the courts as obligatory and conclusive, and how great the number is of those who deny any moral or conscientious reason for obedience to the present government, your Highness needs not be informed. These men, however at present subjected, are at least formidable by their multitudes, and it is always more eligible to procure a chearful and willing, than constrain an involuntary and reluctant obedience. All these men

---

1. *Margin:* Wolseley   3. *Margin:* Wolseley
2. *Margin:* Wolseley

allow the authority[4] of regal government, and profess their willingness to submit to it; so that all opinions unite in this point, and all parties concur to make a compliance with this request necessary to your Highness.

Nor is it only for your own sake that this[5] desire is so warmly press'd, but for the security of those whose endeavours have contributed to the establishment of the present government, or shall hereafter act by your authority. All those who receive commissions from the King, by whatever means exalted to the throne, are secured from prosecution and punishment in any change[f] of affairs, by the statute of the eleventh year of Henry the Seventh;[6] but the name of Protector can confer no such security, and therefore the cautious and vigilant will always decline your service, or prosecute your affairs with diffidence and timidity, even the honest and scrupulous will be fearful of engaging where they have nothing but their own opinion to set in ballance against the law; and the artful and the avaritious, the discontented and the turbulent, will never cease to contrive a revolution, by which they may revenge the wrongs that they imagine themselves to have received, and riot in the spoils of their enemies.

The present alienation of the Crown of these realms from him who pretends to claim them by his birth, may be compared to a divorce, which may, by the mutual consent of both parties, be set aside. It is therefore necessary, to prevent any future reunion, that the Crown[g] be consigned to another.

Were the reasons for your assumption of this title less weighty than they appear, the desire of Parliament ought to add[7] to their efficacy. It is not to be conceived that we are able to assign all the arguments that might be formed by the united and concurrent wisdom of so numerous and discerning an assembly, an assembly deputed by the whole people to judge and to act for them. The desires of a Parliament are never to be considered as sudden[8] starts of imagination, or

f. charge *1741a*   g. Crown *emend.*] Crown, *1741, 1741a*

---

4. *Margin:* Broghill
5. *Margin:* Broghill
6. Cap. 1 [1494]: "None that shall attend upon the King and do him true service shall be attainted, or forfeit any thing."
7. *Margin:* Glynne
8. *Margin:* Wolseley

to be rejected as trivial, or unworthy of consideration; the desire of the Parliament, is the voice of the people; nor can it, indeed, be now disregarded, without breaking all the rules of policy, and neglecting the first opportunity of reinstating[h] the nation in tranquillity.[9] The Parliament, the only authority which the nation reverences, has now first attempted to establish a legal and settled government, by conferring on your Highness the title of King, which you therefore cannot refuse without encouraging the enemies of our government, by showing[1] not only, that the chief magistrate of the nation bears a title unknown to the law, but even such as is disapproved by the Parliament, that Parliament which himself called.

But the Parliament is far from desiring that their authority alone should enforce their desire, for which they have so many and so strong reasons to alledge; nor are their own reasons alone to be considered, but the authority of all former parliaments, who have ever been to the last degree cautious of admitting the least change in any thing that related to the constituent part of our government.

When King James, after his accession to[2] the Crown of England, was desirous of changing his title to that of King of Great Britain, the Parliament refused to admit any alteration in the regal stile; not that they discovered any apparent ill consequences arising from it, but because they did not know how far it might affect the constitution, nor to what farther alterations it might make way.

In the late Parliament, when it was proposed that the name of Parliament should[3] be changed to that of Representative of the People, the proposal was for the same reason disapproved. *Nolumus leges Angliae mutari* was a fixed principle of the antient barons, and certainly nothing can shew greater weakness than to change without prospect of advantage. Long prescription is a sufficient argument in favour of a practice against which nothing can be alledged; nor is it sufficient to affirm that the change may be made without

h. restraining *1741a*

---

9. *Margin:* Glynne
1. *Margin:* Broghill

2. *Margin:* Lenthal
3. *Margin:* Lenthal

inconvenience, for change itself is an evil, and ought to be ballanced by some equivalent advantage,[4] and bad consequences may arise tho' we do not foresee them.

But the consequences of the change now proposed are neither remote nor doubtful; by substituting the name and office of Protector in the place of those of King, we shall immediately alarm the people, we shall awaken the jealousy of the wise, and the fears of the timorous, there[5] will be indeed some reasons for[6] apprehension and suspicion, which designing men will not fail to exaggerate for their own purposes. The first question that will naturally arise will be, What is this new office of Protector, upon what law is it founded, and what are the limits of his authority? To these enquiries what answer can be returned? Shall it be said that his authority is independent, despotick, and unlimited? Where then is the liberty for which the wisest and best men of this nation have been so long contending? What is the advantage of all our battles and all our victories? If we say that the authority of the Protector is bounded by the laws, how shall we prove[7] the assertion? What law shall we be able to cite, by which the duties of the Protector[i] to the people, or those of the people to the Protector, are marked out?

This then is the great reason upon which the Parliament have made their request. The people are to be governed[8] according to the law, and the law acknowledges no supreme magistrate but the King. It is necessary to the good administration of the state, that the duty both of governors and subjects should be known, limited,[9] and stated, that neither

i. Protector *emend.*] Protector, *1741, 1741*a

4. "All change is of itself an evil, which ought not to be hazarded but for evident advantage" (*Plan of a Dictionary*, 1747); " 'Change,' says Hooker, 'is not made without inconvenience, even from worse to better.' There is in constancy and stability a general and lasting advantage, which will always overbalance the slow improvements of gradual correction" (Preface to the *Dictionary*). This observation, so dear

to SJ, is apparently his own contribution to the debate; there seems to be no passage corresponding to it in *Monarchy Asserted*.

5. *Margin:* Fines
6. *Margin:* Lisle
7. *Margin:* Whitlocke Glynne Fines Broghill
8. *Margin:* Glynne
9. *Margin:* Wolseley Whitlocke Broghill Glynne

the governors may oppress the people, nor the people rebel against the governors; the Parliament therefore desires that the office and title of King may be restored as they are understood in their whole extent, and in all their relations; every man is well informed when the King acts in conformity to the law, and when he transgresses the limits of his authority. But of the power of the Protector they know nothing, and therefore will suspect every thing;[1] nor indeed can their suspicions be reasonably censured, for till they are informed what are the claims of this new magistrate, how can they know their own rights?

If your Highness should injure, or oppress[2] any man, to what law can he appeal? He may, indeed, discover that the King could not have attacked his property, but will never be able to prove that the Protector is subject to the same restraint; so that neither your Highness is protected by the law when you do right, nor the subject redressed if you should do wrong.

The end for which monarchy has been[3] for some time suspended, is the happiness of the people, and this end can only now be attained by reviving it. The question may indeed be brought to a short issue, for either the office of Protector[4] is the same with that of King, or something different from it; if it be the same, let us not be so weak as to impose upon ourselves, or so dishonest as to endeavour to deceive others, by rejecting the name while we retain the thing; let not an aversion[5] to an idle sound, to a name reverenced by the people, and approved by the Parliament, incite you to reject the petition of the whole nation, to raise difficulties in the distribution of justice, and awaken themselves[6] in the minds of all those who attend more to names than things,[7] who will always be the

---

1. *Margin:* Fines Lisle Broghill
2. *Margin:* Glynne
3. *Margin:* Broghill
4. *Margin:* Fines
5. *Margin:* Fines Lisle Glynne
6. The text of *Monarchy Asserted* gives no clue as to how this imperfect sentence should be corrected.

7. "I am not yet so lost in lexicography as to forget that 'words are the daughters of earth, and that things are the sons of heaven.' Language is only the instrument of science, and words are but the signs of ideas" (Preface to the *Dictionary*).

greatest number, and whose satisfaction ought therefore to be
endeavoured by all lawful compliances.

It is a certain truth that old institutions[8] are, merely because they are old, preferable to new plans, in their nature
equally good, because a very small part of mankind judges
from any other principle than custom, and it will be long
before new titles attract their regard, esteem and veneration.

But if the office of Protector be not only in its denomination,
but in nature also, absolutely new, we are then yet in a state
of uncertainty, confusion and misery; we have the bounds of
his authority to settle, the rights of Parliament to state, all
our laws to new model, and[9] our whole system of government
to constitute afresh. An endless and insuperable task, from
which we intreat your Highness to exempt us, by assuming,
according to the advice of Parliament, the office and title of
King.

The Protector having desired some time to consider the arguments that had been offered, returned on April the 13th (the
7th as may be collected from Whitlocke) his answer to this
effect.

My Lord,[1]

Though I am far from imagining myself qualified to con-
trovert a question of so great importance, with the learned
members of this Committee, especially as the arguments have
been founded chiefly upon the laws and antient constitution
of this nation, with which I have had no opportunity to be
well acquainted, yet, since it may be reasonably required of
me either to yield to your reasons,[j] or to assign the difficulties

j. reason *1741a*

8. *Margin:* Broghill Fines Wolseley
9. *Margin:* Fines
1. Printed "Lords" in *1741a*; at
first glance, the plural seems more
suitable to the context, and perhaps
this is what the compositor of the
reset 1741 issue thought. But both
the 1660 and 1742 editions of *Monarchy Asserted* and the earlier setting

of *1741* have the singular; moreover, it
is used at the beginning of Cromwell's
second speech, p. 106 below; and it
seems safer to assume that this was
SJ's intention. Cromwell may be
thought of as addressing himself to
the chairman, or senior member, of
the committee.

and objections that hinder me from yielding, I shall attempt to consider and discuss them diligently and distinctly.

It has been urged, with great appearance of strength, that the title of King is the only title by which the laws acknowledge the chief magistrate of this nation, that the title cannot be changed without supposing a change in the office, and that a change in the office would be a dangerous innovation, productive of debate, jealousy, and suspicion; that the limits of this new-erected authority would be unknown to the people, as being unsettled by the law; that the people are best pleased with institutions which they have long known, and that therefore it would neither contribute to the public happiness, nor to our own security, to obtrude upon the nation titles and offices either new in reality or in appearance.

The apprehension that the parliaments have always expressed of changes and innovations, has been made appear by two remarkable instances, and to shew the necessity of restoring the title of King it has been alledged, that not only the dangers and discontents that novelty produces will be escaped by it, but that both the chief magistrate, and those that act by his authority, will be more effectually protected by the laws of the nation.

These are the chief arguments that have dwelt upon my memory. Arguments doubtless of force, and such as do not admit of an easy confutation, but which, however, in my opinion, prove rather the expediency than necessity of reviving[k] monarchy under its ancient title, and as such I shall consider them, for where absolute inevitable necessity is contended for, the controversy will be very short; absolute necessity will soon appear by the impossibility of shewing any method of avoiding it, and where any expedient may be proposed that may probably produce the same effects, necessity vanishes at once. Very few actions are really necessary, most of them are only expedient, or comparatively preferable to other measures that may be taken. Where there is room for comparisons there is room for diversity of opinions.

That the title of King is not necessary, how long soever it may have been in use, or what regard soever may have been

k. reviving of *1741a*

paid it, is plain from the very nature of language: Words have not their import from the natural power of particular combinations of characters, or from the real efficacy of certain sounds, but from the consent of those that use them, and arbitrarily annex certain ideas to them which might have been signified with equal propriety by any other.[2] Whoever originally distinguished the chief magistrate by the appellation of King, might have assigned him any other denomination, and the power of the people can never be lost or impaired. If that might once have been done, it may be done now; for surely words are of no other value than their significations, and the name of King can have no other use than any other word of the same import.

That the law may be as regularly executed, and as chearfully obey'd, tho' the name of King be entirely rejected, is, in my opinion, plain, from the experience both of the time in which I have administered the government, and of that when the execution of the laws was intrusted to the (*Custodes Libertatis Angliae*) Keepers[1] of the Liberties of England, in which justice has been as regularly, as equally, and as expeditiously distributed as in the happiest days of the most celebrated kings. The judges did, indeed, hesitate for some time about the legality of their commissions, but a short deliberation freed them from their doubts, and certainly their authority ought to be of weight, as they have been excelled by none of their predecessors in learning or abilities.

That I have never interrupted the course of justice, all the judges can attest, and, I believe, affirm with equal confidence, that it has not been more obstructed by any other impediment than in former times; so that the title of King appears by no means necessary to the efficacy of the law.

Such obedience has been paid to the supreme magistracy under two different denominations, neither of which were established by a parliamentary sanction; and why should we

1. keeper *1741a*

---

2. See n. 7, p. 87 above. This is perhaps the most explicit of SJ's many statements of his "nominalist" view of language. Although the point is frequently made in *Monarchy Asserted* that "king" is only a name, there is nothing like this Lockean or Berkeleyan exposition.

imagine any other title would obtain less regard when confirmed by the power to which[m] the title that you now contend
for owes its validity?

There was once a time when every office, and the title
annexed to that office, was newly invented and introduced,
from what did it derive its legality and its importance at its
first introduction, but from general consent? The great, binding, the inviolable law, is the consent of the people; without
this nothing is right, and supported by this nothing can be
wrong. Antiquity adds nothing to this great sanction, nor
can novelty take away its authority. What is now determined
by the people, or by their proper representatives, is of equal
validity with the earliest institutions, and whether they will
be governed by a supreme magistrate under the name of[n]
King, or any other, the government is equally lawful.

As therefore neither reason nor experience can prove that
this title is absolutely essential to the due administration of
justice, it is proper to enquire how far it may be convenient,
what proportions of advantage or detriment will arise from it.
In this enquiry I hope that the honesty of my intentions, and
the purity of my heart will not be mistaken. I hope that neither
hypocrisy nor artifice will be imputed to my open declarations
and sincere professions; declarations and professions which I
make not hastily and negligently, but with care, reflection,
and deliberate caution, in the presence of the Almighty Power
by whose providence I have been guided, and in whose
presence I stand. I hope it will not be imagined that I reject
the title of King from fondness for that of *Protector*, a name and
an office to which I was far from aspiring, and which I only
did not refuse when it was offered me; nor did I then accept
it as imagining myself qualified to govern others, who find it
sufficiently difficult to regulate my own conduct, nor even
from a confidence that I should be able much to benefit the
nation; the only motive by which I was induced to engage in
so arduous and invidious[o] an employment, was the desire of
obviating those evils which I saw impending over the nation,
and to prevent the revival of those disputes in which so much

m. which *emend.*] *om. 1741, 1741a*   n. name of *emend.*] *om. 1741, 1741a*   o. in-
dividious *1741a*

blood had been already shed, and which must inevitably involve us in endless confusion.

Having these prospects before me, I thought it not lawful to reject an opportunity of preventing calamities, even when there was no hope of promoting happiness; I therefore could not but accept, what at the same time I could not ardently desire. For nothing can deserve to be pursued with eagerness and assiduity but the power of doing good, of conferring real and solid benefits upon mankind. And surely, while the only end for which greatness and authority are desired, is public good, those desires are at least lawful, and perhaps worthy of applause: They are certainly lawful, if he that entertains them has, by a long and diligent examination of his own heart, an examination serious and sincere, without any of those fallacious arts by which the conscience is too frequently deceived, satisfied himself that his ultimate views are not his own honour or interest, but the welfare of mankind, and the promotion of virtue, and that his advancement will contribute to them.

Having informed you by what means I was raised to the Protectorship, and for what reasons I accepted it, I may properly proceed to deliver my own sentiments of the office in which I have engaged, that it may appear, from my own notions of my present situation, how little it can be preferred by me, on account of any personal views, to that which the Parliament now offers, and that whatever arguments I shall make use of in this question are not dictated by private interest, but by a sincere and unfeigned regard for the happiness of the nation.

I have often considered, with a degree of attention suitable to the importance of the enquiry, what is the nature of my present office, and what is the purpose which I am principally to have in view, and could never attain to any farther determination than that I was the chief constable of the nation, and was intrusted with the care of the public peace. This trust I have endeavoured faithfully to discharge, and have been so far successful, that peace has never been long interrupted, and whatever miseries have been feared or felt, we have enjoy'd the blessing of quiet, a blessing, in my opinion, too valuable to be hazarded by any unnecessary or inconsiderate[p] innovations, and for the sake of which I think it therefore necessary to decline the title which is now offered me.

This argument will not, perhaps, be immediately understood, nor is it easy for me to make it intelligible without giving an account of some past transactions, too long to be excused but by the importance of the subject.

At the beginning of the late war between the King and Parliament, I observed that in all encounters the Royalists prevailed, and our men, tho' superior in number, or other advantages, were shamefully routed, dispersed, and slaughtered; and discoursing upon this subject with my worthy friend Mr. John Hampden, a name remembered by most of you with reverence, I told him that this calamity, formidable as it was, admitted, in my opinion, of a remedy, and that by a proper choice of soldiers the state of the war must soon be changed. You are, says I, in comparing our forces with those of the enemy, to regard, in the first place, the difference between their education and habitual sentiments. Our followers are, for the most part, the gleanings of the lowest rank of the people, serving-men[q] discarded, and mechanics without employments, men used to insults and servility from their cradles, without any principles of honour, or incitements to overbalance the sense of immediate danger. Their army is crowded with men whose profession is courage, who have been by their education fortified against cowardice, and have been esteemed throughout their lives in proportion to their bravery. All their officers are men of quality, and their soldiers the sons of gentlemen, men animated by a sense of reputation, and had rather die than support the ignominy of having turned their backs; can it be supposed that education has no force, and that principles exert no influence upon actions? Can men that fight only for pay, without any sense of honour from conquest, or disgrace from being overcome, withstand the charge of gentlemen, of men that act upon principles of honour, and confirm themselves and each other in their resolutions by reason and reflection. To motives such as these, what can be opposed by our men that may exalt them to the same degree of gallantry, and animate them with the

p. inconsiderable *1741a*   q. serving-men, *1741a*

same contempt of danger and of death? Zeal for religion is the only motive more active and powerful than these, and that it is in our power to inculcate. Let us chuse men warm with regard for their religion, men who shall think it an high degree of impiety to fly before the wicked and profane, to forsake the cause of heaven, and prefer safety to truth, and our enemies will quickly be subdued.

This advice was not otherways disapproved than as difficult to be put in execution: This difficulty I imagined myself in some degree able to surmount, and applied all my industry to levy such men as were animated with the zeal of religion, and to inflame their fervour; nor did the effect deceive my expectation, for when these men were led to the field, no *Veterans* could stand before them, no obstructions could retard, or danger affright them; and to these men are to be attributed the victories that we have gained, and the peace that we enjoy.

Of this account there may be many uses; it may contribute to confirm us in our perseverance in this cause, that it has hitherto succeeded by the endeavours of good men; it may tend to the confirmation of religious men in their purposes of an holy life, that those principles are more efficacious and powerful than any other, but with regard to the present dispute, I mean only to observe how highly these men are to be valued, how much of our regard they may justly claim, and how weak it would be to alienate them from us by reviving a title which they have been taught to abhor.

It may be urged, that to refuse obedience to lawful authority, under whatsoever name, is not consistent with the character of piety; and that to abhor the title and office of King, the title lawfully conferred, and the office justly administered, is not so much religion as prejudice, and rather folly than conscience. Nor can I deny either of these assertions, I am far from thinking it lawful to withold obedience from lawful government, and freely confess, that to reverence or detest a mere name, is equally weak. And I am confident that those good men of whom I have been speaking, will obey the legislative power by what title soever exercised; and with regard to their scruples, however unreasonable, it is my opinion that they who have done and suffered so much, deserve that some indulgence should be shewed, even to their weakness, and that they should not be grieved with imaginary hardships, or perplexed with tormenting scruples without necessity; their readiness to comply with authority is a plea for tenderness and regard, which will contribute to unite their endeavours with ours, for the suppression of those who seem to look upon it as their duty to oppose all government, and whose opinions lead them to imagine all human authority impious and detestable.

The reason for which these men will be offended at the revival of the title and office of King, a reason which, I confess, has some weight with me, and may, perhaps, more strongly affect weaker minds, if any such there are, is this: We are, indeed, principally to consult the Scriptures as the rule of our consciences, but we are likewise to have regard to the visible hand of God, and the dispensations of providence, by which the Scripture may be often very clearly and usefully explained; in these explications, indeed, we may easily be deceived; and therefore ought not to depend upon them with a presumptuous degree of confidence, but to use them with caution, modesty, and a careful attention to every circumstance that may rectify our mistakes, but we certainly ought not to pass great events over without reflection, observation, or regard.

When, in conformity to this rule, I consider the late revolution that has happened in this nation, and see that, not only the royal family is subdued and exiled, but the name and title eradicated by the providence of God, it appears to me no less than presumption to attempt to restore it. How just these proceedings were with regard to those that transacted them, I am not[r] to dispute, nor need I say how I would act were the same circumstances to recur, I only desire you to remember, that neither by me, nor by those who invested me with this authority, was the title abolished, but by the long Parliament. It is sufficient for my purpose to remark, that the title was not laid aside by caprice, or accidental disgust, but after ten years' war, by long and sober deliberation, and what is this less than the hand of God? When I see that by these instruments of vengeance he has not only ex-

r. not *emend.*] now *1741, 1741a*

pelled the family, but blasted the title; would not an attempt
to restore it be like an endeavour to build up Jericho, to
defeat the designs of Providence, and oppose the great Ruler
of the Universe?

These are the reasons for which I think the office and title
of King neither necessary nor expedient; whether they ought
to convince you I am not able to determine, nor wish that
they should have any force which their own weight does not
give them. In the desire of a firm and settled form of government, the great end for which this proposal is made, I concur
with the Parliament, and hope that no reasons or resolution
of mine will in the least tend to obstruct it; for a firm and
legal establishment, as it is the only method by which happiness and liberty can be secured, is equally the concern of
every wise and honest man, and whoever opposes it, deserves
nothing less than to be marked out as an enemy to his country.
I would not wish that this great design should be frustrated
by a compliance with my inclinations, for settlement and
order are surely necessary, whether royalty be necessary or
not; whatever may contribute to this, I intreat you steadily
to pursue, nor should I advise even to deny that gratification
to the particular prejudices or passions of private men, that
may secure their affections to good for the advancement of it.
For my part, could I multiply my person, or dilate my power,
I should dedicate myself wholly to this great end, in the
prosecution of which I shall implore the blessing of God upon
your counsels and endeavours.[3]

On the 13th of April, (according to Whitlock) the Committee attended the Protector, and offered the following reply.

As the request of the Parliament is of too great importance
to be either granted or refused without long deliberation, we
have thought it necessary to attend your Highness a second
time, that this great question, after having been on both
sides attentively consider'd, may at last be diligently discuss'd, and determin'd with that caution which is always to
be used, where the happiness and tranquility of the publick
is evidently concern'd.

---

3. The February instalment ends here.

That the title of King is not absolutely and physically necessary to government, will be readily admitted; for, if government can subsist an hour, or a day,[s] without it, no man can affirm that it is absolutely necessary. Necessity in this sense has no place in political transactions. Laws themselves[4] are not absolutely necessary, the will of the prince may supply them, and the wisdom and vigilance of a good prince make a people happy without them. Natural necessity allows no room for disputation, being always evident beyond controversy, and powerful beyond resistance. Therefore in all debates of this kind, by necessity, moral necessity is to be understood, which is nothing more than a high degree of expedience, or incontestable reasons of preference.

That the title of King is in this sense necessary to the government of these nations may perhaps be proved, but an attempt to prove it seems in the present state of the question superfluous, because the request of the Parliament is in itself a reason sufficient to over ballance all that has been urged in opposition to it. And it may therefore be rather requir'd of your Highness to prove the necessity of rejecting that title which the whole people of England entreat you to accept.

For nothing less than necessity ought to[5] be put in balance with the desires of the whole people legally represented. But how can such necessity be evinced? Or whence can it arise? That either monarchy, or any other form of government is contrary to the reveal'd will of God cannot be pretended. No kind of government is unlawful in its own nature, nor is any one dignified with a higher degree of the divine approbation than another;[6] political institutions are like other contracts, in which such stipulations are to be made as the contracting parties shall judge conducive to their happiness, and they must therefore vary according to the various opinions of those that make them; but when[7] made they are all obligatory and inviolable. There is therefore no necessity from the divine commands either of accepting this title, or refusing it; there is nothing in the name of a King either *sacred* as some have had

s. day, *emend.*] day *1741*

4. *Margin:* Fines
5. *Margin:* Fines

6. *Margin:* Lenthal
7. *Margin:* Fines

the weakness to assert, or *profane* as others have imagined
with no better reason. The necessity on either side must
therefore be accidental, and arise from circumstances and
relations. And surely the prescription of many hundred
years, the authority of the law, and the approbation of the
people, are circumstances that will constitute the highest
degree of political necessity.

That monarchy under the title of King has[8] all the sanction
that antiquity can give, is too evident for controversy, but it
may perhaps be questioned how far the sanction of antiquity
deserves to be regarded. The long continuance of any practice
which might have been altered or disused at pleasure, is at
least a proof that no inconveniences have been found to arise
from it, and a custom not in itself detrimental becomes every
day better established, because the other part of life will be
regulated with relation to it, till what was merely arbitrary
at first, appears in time essential and indispensible. The nation
might doubtless when government was first instituted here,
have chosen any other constitution no less lawfully than that
of monarchy, but monarchy either by deliberation or chance
was established, and the laws have all been made in consequence of that establishment, and so strongly connected
with it that they must stand or fall together. The King is
obliged to act in conformity to the laws, and the law can only
act by commission from the King. The prerogative of our
monarchs, and the authority of[9] our laws, it has been already
the task of several ages to regulate and ascertain, a task which
must be again begun, if the supreme magistrate has another
title.

If it be urged that this labour may be spared by one general
act, declaring the power of the Protector the same with that[1]
of our former Kings, what then have we been contending for?
a meer name! an empty sound! yet a sound of such importance
to be preferred to the voice of the whole people. But this
certainly will not be proposed, because if such an act be
publick, all must be immediately convinced that they are
governed as before by a King, and therefore all objections to
our ancient constitution remain in their full strength.

---

8. *Margin:* Glynne Fines   1. *Margin:* Fines Broghil
9. *Margin:* Fines Glynne Broghil

But indeed the long continuance of monarchy is an irrefragable proof, that in the opinion of the people, there have hitherto arisen no lasting or heavy calamities from it, and that therefore nothing can reasonably be feared from reviving it, at least nothing equivalent to the discontent that will be produced by a total alteration of our constitution, and the apprehensions which a new power, or new title, must certainly create; a title of which the import is unknown, and a power of which the limits are unsettled.

Antiquity, which to the wise and inquisitive is often only a proof of general approbation, becomes to the vulgar a foundation for reverence. Institutions and customs are long continued because they are good, and are reverenced because they have been long continued. Thus the danger of changing them, grows every day greater, as the real usefulness is always the same, and the accidental esteem of them is always increasing. To shew how much this regard to antiquity contributes to the good order of the world, and how inevitably it arises from the present state of things, is not at present requisite; since experience may convince us of its influence, and the experience of our own times above any other, in which we have almost every day been changing[2] the form of government, without having been able to satisfy either our selves or the people. Whether any of the schemes that have been tried were, in themselves,[t] preferable to that of monarchy, it is difficult to determine, but this at least is obvious, if they were not preferable, monarchy ought to be restored, and if they were, there needs no farther proof of the affection of the people to the ancient constitution, since they wou'd be content with no other, tho' of greater[3] excellence; but after years spent in fruitless experiments, have returned back to monarchy with greater eagerness.

Nor was the disapprobation of these new forms merely popular, but the result[4] of long deliberation, and careful enquiry in those whose opinions ought most to be regarded in questions of this kind. Some of the judges themselves, even

t. tried . . . themselves, *emend.*] tried, were, in themselves *1741*

---

2. *Margin:* Jones
3. *Margin:* Jones Lenthal

4. *Margin:* Lenthal

of those whose learning and integrity are above distrust, refused to act by any other commission than that of the King, and, as it was observed in our last conference, those that complied, pleaded no other reason[5] for their conduct, than necessity, a reason which can last no longer, since that necessity is now at an end.

Nor can it be wonder'd, that those whose lives have been laid out upon the study of the laws, have conceived the strongest ideas of the necessity of this title; a title supposed by the law so essential to our constitution, that the cessation of its influence, even for a few days, might subvert or endanger it, as the destruction of one of the elements would throw the natural world into confusion. For this reason[6] it is a fix'd principle, *That the King never dies*, that the regal authority is never extinct, and that there has in effect been no more than one King since the first establishment of monarchy. For, during the time that the regal authority shou'd be suspended, the law must cease from its operations; no crime cou'd be punish'd, nor any question of property be decided; all power to punish, and all authority to decide, being derived immediately from the King, whose office therefore cannot be abrogated; for no authority can be taken away but by a superior power, and this nation has never known or acknowledged any power independent on that of the King. The authority of Parliament, and the rights of the people, can boast no deeper foundation, or stronger establishment. The power of Parliament has no efficacy but as it co-operates with that of the King, nor can one destroy the other without a general dissolution of our government: These two concurrent powers are the essential parts of our constitution, which, when either of them shall cease, is equally destroyed.

These considerations are surely sufficient to vindicate the judges, whom it would be to the last degree unreasonable to blame, for their steady adherence to the laws, which it is the business of their office to maintain; but it is not to be imagined that the same motives influenc'd the bulk of the people to this general desire which was so apparently prevalent throughout the nation. General effects must have general causes, and

5. *Margin:* Broghil   6. *Margin:* Lenthal

nothing can influence the whole nation to demand the restoration of monarchy, but universal experience of the evils
produced by rejecting it; evils too evident to be concealed,
and too heavy to be borne. One of these, and perhaps not the
least, is the interruption[7] of justice, which has not been ad-
ministred but by the assistance of the army, the last expedient
that ought to be made use of.

That the laws did not lose more of their authority,[8] and
justice was not more evaded, is indeed not to be ascribed to
the forms of government which these years of distraction
have produc'd, but to the care, integrity, and reputation of
those men in whose hands the great offices were placed; who
were reverenc'd by the people on account of their own characters, rather than from any regard to the powers by whom
they were commissioned. Powers which yesterday produc'd,
and which were expected to perish to-morrow. For every title,
except that of King, which antiquity had made venerable, is
considered only as the issue of a momentary caprice, and
subject to be changed by the inconstancy that erected it,[9]
as soon as any inconvenience shall be discovered to arise from
it; because what is raised by one act of Parliament, may, by
another, be destroyed, and such alterations it is reasonable
to expect; for as no form of government is without its defects,
while it remains part of every man's right to propose a new
scheme, which he will always think more beneficial than any
other, every man that has any real or fancied amendments to
offer, will be impatient till they have been try'd, and will
endeavour to facilitate the reception of them, by exaggerating
the disadvantages of the present plan, and heightening the
discontents that arise from them. Thus shall we go on from
change to change, from expedient to expedient. Thus shall
we attempt to remove one evil by introducing another, and
gain nothing by all our fatigues, perplexities, and sufferings,
but new conviction of the necessity of complying with the laws
and the people.

It is indeed no great proof of regard to the nation, to deny
any legal request; perhaps more may be said without the

---

7. *Margin:* Lenthal Fines   9. *Margin:* Lenthal
8. *Margin:* Jones

least[1] deviation from truth and justice. The people, for whose
sake only government is constituted, have a right to settle
the forms of it, and this petition is only an exertion of that
natural privilege which cannot be forfeited. All government
must derive its legality either from the choice of the people
by whom it was established, or from their consent after its
institution, the present government was erected without their
concurrence, and it is to be enquired whether it be not now
dissolved by their petition to dissolve it.

But whether this petition may be lawfully refused or not,
prudence at least requires that it be complied with; for it's
always absolutely necessary to the happiness of any administration, that the people love and esteem their governors. The[2]
supreme magistrate must therefore assume the title of King
for no title that has not the sanction of the Parliament, and is
therefore subject to an immediate change, can be equally
reverenced[3], with that which has been establish'd by the
approbation of many generations, the authority of many
parliaments, and which the experience of the whole[4] nation
has proved to be without those dangers that may be justly
suspected in any new institution, which can never be consider'd in its whole extent, or pursued to all its consequences.

Nor can the nation in this demand be charged with inconstancy in their resolutions, or inconsistency in their conduct; for that the war was begun not against the[5] office of
King, but against the person of him who was then invested
with it, and discharged it in a manner contrary to the intention
for which[6] he was intrusted with it, is apparent from four
declarations of Parliament; nor is it less known that the first
breach of unanimity amongst the[7] friends of liberty was produced by the abolition of this title, and may therefore be
probably repaired by the revival of it.

If it be urged that the question, which relates only to a
name, be trifling and unimportant, it may be replied, that the

---

1. *Margin:* Fines
2. *Margin:* Fines
3. *Margin:* Fines Whitlock Lenthal
("Whitlock" is an emendation of
"Whiihouse" *1741*.)
4. *Margin:* Jones Glynne Broghil

("Broghil" is an emendation of
"Bright" *1741*).
5. *Margin:* Lenthal
6. *Margin:* Jones
7. *Margin:* Broghil

less is demanded, the greater contempt is shown by a refusal. That titles are more than empty sounds, may be proved not only from the present dispute, but from the ancient constitutions, and the determinations of former[8] parliaments, by which the title of King was declared essential to the constitution, in the reigns of Edward IV and Henry VII; and yet a stronger proof of regard to titles, was given to the Parliament of Henry the VIII in which it was enacted, that the title[9] of Lord of Ireland should be changed to that of King; that the difficulties arising from the ambiguity of the title might be removed. Even the late convention called together without the election or concurrence of the people, found the prejudice arising from mere titles of so great force, that they were obliged to assume the name of a Parliament, that their determinations might escape contempt.

Thus the request of the Parliament appears not only reasonable, but necessary; not only consistent with the present disposition of the people, but conformable to the sentiments of all former acts; and certainly nothing should produce a refusal of such a request except the impossibility of granting it.

But the objections raised by your Highness seem very far from implying any necessity of declining the title so unanimously offer'd you, and so earnestly pressed upon you, being founded upon suppositions merely conjectural. For your first assertion, that the office does not necessarily require the same title, has been already consider'd, and it has been shewn, that there can be no reason in altering the title, if the power be the same; and that the supreme magistrate cannot be invested with new powers without needless confusion and incredible jealousies. It is therefore of no great force to object, that many good men will be dissatisfied with the revival of the title; for tho' it must be granted, that those who have assisted us in shaking off oppression, have a claim to our gratitude, and that piety, tho' erroneous, deserves indulgence, yet both gratitude and indulgence ought to be[u] limited by[1]

u. be *emend.*] *om. 1741*

---

8. *Margin:* Onslow   1. *Margin:* Jones
9. *Margin:* Whitlock

reason. In things indifferent,[2] considerations of tenderness and respect may turn the balance; but we have not a right to consult the satisfaction of a few, however great their merits may have been, at the expence of the publick tranquillity, and the happiness of[3] succeeding generations. The satisfaction of particulars may be endeavoured by particular provision; but if, in questions of universal importance, we have regard to any thing but universal good, and the great laws of reason and justice, we shall be tossed in endless uncertainty. "He that observeth the wind[4] shall never sow and he that regardeth the clouds shall never reap."[5] He that attends to mutable circumstances, and waits till nothing shall oppose his intention, shall design for ever without execution. When are we to hope for settlement, if general unanimity must introduce it? Whatever shall be determined,[6] multitudes will still remain dissatisfied, because men's opinions will always be various.[7] It was not with universal approbation that the title of Protector was assumed, or that any change has hitherto been made; but since some discontent will always be found, whatever[8] measures shall be taken, let not the satisfaction of private[9] men be preferr'd to that of the Parliament, to the determination[1] of which all good men will readily submit.

Still less weight has the objection drawn by[2] your Highness from the visible dispensations[v] of Providence, of which we know too little to direct our actions by them, in opposition to evident reason, to certain facts and revealed precepts; lights which we always are commanded to use, and of which the two first can seldom, and the last never deceive us. If we consider this position, that because Providence has once blasted the title of King, or suffer'd it to be blasted, it is therefore never to be revived, it will soon appear that we cannot admit it in its whole extent and pursue it through all

---

v. dispensations *emend.*] dispensation *1741*

2. ἀδιάφορα, an important term in the religious controversies of the seventeenth century.
3. *Margin:* Jones
4. *Margin:* Jones
5. Ecclesiastes xi. 4.

6. *Margin:* Fines Onslow
7. *Margin:* Fines
8. *Margin:* Broghil
9. *Margin:* Whitlock
1. *Margin:* Broghil
2. *Margin:* Fines Onslow

its consequences, without involving ourselves in endless difficulties and condemning our own conduct.

If Providence hath blasted the office of King,[3] how can it be proved that the supreme power, in any single head, under whatsoever title, even the power which you now possess, is not equally interdicted?[4] The acts of Parliament extend equally to all titles, and declare against monarchy under every name.

But the consequences of this proposition do not terminate in this inconsistency of conduct, but extend equally to every determination;[5] for if what has been once destroy'd by Providence be for ever after interdicted, what will remain of which the use is lawful? what is there of which we have not at some time been deprived by Providence, or which Providence has not some time made the instrument of our punishment?[6] May not the dissolution of the long Parliament be interpreted as a blast from Heaven with equal justice, and the people be represented no more? But in reality, the proceedings of Providence are not intended as rules of action, we are left to govern our own lives by virtue and by prudence; when a form of government is destroyed,[7] for just reasons it is blasted by Providence, and loses its efficacy; when with equal reason it is restored, then Providence again smiles upon it, and the sanction of heaven renews its validity. If royalty was destroyed[8] by Providence, who can deny that the same Providence directs it to be revived? Is not the resolution of the Parliament equally a proof on either side; or have we any arguments to prove that the people co-operate with Providence less when they require than when they reject a King? Let us wave such inconclusive arguments and dubious conjectures, and guide ourselves by the steady light of religion, reason and experience. That a just demand is not to be refused, religion[9] will inform us: reason will teach us that the magistrate is to conform to the laws, and not the laws yield to the magistrate: and the experience[1] of many ages may instruct us, that the King has

---

3. *Margin:* Jones Onslow Fines Broghil

4. *Margin:* Fines Broghil

5. *Margin:* Fines Jones

6. *Margin:* Broghil Fines

7. *Margin:* Fines

8. *Margin:* Onslow Broghil Fines

9. *Margin:* Broghil

1. *Margin:* Broghil

nothing to fear from compliance with the Parliament. At least if any danger should arise from the measures now proposed, it will arise from the performance, not neglect[2] of our duty; and we may therefore encounter it with that resolution which a consciousness of the approbation of God ought to inspire.

The Protector's Reply.

[The reply is in many parts remarkably obscure, as well from the negligence and ignorance of the copiers and printers, as from frequent allusions to occurrences known to the persons with whom Cromwell was conferring, but not mentioned in any history which it is now in our power to consult; we have therefore collected such of the arguments as we can apprehend the full meaning of, and have omitted some unintelligible passages, and others which related to other articles in the petition.]

On the 26th of April, (and in another conference May 11,) the Protector made the following reply.

My Lord,

Having seriously reflected on the demand of the Parliament, and the learned arguments produced by the Committee to support it, I think it unreasonable any longer to delay such a reply as it is in my power to make, because it is both due to the great body by whom you are deputed, and necessary to the dispatch of publick affairs, which seem to be entirely suspended, and to wait for the decision of this question; a question which I cannot yet think of so much importance as it is represented and conceived.

The arguments produced in the last conference, I shall not waste time in repeating, because they were little different from those formerly produc'd, only graced with new decorations, and enforced with some new instances. With respect to the chief reason, the known nature of the title of King, the fix'd and stated bound of the authority imply'd by it, its propriety with regard to the laws, and the veneration paid to it by the people, I have nothing to add, nor think any thing

---

2. *Margin:* Broghil

necessary beyond what I have already offered. I am convinced that your authority is sufficient to give validity to any administration, and to add dignity to any title, without the concurrence of ancient forms, or the sanction of hereditary prejudices.

All government intends the good of the people, and that government is therefore best by which their good may be most effectually promoted; we are therefore, in establishing the chief magistracy of these kindgoms, chiefly to enquire, what form or what title will be most willingly admitted, and this discovery being once made, it will easily be established by a single Act of Parliament, concurring with the general desire of the people.

It may indeed be urged, that in rejecting the title of King, I deny the request of the Parliament, and treat the representatives of the people with a degree of disregard, which no King of England ever discover'd. But let it be considered how much my state differs from that of a legal King, claiming the crown by inheritance, or exalted to supreme authority by the Parliament, and governing by fix'd laws in a settled establishment. I hold the supreme power by no other title than that of necessity. I assumed the authority with which I stand invested at a time when immediate ruin was falling down upon us, which no other man durst attempt to prevent, when opposite factions were rushing into war, because no man durst interpose and command peace. What were the dangers that threaten'd us, and upon what principles the factious and disobedient attempted to interrupt the publick tranquillity, it may not be at this time improper to explain.

The Parliament which had so vigorously withstood the encroachments of the regal power, became themselves too desirous of absolute authority, and not only engross'd the legislative, but usurp'd the executive power. All causes, civil and criminal, all questions of property and right, were determined by committees, who being themselves the legislature, were accountable to no law; and for that reason their decrees were arbitrary, and their proceedings violent; oppression was without redress, and unjust sentence without appeal; all the business of all the courts of Westminster was transacted in this manner, and the hardships were still more lamented, because there was no prospect of either end or intermission. For the Parliament was so far from intending to resign this unlimited authority, that they had formed a resolution of perpetuating their tyranny; and apprehending no possibility of a dissolution by any other power, determin'd never to dissolve themselves.

Such and so oppressive was the government plann'd out to us, and for our posterity, and under these calamities must we still have languish'd, had not the same army which repress'd the insolence of monarchy, relieved us with the same spirit from the tyranny of a perpetual Parliament, a tyranny which was equally illegal and oppressive.

When, after their dangers and labours, their battles and their wounds, they had leisure to observe the government which they had establish'd at so much expence, they soon perceiv'd that unless they made one regulation more, and crush'd this many headed tyranny, they had hitherto ventured their lives to little purpose, and had, instead of asserting their own and the people's liberty, only changed one kind of slavery for another.

They therefore dissolved the Parliament which wou'd never have dissolved itself, and that the nation might not fall into its former state of confusion, intreated me to assume the supreme authority, under the title of Protector; a title which implies not any legal power of governing in my own right, but a trust consign'd to me for the advantage of another; this trust I have faithfully discharged, and, whenever the means of settling the publick shall be found, am ready to give an account of it, and resign it.

The necessity which compelled me to accept it, was, indeed,[w] not wholly produced by the illegal resolutions of the Parliament, but was much heightened by the ungovernable fury of wild fanaticks and tumultuous factions, who, to establish their new schemes, wou'd have spread slaughter and desolation through the kingdom, and spared nothing, however cruel or unjust, that might have propagated their own opinions.

Of these, some were for abrogating all our statutes, and abolishing all our customs, and introducing the judicial law

w. indeed, *emend.*] indeed *1741*

of Moses as the only rule of judgment, and standard of equity. Of this law every man was to be his own interpreter, and consequently was allowed to judge according to his passions, prejudices, or ignorance, without appeal. Every man was then to commence legislator: For to make laws, and to interpret them for his own use, is nearly the same.

Another set of men there was, who were yet more professedly for investing every man with the power of determining his own claims, and judging of his own actions; for[x] it was among them a principle fix'd and uncontrovertible, that all magistracy was forbidden by God, and therefore unlawful and detestable.

It is unnecessary to say what must have been the state of a nation, in which either of these parties had exalted themselves to power, and how usefully that man was employ'd, who stepping on a sudden into the seat of dominion, had spirit to controul, and power to suppress them.

The reproaches thrown upon my conduct by the ignorant or ill affected, I sometimes hear, but with the neglect and scorn which they deserve; I am acquitted by my own conscience, and I hope by the best and wisest men; I am convinc'd that I was called by Providence to the power which I possess, and know that I desire it no longer than is necessary for the preservation of peace, and the security of liberty, that liberty which I have never violated, and that peace, which amidst murmurs, and discontents, threats, and complaints, I have yet never suffer'd to be broken. That I aspire to unlimited authority, and therefore assume a title unknown to the nation, is a reproach easily cast, and as easily contemned; my power has been the offspring of necessity, and its extent has been bounded only by the occasions of exerting it. If a settlement is now proposed, and previously to it, a legal establishment of my authority, it may be limited by you, under whatever title it shall be conferr'd upon me, that title will then be valid, and those limitations cannot be transgress'd.

May 11.] With regard to the particular *title* which you have so warmly recommended to me, I cannot yet prevail upon myself to accept it, when I consider your arguments I cannot

x. for *emend.*] for, *1741*

find them inevitably conclusive; and when I examine my own conscience in solitude, I find it yet unsatisfy'd. The desire of Parliament is indeed a powerful motive, but the desire of Parliament cannot alter the nature of things; it may determine me in things indifferent, to chuse one rather than another; but it cannot make those actions lawful which God has forbidden, nor oblige me to do what, though perhaps lawful in itself, is not lawful in my private judgment.

Upon the calmest reflection, I am convinced that I cannot, without a crime, comply with their demand; and therefore, as I am far from believing that those who sit for no other end than to preserve the liberty of the nation, can design any infraction of mine, *I declare that I cannot undertake the administration of the government, under the title of King.*

N.B. The whole debate, as printed in 1660, whence this foregoing is extracted,[3] will soon be publish'd with some remarks and necessary illustrations.

---

3. The *Dictionary* defines *extract* (n., def. 2) as "The chief heads drawn from a book; an abstract; an epitome."

"O.N." ON THE FIREWORKS FOR THE PEACE OF AIX-LA-CHAPELLE. 1749.

After Walpole's fall in 1742, and his replacement by a coalition of his allies and the enemies who had been baying at his heels, Johnson and most other Englishmen had had their fill of politics for a time.[1] Macaulay describes the revulsion in terms which sound more like Johnson—the later Johnson—than Macaulay:

> The Opposition reaped what they had sown. . . . Constantly talking in magnificent language about tyranny, corruption, wicked ministers, servile courtiers, the liberty of Englishmen, the Great Charter, the rights for which our fathers bled, Timoleon, Brutus, Hampden, Sydney, they had absolutely nothing to propose which would have been an improvement on our institutions. Instead of directing the public mind to definite reforms . . . they excited a vague craving for change, by which they profited for a single moment, and of which, as they well deserved, they were soon the victims. . . . The name of patriot had become a by-word for derision. [Review of Horace Walpole's *Letters to Mann* (1833)]

Johnson, of course, had been, for a time, one of those "patriots," and there can be little doubt that he became very angry, with an anger that endured all his life, at those who had thus taken him in.[2] Later, when the "patriotic" idiom began to be heard in the land again, on the lips of Pitt and Wilkes and, above all, the publicists of the American Revolution, he dedicated himself to trying to open the eyes of those who were likely to be deluded, as he had been deluded, by talk of this kind.

Johnson's own valediction (for the time being) to serious political writing may be found in his preface to the *Gentleman's Magazine* for 1743 (published early in 1744):

> It has been for many years lamented . . . that the struggles of opposite parties have engrossed the attention of the public, and that all subjects of conversation and all kinds of learning have given way to politics. . . . Life requires many other considerations and . . . politics may be said to usurp the mind when they leave no room for any other subjects.

1. Good accounts of the political history of the time will be found in John B. Owen, *The Rise of the Pelhams* (1957), dealing with the period 1741 to 1747, and John W. Wilkes, *A Whig in Power: The Political Career of Henry Pelham* (1964), which goes up to 1754.

2. Elsewhere (*Politics*, ch. 5) I argue that the curious ambivalent tone of the "Life of Savage" (1744)—Savage was clearly SJ's early mentor in patriotism—may be due to such a revulsion.

So Johnson, like the magazine, turned for a while to other considerations—working with the Harleian library, making an abortive start at an edition of Shakespeare, and then, from 1747 on, compiling his *Dictionary of the English Language*. Not until its completion, in 1755, was he again to employ his pen at any length on political subjects, though even during this period, he found occasional opportunity for brief and sometimes acute *obiter dicta* on politics: in the prefaces he wrote for various periodical publications; in the fine introduction to that very political collection, the *Harleian Miscellany*, and some brief editorial notes in it;[3] even in the preliminary matter to the *Dictionary* itself, where he quotes Hooker, "Change is not made without inconvenience, even from worse to better," and comments on the inevitably increasing economic and social complexity of the modern world.

Of Johnson's writings of this decade, only one isolated piece is primarily political, the letter to the *Gentleman's Magazine* printed immediately below. It was attributed to him (on "internal evidence") by Alexander Chalmers, in his edition of Boswell's *Life* (1822), I.xxxv, and reprinted in his edition of Johnson's *Works* (1823). Although one would like to have further confirmation of Johnson's authorship of the piece, it has not been challenged. Both the style and the sentiments are very convincing.[4] The signature, "O. N.," is made up of the last two letters of Johnson's name: this fact can hardly be called evidence, but equally ingenious methods of concocting pseudonyms did exist at the time.

The Treaty of Aix-la-Chapelle, which brought the War of the Austrian Succession to a momentary halt before it resumed in what was to become the Seven Years' War, was signed late in 1748, to everyone's dissatisfaction ("Bête comme la paix" is said to have been a common French proverb). For some reason, it was decided that the official celebration of it in London should take the form of a display of fireworks in the Green Park. It is the best-known pyrotechnical performance in history. The project succeeded in tickling various exuberant aspects of the eighteenth-century Londoner's fancy. The great Handel set himself to make George II's pacific genius resound from the dome of London's night sky; providing himself with an orchestra of twenty-four oboes, twelve bassoons, nine trumpets, nine horns, with strings and kettle-drums in proportion (and a battery of 101 cannon to fill in during intervals of unavoidable silence), he composed for it the splendid and still deservedly popular *Musick for the Royal Fireworks*. The French stage-designer Servandoni was commissioned to erect in the Park a Temple of Peace, from which the fireworks were to be let off; and he did

3. See D. J. Greene, "Johnson and the *Harleian Miscellany*," *Notes & Queries*, CCIII (July 1958), 304.

4. The piece was composed specifically for the *Gentleman's Magazine*. This is made clear by a passage in the Preface to the volume for 1749, where the *Gentleman's Magazine* is fulminating against the copying of its contents by other periodicals: "One ingenious collector, entirely to conceal it, pretends that he took the pyrotechnical remarks from the Hague gazette, though they are not to be found in it, and we have the original MS to produce."

so with all the profusion of the baroque imagination let loose on the allegorical. A great masquerade ball was given at Ranelagh, attended in fancy dress by all the fashionable, headed by George II himself, in "Old English" costume (no doubt symbolizing primitive patriotic virtue). A rehearsal drew enormous crowds, created a traffic jam of three hours on London Bridge, and caused untold injury and disorder. Horace Walpole's epistolary genius rose to the occasion, and even the formidably correct Mrs. Montagu was moved to wit as she reported that at the masquerade the notorious Miss Chudleigh (later bigamously Duchess of Kingston and Countess of Bristol) had come dressed as "Iphigenia for the sacrifice, but so naked that the high priest might easily inspect the entrails of the victim," and that His Sacred Majesty could not tear his lewd gaze from the spectacle.

On 27 April 1749, after four months of anticipation and hectic preparation, the great night arrived, and the *fête* went off in a manner that could not have been bettered in a Marx Brothers scenario. The timing of everything went hopelessly wrong; a gunner was killed preparing the cannon; at first the fireworks could not be persuaded to ignite at all; but when at last they did, they went up in a mighty burst that set the Temple of Peace on fire and put the close-packed mob of spectators to hysterical, trampling flight. The one piece of comfort was the news that a similar and larger display at Paris had been an even greater fiasco. All together, the affair was a wonderfully satisfying orgy, and must have had as useful a cathartic effect on the public mind as a dozen of the public hangings that Johnson extolled.

It is pleasant to know that the event which inspired the artistry of Handel, Horace Walpole, and others drew a response from Johnson too, though an unexpected one—with the sour denunciations of a Cato (or Milton), he shook his head ominously over such extravagant frivolity. Twelve years later, in his introduction to Gwynn's *Thoughts on the Coronation*, he was to express himself more graciously toward such shows—for the king involved was now George III, not George II—though he still insisted on the sound principle he laid down in 1749, that those who pay for a spectacle should have a chance to see it. There is not much to be said about the letter itself, except that the skepticism about foreign wars, especially wars conducted by George II, is consonant with Johnson's "old Toryism," as are the preference expressed for local to centralized administration, and the solicitude for starving sailors (though not soldiers); this, and the fact that it is, as usual, very competently written—the amusingly elaborate imagery is evidence that Johnson was by no means immune from the metaphysicals' attraction to a conceit.

The text is that of the original publication in the *Gentleman's Magazine*, XIX (Jan 1749), 8.

["O.N." on the Fireworks for the Peace of Aix-la-Chapelle]

MR. URBAN,

Among the principal topics of conversation, which now furnish the places of assembly with amusement, may be justly numbered the Fireworks, which are advancing, by such slow degrees, and with such costly preparation.

The first reflection that naturally arises is upon the inequality of the effect to the cause. Here are vast sums expended, many hands, and some heads employed, from day to day, and from month to month, and the whole nation is filled with expectations, by delineations and narratives. And in what is all this to end? in a building that is to attract the admiration of ages? in a bridge, which may facilitate the commerce of future generations? in a work of any kind which may stand as the model of beauty, or the pattern of virtue? To shew the blessings of the late change of our state, by any monument of these kinds, were a project worthy not only of wealth, and power, and greatness, but of learning, wisdom, and virtue. But nothing of this kind is designed, nothing more is projected, than a crowd, a shout and a blaze; the mighty work of artifice and contrivance, is to be set on fire, for no other purpose, that I can see, than to shew how idle pyrotechnical virtuosos have been busy. Four hours the sun will shine, and then fall from his orb, and lose his memory and his lustre together, the spectators will disperse as their inclinations lead them, and wonder by what strange infatuation they had been drawn together. In this will consist the only propriety of this transient show, that it will resemble the war of which it celebrates the period. The powers of this part of the world, after long preparations, deep intrigues, and subtile schemes, have set Europe in a flame, and, after having gazed awhile at their fireworks, have laid themselves down where they rose, to enquire for what they have been contending.

It is remarked likewise, that this blaze, so transitory and so useless, will be to be paid for, when it shines no longer; and many cannot forbear observing, how many lasting advantages might be purchased, how many acres might be

drained, how many ways repaired, how many debtors might
be released, how many widows and orphans, whom the war
has ruined, might be relieved, by the expence which is now
about to evaporate in smoke, and to be scattered in rockets;
and there are some who think not only reason, but humanity
offended, by such a trifling profusion, when so many sailors
are starving, and so many churches sinking into ruins.

It is no improper enquiry by whom this expence is at last
to be born; for certainly nothing can be more unreasonable
than to tax the nation for a blaze, which will be extinguished
before many of them know it has been lighted; nor will it
be consistent with the common practice, which directs that
local advantage shall be procured at the expence of the
district that enjoys them. I never found in any records, that
any town petitioned the Parliament for a maypole, a bull-ring,
or a skittle-ground; and, therefore, I should think fireworks,
as they are less durable, and less useful, have at least as little
claim to the publick purse.

The fireworks are, I suppose, prepared, and therefore it
is too late to obviate the project; but, I hope, the generosity
of the great is not so far extinguished, as that they can for
their[a] diversion drain a nation already exhausted, and make
us pay for pictures in the fire, which none will have the poor
pleasure of beholding, but themselves.

O.N.

a. the is *1749*.

FURTHER THOUGHTS ON
AGRICULTURE. 1756.

No one who thinks seriously on political matters gets far without having to come to grips with basic questions of economic theory. Even though political economy was not recognized as a separate discipline in Johnson's day—it was an age when, as has been said, every man was his own economist—Johnson was well enough aware of the important economic problems implicit in many of the political questions with which he concerned himself. Rather surprisingly so, perhaps: the twentieth-century reader who flatters himself that the economic interpretation of history is something of recent invention, stemming from the time of Karl Marx, will be astonished by the frank economic determinism of some of Johnson's historical essays of 1756 (pp. 120–212 below). Part of Johnson's readiness to adopt such a position may be a reaction to the gaudy but flimsy idealism of "patriot" writers of his time, a desire to bring such questions down to hard earth out of the clouds of rhetoric where Bolingbroke, Pitt, and others placed them. At the same time, Johnson was not the first, by any means, to display an unsentimental attitude towards the materials of political history; one finds a similar tone of "objectivity" in the writings of his French contemporaries, such as Raynal; and indeed the whole tradition of *Realpolitisch* historiography, from Machiavelli to Charles Beard, is probably a continuous manifestation of the Renaissance empirical spirit, a rebuttal of the jejune moralism of a Livy, just as Johnson's theory of biography (a branch of history), his insistence on getting the facts, however inelegant, and letting them speak for themselves, is a rebuttal of the crude propagandist purpose of the Plutarchan school.

Johnson paid his respects to the study of economics (as we should now call it) in his preface to *The Preceptor*, 1748.

> It is . . . necessary that it should be universally known among us, what changes of property are advantageous, or when the balance of trade is on our side; what are the products or manufactures of other countries; and how far one nation may in any species of traffic obtain or preserve superiority over another. The theory of trade is yet but little understood, and therefore the practice is often without real advantage to the public; but it might be carried on with more general success, if its principles were better considered.

The terms Johnson uses in this account are those of the "mercantilism" of the seventeenth century, and the books Johnson goes on to recommend for study are those of the standard mercantilist authors—Child, Mun, Davenant, Gee. It is possible that Johnson had himself contributed previously to the literature of trade. For several years, from around 1739 to 1744, the *Gentleman's Magazine* had made a point of following the controversies that were going on about whether the legislation intended to protect British wool growers and manufacturers was actually accomplishing that purpose or whether it should be modified. The subject was a vast and complex one: the wool trade had been regarded for centuries as the keystone of English economic life (symbolized by the Woolsack on which the Lord Chancellor sits when he presides over the House of Lords), and the criticisms being made of the traditional methods of government regulation of it were symptomatic of the new "free trade" ideas (as they later came to be called) that were beginning to be in the air. Johnson, in his 1743 *Preface*, makes the *Gentleman's Magazine* congratulate itself on this enterprise; it was likely Johnson himself, who had an important voice in the direction of the magazine at the time, who was responsible for the undertaking; and there are passages of editorial commentary in the series that are written in a very Johnson-like style. This commentary frequently follows the involved arguments of the controversy with considerable technical competence, and appears generally to take a "protectionist" attitude—that is, it seems to be in favour of embargoes and subsidies and similar forms of government control, and to oppose suggestions of relaxing it. A similarly Johnsonian-sounding commentary appears in the *Gentleman's Magazine* in 1741 rebutting an attack on the principle of government control of the grain trade.[1]

The question of the extent of government intervention in economic matters—the issue between the Manchester school's *laissez-faire*, "free enterprise" concept of the function of government, and the older (and newer) school of thought, that lays on the government of a country heavier responsibilities for the supervision of the economic welfare of the state and of the individuals in it[2]—is basic to the political history of Britain in the eighteenth century, and Johnson sensed its fundamental importance. The situation deserves more study than has been done on it; but one possible summary is this: The question underlying political controversy in the mid-eighteenth century was, what kind of country was Britain going to be in the modern world whose outlines were beginning dimly to be discerned? Should it remain a small, economically self-contained state, the balance among manufacturing, commerce, and agriculture maintained by government action so that its population could continue to feed and clothe itself, if necessary, without dependence on the uncertain ministration of foreign countries? Or should it take advantage of its current superiority over the rest of the world in technology and navigation, and put all its eggs in the one basket of unrestricted commercial (and, if necessary, imperial)

1. D. J. Greene, "Some Notes on Johnson and the *Gentleman's Magazine*," *PMLA*, LXXIV (Mar 1959), 75–84.
2. The issue is still, of course, very live. It has seemed to me preferable here to give a candidly sympathetic account of Johnson's attitude toward it, than to adopt a façade of "impartiality" that must inevitably conceal a bias in one direction or the other.

expansion? Johnson and the smaller Tory landowners believed the first course was right. And the main stream of Whiggism, the Walpole-Newcastle-Rockingham-Fox-Burke "connexion," seems on the whole to have felt much the same way: though closely connected with the great chartered trading corporations, the East India Company, the South Sea Company, the Bank of England, the Hudson's Bay Company, that fact in itself put them on the side of a *controlled* national economy, for these were government-authorized monopolies, their charters subject to revision or cancellation by legislation at any time.

On the other side of the question were the Pitts, elder and younger, their dissident Whig allies, and the independent trading interests of London and Bristol. They were filled with a hot conviction of the rightness of free economic enterprise. It is significant that Thomas Pitt founded the fortunes of the family as an "interloper" in the East India trade, and forced the great Company to come to terms with him. In 1739, the elder William Pitt was in the forefront of the hue-and-cry that forced Walpole to declare war on Spain in order to facilitate the expansion of British trade into the South Seas: "enemy of commerce" was a frequent objurgation hurled against Walpole by Pitt, Sandys, and the rest. In 1757, it was Pitt again who took over the conduct of the Seven Years' War from the hands of the unenterprising Newcastle, and led it to the glorious conclusion of opening almost the whole of North America and the subcontinent of India to the free expansion of British, and colonial American, commercial power. The younger William Pitt, coming into power in 1783 and retaining it for the rest of the century, was an admirer of Adam Smith, and made a start at introducing those economic policies that culminated in 1846 with the abandonment of government control of the economy by means of protective tariffs. In short, the battle was decisively won by the Pittite forces; and the result of their victory was the Britain of the nineteenth century—a magnificent spectacle, on the surface at least. In the nineteenth century, the elder Pitt received his full share of acclaim for the feat;[3] and there was considerable sneering at short-sighted fuddy-duddies of the eighteenth century, like Johnson, who tried to obstruct the march of progress.

In the twentieth century, we are perhaps not so sure where the short-sightedness lay. In the twentieth century, the prediction made by Johnson in the piece printed immediately below finally came true: "the natives of Lombardy" (or their equivalent), having caught up with, and in some cases overpassed, the superiority in technological skill that had given Britain the advantage between 1750 and 1850 or thereabouts, did "resolve to retain their silk at home, and employ workmen of their own to weave it," rather than to sell the raw material to the British weavers, and buy the finished product back at a price high enough to pay for the livelihood of the British operatives. A few years after Johnson's death, at the time when the

3. "Pitt, the first real Imperialist in modern English history, was the directing mind in the expansion of his country, and with him the beginning of empire is rightly associated" ("Chatham," *Encyclopaedia Britannica*, 11th ed., 1910).

First Lord of the British Treasury, the younger Pitt, was beginning to "free" British trade, the Secretary of the Treasury of the United States, Alexander Hamilton, submitted to Congress his famous "Report on Manufactures," which recommended that the young Republic adopt the basic principle of economic policy that Johnson here recommends—the principle of maintaining, through government action, a diversified, self-contained economy, independent of the vagaries of the rest of the world.[4] Hamilton's advice was followed. It is no doubt too simple a question to ask which policy the results, as observed in the mid-twentieth century, have justified. But it is hard to avoid at least reflecting on the question. At any rate, after eighty years, Britain finally abandoned free-trade doctrine, with the reimposition in 1931 of substantial tariffs; and subsequent administrations, Socialist or Conservative, have shown no sign of wishing to return to it. Even the remnant of the British Liberal party, whose glory that doctrine once was, keeps very quiet about it.

In his economic thinking, Johnson is no doubt to be classed as an adherent of "mercantilism," that grab-bag term for most economic thought before Adam Smith. In connexion with the following piece, however, the distinction made by C. R. Fay[5] between "mercantilism" proper, and "Colbertism" (a term invented by William Cunningham) might be noted: simple mercantilism, Fay thinks, does not rule out "interloping"—free-trading. Colbertism, on the other hand, means economic nationalism— the acceptance by national governments of the responsibility of seeing that a country's economic resources are disposed to best advantage. Johnson's expressed admiration for Colbert as an administrator—Johnson seldom expresses admiration for statesmen—is probably significant. Whether or not we like the sound of "economic nationalism," it is what prevails in the world today. As Johnson clearly saw, while there is nationalism, there will be national economies, and all each country can do is to make its own as efficient and secure as possible. It is by no means clear that Johnson liked modern nationalism, in itself; but he saw well enough, in the 1750's,

4. Hamilton argues for the encouragement of manufactures in a hitherto almost entirely agricultural nation, as Johnson argues for the encouragement of agriculture in a nation where (he thinks) manufacturing and commerce are becoming relatively too important. (*Alexander Hamilton's Papers on Public Credit, Commerce, and Finance*, ed. Samuel McKee, Jr., 1957, pp. 197–8, 200–202.)

5. *English Economic History, Mainly Since 1700* (1948), p. 13. William Cunningham's *The Growth of English Industry and Commerce in Modern Times* (Cambridge [England], 1882; 3rd ed., 1896–1903) is still probably the best account for the student of Johnson. Archdeacon Cunningham was a vigorous and acute critic of *laissez-faire*, though his discussion is sometimes made confusing by his use of the older concept of party-structure in the eighteenth century. The scanty list of studies of Johnson's economic views includes Earl R. Miner, "Dr. Johnson, Mandeville, and 'Publick Benefits,' " *Huntington Library Quarterly*, XXI (1958), 159–66; John H. Middendorf, "Dr. Johnson and Mercantilism," *Journal of the History of Ideas*, XXI (1960), 66–83, and "Johnson on Wealth and Commerce" in *Johnson, Boswell, and Their Circle* (1965); and Greene, *Politics*, pp. 280–84.

that it is here to stay for some time. Whether or not Johnson had ever
written a sentence on specifically economic matters, it might have been
predicted from his other expressions of opinion that the doctrine of strict
laissez-faire, as erected later into an ethic by the Manchester school, would
have had little appeal for him. It smacks too much of "Whatever is, is right,"
"Partial evil is universal good," and the other dreary maxims of eighteenth-
century optimism, of which, indeed, Cobdenism may be the direct intellectual descendant.

"Further Thoughts on Agriculture" was one of Johnson's contributions to
Christopher Smart and Richard Rolt's *Universal Visiter*. It purports to be
the sequel to a worthless essay by Rolt entitled "Some Thoughts on Agriculture," published in the preceding number of the *Visiter*. Both pieces
were regularly reprinted in the older collections of Johnson's *Works*, and
were frequently confused. The confusion began in 1773, when Tom Davies,
attempting to collect Johnson's smaller prose works in his *Miscellaneous
and Fugitive Pieces* (II.161), reprinted Rolt's essay but not Johnson's. The
notice of Davies's work in the *Gentleman's Magazine*, Nov 1774, p. 525, a
piece that is usually fairly accurate, repeats Davies's error by assigning
the Rolt essay to Johnson. The matter was set right in the *European Magazine*,
Feb 1785, p. 82, which assigns the "Thoughts on Agriculture" in No. 3
(i.e., March 1756) of the *Universal Visiter* to Johnson. But Hawkins (*Life*,
p. 351) is still confused: "He [Johnson] wrote for the *Universal Visiter* . . .
two of three letters therein inserted, on the subject of agriculture" (I know
of no third letter: perhaps "of" is a misprint for "or"). Finally, in 1791,
Boswell pointed out the discrepancy in quality between the two essays,
and argued for the authenticity of the "Further Thoughts" as against
"Some Thoughts"—as he says, on "internal evidence."

The text given here is that of the *Universal Visiter*, March 1756, pp. 111–15.

Further Thoughts on Agriculture

At my last visit[1], I took the liberty of mentioning a subject,
which, I think, is not considered with attention proportionate
to its importance. Nothing can more fully prove the ingratitude of mankind, a crime often charged upon them, and
often denied, than the little regard which the disposers of
honorary rewards have paid to agriculture; which is treated
as a subject so remote from common life, by all those who do
not immediately hold the plough, or give fodder to the ox,
that I think there is room to question, whether a great part

---

1. I.e., in Rolt's "Some Thoughts   February issue of the *Universal Visiter*
on Agriculture," published in the   (see headnote).

of mankind has yet been informed that life is sustained by the fruits of the earth. I was once indeed provoked to ask a lady of great eminence for genius,[2] "Whether she knew of what bread is made?"

I have already observed, how differently agriculture was considered by the heroes and wise men of the Roman commonwealth, and shall now only add, that even after the emperors had made great alteration in the system of life, and taught men to portion out their esteem to other qualities than usefulness, agriculture still maintained its reputation, and was taught by the polite and elegant Celsus[3] among the other arts.

The usefulness of agriculture, I have already shewn; I shall now, therefore, prove its necessity: and having before declared, that it produces the chief riches of a nation, I shall proceed to shew, that it gives its only riches, the only riches which we can call our own, and of which we need not fear either deprivation or diminution.

Of nations, as of individuals, the first blessing is independance. Neither the man nor the people can be happy to whom any human power can deny the necessaries or conveniencies of life. There is no way of living without need of foreign assistance, but by the product of our own land, improved by our own labour. Every other source of plenty is perishable or casual.

Trade and manufactures must be confessed often to enrich countries; and we ourselves are indebted to them for those ships by which we now command the sea, from the equator to the poles, and for those sums with which we have shewn

---

2. Perhaps Elizabeth Carter. One is strongly tempted to assign this piece of ignorance to Johnson's *bête noire*, the egregious Catharine Macaulay, whom Johnson had known as early as 1752. But she had not yet attained the "great eminence" that was to come with the publication of her *History of England* (Vol. I, 1763), even if one could imagine Johnson testifying to her "genius."

3. Aulus (or Aurelius) Cornelius

Celsus, encyclopaedist of the first century. He is usually known more specifically as a writer on medicine, but Columella *De Re Rustica* (referred to in Rolt's essay) speaks (II.2) of *"Cornelium Celsum non solum agricolatione sed universae naturae prudentem virum." Celsi opera* (Leyden, 1746) was in Johnson's library (*Sale Catalogue of Dr. Johnson's library* [facsimile, 1925], item no. 259).

ourselves able to arm the nations of the north[4] in defence of
regions in the western hemisphere. But trade and manufactures, however profitable, must yield to the cultivation
of lands in usefulness and dignity.

Commerce, however we may please ourselves with the
contrary opinion, is one of the daughters of fortune, incon-
stant and deceitful as her mother; she chuses her residence
where she is least expected, and shifts her abode, when her
continuance is in appearance most firmly settled. Who can
read of the present distresses of the Genoese,[5] whose only
choice now remaining, is from what monarch they shall
solicit protection? Who can see the Hanseatick[6] towns in
ruins, where perhaps the inhabitants do not always equal the
number of the houses; but he will say to himself, These are
the cities, whose trade enabled them once to give laws to
the world, to whose merchants princes sent their jewels in
pawn, from whose treasuries armies were paid, and navies
supplied? And who can then forbear to consider trade as a
weak and uncertain basis of power, and wish to his own
country greatness more solid, and felicity more durable?

It is apparent, that every trading nation flourishes, while
it can be said to flourish, by the courtesy of others. We cannot
compel any people to buy from us, or to sell to us. A thousand
accidents may prejudice them in favour of our rivals; the
workmen of another nation may labour for less price, or some
accidental improvement, or natural advantage, may procure
a just preference to their commodities; as experience has
shewn, that there is no work of the hands, which, at different
times, is not best performed in different places.

Traffic, even while it continues in its state of prosperity,

---

4. Specifically, Russia and (though
hardly northern) Hesse-Cassel,
through the treaties of 1755. See
below, p. 177, Johnson's "Observations" on these treaties.

5. The decline of the power of
Genoa (as of Venice) dated from the
discovery by the Portuguese, in the
late fifteenth century, of the sailing
route to India around the Cape of

Good Hope. This led to the decay of
the old trade route between Asia
and Europe, across Asia Minor and
then by Mediterranean shipping,
dominated by the two Italian cities.

6. The Hanse towns, on the Baltic
and North Seas, reached the height
of their prosperity in the fourteenth
century. The cause of their decline
is obscure.

must owe its success to agriculture; the materials of manufacture are the produce of the earth. The wool which we weave into cloth, the wood which is formed into cabinets, the metals which are forged into weapons, are supplied by nature with the help of art. Manufactures, indeed, and profitable manufactures, are sometimes raised from imported materials, but then we are subjected a second time to the caprice of our neighbours. The natives of Lombardy might easily resolve to retain their silk at home, and employ workmen of their own to weave it[7]. And this will certainly be done when they grow wise and industrious, when they have sagacity to discern their true interest, and vigour to pursue it.

Mines are generally considered as the great sources of wealth, and superficial observers have thought the possession of great quantities of precious metals the first national happiness. But Europe has long seen, with wonder and contempt, the poverty of Spain, who thought herself exempted from the labour of tilling the ground, by the conquest of Peru, with its veins of silver. Time, however, has taught even this obstinate and haughty nation, that without agriculture, they may indeed be the transmitters of money, but can never be the possessors. They may dig it out of the earth, but must immediately send it away to purchase cloth or bread, and it must at last remain with some people wise enough to sell much, and to buy little; to live upon their own lands, without a wish for those things which nature has denied them.

Mines are themselves of no use, without some kind of agriculture. We have, in our own country, inexhaustible stores of iron which lie useless in the ore for want of wood. It was never the design of Providence to feed man without his own concurrence; we have from nature only what we cannot provide for ourselves; she gives us wild fruits which art must meliorate, and drossy metals which labour must refine.

Particular metals are valuable, because they are scarce; and they are scarce, because the mines that yield them are

---

7. An important silk-weaving industry had been established in Spitalfields (London) by French workmen who immigrated there after the revocation of the Edict of Nantes, 1685.

emptied in time. But the surface of the earth is more liberal than its caverns. The field, which is this autumn laid naked by the sickle, will be covered, in the succeeding summer, by a new harvest; the grass, which the cattle are devouring, shoots up again when they have passed over it.

Agriculture, therefore, and agriculture alone, can support us without the help of others, in certain plenty and genuine dignity. Whatever we buy from without, the sellers may refuse; whatever we sell, manufactured by art, the purchasers may reject: but, while our ground is covered with corn and cattle, we can want nothing; and if imagination should grow sick of native plenty, and call for delicacies or embellishments from other countries, there is nothing which corn and cattle will not purchase.

Our country is, perhaps, beyond all others, productive of things necessary to life. The pine-apple thrives better between the tropics, and better furs are found in the northern regions. But let us not envy these unnecessary privileges. Mankind cannot subsist upon the indulgencies of nature, but must be supported by her more common gifts. They must feed upon bread, and be cloathed with wool; and the nation that can furnish these universal commodities, may have her ships welcomed at a thousand ports, or sit at home and receive the tribute of foreign countries, enjoy their arts, or treasure up their gold.

It is well known to those who have examined the state of other countries, that the vineyards of France are more than equivalent to the mines of America; and that one great use of Indian gold, and Peruvian silver, is to procure the wines of Champaigne and Burgundy. The advantage is indeed always rising on the side of France, who will certainly have wines, when Spain, by a thousand natural or accidental causes, may want silver. But surely the vallies of England have more certain stores of wealth. Wines are chosen by caprice; the products of France have not always been equally esteemed; but there never was any age, or people, that reckoned bread among superfluities, when once it was known. The price of wheat and barley suffers not any variation, but what is caused by the uncertainty of seasons.

I am far from intending to persuade my countrymen to

quit all other employments for that of manuring the ground. I mean only to prove, that we have, at home, all that we can want, and that therefore we need feel no great anxiety about the schemes of other nations for improving their arts, or extending their traffic. But there is no necessity to infer, that we should cease from commerce, before the revolution of things shall transfer it to some other regions! Such vicissitudes the world has often seen; and therefore such we have reason to expect. We hear many clamours of declining trade, which are not, in my opinion, always true; and many imputations of that decline to governors and ministers, which may be sometimes just, and sometimes calumnious. But it is foolish to imagine, that any care or policy can keep commerce at a stand, which almost every nation has enjoyed and lost, and which we must expect to lose as we have long enjoyed it.

There is some danger, lest[a] our neglect of agriculture should hasten its departure. Our industry has for many ages been employed in destroying the woods which our ancestors have planted. It is well known that commerce is carried on by ships, and that ships are built out of trees; and therefore, when I travel over naked plains, to which tradition has preserved the names of forests, or see hills arising on either hand, barren and useless, I cannot forbear to wonder, how that commerce, of which we promise ourselves the perpetuity, shall be continued by our descendants; nor can restrain a sigh, when I think on the time, a time at no great distance, when our neighbors may deprive us of our naval influence, by refusing us their timber.[8]

By agriculture only can commerce be perpetuated; and by agriculture alone can we live in plenty without intercourse with other nations. This, therefore, is the great art, which every government ought to protect, every proprietor of lands to practice, and every enquirer into nature to improve.

* *

a. lest *emend.*] least *1756*

---

8. The importance to a maritime country like Britain of a supply of timber for shipbuilding (coupled with the traditional Tory emphasis on the navy) helps to explain Johnson's notorious concern over the treelessness of Scotland.

AN INTRODUCTION TO THE POLITICAL STATE OF GREAT-BRITAIN. 1756.

The importance in Johnson's intellectual life of the remarkable half-year (April to October or November 1756) that he spent as founding editor and overwhelmingly the leading contributor to the *Literary Magazine, or Universal Review* has seldom been fully appreciated. Nothing whatever is known of how he came to be associated with this undertaking; as to why he left it, we can only speculate[1]. But in those few months his creative powers were exercised with a sustained intensity equalled during few other periods of his life. Between forty and fifty pieces of writing in the *Literary Magazine* have been attributed to his pen, most of them appearing in the first six or seven monthly issues; as well, he probably acted as editorial director of the first four or five. Some of these pieces are extremely short, of course, an introductory paragraph or two of a review that consists largely of extracts from the book being noticed—though even this would require some expenditure of time reading the book. Others, like the essay printed here, are very substantial.

Some of this sudden burst of creative energy may have been a natural reaction from many years of "drudgery" on the *Dictionary*, completed the year before, and perhaps on the Shakespeare edition, for which he published new proposals in the spring of 1756. After so much minute and scholarly work, an urge to write in more extended form and on wider topics would be understandable; and certainly the acceptance of an offer to "superintend and contribute largely" to a new monthly magazine would be an excellent way of satisfying it. But a more urgent stimulus was the occurrence of an historical event which Johnson knew to be of immense importance and about which he had very strong feelings. This was the official commencement of the Seven Years' War—"the Great War for the Empire," as its latest historian, L. H. Gipson calls it.[2] For in spite of its name, the *Literary Magazine* was pre-eminently a journal of current political history; and significantly the appearance of its first number coincided with the formal declaration of war by England on France.

The early numbers of the *Literary Magazine* form as good an introduction as any that exists to the history of the origin of that war. Johnson is evidently trying to create (as I believe he was also trying to do in his parliamentary reporting in the early 1740's) a piece of substantial and serious historiography, with a concern for careful documentation much closer to that of the better historians of the twentieth century than to those of his own day. As an

1. See D. J. Greene, "Johnson's Contributions to the *Literary Magazine*," *Review of English Studies*, n. s. VII (Oct 1956), 367–92.

2. *The British Empire before the American Revolution* (Caldwell, Idaho, and New York, 1936–70).

important part of his editorial policy, Johnson publishes in full the texts of relevant diplomatic exchanges, treaties, declarations—"*materials for the history of the present times* [italics in the original], which is one part of our plan to preserve. To these the inquisitive reader will find frequent occasion hereafter to refer; though perhaps they may convey no new information at this particular juncture." In the monthly "Historical Memoirs" he prints a detailed listing of military and diplomatic events as they occur. He includes in the magazine numerous pieces relevant to contemporary events— a long review of, or rather commentary on, John Armstrong's *History of Minorca* (1752), then being invested by the French; a long review of Lewis Evans's *Geographical, Historical, Political . . . Essays* (1755), giving a detailed account of the regions in America over which the British and French (and Americans) were already bitterly fighting (see p. 197); a series of notices, and comments, on the pamphlet war that raged over the execution of Admiral Byng (see p. 213); a biography, extending over three issues of the magazine, of Frederick of Prussia, the key figure in the war on the continent. And the first article printed in the magazine (after the opening manifesto of editorial policy) is the long and acute summary of history reprinted here—an account which was, in effect, continued in the "Observations on the Present State of Affairs" in the fourth issue of the magazine, and was to have been continued beyond that. It is not every historian, let alone journalist, who feels it incumbent on him to begin his study of the origins of a war at a point two hundred years before the actual commencement of hostilities.

A recent student of the events of this time has remarked, "National historians are rarely honest in their estimates of the causes that lead to war, because they are the victims and sometimes the perpetrators of the legends that mould history to suit national prejudice. Ideas have played and, at the risk of controversy, still do play a very small part in bringing about a war. Ideas rationalise and justify the fiercer and uglier antagonisms fighting under the surface. They form, metaphorically, the splendid clothing that conceals the deformed figure beneath."[3] It is to the task of stripping off the splendid ideological clothing with which the Seven Years' War was invested by the rhetoric of Pitt, first of the great modern national "war leaders," that Johnson dedicates himself in his writings for the *Literary Magazine*.

A sketch of the political scene at the time of Johnson's involvement with the *Literary Magazine* may help the reader to detect certain nuances which

3. V. H. H. Green, *The Hanoverians, 1714-1815* (1948), p. 190. After this admirable statement in recommendation of skepticism and detachment, however, Green goes on to give an account of the war that is the customary paean to Pitt's genius. He lauds Pitt's "great honesty of purpose"; quoting one of Pitt's speeches in the House of Commons, he comments, "These last few sentences were typical of Pitt; they may not be dismissed as rhetoric, for they breathe an intense moral earnestness. Whatever Pitt's defects, he cannot be charged with frivolity or irresponsibility" (p. 187). Unfortunately the sentences that provide the evidence for this judgement were composed by Johnson.

he might otherwise miss in the essays from it reprinted below. The ineffective Peace of Aix-la-Chapelle in 1748 had done nothing to resolve the basic conflict between France and Britain. Hostility between the garrisons of the two powers in India and America continued, and soon broke out again into open, though undeclared, warfare. And the French, for the reasons suggested by Johnson—the superior efficiency of a powerful central administration, and the greater friendship existing between the French and the Indians in America—were getting the better of it. Henry Pelham, Walpole's political heir, unexpectedly died in 1754, and was succeeded as chief minister by his less astute brother, the Duke of Newcastle. Newcastle was helpless before the course of events; he was no more a convinced imperialist than Walpole had been; but, like Walpole in the Spanish crisis of 1739, found himself unable to control them. Pitt had broken with Newcastle after Henry Pelham's death, and was now leading a vigorous campaign of obstructionism to all the government's activities. "My lord, I am sure I can save this country, and nobody else can," he proclaimed.

It seems likely that the ownership of the *Literary Magazine* was Pittite, and that Johnson was engaged as editor at this time, because of his well-known powers of literary vituperation, which were to be directed against Newcastle's administration. True, Johnson's basic views were even farther removed from Pitt's than from Newcastle's: Johnson condemned Newcastle for having allowed Britain to become involved in a dishonest war, whereas the Pittites condemned him for not having involved her in it sooner. But this was, for the moment, irrelevant. The political situation was virtually a repetition of that of 1741, with (to use a later terminology) the right-wing and the left-wing temporarily allied against the centre; and anything that might embarrass Newcastle was desirable. Later, when the embarrassment had served its purpose in getting Newcastle out and Pitt in, Johnson could be discarded—as I believe he was. All this is pure speculation—we have no evidence but that of the contents of the publication itself as to the nature of Johnson's relations with its proprietors. But at least it is one possible explanation of what we do know to have happened; there may be others.

There are few, if any, parallels in contemporary English sources for Johnson's a-plague-on-both-your-houses attitude towards the War for the Empire. A more likely hunting ground might be the writings of the French *philosophes* of the time. When one reads Johnson's "Canada, a cold uncomfortable uninviting region from which nothing but furrs and fish were to be had ... this region of desolate sterility," one thinks immediately of Voltaire's "quelques arpents de neige" in *Candide* (1759). In Voltaire's *Essai sur l'histoire générale et sur les moeurs et l'esprit des nations, depuis Charlemagne jusqu'à nos jours*, which appeared in the 1750's, there are some remarkable similarities of thought and even expression to those of Johnson's "Introduction": "ces terres stériles et glacées du Canada ... ces mauvais pays ... le Canada, pays couvert de neiges et de glaces huit mois de l'année, habité par des barbares, des ours, et des castors. ... Déjà les Anglais se mettaient en possession des meilleures terres et des plus avantageusement situées qu'on puisse posséder dans l'Amérique."[4] Voltaire's general attitude toward the European enterprise in the Americas is that of Johnson: "Ce mélange de grandeur et de cruauté étonne et indigne. . . . Les Espagnols tiraient déjà du Méxique et du Pérou des trésors immenses, qui pourtant à la fin ne les ont beaucoup enrichis, quand les autres nations, jalouses et excitées par leur exemple, n'avaient pas encore dans les autres parties de l'Amérique une colonie qui leur fût avantageuse."

How unacceptable Johnson's views were may be seen in a revised version of the essay, retitled "An Historical Account of the Policy and Trade of Great Britain," and printed as part of *An Account of the Constitution and Present State of Great Britain* (Newbery [1759]). This version introduces minor changes in punctuation and wording, and omits or softens much of Johnson's strong language. A later edition of the *Account* (Newbery and Carnan, [1765?]) continues the process of softening, most notably by deleting Johnson's last four paragraphs and introducing paragraphs sympathetic to the American objection to "taxation without representation." There is yet no evidence of Johnson's participation in either of these volumes. However, a few textual improvements found in the 1759 version, suggestive of careful attention, have been included in the notes; in two instances the 1759 reading has been incorporated into the text. A full account of these changes will appear in a forthcoming article by Professor F. V. Bernard, who kindly called my attention to the work. For borrowings from the original essay and from "Observations on the Present State of Affairs" in writings dubiously attributed to Goldsmith, see R. W. Seitz, "Goldsmith and the *Literary Magazine*," *Review of English Studies*, v (1929), 410–30.

The text below is that of the *Literary Magazine*, No. 1 (15 Apr–15 May 1756), pp. 1–9. This version was reprinted in Vol. 1 of Thomas Davies's *Miscellaneous and Fugitive Pieces* (1773; 2nd ed., 1774) and attributed to Johnson in the *GM*'s notice of the Davies collection, Nov 1774, p. 524; in Vol. x of the 1787 collected *Works* of Johnson; and in later editions of the collected works.

4. Voltaire, *Oeuvres inédites* (1914), ed. Fernand Caussy, 1. 347f. Johnson was familiar with Voltaire's historical writings: see *Life*, v.272, n. 3 and v.311, and a reference in the "Memoirs of the King of Prussia," published in the *Literary Magazine* later in 1756. Johnson owned a copy of Voltaire's *Siècle de Louis XIV*, 1751 (*Sale Catalogue*, no. 83).

An Introduction to the Political State of Great-Britain

As it is intended to exhibit in the following pamphlet[1] an accurate account of every political debate, it appears necessary to lay before the reader a succinct account of British affairs, from the time in which our present relations to the continent began, and the competitions which keep us at variance with our neighbours arose. Without this previous knowledge, either recollected or acquired, it

1. I.e., the *Literary Magazine*, of which this is the opening article.

is not easy to understand the various opinions which every change
in our affairs produces, or the questions which divide the nation into
parties, and cause divisions in the parliament, and wars among the
pamphleteers.

The present system of English politics may properly be
said to have taken rise in the reign of Queen Elizabeth. At
this time the protestant religion was established, which
naturally allied us to the reformed states,[a] and made all the
popish powers our enemies.

We began in the same reign to extend our trade, by which
we made it necessary to ourselves to watch the commercial
progress of our neighbours; and, if not to incommode and
obstruct their traffick, to hinder them from impairing ours.

We then likewise settled colonies in America, which was
become the great scene of European ambition; for, seeing
with what treasures the Spaniards were annually inriched
from Mexico and Peru, every nation imagined, that an
American conquest or plantation would certainly fill the
mother country with gold and silver. This produced a large
extent of very distant dominions, of which we, at this time,
neither knew nor foresaw the advantage or incumbrance:
We seem to have snatched them into our hands, upon no
very just principles of policy, only because every state,
according to a prejudice of long continuance, concludes
itself more powerful as its territories become larger.[b]

The discoveries of new regions, which were then every day
made, the profit of remote traffick, and the necessity of long
voyages, produced, in a few years, a great multiplication of
shipping. The sea was considered as the wealthy element;
and, by degrees, a new kind of sovereignty arose, called naval
dominion.

As the chief trade of the world, so the chief maritime power
was at first in the hands of the Portuguese and Spaniards, who,
by a compact,[2] to which the consent of other princes was not
asked, had divided the newly discovered countries between

a. states *1759*] state *1756*   b. more extensive *1759*

2. The Treaty of Tordesillas, 1494,   lands west of a line drawn 370 leagues
which gave effect to the famous bulls   west of Cape Verde, and to Portugal
of Pope Alexander VI (4 May 1493)   lands east of the line. On all this,
awarding to Spain all newly discovered   see SJ's lengthy and outspoken study

THE

LITERARY MAGAZINE,

For the Year 1756.

NUMBER I.

An Introduction to the Political State of Great-Britain.

S it is intended to exhibit in the following pamphlet an accurate account of every political debate, it appears necessary to lay before the reader a succinct account of *British* affairs, from the time in which our present relations to the continent began, and the competitions which keep us at variance with our neighbours arose. Without this previous knowledge, either recollected or acquired, it is not easy to understand the various opinions which every change in our affairs produces, or the questions which divide the nation into parties, and cause divisions in the parliament, and wars among the pamphleteers.

THE present system of *English* politics may properly be said to have taken rise in the reign of queen *Elizabeth*. At this time the protestant religion was established, which naturally allied us to the reformed state, and made all the popish powers our enemies.

We began in the same reign to extend our trade, by which we made it necessary to ourselves to watch the commercial progress of our neighbours; and, if not to incommode and obstruct their traffick, to hinder them from impairing ours.

We then likewise settled colonies in *America*, which was become the great scene of *European* ambition; for, seeing with what treasures the *Spaniards* were annually inriched from *Mexico* and *Peru*, every nation imagined, that an *American* conquest or plantation

VOL. I.

would certainly fill the mother country with gold and silver. This produced a large extent of very distant dominions, of which we, at this time, neither knew nor foresaw the advantage or incumbrance : We seem to have snatched them into our hands, upon no very just principles of policy, only because every state, according to a prejudice of long continuance, concludes itself more powerful as its territories become larger.

The discoveries of new regions, which were then every day made, the profit of remote traffick, and the necessity of long voyages, produced, in a few years, a great multiplication of shipping. The sea was considered as the wealthy element; and, by degrees, a new kind of sovereignty arose, called naval dominion.

As the chief trade of the world, so the chief maritime power was at first in the hands of the *Portuguese* and *Spaniards*, who, by a compact, to which the consent of other princes was not asked, had divided the newly discovered countries between them; but the crown of *Portugal* having fallen to the king of *Spain*, or being seized by him, he was master of the ships of the two nations, with which he kept all the coasts of *Europe* in alarm, till the *Armada*, which he had raised at a vast expence for the conquest of *England*, was destroyed, which put a stop, and almost an end, to the naval power of the *Spaniards*.

At this time the *Dutch*, who were oppressed by the *Spaniards*, and feared yet greater evils than they felt, resolved no longer to endure the insolence of their masters : they therefore revolted,

B and

them; but the crown of Portugal having fallen to the king of Spain,[3] or being seized by him, he was master of the ships of the two nations, with which he kept all the coasts of Europe in alarm, till the Armada, which he had raised at a vast expence for the conquest of England, was destroyed, which put a stop, and almost an end, to the naval power of the Spaniards.

At this time the Dutch, who were oppressed by the Spaniards, and feared yet greater evils than they felt, resolved no longer to endure the insolence of their masters: they therefore revolted, and after a struggle, in which they were assisted by the money and forces of Elizabeth, erected an independent and powerful commonwealth.[4]

When the inhabitants of the Low-Countries had formed their system of government, and some remission of the war gave them leisure to form schemes of future prosperity, they easily perceived that, as their territories were narrow and their numbers small, they could preserve themselves only by that power which is the consequence of wealth; and that, by a people whose country produced only the necessaries of life, wealth was not to be acquired, but from foreign dominions, and by the transportation of the products of one country into another.

From this necessity, thus justly estimated, arose a plan of commerce, which was for many years prosecuted with industry and success, perhaps never seen in the world before, and by which the poor tenants of mudwalled villages and impassable bogs, erected themselves into high and mighty states,[5] who put[c] the greatest monarchs at defiance, whose

c. set *1759*

---

of Spanish and Portuguese discovery and expansion in his introduction to *The World Displayed* (1759).

3. Philip II, who, on the extinction of the Aviz dynasty of Portugal in 1580, made good his claim to the throne of that country. Spanish domination was thrown off in 1640, when John IV became the first Portuguese king of the house of Bragança.

4. The Dutch republic may be said to have formally come into existence with the Union of Utrecht, 1579.

5. The English translation of the official style of the States-General, the Dutch sovereign body (*De Edele Groot Mogende Heeren Staaten*). This phrase, or "their high mightinesses," was often used sarcastically by English writers, as SJ is no doubt using it here.

alliance was courted by the proudest, and whose power was dreaded by the fiercest nation. By the establishment of this state there arose to England a new ally and a new rival.

At this time, which seems to be the period destined for the change of the face of Europe, France began first to rise into power, and, from defending her own provinces with difficulty and fluctuating success, to threaten her neighbours with incroachments and devastations. Henry the Fourth[6] having, after a long struggle, obtained the crown, found it easy to govern nobles exhausted and wearied with a long civil war, and having composed the disputes between the protestants and papists, so as to obtain, at least, a truce for both parties, was at leisure to accumulate treasure, and raise forces which he purposed to have employed in a design of settling for ever the balance of Europe. Of this great scheme he lived not to see the vanity, or to feel the disappointment; for he was murdered in the midst of his mighty preparations.

The French however were in this reign taught to know their own power; and the great designs of a king, whose wisdom they had so long experienced, even though they were not brought to actual experiment, disposed them to consider themselves as masters of the destiny of their neighbours; and, from that time, he that shall nicely examine their schemes and conduct will, I believe, find that they began to take an air of superiority, to which they had never pretended before; and that they have been always employed, more or less openly upon schemes of dominion, though with frequent interruptions from domestic troubles, and with those intermissions which human counsels must always suffer, as men intrusted with great affairs are dissipated in youth, and languid in age, are embarrassed by competitors, or, without any external reason, change their minds.

France was now no longer in dread of insults and invasions from England. She was not only able to maintain her own territories, but prepared, on all occasions, to invade others, and we had now a neighbour whose interest it was to be an enemy, and who has disturbed us, from that time to this, with open hostility or secret machinations.

---

6. Reigned 1589–1610.

Such was the state of England and its neighbours, when Elizabeth left the crown to James of Scotland. It has not, I think, been frequently observed by historians at how critical a time the union of the two kingdoms happened. Had England and Scotland continued separate kingdoms, when France was established in the full possession of her natural power, the Scots, in continuance of the league, which it would now have been more than ever their interest to observe, would, upon every instigation of the French court, have raised an army with French money, and harrassed us with an invasion, in which they would have thought themselves successful, whatever numbers they might have left behind them. To a people warlike and indigent, an incursion into a rich country is never hurtful. The pay of France, and the plunder of the northern counties, would always have tempted them to hazard their lives, and we should have been under a necessity of keeping a line of garrisons along our border.

This trouble, however, we escaped by the accession of King James; but it is uncertain, whether his natural disposition did not injure us more than this accidental condition happened to benefit us. He was a man of great theoretical knowledge, but of no practical wisdom; he was very well able to discern the true interest of himself, his kingdom, and his posterity, but sacrificed it, upon all occasions, to his present pleasure or his present ease; so conscious of his own knowledge and abilities, that he would not suffer a minister to govern, and so lax of attention, and timorous of opposition, that he was not able to govern for himself. With this character James quietly saw the Dutch invade our commerce; the French grew every day stronger and stronger, and the protestant interest, of which he boasted himself the head, was oppressed on every side, while he writ, and hunted, and dispatched ambassadors, who, when their master's weakness was once known, were treated in foreign courts with very little ceremony. James, however, took care to be flattered at home, and was neither angry nor ashamed at the appearance that he made in other countries.

Thus England grew weaker, or what is in political estimation the same thing, saw her neighbours grow stronger, without receiving proportionable additions to her own power.

Not that the mischief was so great as it is generally conceived or represented; for, I believe, it may be made to appear, that the wealth of the nation was, in this reign, very much increased, though that of the crown was lessened. Our reputation for war was impaired, but commerce seems to have been carried on with great industry and vigour, and nothing was wanting, but that we should have defended ourselves from the incroachments of our neighbours.

The inclination to plant colonies in America still continued, and this being the only project in which men of adventure and enterprise could exert their qualities in a pacific reign, multitudes, who were discontented with their condition in their native country, and such multitudes there will always be, sought relief, or at least change in the western regions, where they settled in the northern part of the continent, at a distance from the Spaniards at that time almost the only nation that had any power or will to obstruct us.

Such was the condition of this country when the unhappy Charles inherited the crown. He had seen the errors of his father, without being able to prevent them, and, when he began his reign, endeavoured to raise the nation to its former dignity. The French papists had begun a new war upon the protestants: Charles sent a fleet to invade Rhee and relieve Rochelle,[7] but his attempts were defeated, and the protestants were subdued. The Dutch grown wealthy and strong, claimed the right of fishing in the British seas: this claim the king, who saw the increasing power of the states of Holland, resolved to contest. But for this end it was necessary to build a fleet, and a fleet could not be built without expence: he was advised to levy ship-money,[8] which gave occasion to the civil war, of which the events and conclusion are too well known.

While the inhabitants of this island were embroiled among themselves, the power of France and Holland was

---

7. The Duke of Buckingham's unsuccessful expedition to the Île de Ré, off La Rochelle, took place in 1627.

8. SJ adroitly evades the question of Charles I's personal responsibility for the Civil War by use of the formula "was advised," which could mean much or little. Censure of royal activities by Parliament and disgruntled ministers frequently took the form of condemnation of "whoever advised" His Majesty to do so-and-so.

every day increasing. The Dutch had overcome the difficulties of their infant commonwealth; and as they still retained their vigour and industry, from rich grew continually richer, and from powerful more powerful. They extended their traffick, and had not yet admitted luxury, so that they had the means and the will to accumulate wealth, without any incitement to spend it. The French, who wanted nothing to make them powerful, but a prudent regulation of their revenues, and a proper use of their natural advantages, by the successive care of skilful ministers became every day stronger, and more conscious of their strength.

About this time it was, that the French first began to turn their thoughts to traffick and navigation, and to desire like other nations an American territory. All the fruitful and valuable parts of the western world were already either occupied or claimed, and nothing remained for France but the leavings of other navigators, for she was not yet haughty enough to seize what the neighbouring powers had already appropriated.

The French therefore contented themselves with sending a colony to Canada,[9] a cold uncomfortable uninviting region, from which nothing but furrs and fish were to be had, and where the new inhabitants could only pass a laborious and necessitous life in perpetual regret of the deliciousness and plenty of their native country.

Notwithstanding the opinion which our countrymen have been taught to entertain of the comprehension and foresight of French politicians, I am not able to persuade myself, that when this colony was first planted, it was thought of much value, even by those that encouraged it; there was probably nothing more intended than to provide a drain into which the waste of an exuberant[1] nation might be thrown, a place where those who could do no good might live without the power of doing mischief. Some new advantage they undoubtedly saw, or imagined themselves to see, and what

---

9. Samuel de Champlain's settlement of Port Royal in what is now Nova Scotia took place in 1604, and of Quebec in 1608.

1. "Growing with superfluous shoots: over abundant; superfluously plentiful; luxuriant" (*Dictionary*, def. 1).

more was necessary to the establishment of the colony was supplied by natural inclination to experiments, and that impatience of doing nothing, to which mankind perhaps owe much of what is imagined to be effected by more splendid motives.[2]

In this region of desolate sterility they settled themselves, upon whatever principle; and as they have from that time had the happiness of a government by which no interest has been neglected, nor any part of their subjects overlooked, they have, by continual encouragement and assistance from France, been perpetually enlarging their bounds and increasing their numbers.

These were at first, like other nations who invaded America, inclined to consider the neighbourhood of the natives, as troublesome and dangerous, and are charged with having destroy'd great numbers, but they are now grown wiser, if not honester, and instead of endeavouring to frighten the Indians away, they invite them to intermarriage and cohabitation, and allure them by all practicable methods to become the subjects of the king of France.[3]

If the Spaniards, when they first took possession of the newly discovered world, instead of destroying the inhabitants by thousands, had either had the humanity[4] or the policy to have conciliated them by kind treatment, and to have united them gradually to their own people, such an accession might have been made to the power of the king of Spain, as would have made him far the greatest monarch that ever yet ruled

---

2. Cf. *Rasselas*, Ch. 31: "[The Great Pyramid] seems to have been erected only in compliance with that hunger of imagination which preys incessantly on life, and must be always appeased by some employment."

3. The adoption in French Canada of a policy of conciliation of the Indians (with the exception of the Iroquois, the allies of the English) is generally credited to the Comte de Frontenac, governor from 1672 to 1698. But the question of the relations between Eu-

ropeans and Indians in America during the seventeenth and eighteenth centuries is a complex one, still being subjected to investigation by historians. See "Observations on the Present State of Affairs," p. 185 below.

4. "Unanimity" in *1756* is clearly a mistake; but Davies's emendation, "urbanity" (reprinted in *1773* and later editions), is not very satisfactory either. The "humanity" of *1759* is clearly right; SJ's initial "h" can easily be mistaken for "u," his "u" for "n."

in[d] the globe; but the opportunity was lost by foolishness and cruelty, and now can never be recovered.[5]

When the Parliament had finally prevailed over our king and the army over the Parliament, the interest of the two commonwealths of England and Holland soon appeared to be opposite, and the new government declared war against the Dutch. In this contest was exerted the utmost power of the two nations, and the Dutch were finally defeated, yet not with such evidence of superiority as left us much reason to boast our victory; they were obliged however to solicit peace, which was granted them on easy conditions, and Cromwell, who was now possessed of the supreme power, was left at leisure to pursue other designs.

The European powers had not yet ceased to look with envy on the Spanish acquisitions in America, and therefore Cromwell thought that, if he gained any part of these celebrated regions, he should exalt his own reputation, and inrich the country. He therefore quarreled with the Spaniards upon some such subject of contention, as he that is resolved upon hostility may always find, and sent Pen and Venables[6] into the western seas. They first landed in Hispaniola, whence they were driven off with no great reputation to themselves, and that they might not return without having done something, they afterwards invaded Jamaica, where they found less resistance, and obtained that island, which was afterwards consigned to us, being probably of little value to the Spaniards, and continues to this day a place of great wealth and dreadful wickedness, a den of tyrants, and a dungeon of slaves.[7]

d. on *1759*

---

5. For other statements by SJ on the treatment of indigenous peoples by European invaders, see "The State of Affairs in Lilliput" (1738), the "Life of Sir Francis Drake" (1740), and the introduction to *The World Displayed* (1759).

6. Admiral Sir William Penn (1621–70), father of the founder of Penn-

sylvania, and General Robert Venables. The actions referred to took place in 1655.

7. SJ may be drawing upon first-hand information from his friend Dr. Richard Bathurst, a native of Jamaica. The young Jamaican Negro Frank Barber had been a member of SJ's household since 1752.

Cromwell, who perhaps had not leisure to study foreign politics, was very fatally mistaken with regard to Spain and France. Spain had been the last power in Europe, which had openly pretended to give law to other nations, and the memory of this terror remained when the real cause was at an end. We had more lately been frighted by Spain than by France, and though very few were then alive of the generation that had their sleep broken by the Armada, yet the name of the Spaniards was still terrible, and a war against them was pleasing to the people.

Our own troubles had left us very little desire to look out upon the continent, and inveterate prejudice hindred us from perceiving, that for more than half a century the power of France had been increasing, and that of Spain had been growing less; nor does it seem to have been remembred, which yet required no great depth of policy to discern, that of two monarchies,[8] neither of which could be long our friend, it was our interest to have the weaker near us, or that if a war should happen, Spain, however wealthy or strong in herself, was by the dispersion of her territories more obnoxious[9] to the attacks of a naval power, and consequently had more to fear from us, and had it less in her power to hurt us.

All these considerations were overlooked by the wisdom of that age, and Cromwell assisted the French to drive the Spaniards out of Flanders at a time when it was our interest to have supported the Spaniards against France, as formerly the Hollanders against Spain, by which we might at least have retarded the growth of the French power, though I think it must have finally prevailed.

During this time, our colonies which were less disturbed by our commotions than the mother country, naturally increased; it is probable that many who were unhappy at home took shelter in those remote regions, where for the sake of inviting greater numbers, every one was allowed to think and live his own way.[1] The French settlement in the mean

---

8. *1756* and *1759* read "monarchs." SJ would hardly have been guilty of the solecism of using the neuter pronoun "which" to refer to "monarchs," which in any case does not fit the context.

9. "1. Subject. ... 4. Liable; exposed" (*Dictionary*).

1. Certainly a very questionable statement as regards Massachusetts and Connecticut.

time went slowly forward, too inconsiderable to raise any jealousy, and too weak to attempt any incroachments.

When Cromwell died, the confusions that followed produced the restoration of monarchy, and some time was employed in repairing the ruins of our constitution, and restoring the nation to a state of peace. In every change there will be many that suffer real or imaginary grievances, and therefore many will be dissatisfied. This was, perhaps, the reason why several colonies had their beginning in the reign of Charles the Second. The Quakers willingly sought refuge in Pensylvania; and it is not unlikely that Carolina owed its inhabitants to the remains of that restless disposition, which had given so much disturbance to our country, and had now no opportunity of acting at home.

The Dutch still continuing to increase in wealth and power, either kindled the resentment of their neighbours by their insolence, or raised their envy by their prosperity. Charles made war upon them without much advantage; but they were obliged at last to confess him the sovereign of the narrow seas.[2] They were reduced almost to extremities by an invasion from France; but soon recovered from their consternation, and, by the fluctuation of war, regained their cities and provinces with the same speed as they had lost them.

During the time of Charles the Second the power of France was every day increasing; and Charles, who never disturbed himself with remote consequences, saw the progress of her arms, and the extension of her dominions, with very little uneasiness. He was indeed sometimes driven by the prevailing faction into confederacies against her; but as he had, probably, a secret partiality in her favour, he never persevered long in acting against her, nor ever acted with much vigour: so that, by his feeble resistance, he rather raised her confidence, than hindered her designs.

About this time the French first began to perceive the advantage of commerce, and the importance of a naval force; and such encouragement was given to manufactures, and so eagerly was every project received, by which trade could be advanced, that, in a few years, the sea was filled with their ships, and all the parts of the world crowded with their

---

2. The English Channel and the North Sea.

merchants. There is, perhaps, no instance in human story of such a change produced, in so short a time, in the schemes and manners of a people, of so many new^e sources of wealth opened, and such numbers of artificers and merchants made to start out of the ground, as was seen in the ministry of Colbert.[3]

Now it was that the power of France became formidable to England. Her dominions were large before, and her armies numerous; but her operations were necessarily confined to the continent. She had neither ships for the transportation of her troops, nor money for their support in distant expeditions. Colbert saw both these wants, and saw that commerce only would supply them. The fertility of their country furnishes the French with commodities; the poverty of the common people keeps the price of labour low. By the obvious practice of selling much and buying little, it was apparent that they would soon draw the wealth of other countries into their own; and, by carrying out their merchandise in their own vessels, a numerous body of sailors would quickly be raised.

This was projected, and this was performed. The king of France was soon enabled to bribe those whom he could not conquer, and to terrify with his fleets those whom his armies could not have approached. The influence of France was suddenly diffused over all the globe; her arms were dreaded, and her pensions received in remote regions, and those were almost ready to acknowledge her sovereignty, who, a few years before, had scarcely heard her name. She thundered on the coasts of Africa, and received ambassadors from Siam.

So much may be done by one wise man, endeavouring with honesty the advantage of the public. But that we may not rashly condemn all ministers as wanting wisdom or integrity, whose counsels have produced no such apparent benefits to their country, it must be considered, that Colbert had means of acting, which our government does not allow. He could inforce all his orders by the power of an absolute monarch; he could compel individuals to sacrifice their

e. *om. 1759*

---

3. Jean-Baptiste Colbert, Louis XIV's chief minister 1661–83. SJ's use of the myth of Cadmus should be noted.

private profit to the general good; he could make one under-standing preside over many hands, and remove difficulties by quick and violent expedients. Where no man thinks himself under any obligation to submit to another, and, instead of co-operating in one great scheme, every one hastens through by-paths to private profit, no great change can suddenly be made;[4] nor is superior knowledge of much effect, where every man resolves to use his own eyes and his own judgment, and every one applauds his own dexterity and diligence in pro-portion as he becomes rich sooner than his neighbour.

Colonies are always the effects and causes of navigation. They who visit many countries find some in which pleasure, profit or safety invite them to settle; and these settlements, when they are once made, must keep a perpetual correspond-ence with the original country, to which they are subject, and on which they depend for protection in danger, and supplies in necessity. So that a country,[5] once discovered and planted, must always find employment for shipping, more certainly than any foreign commerce, which, depending on casualties, may be sometimes more and sometimes less, and which other nations may contract or suppress. A trade to colonies can never be much impaired, being, in reality, only an intercourse between distant provinces of the same empire, from which intruders are easily excluded; likewise the interest and affection of the correspondent parties, however distant, is the same.[6]

---

4. Locke in his *Second Treatise on Government* (1690) emphasizes the in-nate conservatism of government by popular consent. It would be wrong to deduce, from SJ's remarks here on the "superior efficiency" of the French government, that he had any han-kering for absolutism. As he says, he mentions the fact in defence of administrators under constitutional governments, who have no such means of speedy action as Colbert had. SJ's "The Bravery of the English Common Soldiers" (p. 281 below) might be read in conjunction with this passage.

5. I.e., a country once discovered and planted as a colony.

6. The "mercantilist" theory of colonies stated in this paragraph is basic to SJ's thinking about America, as expressed in his "Observations on a Letter from a French Refugee" (pp. 173–6 below) and his review of Lewis Evans's *Geographical ... Essays* (pp. 210–12 below), and later in *Taxation No Tyranny*. A country, *together with* its col-onies, should form a self-contained economic unit; otherwise colonization is pointless. See also "Further Thoughts on Agriculture" (pp. 120–25 above).

On this reason all nations, whose power has been exerted on the ocean, have fixed colonies in remote parts of the world, and while those colonies subsisted, navigation, if it did not increase, was always preserved from total decay. With this policy the French were well acquainted, and therefore improved and augmented the settlements in America, and other regions, in proportion as they advanced their schemes of naval greatness.

The exact time in which they made their acquisitions in America, or other quarters of the globe, it is not necessary to collect. It is sufficient to observe, that their trade and their colonies increased together; and, if their naval armaments[7] were carried on, as they really were, in greater proportion to their commerce, than can be practised in other countries, it must be attributed to the martial disposition at that time prevailing in the nation, to the frequent wars which Lewis the Fourteenth made upon his neighbours, and to the extensive commerce of the English and Dutch, which afforded so much plunder to privateers, that war was more lucrative than traffick.

Thus the naval power of France continued to increase during the reign of Charles the Second, who, between his fondness of ease and pleasure, the struggles of faction, which he could not suppress, and his inclination to the friendship of absolute monarchy, had not much power or desire to repress it. And of James the Second, it could not be expected that he should act against his neighbours with great vigour, having the whole body of his subjects to oppose. He was not ignorant of the real interest of his country; he desired its power and its happiness, and thought rightly, that there is no happiness without religion; but he thought very erroneously and absurdly, that there is no religion without popery.

When the necessity of self-preservation had impelled the subjects of James to drive him from the throne,[8] there came

---

7. "A force equipped for war; generally used of a naval force" (*Dictionary*).

8. If a Jacobite is one who thinks James II should have retained the English throne, this uncompromising statement may be taken as evidence against the theory that SJ had "Jacobite tendencies."

a time in which the passions, as well as interest of the government, acted against the French, and in which it may perhaps be reasonably doubted, whether the desire of humbling France was not stronger than that of exalting England;[9] of this, however, it is not necessary to inquire, since, though the intention may be different, the event will be the same. All mouths were now open to declare what every eye had observed before, that the arms of France were become dangerous to Europe, and that, if her incroachments were suffered a little longer, resistance would be too late.

It was now determined to reassert the empire of the sea; but it was more easily determined than performed: the French made a vigorous defence against the united power of England and Holland, and were sometimes masters of the ocean, though the two maritime powers were united against them. At length, however, they were defeated at La Hogue;[10] a great part of their fleet was destroyed, and they were reduced to carry on the war only with their privateers, from whom there was suffered much petty mischief, though there was no danger of conquest or invasion. They distressed our merchants, and obliged us to the continual expence of convoys and fleets of observation; and, by skulking in little coves and shallow waters, escaped our pursuit.

In this reign began our confederacy with the Dutch, which mutual interest has now improved into a friendship, conceived by some to be inseparable, and from that time the states began to be termed, in the stile of politicians, our faithful friends, the allies which nature has given us, our protestant confederates, and by many other names of national endearment. We have, it is true, the same interest, as opposed to France, and some resemblance of religion, as opposed to popery; but we have such a rivalry, in respect of commerce, as will always keep us from very close adherence to each other. No mercantile man, or mercantile nation, has any friendship but for money, and alliance between them will last no longer than their common safety or common profit

---

9. That is, in the mind of William III and his supporters. It is noteworthy that SJ concedes the right-ness, in effect, of William's policy, whatever its motives.

10. In 1692.

is endangered; no longer than they have an enemy, who threatens to take from each more than either can steal from the other.

We were both sufficiently interested in repressing the ambition, and obstructing the commerce of France; and therefore we concurred with as much fidelity and as regular co-operation as is commonly found. The Dutch were in immediate danger, the armies of their enemies hovered over their country, and therefore they were obliged to dismiss for a time their love of money, and their narrow projects of private profit, and to do what a trader does not willingly at any time believe necessary, to sacrifice a part for the preservation of the whole.[1]

A peace[2] was at length made, and the French with their usual vigour and industry rebuilt their fleets, restored their commerce, and became in a very few years able to contest again the dominion of the sea. Their ships were well built, and always very numerously manned, their commanders having no hopes but from their bravery or their fortune, were resolute, and being very carefully educated for the sea, were eminently skilful.

---

1. The traditional Tory dislike of the Dutch needs analysis. Swift's detestation of them is frequently assigned to religious motives. SJ discounts these; but his thesis of simple economic rivalry is hardly convincing. If, as SJ argues, the wise observer will allow no sympathetic emotions to be involved in the spectacle of an alliance between two "mercantile" nations, it would seem, conversely, that the mere fact of their economic rivalry should inspire no such emotional antipathy as SJ obviously feels towards the Dutch. Cf. "Remarks on *Considerations on the Embargo upon the Provision of Victual*" (*Gentleman's Magazine*, XI [1741], 634): "It is said that the Dutch have sold to their enemies at night that ammunition which was to be made use of next day against themselves; but surely no man will attempt to justify this conduct, which could be produced only by inveterate habits of avarice, and a closer attention to the love of money than to that of life"; and "Historical Memoirs" in the *Literary Magazine*, No. 4, July–Aug 1756: "Such are the sentiments and such the conduct of a people [the Dutch] who have cost Great-Britain millions to support, and for whose emolument she sacrifices the most beneficial branches of her trade. But ingratitude is and will be the necessary consequence of ill-placed generosity." I have suggested that the first passage is by SJ (*PMLA*, LXXIV [Mar 1959], 79) and possibly the second (*Review of English Studies*, n.s. VII [Oct 1956], 386).

2. The Peace of Ryswick, 1697.

All this was soon perceived, when Queen Anne, the then darling of England,[3] declared war against France.[4] Our success by sea, though sufficient to keep us from dejection, was not such as dejected our enemies. It is, indeed, to be confessed, that we did not exert our whole naval strength; Marlborough was the governor of our counsels, and the great view of Marlborough was a war by land, which he knew well how to conduct, both to the honour of his country and his own profit.[5] The fleet was therefore starved that the army might be supplied, and naval advantages were neglected for the sake of taking a town in Flanders, to be garrisoned by our allies. The French, however, were so weakened by one defeat after another, that, though their fleet was never destroyed by any total overthrow, they at last retained it in their harbours, and applied their whole force to the resistance of the confederate army, that now began to approach their frontiers, and threatned to lay waste their provinces and cities.

In the latter years of this war, the danger of their neighbourhood in America seems to have been considered, and a fleet was fitted out and supplied with a proper number of land forces to seize Quebec, the capital of Canada, or New France; but this expedition[6] miscarried, like that of Anson against

---

3. Cf. SJ's review of the *Account of the Conduct of the Dutchess of Marlborough*, 1742: "[The letters from Anne to the Duchess] will be equally useful for the confutation of those who have exalted or depressed her character. . . . It appears plainly enough from them that she was what she has been represented, little more than the slave of the Marlborough family." Among those who "exalted" Anne's character and regarded her as the "darling of England" was Smollett (*History of England*, Book I, Ch. 11): "She felt a mother's fondness for her people, by whom she was universally beloved with a warmth of affection which even the prejudice of party could not abate. In a word, if she was not the greatest, she was certainly one of the best and most

unblemished sovereigns that ever sat upon the throne of England; and well deserved the expressive, though simple epithet of 'the good Queen Anne'."

4. The War of the Spanish Succession, 1702–13.

5. SJ and Macaulay agree on at least this one point—Marlborough's personal character. The classic defence is Winston Churchill's *Marlborough, His Life and Times* (1933–38). Historians have remained not wholly convinced by it.

6. In 1711, under Sir Hovenden Walker and General Hill, brother of Mrs. Masham, the Tory favourite who replaced Sarah, Duchess of Marlborough, in Anne's affections.

the Spaniards,[7] by the lateness of the season, and our ignorance of the coasts, on which we were to act. We returned with loss, and only excited our enemies to greater vigilance, and perhaps to stronger fortifications.

When the peace of Utrecht was made, which those who clamoured among us most loudly against it,[8] found it their interest to keep, the French applied themselves with the utmost industry to the extension of their trade, which we were so far from hindering, that for many years our ministry thought their friendship of such value, as to be cheaply purchased by whatever concession.

Instead therefore of opposing, as we had hitherto professed to do, the boundless ambition of the house of Bourbon, we became on a sudden solicitous for its exaltation, and studious of its interest. We assisted the schemes of France and Spain with our fleets, and endeavoured to make these our friends by servility, whom nothing but power will keep quiet, and who must always be our enemies while they are endeavouring to grow greater, and we determine to remain free.

That nothing might be omitted which could testify our willingness to continue on any terms the good friends of France, we were content to assist not only their conquests but their traffick; and though we did not openly repeal the prohibitory laws, we yet tamely suffered commerce to be carried on between the two nations, and wool was daily imported[9] to enable them to make cloth, which they carried to our markets and sold cheaper than we.

---

7. This must refer to Commodore George Anson's expedition in 1740, directed against the west coast of South America, which turned into his famous circumnavigation of the world. It seems an odd reference for SJ to make at this point, for instances of ill-conceived military expeditions would have been easy enough to glean from the war of 1701–13 itself. It can only be interpreted as a gratuitous piece of anti-ministerial propaganda, for Anson was now (1756) First Lord of the Admiralty and in charge of the naval war against France. For other in-

stances of SJ's hostility toward Anson, see pp. 217 and 353 below.

8. I.e., the Whigs, who, under Walpole, later made the alliance with France the keystone of their foreign policy during the 1720's and 1730's. Casuistically, SJ omits to notice that the argument applies in reverse—that a Tory opponent of Walpole's conciliatory policy toward France ought to condemn the Tory Peace of Utrecht.

9. I.e., into France, from Great Britain. As SJ says, there was no formal relaxation during this period of the strict embargo on the exportation of

During all this time, they were extending and strengthening their settlements in America, contriving new modes of traffick, and framing new alliances with the Indian nations. They began now to find these northern regions, barren and desolate as they are, sufficiently valuable to desire at least a nominal possession, that might furnish a pretence for the exclusion of others; they therefore extended their claim to tracts of land, which they could never hope to occupy,[1] took care to give their dominions an unlimited magnitude, have given in their maps the name of Louisiana to a country, of which part is claimed by the Spaniards, and part by the English, without any regard to ancient boundaries or prior discovery.

When the return of Columbus from his great voyage had filled all Europe with wonder and curiosity, Henry the Seventh sent Sebastian Cabot[2] to try what could be found for the benefit of England: he declined the track of Columbus, and, steering to the westward, fell upon the island, which, from that time, was called by the English, Newfoundland. Our princes seem to have considered themselves as intitled by their right of prior seizure to the northern parts of America, as the Spaniards were allowed by universal consent their claim to the southern region for the same reason, and we accordingly made our principal settlements within the limits of our own discoveries, and, by degrees, planted the eastern coast from Newfoundland to Georgia.

As we had, according to the European principles which allow nothing to the natives of these regions, our choice of situation in this extensive country, we naturally fixed our habitations along the coast, for the sake of traffick and correspondence, and all the conveniencies of navigable rivers.

---

raw wool from Britain; see Adam Smith's account (*The Wealth of Nations,* Book IV, Ch. 8) of what he calls the Draconian legislation to prevent it. I know nothing of the governmentally condoned clandestine trade that SJ speaks of; but it may well have been described in the pamphlet-war about the wool embargo that the *Gentleman's Magazine* (probably with SJ's assistance and perhaps even under his direction)

devoted much space to reviewing in the early 1740's (see D. J. Greene, *PMLA,* LXXIV [Mar 1959], 75–84).

1. Cf. Voltaire, *Essai sur les moeurs* (1756), Ch. 148: "Peut-être un jour, s'il y a des millions d'habitants de trop en France, sera-t-il avantageux de peupler la Louisiane."

2. In 1497. Actually John (Giovanni), Sebastian Cabot's father, was in charge of the expedition.

And when one port or river was occupied, the next colony, instead of fixing themselves in the inland parts behind the former, went on southward, till they pleased themselves with another maritime situation. For this reason our colonies have more length than depth; their extent from east to west, or from the sea to the interior country, bears no proportion to their reach along the coast from north to south.

It was, however, understood, by a kind of tacit compact among the commercial powers, that possession of the coast included a right to the inland; and, therefore, the charters granted to the several colonies limit their districts only from north to south, leaving their possessions from east to west unlimited and discretional, supposing that, as the colony increases, they may take lands as they shall want them, the possession of the coasts excluding other navigators, and the unhappy Indians having no right of nature or of nations.[3]

This right of the first European possessor was not disputed till it became the interest of the French to question it. Canada or New-France, on which they made their first settlement, is situated eastward[4] of our colonies, between which they pass up the great river of St. Laurence, with Newfoundland on the north, and Nova Scotia on the south. Their establishment in this country was neither envied nor hindered; and they lived here, in no great numbers a long time, neither molesting their European neighbours, nor molested by them.

But when they grew stronger and more numerous, they began to extend their territories; and, as it is natural for men to seek their own convenience, the desire of more fertile and agreeable habitations tempted them southward. There is land enough to the north and west of their settlements, which they may occupy with as good right as can be shewn by the other European usurpers, and which neither the English nor Spaniards will contest; but of this cold region they have enough already, and their resolution was to get a better country. This was not to be had but by settling to the west of our plantations, on ground which has been hitherto

---

3. The classic divisions, in Roman law, of *jus naturale* and *jus gentium*.
4. Probably a mistake for "west-ward," but at least as likely to be SJ's as the printer's.

supposed to belong to us.

Hither, therefore, they resolved to remove, and to fix, at their own discretion, the western border of our colonies, which was heretofore considered as unlimited. Thus by forming a line of forts, in some measure parallel to the coast, they inclose us between their garrisons and the sea, and not only hinder our extension westward, but, whenever they have a sufficient navy in the sea, can harrass us on each side, as they can invade us, at pleasure, from one or other of their forts.

This design was not perhaps discovered as soon as it was formed, and was certainly not opposed so soon as it was discovered; we foolishly hoped, that their incroachments would stop, that they would be prevailed on by treaty and remonstrance, to give up what they had taken, or to put limits to themselves. We suffered them to establish one settlement after another, to pass boundary after boundary, and add fort to fort, till at last they grew strong enough to avow their designs, and defy us to obstruct them.

By these provocations long continued, we are at length forced into a war, in which we have had hitherto very ill fortune. Our troops under Braddock were dishonourably defeated;[5] our fleets have yet done nothing more than take a few merchant-ships,[6] and have distressed some private families,[7] but have very little weakened the power of France. The detention of their seamen makes it indeed less easy for them to fit out their navy; but this deficiency will be easily supplied by the alacrity of the nation, which is always eager for war.

---

5. On 9 July 1755, when attempting to drive the French from Fort Duquesne, at the strategic junction of the Allegheny and Monongahela rivers to form the Ohio. In 1754, the invading French had defeated a Virginian force under Colonel George Washington (who had originally surveyed the site for a British fort, and who was engaged in extensive land speculation in the area); Washington also took part in the recapture of the fort from the French in 1758, when it was renamed Fort Pitt (now Pittsburgh.)

6. In fact, three hundred by the end of 1755, together with 8,000 French seamen, according to Smollett (*History of England*, 1757–58, Book III, Ch. 4, Sect. 6).

7. SJ is probably referring to the expulsion, in 1755, of the Acadian French, some 6,000 in number, from Nova Scotia, commemorated in Longfellow's *Evangeline*.

It is unpleasing to represent our affairs to our own disadvantage; yet it is necessary to shew the evils which we desire to be removed; and, therefore, some account may very properly be given of the measures which have given them their present superiority.

They are said to be supplied from France with better governors than our colonies have the fate to obtain from England. A French governor is seldom chosen for any other reason than his qualifications for his trust. To be a bankrupt at home, or to be so infamously vicious that he cannot be decently protected in his own country, seldom recommends any man to the government of a French colony. Their officers are commonly skilful either in war or commerce, and are taught to have no expectation of honour or preferment, but from the justice and vigour of their administration.[8]

Their great security is the friendship of the natives, and to this advantage they have certainly an indubitable right; because it is the consequence of their virtue. It is ridiculous to imagine, that the friendship of nations, whether civil or barbarous, can be gained and kept but by kind treatment; and surely they who intrude, uncalled, upon the country of a distant people, ought to consider the natives as worthy of common kindness, and content themselves to rob without insulting them. The French, as has been already observed, admit the Indians, by intermarriage, to an equality with themselves, and those nations, with which they have no such near intercourse, they gain over to their interest by honesty in their dealings. Our factors and traders having no other purpose in view than immediate profit, use all the arts of an European counting-house, to defraud the simple hunter of his furs.

These are some of the causes of our present weakness; our planters are always quarreling with their governor, whom they consider as less to be trusted than the French; and our traders hourly alienate the Indians by their tricks and oppressions, and we continue every day to shew by new proofs, that no people can be great who have ceased to be virtuous.

---

8. It will be noted that SJ here concurs in some of the complaints of maladministration later made in the Declaration of Independence. See also the letter from "Gallo-Anglus" (p. 168 below).

REMARKS ON THE MILITIA BILL. 1756.

"A national militia has been the cry of every patriot since the Revolution," explains that most famous of militiamen, Captain Edward Gibbon.[1] The contrasting attitudes, in English-speaking countries, toward the professional and the amateur soldier—toward the idea of national defence by, on the one hand, a permanently constituted, full-time regular army, and, on the other, the general citizenry of the country, carrying on their usual occupations, but trained in military skills during their spare time—have a long history.[2] The effect of the nature of their military institutions on the "spirit"

1. *Memoirs of My Life and Writings, sub anno* 1760.

2. The distinction between the militia (which SJ and Tories generally approved of) and the standing army (of which they disapproved) seems not to have been clear to some students who have written on this period—see, e.g., I. S. Leadam's strange remark about the 1757 Militia Bill, "The tory party, consistently with its attitude since the revolution, vehemently opposed it" (*The Political History of England*, 1909, IX, 448–49), and E. A. Bloom's discussion of the present piece by SJ (*Samuel Johnson in Grub Street*, 1957, pp. 103–04). The distinction is so essential to an understanding of SJ's writings and conversation on military topics that it may be worth while repeating here the excellent summary given by the *Encyclopaedia Britannica*, 11th ed. (art. "militia"):

> Upon this footing [the organization established by the Militia Act of 1662] the militia of England remained for nearly a century with the general approval of the community. It was recognized as an instrument for defence and for the preservation of internal order, while it was especially popular from the circumstance that from its constitution and organization the Crown could not use it as a means of violating the constitution or abridging the liberty of the subject. It was controlled and regulated in the county: it was officered by the landowners and their relatives, its ranks were filled by men not depending for their subsistence or advancement upon the favour of the Crown; its numbers and maintenance were beyond the royal control; its government was by statute. While the supreme command was distinctly vested in the Crown, every practical security was thus taken against its use by the Crown for any object not constitutional or legitimate. It was regarded as, and was, in fact, the army of the state as distinguished from the standing army, which was very much the army of the king personally. The latter consisted of hired soldiers, and was more than once recruited by a conscription, confined, however, to persons of the vagrant class not having a lawful employment, while the former was mainly composed of those having a fixed abode and status. The militia thus enjoyed for many years as compared with the regular forces a social as well as a constitutional superiority.

151

of ancient peoples, particularly the Greeks, the Romans, and the Germans, was the subject of much theorizing by sociologically minded historians from Plutarch and Tacitus to Montesquieu and Gibbon himself; and for a long time great emotional appeal attached to the idea of a community without a special "warrior class," where in time of emergency every able-bodied male, like a Cincinnatus or William Tell, is qualified to leave his plough, take up arms, and beat off an invader. In the eighteenth century it gained renewed force in the young American republic, with the story of the "embattled farmers" of Lexington and Concord putting to rout a foreign tyrant's despicable mercenaries. Of course, the military history of the Revolutionary War is in reality hardly so simple as that: the concept, the myth, existed before the events and coloured the popular picture of them. It came, in fact, from England with the American colonists themselves, and in turn had come to England with the Angles and Saxons, the "national armies" of whose progenitors had overwhelmed the professional troops of "decadent" Rome. Constitutionally, the permanent liability of all able-bodied males in a country to serve as soldiers when called on was affirmed as early as the "Fyrd" or general levy of the time of King Alfred, and, though undergoing many vicissitudes, has never lapsed.

Those vicissitudes were especially numerous in Britain in the seventeenth and eighteenth centuries, when, as the art of war grew more technical, the difficulty of keeping a citizen army competently trained became greater and greater. The ideal suffered its rudest shock at the hands of Oliver Cromwell (ironically, not a soldier by vocation himself, but a country squire), who, losing patience with the inefficient "trained bands" of the mediaeval militia system, organized his virtually professional "New Model," which rapidly crushed the power first of the Crown and then of Parliament. The New Model was the beginning of the British regular army; the restored monarchy saw no reason to abandon an institution so useful to the central executive; in 1688, the action of James II in concentrating a reinforced regular army on Hounslow Heath to overawe, if necessary, the city of London, further emphasized its political significance. Throughout the first century of its existence, the idea of a professional "standing army" continued to be regarded with the deepest distrust by the general populace, especially by the various "country parties," always jealous of any increase in the power of the central administration; and it was with the greatest difficulty, during Walpole's pacific regime, that a small permanent army was kept in being at all. It was annually denounced in Parliament by patriots and Tories, as a threat to civil liberty, and a needless extravagance, frequently subjected to motions calling for a reduction in its already small numbers, and defended only in the feeblest and most apologetic manner by the ministry itself. British troops were little engaged in the war with Spain that began in 1739 and in the War of the Austrian Succession, where the brunt of the war effort was borne by the Royal Navy and the armies of Britain's continental allies. Even the utter ineffectiveness of the militia during the rebellion of 1745 failed to provide a warning. It was not until 1755 that the British, finding themselves committed to a war of global dimensions, had at last to face the unpleasant fact of the inadequacy of their ground forces.

What was to be done? "In the outset of a glorious war, the English people had been defended by the aid of German mercenaries," Gibbon reports further. The subsidization of military assistance from other countries was one means available to Newcastle, when war with France was imminent, of bolstering Britain's military weakness. It was not a popular one. Gibbon's disdain is obvious. The use of Hanoverian troops in the British service had long been the subject of bitter debate; Pitt denounced the treaties of military assistance with Russia and Hesse in one of his most celebrated philippics, full of the old patriot rhetoric about Britain's being exploited for the sake of Hanover, denouncing entangling alliances generally, and concluding, "None but a nation that had lost all signs of virility would submit to be so treated";[3] and Johnson, in his new magazine, seconded Pitt's sentiments.

Pitt (who was still nominally Paymaster-General to the Forces under Newcastle, though actually in the bitterest opposition to him) now took it upon himself to sponsor the only other solution of the defence problem available: the time-honoured one of arming and training, in his spare time, the man in the street. It is hard to say with what genuine seriousness he did so: the Great War, when Pitt finally assumed charge of its conduct, was won, certainly not by citizen soldiers, but by the despised regular army—and by subsidies to allied armies on a far greater scale than those he had attacked in 1755. But at that point it was the obvious political manoeuvre for Pitt to make; and on 8 December 1755 he moved that a committee of the whole House of Commons consider the question of redesigning the militia system. The committee reported favourably, and on 12 March 1756 Colonel George Townshend (a professional soldier, later Field Marshal Marquess Townshend; heir to Walpole's estranged ally, Charles, Viscount Townshend) brought in the bill that Johnson discusses here. It passed the House of Commons, with some amendment but apparently little debate—it would have been a dangerous measure for elected legislators to oppose too vigorously. Indeed it seems to have caused considerable blurring of such party lines as then existed. Gibbon (writing of the Militia Bill of 1757, and after the accession of George III) says, "This measure, both in parliament and in the field, was supported by the country gentlemen or Tories, who insensibly transferred their loyalty to the house of Hanover: in the language of Mr. Burke, they have changed the idol, but they have preserved the idolatry." Certainly Johnson's attitude towards the 1756 bill (though distinctly accompanied by no idolatry of George II) tends to support this judgement. On the other hand, we find "old Horace" Walpole writing to Lord Chancellor Hardwicke, "I think the Tories in general, although some few are engaged in the conduct of it [the 1756 bill], do not approve it extremely." This stalwart old party wheel-horse of Whiggism goes on to plead with Hardwicke not to oppose the bill in the Lords, "for I apprehend it may occasion a great deal of ill humour and clamour, industriously fomented and propagated, not only by the pretended patriots in opposition, but even by the Tories, who do not approve the present plan, as if there was

3. *Parliamentary History*, xv. 660–63.

a design to keep the foreign troops here longer than the defence of the country may require it."[4]

The 1756 bill was, in fact, killed in the House of Lords by Hardwicke, with a statesmanlike disregard of the political consequences outlined by the timorous Horace. His speech[5] is a masterly analysis, by a fine legal mind, of the constitutional and practical implications of the British and American dual army system. A strong professional army, with the command-in-chief vested in the head of the executive branch of government, connotes a strong central administration; a militia, raised and commanded by local authorities (in Britain, the lords lieutenant of counties, in America, the governors of states), connotes decentralization; and when the two forces subsist simultaneously there are grave potential dangers in the ambiguity of command. Hardwicke puts his finger squarely on the sources of danger in this bill. The arrangements whereby, in case of national emergency, the Crown shall assume supreme command over the militia are far from watertight. It is provided that if the Crown wishes to "call out" the militia, it shall report the fact to Parliament and get its sanction for doing so. But suppose Parliament is not sitting at the time? Is it safe to leave known supplies of arms stored in every parish of the kingdom, under the feeble custody of the churchwardens? What kind of discipline can be expected in a force which is not subject to military law, but where lapses of military conduct must be proceeded against before justices of the peace or in other civil courts? In a country which, only ten years before, had suddenly found half its area overrun by an invading force, supported—or thought to be supported—by a formidable "fifth column" within the country itself, these objections were not merely academic ones.

Hardwicke's arguments (or party discipline) prevailed, and the bill was rejected by the Lords, on 24 May 1756, by a vote of 59 to 23. The next year Pitt was in power and Hardwicke out, and a similar militia bill, again introduced by George Townshend, was eventually passed, though the Lords reduced the proposed number of militiamen from the former 61,000 to 32,340. It was under this act that Gibbon served the two-and-a-half years with the Hampshire militia that he so vividly and appreciatively describes. If, as Gibbon complains, the actual turn-out of men was only about half of even the reduced establishment, it can hardly be maintained that the much-publicized project in the end contributed very much to winning the war. But it had served its main purpose in helping to get Pitt into power. And Gibbon's tributes—"my principal obligation to the militia was the making me an Englishman, and a soldier"; "the captain of the Hampshire grenadiers (the reader may smile) has not been useless to the historian of the Roman empire"—are not, indeed, merely to be smiled at. Since the days of Pitt, and perhaps largely because of him, the Anglo-American community has had to accept fully the idea of universal military service for all able-bodied male citizens. Though the role of the institution in military theory has undergone considerable change in recent years, there is still some point

4. Ibid., pp. 705–07.
5. Ibid., pp. 724–40.

in the justification for it that Gibbon suggests—the old argument from "the spirit of a nation"; and it is rather pleasant to remember that the two leading "intellectuals" of their day, Gibbon and Johnson, diverse in temperament and philosophy as they were, and far as they were from being notably "able-bodied," both welcomed the opportunity to serve in the "general levy" of their people.[6]

Johnson's view of the theory of a militia is given at greater length in his "Observations on the Russian and Hessian Treaties" (p. 178 below) than in the piece reprinted here, obviously a rather hasty piece of journalism. His remarks on the subject of "loyalty oaths," however, are of interest, especially since these were again much discussed in the United States in the mid-twentieth century, when they were used as a weapon against Communism, as they were against Jacobitism in eighteenth-century Britain; and the counter-arguments advanced by Johnson were also heard again— "Every man who takes these oaths is or is not already faithful to his king. If he be faithful, how is his fidelity increased? If he be not, how is his loyalty improved by diminishing his honesty?" Johnsonian students, following Boswell, have been accustomed to regard Johnson's aversion to such oaths as a manifestation of his profound religious sensibilities. Religion enters into it, certainly, but quite apart from religion the question has a strictly political significance that Johnson fully appreciated.

The text here follows that of the *Literary Magazine*, No. 2 (15 May– 15 June 1756), pp. [57]–63. Johnson's "remarks" are interspersed among the provisions of the bill, and it seems desirable to reprint the whole article, especially since the "provisions" are paraphrases, not verbatim extracts from the bill, and may well be Johnson's work too. The article is followed in the *Literary Magazine* by a statistical "Estimate for a Militia," in tabular form, which is omitted here. A similar tabulation in the body of the article itself has been omitted, and the place of its omission indicated. The article was first attributed to Johnson by Boswell (*Life*, 1.307) on "internal evidence." It has not hitherto been reprinted.

6. Boswell (*Life*, IV.319) tells the (undated) story of SJ's having been "drawn" for service with the London trained bands (as a resident of the City he was liable for such service), and of his providing himself with a musket, sword, and belt for the purpose.

Extract of the Bill for the Better Ordering the Militia Forces in the Several Counties of That Part of Great-Britain Called England, As Altered and Amended by the Committee, with Remarks.

I know not whether it may deserve notice, that "militia forces" is a very improper expression, not better than the "regular troop forces," or the "army forces." It might have been better to have used the old English word, "trained bands."[1]

Whereas a well-ordered militia is necessary, and the present laws for its regulations are defective.

The prologue to the bill was originally this: "Whereas it is necessary that England be supplied with a militia—of natives —to whom alone under the direction of his majesty, his heirs and successors, the defence of this realm can be legally intrusted." Why this was altered it is easy to find.[2]

Be it enacted, that from the 29th of September, 1756, the lieutenants[3] of counties shall arm and array proper persons, and the lieutenants shall appoint their deputy-lieutenants, and give commissions to lieutenant-colonels, majors, and other officers, whose names shall, within a month, be certified to the king.

The lieutenant of every county shall have the chief command of the militia of that county.

In each county shall be appointed twenty deputy-lieutenants, if so many can be found qualified, each of whom shall possess six hundred pounds a year, of which two thirds shall lie in the county; or shall be heir apparent of a possession of a thousand a year, two thirds of which shall lie in the same county.

Of these deputies either the names or the qualification may seem more than is necessary. But to divide power, or the shew of power, into many hands, is indeed popular and prudent;[4]

1. The name seems to have come into use around the sixteenth century for the groups of able-bodied citizens annually mustered and exercised under the mediaeval militia regulations. It was discontinued under the Militia Act of 1662 except for those of London, which had maintained their efficiency and repute during the Civil War. For SJ's connexion with them, see n. 6, p. 155 above. In 1794, the London trained bands were reorganized as the City of London Militia.

2. "Of natives" reflects on the policy of subsidizing foreign troops for the defence of Britain, and "to whom alone . . . the defence of this realm

can be legally intrusted" is the old Tory contention that the existence of a full-time, professional "standing" army is essentially unconstitutional (see n. 2, p. 151). SJ's point is that the phraseology was amended to secure the support of the administration for the bill in the House of Commons.

3. This is still the official title of the king's representative in each county, although the common designation is "lord lieutenant."

4. A judgement central to SJ's political thinking, and that of "old Toryism" generally. SJ may well be using "popular" here in the sense of the modern "democratic."

and those who have possessions in a county, are most properly trusted with its defence.

The colonels, lieutenant-colonels, and majors, shall be qualified as the deputy-lieutenants. A captain shall possess three hundred a year, or be heir to six. A lieutenant or an ensign shall possess one hundred a year, or be the son of one who possesses, or at his death did possess three hundred a year: Two thirds of the estate in all these cases lying within the county.

The king may displace any deputy-lieutenant or officer, and the lieutenants shall appoint others in their stead.

Every deputy or officer shall give in his qualification to the clerk of the peace, and take the oaths to the government; within six months after he shall begin to act, on penalty of one hundred pounds.

A commission in the militia shall not vacate a seat in parliament.

At the end of every five years a number of officers shall be discharged, equal to the number of those who, duly qualified, shall solicit for admission.

To each regiment, or to each county, an adjutant shall be appointed, who has born a commission in the regular forces, in which he shall still retain his rank; and to every company of the militia shall be appointed four serjeants out of the regular forces, or such as have formerly served in the army, and are recommended by the lieutenant who shall be intitled, at their discharge from the militia, to the hospital of Chelsea, upon the recommendation of the lieutenant, or five deputy-lieutenants.

No person selling liquors by retail shall be capable of being a serjeant of the militia.

The number of private men serving in the militia shall be for Yorkshire, west-riding, with the city and county of York ——— 2500

[A table giving figures for the other counties follows. The total is 62,680.]

The lieutenant of each county, or three or five deputies in the absence of the lieutenant, shall meet once a year to consult upon the execution of their office, and require the head-constable to deliver in a list of all the men between the ages of 18 and 50, in their several districts, except peers, officers of the militia, men residing in either university, clergymen, teachers of separate meetings, peace and parish officers, articled clerks, and apprentices, and seamen; noting in the list the papists, quakers, or men labouring under any bodily infirmity.

Every deputy-constable, or other petty officer, shall transmit to the head-constable the list of his division, having first affixed it to the door of the church or chapel for one Sunday.

On the day appointed for receiving those lists the lieutenants and deputy-lieutenants, shall settle the number to be taken from each hundred, or the division of the county. They shall then subdivide themselves, and one deputy or more with three commissioners of the land-tax, shall meet in every subdivision to hear the complaint of those that think themselves intitled to exemption, and upon any just cause shall correct the lists. They shall then settle the number to be raised in each parish, and choose the individuals by lot; and within three weeks afterwards the person so chosen shall appear before them, each of whom shall take the oaths, and enter into the militia for three years, or bring one to serve as his substitute.

In this part of the act there are several things to be objected. The exceptions are too few. Chirurgeons and apothecaries, and perhaps attorneys ought to be exempted, since they are already exempted from more important duties.[5] It is indeed to be supposed, that the officers will consider the inconsistency of such employment with the duties of a military man, but the exemption will be a favour not a privilege; and therefore no man can be secure of it.

Another objection shall be ventured, however unpopular. It surely cannot be necessary, that every private man should take the oaths. Shall then the defence of the king be intrusted to those who will not swear allegiance? That is undoubtedly absurd. No man disaffected to any government can be trusted by that government with arms; it is enough that he is intrusted with liberty, and with the general rights of the rest of the community. Yet surely nothing has more tendency to make bad subjects than irreligion, and nothing will sooner make men irreligious, than the frequency of oaths. To what purpose is it that any man takes an oath which contains more particulars than he well remembers, which contains positions which he cannot understand? When the obligation of an oath is weakened, the security of property, and of life, is at an end; and oaths will be reverenced less, as they are oftener repeated. Every man who takes these oaths is or is not already faithful to his king. If he be faithful, how is his fidelity increased? If he be not, how is his loyalty improved, by diminishing his honesty? It is undoubtedly intended, that men of disloyal

5. E.g., from serving on juries.

principles should be forced to discover their tenets by refusing their test. But this those who intend it do not expect. They know, what every one knows, that mean men called before those whom they have always regarded with veneration, will be more afraid of man than God, and will take the oath taken and offered by their betters, without understanding, without examining, perhaps without hearing it. We know there was a time when men swore to an *et caetera*.[6] I would not on so serious a subject be thought to write in jest. The frequent imposition of oaths has almost ruined the morals of this unhappy nation, and of a nation without morals it is of small importance who shall be king.

What then is to be done? Let the officers who must be supposed to know the state of their own counties choose those whom the government may trust without an oath.

If any person thirty-two years old, after having served two years, shall desire his discharge, it shall be granted, and another chosen by lot in his room; and the vacation by death shall be filled up in the same manner.

He that cannot apply to a meeting may be discharged by one deputy-lieutenant, if he brings another to serve the time wanting to the expiration of three years.

A militia-man removing to another parish is bound to serve the remainder of his time in the new parish.

Any peer, or heir apparent of a peer, may, by the lieutenant of the county, be appointed a deputy or officer without the qualification of an estate.

In all cities or towns which are counties within themselves, and have been accustomed to raise their own militia, the lieutenant or chief magistrate shall appoint five deputy-lieutenants, who shall exercise the same power as the other deputies. Of these smaller counties the deputies, colonels, lieutenant-colonels, and majors shall possess lands to the value of three hundred pounds a year, or a personal estate of five thousand pounds, or lands and personal estate together of six thousand pounds. Captains one hundred and fifty

---

6. By the notorious canons of the Church of England adopted at the instigation of Laud by the Convocation of 1640, members of the learned professions were required to swear that they would not subvert "the govern- ment of the Church by archbishops, bishops, deans and archdeacons, &c., as it stands established." The enraged Puritans pointed out that the "et cetera" could be used to conceal a pope.

pounds, or two thousand five hundred pounds personal estate, or three thousand mixed estate. Lieutenants and ensigns fifty pounds a year, or seven hundred and fifty pounds personal, or one thousand pounds mixed estate. The estates of the officers of county towns may lie in any part of England, and must be proved by the oath of the possessor.

Here is another hateful oath administered without necessity; the condition of every man is sufficiently known among his neighbours, to make all such evidence useless. It is of no importance to limit qualifications nicely; it is sufficient that an ensign be known to have a considerable property, or to be above want, that a captain be confessedly richer, and a superior officer so much richer still, as that subordination may subsist without the appearance of injury to any.

The regulation of military rank in the national army, by the gradations of property, is rational and just. The man who hazards most has most right to be trusted, and men willingly obey in the field those whom they are accustomed to respect in all other places.

But there seems to be an unreasonable disproportion between the qualifications arising from land and from money. Five thousand pounds in money being absurdly placed as equivalent to three hundred pounds a year in land; and to prove that money is supposed a better pledge of duty than land, the qualifications arising partly from lands, and partly from money, must arise to six thousand. Now every one knows, that five thousand pounds is not of more than half the value of the land required, and therefore, unless money makes a man wiser or honester than land, ten thousand pounds should be required as a qualification, if indeed any money can qualify.

New lists of men qualified for service shall be made every year.

A new body shall be chosen every third year, so that all persons duly qualified may serve in their turns, each for three years.

It would be better to change a certain proportion only every year, for by changing all at once, there will be every third year a new army totally void of discipline and skill.

A list of the persons serving in each parish shall be transmitted to the lieutenant.

Any officer neglecting to return his list, or making a false or partial list shall be committed for a month to the common goal, or be fined five pounds, by a warrant under the seal of the lieutenant, and of two deputies, or of five deputies, or of one deputy and three commissioners of the land-tax.[7]

In this clause without any reason, three commissioners of the land-tax are made equivalent to four deputy-lieutenants, therefore the deputies must have a certain property which is not required for the commissioners.

When any parish extends into two counties, its militia shall serve in that county where the church stands.

A Quaker refusing to serve shall hire another in his stead, and, if he neglects, a sum shall be levied upon him by distress sufficient to hire another man.

Those who are trained and muster'd in the docks, shall not be obliged to serve in the militia.

No officer of the militia shall be obliged to serve as sheriff, nor any private man be compelled to work on the high-ways, or to enter into the fleet, unless he be a seaman.

He that has served three years shall not serve again till it comes to his turn by rotation.

Within one week after the return of the lists, the lieutenant and two deputies, or without the lieutenant, five deputies, shall form the militia of each county into regiments, consisting of not more than ten, nor less than five companies of eighty men each, appointing the commissioned and non-commissioned officers to each company.

They shall be exercised thus. Twenty men at least in a body shall be exercised three Sundays in every month, before and after divine service.

On the fourth Sunday they shall be exercised in half companies.

And once every year on the Tuesday, Wednesday, Thursday, and Friday of Whitsun Week, they shall be exercised in whole regiments.

All, except dissenters, shall duly attend divine service at the place where they are exercised.

No man shall be exercised on Sundays more than six miles from his own house.

Notice of the time and place of every exercise shall be sent by the lieutenant, or his deputy, to the high constables, and by them to the petty constables, who shall fix them upon the door of their respective churches.

---

7. These commissioners were appointed by Parliament (in the annual Land Tax Act) to assess the property in each county.

The lieutenant shall appoint at pleasure a regimental clerk, a serjeant-major out of the serjeants, and a drum-major out of the drummers.

The militia during their annual exercise shall be billeted as regular troops.

In counties where the militia do not amount to four hundred, and therefore cannot make a regiment, they shall be formed into companies under the lieutenant, and one field-officer: one adjutant, who shall be a subaltern in the army, a serjeant-major, a drum-major, and a clerk shall be appointed them, and they shall be exercised as a complete regiment.

Where twenty men cannot be brought together they may be exercised in smaller numbers as the lieutenant or deputies shall direct.

One commissioned officer shall attend the exercise of the half company, and inspect their arms and accoutrements.

The arms and clothes of the militia of each parish shall be carefully kept by the church-wardens. All the arms shall be marked M, with the name of the county.

The officer who superintends the exercise shall, in the presence of the churchwarden or overseer of the poor, call over the list, and certify to a justice the names of those who are absent from exercise or worship. The justice shall examine the excuse offered, and if it be insufficient shall punish the defaulter for the first offence, by fining him one shilling, or setting him in the stocks for an hour; for the second he shall fine him two shillings and six-pence, and send him to the house of correction for four days; for every offence afterwards he shall fine him five shillings, and if it be not paid send him to the house of correction for any time not exceeding a month.

In this clause there seems to be no proportion between the pecuniary and corporal punishment.

If any man shall be convicted upon oath before a justice of being drunk at the time of exercise, he shall forfeit his pay, and sit an hour in the stocks.

This punishment seems too light for the offence.

He that shall be convicted on oath before a justice of insolence or disobedience to his officer shall for the first offence be fined two shillings and six-pence, and in default of payment be sent to the house of correction for four days; for the second be fined five shillings, or committed for seven days; and for every offence afterwards shall be committed to the house of correction for any time not exceeding a month.

If any man shall sell, pawn, or lose his arms or accoutrements, he shall be fined a sum not exceeding three pounds, or in default of payment be committed to the house of correction for one month, and if he cannot then raise the sum required, for three months.

He that shall neglect to leave his arms and accoutrements after exercise with the church-wardens, or to return them after the annual exercise, shall be punished with a fine or by commitment; and the church-warden who shall omit to complain of such neglect shall forfeit twenty shillings.

The soldier or non-commissioned officer, that shall be absent from his annual exercise shall forfeit ten shillings a day, or be committed to the house of correction by a justice for a month.

If any non-commissioned officer shall be negligent in his duty, or disobedient or insolent to the adjutant, or other superior officer, he shall be fined by a justice a sum not exceeding thirty shillings, or in default of payment be committed to the house of correction for fourteen days, and may be discharged by the lieutenant.

This clause seems inconsistent with a former; an officer cannot easily *neglect* his duty more than by being absent from it, yet absence is less severely punished. There is indeed some difference between a soldier's neglect and an officer's.

In a former clause a *crown* and a month's confinement to the house of correction were considered as equivalent; in this thirty shillings and a confinement of fourteen days are placed as alternatives.

By specifying the crime for which the lieutenant of a county may dismiss a serjeant, a reason is given to infer, that he may dismiss him for no other fault, which would certainly be too small a grant of power to the chief commander of the forces of a county.

That the punishment of the militia should be inflicted by a justice of the peace is, I think, proper; that the people may not learn that contempt of the civil power too common among soldiers;[8] but surely some objection may properly be made to

---

8. A venerable cliché used in arguments against a standing army, e.g., Phillips Gybbon, M.P., during the debate on the annual Mutiny Act, 1741, declaims, "Soldiers are governed by particular laws, and subject to particular authority; authority, which, in the manner of its operation, has scarcely any resemblance of the civil power. Thus they soon learn to think themselves exempt from all other laws."

the frequency of oaths, which this law will produce. There is not here indeed any danger of perjury or temptation to it, but the reverence of an oath will be gradually lessened by the necessity of swearing at one time, "that John Trot broke the rank," at another, "that James Budge would not ground his musket." There is such a disproportion between the trifle to be proved, and the awful proof, as must make the solemnity too ludicrous; and what is once ridiculed will quickly be contemned.

I cannot persuade myself that an oath is necessary to prove a fact which must at least have twenty witnesses, which therefore is not very likely to be falsified, and which terminates at last in the penalty of a shilling.

If the crime charged be denied, it may be proper to make farther inquiry of some of the spectators, perhaps one of the parish officers might very properly be required to attend the exercise. But let us not take oaths or offer them on such small occasions.

Whoever shall unlawfully buy or receive any arms or accoutrements belonging to the militia, shall incur the penalty of five pounds, and in default be imprisoned for three months, or publicly whipped at the discretion of the justice.

No man shall be censured for absence occasioned by attending an election.

The militia are to be subject in military affairs to their own officers, and in civil to the civil magistrate.

All fines and forfeitures shall be paid to the regimental clerk, and made a common stock for each hundred, of which an account shall be given to two deputy-lieutenants, and three commissioners of the land-tax, who shall apply it to the erection of buts, and the provision of gun-powder to be used in shooting at marks, and the remainder shall be distributed in prizes to the best marksmen, or employed in any other way for the use of the militia.

This is so important a part of discipline that perhaps more money ought to be employed upon it, than will arise from forfeitures.

All parish officers are required to assist the lieutenants and justices, only Quakers are excused.

In case of actual invasion or upon imminent danger thereof, and in case of rebellion, the king, first notifying the occasion to the parliament if then sitting, or in their recess to the privy council, and to the people by proclamation,[9] may direct the lieutenants or any five deputies to draw out their regiments, beginning with the counties nearest the danger, and proceeding regularly till a sufficient number be brought together who shall march by his majesty's order to any part of England or Wales under the command of such general as he shall appoint, receiving during the service the same pay with the regular regiments of foot, and the officers holding the same rank with the regular officers of the same denomination. The militia during the time of service shall be liable to the law martial then subsisting, and any man wounded shall be intitled to the hospital of Chelsea.

The militia shall not on any occasion be compelled to go out of this kingdom.

The militia and regular troops shall be tried in courts martial each by their own officers.

If any county shall be thought by the lieutenant to be charged with too great a number of men, he may complain to the privy council, who shall redress the grievance by comparing the list of the inhabitants of the county so complaining, with the proportions of other counties.

A manor, of which the reserved rent is thirty pounds a year, shall be considered as equivalent to an estate of three hundred pounds a year.

In counties where twenty deputy-lieutenants with proper qualification cannot be found, it shall be sufficient to appoint so many as can be found.

The lieutenant or two deputies may impower any persons, of whom a commissioned officer and an officer of the parish shall be two, to search for and seize arms in suspected houses. But they shall not search by night except in towns, nor shall the house of a peer be searched except by a warrant under the king's sign manual, or in the presence of the lieutenant or deputy-lieutenant. The arms so seized may be restored by the lieutenant or his deputies, if it shall be thought fit, to the owners.

The other clauses in the act contain provisions respecting the privileges or conveniences of particular places.

All former acts relating to the militia are repealed.

Such was the bill, which having passed through the House of

---

9. In the form of the bill attacked by Lord Chancellor Hardwicke in the House of Lords (see p. 154 above), this part of the clause reads only "the occasion being first communicated to parliament" (*Parliamentary History*, xv.728).

Commons was rejected by the Lords, and rejected by a great majority. It seems to be a good bill in the fundamental parts, to contain the rudiments of a military establishment, which may be of great use in this kingdom, by enabling us to defend ourselves against any insult or invasion, and by placing the sword in the hands of the people.

To such a design it is the duty of every man to contribute what he thinks may be of use, and therefore I shall add to the observations already made, a supplemental clause.

The body of militia established by this act is not very numerous in proportion to the inhabitants or the extent of our country, and perhaps may not always be sufficient for the occasion on which it is raised, but as the whole body is changed[a] every third year, it may be increased upon exigencies by an easy expedient.

Let us suppose the militia in actual exercise to be sixty thousand men, it may always be presumed that of those who were last dismissed at the triennial discharge there are yet fifty thousand fit for service, and of those dismissed at the last general discharge but one, forty thousand.

Be it therefore enacted, that if the number of militia actually subsisting at the time of any exigence shall be deemed insufficient for the defence of the kingdom, it shall be lawful for the king to command the lieutenant or his deputies to recal those to their arms who were discharged at the last triennial dismission, or any part of them; and that if the forces so raised are not yet sufficient, to recal those who were discharged at the last triennial dismission but one, or any part of them, over whom the lieutenant shall set such officers as have formerly served in the militia, or if a sufficient number cannot be found shall appoint others in the same county as nearly approaching to the stated qualification as the county will supply, whose commissions shall determine at the dismission of the regiments.

By this clause the king will be impowered in any time of difficulty or sudden exigence, to raise an hundred and fifty thousand men in a day, of whom part may be stationed to defend their own counties, and part sent to oppose the enemy.[1]

a. changed *emend.*] charged *1756*

---

1. SJ refers again to this proposal in his "Observations on the Russian and Hessian Treaties" (p. 183 below).

OBSERVATIONS ON A LETTER FROM A FRENCH REFUGEE IN AMERICA. 1756

The history of the numerous attempts that have been made to bring this piece to the attention of Johnsonian students forms a wry comment on the vanity of scholarly wishes. Tom Davies had apparently heard Johnson's name vaguely connected with it, for he printed the "Letter" in the third volume of his *Miscellaneous and Fugitive Pieces*, 1774, between two indubitably Johnsonian items from the early numbers of the *Literary Magazine*, the review of Blackwell's *Memoirs of the Court of Augustus*, and the "Observations on the Present State of Affairs"—but he printed only the "Letter." He was emphatically corrected by the reviewer of his book in the *Gentleman's Magazine*, Nov 1774, p. 525: "To this letter the observations on it by Dr. J—— should also, we think, have been annexed." The piece was ignored by Hawkins, but was picked up by the editor of the supplementary Volume xiv of Johnson's *Works* (1788), who reprinted both the letter and the observations, heading the observations "By Dr. Johnson." Then Boswell overlooked it; but it was once more rescued by that assiduous corrector of Boswell, Alexander Chalmers, and listed in a note contributed by Chalmers to Malone's edition of the *Life of Johnson* (1807), i.xxxv. The note was repeated in four subsequent editions of the Malone-Chalmers revision of the *Life*, and in Croker's 1831 edition, and Chalmers's own MS memorandum was printed in facsimile in 1929 (*The R. B. Adam Library*, iii, following p. 56). Yet despite these efforts the piece seems never to have been mentioned in connexion with Johnson by any of his students between 1831 and 1950, when still another attempt was made to bring it to their notice (D. J. Greene, "The Johnsonian Canon: A Neglected Attribution," *PMLA*, lxv [June 1950], 427). But a more recent listing of Johnson's journalistic writings (E. A. Bloom, *Samuel Johnson in Grub Street*, 1957, p. 267) still puts a suspicious question-mark after it.

It is a pity that the "Observations" have been so drastically neglected, for, short as they are, they are well written and provide, not merely reinforcement for what is known from other sources about Johnson's *Weltanschauung*, but the occasional novel clue: one remark in particular deserves a good deal of pondering—"I have not in general a favourable opinion of restraints, which always produce discontent and an habitual violation of laws, and, perhaps, seldom contribute much to the end proposed." Gallo-Anglus's letter (where did it come from? at whose instigation was it published in the *Literary Magazine* at all?) was the kind of thing best designed to make Johnson's hackles rise. It is full of the complaints that the publicists of the American Revolution were later to make—though it should be noted that, here as elsewhere, Johnson grants that many of those complaints are serious ones and deserve attention: neither Gallo-Anglus nor James Otis nor Sam Adams had anything more caustic to say about British colonial governors than what Johnson had said in "An Introduction to the Political State": "To be a bankrupt at home, or to be so infamously vicious that he cannot be decently protected in his own country, seldom recommends any man to the government of a French colony." Johnson's initial concession to Gallo-Anglus—"the foregoing letter . . . contains many just observations and positions, that, though very little to the honour of our country, cannot be disputed"—should be taken in all seriousness. But the tone of maudlin self-pity that informs the letter, the doctrinaire insistence on fictitious and meaningless "rights," the aura of *laissez-faire* ("Whatever is, is right") surrounding the "cant about nature and providence," the view of emigration as a panacea, called down on Gallo-Anglus Johnson's most acid rebuke, and, as frequently happened, impelled Johnson to overstatement of the opposite positions. Such a comment as "What should we sacrifice but a *poor infant colony?*" is the sort of thing with which Johnson delighted to *épater* the liberals when he was in this mood; though if it is placed in the context of current economic theory, or even in that of the whole of the paragraph in which it appears, it is not really so brazenly callous as it sounds.

The text here follows that of the *Literary Magazine*, No. 2 (15 May–15 June 1756), pp. 66–67. It seemed desirable also to reprint Gallo-Anglus's letter (pp. 64–66) unedited. There seems to have been only one early reprinting of the "Observations," that in Vol. XIV of Johnson's *Works* (1788).

[A Letter from a French Refugee in America to His Friend a Gentleman in England

SIR,
The loser must be allowed to speak; you will give us leave therefore, who have already begun to suffer, and who know not what is yet behind, to represent to you some of the instances of neglect on our own part, and of ill-conduct and unkind usage toward us, on the part of our mother country.

I shall begin with the policy of the English in appointing us our GOVERNORS, who are generally strangers and have no *landed interest* here; and who therefore cannot be supposed to have that *natural affection* for us, or that *political attachment* to us, which natives, or those who have a *large landed interest* here, may be supposed to have.

Another consideration, which tends to break the tie between us, is, that they generally reside but a little while among us; or, at least, have no views of continuing for life; and are too often sent hither *only to serve a turn*. Is it therefore any wonder that such persons as these should be but very *indifferent* with regard to *our* interest, however *solicitous* they may be in cultivating what they may call *their own?**

Another hardship is, not being suffered to go into those manufactures, which nature has fitted and designed us for. This restraint, you are sensible, is laid upon us under the pretence, *lest we should rival our mother country.* Whereas God and nature no doubt designed, that every part of the globe should contribute its quota towards the wants and advantages of human life; and to restrain any part of the earth, in this respect, from political considerations, is nothing less than laying an embargo upon nature, and shackling, as it were, divine Providence *itself.* If we rival Europe in some articles, Europe rivals us in others. Nature ought to have its free course in this respect, and not to be check'd, and put out of the direction the God of nature and the great king of kings has given her. Nor, indeed, are princes aware what injuries they do *themselves,* as well as what hardships they lay their *subjects* under, by restraints of this kind; how many countries have revolted, and others been lost and torn from their mother nations by being kept in this bondage. And it will be well, if, by thus *keeping down* the American colonies, and not letting us exert our natural strength, we don't become a prey to a foreign power, instead of being a defence to our mother country, as we might easily have been made ere this in much greater degrees than we are now capable of being, had we been suffered to have exerted ourselves in our *own proper sphere.*

Another instance of gross neglect has been the not repelling, *immediately* and *without any loss of time,* the first incroachments, whether on the sea-coast, or inland, or with regard to islands. As soon as ever advice had been received that the French or Spaniards had invaded our territories, or neutral lands or islands, and were beginning to settle and fortify themselves upon them, we should have gone against these invaders *directly,* and have driven them out sword in hand; and not pretended to have entered into *treaty* with people who will spend year after year in treating with you, and keep all the while *invading* you, and fortifying themselves in those invasions, and then *you may drive them out of their incroach-*

*Without an attendance to the above considerations, it is hard to conceive how such enormous incroachments could have been suffered to have taken place on our territories in America, by the French and Spaniards, more especially by the former; who have in a manner covered that country with their forts, in order to maintain those incroachments. See a map published in the *Gentleman's Magazine* for July, 1755. Where these incroachments appear by inspection, as also the numerous forts built in defence of them, many of which have been erected since the treaty of Aix-la-Chapelle.

ments how you can. If the French or Spaniards had any demands upon us, they should have proposed them to us and made their claims; and if we would not have heard the voice of *treaties*, of *evidence, reason* and *justice*, it would *then* have been time enough for them to have had recourse to *arms*, but to invade us first and then to talk about treating, is all a *mere joke.**

But once more, our mother country has been certainly wanting *to us* as well as to herself, in not directing long since the building a strong squadron of ships here; where we have so many *materials* towards it, and could so easily have *mann'd* them; which would have served as a *fleet of observation* to have watch'd the sea-coasts, and prevented all incroachments upon them, not to say, on the *neutral American islands;*[1] and even the landing of the last late armament from France, which may prove so fatal to us, if not counterwrought by a proper reinforcement from England, might, in all probability, have been prevented.

What shall I say to the giving up Cape-Breton?[2] Had we been suffered to keep *that important* place, it might have prevented the present American war, by breaking in a good measure the *chain*, which the French have formed between Canada and Louisiana. Certainly, as it was an American *conquest* it ought in justice, and more especially, in POLICY, to have been left to America. And if all the powers of Europe CANNOT, or will not make head against France on the European continent; why must America, a poor infant settlement of but about a century or two's standing be the sacrifice? Had we kept the island of Cape Breton it would have been a good step towards *driving the French intirely out of America;* and, it is much to be feared, we shall never have any *solid peace* till that is done. In which case, we had been in condition to have

---

*It was as long ago as July, 1754, that the French had the insolence to attack Colonel Washington, and to drive him out of Fort Necessity in Virginia, murdering a number of his men; at which time the whole garrison narrowly escaped being put to the sword. See *Gentleman's Magazine*, 1754, page 399.

---

1. St. Lucia, St. Vincent, and Dominica, in the West Indies, whose neutrality had been established by the Peace of Aix-la-Chapelle, 1748.

2. Louisbourg, in Cape Breton, the great French fortress controlling the entrance to the Gulf of St. Lawrence, had been captured in June 1745 by a British naval force under Commodore (later Admiral Sir Peter) Warren,

and 4,000 colonial militia, under the command of Colonel (later Sir William) Pepperell, of Massachusetts. The New Englanders were justly proud of their feat; and the British government's action in restoring Louisbourg to the French in 1748 certainly contributed (as this passage shows) to the growing resentment toward Britain that culminated in the Revolution.

lent our mother country *incredible assistance* in a time of war; whereas, now, by being thus reduced again into *bondage*, we stand in need of assistance from her. Louisbourg is the Dunkirk[3] of America.

I come now to an article of much folly and guilt: I mean no other than our *management* of the Indians. These, we should have endeavoured, no doubt by all possible means, to have gained over to, and secured in OUR interest; in opposition to those in the interest of France and Spain. This should have been attempted by all possible applications to their *minds* and their *bodies*. We should have endeavoured to have given them just notions of life, natural, civil, and religious; and shewn them the difference between the *friendship*, the *service*, and the *government* of the English, and of the French and Spaniards. Where *reason* had failed us, I mean where we had found the Indians incapable of the convictions of reason, we should have had recourse to such other considerations as are immediate and palpable; and such as considering them as *mere animals only*, they could not but have been sensible to.

After gaining over as many of the ADULTS as possible into our interest, we should have been particularly attentive to the education of their CHILDREN; in order to have worn out the race of the wild Indians, we should have taught them our language, and the first principles of our *learning, natural, civil*, and *religious:* initiated them into the *mechanical trades;* and shewn them the *conveniences* and *accommodations* of life, in order to have drawn them off from the savage life of their parents; and a few of *genius* selected out from each nation among them, might have been introduced to an acquaintance with the liberal *arts*, who might have been made instruments to have gained others.

But there is the less necessity to enlarge upon this head; as I have observed, from time to time among the advertisements found in the *Gentleman's Magazine* you sent me, a treatise upon *the importance of gaining and preserving the friendship of the Indians to the British interest;*[4] which however, I suppose, like multitude of your other

---

3. A well-worn cliché. Dunkerque, on the French coast of the Straits of Dover, for centuries symbolized to the British a threat to their control of the English Channel. By the Peace of Utrecht, 1713, the French agreed to demolish its fortifications, but much squabbling followed as to the effectiveness with which this agreement was carried out.

4. The following is listed in the *Gentleman's Magazine*, XXII (1752), 46: "The Importance of gaining and preserving the friendship of the Indians of the Six Nations to the British Interest considered. *1* s. Cave." A brief editorial note following the listing of the title comments favourably on the thesis, remarking, "It is absolutely true, that the preservation of the whole

books, has lain by neglected among you, as it has done among us.

Lastly, it is pity, methinks, that a scheme, like that obtaining among the French, was not set on foot *here;* by which an *immediate estimate* might be made of our *natural, civil,* and *military* strength; which, more especially in a time of war, might be of infinite service.

I say nothing at present of the neglect with regard to the *peopling* of us more thoroughly: though there is *room,* it is certain, to *receive,* and *work* enough to *employ* all the *spare hands* of the islands of Great-Britain and Ireland: Nor need you have any single *beggar* or *stroller* left throughout the *three kingdoms.*

Nor do I take any notice of the deficiencies in the forming and training our MILITIA, or those already settled among us. These, together with several other articles *natural, civil* and *religious,* will be the subject of *another* year's letters, if providence shall permit the continuance of the correspondence; which however, considering my *age* and the *troubles* in view, is not, I am afraid, very probable.

Thus, Sir, I have laid before you a specimen of our grievances; some of them occasioned by our own *indolence,* and others by the *neglect* of our *mother country.* You compassionate us, I don't question, harrassed by robbers on either side, the inhabitants of Canada and Louisiana; not to say the French and the Spaniards;* but, Sir,

*It is not long since we had advice that the Spaniards had rebuilt the *forts of incroachment* in Georgia, which had been demolished by General Oglethorpe during his government of that colony; to say nothing of their late conduct in regard to our settlements in the bays of Honduras and Campeachy.

---

continent depends on a proper management of those Indians." A month after Gallo-Anglus's letter was published, Sir William Johnson was reappointed superintendent of Indian affairs in North America, and his highly successful "management" of the Six Nations (the Iroquois) so reinforced their traditional alliance with the English that they later fought on the Loyalist side in the Revolutionary War, and after it many migrated to Canada with Sir William's son, Sir John Johnson. The Johnsons' methods of dealing with the Indians were those recommended by SJ (p. 150 above), including "intermarriage and cohabitation": Sir William married, *au façon du nord,* the sister of the famous Mohawk chief,

Joseph Brant. Number 4 of the *Literary Magazine* (pp. 191–93) carries a notice of *An Account of the Conferences held, and treaties made, between Major-General Sir William Johnson and . . . the Mohawks, Onondagas* [and other Indian tribes], for which SJ may have been responsible. The Johnsons' attitude toward the Indians was looked on with deep suspicion by the New Englanders, who had no wish to assimilate them. SJ's concern over the relations between the Indians and the various groups of whites in North America is not to be regarded as mere academic "humanitarianism": those relations had very real and practical consequences in the history of the continent.

pity alone, give me leave to tell you, will not do. You must send us supplies, *veterans* and *engineers* are the people that we want to mix with our *raw levies*, and to pit against the *veterans* and *engineers* of France; without a *timely* and *powerful supply* of which, God only knows what must be the consequence.

Adieu, dear Sir, and may heaven avert the melancholy appearances, which now threaten us.

Make my compliments to all our common friends, and particularly to the Rev. Mr. ———— and his very agreeable family, letting him know how sincerely glad I now am, that he did not accept my pressing invitations of settling here, offered him when I was last in England. Since, if there are not already *enow* of us to *repel* the French, there are however *enow* of us to *fall* before them, and to be *enslaved* by them: One or the other of which must certainly be the fate of all the inhabitants of every country, where these perfidious and bloody people obtain the mastery.

I am,

Dear Sir, &c.

America, Aug. 1, 1755.   GALLO-ANGLUS

P.S. Don't you think me an unhappy man? Driven out of France, as you know I first was together with my parents, in infancy, by that hoary tyrant Louis XIV into Holland:[5] From thence residing some years in England. And now settling, as I thought, for the last time in order to spend the remainder of my days in these solitudes, to have the repose of my old age broken, by men whom I am ashamed to call my *countrymen:* as they are indeed no other than the *common enemies* and *sworn disturbers* of mankind, resolving that no body shall ever have any *enjoyment* of life, till they become *their subjects;* when it will be *impossible* they should have any.]

Observations on the Foregoing Letter.

It is natural for every man to think highly of his own usefulness and importance, and consequently of the importance of that community, or part of the community, with which he is connected.

From this disposition proceeds much of the right and of the wrong in every man's actions and opinions; and to this

---

5. By the revocation of the Edict of Nantes in 1685. Gallo-Anglus must have been quite an old man.

must be imputed whatever is censurable in the foregoing letter, which contains many just observations and positions, that, though very little to the honour of our country, cannot be disputed.

His complaints of restraints laid upon their manufactures are such as every man makes, who finds himself restrained. But his cant about nature and Providence would prove that no human legislature has a right to make any prudential laws, or to regulate any thing which before such regulation was indifferent. But such is the state of society, that part must be sometimes incommoded for the advantage of the whole. Every nation forbids some importations or exportations, or regulates the buildings, plantations, and agriculture of its own people.

I do not attempt to prove, that all the restraints laid on the Americans are prudent. I have not in general a favourable opinion of restraints,[6] which always produce discontent and an habitual violation of laws, and, perhaps, seldom contribute much to the end proposed. But whether wise or not they may undoubtedly be just.

If the American colonies can support themselves against their enemies, to what do they owe that strength, but to the protection of England, and how can they repay it but by contributing to the wealth of that country which protected them in their helpless state, on condition that they should obey her laws, and promote her interest.

If they yet cannot subsist but by the help and defence which they receive from England, as indeed they cannot for a single year, they may surely be content to purchase that protection by the use of the manufactures of their native country.

When he talks of their importance, he forgets that their importance is the consequence of the restraints which he condemns; for if our colonies did not consume our manu-

---

6. SJ is speaking specifically of economic restraints, of course. Eighteenth-century punctuation gives no guidance as to whether the following "which" clause is to be taken as restrictive or nonrestrictive of "restraints." The more obvious reading is to take it as nonrestrictive, though this gives a statement that seems strangely contradictory of other expressions of SJ's economic thinking.

factures they would be to us of no importance or value, nor should we have any interest in defending them more than any other body of exiles or fugitives.

When he talks of their strength, he in some measure confutes himself: for if they are grown so strong in so short a time, it is evident that they cannot have been much discouraged or oppressed.

With as little reason does he complain of the restitution of Cape-Breton, which, as he knows, was restored only because it could not be kept. Nothing can be more absurd than to claim it as an American *conquest:* which is false, because it was conquered by the help of an English fleet, and which, if it were true, could not be urged without considering the Americans as having an interest distinct from that of their mother country.

"If the powers of Europe," says he, "cannot or will not make head against France, why must America, a poor infant colony, be sacrificed?" If any sacrifice must be made, which we hope to be always able to refuse, what should we sacrifice but a "poor infant colony"? What should we sacrifice but that which is of least value? But this complaint is surely unseasonable, when all the power of Britain is exerted in defence of the American colonies.

One of his arguments, by which he proves the value of our American dominions, is such as deceives many, and gives occasion to many absurd speculations, if not to mischievous practices, and therefore deserves to be considered. There is, says he, so much room in the American regions, "that there needs not be a beggar or stroller in England."

I do not very clearly see the consequence that, because there are lands in America, there need be no beggars in England. Our beggars are not beggars because we want land, but either by impotence, idleness, ignorance of the arts of life, or misfortune. Those who are impotent will not be much mended by the voyage, and, I am afraid, will be coldly received by their fellow-subjects in America. What cure, except hunger, or a whip, there is in America for idleness, the inhabitants of that country must inform us; if idlers can be reformed there by any means which cannot be used at home, they ought certainly to be shipped off with the first wind. Those that have been so unhappily trained as to have no means of earning a livelihood, but by brute labour or bodily strength exercised without art, are, I believe, less wanted in America than in England. And of those who are impoverished, the number, whom misery, terror and want drive into America, is already too great.

It ought to be considered that every inhabitant gained to the colonies, is lost to the mother country. That the people sent into these unbounded regions, are diffused over vast tracts, to such a distance as to be disabled from instructing or helping one another, and are therefore less useful and less happy than at home. The strength of every country consists in the number of people proportionate to its extent, and it is not the populousness of a nation that produces beggars and strollers, but want of due regulation. To free ourselves from beggars and strollers by sending them to America, is to cure an ulcer by cutting off the limb.

OBSERVATIONS ON THE RUSSIAN AND
HESSIAN TREATIES. 1756.

The general political circumstances of this piece have been described in the introductory note to "Remarks on the Militia Bill," above. The piece is preceded in the third number of the *Literary Magazine* by the texts of the three treaties under discussion—the treaty of mutual assistance concluded with the Czarina Elizabeth of Russia on 11 December 1742, at the outset of the War of the Austrian Succession, whereby Russia agreed to supply 12,000 troops for the protection of Hanover in case of attack by France (and Great Britain would reciprocate in case of an attack on Russia); the subsidy treaty concluded with the Landgrave of Hesse-Cassel on 18 June 1755, whereby Britain agreed to pay £54,000 for the services of 8,000 Hessian troops, to be employed on the continent or in the British Isles, but not overseas; and a new treaty with Elizabeth, signed 19/30 September 1755, by which 40,000 Russian troops were to be held in readiness for the protection of Hanover, in return for a payment by Britain of £100,000.

This "system of subsidies" was subjected to violent attack by the Pittites. On 10 December 1755, Pitt's brother-in-law and chief ally in the Lords, Richard Grenville, Earl Temple, moved in that House a vote of censure on the government on the ground that the treaties "tend to involve this nation in an expensive and ruinous war on the continent, to consume our strength and treasure, and to divert us from the exertion of our utmost efforts for the defence of these kingdoms, threatened with invasion, and for the recovery and protection of our possessions in America, encroached upon, and actually invaded, by the arms of France." The motion was supported by Lords Halifax and Pomfret, and was opposed by Chesterfield (who approved the Russian alliance though not the Hessian) and Hardwicke. It was lost, by 84 votes to 11. On 15 December, in the committee of supply of the House of Commons, on the motion for providing the sums of money required by the treaties, Pitt delivered a famous philippic, that resulted in his dismissal from the ministry. The motions of supply were carried, how-ever, by large majorities.

Johnson's "Observations," though purporting to record both the pros and the cons of the debate, are heavily biased on the side of the opposition: the arguments advanced by Pitt, Temple, and Pomfret are given a much more engaging presentation than those of the government. In this, Johnson is acting consistently with traditional "old Tory" isolationist principles—with the theory that Britain, secured by her fleet and her insularity, should remain clear of "entangling alliances" on the continent. That he finds himself for the moment in accord with the Pittites is due to the fact that Pitt found it temporarily expedient to adopt this position; when, a few months later, he took charge of the war himself, Pitt's objections to continental alliances and subsidies speedily vanished. Johnson, however, continued loyal to the concept of an England small, self-contained, and minding its own business, while other, less enlightened nations pursued their internecine strife.

The "Observations," however, form a well-written and satisfying example of Johnson's most competent journalistic writing. His transition at the end to the subject of the Militia Bill, with which the exigencies of a deadline had prevented him from dealing adequately in the previous number of the *Literary Magazine*, is cleverly done: he has now had time to think out more clearly his position on the principle of a militia, and works it in very nicely with his discussion of the subsidy treaties. The authorship of the piece seems to have been first attributed to Johnson in the *European Magazine*, Feb 1785, p. 83. It was first reprinted in Volume xiv of Johnson's *Works* (1788).

The text here follows that of the *Literary Magazine*, No. 3 (15 June–15 July 1756), pp. 119–21.

Observations on the Foregoing Treaties

These are the treaties which for many months filled the senate with debates, and the kingdom with clamours, which were represented on one part as instances of the most profound policy and the most active care of the public welfare, and on the other, as acts of the most contemptible folly and most flagrant corruption, as violations of the great trust of government, by which the wealth of Britain is sacrificed to private views and to a particular province.

What honours our ministers and negotiators may expect to be paid to their wisdom it is hard to determine, for the demands of vanity are not easily estimated. They should consider before they call too loudly for encomiums, that they live in an age when the power of gold is no longer a secret, and in which no man finds much difficulty in making a bargain with money in his hand. To hire troops is very easy to those who are willing to pay their price. It appears therefore that whatever has been done was done by means which every man knows how to use if fortune is kind enough to put them in his power. To arm the nations of the north in the cause of Britain, to bring down hosts against France from the polar circle has indeed a sound of magnificence,[1] which might induce a mind unacquainted with public affairs to imagine that some effort of policy more than human had been exerted, by which distant nations were armed in our defence, and the influence of Britain was extended to the utmost limits of the world. But when this striking phenomenon of negotiation is more nearly inspected, it appears a bargain merely mercantile of one power that wanted troops more than money, with another that wanted money, and was burdened with troops, between whom their mutual wants made an easy contract, and who have no other friendship for each other, than reciprocal convenience happens to produce.

We shall therefore leave the praises of our ministers to others, yet not without this acknowledgment, that if they have done little, they do not seem to boast of doing much,[2] and that whether influenced by modesty or frugality, they have not wearied the public with mercenary panegyrists, but have been content with the concurrence of the Parliament, and have not much solicited the applauses of the people.

In public as in private transactions men more frequently deviate from the right for want of virtue than of wisdom; and those who declare themselves dissatisfied with these treaties impute them not to folly but corruption.

By these advocates for the independence of Britain, who, whether their arguments be just or not, seem to be most favourably heard by the people, it is alleged, that these treaties are expensive without advantage, that they waste the treasure,

---

1. In striking contrast to this offhand attitude toward subsidized military aid are Demetrius's bitter comments, near the opening of *Irene* (1.22–23), on "That wealth, which granted to their weeping prince, / Had rang'd embattled nations at our gates." Demetrius's speech in favour of the principle of military subsidies seems not to be in the "first draft" of *Irene*. If it was added in the 1740's, when the same debate was going on (between the same sides) as in 1756, it forms an effective piece of *government* propaganda. Sir William Yonge, who assisted SJ with at least part of the epilogue to *Irene*, was Walpole's and Pelham's Secretary at War, and particularly concerned with matters of military aid.

2. For the construction, cf. SJ's final version of his quip about George Grenville in *Thoughts on Falkland's Islands*, 1771 (p. 383 below): "If he was sometimes wrong, he was often right."

which we want for our own defence, upon a foreign interest,[3] and pour the gains of our commerce into the coffers of princes, whose enmity cannot hurt nor friendship help us, who set their subjects to sale like sheep or oxen without any enquiry after the intentions of the buyer,[4] and will withdraw the troops with which they have supplied us, whenever a higher bidder shall be found.

This perhaps is true, but whether it be true or false is not worth enquiry. We did not expect to buy their friendship but their troops; nor did we examine upon what principle we were supplied with assistance, it was sufficient that we wanted forces, and that they were willing to furnish them. Policy never pretended to make men wise and good, the utmost of her power is to make the best use of men such as they are, to lay hold on lucky hours, to watch the present wants and present interests of others, and make them subservient to her own convenience.

It is farther urged with great vehemence, that these troops of Russia and Hesse are not hired in defence of Britain; that we are engaged in a naval war for territories on a distant continent, and that these troops though mercenaries can never be auxiliaries; that they increase the burden of the war without hastening its conclusion, or promoting its success; since they can neither be sent into America, the only part of the world where England can, on the present occasion, have any employment for land forces, nor be put into our ships, by which and by which only we are now to oppose and subdue our enemies.

Nature has stationed us in an island inaccessible but by sea, and we are now at war with an enemy, whose naval power is inferior to our own, and from whom therefore we are in no danger of invasion:[5] to what purpose then are troops

---

3. That of Hanover. The paragraph accurately summarizes the charges made in the speeches of Pitt, Temple, and Pomfret. The concern with wasting "the gains of our commerce" should be noted (the treaties will "consume the profits of our trade"— Pitt, in *Parliamentary History*, xv.664).

4. This charge was levied in particular at Hesse, rather than Russia. Perhaps some of the American animus against "the Hessians" in the Revolutionary War is a reminiscence of this earlier debate.

5. On this point, SJ parts company with Pitt and Temple, who played up

hired in such uncommon numbers? To what end do we procure strength which we cannot exert, and exhaust the nation with subsidies at a time when nothing is disputed, which the princes who receive our subsidies can defend. If we had purchased ships and hired seamen, we had apparently increased our power, and made ourselves formidable to our enemies, and, if any increase of security be possible, had secured ourselves still better from invasions: but what can the regiments of Russia or of Hesse contribute to the defence of the coasts of England, or by what assistance can they repay us the sums which we have stipulated to pay for their costly friendship?

The King of Great-Britain has indeed a territory on the continent, of which the natives of this island scarcely knew the name till the present family was call'd to the throne, and yet know little more than that our king visits it from time to time.[6] Yet for the defence of this country are these subsidies apparently paid, and these troops evidently levied. The riches of our nation are sent into distant countries, and the strength which should be employed in our own quarrel consequently impaired, for the sake of dominions the interest of which has no connection with ours, and which by the act of succession we took care to keep separate from the British kingdoms.[7]

---

the threat of invasion. In the next issue of the *Literary Magazine*, SJ (as I think) continues to pooh-pooh it: "This pamphlet is published to prove what nobody will deny, that we shall be less happy if we were conquered by the French. The intention of the author is undoubtedly good, but his labour is superfluous. . . . There is no great danger of invasions while we have the sea covered with our ships, and maintain fifty thousand men in arms on our coasts" (review of Charles Parkin's *An Impartial Account of the Invasion under William, Duke of Normandy, Literary Magazine*, No. 4, pp. 186–87); and again in No. 7 (15 Oct–15 Nov), in his review of *The Conduct of the Ministry Impartially*

Examined (p. 258 below).

6. George II was now 73, and such visits as he still made to Hanover were for military and diplomatic, rather than amorous, purposes. But SJ cannot resist reviving by innuendo the memory of his exploits of the 1730's (see pp. 5f. above). SJ attacked many people during his career, but none more relentlessly and vindictively than the king under whom he lived the longest portion of his life.

7. Provisions against mingling the affairs of Great Britain and Hanover were incorporated in the Act of Settlement, 1701, which conferred the succession to the throne on the Hanoverian electoral family.

To this the advocates for the subsidies say, that unreasonable stipulations, whether in the act of settlement or any other contract, are in themselves void, and that if a country connected with England by subjection to the same Sovereign is endangered by an English quarrel, it must be defended by English force, and that we do not engage in a war for the sake of Hanover, but that Hanover is for our sake exposed to danger.

Those who brought in these foreign troops have still something further to say in their defence, and of no honest plea is it our intention to defraud them. They grant, that the terror of invasion may possibly be groundless, that the French may want the power or the courage to attack us in our own country; but they maintain likewise that an invasion is possible, that the armies of France are so numerous that she may hazard a large body on the ocean, without leaving herself exposed: that she is exasperated to the utmost degree of acrimony, and would be willing to do us mischief at her own peril. They allow that the invaders may be intercepted at sea, or that, if they land, they may be defeated by our native troops. But they say, and say justly, that danger is better avoided than encountered; that those ministers consult more the good of their country who prevent invasion, than repel it, and that if these auxiliaries have only saved us from the anxiety of expecting an enemy at our doors, or from the tumult and distress which an invasion, how soon soever repressed, would have produced, the public money is not spent in vain.

These arguments are admitted by some, and by others rejected. But even those that admit them, can admit them only as pleas of necessity, for they consider the reception of mercenaries into our country as the desperate remedy of desperate distress,[8] and think with great reason, that all means of prevention should be tried to save us from any second need of such doubtful succours.

That we are able to defend our own country, that arms

---

8. Birkbeck Hill remarks (*Life*, I. 308, n. 1) that these "forcible words . . . have been used since by orators." The phrase may contain a reminiscence of *Hamlet*, IV. iii. 9–11: "Diseases desperate grown, / By desperate appliance are relieved, / Or not at all."

are most safely intrusted to our own hands, and that we have strength, and skill, and courage equal to the best of the nations of the continent, is the opinion of every Englishman who can think without prejudice, and speak without influence, and therefore it will not be easy to persuade the nation, a nation long renowned for valour, that it can need the help of foreigners to defend it from invasion. We have been long without the need of arms by our good fortune, and long without the use by our negligence, so long that the practice and almost the name of our old trained-bands is forgotten.[9] But the story of ancient times will tell us, that the trained-bands were once able to maintain the quiet and safety of their country, and reason without history will inform us, that those men are most likely to fight bravely, or at least to fight obstinately, who fight for their own houses and farms, for their own wives and children.

A bill was therefore offered for the prevention of any future danger of[a] invasion, or necessity of mercenary forces, by re-establishing and improving the militia. It was passed by the Commons, but rejected by the Lords. That this bill, the first essay of political consideration on[b] a subject long forgotten, should be liable to objection cannot be strange, but surely, justice, policy, common reason require that we should be trusted with our own defence, and be kept no longer in such a helpless state as at once to dread our enemies and confederates.

By the bill, such as it was formed, sixty thousand men would always be in arms. We have shewn page 63[1] how they may be upon any exigence easily increased to an hundred and fifty thousand, and I believe, neither our friends nor enemies will think it proper to insult our coasts when they expect to find upon them an hundred and fifty thousand Englishmen with swords in their hands.

a. of *emend.*] or *1756*   b. on *emend.*] as *1756*

9. See n. 1, p. 156 above.   1. P. 166 above.

OBSERVATIONS ON THE PRESENT
STATE OF AFFAIRS. 1756.

This essay may be regarded as an expansion and continuation of the latter part of "An Introduction to the Political State of Great-Britain," published in the *Literary Magazine* three months earlier. Its content is also clearly related to the instalment of "Historical Memoirs" (a monthly feature of the *Literary Magazine*) which had appeared in the second number (15 May–15 June), pp. 105–06, and which is subtitled "Of the Rise of the Troubles in America." Some parts of "Of the Rise of the Troubles" sound very Johnsonian: e.g., "That some of our settlements on that vast continent are held by purchase, and others by voluntary concession, is, we believe, universally known; neither will it be disputed that this kind of tenure is preferable to force; yet while we boast the justice of our title let us not forget that our possessions have limits; let us not, because we owe much to the generosity of our Indian friends, be so unreasonably covetous as not to be contented with less than all that they had to give." Johnson puts it more succinctly in the present "Observations": those colonists who obtained their lands from the Indians by negotiation rather than violence "have no other merit than that of a scrivener who ruins in silence over a plunderer that seizes by force"; they ought to "content themselves to rob without insulting them," he had said in the "Introduction to the Political State."

The "Observations" terminate with some abruptness, which makes the reader look forward to the promised continuation. But no such continuation ever appeared. Nor indeed did any further substantial political writing by Johnson ever appear in the *Literary Magazine*. There were, to be sure, his reviews of the pamphlets on the Byng case, in Nos. 6 and 7 (see below, p. 213), which are outspoken in support of Byng against the government, and the "Memoirs of the King of Prussia," in Nos. 7, 8, and 9, which give no very enthusiastic account of the political and military exploits of Britain's great continental ally. But by comparison with the essays of Nos. 1 to 4 these are minor pieces, politically. The question cannot be avoided, why was this brilliant and impressive series of commentaries on the current political situation broken off, in the full spate of some of Johnson's most magnificent invective, with an unfulfilled promise "to be continued"? We have virtually no "external evidence" as to the circumstances of Johnson's employment by the proprietors of the *Literary Magazine*. But until such is forthcoming, the inescapable answer to the question is that which is to be found in the content of the essays themselves, in particular the discontinued "Observations on the Present State of Affairs," for in them Johnson designated a great international war just begun by his country as "only the quarrel of two robbers for the spoils of a passenger"; found the broken treaties that formed his country's *casus belli* analogous to the terms of confederacy of a "gang" of bandits; described his countrymen's activities in the territory for whose possession the war was being fought as "but new modes of usurpation, but new instances of cruelty and treachery"; said of their assertions as to their legal title to it, "There is no great malignity in suspecting that those who have robbed have also lied"; and summed it all up by pronouncing, "Such is the contest that no honest man can heartily wish success to either party." That other forces, with a very different political point of view, exercised control over the *Literary Magazine's* editorial policy is shown clearly enough in the instalment of the "Historical Memoirs" that appeared in No. 5, the issue following the discontinued "Observations": it is a paean, of incredible fatuity and naiveté, to Pitt and his glorious war for the rescue of Britain's priceless honour, etc.

The "Observations," incomplete though they may be, are one of Johnson's finest smaller pieces of writing. The white heat of the underlying indignation against fraud and injustice is as intense as in *Marmor Norfolciense* and the *Vindication of the Licensers;* but, perhaps because the moral basis of Johnson's conviction is deeper—because the subject is more important, more far-reaching—the passion is better controlled and shapes the writing into a stylistically more satisfactory form than in the two early pamphlets. I myself feel that the piece, short as it is, is worthy to be ranked second only, among Johnson's controversial writings, to his supreme achievement, the review of Soame Jenyns, which appeared nine months later in the same periodical.

The "Observations" were reprinted by Thomas Davies in Volume III (1774) of his *Miscellaneous and Fugitive Pieces*, and attributed to Johnson in the *Gentleman's Magazine's* notice of Davies's book, Nov 1774, p. 525. Davies emended the title to "Observations on the State of Affairs in 1756," under which designation it was reprinted in Volume x of Johnson's *Works* (1787), and subsequent editions. The text here follows that of the *Literary Magazine*, No. 4 (15 July–15 Aug 1756), pp. [161]–65. Like "An Introduction to the Political State of Great Britain," it is the first article in the number of the magazine in which it appears.

Observations on the Present State of Affairs[a]

The time is now come in which every Englishman expects to be informed of the national affairs, and in which he has a right to have that expectation gratified.[1] For whatever may

a. *Title:* On the State of Affairs in 1756 *1774, 1787, etc.*

---

1. Equally forthright assertions of the right of the people to know what their government is doing (and to make their opinion of it known), and equally scornful condemnation of official obscurantism, are to be found

be urged by ministers, or those whom vanity or interest make
the followers of ministers, concerning the necessity of confidence in our governors, and the presumption of prying
with profane eyes into the recesses of policy, it is evident,
that this reverence can be claimed only by counsels yet
unexecuted, and projects suspended in deliberation. But when
a design has ended in miscarriage or success, when every
eye and every ear is witness to general discontent, or general
satisfaction, it is then a proper time to disintangle confusion
and illustrate[2] obscurity, to shew by what causes every event
was produced, and in what effects it is likely to terminate:
to lay down with distinct particularity what rumour always
huddles in general exclamations, or perplexes by undigested
narratives; to shew whence happiness or calamity is derived,
and whence it may be expected, and honestly to lay before
the people what inquiry can gather of the past, and conjecture can estimate of the future.

The general subject of the present war is sufficiently known.
It is allowed on both sides, that hostilities began in America,
and that the French and English quarrelled about the boundaries of their settlements, about grounds and rivers to which,
I am afraid, neither can shew any other right than that of
power, and which neither can occupy but by usurpation, and
the dispossession of the natural lords and original inhabitants.
Such is the contest that no honest man can heartily wish
success to either party.

It may indeed be alleged, that the Indians have granted
large tracts of land both to one and to the other; but these
grants can add little to the validity of our titles, till it be
experienced how they were obtained: for if they were extorted
by violence, or induced by fraud; by threats, which the
miseries of other nations had shewn not to be vain, or by
promises of which no performance was ever intended, what

---

in the essay "On . . . Small Tracts and
Fugitive Pieces," *A Compleat Vindication
of the Licensers of the Stage*, the preface
to *The Preceptor*, the "speech" on the
Rochefort expedition, and elsewhere.
The legend of Johnson the blind
authoritarian, the Johnson who wished
to "stem the rising tide of democracy,"
can only continue to be kept alive by
resolutely ignoring the existence of
such writings.

2. "1. To brighten with light . . . 3.
To explain; to clear; to elucidate"
(*Dictionary*).

are they but new modes of usurpation, but new instances of cruelty and treachery?

And indeed what but false hope, or resistless terror can prevail upon a weaker nation to invite a stronger into their country, to give their lands to strangers whom no affinity of manners, or similitude of opinion can be said to recommend, to permit them to build towns from which the natives are excluded, to raise fortresses by which they are intimidated, to settle themselves with such strength, that they cannot afterwards be expelled, but are for ever to remain the masters of the original inhabitants, the dictators of their conduct, and the arbiters of their fate?

When we see men acting thus against the precepts of reason, and the instincts of nature, we cannot hesitate to determine, that by some means or other they were debarred from choice; that they were lured or frighted into compliance; that they either granted only what they found impossible to keep, or expected advantages upon the faith of their new inmates, which there was no purpose to confer upon them. It cannot be said, that the Indians originally invited us to their coasts; we went uncalled and unexpected to nations who had no imagination that the earth contained any inhabitants so distant and so different from themselves. We astonished them with our ships, with our arms, and with our general superiority. They yielded to us as to beings of another and higher race, sent among them from some unknown regions, with power which naked Indians could not resist, and which they were therefore, by every act of humility, to propitiate, that they, who could so easily destroy, might be induced to spare.

To this influence, and to this only, are to be attributed all the cessions and submissions of the Indian princes, if indeed any such cessions were ever made, of which we have no witness but those who claim from them, and there is no great malignity in suspecting, that those who have robbed have also lied.

Some colonies indeed have been established more peaceably than others. The utmost extremity of wrong has not always been practised; but those that have settled in the new world on the fairest terms, have no other merit than that of a scrivener who ruins in silence over a plunderer that seizes by force; all have taken what had other owners, and all have had recourse to arms, rather than quit the prey on which they had fastened.

The American dispute between the French and us is therefore only the quarrel of two robbers for the spoils of a passenger, but as robbers have terms of confederacy, which they are obliged to observe as members of the gang, so the English and French may have relative rights, and do injustice to each other, while both are injuring the Indians. And such, indeed, is the present contest: they have parted the northern continent of America between them, and are now disputing about their boundaries, and each is endeavouring the destruction of the other by the help of the Indians, whose interest it is that both should be destroyed.

Both nations clamour with great vehemence about infraction of limits, violation of treaties, open usurpation, insidious artifices, and breach of faith. The English rail at the perfidious French, and the French at the encroaching English; they quote treaties on each side, charge each other with aspiring to universal monarchy, and complain on either part of the insecurity of possession near such turbulent neighbours.

Through this mist of controversy it can raise no wonder, that the truth is not easily discovered. When a quarrel has been long carried on between individuals, it is often very hard to tell by whom it was begun. Every fact is darkened by distance, by interest, and by multitudes. Information is not easily procured from far; those whom the truth will not favour, will not step voluntarily forth to tell it, and where there are many agents, it is easy for every single action to be concealed.

All these causes concur to the obscurity of the question, by whom were hostilities in America commenced? Perhaps there never can be remembered a time in which hostilities had ceased. Two powerful colonies enflamed with immemorial rivalry, and placed out of the superintendence of the mother nations, were not likely to be long at rest. Some opposition was always going forward, some mischief was every day done or meditated, and the borderers were always better pleased with what they could snatch from their neighbours, than what they had of their own.

In this disposition to reciprocal invasion a cause of dispute never could be wanting. The forests and desarts of America are without land-marks, and therefore cannot be particularly specified in stipulations; the appellations of those wide extended regions have in every mouth a different meaning, and are understood on either side as inclination happens to contract or extend them. Who has yet pretended to define how much of America is included in Brazil, Mexico, or Peru? It is almost as easy to divide the Atlantic Ocean by a line,[3] as clearly to ascertain the limits of those uncultivated, uninhabitable, unmeasured regions.

It is likewise to be considered, that contracts concerning boundaries are often left vague and indefinite without necessity, by the desire of each party, to interpret the ambiguity to its own advantage when a fit opportunity shall be found. In forming stipulations, the commissaries are often ignorant, and often negligent; they are sometimes weary with debate, and contract a tedious discussion into general terms, or refer it to a former treaty, which was never understood. The weaker part[4] is always afraid of requiring explanations, and the stronger always has an interest in leaving the question undecided: thus it will happen without great caution on either side, that after long treaties solemnly ratified, the rights that had been disputed are still equally open to controversy.

In America it may easily be supposed, that there are tracts of land yet claimed by neither[b] party, and therefore mentioned in no treaties, which yet one or the other may be afterwards inclined to occupy; but to these vacant and unsettled countries each nation may pretend, as each conceives itself intitled to all that is not expressly[c] granted to the other.

Here then is a perpetual ground of contest, every enlargement of the possessions of either will be considered as something taken from the other, and each will endeavour to regain what had never been claimed, but that the other occupied it.

b. yet . . . neither *1756*] not yet claimed by either *1774, 1787*, etc.   c. expresly *1756*

---

3. See n. 2, p. 130 above.
4. Perhaps "party," which occurs seven lines below.

Thus obscure in its original is the American contest. It is difficult to find the first invader, or to tell where invasion properly begins; but I suppose it is not to be doubted, that after the last war, when the French had made peace with such apparent superiority,[5] they naturally began to treat us with less respect in distant parts of the world, and to consider us as a people from whom they had nothing to fear, and who could no longer presume to contravene their designs, or to check their progress.

The power of doing wrong with impunity seldom waits long for the will, and it is reasonable to believe, that in America the French would avow their purpose of aggrandising themselves with at least as little reserve as in Europe. We may therefore readily believe, that they were unquiet neighbours, and had no great regard to right which they believed us no longer able to enforce.

That in forming a line of forts behind our colonies, if in no other part of their attempt, they had acted against the general intention, if not against the literal terms of treaties, can scarcely be denied; for it never can be supposed, that we intended to be inclosed between the sea and the French garrisons, or preclude ourselves from extending our plantations backwards to any length that our convenience should require.

With dominion is conferred every thing that can secure dominion. He that has the coast, has likewise the sea to a certain distance; he that possesses a fortress, has the right of prohibiting another fortress to be built within the command of its cannon. When therefore we planted the coast of North-America we supposed the possession of the inland region granted to an indefinite extent, and every nation that settled in that part of the world, seems, by the permission of every other nation, to have made the same supposition in its own favour.

Here then, perhaps, it will be safest to fix the justice of our cause; here we are apparently and indisputably injured, and this injury may, according to the practice of nations, be justly resented. Whether we have not in return made some

---

5. The Peace of Aix-la-Chapelle, 1748. See "Letter on the Fireworks," p. 111 above.

incroachments upon them, must be left doubtful, till our practices on the Ohio shall be stated and vindicated. There are no two nations confining[6] on each other, between whom a war may not always be kindled with plausible pretences on either part, as there is always passing between them a reciprocation of injuries and fluctuation of incroachments.

From the conclusion of the last peace perpetual complaints of the supplantations and invasions of the French have been sent to Europe from our colonies, and transmitted to our ministers at Paris, where good words were sometimes given us, and the practices of the American commanders were sometimes disowned, but no redress was ever obtained, nor is it probable that any prohibition was sent to America. We were still amused with such doubtful promises as those who are afraid of war are ready to interpret in their own favour, and the French pushed forward their line of fortresses, and seemed to resolve that before our complaints were finally dismissed, all remedy should be hopeless.

We likewise endeavour'd at the same time to form a barrier against the Canadians by sending a colony to New-Scotland, a cold uncomfortable tract of ground, of which we had long the nominal possession before we really began to occupy it. To this those were invited whom the cessation of war deprived of employment,[7] and made burdensome to their country, and settlers were allured thither by many fallacious descriptions of fertile vallies and clear skies. What effect these pictures of American happiness had upon my countrymen I was never informed, but I suppose very few sought provision in those frozen regions, whom guilt or poverty did not drive

6. "*To confine.* v.n. To border upon; to touch on different territories, or regions: it has *with* or *on*" (*Dictionary*).

7. The town of Halifax (named after the President of the Board of Trade and Plantations) was founded in 1749; many of its settlers were soldiers demobilized at the conclusion of the War of the Austrian Succession. One of its early inhabitants was John Salusbury, Mrs. Thrale's father, who was a protégé of Lord Halifax's and held a small government post there for some years. He seems to be well characterized as one of those who had become "burdensome to their country," and bore out SJ's thesis by continuing to have little success in Nova Scotia. SJ later annotated some of Salusbury's Nova Scotian journals (J. L. Clifford, *H. L. Piozzi*, 1941, p. 17, n. 1).

from their native country. About the boundaries of this new colony there were some disputes, but as there was nothing yet worth a contest, the power of the French was not much exerted on that side: some disturbance was however given and some skirmishes ensued. But perhaps being peopled chiefly with soldiers, who would rather live by plunder than by agriculture, and who consider war as their best trade, New-Scotland would be more obstinately defended than some settlements of far greater value, and the French are too well informed of their own interest, to provoke hostility for no advantage, or to select that country for invasion, where they must hazard much, and can win little. They therefore pressed on southward behind our ancient and wealthy settlements, and built fort after fort at such distances that they might conveniently relieve one another, invade our colonies with sudden incursions, and retire to places of safety before our people could unite to oppose them.

This design of the French has been long formed, and long known, both in America and Europe, and might at first have been easily repressed had force been used instead of expostulation. When the English attempted a settlement upon the Island of St. Lucia, the French, whether justly or not, considering it as neutral and forbidden to be occupied by either nation, immediately landed upon it, and destroyed the houses, wasted the plantations, and drove or carried away the inhabitants.[8] This was done in the time of peace, when mutual professions of friendship were daily exchanged by the two courts, and was not considered as any violation of treaties, nor was any more than a very soft remonstrance made on our part.

The French therefore taught us how to act, but an Hanoverian quarrel with the house of Austria for some time induced us to court, at any expence, the alliance of a nation whose very situation makes them our enemies. We suffered them to destroy our settlements, and to advance their own, which we had an equal right to attack. The time however came at last, when we ventured to quarrel with Spain, and

8. In 1723. See n. 1, p. 170 above.

then France no longer suffered the appearance of peace to subsist between us, but armed in defence of her ally.

The events of the war are well known, we pleased ourselves with a victory at Dettingen, where we left our wounded men to the care of our enemies,[9] but our army was broken at Fontenoy and Val;[1] and though after the disgrace which we suffered in the Mediterranean we had some naval success, and an accidental dearth made peace necessary for the French, yet they prescribed the conditions, obliged us to give hostages, and acted as conquerors, though as conquerors of moderation.

In this war the Americans distinguished themselves in a manner unknown and unexpected. The New English raised an army, and under the command of Pepperel took Cape-Breton, with the assistance of the fleet.[2] This is the most important fortress in America. We pleased ourselves so much with the acquisition, that we could not think of restoring it, and among the arguments used to inflame the people against Charles Stuart, it was very clamorously urged, that if he gained the kingdom, he would give Cape-Breton back to the French.

The French however had a more easy expedient to regain Cape-Breton than by exalting Charles Stuart to the English throne,[3] they took in their turn Fort St. George, and had our

9. In 1743. George II led his troops in person, the last time a British king has done so. Needless to say, the administration made much of this circumstance; and needless to say, SJ preferred to emphasize the unfavourable aspects of the ambiguous outcome of the battle.

1. The battles of Fontenoy (1745) and Val (Lauffeld) (1747) were severe defeats for the allied armies led by the King's younger son, the Duke of Cumberland.

2. See n. 2, p. 170 above.

3. SJ's references merely to "Charles Stuart" may be taken as further evidence that SJ was no Jacobite. Charles was certainly entitled to the style of "Prince," and many Englishmen firmly loyal to the Hanoverian dynasty felt no qualms in giving it to him. (Cf. Boswell's agonies over the question of how to designate him, *Life*, V. 185, n. 4.) Moreover, a serious Jacobite would not have committed the solecism of talking about "exalting" Charles "to the English throne" in 1745 or 1756. The Stuart claimant to the throne, until his death in 1766, was Charles's father, James Edward. Perhaps the most accurate description of SJ's position *vis-à-vis* the Stuart cause is (to borrow a useful expression from a later situation) that he was an anti-anti-Jacobite.

East-India company wholly in their power, whom they re-stored at the peace to their former possessions, that they may continue to export our silver.[4]

Cape-Breton therefore was restored, and the French were re-established in America, with equal power and greater spirit, having lost nothing by the war which they had before gained.

To the general reputation of their arms, and that habitual superiority which they derive from it, they owe their power in America, rather than to any real strength, or circumstances of advantage. Their numbers are yet not great; their trade, though daily improved, is not very extensive; their country is barren, their fortresses, though numerous, are weak, and rather shelters from wild beasts, or savage nations, than places built for defence against bombs or cannons. Cape-Breton has been found not to be impregnable; nor, if we consider the state of the places possessed by the two nations in America, is there any reason upon which the French should have presumed to molest us; but that they thought our spirit so broken that we durst not resist them, and in this opinion our long forbearance easily confirmed them.

We forgot, or rather avoided to think, that what we delayed to do must be done at last, and done with more difficulty, as it was delayed longer; that while we were com-plaining, and they were eluding, or answering our complaints, fort was rising upon fort, and one invasion made a precedent for another.

This confidence of the French is exalted by some real advantages. If they possess in those countries less than we, they have more to gain, and less to hazard; if they are less numerous, they are better united.

The French compose one body with one head. They have all the same interest, and agree to pursue it by the same

---

4. This somewhat obscure comment seems to be a censure on grounds of mercantilist economic theory of the East India Company—something very seldom found in SJ. He later enrolled himself in defence of the Company against government (Pittite) inter- vention in 1767 (see *Letters* 187.3). Perhaps the fact that the imperially minded Robert Clive, whom SJ detested, was at this time all powerful in Indian affairs has something to do with the rebuke.

means. They are subject to a governor commission'd by an absolute monarch, and participating the authority of his master. Designs are therefore formed without debate, and executed without impediment. They have yet more martial than mercantile ambition, and seldom suffer their military schemes to be entangled with collateral projects of gain: they have no wish but for conquest, of which they justly consider riches as the consequence.

Some advantages they will always have as invaders. They make war at the hazard of their enemies: the contest being carried on in our territories, we must lose more by a victory than they will suffer by a defeat. They will subsist, while they stay, upon our plantations, and perhaps destroy them when they can stay no longer. If we pursue them and carry the war into their dominions, our difficulties will encrease every step as we advance, for we shall leave plenty behind us, and find nothing in Canada, but lakes and forests barren and trackless, our enemies will shut themselves up in their forts, against which it is difficult to bring cannon through so rough a country,[5] and which if they are provided with good magazines will soon starve those who besiege them.

All these are the natural effects of their government, and situation; they are accidentally more formidable as they are less happy. But the favour of the Indians which they enjoy, with very few exceptions, among all the nations of the northern continent, we ought to consider with other thoughts; this favour we might have enjoyed, if we had been careful to deserve it. The French by having these savage nations on their side, are always supplied with spies, and guides, and with auxiliaries, like the Tartars to the Turks or the Hussars[6] to the Germans, of no great use against troops ranged in order of battle, but very well qualified to maintain a war among woods and rivulets, where much mischief may be done by unexpected onsets, and safety be obtained by quick

5. The transportation of artillery had been one of Braddock's difficulties in his disastrous Pennsylvanian expedition of the previous year.
6. A novelty in the War of the Aus-trian Succession. See Gunther Rothenberg, *Notes & Queries*, ccix (Aug. 1964), 296–98, and *The Vanity of Human Wishes*, l. 249.

retreats. They can waste a colony by sudden inroads, surprise the straggling planters, frighten the inhabitants into towns, hinder the cultivation of lands, and starve those whom they are not able to conquer.

(To be continued.)[d]

d. (To be continued.) *1756*] *om. 1774, 1787*, etc.

REVIEW OF LEWIS EVANS, *ANALYSIS OF A GENERAL MAP OF THE MIDDLE BRITISH COLONIES IN AMERICA.* 1756.

Cartography, as Johnson suggests in the opening paragraph of this review, has often been a branch of political action. This was particularly true in the years preceding the declaration of the Seven Years' War in 1756, years in which the struggle between the French and the British (including the American colonists) for the immensely important prize of the Ohio Valley reached its violent climax. The French were charged with

> deliberately revising their maps in this period to show boundaries which confined the English colonies to the narrow Atlantic seaboard between Florida and Nova Scotia. "Boastful," "impudent," "lying" were a few of the adjectives applied to the French cartographical policy. The maps of Bellin, De Lisle, and DeFer were selected for particular vilification. . . . The colonials longed for maps which should show the English side of the argument. In 1755, two productions that seemed sent in answer to their desires appeared respectively in London and Philadelphia. These were the celebrated maps of Dr. John Mitchell of Virginia and London, and that of equal fame by Lewis Evans of Philadelphia.[1]

Mitchell's "great eight-sheet map" of North America was published (in February) under the auspices of the Lords Commissioners of Trade and the Plantations; Mitchell, who had moved to London fifteen years earlier, compiled it from "original surveys in the Plantations Office." It was "an official political document, the most important statement . . . of the British claims regarding America to come from a government source." Later issues of it were used, in 1775, and by the negotiators of the Treaty of Versailles in 1783, to mark out the first official boundaries of the new United States of America.[2]

1. Lawrence C. Wroth, *An American Bookshelf, 1755* (Philadelphia, 1934), pp. 32–35. Most of the information about Evans in this introductory note comes from two useful accounts, Wroth's, and that in Lawrence Henry Gipson's sumptuous *Lewis Evans* (Philadelphia, 1939), which contains facsimiles of both volumes (1755 and 1756) of Evans's *Geographical . . . Essays* and of Evans's maps, including that of the Middle British Colonies, discussed here. Henry N. Stevens, *Lewis Evans: His Map of the Middle British Colonies in America* (1905; 3rd ed., 1924) is a bibliographical study of the very many later states and issues of the map.

2. Mitchell's pamphlet, *The Contest in America* (1757), arguing the British claims to the Ohio territory, was reviewed in the *Monthly Review* by Oliver Goldsmith (*Collected Works*, ed. Arthur Friedman, 1966, 1.150–52).

Lewis Evans's map, "of equal fame" and equally important, was by
contrast an unofficial[3] and local production, but perhaps for that reason
of even greater value in contributing to a knowledge of the region that is now
Ohio, Indiana, southern Michigan, and western New York State and
Pennsylvania, then largely unknown except to its Indian inhabitants and a
few French Canadian and British American fur traders and occupants of
isolated military posts. Not much is known about Evans's early life. He
seems to have been born in Wales around 1700 and to have migrated to
Pennsylvania some time before 1736, where he made a living as a surveyor,
cartographer, and occasional writer and lecturer. He was interested in
science, and delivered pioneering public lectures on electricity and other
scientific topics in New York, New Jersey, and Philadelphia. He associated
with Peter Kalm, the Swedish scientist who visited America, and with
Benjamin Franklin; it has been suggested that Evans's interest in electricity
helped to stimulate Franklin's. He was employed by the government of
Pennsylvania to map the Middle Atlantic region, in the hope of resolving
boundary disputes between Pennsylvania and Maryland; this map was
published in 1749.

As the tension between the French and British in the Ohio country increased, Evans became a dedicated adherent to the party among the
Americans which maintained that the British and American military effort
should be concentrated on expelling the French from the Ohio Valley;[4]
the opposing party advocated that it be directed against Quebec and
Montreal and other centres of French power on the St. Lawrence. No doubt
with this purpose in mind, he embarked on his great project of mapping this
region more thoroughly than it had ever been done before. He industriously
collected information from earlier maps, reports, explorers; not only geographical information, but information about the way of life of the Indian
tribes, their history, the economic possibilities of the country, and much
else which he reports in detail in the "Analysis" constituting the first volume
of his *Geographical, Historical, Political, Philosophical* [i.e., scientific], *and
Mechanical Essays*, the volume under review here. The volume included,
folded in, his fine map. The work was printed by Evans's friend, Benjamin
Franklin, and published on 23 June 1755—too late to reach General
Braddock on his ill-fated expedition to Fort Duquesne (now Pittsburgh),
where he was defeated and killed on 9 July. But Governor Morris of Pennsylvania seems to have sent Braddock an early draft, or engraver's proof,
of the map in February of that year. The volume was distributed in England
by Dodsley, who added his imprint to Franklin's on the title page. Evans's
map remained the standard map of the Ohio region for over fifty years; at
least twenty-seven different issues (mostly pirated) have been identified,

3. Though the Pennsylvania Assembly granted Evans £50 to help with the
completion and publication of the work.
4. Evans puts it wittily in Volume II of his *Essays* (1756): "Some kind reader
may here suggest that were we masters of Frontenac [Fort Frontenac, now
Kingston, Ontario], we might proceed still further and drive the French quite
out of Canada. It would be a much better scheme to drive them all into it"
(p. 28).

the last well into the nineteenth century. Swedish, Dutch, French, and German, as well as British and American, editions appeared. It was "a milestone in American cartography," as L. H. Gipson says.

By the time Johnson's review appeared, Evans was dead. The vehemence with which he put forward the case for mounting the main British-American effort against the Ohio country rather than the St. Lawrence led to bitter controversy. He was vigorously attacked in the New York *Mercury*, and replied in Volume II of his *Geographical . . . Essays*, published in March 1756. During these recriminations he went so far as to accuse Governor Morris of high treason and "to asperse two of his Majesty's ministers as pensioners to France." Morris proceeded against him for slander; Evans fled from Pennsylvania to New York to escape his wrath, but Morris prosecuted him in the New York courts and had him arrested and imprisoned. He was released from prison on a writ of *habeas corpus* by his supporter William Livingston (later Governor of New Jersey). But he died on 11 June 1756, heartbroken, Gipson suggests, by the defeat of Braddock and the imminent capture of Oswego, which seemed to leave the French in complete possession of his beloved Ohio country.

It is understandable that Johnson should have selected for review in the *Literary Magazine* a work of such contemporary relevance to the Great War for the Empire.[5] As in many of his reviews of this time, he prints copious extracts from the work itself, simply as documentation for the use of the readers of the magazine. But his interspersed commentary contains some of Johnson's most pointed expressions of his fundamental political views— for instance, his remark that Evans's arguments about the potential importance of the Ohio Valley "may be of great use in the present system of European policy, but . . . *will not prove that this system is right, or in other words, that it is more productive than any other of universal happiness*" (my italics). Johnson's doubts that the present system of national aggrandizement by European powers was productive of universal happiness had been expressed many times before. Yet the review is not, on the whole, a hostile one, though Johnson's deflation of Evans's enthusiasm for British-American expansion into the Ohio Valley has not appealed to the patriotism of the few students (American historians rather than Johnsonian scholars) who have paid any attention to the work. L. H. Gipson speaks of Johnson's "indulging in various philosophical ramblings," and L. C. Wroth describes the review as a combination of "insular superiority, invincible ignorance, [and] incomparable good sense." ("Invincible ignorance" of what, one wonders? Certainly not of the Ohio Valley's potential as a producer of raw silk, Evans's views of which Johnson justifiably pokes fun at.)

The review appeared in Vol. I, No. 6 (15 Sept–15 Oct 1756), pp. 293–299 of the *Literary Magazine*, the text of which is followed here, though some clear errors of transcription from Evans's volume have been corrected. These

5. Johnson's wish to provide the readers of the *Literary Magazine* with detailed knowledge of the places (and their inhabitants) over which the war was being fought should be noted. The long review of John Armstrong's *History of Minorca* (1752) in the magazine's first number was probably part of the same program.

are noted in the textual notes, together with other variants from Evans's text, some of which suggest deliberate editing (apparently for stylistic reasons), perhaps by Johnson himself. It was reprinted after Johnson's death in the so-called "Volume xv" of Johnson's *Works* (1789), edited by George Gleig (pp. 454–69), and later was listed by Boswell in his *Life*. But, like some of his other reviews in the *Literary Magazine*, it was never included in the various nineteenth-century collections of Johnson's works. Lawrence C. Wroth, in *An American Bookshelf, 1755* (1934), reprints most of the Johnsonian parts of the review, omitting the passages quoted from Evans (pp. 164–166). The extensive quotations from Evans are here printed in smaller type.

Geographical, Historical, Political, Philosophical, and Mechanical Essays: the First Containing an Analysis of a General Map of the Middle British Colonies in America; and of the Country of the Confederate Indians. A description of the face of the country, the boundaries of the confederates; and the maritime and inland navigations of the several rivers and lakes contained therein. By Lewis Evans. Dodsley.

Nothing in this world is simply good. Peace the great blessing of the world, produces luxury, idleness and effeminacy. Scarcely any thing is simply evil. War among its numerous miseries has sometimes useful consequences. The last war between the Russians and Turks[1] made geographers acquainted with the situation and extent of many countries little known before, in the north of Europe, and the war now kindled in America, has incited us to survey and delineate the immense wastes of the western continent by stronger motives than mere science or curiosity could ever have supplied, and enabled the imagination to wander over the lakes and mountains of that region, which many learned men have marked as the seat destined by Providence for the fifth empire.[2]

---

1. Presumably their involvement, on opposite sides, in the War of the Polish Succession, 1736–39. See *Marmor Norfolciense*, p. 38 above.

2. Daniel's interpretation of Nebuchadnezzar's dream (Daniel ii. 36–45), in which four successive imperfect kingdoms are succeeded by one that "shall stand for ever," gave rise to an enormous amount of speculation, from the early Fathers up to Luther, Calvin, Bellarmine, and beyond. Jerome and others interpreted the four kingdoms as those of Babylon, Medo-Persia,

At what time, or whether at any time their prediction will be verified, no human sagacity can discover, but as power is the constant and unavoidable consequence of learning, there is no reason to doubt that the time is approaching when the Americans shall in their turn have some influence on the affairs of mankind, for literature apparently gains ground among them. A library is established in Carolina; and some great electrical discoveries were made at Philadelphia,[3] where the map and treatise which we are now about to consider were likewise printed and engraved.

> Westward the seat of empire takes its way,
>   The four first acts already past,
> The fifth shall end the drama with the day,
>   Time's noblest product is the last.
>   Bp. Berkley.[4]

To this great event the present inland war cannot fail to contribute, as the inhabitants will necessarily become better

Greece, and Rome, and this seems to have been the commonest exegesis. The "Fifth-Monarchy Men" of the Interregnum won notoriety for attempting to realize the final Utopia. Berkeley's verse (next par.) adds an analogy to the conventional five acts of contemporary drama.

3. The Charleston (South Carolina) Library was founded in 1748. Franklin's *Experiments and Observations on Electricity Made at Philadelphia* was published in 1751. He received the Copley Medal of the Royal Society in 1752 and published other reports of electrical experiments in the Society's *Philosophical Transactions*. SJ again praises them in his review in Vol. I, No. 4 (1756) of the *Literary Magazine* of *Phil. Trans.*, Vol. XLIX, Part I. In Vol. I, No. 5 (1756) of the magazine, SJ (probably) also reviewed books on electricity by R. Lovett and by Hoadly and Wilson, writing, "Electricity is the great discovery of the present age,

and the great object of philosophical curiosity. . . . How many wonders may yet lie hid in every particle of matter no man can determine."

4. Berkeley's verses, originally entitled "America or the Muse's Refuge: A Prophecy," were composed in February 1726 (Berkeley, *Works*, ed. A. A. Luce [Edinburgh, 1955], VII.369–73). They were first printed in Berkeley's *A Miscellany* (Dublin, 1752), with many variants from the earlier form, and with the title "Verses by the Author on the Prospect of Planting Arts and Learning in America." SJ, no doubt quoting from memory, gives "seat" for "course," "end" for "close," and "product" for "offspring." This is the last of the six stanzas of the poem, inspired by Berkeley's unrealized project to found a university in Bermuda or Rhode Island. Because of these lines, the site of the young University of California, in the 1870's, was named "Berkeley."

versed in the military arts, and the Indians themselves as they
are courted by one or other of the contending nations, will
learn the use of European weapons, and the convenience of
European institutions. They will at least in time learn their
own importance, and will be incited to attempt something
more than the chase of beavers, when they are once convinced
that something more may be performed.

The map is engraved with sufficient beauty,[5] and the
treatise written with such elegance as the subject admits
tho' not without some mixture of the American dialect,[6] a
tract of corruption to which every language widely diffused
must always be exposed.

The general account which Mr. Evans gives of his map,
may afford some hints for the improvement of geographical
projections.[7]

It comprizes such an extent, as is connected with that very
valuable country on the Ohio, which is now the object of the
British and French policy, and the different routes of both nations
thither. The lake Ontario is equally open to both; to the one by the
river St. Lawrence; to the other by the rivers Hudson, Mohocks,
and Seneca. But the French having, thirty years ago, fixed themselves on the straits of Niagara, by building fortresses on lands
confessedly British, secured the key on that side to all the country
westward. Those in power see at last its consequence, and are
projecting the recovery of it; and with great judgment, for that
purpose, are establishing a naval force on Lake Ontario, as very
necessary in the recovery and securing of it. The issue of this enterprize will have great influence on our affairs, and of all things it
becomes the colonies to push it on with vigour. If they succeed here,
the remainder of the work will be easy; and nothing so, without it.
The English have several ways to Ohio; but far the best is by
Potomack.

By reason of the little acquaintance the public has with these
remoter parts, where the country is yet a wilderness, and the
necessity of knowing the ways of travelling there, especially by
water; in the map is pointed out the nature of the several streams;
as where rapid, gentle or obstructed with falls, and consequently

---

5. By James Turner of Philadelphia.
6. For instance, "pretty sharp" and
"pretty good" (p. 208)? Readers may

be able to discover other examples.
7. "Projection. . . . 2. Plan; delineation" (*Dictionary*).

more or less fitted for inland navigation with canoes, boats or larger vessels; and where the portages are made at the falls, or from one river, creek or lake to another. And for distinguishing the extent of the marine navigation, the places, that the tide reaches, in the several rivers, are pointed out. And in these sheets, both the marine and inland navigation are treated of at length.

As the natures[a] of the soil and streams depend upon the elevation and depression of the land; I have particularly explained here the different stages that it is divided into. It were to be wish'd that we had like accounts of all countries; as such would discover to us great regularity, where an unattentive observer would imagine there was nothing but confusion; and at the same time explain the climates, the healthiness, the produce, and conveniences for habitations, commerce and military expeditions, to a judicious reader in a few pages, better than volumes of remarks on places, drawn without these distinctions.

To render this map useful in commerce, and in ascertaining the boundaries of lands, the time of high-water at the full and change of the moon, and the variation of the magnetical needle are laid down. But as these deserve particular explanations, I have, for want of room, concluded to treat of them at large in a separate essay.

Along the western margin of the map is[b] a line representing the greatest lengths of days and nights (without allowance for the refraction) which will assist travellers, in forming some judgment of the latitude of places, by the help of their watches only.

Tho' many of these articles are almost peculiar to the author's maps, they are of no less importance than any thing that has yet had a place amongst geographers. But want of room in the plate, has obliged me to leave out what would have very much assisted my explanation of the face of the country, I mean a section of it in several directions; such would have exhibited the rising and falling of the ground, and how elevated above the surface of the sea; what parts are level, what rugged; where the mountains rise, and how far they spread. Nor is this all that a perpendicular section might be made to represent; for, as on the upper side, the elevations, depressions, outer appearances and names of places may be laid down; on the lower, the nature of the soil, substrata and particular fossils may be expressed. It was with regret I was obliged to omit it. But in some future maps of separate colonies, I hope to be furnished with more room.

The present, late and antient seats of the original inhabitants are

a. natures *Evans*] nature *LM*   b. is] is drawn *Evans*

expressed in the map; and though it might be imagined that several
nations are omitted, which are mentioned by authors, it may be
remarked, that authors, for want of knowledge in Indian affairs,
have taken every little society for a separate nation; whereas they
are not truly more in number than I have laid down. I have been
something particular in these sheets in representing the extent of
the country of the Confederates or Five Nations;[8] because, whatever
is theirs,[c] is expressly acceded to the English by treaty with the
French.

He has given a short table of latitude which will likewise
be of use to those who shall construct general maps. As he
writes chiefly for America he places his meridian at the
State-house in Philadelphia, but to facilitate the comparison
of his map with others he has added a computation of degrees
from London.

The principal observations of latitude are these,

Boston	42	25	
N. Boundary ⎱ Connecticut ⎰	42	2 ⎫	By Governor Burnet.
New–York	40	42 ⎭	
N. Station Point	41	40	By the Jersey and N. York
Philadelphia	39	57	Commissioners, 1719.
Shamokin	40	40 ⎫	
Owege	41	45 ⎪	
Onandaga	42	55 ⎬	By L. Evans.
Oswego	43	17 ⎪	
Sandy-Hook	40	28 ⎭	
Ray's Town	39	59 ⎫	By Col. Fry.
Shannopen's Town	40	26 ⎭	
S. Side of S. St. Louis	45	18 ⎫	By Champlain, in 1603.
Ville Marie[9]	45	27 ⎭	

As this treatise consists principally of descriptions of roads
disfigured by Indian names, and of authorities on which the

c. theirs] such *Evans*

---

8. The words "Confederates" and
"Five Nations" refer to the group of
tribes then known to the French, and

now generally, as the Iroquois.
9. Montreal.

map depends, it scarcely admits of extract or epitome. There are however interspersed some observations like green spots among barren mountains from which our readers will obtain a just idea of the situation and state of those untravelled countries.

To recount all the surveys of roads, tracts of land and general lines, that I have been favoured with, in the composition of my former map,[1] which makes so considerable a part of this, would be endless: but I must not omit here to repeat, with gratitude, my thanks, not only for the favours many gentlemen did me, but the chearfulness they shewed in assisting in a design intended for public service. It would have been almost impossible to have succeeded in the composition, notwithstanding all these helps, without my personal knowledge also of almost all the country it contained. One of the greatest mistakes in it arose, from my going from Kinderhook to Albany by night, where the skipper deceived me in the distance. An European may be at a loss to know, why there is a necessity for these sorts of helps in making a map of a country; for that reason it must be observed, that all America, east of Mississippi, low lands, hills and mountains, is every where covered with woods, except some interval spots of no great extent, cleared by the European colonists.[d] Here are no churches, towers, houses or peaked mountains to be seen from afar, no means of obtaining the bearings or distances of places, but by the compass and actual mensuration with the chain. The mountains are all almost so many ridges with even tops and nearly of a height. To look from these hills into the lower lands, is but as it were into an ocean of woods, swelled and depressed here and there by little inequalities, not to be distinguished, one part from another any more than the waves of the real ocean.

The uniformity of these mountains, though debarring us of an advantage in this respect, makes some amends in another. They are very regular in their courses, and confine the creeks and rivers that run between; and if we know where the gaps are, that let through these streams we are not at a loss to lay down their most considerable inflections.

On occasion of mentioning the Indians of Ohio, Mr. Evans gives a good account of the French designs and the means of opposing them.

d. colonists *conj.*] colonets *Evans, LM;* colonies *1789*

---

1. That of 1749; see p. 198 above.

I must not omit giving one caution to those in power, in this public manner, for I find from experience, that few are to be benefited from private information. Heretofore we apprehended no greater scheme of the French than making a communication[e] between Canada and the mouth of Missisippi. As this was remote, we thought ourselves but little interested in it. Now they attempt it nigher to us, by the way of Ohio, where they have begun an establishment; if this succeed, it is not Ohio only must fall under their dominion, but the country thence southward to the bay of Mexico. For that reason it becomes the English immediately to establish forts on the Cherokee river, and other passes in the way from Ohio to Moville,[2] before the French attempt to settle there, or draw off the Cherokees, Chicasaws, or Creeks from their friendship to the English. And supposing the French should be beaten off from the Ohio, 'tis ten to one but they will turn their forces, in hopes of better fortune, to the back of Carolina. We charge the Indians with fickleness, but with greater propriety we should charge ourselves with great want of sense or experience, in supposing any nation is to be tied to another, by any other thing[f] than interest. The Welinis[3] cultivated a friendship with the English for the sake of trade, and got leave of the Confederates to remove nigher them. They shewed both affection and resolution in the defence of the English at the Tawightawi town, where they lost out of 70, not less than 22 warriors on the spot: and though the French afterwards offered them very advantageous terms, they still persisted in their affection to us; and in their war with the French, amused[g] with expectation of relief, they were basely abandoned, without arms, and without ammunition, to the resentment of an enraged enemy. 'Tis a custom, established with the English, to purchase the friendship of wavering nations at a great expence, and to abandon their friends. Hence those who know this mixture of weakness and baseness that possesses us, keep members of council in the French interest as well as ours, as the Confederates do, to keep us under a perpetual contribution; while those nations who are truly in our interest are entirely slighted.

If we secure the country back of Carolina in time, we shall yet defeat the very point that it is the French interest to pursue; I mean a communication between the Ohio and Moville. Whatever we

e. a communication] a chain of communication *Evans*   f. any other thing] any thing *Evans*   g. us ... amused *Evans*] us, and in their war with the French. Amused *LM*

2. Mobile, Alabama, founded by   Louisiana until 1720.
the French in 1702, and capital of   3. Illinois.

may surmise in regard to the great river Missisippi being the only channel fitted for the inland commerce of Florida, and no other would suit the French, we shall find ourselves extremely mistaken. Even now the French scarce ever come up that river by water, by reason of its great and uniform rapidity, scarce to be stemm'd in a canoe and six oars in mid-channel. This obliges the French, in coming up, to take to the river Rouge, notwithstanding they are obliged to make one or two very long portages. The edges are less rapid in the Missisippi, but then the enmity of the Indians on its banks prevents their keeping so near the shore. Therefore, to make what use this river is capable of, the French must secure the country of the Chicasaws and Cherokees; and then Moville, and not New Orleans, will be the center of the French trade of Florida; since the latter though scarce forty leagues up the Missisippi, by reason of the rapidity of the river, is not reached with ships in less than 30 or 40 days from the mouth; and Moville is upon Tide-water. If in pursuit of our present point on Ohio, we shew any remissness in our attachment to the safety of those Indians, who are our friends, or we neglect to secure the country back of Carolina, the defection of the Indians there is inevitable; since the French have long known the consequence of it, tho' much to their cost. The public may be amused with a notion that we have forts and settlements there already, as represented in some maps, published with great authority ——I can only say, That I wish either were true. Itinerant trading is not a settlement,[h] in the sense the English use the word, nor a house built of logs of wood, without order or artillery, or garrison a fort in any sense.

The Ontario, on the south-east corner of which stands Oswego, is thus described,

Ontario or Cataraqui is a beautiful lake of fresh water, very deep, and has a moderate steep bank and gravelly shore along the south side: the rivers which fall into it are apt to be sometimes barred at the entrances. This, like the Mediterranean, the Caspian and other large invasated waters, has a small rising and falling of the water like tides, some 12 or 18 inches perpendicular, occasioned by the changes in the state of the atmosphere; rising higher, as the weight of the incumbent air is less, and falling as it becomes greater. This lake is best fitted for the passage of batteaux and canoes, along the south side, the other having several rocks near the surface of the water; but the middle is every where safe for shipping. The snow is

h. settlement *italicized by Evans*

deeper on the south side of this lake, than any other place in these parts; but the lake does not freeze, in the severest winter, out of sight of land. The strait of Oghniágara, between the lake Ontario and Erie, is easily passable some five or six miles with any ships, or ten miles in all with canoes; then you are obliged to make a portage up three pretty sharp hills about eight miles, where there is now cut a pretty good cart-way. This portage is made to avoid that stupendous fall of Oghniágara, which in one place precipitates headlong five or six and twenty fathoms, and continues for six or seven miles more to tumble in little falls, and run with inconceivable rapidity. And indeed the strait for a mile or two is so rapid, above the fall, that it is not safe venturing near it. They embark again at the fishing battery, and thence to Lake Erie it is eighteen miles and the stream so swift, that the stiffest gale is scarce sufficient to stem it in a ship; but it is easily passed in canoes, where the current here, as in all other places, is less rapid along the shore.

Lake Erie has a fine sandy shore on the north side; and in many places such, on the other, especially towards the south-east part. The weather and climate of this is far more moderate than that of Ontario.

He concludes his pamphlet with some observations which may be of great use in the present system of European policy, but which will not prove that this system is right, or in other words, that it is more productive than any other of universal happiness.

Were there nothing at stake between the crowns of Britain and France, but the lands on that part of the Ohio included in this map, we may reckon it as great a prize, as has ever yet been contended for between two nations; but if we further observe, that this is scarce a quarter of the valuable land, that is contained in one continued extent, and the influence that a state, vested with all the wealth and power that will naturally arise from the culture of so great an extent of good land in a happy climate, it will make so great an addition to that nation which wins it, where there is no third state to hold the balance of power that the loser must inevitably sink under his rival. It is not as two nations at war, contending the one for the other's habitations; where the conquered on submission, would be admitted to partake of the privileges of the conquerors; but for a vast country exceeding in extent and good land all the European dominions of Britain, France and Spain, almost destitute of inhabitants, and will as fast as the Europeans settle become more so of its former inhabitants. Had his Majesty been made acquainted with its value, the large strides the French have been making, for several years past, in their incroachments on his dominions; and the measures still taken to keep the colonies disunited, and of impeding the generous attempts of his most zealous subjects, it is impossible to conceive that[i] his Majesty would have sacrificed, to the spleen of a few bitter spirits, the best gem in his crown. It is not yet too late to retrieve the whole, *provided* the British plantations are not thought to be grown already too large—if such an opinion prevails, an opportunity now offers of soon making them less. We may reckon the representation of the extent and power of the plantations being great and that such power may be dangerous to their mother-country, amongst the greatest of vulgar errors. Any person, who knows the nature of the soil, and the extent of our settlements, will confess that all the lands, worth the culture from New Hampshire to Carolina, and extended as far back as there are planters settled within three or four miles of one another, though including nine colonies, is not equal in quantity to half the arable land in England. All the whites in the remainder of the British colonies on the continent scarce amount to 120,000 souls. How different is this from the conceits of those who would represent some single colonies as equal to all England. The Massachusets though made such a bug-bear, as if its inhabitants were so rich and numerous, as that they might one day be able to dispute dominion with England, is not as large as Yorkshire, nor has half so much arable land. Supposing the colonies were grown rich and powerful, what inducement have they to throw off their independency?[4] National ties of blood and friendship, mutual dependencies for support and assistance in their civil and military interests, with England; each colony having a particular form of government of its own, and the jealousy of any one's[j] having the superiority over the rest, are unsurmountable obstacles to their ever uniting, to the prejudice of England, upon any ambitious views of their own. But, that repeated and continued ill usage, infringements of their dear-bought privileges, sacrificing them to the ambition and intrigues of domestic and foreign enemies, may not provoke them to do their utmost, for their own preservation, I would not pretend to say, as weak as they are. But while they are treated as members of one body, and allowed their natural rights, it would be the height of madness

i. it . . . that] *Evans places this clause at the beginning of the sentence*   j. any one's] either's *Evans*

---

4. Both Evans and the *Literary Magazine* give "independency," but surely this is a mistake for "dependency."

for them to propose an independency, were they ever so strong. If they had any ambitious views, a strong colony, of a natural enemy to England, on their borders, would be the only article that would render any attempt of independency truly dangerous; and for that reason it becomes those who would regard the future interest of Britain and its colonies, to suppress the growth of the French power, and not the English, in America.

If his Majesty would be pleased to appoint a colony to be made on the Ohio,[k] with a separate governor, and an equitable form of government, a full liberty of conscience, and the same secured by charter; not all that the French could project would give it any impediment after a few years. The importance of such a colony to Britain would be vastly great, since the climate, and its remoteness from the sea, would turn it immediately to raising raw silk, an article of vast expence to our nation, which[l] we are at continual difficulties and disappointments in procuring. The charge of carriage of this article from the remotest parts to the sea, is too inconsiderable to affect its value. Ohio is naturally furnished with salt, coal, limestone, grindstone, millstone, clay for glass-houses and pottery, which are of vast advantage to an inland country, and well deserving the notice I take of them in the map.

In settling a colony there, let care be taken against the scandalous ingrossing the land by private persons or public companies—and for that purpose, let any piece of land left unimproved three years, after surveying, and containing more than 500 acres to a family, be free for any person to settle on; and the first owner be obliged to go further for land, when disposed to settle—And let[m] all lands appropriated and lying unimproved or unsettled be liable to threefold taxes, compared with the adjacent improved lands of like goodness; for supposing one part be allotted for its true value, the remaining two thirds will be far short, at a mean, from making up the deficiency of the excise, duties, watching, civil and military services of those who truly settle and improve.

Upon these pompous paragraphs let a man whose course of life has acquainted him very little with American affairs, venture to make a few observations.

This great country for which we are so warmly incited to contend, will not be honestly our own though we keep it from the French. It will indeed, he says, be deserted by its inhabitants, and we shall then have an addition of land greater

k. on the Ohio] in Ohio *Evans*   l. which] and that *Evans*   m. let] that *Evans*

than a fourth part of Europe. This is magnificent in prospect, but will lose much of its beauty on a nearer view. An increase of lands without increase of people gives no increase of power or of wealth, but lies open to assaults without defenders, and may disgrace those who lose it without inriching those that shall gain it.

It is indeed supposed by our author to receive inhabitants from Europe; but we must remember that it will very little advance the power of the English to plant colonies on the Ohio by dispeopling their native country. And since the end of all human actions is happiness, why should any number of our inhabitants be banished from their trades and their homes to a trackless desart, where life is to begin anew, and where they can have no other accommodation, than their own hands shall immediately procure them. What advantage even upon supposition of, what is scarcely to be supposed, an un-interrupted possession and unimpeded improvement, can arise equivalent to the exile of the first planters, and difficulties to be encountered by their immediate descendants.[5]

We have at home more land than we cultivate, and more materials than we manufacture; by proper regulations we may employ all our people, and give every man his chance of rising to the full enjoyment of all the pleasures and advantages of a civilised and learned country.

I know not indeed, whether we can at home procure any great quantity of raw silk, which we are told is to be had in so great plenty upon the banks of the Ohio. Away therefore with thousands and millions to those dreadful desarts, that we may no longer want raw silk. Who that had not often observed how much one train of thought sometimes occupies the mind could think so wild a project seriously proposed?

The fear that the American colonies will break off their dependence on England, I have always thought, with this writer, chimerical and vain.[6] Yet though he endeavours for

---

5. Later expressions of SJ's views on the undesirability of emigration are found in his *Journey to the Western Islands of Scotland* (Vol. IX of this edition).

6. Gipson and others have accused SJ of being a bad prophet here, but this is unjust. SJ makes it clear that his prediction that the American colonies will not break away rests on

his present purpose to shew the absurdity of such suspicions, he does not omit to hint at something that is to be feared if they are not well used. Every man and every society is intitled to all the happiness that can be enjoyed with the security of the whole community. From this general claim the Americans ought not to be excluded, but let us not be frightned by their threats, they must be yet dependent, and if they forsake us, or be forsaken by us, must fall into the hands of France.

---

the assumption of the continuation of the French threat to their security. When that threat had been eliminated by the war just commencing, and the Americans no longer needed military protection by Britain, these terms no longer applied.

REVIEWS OF PAMPHLETS ON THE CASE
OF ADMIRAL BYNG. 1756.

"The trial and execution of Admiral the Honourable John Byng was one of the most cold-blooded and cynical acts of judicial murder in the whole of British history."[1] So begins a recent book recounting the affair, and there have been few of the many commentators on it, from the time it took place to the present, who have not arrived at a similar verdict. One has at least to go back to such political executions of the seventeenth century as those of Sir Walter Raleigh and Lord Russell for an analogy, and even in these the victims were thought to offer some kind of potential danger to the government of the day. Nothing of the sort can be alleged of Byng; he was an utterly harmless, well intentioned, not very distinguished professional sailor whom the Prime Minister, the Duke of Newcastle, and the First Lord of the Admiralty, Anson, picked as a sacrifice to try to distract the British public from their own administrative inefficiency and faulty judgement.

That they failed conspicuously to do so is a tribute to the independence of mind of the more literate British public of the eighteenth century, and to the freedom of the British press. The British Museum library catalogue lists somewhere in the neighbourhood of sixty contemporary pamphlets on the affair, and the newspapers and magazines were full of it for many months. Even in the twentieth century, judging by the amount that still continues to be published about it, it has not yet lost its interest as a warning example of what arbitrary governmental power is capable of perpetrating.

Credit too is due to two great publicists of the eighteenth century, one French and one English, in arousing public indignation over the matter. Voltaire immortalized it, two years later, in an unforgettable passage in *Candide*, with an apothegm that has become a proverb: "Dans ce pays-ci il est bon de tuer de temps en temps un amiral pour encourager les autres." Less well known is Voltaire's attempt, though France and England were

---

1. Dudley Pope, *At Twelve Mr. Byng Was Shot* (1962), p. xi. Pope's is the fullest account yet given. See also W. C. B. Tunstall, *Byng and the Loss of Minorca* (1928) and E. G. French, *The Martyrdom of Admiral Byng* (1961). Tunstall devotes considerable space to Johnson's part in the affair, space largely wasted, however, since he is under the misapprehension that Johnson wrote the pamphlets, rather than the reviews of them. The motive for French's book is to draw a parallel between Byng's victimization and the supersession, in 1916, of the author's father, Sir John French, as commander-in-chief of the British forces in World War One. James A. Butler, "Johnson: Defender of Admiral Byng," *Cornell Library Journal*, No. 7 (Winter, 1969), pp. 25–47, sheds useful light on the circumstances surrounding the composition of *The Conduct of the Ministry Impartially Examined* (1756), the last of the pamphlets reviewed by Johnson.

then at war, to help Byng by writing to him during his trial by court martial, enclosing a letter from the Maréchal Duc de Richelieu, commander of the French forces that had opposed him at Minorca, testifying in glowing terms to Byng's conduct there.[2] But even this chivalric action had no effect on those who had determined on his death—primarily Anson, one supposes, rather than the weaker-minded Newcastle.

Johnson's endeavours are still less well known. The reviews below, which appeared in the *Literary Magazine* during his editorship of it in the first year of the Seven Years' War, have seldom been reprinted (one has apparently never been reprinted until now). To the modern student they are not particularly interesting reading. Johnson's own comments, when they do appear, are pungent enough—"Mr. Byng is stigmatized with infamy, and pursued with clamours artfully excited to divert the public attention from the crimes and blunders of other men, and . . . while he is thus vehemently pursued for imaginary guilt, the real criminals are hoping to escape." But they appear rarely, and the bulk of the reviews consists in long extracts from the pamphlets under review, setting out in detail the relative strengths of Byng's fleet and the opposing French one, printing in full documents suppressed or mutilated by the government, and the like. It must be remembered that the case of Byng was still *sub judice*—his execution did not take place until March 1757—and Johnson, as a responsible journalist, is concerned to put before his readers, with full documentation, the evidence in the case, which the government was anxious to hide, so that they can scrutinize it and judge for themselves. In the end, of course, Johnson's efforts were no more successful than Voltaire's, or than Johnson's later crusade (1777) to save William Dodd from the barbarous punishment of death by hanging for forgery.

To go into all the ramifications of the Byng affair would require a substantial book—and indeed such books continue to be published. A brief outline may help the reader to follow the sequence of events. Throughout 1755 and early 1756, the outbreak of fully declared war with France appeared inevitable. The actual declaration took place on 18 May 1756, but hostilities had already commenced in America, where Braddock had been disastrously defeated in July 1755, and in India. In Europe, an uneasy peace still prevailed, but alarming reports were received from British intelligence agents on the Continent of massive French preparations for an invasion of England across the Channel. In the end, nothing of the kind was attempted, and Johnson was presently to pooh-pooh "the flat-bottomed boats, built, I suppose, in the clouds, and now lost in the clouds again."[3] But the reports were sufficiently disturbing in an island where, only a decade before, the Young Pretender, with French aid, had for a time looked as if he were carrying out a successful conquest. There were also reports that a French fleet was massing at Toulon, with a view to an assault on the

2. Pope, pp. 246–49. Voltaire's letter was opened by the Post Office and circulated among the ministry before being transmitted to Byng. See also Voltaire, *Correspondence*, ed. Theodore Besterman (1958), Nos. 6400, 6413.

3. See p. 258 below.

strategic British naval base in Minorca, protected only by a tiny squadron and garrison. For defence against this double-pronged threat, a cross-Channel attack and one in the Mediterranean, Newcastle and Anson were in a dilemma about how to distribute their limited naval forces. They made what turned out to be the wrong decision—to keep the bulk of the Royal Navy in home waters for protection against the invasion that never materialized, and to send only a skimpy force to the Mediterranean. The command of this force was given, in March 1756, to the fifty-two-year-old John Byng, a younger son of a most distinguished figure in British naval history, Admiral George Byng, first Viscount Torrington, hero of the Battle of Cape Passaro in 1718, and later Walpole's First Lord of the Admiralty. Young John, only fourteen, had been present as a midshipman at that battle (as had young George Anson, a twenty-one-year-old lieutenant); and, though he failed to duplicate his father's brilliance, had had a respectable enough professional career in the Navy, having risen by 1756 to the rank of Vice-Admiral of the Red Squadron (highest of the three grades of vice-admiral); on his appointment to command the Minorca force, he was promoted to Admiral of the Blue. The quantity and quality of the ships, men, and supplies allotted him later became the subject of much controversy; but obviously Anson, the First Lord, was husbanding his resources for the threatened invasion, and they were not generous. Difficulties of manning, fitting, and supplying his ships delayed Byng in Portsmouth, and his force did not set sail for the Mediterranean until 5 April. Four days later, in Toulon, the French admiral, the Marquis de la Galissonière, sailed for Minorca with a fleet about equal in number of ships to Byng's (but, as was later argued, considerably stronger in man- and fire-power), convoying 15,000 troops commanded by Richelieu. The tiny British squadron off Minorca could not prevent the force from landing (on 17 April) and laying siege to the British garrison of 2,500, under old General Blakeney, who had fortified themselves in Fort San Felipe (St. Philip), overlooking the harbour of Port Mahon. Blakeney's force defended themselves gallantly, while La Galissonière's fleet patrolled the waters around the island.

Byng encountered foul weather in the Bay of Biscay, and did not succeed in reaching Gibraltar until 2 May. There he discovered the dockyard, where he had hoped to refit his battered ships, in disrepair. Moreover, the Governor, Lieutenant-General Thomas Fowke, afraid that after Minorca the French would turn their strength against Gibraltar, was reluctant to supply him with additional forces from his garrison. From Gibraltar Byng sent the Admiralty his dispatch of 4 May, printed in the first review below, warning it of the strong position of the French and the unlikelihood of his being able to retake Minorca with the forces at his disposal. He mentioned the probability of the French then making an attempt on Gibraltar, and wrote, "If I should fail in the relief of Port Mahon, I shall look upon the security of Gibraltar as my next object, and shall repair down here with the squadron." Byng then set sail for Minorca, encountered the French fleet, and fought the action described in his dispatch of 25 May, in which, after receiving some damage from the French, he broke it off and returned to

Gibraltar. In the circumstances an argument can be made for Byng's caution; to have imperilled the existence of his fleet might well have meant the loss of Gibraltar as well as Minorca.

Meanwhile, the ministry in London had obtained a copy of La Galissonière's report of the action to his own government, which tended to glorify his own aggressiveness and minimize Byng's. Without waiting to learn more, Anson and Newcastle seized on this vague hint that Byng was wanting in courage as an escape from their own responsibility for the loss of Minorca (Blakeney surrendered Fort San Felipe on 29 June). Anson immediately relieved Byng of his command and ordered his return to England, where he was put under arrest and a court martial convened. Some of the four admirals and nine captains of the court were obviously selected because they had professional or political reasons for hostility to Byng.

Because of the need for bringing back witnesses from the Mediterranean and elsewhere, the trial did not begin until 28 December 1756. Meanwhile, the ministry did what it could to prejudice the public against Byng. His dispatch of 4 May, in which he described his inability to get his ships properly repaired and supplied at Gibraltar and expressed his concern for losing Gibraltar, was not made public; what was printed instead in the *London Gazette*, the vehicle for official government notices, was his dispatch of 25 May, unscrupulously edited so as to distort the truth of the situation. For instance, where Byng had written, "I am making the best of my way to cover Gibraltar," the word "cover" was deleted, so as to make the sentence appear a weak confession of fear instead of the announcement of a valid strategical plan. As a result of these tactics, there was much public outcry against Byng, some of it instigated, according to Byng's defenders, by government agents. Byng was burnt in effigy, mobs threatened to destroy his country seat, lampooning ballads were sold. But presently the truth began to emerge, in such pamphlets as the first three reviewed by Johnson below, and public indignation began to turn away from Byng and toward the ministry. Nevertheless, Anson and Newcastle held on their course, with Pitt, now in and now out of the ministry, playing an ambiguous role. On 27 January 1757, the court martial found Byng guilty on various counts, including that of a breach of the 12th Naval Article of War, by failing "through cowardice, negligence, or disaffection" to "do his utmost to take or destroy every ship which it shall be his duty to engage." For this there was only one penalty prescribed, death. The court nevertheless added a plea for mercy. But attempts to secure a pardon or a reconsideration of the verdict were resisted by the ministry, and Byng was put to death by a firing squad on the quarterdeck of H.M.S. *Monarch* in Portsmouth harbour at noon on 14 March 1757—"To the perpetual disgrace of public justice," as the tablet in his family vault reads; "A martyr to political persecution."

Johnson's involvement in the affair needs no other explanation than his detestation, like Voltaire's, of such callous and cynical injustice, and the fact that he was then in charge of a journal which he had dedicated to relentless criticism of the government then in power and of the savage world war which that government had embarked on. But there were two personal connexions that might have reinforced his views. Lord Anson, the chief persecutor of Byng, was a native of Shugborough, near Lichfield. Though famous for his voyage round the world in the 1740's, he was also an active Whig politician, an unscrupulous infighter, who had allied his family with the powerful Staffordshire Whig magnates, the Leveson Gowers ("*Renegado —sometimes* we say a *Gower*"), to wrest the parliamentary representation of Johnson's native Lichfield from the Tories in the bitterly fought election of 1747. Johnson's hostile stepson, Captain Jervis Porter, R.N., seems to have been one of Anson's henchmen. Later, the Anson family were rewarded with the title of Earls of Lichfield, as the Gowers were with that of Marquesses of Staffordshire.[4]

On the other side, Captain the Honourable Augustus Hervey, later third Earl of Bristol, had served under Byng at Minorca, was his personal friend, and one of his most vigorous defenders, giving copious evidence on his behalf during the trial, writing pamphlets in his defence, organizing petitions, even contemplating a scheme to help Byng escape to freedom after the death sentence had been passed. Johnson's affection for the Hervey family is well known—"If you call a dog Hervey, I shall love him." For one of Augustus's brothers, the Reverend Henry Hervey Aston, Johnson composed a charity sermon delivered in St. Paul's, and to another, Thomas, gave good advice regarding his unfortunate marital affairs.[5]

4. See *Politics*, pp. 39–40, 297–98. The editors of SJ's poems (Vol. VI of this edition, pp. 256–57) speculate that a sardonic epigram on Anson composed by SJ may be accounted for by the Admiralty's ignoring Zachariah Williams's scheme for determining the longitude, or, as an earlier writer suggested, the fact that "providence is not mentioned in Anson's *Voyage*." SJ's hostility toward Anson is more easily explained in terms of their Lichfield backgrounds. See p. 353 below for a slighting reference by SJ to Anson's voyage.

5. For the sermon for Henry Hervey Aston, see James L. Clifford's introduction to *A Sermon Preached at the Cathedral Church of Saint Paul, Before the Sons of the Clergy* ([Augustan Reprint Society], 1955). For Thomas Hervey, see *Mr. Hervey's Answer to a Letter He Received from Dr. Samuel Johnson, wherein he had endeavoured to dissuade him from parting with his supposed wife* (1772). *Augustus Hervey's Journal*, ed. David Erskine (1953), contains a great deal about the Byng affair. Horace Walpole was also active: he collected numerous pamphlets about Byng, and he wrote "Queries" that Augustus Hervey published in the *London Chronicle*.

REVIEW OF *A LETTER TO A MEMBER OF PARLIAMENT* AND *AN APPEAL TO THE PEOPLE.* 1756.

The two pamphlets that Johnson deals with here were published early in October 1756 and were the opening of the counter-attack on the ministry by Byng's friends. The first, *A Letter to a Member of Parliament in the Country from his friend in London Relative to the Case of Admiral Byng: With Some Original Papers and Letters Which passed during the Expedition,* is thought to be by Paul Whitehead, a somewhat disreputable minor poet and hack writer, who was apparently commissioned by Byng's defenders (headed by Augustus Hervey) to act as their chief "public relations" man. Whitehead remained close to Byng and Hervey throughout the months before, during, and after the trial by court martial, helping Byng to prepare his defence and generally organizing publicity on his behalf. The second, *An Appeal to the People* (its full title is given in the heading to the review itself, except for its conclusion, "Part the First"), was apparently by the perennial opposition gadfly, Dr. John Shebbeare, a little later to be imprisoned and pilloried by the Pitt-Newcastle administration for sedition, but still later, under George III and Bute, to be rewarded by a pension at the same time that Johnson was. Johnson does a competent job of combining the contents of the two into a masterly statement of the case against Anson and Newcastle.

The review was first attributed to Johnson in the supplementary "Volume xiv" of his *Works* (1788), where it is reprinted, pp. 427–55, with a footnote, "Both this and the subsequent article [the review of *The Conduct of the Ministry*] were originally printed in the *Literary Magazine.* They are ascribed to Dr. Johnson on conjecture." The attribution has never been questioned. The text below follows that of the *Literary Magazine,* No. 6 (15 Sept–15 Oct 1756), pp. 299–309. Quotation, generally indicated in the *LM* by the use of inverted commas in the margin, is indicated here by smaller type. The *LM*'s quotations show some variants from the texts in the *Letter* and *Appeal,* some of them probably the result of haste and carelessness, others for the purpose of condensation. (And the texts in the *Letter* and *Appeal* themselves show small variants from the original printings of the documents they quote.) Only those of some significance are indicated in the notes; they nowhere give the impression of having been made deliberately to strengthen the writer's arguments.

218

A Letter to a Member of Parliament in the Country,
from His Friend in London, Relative to the
Case of Ad. Byng. Cook.

Also an Appeal to the People, Containing the
Genuine and Entire Letter of Admiral Byng to the
Secr. of the A——y: Observations on Those Parts of It
Which Were Omitted by the Writers of the *Gazette:*
And What Might Be the Reasons for Such Omissions.
Morgan.

To hear both parties, and to condemn no man without
a trial are the unalterable laws of justice. The man who
lately commanded the English fleet in the Mediterranean;
after having had his effigies burnt in a hundred places, and
his name disgraced by innumerable lampoons; after having
suffered all that the malice of wit or folly could inflict on his
reputation, now stands forth, and demands an audience
from those who have almost universally condemned him,
but condemned him in his own opinion without justice,
and certainly without any calm or candid examination.

In this extract we shall join the two apologies together,
and give the argument which shall result from their con-
currences.

The general position which both pamphlets endeavour
to prove is, that Mr. Byng is stigmatised with infamy, and
pursued with clamours artfully excited to divert the public
attention from the crimes and blunders of other men, and
that while he is thus vehemently pursued for imaginary
guilt, the real criminals are hoping to escape. To make this
probable, a detail is given of the conduct of the admiral,
and the practices of his enemies, and reasons at least specious
are offered why the persecution has exceeded the crime.

The first offence which the admiral is supposed to have
given the ministry was by the following letter.

Ramillies,[1] in Gibraltar-Bay, May 4, 1756.

Sir,

This comes to you by express from hence by the way of Madrid, recommended to Sir Benjamin Keene, his Majesty's minister at that place, to be forwarded with the utmost expedition.

I arrived here with the squadron under my command, the 2d instant in the afternoon, after a tedious passage of twenty-seven days, occasioned by contrary winds and calms, and was extremely concerned to hear from Capt. Edgcumbe[2] (who I found here with the *Princess Louisa* and *Fortune* sloop) that he was obliged to retire from Minorca, the French having landed on that island by all accounts from thirteen to fifteen thousand men.

They sailed from Toulon the 10th of last month, with about one hundred and sixty, or two hundred sail of transports, escorted by thirteen sail of men of war; how many of the line[3] I have not been able to learn with any certainty.

If I had been so happy to have arrived at Mahon, before the French had landed, I flatter myself, I should have been able to have prevented their getting a footing on that island; but as it has so unfortunately turned out, I am firmly of opinion, from the great force they have landed, and the quantity of provisions, stores and ammunition of all kinds they brought with them, that the throwing men into the castle,[4] will only enable it to hold out but a little longer,[a] and add to the numbers that must fall into the enemy's[b] hands; for the garrison in time will be obliged to surrender, unless a sufficient number of men could be landed to dislodge the French, or raise the siege: however, I am determined to sail up to Minorca with the squadron, where I shall be a better judge of the situation of affairs there, and will give General Blakeney all the assistance he shall require; though I am afraid all communication will be cut off between us, as is the opinion of the chief engineers of this garrison (who have served in the island) and that of the other officers of the artillery, who are acquainted with the situation of the harbour; for if the enemy have erected batteries on the two shores near the entrance of the harbour (an advantage scarce to be supposed they have neglected) it will render it impossible for our boats to have a passage to the sallee port of the garrison.

a. little longer] little time longer *Letter*   b. enemy's *Letter*] enemies *LM*

1. Byng's flagship. Following modern practice, names of ships are italicized in the present text. Usage in the copy-text is inconsistent.

2. The Hon. George Edgcumbe, commander of the small British squadron that had been at Minorca.

3. Line-of-battle ships (later abbreviated to "battleships").

4. Fort San Felipe (or St. Philip), now occupied by four British regiments commanded by General William Blakeney.

By the inclosed list, delivered to me by Capt. Edgcumbe, their lordships[5] will observe the strength of the French ships in Toulon, and by the copy of a letter from Marseilles to General Blakeney, which I herewith transmit to you, their lordships will perceive the equipment the French have made on this occasion. It is to be apprehended, when they have got all the ships they possibly can ready for service, they may think of turning their thoughts this way.[6]

If I should fail in the relief of Port-mahon, I shall look upon the security of Gibraltar as my next object, and shall repair down here with the squadron.[7]

The *Chesterfield*, *Portland* and *Dolphin* are on their passage from Mahon for this place. The *Phoenix* is gone to Leghorn by order of Capt. Edgcumbe for letters and intelligence; and the *Experiment* is cruising off Cape Pallas, whom I expect in every hour.[8]

By a letter from Mr. Banks, our consul at Carthagena, to General Fowke,[9] dated the 21st of April, it appears that twelve sail of Spanish men of war are ordered for Cadiz and Ferrol, which are expected at that port, but on what account he could not tell the Governor.

We are employed in taking in wine and compleating our water, with the utmost dispatch, and shall let no opportunity slip of sailing from hence.

Herewith I send you inclosed a copy of such papers as have been delivered me, which I thought necessary for their lordships' inspection.

I am, Sir,
Your most humble servant,
J. B.

Hon. J——n C——d, Esq;[1]

---

5. The Lords Commissioners of the Admiralty, headed by Anson. All operation orders from the Admiralty were issued in their collective name, and all dispatches addressed to them, through the Secretary of the Admiralty.

6. I.e., to Gibraltar.

7. Three paragraphs that follow in the *Letter to a Member of Parliament* are omitted in the *LM*. In them Byng complains of his inability to get his ships repaired and supplied in Gibraltar.

8. The ships listed in this paragraph, together with the *Princess Louisa*, mentioned above, constituted Edgcumbe's Minorca squadron. None carried as many as sixty-four guns, then generally considered the minimum for a line-of-battle ship. The *Phoenix* was commanded by Captain Augustus Hervey.

9. Lieutenant-General Thomas Fowke, Governor of Gibraltar. He too was later recalled and court-martialled for disobeying the War Office's order to send reinforcements from his garrison to Minorca with Byng. He was cashiered from the service.

1. John Clevland (or Cleveland), Secretary of the Admiralty.

This letter was carefully suppressed, it being not convenient that the people should know that he already found "his arrival too late" and "his force too weak," that his "ships were foul" or "his stores short," or the "works of Gibraltar neglected and ruinous."[2] However, he was punished for this uncertain intelligence by an oraculous anticipation of cowardice, and a report diligently spread that "he would not fight."

To prove that what he asserted of the superiority of the French to the English squadron is not the fiction of art or the double sight of cowardice, he gives the following table of their different strength.[3]

In the first place, the number of ships was equal on each side; from this then no advantage was to be drawn by one party above another. As the frigates on either side did not engage, notwithstanding the French exceeded the English, greatly in number of men and weight of metal, I shall not attempt to derive from that circumstance any argument of the superiority of the French fleet to that of the English, but consider those ships which were drawn up in line of battle, only[4] remarking the weakness of that objection to the conduct of the admiral, in leaving the *Deptford* out of the line; when the same thing was done by Monsieur La Gallissonniere in not taking the *Junon* into his line; the first being of forty-eight guns, and the latter of forty-six.

The number of ships being equal, the next consideration is the number of guns; and in this article, according to this list, which was received from a person the best enabled to give a just account, and the least to be suspected of doing the contrary, the French fleet exceeded the English by fifty cannon, the number of the first being eight hundred twenty-eight, and of the second seven hundred seventy-eight, which gives a majority of fifty on the side of the French; but as it may be objected, that, according to other lists printed by authority, the *Hipopothame* and *Fier* are given as fifty gun ships only, we will suppose that to be the right, and then the

---

2. Though, oddly, SJ (or the printer) omits the portion of Byng's letter from which the quoted phrases are taken (see n. 7, p. 221).

3. The Table on the opposite page appears in *LM* at this point; both the

Table and what follows are quoted from *An Appeal to the People*, pp. 26–32.

4. Perhaps the punctuation here should be "battle only, remarking."

The honourable Admiral Byng's Squadron, when he engaged M. De La Galassonniere's off Cape Mola, 20 May, 1756.

Ships Names.	Guns	Wt of metal on the			men.
		low dec. (lb.)	mid dec. (lb.)	upp dec. (lb.)	
Ramilies -	90	32	18	12	780
Culloden -	74	32		18	600
Buckingham -	68	32		18	535
Lancaster -	66	32		18	520
Trident -	64	24		12	500
Intrepid -	64	32		18	480
Captain -	64	24		12	480
Revenge -	64	24		12	480
Kingston -	60	24		9	400
Defiance -	60	24		12	400
Princess Louisa -	56	24		12	400
Portland -	48	24		12	300
	778				5875
Frigates.					
Deptford -	48				280
Chesterfield -	40				250
Phoenix -	22				160
Dolphin -	22				160
Experiment -	22				160
Total	932				6885

M. De La Galassonniere's Squadron, when he landed the troops at Minorca 18 April, and at the engagement with Admiral Byng's Squadron off Cape Mola 20 May, 1756.

Ships Names.	Guns	wt of met. on the		Number of		Total men on board each ship.
		low dec. (lb.)	upp dec. (lb.)	Seamen	Soldiers	
Foudroyant	84	52	24	700	250	950
La Couronne	74	42	24	650	150	800
Le Guerrier	74	42	24	650	150	800
Le Temeraire	74	42	24	650	150	800
Le Redoutable	74	42	24	650	150	800
l'Hipopothame	64	36	24	500	100	600
Le Fier	64	36	24	500	100	600
Le Triton	64	36	24	500	100	600
Le Lion	64	36	24	500	100	600
Le Contant	64	36	24	500	100	600
Le Sage	64	36	24	500	100	600
L' Orphée	64	36	24	500	100	600
	828			6800	1550	8350
Frigates.						
La Juno	46			300		300
La Roze	30			250		250
La Gracieuse	30			250		250
La Topaze	24			250		250
La Nymphe	24			200		200
Total	982			8050	1550	9600

number of French cannon exceeds the English by twenty-two guns only.

The next article which comes in^e consideration is the weight of metal; and in this place it seems necessary to remark, that it is the usual custom to denominate the weight of metal by the guns which are on the whole decks only; hence it happens, tho' three sizes are only mentioned in the list of the *Ramillies*, and two in that of the *Foudroyant*, that there were ten of the number on board the *Ramillies* on the quarter deck and forecastle, which carried six pounds only, and on board the *Foudroyant* twenty-four, which placed in the same parts mentioned in the *Ramillies*, carried only shot of twelve pounds.

The *Foudroyant* and *Ramillies* then may be thus considered with respect to the cannon which each carried.

	Foudroyant.			*Ramillies.*	
Guns.	Weight of shot.		Guns.	Weight of shot.	
30	of	52 pounds.	26	of	52 pounds.
30		24	26		18
24		12	28		12
—		——	10		6
84		2268 lb. each charge.	—		——
—		——	90		1696 lb. each charge.
			—		——

Deducting then the lesser from the greater number, the weight of the shot fired by the *Foudroyant* in a discharge of all the cannon,[5] exceeds that of the *Ramillies* by five hundred seventy-two pounds, almost a third of the whole quantity. The number of men on board the English ship, was seven hundred and thirty:[6] on board the French, nine hundred and fifty: which gives a majority of two hundred and twenty men to the French ship. Now, on a medium,[7] we may allow eight men to a gun on board the *Foudroyant*, as her metal is heavier, and six to a gun on board the *Ramillies;* this will make six hundred seventy-two at the great guns, and two hundred and seventy-eight at the small arms, on board the French ship;

c. in] under *Appeal*

---

5. The standard form of engagement in eighteenth- to twentieth-century naval warfare was by broadside salvos of line-of-battle ships; total weight of metal discharged in a salvo was therefore of prime importance.

6. The table in the *Appeal*, as in the *LM*, reads "780."

7. Average.

and five hundred and forty at the great guns, and one hundred and ninety at the small arms, on board the *Ramillies*, which gives a majority of eighty-eight small arms men to the *Foudroyant*, almost a third superior to the *Ramillies*. In this account we have computed the officers and others employed in various duties, amongst the small arms; and as each ship has probably an equal number engaged in these services, whatever is allowed, being allowed alike on board each ship, it leaves the same proportion amongst the small arms men; this then effects nothing on the validity of the reasoning.

Let me then imagine them all engaged on board each ship, the *Foudroyant* discharging from the small arms, two hundred and seventy-eight balls, and the *Ramillies* one hundred and ninety, the French ship's fire in this respect exceeds the English by eighty-eight balls in each general volley; let me suppose also, that a number of cannon equal to the whole sum in each ship, be discharged in a minute, which seems no improbable supposition, since cannon are fired twelve times in a minute in land service; the excess of weight of metal in the *Foudroyant*, compared with that fired by the *Ramillies* in one hour, will be thirty-four thousand three hundred and twenty pounds, a most amazing superiority. If we allow at the same time, four discharges of the small-arms in each minute, then the number of small shot fired from the *Foudroyant*, more than from the *Ramillies* in one hour, will be twenty-one thousand one hundred and twenty, which increases the chance of the men being killed on the upper decks on board the English ship equal to that number. The advantage drawn from the small arms, is then exactly in proportion to the number in which one ship exceeds another, and the advantage of the heavier shot discharged from the cannon, is as the diameter of each exceeds the other; let me suppose a thirty-two pound ball to be ten inches in diameter, such a shot can pass between two objects eleven inches distant from each other, and touch neither of them; whereas, allowing a ball of fifty-two pounds, to be twelve inches diameter, and to pass in the same direction with the former, this last ball may[d] destroy, but must[d] inevitably wound both objects: again, if you suppose a ball of ten inches diameter, to pass within half an inch of any single object, that of twelve passing in the same line by the increased diameter, must destroy or injure it: in like manner as the diameter in shot increases, the holes which are made in the sides will be increased also; thus two men may be killed by the biggest ball, and not touched by the lesser; two ropes cut by the biggest, and not touched

d. *Appeal italicizes* may *and* must

by the lesser; and masts and yards carried away by the increased diameter of the heavy ball, which will be untouched or less affected by the lighter; besides this, holes between wind and water,[8] which are made by heavy balls, being proportioned to the diameter also, the danger of sinking is increased, as the water which flows through the great aperture, is more than that through the lesser; every broadside then fired from the *Foudroyant*, carries a probability of doing more mischief than that from the *Ramillies*, as the diameters of all the balls taken together, fired from the French ship, exceeds that of the English; and for this reason it is in a great measure, that the masts, yards, and rigging, are more damaged on board English ships in battle than on board French.

Hence in every view, except number of cannon, which are only six small guns of six pounds, the *Foudroyant* is superior to the *Ramillies*, almost as three to two, in this manner of computing the superiority, which appears to me to be just, if for three to two in force, we put three to two in ships, which amounts to the same thing, on which side ought a prudent man to expect the victory.[9]

I do not, by this manner of computing each force, propose to reduce the different degrees in strength of each ship to a mathematical and demonstrative exactness, but only to show nearly,[1] how much the superiority of the French ship was greater than that of the English; as to the size of the ships, the *Foudroyant* is the largest.

It may be objected, probably, that the charge and discharge of a cannon, instead of taking up one minute, may take up five or perhaps ten, and each man at the small arms employ a like time to charge and fire his fusee; even then this will create no difference, the same time being allowed alike to each ship, the superiority of powers on board the *Foudroyant* to those on board the *Ramillies* will be still preserved the same; and the sole alteration arising from this is, that by less firings the superiority is not so often exerted, and the proportion of four to three still remain.

In this manner of comparing the different strengths of the two fleets, I have pitched upon the two ships which were the nearest a match for each other, and here the odds were as four to three. Between the *Couronne* and *Culloden*, it is still greater, and when you descend lower, and compare the seventy-four and sixty-four gun French ships, against the sixty-eight, sixty-six, sixty-four, and sixty gun ships of England, it is three to two; so that the proportion of

---

8. Partly above and partly below the ship's waterline.

9. Sense requires a question mark here.

1. Approximately.

four to three, is a very inferior allowance for the superiority of
the French fleet over the English as they met in the Mediterranean.
Hence it evidently appears, that if this third part of superiority
was taken from the twelve French ships, leaving each an equal to
the English, there would remain a sufficient force to equip four
ships more, then the number would be sixteen French ships to
twelve English, a superiority not to be attacked by a prudent man.

Mr. Byng's next complaint is of the injury done to his
character by mutilations of his letter published in the *Gazette*,[2]
and it is now given to the public complete, that the public
may freely examine it.
The parts printed in comma's,[3] are the parts omitted in
the *Gazette*.

Ramillies, off Minorca, 25 May, 1756.

Sir,
I have the pleasure to desire you will acquaint their lordships,
that having sailed from Gibraltar the 8th, I got off Mahon the 19th,
having been joined by his majesty's ship *Phoenix*, off Majorca,
two days before, *by whom I had confirmed the intelligence I received at
Gibraltar, of the strength of the French fleet, and of their being off Mahon. His
majesty's colours were still flying at the castle of St. Philip's, and I could
perceive several bomb batteries playing upon it from different parts; French
colours we saw flying on the west part of St. Philip's. I dispatched the
Phoenix, Chesterfield, and Dolphin a-head, to reconnoitre the harbour's
mouth, and Captain Hervey, to endeavour to land a letter for General Blakeney,
to let him know the fleet was here to his assistance, though every one was
of opinion, we could be of no use to him, as by all accounts no place was
secured for covering a landing, could we have spared any people. The Phoenix
was also to make the private signal between Captain Hervey and Captain
Scrope, as this latter would undoubtedly come off, if it were practicable,
having kept the Dolphin's barge with him; but the enemy's fleet appearing
to the south-east,*[4]* *and the wind at the same time coming strong off the land,
obliged me to call those ships in, before they could get quite so near the entrance
of the harbour, as to make sure what batteries or guns might be placed to
prevent our having any communication with the castle.* Falling little wind,
it was five before I could form my line, or distinguish any of the

---

2. *London Gazette*, No. 9594, 22–26
June 1756.
3. Here printed in italics.
4. The *Gazette* printed "when the
enemy's fleet appeared to the south-
east" following "Majorca, two days
before," thus forming a conclusion
to the sentence.

enemy's motions, and not at all to judge of their force more than by their numbers, which were seventeen, and thirteen appeared large. They at first stood towards us in a regular line, tacked about seven, which I judged was to endeavour to gain the wind of us in the night; so that being late, I tacked, in order to keep the weather-gage of them, as well as to make sure of the land wind,[5] in the morning, being very hazy and not above five leagues off Cape Mola. We tacked off towards the enemy at eleven; and at day-light had no sight of them. But two tartans[6] with the French private signal being close in with the rear of our fleet, I sent the *Princess Louisa* to chase one, and made the signal for the rear-admiral, who was nearest the other, to send ships to chase her; the *Princess Louisa*, *Defiance*, and *Captain*, became at a great distance, but the *Defiance* took hers, which had two captains, two lieutenants, and one hundred and two private soldiers, who were sent out the day before with six hundred men on board tartans to reinforce the French fleet, on our then appearing off the place. The *Phoenix*, on Captain Hervey's offer, prepared to serve as a fire-ship, but without damaging her as a frigate, till the signal was made to prime, when she was then to scuttle her decks, every thing else being prepared, as[e] the time and place allowed of. The enemy now began to appear from the mast-head; I called in the cruisers, and when they had joined me, I tacked towards the enemy, and formed the line a-head. I found the French were preparing theirs to leeward, having unsuccessfully endeavoured to weather me: they were twelve large ships of the line, and five frigates. As soon as I judged the rear of our fleet[f] to be the length of their van, we tacked all together, and immediately made the signal for the ships that led, to lead large, and for the *Deptford* to quit the line, that ours might become equal in number with theirs. At two I made the signal to engage, as I found it was the surest method of ordering every ship to close down on the one that fell to their lot. And here I must express my great satisfaction at the very gallant manner in which the rear-admiral set the van the example, by instantly bearing down on the ships he was to engage with his second, and who occasioned one of the French ships to begin the engagement, which they did, by raking ours as they went down; I bore down

e. as] at *Gazette*   f. our fleet] ours *Gazette*

---

5. The *Gazette* punctuates "wind; in the morning, being very hazy and not above five leagues off Cape Mola, we tacked."

6. "A small one-masted vessel with a large lateen sail and a foresail, used in the Mediterranean" (*OED*).

on the ship that lay opposite me, and began to engage him, after having received the fire for some time in going down. The *Intrepid unfortunately* (in the very beginning) had his fore-top-mast shot away, and as that hung on his fore-sail and backed it, he had no command of his ship, his fore-tack and all his braces being cut at the same time, so that he drove on the next ship to him, and obliged that, and the ships a-head of me to throw all aback; this obliged me to do so also for some minutes to avoid their falling on board me, though not before we had drove our adversary out of the line, who put before the wind, and had several shot fired at him from his own admiral. This not only caused the enemy's center to be unattacked, but left the rear-admiral's division rather uncovered for some little[g] time. I sent and called to the ships a-head of me to make sail on, and go down on the enemy, and ordered the *Chesterfield* to lay by the *Intrepid*, and the *Deptford* to supply the *Intrepid's* place. I found the enemy edged away constantly, and as they went three feet to our one, they would never permit our closing with them, but took the advantage of destroying our rigging; for though I closed the rear-admiral fast, I found I could not again close the enemy, whose van were fairly drove from their line; but their admiral was joining them by bearing away. By this time 'twas past six, and the enemy's van and ours were at too great a distance to engage; I perceived some of their ships stretching to the northward, and I imagined they were going to form a new line; I made the signal for the headmost ships to tack, and those that led before with larboard tacks, to lead with the starboard, that I might by the first keep, (if possible) the wind of the enemy, and by the second, be between the rear-admiral's division and the enemy, as his had suffered most, as also to cover the *Intrepid*, which I perceived to be in a very bad condition, and whose loss would very greatly give the balance against us, if they had attacked us the next morning as I expected. I brought to about eight that night to join the *Intrepid*, and to refit our ships as fast as possible, and continued so all night. The next morning we saw nothing of the enemy, though we were still lying to; Mahon was N. N. W. about ten or eleven leagues. I sent cruisers out to look for the *Intrepid* and *Chesterfield*, who joined me the next day; and having, from a state and condition of the squadron brought me in, found that the *Captain*, *Intrepid*, and *Defiance*, (which latter has lost her captain) were much[h] damaged in their masts, *so that they were endangered of not being able to secure their masts properly at sea; and also, that the squadron in general were very sickly, many killed and wounded,*

g. some little] some very little *Gazette*   h. were much] were very much *Gazette*

and no where to put a third of their number, if I made an hospital even of
the forty gun ship, which was not easy at sea. I thought it proper in
this situation, to call a council of war before I went again to look
for the enemy. I desired the attendance of General Stuart, Lord
Effingham, and Lord Robert Bertie, and Colonel Cornwallis, that
I might collect their opinions upon the present situation *of Minorca
and Gibraltar, and make sure of protecting the latter, since it was found
impracticable to either succour or relieve the former with the force we had;
for though we may justly claim the victory, yet we are much inferior to the
weight of their ships, though the numbers are equal, and they have the advantage of sending to Minorca their wounded, and getting reinforcements
of seamen from their transports, and soldiers from their camp; all which,
undoubtedly has been done in this time that we have been laying to to refit,
and often in sight of Minorca; and their ships have more than once appeared
in a line from our mast-heads, I send their lordships the resolution of the
council of war,* in which there was[7] not the least contention or doubt
arose. *I hope indeed we shall find stores to refit us at Gibraltar, and if I have
any reinforcement, will not lose a moment's time to seek the enemy again, and
once more give them battle, though they have a great advantage in being
clean ships, that go three feet to our one, and therefore have the choice how
they will engage us, or if they will at all, and will never let us close them,
as their sole view is the disabling our ships, in which they have but too well
succeeded, though we obliged them to bear up.* I do not send their lordships
the particulars of our losses and damages by this, as it would take
me much time, and that I am willing none should be lost in letting
them know an event of such consequence. *I cannot help urging their
lordships for a reinforcement, if none are yet sailed, on their knowledge of
the enemy's strength in these seas, and which, by very good intelligence,
will in a few days be strengthened by four more large ships from Toulon,
almost ready to sail, if not now sailed to join these.* I dispatch this to Sir
Benjamin Keene by way of Barcelona, and am making the best
of my way to *cover* Gibraltar; from which place I propose sending
their lordships a more particular account.

I am, Sir, your most humble servant,
J. B.

Hon. John Cleveland, Esq;
    P. S. I must desire you will acquaint their lordships, that I have
appointed Captain Hervey to the command of the *Defiance*, in the
room of Captain Andrews slain in the action.
    I have just sent the defects of the ships, as I have got it made
out, whilst I was closing my letter.

---

7. The *Gazette* bridges the gap by substituting "at which council" for "in
which there was."

The passages omitted are here specified, and why they were omitted it is now time to conjecture.[8]

The first mutilation concealed an allusion made to his former letter from Gibraltar, which it was apparently the interest of the ministry to keep in darkness. It seems likewise intended by this omission to insinuate that Byng never came into sight of Minorca, and that he was caught unexpectedly by the French. The words could "we have spared any people" would have discovered the weakness of the armament; and the opinion of the officers that the "landing place was covered," would have shewn the folly of those who contrived the expedition, and sent out a fleet too weak to encounter the enemy at sea, and not expected that this should at the same time drive away an army intrenched on the land. Who sent out a weak fleet, when they might have made it stronger by adding the ships of which the crews were uselessly devouring their provisions at Spithead, and amused the nation with an attempt to relieve Minorca, while they sent no land forces or none proportioned to the purpose, and sent them out at a time when they could not be landed.

The next omission was likewise equally unfair, and equally malignant, and appears designed partly to cast reproach on the admiral, and partly to hide the faults of the ministry. To conceal the fitness of Byng's retreat, they suppress the damage done to the ships; to conceal their own negligence, they omit the mention of the wounded, and the want of an hospital ship for their reception. Surely the men who sent out a fleet without provision for the wounded, had no design that there should ever be a battle, and meant only to deceive the nation by an expedition purposely contrived to be vain.

This is the first time that a fleet was fitted out for such an enterprize, without store-ships, fire-ships, hospital-ships, or tenders; and why this fleet was thus imperfectly furnished, what reason can be given, but that the relief of Minorca was never intended?

The intent of this omission being principally to fix upon Byng the reproach of returning without necessity, it may now be enquired whether it was proper to have hazarded a second

---

8. The following eight paragraphs are largely a paraphrase of arguments in *An Appeal to the People*.

engagement. No man was ever expected to fight without
hope of victory, or without prospect of advantage proportionate to the danger of defeat. Hope of victory he could
have none, the French fleet was at first superior, and was far
more superior after the battle; prospect of advantage was
now at an end, for he could not now relieve St. Philip,
though Galissonniere had delivered up his ships without a
shot, it was already invested by an adequate force, and though
the siege might have been prolonged it could not have been
raised.

It is much harder to discover why Galissonniere suffered
our shattered ships to escape. Was[i] it by a secret convention
with our ministry, that Minorca was given up on one side,
and our defeated fleet spared on the other? What other
reason can be given why the ministry, who knew the superiority of the French fleet early enough, did not order Byng by
dispatches sent over-land to wait at Gibraltar for reinforcements? What can be alleged but that of this fleet, they had
either covenant for the safety or intended the loss.

The next mutilation suppresses the account of the enemy's[j]
superiority, such an account as surely cannot be contradicted.
The French had an army from which the fleet was supplied
with fresh men: Byng had more than a thousand sick without
an hospital ship for their reception.

The next passage omitted describes another advantage
enjoyed by the French, that their ships were *clean*, to which
it might have been added, to the honour of our ministers,
that "their ships were better." A clamour has been raised by
the assertion, that they sailed "three feet to one": a seaman's
phrase never designed to be understood literally, nor ever
interpreted literally before, by which nothing is implied but
that they sailed faster, and had great advantage by superior
celerity.

He "hoped" to find stores "to refit him at Gibraltar,"
where in effect, from the state in which he had left it, and
which was carefully concealed from the public, he had
"little hopes" of finding them, yet this delay which the

i. escape. Was *1788*] escape, was *LM*   j. enemy's *1788*] enemies *LM*

ministers knew to be unavoidable was imputed to him as a new crime.[9]

The next paragraph which is omitted, is the urging the Ad——y to a speedy reinforcement, if none was already sent, a request which he had before made; at the same time acquainting them with the increasing strength of the enemy at Toulon, by four large ships; which circumstance, though it tends not to justify the admiral's behaviour, gives a favourable idea of his zeal for success, and a contemptible one of those, who, presiding at the head of affairs, had been totally ignorant of what was preparing at Toulon, and negligent at best of what happened to Minorca: unless you may possibly by this time be apprehensive, that some other motives conduced to this behaviour in them.

The last paragraph has but one word omitted, which, instead of "making the best of my way to Gibraltar," is to "cover" Gibraltar; a very material alteration; the going to cover a place being very different from going to a place, the one signifying an act of prudence, and of a soldier; the other, in such instances, of flight, and of a fugitive. Was not this word premeditately left out, to prevent you from asking what danger Gibraltar was in, and to what part of the letter this referred? Does it not seem to be the present employment of the *Gazette* to misrepresent, and of the writers or directors of it, to keep the people of England as ignorant as possible of the real situation of any place, which may be designed to be given up to your declared enemies, by those who are your concealed, if men can be denominated concealed, who are thus open in pursuing a nation's ruin?

To the end of the letter were added lists of the two fleets, of which even our own list was false; our cannon were increased and the French diminished. The admiral's account of the damage suffered by his fleet was omitted, and a list only given of the killed and wounded as if sent by him not only for his own, but for the French fleet.

Having thus deprived him of his reputation, they proceed to divest him of his command, and the following letter was sent.[1]

---

9. The next two paragraphs are quoted from the *Appeal*, p. 60.

1. The two letters are quoted from

A Letter to a Member of Parliament, pp. 22–27.

Sir,

His Majesty having received an account that the squadron under
your command, and that of the French under the command of
Monsieur Galissonniere, came to action off the harbour of Mahon,
the 20th of last month, and that the French (tho' inferior to you
in force) kept before the harbour, and obliged you to retreat; I
am commanded by my Lords Commissioners of the Admiralty, to
send you herewith an extract of Monsieur Galissonniere's letter
to his court, giving an account of the action, and to acquaint
you, that his Majesty is so much dissatisfied with your conduct,
that he has ordered their lordships to recal yourself and Mr. West,[2]
and to send out Sir Edward Hawke, and Rear-Admiral Saunders,
to command the squadron.

I am extremely sorry to be obliged to inform you of such a
disagreeable event, being with great regard,
     Sir,
        Your most obedient humble servant,
                              * * *

Admiralty-Office, June 8, 1756.

To this he returned a letter which neither betrayed consciousness of guilt, dread of resentment, nor confusion of mind.

                        Gibraltar-Bay, July 4, 1756.
Sir,

By Sir Edward Hawke I have received their lordships orders,
and your letter of the 8th of June, which I have immediately
complied with, and have only to express my surprize at being so
ignominiously dismissed from my employment, in the sight of the
fleet I had commanded, in sight of the garrison, and in sight of
Spain, at such a time, in such a manner, and after such conduct,
as I hope shall shortly appear to the whole world. 'Tis not now

---

2. Rear-Admiral Temple West,
Byng's second-in-command and commander of the rear of the squadron
in the Minorca engagement. A cousin
of the Earl Temple, head of the
Temple-Grenville-Pitt clan, he was
promoted, after his return to London,
to Vice-Admiral and a seat on the
Admiralty Board (where, late in
October, Temple replaced Anson
as First Lord, during the short-lived
Devonshire-Pitt ministry). By far the
most important witness at Byng's
trial, his evidence was studiously
ambiguous, giving "the impression
that he really blamed Byng, but was
too loyal to say so" (Dudley Pope,
p. 219). When the verdict was
announced, he sent in a letter of
protest, resigning his command, but
shortly afterward was persuaded to
withdraw his resignation.

for me to expostulate; I flatter myself that Mr. West and I shall make evident the injury done to our characters, which I know of nothing in the power of any being whatever that can atone for; so high an opinion I have of that, which was ever unsullied before, and which I hope to make appear has been most injuriously and wrongfully attacked now, on the grounds of a false gasconade of an open enemy to our king and country, and which would have evidently appeared, had the possible time been allowed for my own express's arrival, in which there was nothing false, nothing vaunting, nothing shameful, nor any thing which could have prevented our receiving his Majesty's royal approbation, for having, with a much inferior force, fought, met, attacked, and beat the enemy: of this, it is needless for me to say more at present, than that I am sorry to find Mr. West, with the captains, lieutenants, and officers of the ships we had our flags on board of, are to be sufferers for what I alone, as commander in chief, am answerable: but it is so much of a piece with the whole unheard of treatment I have met with, that neither they, the fleet, or myself can be more astonished at that particular than at the whole.

I am, Sir,

Your very humble servant,

J. B.

To The Hon. J——n C——d, Esq;

Let us now review this whole transaction.[3]

First, then how came the French to form the idea of taking St. Philips, when the fleet of England, known to be so superior, might have prevented the embarkation; if not that, their descent on Minorca; if that could not have been done, reinforced St. Philips, beat the French fleet, and taken the whole embarkation prisoners. Is the Duke of Richlieu so mad, that he would have undertaken to command in an expedition which had been preparing for five months, known to all Europe, and open to be disconcerted in all the above different manners? Would the directors of our marine preparations, had they been in earnest to preserve St. Philips, have sent out an inferior squadron? delayed it at Spithead during so many months? and given the Admiral absolute orders to expedite other services, by not taking men from any ship fit for service, to man his own squadron, but to wait the coming of tenders

---

3. The following quotation is from the *Appeal*, pp. 64–71, with a fair amount of not always skilful cutting.

with pressed men from Liverpool? And before the arrival of more than two, he was obliged to sail.

Had the planners of the expedition been truly animated with the interest of their country, why, when all England and all Europe was exclaiming against their delay, did they continually give out, that there was no fleet preparing at Toulon? That the French had no sailors nor military stores: Was it not to give the air of relieving St. Philips only that the English fleet set sail a few days before the French?

When the popular clamor now began to be very loud, were not ten thousand stories invented to draw off the public attention from the planners of the expedition, and to throw it on him who commanded, and who they concluded would miscarry? Was it not owing to a design of ill success in them that the fleet was sent out so small, and that he was assured the French armament could not possibly exceed seven ships, and probably would not be more than five? Was it not constantly asserted, that no fleet was ever so well manned, equipped, and powerful, for the number, as this English fleet? And that the French consisted of old ships not fit for service, ill-manned, and worse provided; whereas one moment's thought would have told them, that a fleet however ill-furnished with men, when it left Toulon, must be abundantly provided with hands from two hundred transports, which after landing the troops spare[4] two thirds of their crews; as to their ships being feeble or ill-fitted out, the falshood of that assertion is now known. To those spurious accounts of the different strength of the two fleets, was it not constantly added that Mr. Byng could blow the French out of the water? With what intent but to aggravate the miscarriage of the Admiral, by creating an opinion of his superior force the more effectually to inflame resentment against him, when the ill news of his not prevailing should arrive?

The citadel of Mahon being attacked, it now became the common conversation amongst the planners of the voyage, that the fortification could not hold out a week, with a design to lessen the surprize of its being taken; or if it was defended any considerable time, to give an idea of its being well provided; does it not therefore seem evident, from the fleet of England being appointed so inferior, so long delayed after it was ready, sent so late, without a soldier but those who acted as marines, without an hospital-ship, fire-ship, transports, or tenders; that no battle was intended to be fought,

------

4. Inept cutting. The *Appeal* reads, "troops, and ammunition, and at anchor, could very well spare."

nor St. Philips relieved? But by this delay, to give time to Marshal Richlieu to take the fortification, return with his fleet, and leave Mr. Byng to cruise ineffectually round Minorca; indeed the brave Irishman[5] disappointed the expectations of those who had thus designed the whole transaction, by defending the place becoming the duty of British subjects, and not according to sinister intention.

By this contemptible cunning, a quality often connected with ignorance in little minds, it seems contrived, that if General Blakeney gave up the citadel before Mr. Byng's arrival, then *he* was to be exclaimed against, and charged with cowardice; and if *he* held out, as the *Admiral* was insufficient, then that imputation was to fall on the latter.

Was it not therefore owing to the daily disappointment of hearing[6] that the citadel had surrendered, that no fleet was sent to reinforce Mr. Byng; apprehending that with a reinforcement he would raise the siege, which seems so contrary to the intent of sending him? Was it not on this account that they did not stop him by express at Gibraltar, to wait for more ships of war? And at last, was not the reinforcement sent when it could not possibly arrive 'till after the Admiral had succeeded or miscarried.

At length comes a letter from Monsieur La Galissonniere, of the English fleet having retired, when immediately a report prevailed, that from a letter sent by Admiral Byng from Gibraltar, it was foreseen that he would not fight: After some time a letter from Admiral Byng arrives, printed in the *Gazette*, where the most material passages in vindication of his conduct are cut out; to preserve the former impressions of his having behaved like a coward, at the same time condemning the resolutions of the whole council of war unheard, a most flagrant affront on men of superior birth, by one who had undeservedly started into nobility.[7]

It was now necessary to continue inventing more tales against Mr. Byng; one day it was given out, that he had sold out of the stocks forty-four thousand pounds before he sailed, which was to insinuate, that he left England with a design never to return: the falshood of this report may be seen in the stock books. Then it was reported, that this was the man who cruised before Genoa last war, and took money to let vessels with provisions and men

---

5. The *Appeal* reads "Irishmen." Either reading is possible. "Irishman" would be General Blakeney, born in Limerick. "Irishmen" could mean, in addition, the 24th regiment of foot, one of the four regiments of the gar-

rison, recruited in Ireland. "Subjects," later in the garbled sentence, seems to indicate the plural.

6. "Disappointment of hearing," i.e., "failure to hear."

7. I.e., Anson.

pass to the relief of the town; a known falshood, and were not the ashes of the dead sacred, I would tell you his name: was not this to hint the idea of venality?

Then it seems it was discovered, that a ship with provisions had gotten into Mahon the very day before the action, which ship arrived at the port a month before the investing the citadel; was not this to insinuate that he might have landed his soldiers also?

Ballads[k] were made to keep up your resentment, and the admiral hanged and burnt in effigy at the national expence, by the clerks and officers of public offices, amongst whom one Mr. Glover,[8] belonging to the Victualling-Office, burning him in White-Chapel road, was rewarded with a broken leg by the Barking stage-coach.

It was now thought necessary to assert, that Mr. Byng was attempting to escape in women's cloaths, to impart the idea of conscious guiltiness, which is likewise an invention of falshood; and yet this idea was to be continued by fixing iron bars to the windows,[9] to prevent a man from escaping, whom they wish to be well rid of, and who would not leave the place if they would permit him.

At one time he is represented as mad, and then as killing himself with drinking: then, that it is to be feared he may attempt suicide. Believe me, he has not lost his senses, as his accusers will find, nor will he destroy himself with his own hands;[1] and it is the duty of the people to preserve his life, for the sake of more perfectly knowing what influenced his pursuers to contrive and conduct the expedition in so preposterous a manner.

And lastly, these contemptible artifices are followed by a letter to Ad——l B——g, published at the expence of his enemies, and hawked through the streets for the sake of universal publication.[2]

k. Balads *LM*

---

8. No doubt the poet Richard Glover, a hanger-on of the Temples, author of stridently "patriotic" works like *Leonidas* (1737) and *Boadicea* (1753).

9. The bars were actually installed; see Dudley Pope, p. 188.

1. The *Appeal* italicizes "with his own hands."

2. The editor of Johnson's *Works* (1788), Vol. XIV, has the following note here: "This was probably the performance mentioned by Dr. John-son in the life of David Mallet. 'In the beginning of the last war, when the nation was exasperated by ill success, he was employed to turn the public vengeance upon Byng, and wrote a letter of accusation under the character of a Plain Man. The paper was with great industry circulated and dispersed; and he for his season-able intervention had a considerable pension bestowed upon him, which he retained to his death'" (p. 454). G. B. Hill's note on the passage in the

But the whole is an entire declamation, intended to inflame, founded on no one argument, and concludes with a confession, which his adversaries would do extremely well to learn by heart, against that day when public justice will demand them to their trials.

Such is the plea of the persecuted Byng, on which, though we do not suppose that the public will pay much regard to our determination, we shall give our opinion with the freedom of men uninfluenced by dependence or expectation.

It appears to us that Byng has suffered without sufficient cause.

That he was sent to the relief of Minorca, when relief was known to be no longer possible.

That he was sent without land forces, the only forces that could raise the siege.

That his fleet was inferior, and long before the battle was known at home to be inferior to that of the French.

That he fought them, and retreated only when he could fight no longer.

That a second engagement would only have increased the loss suffered in the first.

---

life of Mallet (*Lives*, iii.408, par. 21) identifies the work referred to there as *Observations on the Twelfth Article of War . . . By a Plain Man* (1757), attributed to Mallet by Halkett and Laing and others. James A. Butler ("Samuel Johnson: Defender of Admiral Byng," *Cornell Library Journal*, No. 7, Winter, 1969, pp. 25–47) argues that the Mallet pamphlet SJ is referring to is *The Conduct of the Ministry Impartially Examined* (1756) (p. 253 below), pointing out that *Observations on the Twelfth Article* was not published until after Byng's execution. Neither pamphlet however quite answers the description given in Johnson's life of Mallet ("a letter of accusation" and a "paper") or here ("a letter to Ad——l B——g"). *The Conduct of the Ministry* is not a letter of accusation but one of apology for the ministry's actions. Another guess might be a two-page broadsheet, *Some Friendly and Seasonable Advice to Admiral Byng*, signed "Isaac Barclay" and dated "From my house at Redriff, this 22nd of October, 1756." It is an attack and is written in the manner of a simple, rough, frank sailor. As a broadsheet it would be more likely to be "hawked through the streets" and "circulated and dispersed" than a pamphlet. But its date, if authentic, seems too late for Shebbeare's pamphlet and the *LM* quotation. The "confession" mentioned by Shebbeare may provide a clue to the identification. SJ, writing the life of Mallet a quarter-century later, may of course be conflating memories of several publications of the time.

That a victory at sea would not have saved Minorca.
That there was no provision for the chances of a battle.[3]
That the nation has been industriously deceived by false
and treacherous representations.
That Minorca if not betrayed has been neglected.
That Byng's letter has been mutilated injuriously, fraud-
ulently mutilated.
That every act of defamation has been practised against
him.
That unless other evidence can be produced, Byng will
be found innocent.

----

3. I.e., presumably, no hospital ships, tenders, etc.

REVIEW OF *SOME FURTHER PARTICULARS IN RELATION TO THE CASE OF ADMIRAL BYNG.* 1756.

James A. Butler (see n. 1, p. 213 above) thinks the pamphlet reviewed here "possibly by Paul Whitehead" (p. 38). The title does vaguely suggest that it is a sequel to *A Letter to a Member of Parliament . . . relative to the Case of Admiral Byng* (p. 219 above). Whitehead of course had no connexion with Oxford (nor was he much of a gentleman); perhaps Johnson, who had no great personal regard for him, hints as much in the dry opening sentence of the review ("such a title, *whether truly or not bestowed* upon his advocate"). The review, or rather "extract," is immediately followed in the *Literary Magazine* by that of *The Conduct of the Ministry Impartially Examined* (1756), thus "opposing," as he says, the two sides of the argument (though Johnson takes good care not to let the ministerial dogs have the best of it). The sole original contribution by Johnson to the article is the opening paragraph; all the rest is a severely and sometimes ineptly cut version of the forty-odd pages of the pamphlet.

The text below follows the *Literary Magazine*, No. 7 (15 Oct–15 Nov 1756), pp. 336–40 (the second set of pages so numbered; correct numbering would be 344–48).

Some Further Particulars in Relation to the Case of Admiral Byng,[1] by a Gentleman of Oxford.

8vo. Lacey 1 s.

Why a gentleman of Oxford should be supposed particularly qualified to examine and defend the conduct of Mr. Byng, or how his defence is much recommended by such a title, whether truly or not bestowed upon his advocate, we are not able to discover. But as we are willing to hear every pleader in this important cause, we shall make a faithful extract from this pamphlet, and oppose to it what the friends of the ministry have offered, however denominated, or wherever educated.[2]

---

1. The title of the pamphlet continues, "From original papers, &c. *Fiat Justitia!*"

2. SJ may be suggesting that the "friend of the ministry" who offers the "opposing" pamphlet, *The Con-*

On the 17th of March the Admiral receiv'd his commission, as Admiral of the blue: on the 20th he arriv'd at Portsmouth, and found letters from the Board, forbidding him to meddle with any men belonging to the *Torbay, Essex, Nassau, Prince Frederick, Colchester* and *Grayhound* (all which ships were said to be wanted for the most pressing service) or, if it was possible to be avoided, with any men belonging to any other ship in a serviceable condition.

On the 21st at sun-rising, he hoisted his flag on board the *Ramillies:* six other ships of his squadron, viz. The *Buckingham, Culloden, Captain, Revenge, Kingston,* and *Defiance* were at Spithead; two, the *Trident* and *Lancaster* were fitting for sea; the *Intrepid* was not sail'd from the Nore.

For these nine ships, 723 men were wanting, of which 240 were short of complement,[3] 291 lent to ships at sea, and 192 sick in the hospital.

In the evening of this day he received a letter pressing the utmost diligence in getting his squadron into sailing order, communicating a design of the French to make a descent on Minorca.

The Admiral the next day return'd the assurances requir'd, that he was using all possible dispatch: specifying, that in seven or eight days he hoped all the ships under his command would be ready in every respect, excepting men.

There lay at Spithead, at that instant, no less than twelve men of war of the line.

All these ships were either full mann'd, or nearly so, and four of them were mann'd above their complements. And those in the harbour were thirteen more, all of which, except the four first, were also full mann'd, or nearly so.

But no orders came for supplying the defect of men till the 25th, when the Admiral was directed to take them out of the (*a*) tenders and hospitals; and then not till the complement of the *Stirling-Castle* had been compleated first; which is so much the more remarkable, as he received an express the day before to dispatch Mr. Keppel[4]

(*a*) Tenders expected to arrive from Liverpool and Ireland, two only of which arrived before the fleet sailed, the greatest part of the men from them put on board the *Sterling-castle;* the whole number 198.

---

duct of the Ministry—David Mallet—had few claims to the denomination "gentleman"; Mallet of course was educated in Scotland.

3. Spelled "compliment" in *LM*, here and below; a spelling generally in disuse before 1756 (see *OED*).

4. Captain the Hon. Augustus Keppel, son of the 2nd Earl of Albemarle, later became a distinguished admiral (and was a central figure in a notorious court martial). Keppel and the two ships were thus detached from Byng's service and

in the *Essex* and *Gibraltar* to sea, as soon as possible, and to supply the said ships with what number of men they wanted out of the *Nassau*.

However[5] on the 26th the *Ludlow-castle* was order'd to Spithead from her cruise, with the men borrow'd from the *Ramillies;* he was directed to take from aboard the *Stirling-castle* the men on board her towards compleating the complements of his squadron. He was also directed by the same express, to distribute all the marines he had on board among the several ships at Spithead and in Portsmouth harbour, and to receive Lord Robert Bertie's regiment[6] of royal English fuziliers in their room.

April the first the Admiral received a letter, that required him to proceed without loss of time to the Mediterranean.

In obedience to these orders, he directed the captains to take on board all the men, that he might know exactly the number wanting to compleat his complement; which were found to be 336; the greatest part of them lent to the *Ludlow-castle*, (*b*) *Hampton-court*, and *Tilbury*, which were still at sea.

However, the *Ludlow-castle* about four in the afternoon repaid the borrow'd men: with her also came in the *Intrepid*, Captain Young, having 261 supernumeraries on board, but then 156 of these were wanting to make up the complement of that very ship: so that there was still a necessity to take 30 from the *Sterling-castle*, and 70 supernumeraries from the *Cambridge*.

By these shifts the deficiency of men was supply'd: but Captain Young, upon receiving orders to put himself under the Admiral's command, waited upon him, with a representation, that the *Intrepid* was not fit for a foreign voyage, having made so much water in her passage from the Nore[7] to let the water down, in order to

(*b*) The *Hampton-Court* then at Lisbon, the *Tilbury* at Cork in Ireland.

---

did not take part in the Minorca engagement. Keppel was later a member of Byng's court martial, but seems to have tried to save him from the death penalty.

5. SJ omits the sarcastic preamble to this sentence in the pamphlet (p. 7): "To shew, however, how well their Lordships [of the Admiralty] understood business, and how notably they could conduct it."

6. The Royal Marines are under the command of the Admiralty;

Colonel Lord Robert Bertie's regiment of fusiliers, intended to take part in the defence of Minorca, were, as a unit of the army, under the command of the War Office, whose muddled and contradictory orders concerning the regiment "became one of the contributing factors in the loss of Minorca" (Dudley Pope, p. 62).

7. The sense is ruined here by the omission of "that he was forc'd to scuttle the lower deck" (*Some Further Particulars*, p. 12).

have it pump'd out: that he had receiv'd no notice of his being destin'd for any such voyage, and that he had neither water, provisions, or stores for it.

However, as there was now no remedy, her boats were employed in procuring and taking in the necessary stores, provisions, &c.

April 5 the Admiral having issued out the line of battle signals, made the signal at 11 o'clock to weigh, and stood to sea, but was forc'd by the tide of ebb, accompany'd with a calm, to anchor again at three in the afternoon.

With the squadron already particularis'd, then, on the 6th of April, he again put to sea, palpably as soon as it was possible for him to do so, and after a tedious voyage, occasion'd as well by calms as contrary winds, arriv'd at Gibraltar, May the 2d.

The Admiral's instructions were, in general, founded on a persuasion, that the French armament at Toulon, was destin'd to North-America, so it was declar'd with the utmost confidence, by those who ought to have known better, that, for want of seamen, six or eight ships of the line at most, was the greatest number the enemy could possibly put to sea from that port.

For hence it is apparent: First, that we had no true intelligence at home of what was really in agitation at Toulon. Secondly, that instructions unprecise in their nature, because founded on mistakes and uncertainties, accompany'd with orders yet more unprecise and embarrassing, could not but be productive of perplexities in every question, consequently of snares and dangers in every resolution. Thirdly, that from the very different aspect of things[8] a difference of conduct became absolutely necessary; and thence-forward, he was either to proceed discretionally, or not to proceed at all.

Instead of six or eight men of war of the line, he was informed the enemy had put to sea on the 13th of April; with a squadron of twelve ships from sixty to eighty guns; five frigates from twenty to fifty; two xebeques of eighteen, four gallies, two galliots, four bombs, escorting 233 transports, with 18000 soldiers on board, and 50 vessels freighted with cattle, stores, &c. And that they had made a descent on Minorca.

From Mr. Edgecumbe himself, whom he found at Gibraltar, with the *Deptford, Princess Louisa,* and *Fortune* sloop, part of his squadron, he receiv'd the information, and having now one positive fact to reason upon, that Fort St. Philip was besieged, with a great

---

8. The pamphlet (p. 15) reads "things on the Admiral's arrival at Gibraltar from that which they had been made to wear in England."

force, and the siege cover'd with a squadron abundantly stronger and better appointed, than had enter'd into any of the supposers heads to suppose possible, who dictated his orders; his first concern was to consider, how he was best to conduct himself.

He was now to use all possible means in his power for the relief of the place, taking proper care, nevertheless, to exert his utmost vigilance to protect Gibraltar from any hostile attempt; which is not only understood, but expressed in his orders.

And now what his conduct really was, we shall endeavour to shew.

He issued immediate orders, for all the ships of his squadron to compleat their provisions and water.[9]

The winds proving variable, and often interrupted by calms, it was the 16th before the squadron could get up as far as Palma, the capital of Majorca; and here the Admiral thought fit to send the *Experiment* to that port, with a letter to the consul for what intelligence he could supply him with; about which time, a ship close in with the shore (discovered afterwards to be the *Gracieuse*, a frigate of thirty guns; that together with another ship, suppos'd to be the *Amphion* of fifty, which quitted that station the day before, had cruiz'd off that port, and kept in the *Phoenix* for near three weeks) was observ'd to stand away to the eastward, with a fine breeze, whilst the squadron in the offing was in a manner becalm'd: and the next day in the afternoon, the *Experiment* rejoin'd the squadron, (which was standing to the eastward) with the *Phoenix* in company, which last brought the Admiral some intelligence of the quantity of cannon, ammunition, and provision, landed at Minorca by the enemy, as also of their manner of landing, and of treating the inhabitants.

The wind still continued easterly, until the 18th at nine in the evening, when a fine breeze sprung up northerly, and the fleet sailed large all night.

The 19th at day break, the squadron being off the coast of Minorca, about five o'clock in the morning, the Admiral sent the *Phoenix*, Captain Hervey, with the *Chesterfield* and *Dolphin*, Captain Lloyd, and Captain Marlow, to reconnoitre as closely as possible, the harbour's mouth, and the situation both of the enemy and their batteries.

Captain Hervey was also charged with the following letter from the Admiral to General Blakeney.

9. Eight pages of the pamphlet (20–27), describing the activities at Fort San Felipe, are here passed over.

Ramillies off Minorca, May 19, 1756.

Sir,

I send you this by Captain Hervey of his majesty's ship *Phoenix*, who has my orders to convey it to you if possible, together with the inclosed packet, which he received at Leghorn.

I am extremely concerned to find that Captain Edgecumbe has been obliged to retire to Gibraltar with the ships under his command, and that the French are landed, and St. Philip's castle is invested; as I flatter myself had I fortunately been more timely in the Mediterranean, that I should have been able to have prevented the enemy's getting a footing on the island of Minorca.

I am to acquaint you that General Stuart, Lord Effingham and Colonel Cornwallis, with about thirty officers and some recruits belonging to the different regiments now in garrison with you, are on board the ships of the squadron, and shall be glad to know by the return of the officer, what place you will think proper to have them landed at.

The royal regiment of English fuziliers, commanded by Lord Robert Bertie, is likewise on board the squadron destined, agreeable to my orders, to serve on board the fleet in the Mediterranean, unless it should be thought necessary upon consultation with you to land the regiment for the defence of Minorca; but I must also inform you, should the fuziliers be landed, as they are part of the ships complements; the marines having been ordered by the lords commissioners of the Admiralty on board of other ships at Portsmouth, to make room for them, that it will disable the squadron from acting against that of the enemy, which I am informed is cruising off the island; however I shall gladly embrace every opportunity of promoting his majesty's service in the most effectual manner, and shall assist you to distress the enemy, and defeat their designs to the utmost of my power.

Please to favour me with information how I can be of most effectual service to you and the garrison; and believe me to be, with great truth and esteem, Sir,

Your most obedient
humble servant,
J. B.

Captain Hervey's orders were to deliver this letter if possible to the general.

The frigates fell into light airs of wind and calms, but nevertheless continued to make the best of their way for the harbour's mouth.

After an hour after the squadron also got within two or three miles of St. Philip's castle, (which was full in sight, with the French colours flying before it at a small distance, and both sides at intervals exchanging shots as well as shells) it[a] fell in, as the frigates had done before, with light breezes and calms.

And now it was that Captain Hervey in the *Phoenix*, made his private signals. No answer was made: no boat came off: and the enemy's squadron appearing in the S.E. quarter, the Admiral call'd in his frigates.

Both squadrons made sail towards each other, and about two in the afternoon, the Admiral made the signal for the line of battle a head, which for want of sufficient wind could not be form'd.[10] His next care was to furnish such of his ships as were sickly, and ill-mann'd with seamen from the frigates.

Upon Captain Hervey's representation, that there were proper materials on board the *Phoenix* (long ago reported home unfit for service) to convert her into a fireship, he issued orders accordingly.

A fine breeze about seven in the evening, brought the two squadrons within about two leagues of each other; when almost at the same instant both tack'd, to avoid the confusion of a night engagement; as also, the English to gain, and the French to keep the weather-gage.

Night now came on, and the wind freshening, the Admiral stood in towards the shore, till half an hour after eleven, when he made the signal for tacking, and then stood off for the remainder of the night.

On the 20th, the morning proving hazy, the enemy were not to be seen; and two of their tartans,[1] falling in with our rear by mistake; one of them (having on board upwards of 100 soldiers, part of 600, embarked from the enemy's camp the day before to re-inforce the fleet) was taken by the *Defiance*.

About seven, however, the enemy were descry'd to the south-east, and the Admiral made the signal for calling in his cruizers.

About ten he tack'd, and stood towards the enemy; and having by the dint of seamanship, not only kept the wind against all the efforts of the French commander to weather him, but form'd as compleat a line as could be form'd, began the attack, which the enemy lay to, to receive.——The particulars of what followed

---

a. it *emend.*] *om. LM*

10. The pamphlet (p. 33) adds "so properly as it ought to have been."

1. See n. 6, p. 228.

cannot be expected here. The Admiral has now more dangerous enemies to combat with, than he had then. And for the sake of a compleat narrative, must not throw away the materials of his defence.——When the proper time comes, every man that is open to conviction, will be convinced, that he acted in all respects suitably to the great trust repos'd in him; that without impairing the honour, he never once lost sight of the real interest of his country;——that in every order he gave, he made the best use that he could possibly make of his understanding;——that even what seems to be so inexplicable, with regard to his ordering the *Deptford* out of the line, will receive the most clear and satisfactory explanation;——that the odious imputations thrown on his personal behaviour, are as groundless as wicked;——that he had indeed the pleasure to see the enemy give way to the impressions made upon them;——and that nothing could equal his mortification in not being in a condition to follow them.

Instead of encountering six or seven ships at most, he had met with twelve, far superior in strength, far better mann'd, and far better sailors[2] than his own.——These had suffered less in the engagement, could be supply'd perpetually with fresh men from the camp on shore, as had already been the case; were near their own ports; could return to the charge with these advantages whenever they pleased, and if they pleased to retreat could not be overtaken. His own ships, on the contrary, such at least as had borne the brunt of the action, had sustained more damage, than could easily be repair'd. The *Intrepid* from the very beginning, was not fit for the service she had been allotted to, on the evidence of her own commanders; the *Portland* had not been cleaned for upwards of ten months, nor the *Chesterfield* for twelve: and as to the careening-wharfs, storehouses, pits, &c. (c) at Gibraltar, they were entirely decay'd.——The wounded were now moreover to be added to the sick; and no hospital ship had been appointed for the reception of either.——And as to the relief of Minorca, he had neither the battalion on board; which was to have been sent on that service; nor could he have spared the fuziliers, if they had been a number sufficient for it, which it is notorious they were not, without exposing the squadron to utter perdition, either in the attempt to land them, if it could have been made, or in venturing on a second engagement without their assistance.

That however he might not rely on his own judgment he called a

(c) See the Admiral's first letter to the admiralty board, already publish'd.[3]

2. I.e., better able to sail (since fresh from the dockyards at Toulon).
3. That of 4 May 1756 (p. 220 above). The placement of note (c) is conjectural; *LM* does not print the key for the note.

council of war on board the *Ramillies;* the result of which is here submitted to the impartial world.

At a council of war assembled, and held on board his Majesty's ship the *Ramillies*, at sea, on Monday the 24th of May, 1756. Present, &c.

Having read to the council of war the opinion of the engineers, in regard to throwing in succours in the castle of St. Philips, the result of a council of war held by General Fowke at Gibraltar, with regard to embarking a detachment on board the fleet; likewise Admiral Byng's instructions for his proceedings in the Mediterranean; likewise the order with regard to the disposal of the regiment of fuziliers, commanded by the right honourable Lord Robert Bertie, and the defects of the ships which received damage in the action with the French squadron, the 20th instant; as also having laid before the council the state of the sick, and wounded men on board the ships of the fleet, propos'd to the council the following questions, viz.

1. Whether an attack upon the French fleet gives any prospect of relieving Minorca?
   Unanimously resolved that it would not.
2. Whether, if there was no French fleet cruising off Minorca, the English fleet could raise the siege?
   Unanimously of opinion that the fleet could not.
3. Whether Gibraltar would not be in danger, by any accident that might befal this fleet?
   Unanimously agreed that it would be in danger.
4. Whether an attack with our fleet in the present state of it upon that of the French, will not endanger the safety of Gibraltar, and expose the trade of the Mediterranean to great hazard?
   Unanimously agreed that it would.
5. Whether it is not most for his Majesty's service that the fleet should immediately proceed for Gibraltar?
   We are unanimously of opinion, that the fleet should immediately proceed for Gibraltar.

J. Byng	Geo. Edgcumbe
Ja. Stuart	William Parry
Temple West	John Amherst
Henry Ward	Arthur Gardiner
Phil. Durell	Effingham
Edward Cornwallis	A. Hervey
Ja. Young	Mich. Everitt
Cha. Catford	William Lloyd
Fred. Cornewall	Robert Bertie.

Here then we have authority as well as reason, to justify the Admiral's conduct in every particular; and at any other period but this, the unanimous suffrages of so many persons of distinguish'd worth and honour, would have commanded an universal acquiescence.

The fleet stood to the westward in the afternoon, and after a tedious passage (occasion'd partly by contrary winds, and partly by the tardiness of the crippled ships) arriv'd at Gibraltar on the 19th.

Here the Admiral found Commodore Broderick, who had arriv'd four days before with five line of battle ships from England, it is to be observed, notwithstanding what has been given out, that the necessity of re-inforcing Admiral Byng was known soon after his sailing from England, if not before, as may be seen by the secretary of the Admiralty's letter to him by Mr. Broderick; and it is indubitable, that Mr. Broderick received his orders (May 17) and sailed before there was a possibility of receiving any letters from Admiral Byng, or any authentic intelligence relating to his squadron.

The Admiral's first care was to order the sick men of the fleet, amounting to near 1000, into the hospital; after which he issued the following orders. To all the captains to refit their ships, to complete their water, &c.

All these services were prosecuted with the utmost diligence, till July the first, when the fleet being nearly ready for the sea, excepting the *Portland*, unfit for service till careen'd, and the *Intrepid*, in no great likelihood of being rendered fit for service, the Admiral came to a resolution to put to sea on the 6th following, in quest of the enemy, and to attempt the relief of Fort St. Philip, which, according to the intelligence he had receiv'd, still continued to hold out: and whereas most of the sick-seamen were still in the hospital, incapable of service, he proposed to supply that defect as well as he could, out of the companies of the *Portland* and *Intrepid*, and by unmanning several of the frigates, which were to have been left behind: as also to apply to the Gibraltar[4] for two detachments of soldiers, each equal to a battalion, as specify'd in Mr. Broderick's orders, which now could have been spar'd; seeing the garrison had already been re-inforc'd with one regiment brought on board his squadron, and two more were daily expected from England.

But these resolutions of his, he was not permitted to have the honour of carrying into execution: for on the 2d of July arrived Sir

---

4. Supply "garrison"?

Edward Hawke in the *Antelope*, with orders to supersede him, which were executed the same day in the manner already communicated to the public.

REVIEW OF *THE CONDUCT OF THE MINISTRY IMPARTIALLY EXAMINED.* 1756.

James A. Butler (see n. 1, p. 213) has given a most useful account of how the pamphlet under review here came to be composed. It was one of a number commissioned by the Newcastle ministry from David Mallet (who had patriotically volunteered his services), to present the ministry's case against Byng, or rather against those who were attacking the ministry on behalf of Byng. The member of the ministry who made himself responsible for organizing the pamphlet counter-attack was the astute Lord Chancellor, Hardwicke. Butler quotes a letter from Hardwicke to Mallet (9 October 1756) in which Hardwicke instructs Mallet to make certain additions to the manuscript of *The Conduct of the Ministry*—they duly appear—and one from Hardwicke to Anson the following day, telling him that he has read Mallet's manuscript ("I must own I am not much enamoured with it. But this *entre nous*, for authors of this kind must not be discouraged by too much criticism") and forwarding it to Anson for further revision from the Admiralty point of view. It was published on 30 October. Strahan printed 3,000 copies, an enormous number for such a publication, but testimony to the ministry's eagerness to rebut the supporters of Byng. To keep up the publicity, a "second edition" was advertised on 11 November—actually, only the first with a new title page. On 9 November, Newcastle paid Mallet £300 out of the secret service funds.

The pamphlet is primarily an answer, as Johnson notes in his review, to Shebbeare's *A Fourth Letter to the People of England on the Conduct of the M——rs in Alliances, Fleets, and Armies, since the first Differences on the Ohio, to the taking of Minorca by the French*,[1] a blistering omnibus review of the past four or five years, concluding with the Byng affair. Shebbeare is a highly competent writer of invective; Johnson must have relished such a comment as this on Anson, "A parrot which could have pronounced by authority, 'Equip ten ships at Chatham, ten at Portsmouth, and ten at Plymouth,' would as effectually and as speedily have produced a fleet ready for the seas as the voice of the First L——d of the Ad——y." Johnson's generally low opinion of Mallet is well known from his *Life* of him and from Boswell; he was well aware that Mallet was engaged on the ministerial side in the Byng controversy, and very probably, when he wrote the review, that Mallet had been hired to write the pamphlet under review. At any rate, the result is one of Johnson's more memorable expressions of contempt. The review appeared in the *Literary Magazine*, No. 7 (15 Oct–15 Nov 1756), pp. 340 [*sic*; it should

1. Butler argues that it is also an answer to *A Letter to a Member of Parliament* (p. 219 above), but this is a little hard to see. Certainly Johnson in his review regards it as simply an answer to Shebbeare's *Fourth Letter* (1756).

be 348]–351, the text of which is followed here. It was reprinted in Johnson's *Works* (1788), xiv. 456–66, and there attributed to him "on conjecture."

The Conduct of the Ministry Impartially Examined, in a Letter to the Merchants of London. Bladon, 1 s.

Of this pamphlet the eight first pages contain only the general declarations of every writer of every party, with a little flattery, not gross or indecent, of the merchants, an exhortation to impartiality, and an encomium on the purity of his own intention. When a man appeals to himself for what only himself can know, he may be very confident of a favourable sentence. This author may perhaps think as he writes, for there are men who think as they are bidden. He then takes into consideration a pamphlet which he does not name, because, I suppose, he would not help to advertise it. This is artful, but it is not dishonest. The pamphlet is, I think, one of the *Letters to the People of England*,[1] from which he gives the following quotation, with his answer.

In the year one thousand seven hundred and forty nine, or fifty, some American traders, subjects of the king of Great Britain, travelled to the borders of the Ohio to traffick with the natives of those parts; this being known to the Canadian French, messengers were dispatched to acquaint them, that, unless they withdrew from their master's territories, their effects would be confiscated, and themselves carried to prison at Quebec. This message the traders thought fit to obey, and withdrew in consequence of it.

The succeeding season, another company of British subjects came to trade on the Ohio: and not withdrawing on a like message with the former, their goods were confiscated, and themselves carried prisoners to Quebec, from whence they were brought to Rochelle[2] in France, and still detained in prison. Not conscious of having violated the laws of nations,[3]

---

1. Shebbeare's *Fourth Letter to the People of England*. See headnote.
2. One state of Shebbeare's *Fourth Letter* reads "Bordeaux" instead of "Rochelle."
3. International law.

or traded on any ground to which the king of Great Britain had not an undoubted right, they remonstrated to the British ministry, insisted upon being claimed as British subjects, and honourably discharged from prison, as persons unoffending the laws of nations; nay, they entertained the honourable hopes of Englishmen, that the ministry of England would not cease to demand an indemnification for the loss of that merchandize, which had been unjustly taken from them; and reparation for the insult and long imprisonment of their persons: expectations becoming men, who value their liberties, properties, and nation's honour: in this they were deceived, the true spirit of an English minister no longer dwelt amongst us. The ambassador at Paris,[4] instead of demanding these subjects of his master, as men unjustly held in prison, and reparation for the wrongs they had received, was ordered by the ministry to sollicit, as a favour from the court of France, the discharge of them only, acknowledging their offence.

Thus he relates and circumstantiates the fact: and here I beg leave to remark, that when the circumstances, on which alone a charge is founded, are absolutely false, all reflections upon them must be utterly absurd and impertinent. But when those reflections, aimed too at persons of the highest rank, of the greatest eminence in this nation, are delivered in a stile of the most indecent and furious railing; what name, gentlemen, shall we bestow on their author? or what shall be said in reply to them? No more, I think, than what Beralde, in the *Malade Imaginaire* of Moliere, answers to the apothecary. Allez, Monsieur; on voit bien que vous[a] n'avez pas accoutumé de parler a des visages.[5] Here, however, they follow in his own words still:

> Were not your sovereign's rights and your own privileges shamefully given up? Were not the lands on the Ohio confessed

a. nous *LM*

---

4. William Anne Keppel, 2nd Earl of Albemarle.

5. Act III, Scene 4. A famous off-colour witticism (often expunged from school editions of the play). The apothecary, M. Fleurant, appears with syringe in hand to administer to the *malade*, Argan, another in his frequent series of enemas. Béralde, who is trying to cure his brother of his addiction to medical treatment, prevents Fleurant from doing so. Fleurant objects in indignant and impertinent language. Béralde then makes this comment, "Obviously you aren't used to talking to people's faces."

to belong to France? Were not the French justified in imprisoning your fellow-subjects, and confiscating their effects, by this tame behaviour of the British minister?

He resumes the same subject, page 8, and asserts, "That the minister's timidly beseeching as a favour what he had a right to demand as justice from the French, has given that nation a better foundation to the claim of the Ohio." In about fifteen lines lower, he asserts again, "That the timidity of the minister gave the French no foundation at all." But he has not yet done with this favourite topic. He goes on to say,

If it be asked whence it comes to pass that this behaviour of the British minister has never been mentioned in the French memorials, relative to the disputes in America? It may be answered, with truth, that they reserve it only between the British minister and themselves; lest a public declaration of this affair might remove him from the administration, and the French monarch lose an ally of greater consequence to his success, than any potentate in Europe.[6]

Here then we join issue: and let his credit with the public for veracity and candour, in whatever else he asserts through his libel, be determined by the truth or falshood of the fact before us. This demand, gentlemen, is fair and equitable: you see he affirms it in the most undoubting terms, and remarks upon it in a language that not even certainty itself could warrant. But to the point:

On a motion made to the peers, the twentieth of February, one thousand seven hundred and fifty-six, certain papers and letters concerning the incroachments of the French on his Majesty's subjects in North America, were laid before the House. As their authenticity is incontrovertible, I have only the easy task of copying them faithfully for your full satisfaction.

Extract of a letter from the Earl of Albermarle to the Earl of Holdernesse.[7]

Paris, 19th February, 1 March,[8] 1752.

I must acquaint your lordship, that, in the month of November, I received a letter from three persons, signing themselves,

6. *The Conduct of the Ministry* here (p. 9) does some cutting and paraphrasing in its quotations from the *Fourth Letter*.
7. Robert D'Arcy, 4th Earl of Holdernesse, Secretary of State.

8. Britain did not adopt the Gregorian calendar until September of this year. Hence the double date (Old Style in London, New Style in Paris).

John Patton, Luke Erwin, and Thomas Bourke; representing to me, that they were Englishmen, who had been brought to Rochelle, and put into prison there, from whence they wrote: having been taken by the French subjects, who seized their effects as they were trading with the English and other Indians on the river Ohio, and carried them prisoners to Quebec; from whence they have been sent over to Rochelle, where they are hardly used. Upon this information I applied to Mr. St. Contest,[9] and gave him a note of it, claiming them, as the king's subjects, and demanding their liberty and the restitution of their effects that had been unjustly taken from them.

These three persons, I find by the paper your lordship has sent me, are of the number of those demanded of the French by Mr. Clinton,[1] and named in Mr. de la Jonquiere's[2] letter. I have wrote to a merchant at Rochelle to enquire after them, and to supply them with money to make their journey hither, if they are not gone; that I may receive from them all the informations necessary. On my seeing Mr. St. Contest, next Tuesday, I will represent the case to him, in obedience to his Majesty's commands, that la Jonquiere may have positive orders to desist from the unjustifiable proceedings complained of; to release any of his Majesty's subjects he may still detain in prison, and make ample restitution of their effects. And I shall take care to shew him the absolute necessity of sending instructions to their several governors not to attempt any such incroachments for the future.

Extract of a letter from the Earl of Albemarle to the Earl of Holdernesse.

26th February, 8th March, 1752.

I am now to acquaint your lordship, that I saw Monsieur Rouillé[3] yesterday; and that having drawn up a note of the several complaints I had received orders to make of la Jonquiere's conduct, I delivered it to him, and told him, in general,

---

9. François-Dominique Barberie, Marquis de St. Contest, French foreign minister.

1. Admiral George Clinton, Governor of the Province of New York, in whose territories (according to the British claim) the men had been seized.

2. Pierre-Jacques de Taffanel, Marquis de la Jonquière, Governor of New France (Canada).

3. Antoine-Louis Rouillé, Comte de Jouy, minister for the *Marine* (naval and overseas affairs), later foreign minister.

the contents of it; insisting on the necessity, for preserving the good understanding betwixt his Majesty and the Most Christian King,[4] of sending such positive orders to all their governors, as might effectually prevent, for the future, any such incroachments on his Majesty's territories, and committing such violences[b] on his subjects as had been done in the past. I added to my remonstrance, that I hoped they would be taken into consideration quickly; that he might be able to give me an answer next week, or as soon afterwárds as he possibly could. This minister told me, he would use his best endeavours for that purpose; assured me it was the intention of his court to prevent any disputes arising that might tend to alter the present correspondence between the two nations; and that I might depend upon such orders being sent to their governors accordingly.

Of the three men I mentioned to your lordship in my letter of last week, that had been brought prisoners from Canada to Rochelle, whom I sent for to come to Paris, two of them are arrived, and the third is gone to London. I will take such informations from them as may be necessary for my own instruction, to support their receiving satisfaction for the injuries that have been done them.

Translation of part of the Memorial delivered by Lord Albemarle to Mr. Rouillé, on the 7th of March, 1752.

As to the fort which the French have undertaken to build on the river Niagara, and as to the six Englishmen who have been made prisoners; Lord Albemarle is ordered by his court to demand[c] that the most express orders be sent to Mr. de la Jonquiere, to desist from such unjust proceedings, and in particular to cause the fort above-mentioned to be immediately razed; and the French and others in their alliance, who may happen to be there, to retire forthwith: as likewise to set the six Englishmen at liberty, and to make them ample satisfaction for the wrongs and losses they have suffered; and lastly, that the persons who have committed these excesses, be punished in such a manner as may serve for an example to those who might hereafter venture on any like attempt.

I have now, gentlemen, let you into the truth of this transaction; which the pamphleteer assures you was little known, till he ex-

b. violencies *LM*   c. demand *italicized in Conduct*

---

4. The official style of the French monarch, *le Roi Très Chrétien.*

plained, that is, till he falsified it in every particular but one, and that nothing at all to the purpose of calumny. Is this then the advocate of the people of England? Is it thus he informs our judgments first, to set our passions afterwards on the side of truth and public spirit?

Of these two accounts thus set in opposition to each other, it is not very apparent but that both may be near the truth. That some men taken prisoners were once "demanded" with some degree of spirit is evident, but it does not appear whether they were restored on "demand" or on supplication; nor can it be found that any restitution was made of their goods, or was required a second time. The "three" men who are mentioned in the first paper seem to be different from those mentioned in the other, of whose fate there is no account.

He next mentions an assertion of the same author relating to the lands on the Ohio, but does not quote the passage, nor does the answer contain any facts of much importance.

In the next pages of this pamphlet, is a pompous detail of the ships, which under the command of different admirals went out, did nothing, and came home to be refitted. Some reasons are indeed given why they did nothing, while our enemies did every thing. It is very possible to be unfortunate, but it is full as common to be foolish and dishonest.

In one of his pages he just mentions the invasion with which we were threatened in the beginning of the year,[5] over which however "he chuses to throw a total veil."[6] Surely he would not have us forget the alarm which frighted some of our women to strong waters, and our Parliament to Hanoverian troops.[7] Let us not forget the flat-bottomed boats, built, I suppose, in the clouds, and now lost in the clouds again. Again let us not forget that when any nation is to be fleeced, it is first to be frighted.

The latter part of this pamphlet relates to the case of the unfortunate Byng, whom he treats, as the other ministerial writers have treated him, with the utmost malevolence.

---

5. See pp. 180, 214 above.
6. *Conduct*, p. 49: "Had a descent been then attempted; had they even sacrificed fifteen or twenty thousand men in the attempt, what must have been the consequences to this great capital? I chuse, however, to throw a total veil over the scene in my eyes."
7. See p. 153 above.

He first begins with telling us in a manner very little satisfactory, why more ships were not sent to Minorca. After Byng's squadron, and others were sent out, we had but thirty four ships fitted and manned, of which "it was now judged indispensably necessary to have nineteen cruising before Brest and Rochfort."[8] This is nothing, the question is whether such judgment was right. Of the other fifteen he gives no account. The whole of his argument is this, that more ships were not sent to Minorca because they were at some other place; for what reason they were at a place where they were less needed he has not informed us. He then tells us that Byng's fleet was remarkably well manned and equipped, and that the French fleet carried only "the sweepings of Toulon, old men past service, or boys not yet grown up to it."[9] I will not positively deny what I do not certainly know to be false, but as a writer of this kind has no claim to credit on his own word, he should have told us by what intelligence he knows it to be true. The French seldom want men, a few practised seamen were sufficient for such a short and safe navigation, and the rest of the crew might easily be supplied. I am therefore apt to suspect that he has distributed youth and age according to his pleasure.

He goes on in the stile of his brethren to tell us, that "the disgrace of the British flag, and the fatal disasters consequent on that disgrace, were the effect[d] of *one man's*— But let the justice of the Nation give it a name."[1]

To name a crime is easy. If Byng be criminal, there are but two names for his crime, it was either treachery or cowardice. The crime of a writer of falsehood is either malice or prostitution. I accuse this writer of neither, but as I am very ambitious of imitating every one who has intimacies with men of power, will leave the justice of the nation to give a name to the man who declares that Byng could not only have relieved Fort St. Philip, tho' he had but one regiment on board, who were in the battle to serve him as marines, and was called back even from observing the place by a

d. effect *conj.*] effort *LM*

---

8. Quoted from *Conduct*, pp. 52–53.   1. *Conduct*, p. 55 (slightly altered).
9. *Conduct*, p. 54.

superior fleet, but "that he might have brought back a marshal of France and his army prisoners."[2]

To what has been said already on the case of Mr. Byng, I shall add,[3]

That his enemies have, since the appearance of his defence, endeavoured to change the state of the question.

That the most forward of the ministerial writers dare no longer charge him as the loser of Minorca.

That the only question now is concerning his conduct in the battle.

That this is a question relating no otherwise to the nation, than as the nation is interested in the discipline of the navy.

That by his cowardice, if we prejudge him a coward, he lost no ground, for Minorca could not be saved; no ship, for he brought his whole fleet away; no honour, for the enemy retired before him.

That if Byng's general character be infamous, those must share the infamy, that selected him for an undertaking so important.

That Byng has been treated since his return with indignities and severities, neither decent nor needful.

That papers have been industriously given away to inflame the populace against him.[4]

That since the prosecution of Laud, no such zeal for vindictive justice has been ever shewn.

That from such diligence of persecution there is reason to believe some latent enemies interested in the accusation, who defame him that he may be less invidiously destroyed.

That whatever be the fate of Byng, the justice of the nation ought to hunt out the men who lost Minorca.

---

2. *Conduct*, p. 67
3. No doubt intended as a continuation of SJ's peroration to his

Byng reviews in the previous number of the *Literary Magazine* (p. 239 above).
4. See n. 2, p. 238.

SPEECH ON THE ROCHEFORT
EXPEDITION. 1757.

The Pitt-Newcastle coalition finally came into existence in the summer of 1757, but its formation did not immediately result in a flood of military victories. Indeed, the first operation (a "combined" one) under its auspices was an inglorious fiasco. In September, a naval expedition under the command of Sir Edward Hawke, escorting a military force under that of Sir John Mordaunt, was dispatched, with an attempt at secrecy, against the west coast of France—in particular, against the important arms depot of Rochefort. The fleet approached the coast, and overcame the small and unimportant island of Aix. But after considering the problems of attacking Rochefort itself, a council of war of the senior officers of the expedition came to the conclusion that it would be unwise to do so, and the expedition returned to England. The affair could no longer be kept secret, and the public reaction was one of the greatest chagrin and anger.

One of its most vivid expressions is the piece below, whose existence was not known until it was printed in the *Gentleman's Magazine*, October 1785. There is no indication of its provenance. Nichols had printed many small pieces of Johnsoniana in the magazine in the months after Johnson's death, but something of this nature would more probably have been contributed from someone outside the regular *Gentleman's Magazine* circle. Nothing whatever is known of the circumstances in which it was composed, except what we are told in the text itself and the heading. The italics in the heading, "a certain respectable *talking* Society," seem designed to make the reader think that it was a parliamentary occasion (with the old joke about the derivation of "parliament" from *parler*), and Nichols may have thought that it was. But, as the text itself clearly states, Parliament was not in session—it had been prorogued in July 1757, and the new session opened on 1 December.

The one public assembly which seems to have contemplated addressing the King on the occasion was the Common Council of the City of London. "The City talk treason," Horace Walpole wrote his friend General Conway on 13 October—Conway had been involved in the expedition—and "they intend in a violent manner to seek redress." What happened is reported in the *Gentleman's Magazine*, Nov 1757, p. 527:

> Friday, Nov. 4. At a court of common council held at Guildhall, a motion was made to address his majesty on the miscarriage of the late expedition to the coast of France. After some debate, the Lord Mayor being asked whether any intimation had been given his lordship of such an inquiry being intended, his lordship informed the court that on Monday, Oct. 31, Wm. Blair, Esq., one of the clerks of his majesty's

most hon. privy council, came to the Mansion-house and acquainted him that he waited on the Lord Mayor to let him know that his majesty had given directions that such inquiry should be prosecuted with the utmost expedition and vigour, or to that effect; on which, after a short debate, the motion was withdrawn.

The result of the governmental inquiry was that a court martial of Mordaunt was convened; but, as Johnson had as much as predicted, the court martial found him guiltless. Nor did a great deal happen after Parliament met on 1 December: the *Parliamentary History* records (xv.835) a skilful speech on the address in reply to the Speech from the Throne by Philip Yorke, Lord Royston, Hardwicke's son and heir, in which the affair is alluded to with proper regret, but confidence in the ministry is called for. Royston was supported by a large majority: Parliament was not prepared to call for the dismissal of Pitt, which Johnson broadly hints is one solution to the problem.

The most puzzling question is who was the "friend" who delivered Johnson's diatribe? I have been able to find no detailed report of the debate in the Common Council. The one M.P. who (according to the *Parliamentary History*) appears to have taken issue with Royston was William Beckford, who was also of course a prominent member of the City Corporation. Beckford seems an unlikely candidate for Johnson's assistance, considering his later career as a "patriot" in the reign of George III. But then the terms of politics were very different (especially for Johnson) in the reign of George II.

The text is that of the *Gentleman's Magazine* (Oct 1785), 764–65.

A Speech *Dictated* by Dr. Johnson, without Premeditation or Hesitation, on the Subject of an Address to the Throne, after the Expedition to Rochfort, in September, 1757, at the Desire of a Friend, Who Delivered It, the Next Day, at a Certain Respectable *Talking* Society

The present question is not, whether the people have a right to address his Majesty, for an enquiry into the conduct of the late expedition? but, whether, at this time, it be expedient to address him? There is, perhaps, no nation in the world where individuals have not the right to address their king, if they think themselves injured; and what may be done by every single man, may be done, with yet greater propriety, by communities and corporations.[1] The question, therefore,

---

1. This statement seems to confirm the hypothesis that the speech was delivered to a body representing a "community or corporation"—e.g., the Common Council of the City of London.

is, whether this privilege shall be exerted on this occasion? but, if not on this occasion, on what occasion shall we exert it? We have raised a fleet, and an army; we have equipped them; we have paid them; they set out with the favour and good wishes of the whole nation. Great advantage was expected from the secrecy of our counsellors, and the bravery of our commanders. They went out, and they are come back again, not only without doing, but without attempting to do anything; and, therefore, not without suspicion of treachery or cowardice, since no reason has yet been given, why they desisted from the design, at the moment of execution. A wise man may be deceived in forming a scheme; and, in executing it, a brave man may miscarry; and it has been the custom of all wise nations, to honour the man who has done his duty, even when he wanted success. But no nation has yet suffered themselves to be exhausted, in sending out fleets and armies, without enquiring what they have done; and why they have done nothing. Caligula once marched to the sea-coasts, and gathered cockle-shells:[2] our army went to the coast of France, and filled their bellies with grapes.[3] Caligula's expedition has been, to this day, the subject of merriment; and we can only avert, from ourselves, the like contempt, by enquiring rigorously, by whose fault our troops and ships have been equally ridiculous. If contempt, indeed, were the only consequence of the miscarriage, we might sit quietly down, and join in the laugh; but, since a war with France is more than sport; and, since they who betrayed us once, will, if they are not punished, betray us again; or, by the example of their impunity, teach others to betray us; it is fit, that this miscarriage, whether it be the effect of treachery or cowardice, be detected and punished, that those whom, for the future, we shall employ and pay, may know they are the servants of a people, that expect duty for their money, that will not be mocked with idle expeditions, or satisfied with an account of walls that

---

2. Suetonius, *Lives of the Caesars*, IV.46 ("Caligula").

3. Considerable plundering of the property of local inhabitants was reported among the British troops who landed on Aix. In *Idler* 5 (13 May 1758), SJ, sarcastically suggesting that women be enrolled in the army (they can hardly do worse than the men are now doing), writes, "I cannot but think, that seven thousand women might have ventured to look at Rochfort, sack a village, rob a vineyard, and return in safety."

were never seen, and ditches that were never tried. To this address I have heard some objections, which appear to me of no great force, and which, I believe, a few words will be sufficient to obviate. It is said, an objection expresses some distrust of the king, or may tend to disturb his quiet. An English king, Mr. President, has no great right to quiet when his people are in misery; nor does he shew any great respect to his sovereign, who imagines him unwilling to share the distresses, as well as the prosperities, of his subjects. To express distrust, is not intended: we distrust not the king, but those who may have an interest to deceive him. It is the misfortune of a king, that he seldom, but in cases of public calamity, knows the sentiments of his people.[4] It is commonly the interest of those about him to mislead him by false intelligence, or flatter him by soft representations. It is therefore fit, when the people are injured, the people should complain, and not trust the sycophants of a court with their cause or their sentiments. It is said this affair will soon be examined by a court martial; but of court martials the people have no high opinion; they expect justice from them, only when justice is their interest; and it is their interest, only when they find it cannot be refused but by incurring the resentment of the public. Others are of opinion the Parliament, when they meet, will spend the first part of the session in the examination of this event. The proposers of this objection appear to fall upon a dilemma, of which either supposition will conclude against them. If the Parliament will not enquire of themselves, the address is necessary; if they would enquire without the address, the address would be harmless. There is one objection behind still weaker; that such addresses give uneasiness to the minister:[5] but I should not conceive that this objection was made by those who wish the minister's continuance: for, if our

---

4. Cf. SJ's "Memoirs of the King of Prussia," *Literary Magazine*, No. 7 (15 Oct–15 Nov 1756)–No. 9 (15 Dec 1756–15 Jan 1757): "Kings, without this help [i.e., of an acquaintance "with the various forms of life"], from temporary infelicity, see the world in a mist, which magnifies everything near them, and bounds their view to a narrow compass, which few are able to extend by the mere force of curiosity."

5. I.e., the "chief minister." It is a nice question whether Pitt or Newcastle was intended—perhaps the reader could take his choice.

ministers are wise and honest, the address will only afford them an opportunity to put their wisdom and integrity beyond dispute: and, if they are ignorant or treacherous, I hope nobody will wish they should be kept easy at the expence of their country.

"OBSERVATIONS" AND CORRESPONDENCE IN THE *UNIVERSAL CHRONICLE*. 1758.

A full account of what is known of Johnson's connexion with the *Universal Chronicle* (based to a large extent on a study by Boylston Green in 1941, an unpublished dissertation for Yale University) is given in the Introduction to Volume II of this edition, and need not be repeated here. As well as contributing *The Idler*, which commenced in the second number, Johnson has been credited (by Allen T. Hazen, *Johnson's Prefaces and Dedications*, 1937, pp. 205 ff.) with the opening manifesto of the periodical and the essay which immediately follows it, "Of the Duty of a Journalist," in the first number. In addition, Boylston Green, in the study mentioned above, attributes to him the five pieces, four "Observations" and a letter to the *Universal Chronicle*, which Green calls "Observation V," printed below.

Green's attribution is based, as well as on the known fact of Johnson's connexion with the *Chronicle*, on such internal evidence as the following:

> In the *Observations* are several opinions that he had voiced during the preceding months. The derisive references to attacks on unfortified towns and the shameful surrender of Minorca that are in *Observations* IV and V echo the final sentence of *Idler* 5, which was published May 13, 1758. And the same sentiments are reiterated in the conclusion to *Idler* 39, that appeared some months later, January 13, 1759. The coupling of Toulon and Paris when speaking of French strongholds in *Observations* IV and V is a device Johnson utilized in *Idler* 8, June 3, 1758. The refusal to estimate the capture of Louisbourg as a major military triumph in *Observations* II coincides exactly with the opinion voiced in *Idler* 20, published the same day. The interest in Frederick the Great manifest in *Observations* III reminds the reader of the *Memoirs of Frederick* that Johnson wrote for the *Literary Magazine* in 1756.

To these might be added such parallels as that with the notice of Armstrong's *History of Minorca* published in the first number of the *Literary Magazine* a year earlier—

> If the distribution of empire were in my hands, I should indeed rather give up Gibraltar . . . than Minorca. . . . But I know not whether either is worth its charge, and by losing them, I am not sure that we shall suffer anything more than that vexation which accompanies disgrace—

and (with the conclusion of *Observation* III) this, from the "Foreign History" section of the *Gentleman's Magazine* during the period of Johnson's greatest activity on that journal—

Upon these marches and counter-marches, it has been observed that the maxims of war have been much changed by the refinements of the present times. In the ruder and more heroic ages, it was the standing practice to take at all events the first opportunity of fighting: the great rule of conduct at present is never to fight without a visible advantage, which rule, if it be observed on both sides, will for ever prevent a battle.

The point is that it is somewhat remarkable that squibs like these, strongly expressing, in most vivid and incisive prose, a sardonic attitude toward military glory and imperial aggrandizement unusual at the time, have a habit of turning up in periodicals during the time Johnson is otherwise actively involved in them. Conceivably, of course, some other writer, so far unknown, may be discovered whose style and views on these matters are closely similar to Johnson's and who was employed on the same periodicals at the same time he was. Green's attribution of these "Observations," however, has now been public for a quarter of a century and has not been challenged (Hazen's attribution of pieces in the *Universal Chronicle*, likewise based on internal evidence, is only five years older, and has already won the accolade, from the editors of Volume ii of the Yale Edition, "Johnson, as Allen Hazen has shown . . . wrote the two introductory essays"), and it seems safe enough to print these as Johnson's. A remarkable proportion of the accepted Johnson canon owes its existence to such a prescriptive process.

One might almost say that these short "Observations," published in the midst of the Great War for the Empire, deserve reprinting whoever wrote them, for their boldness in opposing the current cant. In fact, the *Universal Chronicle*'s "Observations" managed to survive for only four numbers. Number 4 was too much for its patriotic readers. The indignant response of one is printed below, in proper sequence, in order to make the "Observator's" reply comprehensible. That reply is an utterly devastating counter-attack—one of Johnson's best pieces of controversial writing, as fine in its vigour as the letters to Chesterfield and Macpherson. But evidently Newbery (if his was the controlling hand behind the *Chronicle*) had had enough—as the proprietors of the *Literary Magazine* had had, the year before—and there were no more disturbing "Observations" published on the great patriotic war.

The text here follows that of the first edition in the *Universal Chronicle* (retitled *Payne's Universal Chronicle* after No. 5, 29 Apr–6 May). The "Observations" have hitherto been reprinted only in Boylston Green's article, "Possible Additions to the Johnson Canon," *Yale University Library Gazette*, xvi (1942), 70–79, and in *The Political Writings of Dr. Johnson: A Selection* (1968), ed. J. P. Hardy, pp. 32–38. Green entitles the pieces "*Observation I . . . Observation V.*" The numbering does not appear in the original but for convenience is inserted here, in brackets, for the first four pieces. The fifth, however, is a letter, not an "Observation," and should not be so designated.

Observations. [I][1]

Our troops have at last taken a French town; Cherbourg is in the possession of the English.[2] To celebrate a conquest of so small importance with any ostentation of triumph, would be ridiculous; but it is no less unreasonable to repress the joy which the gleam of success naturally gives, after a long continuance of the clouds of disappointment. This is the first attempt by which all has been done which was expected or desired, and from this we may hope for more advantages. Victory naturally produces elation of spirit, and elation reciprocally invites enterprize, and ensures victory.

It may be asked by those who affect, for some reason or other, to despise all the schemes of the government, what we propose to gain by invading France with seven thousand men; a force which, to a nation so numerous and warlike, must appear contemptible as a troop of wolves descending from the mountains? It may be asked, why we take a town which we cannot keep, and land only to embark again?

To all this, the answer is easy. We invade the French not to conquer, but to harrass and alarm them. We do not suppose that we put Paris or Versailles in any immediate terror, but we know that the maritime provinces are kept in perpetual disturbance, and distraction; that wherever we land the inhabitants are distressed by their fears, if not by their sufferings. The distress of one part is not felt without inconvenience to the rest, and inconvenience long continued will make a people weary of war.

By taking and quitting, at pleasure, the towns of France, we convince all Europe of our naval superiority; we shew to other nations that the French have no fleets that can oppose us on the sea, and to the French themselves, that they have no troops that can guard the coast. We diminish the reputa-

---

1. *Payne's Universal Chronicle*, No. 20 (12–19 Aug 1758), p. 160.

2. This heavily fortified French seaport was captured 7 Aug by a force led by Commodore Richard Howe and General Thomas Bligh. In an

unsuccessful subsidiary action at St. Cas a short time later, Bennet Langton's uncle-in-law, General Alexander Dury, was killed, and SJ wrote to console him (*Letters* 116).

tion of the French for ever among foreigners, and of the French government among the French themselves. We destroy that prejudice which gave every petty people courage to treat us with contempt at the beginning of the war. Those nations that, two years ago, saw us trembling at home, and calling out for succour from the Continent to protect us from an invasion, which it must always be remembred, the French had neither power nor design to execute,[3] now see us insulting the coast of France, not only without repulse, but without resistance. We have had indeed no opportunity to exert our valour nor can boast of no[4] routed armies, but that we ravage the country unopposed, if it does not give any new specimen of English courage, gives at least a proof of the weakness of France.

Observations. [II][1]

It is natural to pass from dejection to exultation. He that thought his danger more than it was, will set more value than he ought upon every glimpse of deliverance. When we lost Minorca[2] a general panick fell upon the nation, and every man met his neighbour with a clouded forehead, and a down cast eye, as if London had been besieged. Louisbourg is now taken,[3] and our streets echo with triumph, and blaze with illumination, as if our King was once more proclaimed at Paris. Surprizes both of grief and joy are natural, but let us recover from them as soon as we can, and estimate every event according to its importance, and every acquisition according to its value. The siege of Louisbourg has been so happily conducted, that perhaps there are few examples in history of a place so strong, conquered in so short a time, with

---

3. See pp. 214 and 258 above.
4. A double negative, rare in SJ.
1. *Payne's Universal Chronicle*, No. 21 (19–26 Aug 1758), p. 168. This number also contains *Idler* 20, satirically imagining the differing accounts an English and a French historian would give of the capture of Louisbourg.

2. Minorca fell to the French in June 1756 after the naval force led by Admiral John Byng failed to drive them away. See above pp. 213–17.
3. By an expedition under the command of Major-General Jeffrey Amherst, a protégé of Pitt, on 26 July. The news reached London 18 Aug.

so little loss. Whether this facility of success be attributed to English skill, or to French timidity, it is equally pleasing. If our military skill be great, we may hope to conquer men who, tho' they have equal bravery, have less knowledge; if our enemies be timorous, they can never be formidable whatever be their skill. The French seem to have placed too much confidence in their ships, which made the harbour inaccessible by sea, and which they did not consider that the besiegers might destroy by their batteries. Human caution is never able to guard all sides, and danger, when it comes unexpected, comes with double force. When the French saw their ships destroyed by shot from the land, they lost their courage, and forgot that their walls were yet undemolished. Thus Louisbourg was taken and the reputation of our arms restored, which is indeed one great effect, if not the greatest of this boasted conquest. Louisbourg is not useful to us, in the same degree as its loss is detrimental to our enemies. They value it as a port of security for their ships, as the place where their American forces may safely assemble, sheltered alike from hostilities and tempests. We can desire it only that we may deprive them of an advantageous station, for we do not want ports in that part of the world; so that much is taken from our enemies, but little gained to ourselves. But this is the condition of war; to make one part weaker, is to strengthen the other; and this advantage we have obtained not only by the capture of the fortress, but by the destruction of 11 ships, by which the French navy that was weak from the beginning of the war, is reduced to a state in which it can no longer hope to oppose us.

Observations. [III][1]

Since the siege of Olmutz[2] was raised, there is little mention of the King of Prussia; we know only that he is retreating to his own dominions, and that the Austrian provinces are in some measure delivered from the terrors of the sword, and

---

1. *Payne's Universal Chronicle*, No. 22 (26 Aug–2 Sept 1758), p. 176.
2. In northern Austria. Frederick had besieged it since April, but on 1 July abandoned the siege.

the burthen of contributions. Our fears are again returning upon us, and whenever the affairs of the Continent are mentioned, the King of Prussia is commiserated as a potentate upon whom destruction is opening her jaws, upon whose dominions all the surrounding powers are bursting at once, and whose provinces are already allotted to his enemies. That he has indeed enemies on all sides is evident, but his enemies have greater names than forces. He has little to fear except from the Austrians, and from them he has not suffered much.

It seems to have been the expectation of his English allies, that his troops should conquer whatever they invade, that his name should disarm every hand that was raised against him; that he should pass without obstruction from province to province, and from city to city; that he should do all, and his enemies do nothing. Elated with this hope, contrary to reason, contrary to experience, we saw him enter the field, expecting that every day would produce new acquisitions; and since we have seen his first enterprize fail of success, we descend at once from our elevation, consider miscarriage as an overthrow, and resign our hero to death or captivity. But what has happened to the King of Prussia, which does not happen to the most successful generals? He besieged a city, his ammunition was intercepted, he could not batter it without bullets, and therefore raised the siege. He was advancing into the enemies' provinces, and encountered little opposition; his territories are invaded on the other side, and he finds it necessary to post his army nearer the center. The gain of a battle would re-establish him in his former superiority, and convince us once more that he is invincible; but perhaps he may think a battle too hazardous in his present situation, when his enemies are all so near him, and so ready to improve any advantage which he might give them by suffering a defeat. The truth is, that a battle is scarcely to be expected unless the King of Prussia should snatch some casual opportunity, or should be so confined on all sides as to find himself obliged to force open a passage; for the condition of the Austrians, after so many losses, is likewise such, that they cannot suffer another overthrow, without the utmost danger and distress. It is therefore not unlikely, that the remaining part of the summer will be spent in marches and counter-

marches, excursions into the open country, and petty skirmishes of small parties.[3]

Observations. [IV][1]

Every public act either raises or sinks the honour of a people,
and is therefore a proper subject of praise or reprehension.
The pomp with which a few French colours were, on Wednesday, carried to St. Paul's,[2] since perhaps it was very little considered before the exhibition may be fitly reviewed after it.

To celebrate victories by triumphs, to notify, by some
publick festivity, the happy success of military enterprizes, has
been the practice of all civilized nations. State-craft has
sometimes inverted this practice, and the people have been
taught to rejoice when the army has been defeated. This is
the grossest stratagem of political fraud; and this, I hope, our
governors will never be reduced to practise; but some approaches to it are made, when we are taught to think our
acquisitions greater than they are, or to express our joy in a
manner disproportionate to the sorrow felt by our enemies.

The display of these captive colours, if not a triumph, was
at least an *ovation*,[3] and was to be understood by the gazing
populace as an undoubted proof of the inferiority of France.
But what has France yet suffered from the British arms, or
what did we gain but the colours, when these colours fell into
our hands? When the trophies of Blenheim were displayed,
one spectator was able to tell another, that the French were
driven out of the Empire, and had lost, perhaps three hundred
miles of territory; when the spoils of Ramillies were carried
thro' the city, it might have been truly proclaimed, that

---

3. SJ's prediction proved untrue: on
25 August Frederick successfully fought
the important battle of Zorndorf
against the Russians.

1. *Payne's Universal Chronicle*, No. 23
(2–9 Sept 1758), p. 184. The *Idler* that
appeared in this number was the
terrible "original No. 22," with the
vultures' reflections on the carnage of
a human battlefield.

2. On 6 Sept they were paraded
before the King and taken to St.
Paul's, where a service of thanksgiving
was conducted by the Bishops of Oxford and Bristol.

3. SJ expects his readers to be
familiar with the difference between
the greater form of Roman public
tribute to a military victor ("triumph") and the lesser ("ovation").

Flanders lay open to our army. But how were these colours got, whence did they come, and what did they cost? They were not gained by a decisive victory; there is no army defeated, France is not much weaker than she was before, and the war, however successful, is not much nearer to an end. They were not torn down from the walls of Paris or Toulon; they were not brought from Minorca, in return for those which we lately lost. They came from a place so obscure and inconsiderable, that its name is known only to the French and English; and are purchased at an expence, which would be barely countervailed by the conquest of a province on the Continent, or the defeat of a royal army.

Surely our understandings are treated with too much contempt, when these fallacies are practised upon us; when we are entertained with such despicable processions, as equivalent to the expence of millions, and the death of thousands.

Let us no more boast, till something is performed; let us not exalt our enemies, by telling mankind how highly we rate this petty conquest, and by confessing how much the slightest advantage has exceeded our hope.

[To the Publisher of the *Universal Chronicle*.[1]

Saturday, Sept. 9, 1758.

Sir,

The freedom with which the remarks in your paper, under the title of *Observations*, are given every week, is not, I suppose, assumed as the unalienable privilege of the Observator himself, but may be exercised by any one who finds him drawing conclusions apparently true, from premises that are certainly false; and I dare say you have candour enough to print, in the next number of your Chronicle, this answer to his paper of to-day.

I shall take no notice of the nature of that spirit with which his pompous composition is animated; but, leaving it to be guessed at by its complexion, shall only rescue a fact from that cover of falshood which inexcusable ignorance has thrown over it.

The Observator, then, must be told, what he might have fully known from the public papers, that the "*few* French colours which,

---

1. *Payne's Universal Chronicle*, No. 24 (9–16 Sept 1758), p. 192.

with so much pomp, were on Wednesday carried to St. Paul's,"
were *all* the colours that the French had to surrender to our victorious troops, when, upon terms of capitulation which themselves
dictated, they took possession of the important fortress of Louisbourg.

"The display of these captive colours was, therefore, not an ovation, but a noble and necessary triumph; an undoubted proof of the
inferiority of France." And, with the same joy that was felt "when
the trophies of Blenheim were displayed, and the spoils of Ramillies carried through the city," one spectator of this triumph
might say to another, That *the whole continent of North America now lies
open to our army;* that though these colours were not "torn down from
the walls of Paris or Toulon," they were yet taken at a place, the
possession of which is of ten times more importance to the welfare
of Great Britain, and an ample recompence for "the loss of Minorca";
and that "they were gained by a *decisive* victory," which has made
"France *much weaker* than she was before"; and, which, if properly
improved by us, and mercifully supported by a continuance of the
Divine Favour, must put "a *speedy end* to the war," with honour and
safety to our King and country.

Those, to whose wisdom and spirit in forming the plan of this
conquest, and to whose resolution and integrity in the execution of it,
we owe the only means of establishing our trade and power in
North America (and the same wisdom, and spirit, and integrity
will, I trust, for ever oppose a *second inglorious surrender*[2] of such an
acquisition as a condition of peace, which would a *second time* be the
cause of a bloody war;) those Patriot Ministers, I say, at the same
time, that by "setting a just value on this conquest," they gratified
every eye, and every heart, with "an undoubted proof of the *inferiority* of France," "convinced every understanding," also, how
highly qualified they are to conduct the business of this kingdom,
in the most critical and dangerous situation.

And now, as the Observator must acknowledge, that so far from
"overrating our conquests, and boasting where we have not performed," we have only made a decent triumph upon a most important victory, he will not, I trust, *take offense* at an ovation; but when
the cannon of Cherbourg[3] (a place which, tho' "so obscure and
inconsiderable that its name is known only to the French and English," was yet found to be rising to the formidable state of another

2. Louisbourg, captured in 1745,   3. A triumphal parade of the French
had been restored to the French under   cannon taken at Cherbourg was to be
the terms of the Peace of Aix-la-   held 16 Sept.
Chapelle in 1748.

Dunkirk)[4] are carried through the streets of London, he will himself be a spectator of the procession, and heartily join in the acclamations of the people.]

To the Author of the Universal Chronicle.[1]

Sir,

It was often said by the Earl of Oxford, that "a knot of idle fellows made a noise in one another's ears at a coffee-house, and imagined the nation to be filled with the same clamour."[2] This seems to have been lately the case of the English rabble; they have drank to the conquest of Louisbourg, till they take Louisbourg to be the seat of the Empire, and believe the rest of the world to be of the same opinion. When any of them are told, that the name of Louisbourg is not known but to the nations to whom a local and accidental interest make it important, they stare, and gape, and wonder, and drink again, and talk what neither themselves nor their hearers can understand, of "premises and conclusions," "inexcusable ignorance," "certain falsehood," "spirit and complexion."

The madness of a nation, at least of the English, seldom lasts long; a week is commonly sufficient to restore them to their senses. They begin already to be ashamed of the acclamations with which the French colours were attended; and, perhaps he that with so much vehemence, attacked my honest Observations, has, before this time, recovered from his delirious elevation of heart, and begins to wonder, what himself meant, when he called the capture of a poor fortress, a "decisive victory," and the display of a few colours, an "undoubted proof of the inferiority of France."

4. In the Peace of Utrecht, 1713, the French agreed to dismantle the fortifications of Dunkirk; but this was not effectively done, and the fortress remained a source of concern to the British for several decades.

1. *Payne's Universal Chronicle*, No. 26 (23–30 Sept 1758), p. 208.

2. Cf. Swift, *Thoughts on Various Subjects:* "When someone was telling a certain great Minister that the People were discontented: 'Poh, said he, half a dozen Fools are prating in a Coffee-house, and presently think their own Noise about their Ears is made by the World' " (*Prose Works*, ed. Herbert Davis, IV.250). I am indebted to Professor Morris Golden for this reference.

These colours, he confesses not to be torn down from Paris or Toulon, "but they were taken," he says, "at a place, the possession of which is of ten times more importance to Great Britain, and an ample recompence for the loss of Minorca." This was suitable to the madness of the first hour, when the news was brought of our conquest. But the people are now sober again, and nothing but strong drink will ever persuade them to believe, that Louisbourg and Paris are to be named together. The writer himself seems to have soared above the strength of his own credulity, and comes down from his height with very dangerous precipitation. "Louisbourg is of ten times more importance than Paris, and an ample reccompence for the loss of Minorca." The latter part of this sentence affirms very little in comparison with the former; and yet, I am afraid, it affirms more than is true. I shall not stay to compare the two places. At Minorca the disgrace was to us greater than the loss; we were overcome in the sight of every nation whose respect is to be desired: At Louisbourg the loss is to the French greater than the disgrace, for our victory has happened in a remote part of the world, at a place which nothing but this contest could make known, and for which, when the enquirer has found it in the map, he wonders what can tempt us to dispute.

My censurer has proceeded to prove the importance of the acquisition, by informing us, "that the whole continent of North America now lies open to our army."—Surely not all the wide continent. Ticonderoga[3] must at least be excepted. I do not indeed see, how the state of the continent is much changed, by the capture of an island: I hope this zealous writer knows, that Cape Breton is only an island.[4] The coasts of America are more open, but the continent is as it was before, nor have we yet made any further progress since Louisbourg was taken.

The real value of this conquest I have, in a former remark,

---

3. A shrewd hit. In July 1758 a British force had been repelled by the French, with heavy casualties, in an attack on Fort Ticonderoga, and its commander, Lord Howe (brother of the naval commander at Cherbourg) killed.

4. Perhaps a glance at the famous story (narrated by Horace Walpole) of the Duke of Newcastle's astonishment at learning that Cape Breton is an island.

endeavoured to shew. It is a loss to the French, but no great gain to the English. The expedition has been honourable and useful; but for the "wisdom and spirit required in the plan, or the resolution and integrity in the execution," we must have another night of madness before they will be found. Narrow minds are always engrossed by the present scene.[5] Where is the wisdom of knowing, that we are to take those fortresses of the enemy that annoy us, particularly that fortress which was taken in the last war. What integrity can be exerted in the capture of a castle, or what resolution has been shewn above the courage required in all the ordinary operations of war?

Let us do ourselves justice, and no more than justice; we had no need, and made no use of the resolution shewn by the French in the attack of Minorca.

It is the fate of great and of brave men to be made ridiculous, by idle processions, and ignorant panegyrists. I am pleased, like others, with every prosperous event; as having, like others, my interest involved in that of the nation. I was the first who congratulated my countrymen on our success at Cherburg; but I did not magnify it to another Dunkirk. I praise when I can praise with truth, and hope, that there will never again be need of swelling trifles into dignity, or of covering deficiency with splendid falshood.[6]

I am, Sir,

Your humble servant.

---

5. *Idler* 24, published in the same number of the *Universal Chronicle*, is a mordant comment on such "narrow minds."

6. Horace, *Odes*, III.XI. 35: *Splendide mendax*.

THE BRAVERY OF THE ENGLISH
COMMON SOLDIERS. 1760(?).

The editorial history of this short but admirable piece has been somewhat of a comedy of errors. It was first publicly connected with Johnson's name (or rather with the sobriquet "The Author of the Rambler") in 1767, when it was appended, with two other early journalistic pieces by Johnson, to the "third" (i.e., second collected) edition of *The Idler*. It was then included in Johnson's collected *Works* (1787), and later editions. Boswell, however, confused matters by listing it, illogically, in the "Chronological Catalogue" of Johnson's prose writings prefixed to his *Life* under "1758," the year *The Idler* began, and confused them further by saying, in the text of the *Life*, that Johnson "added" it "to the Idler, when collected in volumes"—i.e., the reader might suppose, in 1761.

Presently students of Goldsmith discovered the piece printed in the first number, January 1760, of the *British Magazine*, a periodical to which Goldsmith contributed a good deal, and noted that in subject and spirit it had much in common with his fine essay on "The Distresses of a Common Soldier," printed in the June 1760 issue. Sir James Prior, investigating the matter in his *Life of Goldsmith* (1837), read Boswell's account, but, turning to the first collected edition of *The Idler*, 1761, found that the essay was not there. Concluding that Boswell had been misled, he had no hesitation in claiming it for Goldsmith (I.349). A later Goldsmith editor, J. W. M. Gibbs (*Works of Goldsmith*, 5 vols., 1884–86), was likewise unable to find it printed along with *The Idler*. He did find it in the Oxford 1825 edition of Johnson's *Works*, but there, Gibbs said, "The editor . . . states that the essay was added to *The Idler* after Johnson's death, and he seems doubtful of its being by Johnson." On this basis, Gibbs too was willing to print it as Goldsmith's (III.447). In fact, the editorial note in the 1825 Johnson does not say what Gibbs says it says, but what it does say is sufficiently confusing: "This short paper was added to some editions of *The Idler*, when collected into volumes, but not by Dr. Johnson, as Mr. Boswell asserts, nor to the early editions of that work." It is true that the title-page of the 1767 *Idler* does not state specifically that the added essays are by Johnson or that Johnson added them ("The Idler, by the Author of the Rambler. The Third Edition. With Additional Essays"). But the 1767 *Idlers* contain some corrections that *may* be by Johnson; one of the publishers of the 1767 volumes was Newbery, who had been connected with *The Idler* perhaps from the beginning and at least at a very early stage; the other two "additional" essays (the 1740 "Essay on Epitaphs" and the 1756

"Dissertation on the Epitaphs of Pope") are indubitably Johnson's.[1] All
this seems at least as good presumptive evidence of Johnson's authorship
of this piece as exists for many other "accepted" items in the Johnson
canon. At any rate, later Goldsmith scholars (e.g., R. S. Crane, *New
Essays by Goldsmith*, 1927, p. 1, n. and *Collected Works of Oliver Goldsmith*,
ed. Arthur Friedman (1966), III.89) seem content to relinquish Goldsmith's claim to it.

Since D. Nichol Smith listed the *British Magazine* printing of the essay
in the "Johnson" section of the *Cambridge Bibliography of English Literature*
in 1940, Johnsonian students have gone on the assumption that this was the
essay's first appearance in print, although nothing else of Johnson's seems
to have been published for the first time in that periodical. It is conceiv-
able that a still earlier printing may turn up in some obscure place.[2] Nevertheless, the notice in the same number of the *British Magazine* that it is
reprinting *Idler* 89 "by permission of the author, whose great genius and
extensive learning may be justly numbered among the most shining ornaments of the present age" seems to indicate some personal contact between
the editorial direction of the *Magazine* and Johnson. One might wonder,
of course, why, if Smollett, the editor, had such a treasure as an *original*
essay by this ornament of the age, he did not publicize the fact; indeed,
Prior uses the omission to do so as an argument against Johnson's authorship
of it—"It would appear . . . that Smollett, or whoever officiated as editor,
knew not or considered it not to be written by Johnson, or they would have
proclaimed the honour for the credit of their work." But Johnson, with his
curious obsession about (official) anonymity, may have forbidden them to
do so. As to why Johnson, at other periods no great friend of Smollett's,
should have chosen just this time to present him, instead of some other
editor, with this fine and topical essay, one cannot help recalling the fact
that some months earlier (March 1759) Smollett had been instrumental
in getting Johnson's runaway servant, Frank Barber, returned to him by
the Navy. Johnson's gratitude would have been suitably expressed by
this offer of one good essay, to help the new periodical get on its feet, but
need not have extended itself to the point of contracting to become a
regular contributor to it.

The length and tone of the piece suggests that it may have originally
been conceived as a sketch for an *Idler;* and certainly the earlier *Idlers*
contain a good deal on the subject of the "military mind," all of it scathingly

1. It seems strange that Tom Davies, who was one of the publishers of the
1767 *Idler* volume, did not include this essay in his *Miscellaneous and Fugitive
Pieces*, 1773–74. He did include the "Dissertation on Pope's Epitaphs," though
not the 1740 "Essay on Epitaphs." But Davies's is such an erratic collection
that there is probably no significance in the omission.
2. It might be argued, in favour of an earlier date of composition, that the
Comte [Lancelot] Turpin de Crissé's *Essai sur l'Art de la Guerre*, quoted in the
essay and referred to there as "lately published," was in fact published in 1754.
An English translation by Joseph Otway was published in 1761.

hostile.[3] There were a number of reasons for this attitude: Johnson shared
with most of his fellow Englishmen of the time a suspicion of a professional army that went back to the time of Cromwell;[4] as a Tory, he held
that suspicion in an intensified form, for the traditional Tory position,
since the War of the Spanish Succession, was that Britian's defence could
be adequately secured by her naval forces and that she could only need
a large army if she abandoned her old "isolationism" and immorally
engaged in interventionist activities in other parts of the world; the war
in which the British troops were now engaged was conspicuously a war of
intervention, for imperial aggrandizement and commercial gain, and Johnson was bitterly opposed to it; finally, for all the "patriot" fanfare of the
Pittites, Britain's military operations in the opening stages of that war
had been notoriously unsuccessful,[5] and this fact seemed to Johnson to
reduce the whole nonsensical business of the war to its ultimate absurdity.

But by the time this piece was (presumably) written, Pitt's dreams
were beginning to come true, and under his inspired direction, the British
army had magnificently redeemed its earlier failures with the great victories
of Minden in July, and at Quebec in September, 1759. The essay clearly
represents some serious rethinking by Johnson of his earlier scorn of "the
military"—at least, at the level of the common soldier. Not that Johnson
goes into raptures over the noble gallantry of our brave lads—the armies
of Minden and Quebec were still, by modern standards, small professional
armies, their ranks drawn, as Johnson and Goldsmith point out, from
"clowns" and "peasantry," men to whom the King's shilling was a powerful
attraction; the massive citizens' armies of the twentieth century were still
to be invented. But Johnson is clearly moved, as Goldsmith was—as "intellectuals" in all ages tend to be when they become aware of it—by the
capacity for heroism and self-sacrifice of the illiterate and semiliterate,
who have, as Johnson points out, apparently very little to fight for. His
conclusion, that this is the psychological effect of life in a "free society"—in
defining which, he stresses the economic rather than the political elements—
is a shrewd and even "modern" one. Does Johnson himself, in the end,
approve or disapprove of this state of affairs? He expresses himself so
carefully, merely stating dryly that it has its advantages as well as its disadvantages, that it is difficult to give a categorical answer on the basis of
this one piece alone. But when combined with many other statements
in Johnson's writings in which he firmly rejects "absolutism" and "dependance," for all their evident "advantages"—and with his own practice

3. Another amusing thrust on the subject is found in SJ's "Reflections on the
Present State of Literature," in the *Universal Visiter*, 1756 (reprinted in older
collections of his works under the title "A Project for the Employment of Authors"), where he suggests that authoresses (who "are seldom famous for clean
linen") would make satisfactory garrisons for towns supposed to be in danger
of a French invasion (a threat always pooh-poohed by SJ).

4. See the headnote to "Remarks on the Militia Bill," p. 151 above, and
p. 300 below.

5. See "Speech on the Rochefort Expedition," p. 261 above.

when confronted with "lace or titles" in the person of a Lord Chesterfield or Lord Lyttelton—the piece leaves little doubt that he was quite willing to put up with its "disadvantages."

The text given here follows that of the *British Magazine*, 1760. The 1767 reprint shows no substantial differences.

The Bravery of the English Common Soldiers

By those who have compared the military genius of the English with that of the French nation, it is remarked, that "the French officers will always lead, if the soldiers will follow"; and that "the English soldiers will always follow, if their officers will lead."[1]

In all pointed sentences some degree of accuracy must be sacrificed to conciseness; and, in this comparison, our officers seem to lose what our soldiers gain. I know not any reason for supposing that the English officers are less willing than the French to lead; but it is, I think, universally allowed, that the English soldiers are more willing to follow. Our nation may boast, beyond any other people in the world, of a kind of epidemick bravery, diffused equally through all its ranks. We can shew a peasantry of heroes, and fill our armies with clowns, whose courage may vie with that of their general.

There may be some pleasure in tracing the causes of this plebeian magnanimity.[2] The qualities which commonly make an army formidable, are long habits of regularity, great exactness of discipline, and great confidence in the commander. Regularity may, in time, produce a kind of mechanical obedience to signals and commands, like that which the perverse Cartesians impute to animals:[3] discipline may impress such an awe upon the mind, that any danger shall be less dreaded than the danger of punishment; and con-

1. Not traced; perhaps SJ's own phraseology.

2. "Greatness of mind; bravery; elevation of soul" (*Dictionary*).

3. Descartes's view that animals are without souls and therefore merely in-sensible automata (together with its corollary, the legitimacy of vivisection) is a frequent subject of bitter attack by SJ: cf. *Idlers* 10, 17, and ("original") 22.

fidence in the wisdom or fortune of the general, may induce the soldiers to follow him blindly to the most dangerous enterprize.

What may be done by discipline and regularity, may be seen in the troops of the Russian Empress, and Prussian Monarch.[4] We find that they may be broken without confusion, and repulsed without flight.

But the English troops have none of these requisites, in any eminent degree. Regularity is by no means part of their character: they are rarely exercised, and therefore shew very little dexterity in their evolutions as bodies of men, or in the manual use of their weapons as individuals: they neither are thought by others, nor by themselves, more active or exact than their enemies, and therefore derive none of their courage from such imaginary superiority.

The manner in which they are dispersed in quarters over the country, during times of peace, naturally produces laxity of discipline: they are very little in sight of their officers; and, when they are not engaged in the slight duty of the guard, are suffered to live every man his own way.[5]

The equality of English privileges, the impartiality of our laws, the freedom of our tenures,[6] and the prosperity of our trade, dispose us very little to reverence of superiours. It is not to any great esteem of the officers that the English soldier is indebted for his spirit in the hour of battle; for perhaps it does not often happen that he thinks much better

---

4. The Czarina Elizabeth and Frederick II (or III), "Frederick the Great."

5. On the general English suspicion of regular troops in the eighteenth century, see Sir John Fortescue, "The Army," in A. S. Turberville, ed., *Johnson's England* (1933); SJ's "Remarks on the Militia Bill," p. 163 above ("that contempt of the civil power too common among soldiers"); and SJ's reports of the House of Commons debate on the Mutiny Bill, 1741 (e.g., Phillips Gybbon, M.P., "Soldiers shut up in a barrack . . . will lose all sense of social duty and of social happiness, and think nothing illustrious but to inslave and destroy," and Henry Pelham, Secretary at War, "With regard to barracks, I cannot deny that they are justly names of terror to a free nation, that they . . . may contribute to infuse into the soldiers a disregard of their fellow-subjects, and an indifference about the liberties of their country").

6. I.e., of the English system of tenure of land and other property, by contrast with the feudal tenure still common on the Continent, especially in France.

of his leader than of himself. The French Count, who has lately published the *Art of War*, remarks how much soldiers are animated, when they see all their dangers shared by those who were born to be their masters, and whom they consider as beings of a different rank.[7] The Englishman despises such motives of courage: he was born without a master; and looks not on any man, however dignified by lace or titles, as deriving from Nature any claims to his respect, or inheriting any qualities superior to his own.

There are some, perhaps, who would imagine that every Englishman fights better than the subjects of absolute governments, because he has more to defend. But what has the English more than the French soldier? Property they are both commonly without. Liberty is, to the lowest rank of every nation, little more than the choice of working or starving; and this choice is, I suppose, equally allowed in every country.[8] The English soldier seldom has his head very full of the constitution; nor has there been, for more than a century, any war that put the property or liberty of a single Englishman in danger.[9]

Whence then is the courage of the English vulgar? It proceeds, in my opinion, from that dissolution of dependance which obliges every man to regard his own character.[1] While every man is fed by his own hands, he has no need of

---

7. Comte [Lancelot] Turpin de Crissé, *Essai sur l'Art de la Guerre* (Paris, 1754), I.14; "Il est avantageux que des Princes soient employés dans les armées en attendant que l'âge, l'étude, et l'expérience les mettent en état de commander en chef; le danger disparaît aux yeux du soldat, lorsque de tels Généraux, qu'il regarde comme au-dessus de l'humanité, le partagent avec lui. Le François chez qui l'honneur est le premier mobile des vertus, obéit avec plus de zèle et d'intrépidité lorsqu'il a pour compagnons des hommes nés pour être ses maîtres. . . ."

8. An allusion to the famous Lockean phrase, "Life, liberty, and property." Cf. Goldsmith's pathetic sol-

dier (in the version of "The Distresses of a Common Soldier" given in his *Essays*, 1756), "I enjoy good health, and will for ever love Liberty and Old England, Liberty, property, and Old England for ever, huzza!"

9. I.e., since the Civil War of the 1640's.

1. The insertion of "economic" before "character" in *Politics*, p. 177, is an error, the result of misreading a note. Nevertheless, it is clear from what follows that SJ is using "dependance," "character," and "subordination" in primarily an economic sense: he is talking about the condition of the individual in a system of "free enterprise."

any servile arts: he may always have wages for his labour; and
is no less necessary to his employer, than his employer is to
him. While he looks for no protection from others, he is
naturally roused to be his own protector; and having nothing
to abate his esteem of himself, he consequently aspires to the
esteem of others. Thus every man that crowds our streets
is a man of honour, disdainful of obligation, impatient of
reproach, and desirous of extending his reputation among
those of his own rank; and as courage is in most frequent
use, the fame of courage is most eagerly persued. From this
neglect of subordination I do not deny that some inconveniences may from time to time proceed: the power of the
law does not always sufficiently supply the want of reverence,
or maintain the proper distinction between different ranks:
but good and evil will grow up in this world together; and
they who complain, in peace, of the insolence of the populace,
must remember, that their insolence in peace is bravery in
war.

INTRODUCTION TO PROCEEDINGS OF THE COMMITTEE ON FRENCH PRISONERS. 1760.

By the end of 1759, Britain's fortunes in the Seven Years' War had risen to the point where she had the task of supporting several thousand French prisoners of war in her territories. There existed, of course, no such international regulations for the custody of prisoners of war as were later adopted in the Geneva Convention, and no governmental budget item for their maintenance. G. B. Hill, in his excellent note on this piece (*Life*, 1.353, n. 2), quotes John Wesley's description in his journal of 15 October 1759:

> I walked up to Knowle, a mile from Bristol, to see the French prisoners. Above eleven hundred of them, we were informed, were confined in that little place, without any thing to lie on but a little dirty straw, or any thing to cover them but a few foul, thin rags, either by day or night, so that they died like rotten sheep. I was much affected, and preached in the evening on Exod. xxiii. 9 ["Also thou shalt not oppress a stranger: for ye know the heart of a stranger, seeing ye were strangers in the land of Egypt"].

Moved by such conditions, a large group of respectable Londoners assembled on 18 December 1759, at the Crown and Anchor Tavern in the Strand, and constituted themselves a committee to receive and disburse charitable contributions for the relief of the prisoners. As treasurer, they named Serjeant (afterward Sir George) Nares, a distinguished lawyer and later judge. The Committee met weekly throughout the next few months, and by June 1760, had collected and expended £4,139/7/11. Administrative expenses, including advertising, postage, and the like, amounted to only £63/19/7¾ (an astonishingly small sum by modern standards of organized charity). Meticulous accounts were kept, showing that 3,131 greatcoats, 6,146 shirts, 3,006 caps, and 3,158 pairs of shoes, to mention some of the items, had been purchased and distributed.

On 4 June 1760 the Committee resolved to prepare and publish a detailed report of these transactions, and to deposit copies in the British Museum and the universities of the British Empire (the deposit copies are still to be found in some of the older American university libraries). Perhaps the decision to do so resulted from some criticism of the Committee's activities. At any rate, it was also decided to print a preface to the report; though whether the fact that Johnson's introduction is in the nature of an apologia was the Committee's idea or Johnson's own, we do not know.

The request to Johnson to write the introduction came from a prominent member of the Committee, Thomas Hollis, the naïvely ardent, good-hearted

"Republican," whom Johnson later defended against Elizabeth Carter's strictures: "Mrs. Carter said, 'He was a bad man. He used to talk uncharitably.' JOHNSON. 'Poh! poh! Madam; who is the worse for being talked of uncharitably? Besides, he was a dull poor creature as ever lived. And I believe he would not have done harm to a man whom he knew to be of very opposite principles to his own" (*Life*, IV.97). How much more the common Christian compassion of the two men counted than their differences in political "principles" is evident in the story of this commission of Johnson's. For another introduction had already been prepared, and agreed to by the Committee—"for want of a better," Hollis recorded in his diary. The author of the earlier introduction was a Mr. Smith, presumably the "Samuel Smith, Esq." whose name appears in the list of the members of the Committee. But Hollis was convinced that Johnson was the man to do the assignment justice. On 19 June he received from John Payne, who was in charge of getting the report printed (the same John Payne, of the Bank of England, for whose *New Tables of Interest* (1758) Johnson had written a preface a short time before),

> a MS of Mr. Johnson's, composed at my request and for which I have presented him with five guineas, which MS I hope will be allowed to serve as an introduction to the before mentioned publication, notwithstanding that another introduction had been already agreed upon by the Committee.

Hollis then went about assiduously showing the manuscript to other members of the Committee, by all of whom—even by Dr. George Macaulay, husband of Catharine the Whig historian—it was highly approved. Mr. Smith, the author of the rejected introduction, did the gentlemanly thing, and agreed to Johnson's, if "uneasily." The Committee formally accepted Johnson's piece at its meeting of 23 July, and it was published, with the *Proceedings*, the next month.[1]

Hollis and the Committee did well, for the short work is a perfect gem of English prose—economical, precise, carrying complete emotional conviction. The analogy of Lincoln's Gettysburg Address comes to mind. As to how "advanced" and "liberal" (or, rather simply "Christian") Johnson's thinking is on the matter of national attitudes toward "the enemy" in war ("With malice toward none, with charity for all," to quote another of Lincoln's addresses), no better testimony could be desired than the fact that two centuries later, the official journal of the International Red Cross reprinted it in French translation, noting it (under the significant title "Un Siècle avant Solférino") as the expression of an ideal that was only to begin to come to realization, through the efforts of Henri Dunant, in the

1. The sources for this account are the *Proceedings* themselves; James L. Clifford, "Some Problems of Johnson's Obscure Middle Years," *Johnson, Boswell, and Their Circle* (1965); and Professor Clifford's transcripts of Thomas Hollis's diary, which he kindly let me use.

later nineteenth century.[2] It is the perfect epitaph on Johnson's long and troubled involvement with the "Great War for the Empire."

The Introduction was reprinted in 1773 in Volume II of Tom Davies's *Miscellaneous and Fugitive Pieces*, and identified as Johnson's in the notice of that work in the *Gentleman's Magazine*, Nov 1774, p. 525. It was included in supplementary Volume XIV of Johnson's *Works* (1788), and in Volume XI of Chalmers's edition of the *Works* (1823).

The text, which presents no difficulties, is given here from the first edition, 1760.

2. *Revue Internationale de la Croix Rouge* (Geneva), XXXIII (Dec 1951), 969–71.

Proceedings of the Committee Appointed to Manage the
Contributions Begun at London Dec. XVIII
MDCCLVIIII for Cloathing French Prisoners of War
Homo sum: humani nihil a me alienum puto. Ter.[1]

Introduction

The Committee intrusted with the money contributed to the relief of the subjects of France, now prisoners in the British Dominions, here lay before the public an exact account of all the sums received and expended; that the donors may judge how properly their benefactions have been applied.

Charity would lose its name, were it influenced by so mean a motive as human praise: it is, therefore, not intended to celebrate, by any particular memorial, the liberality of single persons, or distinct societies; it is sufficient, that their works praise them.[2]

Yet he who is far from seeking honour, may very justly obviate censure.[3] If a good example has been set, it may lose its influence by misrepresentation; and to free charity from reproach, is itself a charitable action.

Against the relief of the French, only one argument has been brought; but that one is so popular and specious, that if it were to remain unexamined, it would by many be thought

1. *Heauton Timorumenos*, 77.
2. "All thy works shall praise thee, O Lord": Psalm cxlv.10.
3. No printed expression of this censure has been found.

irrefragable. It has been urged, that charity, like other virtues, may be improperly and unseasonably exerted; that while we are relieving Frenchmen, there remain many Englishmen unrelieved; that while we lavish pity on our enemies, we forget the misery of our friends.

Grant this argument all it can prove, and what is the conclusion?—that to relieve the French is a good action, but that a better may be conceived. This is all the result, and this all is very little. To do the best, can seldom be the lot of man; it is sufficient if, when opportunities are presented, he is ready to do good. How little virtue could be practised, if beneficence were to wait always for the most proper objects, and the noblest occasions; occasions that may never happen, and objects that never may be found?

It is far from certain, that a single Englishman will suffer by the charity to the French. New scenes of misery make new impressions; and much of the charity which produced these donations, may be supposed to have been generated by a species of calamity never known among us before. Some imagine that the laws have provided all necessary relief in common cases, and remit the poor to the care of the public; some have been deceived by fictitious misery, and are afraid of encouraging imposture; many have observed want to be the effect of vice, and consider casual almsgivers as patrons of idleness.[4] But all these difficulties vanish in the present case: we know that for the prisoners of war there is no legal provision; we see their distress, and are certain of its cause; we know that they are poor and naked, and poor and naked without a crime.

But it is not necessary to make any concessions. The opponents of this charity must allow it to be good, and will not easily prove it not to be the best. That charity is best, of which the consequences are most extensive: the relief of enemies has a tendency to unite mankind in fraternal affection; to soften the acrimony of adverse nations, and dispose them to peace and amity: in the mean time, it alleviates captivity, and takes away something from the miseries of war. The rage of war, however mitigated, will always fill

---

4. As Sir Andrew Freeport in *The Spectator* does (cf. *Life*, II.212).

the world with calamity and horror:[5] let it not then be unnecessarily extended; let animosity and hostility cease together; and no man be longer deemed an enemy, than while his sword is drawn against us.

The effects of these contributions may, perhaps, reach still further. Truth is best supported by virtue: we may hope from those who feel or who see our charity, that they shall no longer detest as heresy that religion, which makes its professors the followers of Him, who has commanded us to "do good to them that hate us."[6]

---

5. This sentence must not be carelessly read as an assertion by SJ that there will always be wars. He is saying that *while* there are wars, their rage, however mitigated, will always produce calamity and horror.

6. Luke vi.27.

THOUGHTS ON THE CORONATION. 1761.

George III acceded to the throne on 25 October 1760, and his coronation took place 22 September the following year. Like many other Englishmen at the time, Johnson pleased himself with the prospect of a "new deal" under a young, virtuous, and "British" ruler instead of the old, raffish, and "foreign" George II, with his support or at least toleration of the long-entrenched Walpole-Pelham oligarchy. "You know that we have a new King," he wrote to Baretti in Italy, in June 1761. "We were so weary of our old King that we are much pleased with his successor; of whom we are so much inclined to hope great things that most of us begin already to believe them."

Towards the expenditure of taxpayers' money on official public ceremonies Johnson had expressed a fairly jaundiced attitude in his letter on the display of fireworks celebrating the Peace of Aix-la-Chapelle in 1749 (p. 111 above). It would have been much better, he declared, to spend the money for public works, or for the relief of war widows and orphans or starving sailors (he does not mention soldiers). That, of course, was under George II. One might have thought that under George III and in connexion with so old and hallowed a ceremony as the coronation, his mood would have relented. It did not do so immediately. He was inclined (some readers may be surprised to learn) to discount the religious aspects of the coronation ceremony as an anachronism, and liked to use the secular term "inauguration," as though George III were an American president. He uses it in the piece printed below, and in 1766 wrote in the script for Chambers's Vinerian law lectures, "The inauguration of a king is by our ancient historians termed consecration; and the writings, both fabulous and historical, of the middle ages connected with royalty some supernatural privileges and powers"[1]—the implication being that they are no longer considered so connected. In December 1760, writing for the *Public Ledger*,[2] he still harps on the subject of cost, a somewhat surprising attitude for one who was to argue, against Milton's contention that "the trappings of monarchy" were too expensive, "It is surely very shallow policy, that supposes money to be the chief good":[3]

> Among other changes which time has effected, a new species of profusion has been produced. We are now, with an emulation never known before, out-bidding one another for a sight of the coronation; the annual rent of palaces is offered for a single room for a single day.

1. E. L. McAdam, Jr., *Dr. Johnson and the English Law* (1951), p. 93.
2. *The Weekly Correspondent*, No. 2, 9 Dec.
3. "Milton," *Lives*, I.156f. (par. 168).

Yet he eventually concedes, "I am far from desiring to repress curiosity
... nor ... think all pomp and magnificence useless or ridiculous"; and
the one positive precept that emerges from these two earlier essays is that
if there are to be ceremonies at public expense, as many members of the
public as possible should be enabled to view them. This is his chief text
in the piece printed below. Its origin is as obscure as that of anything in
the Johnson canon. Its first public association with Johnson's name was
in the supplementary Volume XIV of Johnson's *Works* (1788). There it
was printed in full, as though it were entirely Johnson's, and nothing is
said, in either the preface or an editorial note, to suggest that anyone else
had anything to do with its composition. Later Boswell was to assert (*Life*,
I. 361), "He this year [1761] lent his friendly assistance to correct and
improve a pamphlet written by Mr. Gwyn, the architect, entitled 'Thoughts
on the Coronation of George III.' " (John Gwynn and Johnson were
friends; in 1759 Johnson had written in support of Gwynn's design for
Blackfriars Bridge, and in 1766 furnished a dedication for his *London and
Westminster Improved*.) On the strength of Boswell's statement, later students
have assumed that the text of the pamphlet was originally and mainly by
Gwynn, and there have been various guesses about how much Johnson
added to it or in what way he revised it. But it appears that Boswell's
source for the statement was a list of Johnson's writings furnished by Percy,
which recorded merely "Thoughts on the Coronation of Geo. 3, 1761,
folio (the facts by Gwynne an architect). Mr. J. corrected it."[4] The only
"facts" contained in the work are topographical detail about the streets
of Westminster contained in the short paragraphs numbered I to IX and
in the handsome street map bound in the pamphlet (and, of course, the
long quotations from Stowe and Clarendon about the coronation processions of Anne Boleyn and Charles II). The actual text of the pamphlet
seems wholly consistent in style and content, being an effectively written
plea for a greater opportunity for the people to see their new king cheaply
and commodiously (and without a barrier of "insolent" soldiery interposed
between them and the monarch), in order to stimulate loyalty on their
part and, in the king, "a due sense of the duties" he is to undertake when
"the happiness of" the nation is put into his hand. There seems no reason
for attributing to Gwynn the initial impulse to lay such views before the
public or any hand in the actual composition of the text. Percy and the 1788
editor are undoubtedly right in ascribing to Gwynn nothing but the "facts"
and to Johnson the whole of the actual text (apart, of course, from the
long quotations, and the Advertisement, which is perhaps by the "proprietor"—i.e., Gwynn?).

The insistence in the Advertisement that the work is copyright, and the
relatively high price for so short a work (one shilling and sixpence) makes
one suspect that the chief attraction of the pamphlet for the buyer was
intended to be the map and the sketch of the order of the coronation

---

4. Marshall Waingrow, *The Correspondence and Other Papers of James Boswell
Relating to the Making of the Life of Johnson* (1968), p. 8.

procession—that is, that Gwynn (and Johnson?) hoped to make some money by providing spectators of the ceremony with a handy guide to what was going on. This would also help to explain the late date of publication,[5] only a few weeks before the actual ceremony, when there could be little hope of effecting any very drastic changes in the arrangements. Gwynn and Johnson could hardly have expected that between the appearance of the pamphlet and the date of the coronation the old Gate-House would be removed and the scaffolding for the spectators would be raised four feet. The main interest of the text, then, must have been, and still is, its expression of Johnson's wish to encourage a greater *rapport* between king and people than there had been in the days of George I and George II. The text given is that of the 1761 folio.

5. It was advertised in the *London Chronicle* as published on 8 Aug. As Allen T. Hazen (*SJ's Prefaces and Dedications*, p. 41, n. 1) points out, it is advertised there as the "Second Edition." But nothing is known of any earlier edition. The *Public Advertiser* (5 Aug) makes no mention of a second edition.

Thoughts on the Coronation of His Present
Majesty King George the Third. Or,
Reasons Offered against Confining the Procession
to the Usual Track, and Pointing Out Others More
Commodious and Proper. To Which Are Prefixed,[1]
a Plan of the Different Paths Recommended,
with the Parts Adjacent, and a Sketch of the
Procession. Most Humbly Submitted to Consideration.
London: . . . MDCCLXI. [Price one shilling and six-pence.]

Advertisement.

The Proprietor having been at some expence and trouble in this undertaking, (trifling as the work may appear,) he hopes he shall be suffered to reap the fruits of his labour, by an unmolested enjoyment of the profits (whatever they may be) that may accrue from the sale of it. And in order thereto, he has taken care to comply with every injunction directed by the Act of Parliament provided for the security

1. As Chapman-Hazen point out (p. 144), one of the two British Museum copies (shelf mark 604.i.30) reads "perfixed."

of copies, of which the compilers of news-papers, and all others, are desired to take notice.

The reader is also hereby informed,

That the usual method of passing in procession at coronations, is four a-breast, tho', for want of room, there are but two marked on the print. And that the several new tracks proposed, are distinguished on the plan by a red line, and the old path by a yellow.

Thoughts on the Coronation, &c.

All pomp is instituted for the sake of the public. A shew without spectators can no longer be a shew. Magnificence in obscurity is equally vain with "a sun-dial in the grave."[2]

As the wisdom of our ancestors has appointed a very splendid and ceremonious inauguration of our kings, their intention was that they should receive their crown with such awful rites, as might for ever impress upon them a due sense of the duties which they were to take, when the happiness of nations is put into their hands; and that the people, as many as can possibly be witnesses to any single act, should openly acknowledge their sovereign by universal homage.

By the late method of conducting the coronation, all these purposes have been defeated. Our kings, with their train, have crept to the temple through obscure passages; and the crown has been worn out of sight of the people. Of the multitudes, whom loyalty or curiosity brought together, the greater part has returned without a single glimpse of their prince's grandeur, and the day that opened with festivity ended in discontent.

This evil has proceeded from the narrowness and shortness of the way through which the procession has lately passed. As it is narrow, it admits of very few spectators; as it is short, it is soon passed. The first part of the train reaches the Abbey before the whole has left the palace; and the nobility of England, in their robes of state, display their riches only to themselves.

---

2. Donne, "The Will": "And all your graces no more use shall have / Than a sun-dial in the grave."

All this inconvenience may be easily avoided by chusing a wider and longer course, which may be again enlarged and varied by going one way, and returning another. This is not without a precedent; for, not to enquire into the practice of remoter princes, the procession of Charles the Second's coronation issued from the Tower, and passed through the whole length of the City to Whitehall.*

The path in the late coronations has been only from Westminster-Hall, along New Palace-Yard, into Union-street, through the extreme end of King-street, and to the Abbey door, by the way of St. Margaret's church-yard.

The paths which I propose the procession to pass through are,

I. From St. James's Palace, along Pall-Mall and Charing-Cross, by Whitehall, through Parliament-street, down Bridge-street, into King-street, round St. Margaret's church-yard, and from thence into the Abbey.

*The King went early in the morning to the Tower of London in his coach, most of the lords being there before. And about ten of the clock they set forward towards Whitehall, ranged in that order as the heralds had appointed; those of the long robe, the King's council at law, the masters of the Chancery, and judges, going first, and so the lords in their order, very splendidly habited, on rich footcloths; the number of their footmen being limited, to the dukes ten, to the lords eight, and to the viscounts six, and the barons four, all richly clad, as their other servants were. The whole show was the most glorious in the order and expence, that had been ever seen in England; they who rode first being in Fleet-street when the King issued out of the Tower, as was known by the discharge of the ordnance: And it was near three of the clock in the afternoon, when the King alighted at Whitehall. The next morning the King rode in the same state in his robes and with his crown on his head, and all the lords in their robes, to Westminster-Hall; where all the ensigns for the coronation were delivered to those who were appointed to carry them, the Earl of Northumberland being made High Constable, and the Earl of Suffolk Earl Marshal for the day. And then all the lords in their order, and the King himself, walked on foot upon blue cloth from Westminster Hall to the Abbey Church, where after a sermon preached by Dr. Morley (then Bishop of Worcester) in Henry the Seventh's Chapel, the King was sworn, crowned and anointed, by Dr. Juxon Archbishop of Canterbury, with all the solemnity that in those cases had been used. All which being done, the King returned in the same manner on foot to Westminster-Hall, which was adorned with rich hangings and statues; and there the King dined, and the lords on either side at tables provided for them: And all other ceremonies were performed with great order and magnificence.

Life of Lord Clarendon, p. 187.

II. From St. James's Palace a-cross the Canal, into the Bird-Cage-Walk, from thence into Great George-street, then turning down Long Ditch, (the Gate-house previously to be taken down) proceed to the Abbey. Or,

III. Continuing the course along George-street, into King-street, and by the way of St. Margaret's Church-yard to pass into the west door of the Abbey.

IV. From St. James's Palace, the usual way his Majesty passes to the House of Lords, as far as to the Parade, when, leaving the Horse-Guards on the left, proceed along the Park, up to Great George-street, and pass to the Abbey in either of the tracks last mentioned.

V. From Westminster-Hall into Parliament-street, down Bridge-street, along Great George-street, through Long Ditch, (the Gate-house, as before observed, to be taken down) and so on to the west door of the Abbey.

VI. From Whitehall up Parliament-street, down Bridge-street, into King-street, round St. Margaret's Church-yard, proceed into the Abbey.

VII. From the House of Lords along St. Margaret's-street, a-cross New Palace-yard, into Parliament-street, and from thence to the Abbey by the way last mentioned.

But if, on no account, the path must be extended to any of the lengths here recommended, I could wish, rather than see the procession confined to the old way, that it should pass,

VIII. From Westminster-Hall along Palace-yard, into Parliament-street, and continued in the last mentioned path, viz. thro' Bridge-street, King-street, and round the Church-yard, to the west door of the Cathedral.

IX. The return from the Abbey, in either case, to be as usual, viz. round St. Margaret's Church-yard, into King-street, through Union-street, along New Palace-yard, and so into Westminster-Hall.

It is almost indifferent which of the six first ways now proposed be taken; but there is a stronger reason than mere convenience for changing the common course. Some of the streets in the old track are so ruinous, that there is danger lest the houses, loaded as they will be with people, all pressing forward in the same direction, should fall down upon the procession. The least evil that can be expected is, that in so close a crowd, some will be trampled upon, and others smothered; and surely a pomp that costs a single life is too dearly bought. The new streets, as they are more extensive, will afford place to greater numbers, with less danger. In this proposal I do not forsee any objection that can reasonably be made. That a longer march will require more time, is not to be mentioned, as implying any defect in a scheme of which the whole purpose is to lengthen the march and protract the time. The longest course which I have proposed is not equal to an hour's walk in the Park. The labour is not such, as that the King should refuse it to his people, or the nobility grudge it to the King. Queen Anne went from the Palace through the Park to the Hall, on the day of her coronation; and when old and infirm, used to pass on solemn thanksgivings from the Palace to St. Paul's Church.*

---

*In order to convey to the reader some idea how highly parade and magnificence was estimated by our ancestors, on these solemn occasions, I shall take notice of the manner of conducting Lady Anne Boleyn from Greenwich, as it is recited by Stow.

King Henry VIII. (says that historian) having divorced Queen Catherine, and married Anne Boleyn, or Boloine, who was descended from Godfrey Boloine, Mayor of the City of London, and intending her coronation, sent to order the Lord Mayor, not only to make all the preparations necessary for conducting his royal consort from Greenwich, by water, to the Tower of London, but to adorn the City after the most magnificent manner, for her passage through it to Westminster.

In obedience to the royal precept, the Mayor and Common Council not only ordered the company of haberdashers, of which the Lord Mayor was a member, to prepare a magnificent state barge; but enjoined all the City corporations to provide themselves with barges, and to adorn them in the most superb manner, and especially to have them supplied with good bands of music.

On the 29th of May, the time prefixed for this pompous procession by water, the Mayor, Aldermen and commons assembled at St. Mary Hill; the Mayor and Aldermen in scarlet, with gold chains, and those who were knights, with the collars of SS. At one they went on board the City barge at Billingsgate, which was most magnificently decorated, and attended by fifty noble barges, belonging to the several companies of the City, with each its own corporation on board; and, for the better regulation of this procession, it was ordered, that each barge should keep twice their lengths asunder.

Thus regulated, the City barge was preceded by another mounted with ordnance, and the figures of dragons and other monsters, incessantly emitting fire and smoke, with much noise. Then the City barge, attended on the right by the Haberdashers state barge, called the Bachelors, which was covered with

Part of my scheme supposes the demolition of the Gate-house,[3] a building so offensive, that, without any occasional reason, it ought to be pulled down, for it disgraces the present magnificence of the capital, and is a continual nuisance to neighbours and passengers.

---

gold brocade, and adorned with sails of silk, with two rich standards of the King's and Queen's arms at her head and stern, besides a variety of flags and streamers containing the arms of that company, and those of the Merchant Adventurers; besides which the shrouds and ratlines were hung with a number of small bells: On the left was a barge that contained a very beautiful mount, on which stood a white falcon crowned, perching upon a golden stump enriched with roses, being the Queen's emblem; and round the mount sat several beautiful virgins, singing, and playing upon instruments. The other barges followed in regular order, till they came below Greenwich. On their return the procession began with that barge which was before the last, in which were the Mayor's and Sheriff's officers, and this was followed by those of the inferior companies, ascending to the Lord Mayor's, which immediately preceded that of the Queen, who was attended by the Bachelors or state barge, with the magnificence of which her Majesty was much delighted; and being arrived at the Tower, she returned the Lord Mayor and Aldermen thanks, for the pomp with which she had been conducted thither.

Two days after, the Lord Mayor, in a gown of crimson velvet, and a rich collar of SS, attended by the Sheriffs and two domestics in red and white damask, went to receive the Queen at the Tower of London, whence the Sheriffs returned to see that every thing was in order. The streets were just before new gravelled from the Tower to Temple-Bar, and railed in on each side, to the intent that the horses should not slide on the pavement, nor the people be hurt by the horses; within the rails near Grace-church, stood a body of Anseatic merchants, and next to them the several corporations of the City in their for-malities, reaching to the Aldermen's station at the upper end of Cheapside. On the opposite side were placed the City constables dressed in silk and velvet, with staffs in their hands, to prevent the breaking in of the mob, or any other disturbance. On this occasion, Gracechurch-street and Cornhill were hung with crimson and scarlet cloth, and the sides of the houses of a place then called Goldsmith's Row, in Cheapside, were adorned with gold brocades, velvet and rich tapestry.

The procession began from the Tower with twelve of the French ambassador's domestics in blue velvet, the trappings of their horses being blue sarsnet, in-terspersed with white crosses; after whom marched those of the equestrian order, two and two, followed by the judges in their robes, two and two; then came the Knights of the Bath in violet gowns, purfled with menever. Next came the abbots, barons, bishops, earls, and marquises, in their robes, two and two. Then the Lord Chancellor, followed by the Venetian ambassador and the

---

3. Shown on the "Plan" as "Stories Gate," at the west end of Great George Street.

A longer course of scaffolding is doubtless more expensive than a shorter; but it is hoped that the time is now past, when any design was received or rejected according to the money that it would cost. Magnificence cannot be cheap, for what

Archbishop of York: Next the French ambassador and the Archbishop of Canterbury, followed by two gentlemen representing the Dukes of Normandy and Aquitain; after whom rode the Lord Mayor of London with his mace, and Garter in his coat of arms; then the Duke of Suffolk, Lord High Steward, followed by the Deputy Marshal of England, and all the other officers of state in their robes, carrying the symbols of their several offices: Then others of the nobility in crimson velvet, and all the Queen's officers in scarlet, followed by her Chancellor uncovered, who immediately preceded his mistress.

The Queen was dressed in silver brocade, with a mantle of the same furred with ermine; her hair was dishevelled, and she wore a chaplet upon her head set with jewels of inestimable value. She sat in a litter covered with silver tissue, and carried by two beautiful pads cloathed in white damask, and led by her footmen. Over the litter was carried a canopy of cloth of gold, with a silver bell at each corner, supported by sixteen knights alternately, by four at a time.

After her Majesty came her Chamberlain, followed by her Master of Horse, leading a beautiful pad, with a side-saddle and trappings of silver tissue. Next came seven ladies in crimson velvet, faced with gold brocade, mounted on beautiful horses with gold trappings. Then followed two chariots covered with cloth of gold, in the first of which were the Dutchess of Norfolk and the Marchioness of Dorset, and in the second four ladies in crimson velvet; then followed by another chariot all in white, with six ladies in crimson velvet; this was followed by another all in red, with eight ladies in the same dress with the former: Next came thirty gentlewomen, attendants to the ladies of honour; they were on horseback, dressed in silks and velvet; and the cavalcade was closed by the Horse Guards.

This pompous procession being arrived in Fenchurch-street, the Queen stopped at a beautiful pageant, crowded with children in mercantile habits; who congratulated her Majesty upon the joyful occasion of her happy arrival in the City.

Thence she proceeded to Grace-church Corner, where was erected a very magnificent pageant, at the expence of the company of Anseatic merchants, in which was represented Mount Parnassus, with the fountain of Helicon, of white marble, out of which arose four springs about four feet high, centering at the top in a small globe, from whence issued plenty of Rhenish wine till night. On the mount sat Apollo, at his feet was Calliope, and beneath were the rest of the Muses, surrounding the mount, and playing upon a variety of musical instruments, at whose feet were inscribed several epigrams suited to the occasion, in letters of gold.

Her Majesty then proceeded to Leadenhall, where stood a pageant, representing a hill encompassed with red and white roses; and above it was a golden stump, upon which a white falcon, descending from above, perched, and was quickly followed by an angel, who put a crown of gold upon his head. A little lower on the hillock sat St. Anne, surrounded by her progeny, one of

is cheap cannot be magnificent. The money that is so spent, is spent at home, and the King will receive again what he lays out on the pleasure of his people. Nor is it to be omitted, that if the cost be considered as expended by the public, much

whom made an oration, in which was a wish that her Majesty might prove extremely prolific.

The procession then advanced to the Conduit in Cornhill; where the Graces sat enthroned, with a fountain before them incessantly discharging wine; and underneath, a poet, who described the qualities peculiar to each of these amiable deities, and presented the Queen with their several gifts.

The cavalcade thence proceeded to a great conduit that stood opposite to Mercers Hall in Cheapside, and, upon that occasion, was painted with a variety of emblems, and during the solemnity and remaining part of the day, ran with different sorts of wine, for the entertainment of the populace.

At the end of Wood-street, the standard there was finely embellished with royal portraitures and a number of flags, on which were painted coats of arms and trophies, and above was a concert of vocal and instrumental music.

At the upper end of Cheapside was the Aldermen's station, where the Recorder addressed the Queen in a very elegant oration, and, in the name of the citizens, presented her with a thousand marks in a purse of gold tissue, which her Majesty very gracefully received.

At a small distance, by Cheapside Conduit, was a pageant, in which were seated Minerva, Juno, and Venus; before whom stood the god Mercury, who, in their names, presented the Queen a golden apple.

At St. Paul's Gate was a fine pageant, in which sat three ladies richly dressed, with each a chaplet on her head, and a tablet in her hand, containing Latin inscriptions.

At the east end of St. Paul's Cathedral, the Queen was entertained by some of the scholars belonging to St. Paul's School, with verses in praise of the King and her Majesty, with which she seemed highly delighted.

Thence proceeding to Ludgate, which was finely decorated, her Majesty was entertained with several songs adapted to the occasion, sung in concert by men and boys upon the leads over the gate.

At the end of Shoe-lane, in Fleet-street, a handsome tower with four turrets was erected upon the conduit, in each of which stood one of the cardinal virtues, with their several symbols; who, addressing themselves to the Queen, promised they would never leave her, but be always her constant attendants. Within the tower was an excellent concert of music, and the conduit all the while ran with various sorts of wine.

At Temple-Bar she was again entertained with songs, sung in concert by a choir of men and boys; and having from thence proceeded to Westminster, she returned the Lord Mayor thanks for his good offices, and those of the citizens, that day. The day after, the Lord Mayor, Aldermen, and Sheriffs, assisted at the Coronation, which was performed with great splendor.

Stow's Annals.

Note. The same historian informs us, that Queen Elizabeth passed in the like manner, through the City, to her coronation.

more will be saved than lost; for the excessive prices at which windows and tops of houses are now let, will be abated, not only greater numbers will be admitted to the shew, but each will come at a cheaper rate.

Some regulations are necessary, whatever track be chosen. The scaffold ought to be raised at least four feet, with rails high enough to support the standers, and yet so low as not to hinder the view.

It would add much to the gratification of the people, if the Horse-Guards, by which all our processions have been of late encumbered, and rendered dangerous to the multitude, were to be left behind at the coronation; and if, contrary to the desires of the people, the procession must pass in the old track, that the number of foot soldiers be diminished; since it cannot but offend every Englishman to see troops of soldiers placed between him and his sovereign, as if they were the most honourable of his people, or the King required guards to secure his person from his subjects. As their station makes them think themselves important, their insolence is always such as may be expected from servile authority; and the impatience of the people, under such immediate oppression, always produces quarrels, tumults, and mischief.

FINIS

CONSIDERATIONS ON CORN. 1766(?).

As Edmond Malone recounts in the preface to his edition of William Gerard Hamilton's *Parliamentary Logick* (1808), he discovered the manuscript of this piece, in Johnson's hand, among Hamilton's papers after his death in 1796. It was in one of "several books filled with ADVERSARIA, written by himself [Hamilton], on many political topicks," which Malone suggests Hamilton composed while "intending, or at least meditating, to take a part in the debates that arose [in Parliament] on several important questions during his time." Malone printed the "Considerations" as an appendix to the *Parliamentary Logick* volume, and the text as given by Malone was included by Alexander Chalmers in his 1823 edition of Johnson's *Works* and in subsequent reprintings of the *Works*. The manuscript passed into the hands of R. B. Adam of Buffalo, New York, who printed a facsimile of it in Volume III of *The R. B. Adam Library* (1929), following page 118. It is now in the Hyde collection at Somerville, New Jersey, where Mr. and Mrs. Donald Hyde kindly permitted me to examine it. It contains eight quarto leaves, 17.5 by 23 centimeters, written on on both sides. The pages are numbered, in what looks like Johnson's hand, from 1 to 15; the last page is not numbered. Page 14 contains only two lines of writing, at the top, and the rest is blank. Malone here instructs the printer, "Let what stands in the next page, follow here," ignoring the gap. Although the text makes good enough sense when treated this way, it may be that what we have is not one complete and continuous essay but two fragmentary memoranda. The handwriting gives no clue to the date of the manuscript, except that it was written during Johnson's "middle period," nor does the watermark (of the "post horn" type, with the initials "L V G"—i.e., Lubertus van Gerrevink— which is that of a Dutch paper widely used throughout the whole of the eighteenth century). The manuscript is fairly heavily "corrected" in another hand—presumably Malone's, since the changes are incorporated in the 1808 printing; but fortunately, since his hand is very different from Johnson's and he used a darker ink, it is relatively easy to distinguish between the edited and the unedited "states" of the work.

Malone's edition of the "Considerations" contains a number of errors, perpetuated in the reprintings in the various collected *Works* of Johnson. There is no authority or justification for the title "Considerations on the Corn Laws," which Malone gives on the title page and in the table of contents of *Parliamentary Logick* and under which it appears in the collections of Johnson's *Works:* Johnson's title, "Considerations on Corn," stands at the head of the piece in his own hand, describes his intention in the piece more accurately than Malone's, and is the only one that should be used. Malone takes some bold liberties with Johnson's text: when Johnson repeats the word "small" at an interval too short to suit Malone's fastidious

301

ear, he strokes out the second "small" and substitutes his own "little" (n. i, p. 305 below); in the penultimate paragraph, he is baffled by Johnson's involved syntax and attempts to correct it by changing "of which" to "in which" (n. h, p. 311); but a careful reading shows that Johnson was right and Malone wrong. More excusably, Malone drastically repunctuates the text, sprinkling it with commas where Johnson had none, and changing many of Johnson's commas to semicolons. He makes one half-hearted attempt to improve Johnson's old-fashioned spelling, striking out one of the *l*'s in the word "ballance" when it first appears; but by its second appearance, near the end of the piece, he has become careless, or discouraged, and leaves it "ballance." Here, however, his printer in 1808 preserves his consistency for him, and changes the second one to "balance" too. It is also the printer, not Malone (unless, of course, Malone did so in proof), who reduces Johnson's occasional use of a capital letter on a common noun to lower case. I venture to disagree with Malone's (or the printer's) reading of a few words in Johnson's difficult hand, though one does not wish to be too dogmatic about such a matter, and readers doubtful about the new readings can check them in the Adam facsimile, which is accessible in most large reference libraries.

Malone also provides the piece with a history, of which the best that can be said is that it is highly speculative. He notes Johnson's prayer headed "Engaging in Politicks with H——n" and dated "Nov. 1765," insists that it "alludes to Johnson's having at that time entered into some engagement with Mr. Hamilton, occasionally to furnish him with his sentiments on the great political topics that should be considered in Parliament," and implies that "Considerations on Corn" was written to fulfil such an engagement to Hamilton. Having established the purpose of the document, Malone then proceeds to date it: the "Considerations"

> certainly were written in November, 1766, when the policy of the parliamentary bounty on the exportation of Corn became naturally a subject of discussion. The harvest in that year had been so deficient, and corn had risen to so high a price, that in the months of September and October there had been many insurrections in the midland counties, to which Johnson alludes; and which were of so alarming a kind, that it was necessary to repress them by military force. In these tumults several persons were killed. The Ministry therefore thought it expedient to accelerate the meeting of Parliament, which was assembled in November; and the King's Speech particularly mentions the scarcity that had taken place (which had induced his Majesty to prevent the further exportation of corn by an embargo), and the tumultuous and illegal conduct of the lower orders of people in consequence of the dearth.

This is all very circumstantial, but the date of the paper is not to be pinned down so closely as this. There were deficient harvests and high prices and riots and suppression of riots and discussion of policy for the regulation of the supply of corn at many other times during the period Johnson and Hamilton were acquainted; D. G. Barnes, in his exhaustive *History of the*

English Corn Laws (1930, Ch. 3), mentions the periods 1756–58, 1766–67, and 1772–73 as particularly troubled ones. Discussion, in the form of pamphlets and articles and letters to periodicals, was continuous from the 1750's to the end of the century and beyond: "The third quarter of the eighteenth century," Barnes writes, "saw a large output, both of periodicals and pamphlets, on the merits of the bounty on the exportation of corn" (p. 27), and his bibliography of pamphlets alone, between 1751 and 1775, runs to 76 titles. According to the "Considerations," both the export bounty and exportation were suspended at the time it was written; Malone speaks of the embargo of 1766 as though it were something unusual; but in fact exportation had been forbidden in 1757, 1758, 1759, 1766, and several following years in succession, and the bounty had been suspended in 1758, 1759, 1766, 1768, and subsequent years (Barnes, Appendix A, p. 196). And the great topic of discussion of the parliamentary session that began in November 1766 was not so much what policy was to be pursued in the regulation of the corn trade as the constitutionality of the Chatham administration's action in imposing an embargo on exportation by Order-in-Council ("executive order") in September 1766 when the Act of Parliament forbidding exportation had expired; Parliament had been summoned early in order to regularize this action and indemnify the ministry for any possible illegality on its part. This was a question that interested Johnson, for it forms the subject of a letter to Robert Chambers 19 November 1766 (*Letters* 187.1), in which Johnson seeks Blackstone's opinion of the constitutionality of the Order-in-Council. Yet this question (of the legality of the embargo) is nowhere mentioned or alluded to in "Considerations on Corn," as it almost certainly would be if it had been written in November 1766.

On the basis of the long history of the discussion of the regulation of the grain trade in England, then, Johnson's piece might have been written at any time after about 1755. There is nothing in the least novel in the content of the piece; Johnson's arguments are the stock ones of the proponents of the bounty, such as Arthur Young and Charles Smith, both of whom wrote extensively in favour of its continuance. (It might be noted, incidentally, that the policy Johnson argues for—governmental "support" of the price of farm products by means of subsidies—is still subscribed to by modern governments, notably that of the United States.) In the absence of other evidence, one might be tempted to assign the piece to 1772, when Burke (who had been Hamilton's assistant) sponsored a bill in the House of Commons regularizing the import and export of wheat and the bounty to be paid on exported wheat. There was much discussion at the time of the theory of agricultural subsidies. The bill passed the Commons, but was returned by the House of Lords with an amendment eliminating the bounty provisions. The Commons were so angry at this interference by the Lords with their exclusive right to handle money legislation—daring to "lay their sacrilegious hands upon this holy of holies, this palladium of the constitution," as Burke declaimed—that they (literally!) kicked the amended bill out of their chamber.

There is one piece of evidence, however, in the text of the "Considerations" that does perhaps justify our dating it somewhere near the time that

Malone (for the wrong reason) dates it. This is Johnson's statement, near the end of the piece, that the French have now come around to adopting the British policy with regard to the control of corn—they "have at last submitted to learn of us how to ensure the bounties of Nature" (p. 310 below). This must refer to the famous *édit* of 10 July 1764 by which, for the first time, the exportation of grain from France was permitted. Arthur Young exults over it:

> This measure was founded on the truest policy; and the wisest attention to the conduct of the English. That people became *great* from their exportation of corn; but such exportation was chiefly owing to a bounty granted by parliament—and this is the last point of encouragement which France (in that respect) wants, to render her more powerful. . . . There is . . . great reason to believe that a bounty on exportation will next ensue (*Letters Concerning the Present State of the French Nation*, 1769, pp. 42–43).

Johnson's "have at last" makes the edict of 1764 sound very recent. However, the rioting and the use of military force to suppress it mentioned in the piece were particularly notable in 1766 and 1767, so that Malone's date of 1766 (though not November) seems as good a guess as any.

We do not have too many illustrations of the changes a contemporary (or nearly contemporary) editor and printer made to a Johnsonian manuscript in setting it up in type, and Malone's changes may give us some guidance on occasions when we wish to work backward from a printed text and try to reconstruct what Johnson may have written in manuscript. The addition of so many commas and semicolons is interesting. Johnson seems to have been in the habit of punctuating more "lightly" than was general eighteenth-century printing house style, and the modern editor, when working from printed editions of Johnson, might possibly be justified in repunctuating the text in a way closer to modern usage in this respect. In editing this piece from Johnson's manuscript (unlike the other pieces in this volume, which are edited from a printed text), I have reproduced Johnson's capitalization.

In the textual apparatus I use the symbols employed in Volumes I and VI of the Yale Edition—⟨ ⟩ to indicate a deletion in the MS, ∧ ∧ to indicate an interlinear insertion. I distinguish changes made by Malone in the MS itself (and followed by the 1808 printer), and (by "*1808*") changes found in the 1808 edition, but not in the MS.

Considerations on Corn

By what causes the necessaries of life have risen to a[a] price at which a great part of the people are unable to procure

a. ⟨the⟩ a

A page from the manuscript of "Considerations on Corn," with corrections in Johnson's hand and alterations by Malone. By kind permission of Mrs. Donald F. Hyde.

them, how the present scarcity may be remedied, and calamities[aa] of the same kind may for the future be prevented,
is an enquiry of the first importance; an enquiry before
which all the considerations which commonly busy the legislature vanish from the view.

The interruption of trade, though it may distress part of
the Community, leaves the rest power to communicate relief;
the decay of one manufacture may be compensated by the
advancement of another; a defeat may be repaired by victory;
a rupture with one Nation may be balanced[b] by an alliance
with another. These are partial and slight misfortunes, which
leave us still in the possession of our[c] chief comforts. They[d]
may lop some of our superfluous[e] pleasures, and[f] repress
some of our exorbitant hopes, but we may still retain the
essential part of civil and of private happiness,—the security
of Law, and the tranquillity of content. They[g] are small
obstructions of the Stream, which raise a foam[h] and noise
where they happen to be found, but at a small[i] distance
are neither seen nor felt, and suffer the main current to
pass forward in its natural course.

But scarcity is an evil that extends at once to the whole
community; that neither leaves quiet to the poor nor safety
to the rich; that in[j] its approaches distresses all the subordinate
ranks of Mankind, and in its extremity must subvert government, drive[k] the populace upon their rulers and end in
bloodshed and massacre. Those who want[l] the supports of
life will seize them wherever they can be found. If in any
place there are more than can be fed, some must be expelled,
or some must be destroyed.

Of this dreadful scene there is no immediate[m] danger,
but there is already evil sufficient to deserve and require
all our diligence and all our wisdom. The miseries of the
poor are such as cannot easily be born; such as have already
incited them in many parts of the kingdom to an open de-

aa. and ⟨any⟩ calamities *MS*   b. *Second* l *deleted by Malone MS*   c. ⟨the⟩ ∧our∧
MS   d. comforts. ⟨of life.⟩ They *MS*   e. superfuous *MS*   f. pleasures, ⟨but⟩
and *MS*   g. The *MS*   h. ⟨tumult⟩ ∧ foam ∧ *MS*   i. ⟨small⟩ ∧ little ∧ (*changed
by Malone*) *MS*   j. *Inserted by Malone MS*   k. government, ⟨and at last⟩⟨must
begin with⟩⟨produce insur⟩ drive *MS*   l. massacre. ⟨While those⟩ ∧Those who∧
want *MS*   m. is ⟨yet⟩ no immediate *MS*

fiance of government, and produced one of the greatest of political evils,—the necessity of ruling by immediate force.

Caesar declared after the Battle of Munda,[1] that he had often fought for victory, but that he had that day fought for life. We have often deliberated how we should prosper; we are now to enquire how we shall subsist.[n]

The Present scarcity is imputed by some to the Bounty for exporting corn, which is considered as having[o] a necessary and perpetual tendency to pour the Grain of this country into other nations.

This position[p] involves two questions, whether the present scarcity has been caused by the bounty, and whether the Bounty is likely to produce scarcity in future[q] times.

It is an uncontroverted principle that *Sublatâ causâ tollitur effectus:* if therefore the effect continues when the supposed cause has ceased, that effect must be imputed to some other agency.

The Bounty has ceased, and the exportation would still continue, if exportation were permitted. The true reason of the scarcity is the failure of the harvest, and the cause of exportation is the like failure in other countries, where they grow less, and where they are therefore always nearer to the danger of want.

Their want is such that in countries where money is at a much higher value than with us, the inhabitants are[r] yet desirous to buy our corn at a price to which our own markets have not risen.

If we consider the state of those countries which being accustomed to buy our corn cheaper than ourselves when it was cheap, are now reduced to the necessity of buying it dearer than ourselves when it is dear, we[s] shall yet have reason to rejoice in our own exemption from the extremity of this wide extended calamity: and if it be necessary to[t] enquire why we suffer scarcity, it may be fit to consider

n. shall ⟨exist⟩⟨subsist *blotted*⟩ subsist *MS*   o. considered ⟨thu⟩ ∧ as ∧ having *MS*
p. This ⟨question⟩ position *MS*   q. in ⟨any⟩ future *MS*   r. us, the⟨y⟩ ∧ inhabitants ∧ are *MS*   s. dear, we *1808*] dear. We *MS SJ's ink;* dear, We *MS as altered by Malone*   t. be ⟨to be⟩ ∧ necess ∧ ary to *MS*

1. Plutarch, *Lives* ("Julius Caesar").

likewise, why we suffer yet less scarcity than our Neighbours.

That the Bounty upon Corn has produced plenty is apparent,

Because ever since the grant of the bounty agriculture has encreased; scarce a sessions has passed without a law for enclosing commons and waste grounds:

Much land has been subjected to tillage which lay uncultivated with little profit.

Yet, though the quantity of Land has been thus encreased, the rent which is the price of land generally encreased[u] at the same time.

That[v] more land is appropriated to tillage is a proof that more corn is raised, and that the rents have not fallen, proves that no more is raised than can readily be sold.

But it is urged, that exportation though it encreases our produce, diminishes our plenty: That the merchant has more encouragement for exportation, than the farmer for agriculture.

This is[w] a paradox which all[x] the principles[y] of commerce and all the experience of policy concur to confute. Whatever is done for gain, will be done more as more gain is to be obtained.

Let the effects of the Bounty be minutely considered.

The state[z] of every country with respect to corn is varied by the chances of the year.

Those to whom we sell our corn must have every year either more corn than they want, or as much as they want, or less than they want. We likewise are naturally subject to the same varieties.[2]

When they have corn equal to their wants, or more, the bounty has no effect for they will not buy what they do not want, unless our exuberance be such as tempts them to store it for another year. This case must suppose that our[a] produce is redundant and useless to ourselves, and therefore the profit of exportation produces no inconvenience.

u. land ⟨has⟩ ∧ generally ∧ encreased *MS*   v. ⟨For a greater⟩ That *MS*   w. *Inserted by Malone.*   x. which ⟨the⟩ all *MS*   y. the ⟨rules⟩ principles *MS*   z. The ⟨Nation [?]⟩ state *MS*   a. *Four or five words deleted after* our *MS*

---

2. "*Variety*. . . . 4.   Variation; deviation; change from a former state" (*Dictionary*).

When they want corn, they must buy of us, and buy at a higher price, in this case, if we have corn more than enough^b for ourselves, we are again benefited by supplying them.

But they may want, when we have no superfluity. When our markets rise, the bounty ceases, and therefore produces no evil. They cannot buy our corn but at an higher rate than it is sold at home. If their necessities, as now has happened, force them^c to give an higher price, that event is no longer to be charged upon the bounty. We may then stop our corn in our ports and pour it back upon our own markets.

It is in all cases to be considered what events are physical and certain, and what are political and arbitrary.

The first effect of the Bounty is the encrease of agriculture, and by consequence the promotion of plenty. This is an effect physically good and morally certain. While men are desirous to be rich, where there is profit there will be diligence. If much corn can be sold much will be raised.

The second effect of the bounty is the diminution by exportation of that product which it occasioned. But this effect is political and arbitrary; we have it wholly in our own hands; we can prescribe its limits and regulate its quantity. Whenever we feel want or fear it, we retain our corn, and feed ourselves upon that which was sown and reaped to feed other nations.

It is perhaps impossible for human wisdom to go further, than to contrive a law of which the good is certain and uniform, and the evil though possible in itself yet always subject to certain and effectual restraints.

This is the true state of the bounty upon corn;^d it certainly and necessarily encreases our crops, and can never lessen them but by our own permission.

That notwithstanding the Bounty there have been from time to time years of scarcity, cannot be denied. But who can regulate the seasons? in the dearest years we owe to the bounty that they have not been dearer. We must always suppose part of our ground sown for our own consumption, and part in hope of a foreign sale. The^e time sometimes

b. corn ∧ more than ∧ enough *MS*   c. ∧ them ∧ *inserted by Malone MS*
d. bounty ⟨of⟩ ∧ upon ∧ corn *MS*   e. sale. The *1808*] sale, the *MS*

comes when the product of all this Land is scarcely sufficient, but if the whole be too little, how[f] great would have been the deficiency if we had sown only that part which[g] was designed for[h] ourselves.

But perhaps if exportation were less encouraged, the superfluous stores of plentiful years might be laid up by the farmer against years of scarcity.[i]

This may be justly answered by affirming that if exportation were discouraged, we should[j] have no years of plenty. Cheapness is produced by the possibility of dearness. Our farmers at present plow and sow with the hope that some country will always be in want, and that they shall grow rich by supplying. Indefinite hopes are always carried by the frailty of human nature beyond reason. While therefore exportation is encouraged, as much corn will be raised as the[jj] farmer can hope to sell, and therefore generally more than can[k] be sold at the price[l] of which he dreamed when he plowed and sowed.

The greatest part[m] of our corn is well known to be raised by those who pay rent for the ground which they employ, and of whom few can bear to delay the[n] sale of one years produce to another.

It is therefore vain to hope that large stocks of grain will ever remain in private hands: he that has not[o] sold the corn of last year will with diffidence and reluctance till his field again, the[p] accumulation of a few years would end in a vacation of agriculture, and the[q] husbandman would apply himself to some more profitable calling.

If the exportation of corn were totally prohibited, the quantity possible to be consumed among us would be quickly known, and being known would rarely be exceeded, for why should corn be gathered which cannot be sold. We should therefore have little superfluity in the most favourable seasons, for the farmer like[r] the rest of mankind acts in hope of success,

f. little, ⟨who⟩ how *MS*   g. only ⟨a⟩ ∧that∧ part ⟨that⟩ which *MS*   h. designed ⟨both [?]⟩ for *MS*   i. *Malone places quotation marks around this paragraph MS*   j. sh ⟨all⟩ ∧ould∧ *MS*   jj. the ⟨hop⟩ *MS*   k. *Inserted by Malone MS*   l. price ⟨[?]⟩ of *MS*   m. The ⟨farmer [?]⟩ ∧greatest∧ part *MS*   n. to ⟨wait [?]⟩ ∧delay∧ the *MS*   o. *Inserted by Malone MS*   p. again, ⟨and⟩ ∧the∧ accumulation *MS*   q. ∧the∧ *MS*   r. for ⟨the . . . [?] world⟩ ∧the farmer∧ like *MS*

and the harvest seldom changes[38] the expectation of the spring. But for Droughts or blights we should never be provided, any intemperature of seasons would reduce us to distress[ss] which we now only read of in our histories, what is now scarcity would then be famine.

What would be caused by prohibiting exportation,[t] will be caused in a less degree by obstructing it, and in some degree by every deduction of encouragement; as we lessen hope we shall lessen labour, as we lessen labour, we shall lessen plenty.

It must always be steadily remembred, that the good of the bounty is certain, and evil avoidable, that by the hope of exportation[u] corn will be encreased, and that this encrease may be kept at home.

Plenty can only be produced by encouraging agriculture, and agriculture can be encouraged only by making it gainful. No influence can dispose the farmer to sow what he cannot sell, and if he is not to have the chance of scarcity in his favour he will take care that there never shall be plenty.

The truth of these[v] principles our Ancestors discovered by reason, and the French have now found it by experience.[4] In this regulation we have the honour of being Masters of those who in commercial policy have[w] been long accounted the Masters of the world. Their prejudices, their emulation, and their vanity have at last submitted to learn of us how to ensure the bounties of Nature, and it seems[x] a strange vicissitude of opinions that should incline us to repeal the law which our rivals are adopting.

s. outgoes *1808*   ss. to ⟨the⟩ distress *MS*   t. by ⟨the⟩ prohibi ⟨tion of⟩ ∧ ting ∧ exportation *MS*   u. that ⟨corn for⟩ ∧ by the hope of ∧ exportation *MS*   v. Th ⟨is our An⟩ ∧ e truth of ∧ these *MS*   w. policy ⟨are⟩ have *MS*   x. forms *1808*

---

3. The beginning of this word in the MS cannot possibly be "out-" as the printer of *1808* gives it. SJ is saying that a farmer will always plan his sowing in the spring in the expectation of a normal yield, and the accident of an abnormal yield the previous autumn will not change those plans. That is, he will consistently sow only as much as, at a normal rate of yield,

he can hope to market; and hence, in a year when there is a poor crop, the consumer will be faced with a shortage. (By "success," SJ seems to be thinking in terms of success in marketing, not success in production.)

4. The reference is undoubtedly to the French royal edict of 1764, permitting exportation of grain from France for the first time.

It may be speciously enough proposed that the bounty should be discontinued sooner. Of this every man will have his own opinion; which, as no general principles can touch^y it, will always seem to him more reasonable than that of another. This is a question of which the state is always changing with time and place, and which it is therefore very difficult to state or to discuss.

It may however be considered, that the change of old establishments is always an evil[5] and that therefore where the good of the change is not certain and constant, it is better to preserve that reverence and that confidence which is produced by consistency of conduct and permanency^z of laws:—

That since the Bounty^a was so fixed the price of money has been much diminished,^{b} so that the^c Bounty does not operate^d so far as when it was first fixed, but the price at which it ceases, though^{dd} nominally the same, has in effect and in reality gradually diminished.[6]

It[7] is difficult to discover any reason why that Bounty which has produced so much good and has hitherto produced no harm should be withdrawn or abated. It is possible that if it were reduced lower, it would still be^e the motive of^f agriculture and the cause of plenty; but why we should desert experience for conjecture, and exchange a known for a possible good will not easily be discovered. If by a ballance of probabilities, in which a grain of dust^g may turn the scale, or by a curious scheme of calculation of^h which if one postulate in a thousand be erroneous, the deduction which^i promises

y. reach *1808*   z. and ⟨[?]⟩ permanency *MS*   a. the ⟨the⟩ Bounty *MS*   b. of ⟨*three words*⟩ ∧ money has been much ∧ diminished *MS*   c. that ⟨if⟩ the *MS* d. Bounty ⟨[?] not⟩ ∧ does not ∧ operate *MS*   dd. ceases, ⟨has⟩ though *MS* e. still ⟨[?]⟩ be *MS*   f. the ⟨cause⟩ ∧ motive ∧ of *MS*   g. which ∧ a grain of ∧ dust *MS*   h. of *deleted by Malone MS;* in *1808*   i. erroneous, ⟨famine may⟩ ∧the deduction∧ which *MS*

5. Cf. n. 4, p. 86.
6. When the export bounty was established, in the late seventeenth century, the regulation was that it should cease to be granted when the price of wheat rose above 4 shillings, 8 pence a quarter. Since that time,

however, SJ points out, there has been considerable inflation of currency.
7. Page 15 of the MS begins here, following a long blank occupying most of p. 14.

plenty[j] may end in Famine, if by a specious mode of uncertain ratiocination, the critical point at which the bounty should stop[k] might seem to be discovered, I shall still continue to believe that it is more safe to trust what we have already tried and cannot but think Bread a product of too much importance to be made the sport of subtilty, and the topick of hypothetical disputation.

The advantage of the Bounty is evident and irrefragable. Since[l] the Bounty was given multitudes eat Wheat who did not eat it before and yet the price of wheat has abated. What more is to be hoped from any change of practice? An alteration cannot make our condition better and is therefore very likely to make it worse.

j. (abundance) ∧ plenty ∧ *MS*   k. ∧ stop ∧ *inserted by Malone MS*   l. ⟨No⟩ ∧ Since ∧ *MS*

THE FALSE ALARM. 1770.

The composition of *The False Alarm* can be exactly dated. It "was written at our house," Mrs. Thrale reported, "between eight o'clock on Wednesday night and twelve o'clock on Thursday night; we read it to Mr. Thrale when he came very late home from the House of Commons."[1] As the Speech from the Throne alluded to near the end of the work was delivered on Tuesday, 9 January 1770, and as the pamphlet was published on Wednesday, 17 January, Johnson must have written it on 10 and 11 January. Four impressions were issued between 17 January and 12 March, the second, third, and fourth, which incorporated a few very minor revisions, being designated "The Second Edition."[2] Together with Johnson's three other political pamphlets of the 1770's, *The False Alarm* was reprinted in *Political Tracts*, 1776, with somewhat more extensive revision by Johnson.[3]

The political history of the first ten years of the reign of George III is complex.[4] Like others who had opposed the Walpole and Newcastle regimes during the reign of George II, Johnson welcomed the advent of a "New Deal" in the person of George's young grandson, heir to his father's tradition of opposition to those regimes, and looked forward to an administration that would be at once more stable and energetic, and yet less cynical, than its predecessors. Like others, he was to become disillusioned over the years,

1. *Miscellanies*, I. 173.
2. For details about the printing of *The False Alarm*, see William B. Todd, "Concealed Editions of Samuel Johnson," *The Book Collector*, II (1953), 59–65. and D. J. Greene, "*The False Alarm* and *Taxation No Tyranny:* Some Further Observations," *Studies in Bibliography*, XIII (1960), 223–31.
3. Added to the title page of *Political Tracts* is a quotation from Claudian,
> Fallitur, egregio quisquis sub principe credit
> Servitium; nunquam libertas gratior extat
> Quam sub rege pio—
"Whoever thinks it slavery to be under an outstanding monarch is mistaken; no more delightful liberty exists than under a virtuous king" (*De Laudibus Stilichonis* Book III—sometimes called *De Secundo Consulatu Stilichonis*—ll. 113–115).
4. J. Steven Watson, *The Reign of George III, 1760–1815* (1960), is recommended as an introduction to the view of the political history of the time that is now accepted as a result of the researches of Sir Lewis Namier and others. Older general histories of the period, such as Green, Lecky, and Trevelyan, should be distrusted when they deal with the political structure of the period. On the background of Johnson's pamphlets of the 1770's George Rudé, *Wilkes and Liberty* (Oxford, 1962), and Lucy S. Sutherland, *The City and the Opposition to Government, 1768–1774* (1959), are valuable.

when the new king found he had to govern in much the same old way, through a set of compromises and fluctuating alliances with the same old groups of politicians. As the Seven Years' War drew to a victorious close, Newcastle and Pitt were discarded, and the Peace of Paris was negotiated by the administration of Lord Bute, George's personal choice. But the Bute administration lasted only a year, and was replaced in 1763 by the unpopular one of George Grenville, who assumed the unenviable task of paying off the heavy debts Britain had contracted during the war; in 1765, the Rockingham group, heirs to the Walpole-Newcastle Whig succession, had a short term of office; then in 1766, Pitt, now Earl of Chatham, undertook to form an administration, which gradually evolved into one headed by the Duke of Grafton (whom Chatham had detached from the Rockinghams), and finally, three weeks after *The False Alarm* was published, one headed by Lord North, which, unexpectedly, was to endure for twelve years. At one time or another Johnson commented scathingly on all these political leaders; but the exact details of his relationship with them and their factions are obscure. Why Bute in 1762 offered, and Johnson accepted, the famous pension of £300 a year remains something of a mystery, but it seems safe to assume that Bute did so primarily because he wanted to enhance the "image" of the new administration as a patron of the arts, and Johnson because he was willing for it to be enhanced. We know little about what his "engaging in politics" with William Gerard Hamilton in 1765 consisted in, apart from the possibility that it resulted in the writing of his *Considerations on Corn*. His correspondence in 1767 shows him highly concerned about the Chatham administration's proposed investigation of the East India Company, and preparing to do some writing on the Company's behalf. His acquaintance with other active politicians, Lord Elibank, George Dempster, the Johnstones, and the Vansittarts, seems to date from this time. Most important, so does his friendship with the brewer Henry Thrale, M.P. for Southwark between 1765 and 1780, once a Grenvillite, but now and for the future a dutiful supporter of North. No doubt his intimacy with Thrale, together with his general desire for a stable and cant-free government, was what chiefly impelled Johnson to write *The False Alarm*, the first of the series of Johnson's four political pamphlets of the 1770's.

The story of the Wilkes affair, which provides the background for the piece, has often been told. John Wilkes, as he himself was later to say, was no Wilkite—that is, not primarily a politician or political reformer, but an astute, witty, and unscrupulously self-seeking individual who saw a way to retrieve his ruined personal fortunes by making clever use of the political situation of the time. In 1763 he had acted as "front man" for Chatham's brother-in-law, the malevolent Earl Temple, in Temple's vendetta against Bute; Temple supported Wilkes financially. The inept attempt of the government to throttle his *North Briton* by means of a "general warrant" was thwarted in the courts by Chatham's legal ally, Charles Pratt, Lord Camden, but Parliament nevertheless voted *North Briton* No. 45 a seditious libel. In February 1764 Wilkes fled to France to avoid trial on this charge and on that of publishing the pornographic *Essay on Woman*, and was pronounced an outlaw. By 1768, his financial condition impelled him to risk returning to England and trying (again with Temple's assistance) to secure a parliamentary seat in the general election of that year (a Member of Parliament was immune from arrest for debt). He stood for one of the four City of London seats but was at the bottom of the poll. He then announced his candidature for one of the two seats for the county of Middlesex, which had a large and restless electorate, and was returned at the head of the poll, with nearly 1,300 votes.

This was in March 1768. In April, Wilkes submitted to arrest on the old outlawry (which was dismissed by Mansfield on technical grounds) and the charges of seditious libel and obscenity, for which he was fined a total of £1,000 and sentenced to twenty-two months imprisonment. But he was still M.P. for Middlesex. His presence in prison in the summer and autumn of 1768 formed a focus for considerable mob violence, and it was perhaps because of this that Grafton—most injudiciously, as it turned out—decided that his influence would be diminished by depriving him of his Membership of Parliament. This was accomplished, when Parliament met in February 1769, by a resolution of the House of Commons.

The story of what ensued after this, Johnson tells in his pamphlet—the re-election of Wilkes, the resolution declaring him incapable of sitting, the two further re-elections, and finally the seating of Wilkes's opponent Luttrell, in spite of the fact that he had received only a minority of the votes, on the grounds that he was the *qualified* candidate with the highest number. This action set off the frenzy of petitioning and agitation that Johnson describes and that continued throughout late 1769 and early 1770. Wilkes's cause was supported by the vociferous Society for the Defence of the Bill of Rights, led by Wilkes's friends John Horne Tooke and Serjeant Glynn; by the trading community of the City, led by Lord Mayor Beckford (Wilkes himself, the son of a wealthy distiller, was an alderman); by Chatham and his intimates; and by Junius. A pamphlet war went on; one of the most thoughtful contributions on the Wilkite side was Sir William Meredith's *The Question Stated* (1769), a number of whose arguments Johnson takes up and answers in *The False Alarm*.

When Parliament met on 9 January 1770, the administration severely snubbed the protesters in the Speech from the Throne (see n. 4, p. 341 n. 5 below). But Grafton, confronted with internal difficulties in the ministry, soon resigned, and was succeeded by the more effective North. The reverberations of the affair continued for the next year or two, but it might be said that in the end both sides got their way: Wilkes continued to be debarred from the Parliament elected in 1768 (which was all that the House of Commons resolution of 17 February 1769 had specified), but was re-elected for Middlesex in the general election of 1774, and allowed to retain his seat. Meanwhile, he finished serving his sentence in jail, his supporters (who, as Steven Watson says, were "not a club of poor men") had raised a large sum of money to pay off his debts, and he was able to resume the career that eventually made him a respectable and respected Lord Mayor, winning applause for his efficiency in suppressing mob violence at the time of the Gordon Riots.

The significance of the Wilkes affair is still as arguable as it was in Johnson's time. Nineteenth-century histories tended to follow the Wilkites' own interpretation, and, bracketing "Wilkes and liberty," to insist that

Wilkes, whatever his personal defects, was manfully defending ancient
and basic democratic rights against encroachment by the would-be despot
George III. More recent histories are not so sure, and in their light, the
thesis of Johnson's pamphlet, that the "alarming crisis" caused by the
Commons' resolution of 17 February 1769 was not so very alarming,
appears to have more to be said for it than even Johnsonian students have
been willing to admit in the past. The constitutional issue, which used to be
the one insisted on—whether the House of Commons, in passing the
resolution, was in fact "violating the rights of electors," as one older history
puts it—is just as debatable as it ever was, since it has never been clear,
in the unwritten British constitution, just what the "rights of electors"
are. Parliament still rates very highly its powers to regulate its own membership without interference: this is a normal "Whig" position, and it is not
surprising to learn that Charles James Fox at the time supported the
ministry's position against Wilkes, nor to find Johnson near the end of his
pamphlet complaining of the "frigid neutrality of the Tories," whose
enthusiasm for the exalted power of Parliament was never great (though
some students, familiar only with the simple notion of Johnson as a "bigoted
Tory," will be astonished to find him doing so). Now that the nineteenth-
century myth of George III and his ministers as would-be subverters of the
constitution has been effectively destroyed by recent historiography, it is
hard not to agree with Johnson that "liberty" was in no particular danger
at the time. One may still, however, hold the view that the Wilkite agitation
was significant at least in indicating the great increase of concern with
political matters by the ordinary citizen that is found around the middle
of the eighteenth century (a concern which Johnson, as we have seen in
his earlier writings, encouraged). But perhaps its greatest significance is as
yet another manifestation of the determination of the trading community
and its favourite politician Chatham to hasten the transformation of
England into a world-wide commercial power, a transformation which was
in time effected and to which Johnson was always, and perhaps with reason,
opposed.

Johnson thought *The False Alarm* the best of his political writings, and,
when Boswell expressed a preference for *Thoughts on Falkland's Islands*,
said, "There is a subtlety of disquisition in the first that is worth all the
fire of the second." What he called subtlety must consist in, first, the array
of precedents from parliamentary history which he cites to show how unlimited the power of the House of Commons to regulate its own membership
had been in the past, and, second, his constant refusal, in his discussion
of the case, to grant any of the Wilkite assumptions about vague "rights"
pertaining to electors, or indeed any political entity. He takes the whole
question out of the "natural rights" frame of reference, and makes all
political activity rest on the hard fact of the existence of power.

If political "rights" are a meaningless term—the cant of interested
politicians and their dupes—the question at hand can be decided only on
grounds of expediency; and Johnson has little difficulty in showing that far
greater harm has been caused to the representative principle by the biased
procedure used for decades in deciding controverted elections—an abuse

shortly to be rectified by Grenville's Elections Act—than by the Middlesex affair, and that the "alarm" might be better directed toward it. The pamphlet begins (after the pregnant introductory remark that the increase in scientific knowledge has eliminated much irrational fear, and that it would be well if political knowledge were to increase similarly and with similar effect) with a lucid review of the events in the Wilkes case so far, cites an imposing collection of precedents, and then settles down to an extended course of powerful ridicule and abuse of the agitators, which includes the delightful Hogarthian vignettes of the progress of a petition and of an election year. It does not forget to make the shrewd point (p. 341 below) that what is involved is "an opposition of the pedlars"—i.e., the trading interests—and ends with a compliment to the King. No one who has tried to summarize the pamphlet would maintain that it is well organized—after all, Johnson wrote it in a day and an evening, and one can sense how quickly and spontaneously the exuberant stream of insult flowed from his pen. But unless one is rendered immune by deeply held nineteenth-century Whig assumptions, it is easy and delightful reading, not unworthy, in its vivacity and literary skill, of Johnson's early master in satire, Swift.

The text here is based on the first edition (Todd's first impression) of 1770, incorporating variants from the second edition, 1770 (Todd's second, third, and fourth impressions) and from the collected *Political Tracts*, 1776, when these are unmistakably authorial changes. There is a good deal of routine variation in spelling between the 1770 and 1776 editions—*desireable / desirable, controul / control, to day / to-day, for ever / forever;* these and similar variants I have not recorded. The punctuation of 1770, whether closer to Johnson's own use or not, is so heavily peppered with commas as to inconvenience the modern reader, and in some nine instances where 1770 and 1776 differ in this respect, I have followed 1776, which is closer to modern usage.

The False Alarm[1]

One of the chief advantages derived by the present generation from the improvement and diffusion of philosophy, is

---

1. "Alarming crisis" was one of the favourite expressions of the Wilkites. Cf. petition to the King of the freeholders of Somerset, "If their silence at this alarming crisis would not be construed into an approbation of the measures [of the Ministry] . . ." (*Middlesex Journal, or Chronicle of Liberty*, No. 95, 7–9 Nov 1769); "The Freeholders of the County of Kent are desired to meet . . . to consider the proper steps necessary to be taken on the present alarming crisis," advertisement in *London Chronicle* throughout Nov 1769; "The present dangerous and alarming crisis," "Cicero" in *Public Advertiser*, 20 Oct 1769; "this alarming and dangerous crisis of the public affairs," "Dreadnought" in *Public Advertiser*, 20 Nov 1769.

deliverance from unnecessary terrours, and exemption from false alarms. The unusual appearances, whether regular or accidental, which once spread consternation over ages of ignorance, are now the recreations of inquisitive security. The sun is no more lamented when it is eclipsed, than when it sets; and meteors play their coruscations without prognostick or prediction.

The advancement of political knowledge may be expected to produce in time the like effects. Causeless discontent and seditious violence will grow less frequent, and less formidable, as the science of government is better ascertained by a diligent study of the theory of man.

It is not indeed to be expected, that physical and political truth should meet with equal acceptance, or gain ground upon the world with equal facility. The notions of the naturalist find mankind in a state of neutrality, or at worst have nothing to encounter but prejudice and vanity; prejudice without malignity, and vanity without interest. But the politician's improvements are opposed by every passion that can exclude conviction or suppress it; by ambition, by avarice, by hope, and by terrour, by public faction, and private animosity.

It is evident, whatever be the cause, that this nation, with all its renown for speculation and for learning, has[a] yet made little proficiency in civil wisdom. We are still so much unacquainted with our own state, and so unskilful in the pursuit of happiness, that we shudder without danger,[b] complain without grievances, and suffer our quiet to be disturbed, and our commerce to be interrupted, by an opposition to the government, raised only by interest, and supported only by clamour, which yet has so far prevailed upon ignorance and timidity, that many favour it as reasonable, and many dread it as powerful.

What is urged by those who have been so industrious to spread suspicion, and incite fury from one end of the kingdom to the other, may be known by perusing the papers which have been at once presented as petitions to the King,[2] and

a. has 76] have 70   b. danger, 76] danger, and 70

2. A feature of the Wilkes affair was the multitude of petitions addressed to the King and ministry by groups purporting to represent the freeholders

exhibited in print as remonstrances to the people. It may therefore not be improper to lay before the public the reflections of a man who cannot favour the opposition, for he thinks it wicked, and cannot fear it, for he thinks it weak. The grievance which has produced all this tempest of outrage, the oppression in which all other oppressions are included, the invasion which has left us no property, the alarm that suffers no patriot to sleep in quiet, is comprised in a vote of the House of Commons, by which the freeholders of Middlesex are deprived of a Briton's birth-right, representation in Parliament.

They have indeed received the usual writ of election, but that writ, alas! was malicious mockery; they were insulted with the form, but denied the reality, for there was one man excepted from their choice.

> *Non de vi, neque caede, nec veneno,*
> *Sed lis est mihi de tribus capellis.*[3]

The character of the man thus fatally excepted, I have no purpose to delineate. Lampoon itself would disdain to speak ill of him of whom no man speaks well. It is sufficient that he is expelled the House of Commons, and confined in jail as being legally convicted of sedition and impiety.

That this man cannot be appointed one of the guardians and counsellors of the church and state, is a grievance not to be endured. Every lover of liberty stands doubtful of the fate of posterity, because the chief county in England cannot take its representative from a jail.

Whence Middlesex should obtain the right of being

---

of the various counties, as well as other institutions. Some petitions, like those of the Universities of Oxford and Cambridge and of some counties, affirmed their support of the ministry's actions; many others, like those of Middlesex and the City of London, verged on the scurrilous in their abuse. The texts of many are given in the *Annual Register* for 1769 and 1770. Cf. SJ in *Life*, II.90 (16 Oct 1769): "This petitioning is a new mode of distressing government, and a mighty easy one. I will undertake to get petitions either against quarter-guineas or half-guineas. with the help of a little hot wine. There must be no yielding to encourage this."

3. Martial, VI.19. The epigram ridicules the bombastic lawyer whose oratory makes a suit over the ownership of three goats sound as important as one of murder.

denominated the chief county,[4] cannot easily be discovered;
it is indeed the county where the chief city happens to stand,
but how that city treated the favourite of Middlesex,[5] is not
yet forgotten. The county, as distinguished from the city, has
no claim to particular consideration.

That a man was in jail for sedition and impiety, would,
I believe, have been within memory a sufficient reason why
he should not come out of jail a legislator. This reason,
notwithstanding the mutability of fashion, happens still to
operate on the House of Commons. Their notions, however
strange, may be justified by a common observation, that few
are mended by imprisonment, and that he whose crimes
have made confinement necessary, seldom makes any other
use of his enlargement, than to do with greater cunning what
he did before with less.

But the people have been told with great confidence, that
the House cannot controul the right of constituting representatives; that he who can persuade lawful electors to chuse
him, whatever be his character, is lawfully chosen, and has a
claim to a seat in Parliament, from which no human authority
can depose him.

Here, however, the patrons of opposition are in some
perplexity. They are forced to confess, that by a train of
precedents sufficient to establish a custom of Parliament,
the House of Commons has jurisdiction over its own members;
that the whole has power over individuals; and that this
power has been exercised sometimes in imprisonment, and
often in expulsion.

That such power should reside in the House of Commons
in some cases, is inevitably necessary, since it is required by
every polity, that where there is a possibility of offence,
there should be a possibility of punishment. A member of
the House cannot be cited for his conduct in Parliament
before any other court; and therefore, if the House cannot

---

4. "The first county of the kingdom," *North Briton* No. 131, 21 Oct
1769 (no longer Wilkes's paper, but a
continuation of it).

5. Of the four members of the House
of Commons elected from the City

of London in the general election of
1768, Harley, the Lord Mayor, received the largest number of votes,
3,729. Of the three defeated candidates, Wilkes was at the bottom of
the poll with 1,247.

punish him, he may attack with impunity the rights of the people, and the title of the King.

This exemption from the authority of other courts was, I think, first established in favour of the five members in the Long Parliament.[6] It is not to be considered as an usurpation, for it is implied in the principles of government. If legislative powers are not co-ordinate, they cease in part to be legislative, and if they be co-ordinate they are unaccountable, for to whom must that power account, which has no superiour?

The House of Commons is indeed dissoluble by the King, as the nation has of late been very clamorously told;[7] but while it subsists it is co-ordinate with the other powers, and this co-ordination ceases only when the House by dissolution ceases to subsist.

As the particular representatives of the people[c] are in their public character above the controul of the courts of law, they must be subject to the jurisdiction of the House, and as the House, in the exercise of its authority, can be neither directed nor restrained, its own resolutions must be its laws, at least, if there is no antecedent decision of the whole legislature.

This privilege, not confirmed by any written law or positive compact, but by the resistless power of political necessity, they have exercised, probably from their first institution, but certainly, as their records inform us, from the 23d of Elizabeth, when they expelled a member[8] for derogating from their privileges.

It may perhaps be doubted, whether it was originally necessary, that this right of control and punishment, should extend beyond offences in the exercise of parliamentary duty, since all other crimes are cognizable by other courts. But they, who are the only judges of their own rights, have exerted the power of expulsion on other occasions, and when wickedness

c. people 76] people, 70

---

6. The reference is to Charles I's attempt, on 4 Jan 1642, to arrest Pym, Hampden, Hollis, Strode, and Haselrig within the House of Commons itself, an incident that helped to precipitate the Civil War.

7. Many of the petitions called for the dissolution of the present Parliament and a new general election.

8. Arthur Hall, M.P. for Grantham (*Commons Journals*, 14 Feb 1580, I.127).

arrived at a certain magnitude, have considered an offence against society as an offence against the House.

They have therefore divested notorious delinquents of their legislative character, and delivered them up to shame or punishment, naked and unprotected, that they might not contaminate the dignity of Parliament.

It is allowed that a man attainted of felony cannot sit in Parliament, and the Commons probably judged,[d] that not being bound to the forms of law, they might treat these as felons, whose crimes were in their opinion equivalent to felony; and that as a known felon could not be chosen, a man so like a felon, that he could not easily be distinguished, ought to be expelled.

The first laws had no law to enforce them, the first authority was constituted by itself. The power exercised by the House of Commons is of this kind, a power rooted in the principles of government, and branched out by occasional practice, a power which necessity made just, and precedents have made legal.

It will occur that authority thus uncontrolable may, in times of heat and contest, be oppressively and injuriously exerted, and that he who suffers injustice, is without redress, however innocent, however miserable.

The position is true but the argument is useless. The Commons must be controlled, or be exempt from control. If they are exempt they may do injury which cannot be redressed, if they are controlled they are no longer legislative.[9]

If the possibility of abuse be an argument against authority, no authority ever can be established; if the actual abuse destroys its legality, there is no legal government now in the world.

This power, which the Commons have so long exercised,

d. felony . . . judged 76] felony, is not eligible in Parliament. They probably judged 70

---

9. For the sense of the word, cf. Locke, *Second Treatise of Government,* Sect. 134: "The Legislative is . . . the supreme power of the commonwealth . . . nor can the edict of any body else, in what form soever conceived, or by what power soever backed, have the force and obligation of a law, which has not its sanction from that legislative. . . ."

they ventured to use once more against Mr. Wilkes, and on the 3d of February, 1769, expelled him the House, "for having printed and published a seditious libel, and three obscene and impious libels."[1]

If these imputations were just, the expulsion was surely seasonable, and that they were just, the House had reason to determine, as he had confessed himself, at the bar, the author of the libel which they term seditious, and was convicted in the King's Bench of both the publications.

But the Freeholders of Middlesex were of another opinion. They either thought him innocent, or were not offended by his guilt. When a writ was issued for the election of a knight for Middlesex, in the room of John Wilkes, Esq; expelled the House, his friends on the sixteenth of February chose him again.

On the 17th, it was resolved "that John Wilkes, Esq; having been in this Session of Parliament expelled the House,[2] was, and is, incapable of being elected a member to serve in this present Parliament."

As there was no other candidate, it was resolved, at the same time, that the election of the sixteenth was a void election.

The Freeholders still continued to think that no other man was fit to represent them, and on the sixteenth of March elected him once more. Their resolution was now so well known, that no opponent ventured to appear.

The Commons began to find, that power without materials for operation can produce no effect. They might make the election void for ever, but if no other candidate could be found, their determination could only be negative. They, however, made void the last election, and ordered a new writ.

On the thirteenth of April was a new election, at which Mr. Lutterel,[3] and others, offered themselves candidates. Every method of intimidation was used, and some acts of violence were done to hinder Mr. Lutterel from appearing.

---

1. *Parliamentary History*, xvi.545.

2. In *Parliamentary History*, xvi.576, and *Commons Journals*, 17 Feb 1769, xxxii.228, the phrase is given as "expelled this House."

3. Henry Lawes Luttrell had resigned his seat for a Cornish borough in order to contest Middlesex against Wilkes on behalf of the ministry.

He was not deterred, and the poll was taken, which exhibited
for Mr. Wilkes, ——— ——— 1143
     Mr. Lutterel, ——— ——— 296

The sheriff returned Mr. Wilkes, but the House, on April
the fifteenth, determined that Mr. Lutterel was lawfully
elected.

From this day begun[4] the clamour, which has continued till
now. Those who had undertaken to oppose the ministry,
having no grievance of greater magnitude, endeavoured to
swell this decision into bulk, and distort it into deformity,
and then held it out to terrify the nation.

Every artifice of sedition has been since practised to awaken
discontent and inflame indignation. The papers of every day
have been filled with the exhortations and menaces of faction.
The madness has spread through all ranks and through both
sexes; women and children have clamoured for Mr. Wilkes,
honest simplicity has been cheated into fury, and only the
wise have escaped infection.

The greater part may justly be suspected of not believing
their own position, and with them it is not necessary to dispute.
They cannot be convinced, who are convinced already, and
it is well known that they will not be ashamed.

The decision, however, by which the smaller number of
votes was preferred to the greater, has perplexed the minds of
some, whose opinions it were indecent to despise, and who by
their integrity well[e] deserve to have their doubts appeased.

Every diffuse and complicated question may be examined
by different methods, upon different principles;[f] and that
truth, which is easily found by one investigator, may be
missed by another, equally honest and equally diligent.

Those who enquire whether a smaller number of legal votes[g]
can elect a representative in opposition to a greater, must
receive from every tongue the same answer.

The question, therefore, must be, whether a smaller number
of legal votes, shall not prevail against a greater number
of votes not legal.

e. well 76] will 70   f. principles; 76] principles, 70   g. votes 76] votes, 70

---

4. So in all editions in SJ's lifetime. *OED* lists it as a common variant of
"began" in the eighteenth century.

It[h] must be considered, that those votes only are legal which are legally given, and that those only are legally given, which are given for a legal candidate.[5]

It remains then to be discussed, whether a man expelled, can be so disqualified by a vote of the House, as that he shall be no longer eligible by lawful electors.

Here we must again recur, not to positive institutions, but to the unwritten law of social nature, to the great and pregnant principle of political necessity. All government supposes subjects, all authority implies obedience. To suppose in one the right to command what another has the right to refuse is absurd and contradictory. A state so constituted must rest for ever in motionless equipoise, with equal attractions of contrary tendency, with equal weights of power balancing each other.

Laws which cannot be enforced, can neither prevent nor rectify disorders. A sentence which cannot be executed can have no power to warn or to reform. If the Commons have only the power of dismissing for a few days the man whom his constituents can immediately send back, if they can expel but cannot exclude, they have nothing more than nominal authority, to which perhaps obedience never may be paid.

The representatives of our ancestors had an opinion very different: they fined and imprisoned their members; on great provocation they disabled them for ever, and this power of pronouncing perpetual disability is maintained by Selden himself.[6]

h. *No new paragraph 70*

---

5. In the debate in the House of Commons over the somewhat similar situation in the riding of Mid-Ulster in 1955, the Attorney-General, Sir Reginald Manningham-Buller (later Lord Chancellor Dilhorne) argued, "It seemed a misuse of the English language to say that a person incapable of being elected a Member of this House has, because he has secured a majority of the votes, been elected to this House. The fact is that he never could be elected to this House because he is incapable by Act of Parliament of being elected" (*Hansard*, 18 July 1955).

6. John Selden, distinguished jurist, antiquary, and Member of Parliament. The anonymous reviewer of *The False Alarm* in the *Critical Review*, xxix (January 1770), 54–57, comments, "This writer quotes Mr. Selden as an advocate for the power of perpetual disability being lodged in the com-

These claims seem to have been made and allowed, when the constitution of our government had not yet been sufficiently studied. Such powers are not legal, because they are not necessary; and of that power which only necessity justifies, no more is to be admitted than necessity obtrudes.

The Commons cannot make laws, they can only pass resolutions, which, like all resolutions, are of force only to those that make them, and to those only while they are willing to observe them.

The vote of the House of Commons has therefore only so far the force of a law, as that force is necessary to preserve the vote from losing its efficacy, it must begin by operating upon themselves, and extends its influence to others, only by consequences arising from the first intention. He that starts game on his own manor, may pursue it into another.[7]

They can properly make laws only for themselves: a member, while he keeps his seat, is subject to these laws; but when he is expelled, the jurisdiction ceases, for he is now no longer within[i] their dominion.

The disability, which a vote can superinduce to expulsion, is no more than was included in expulsion itself; it is only a declaration of the Commons,[j] that they will permit no longer him whom they thus censure to sit with them[k] in Parliament; a declaration made by that right which they necessarily

i. within *76*] in *70*   j. Commons *76*] House *70*   k. with them *76*] *om. 70*

---

mons. As he does not quote the particular passage of Selden where this doctrine is found, we must suppose that he alludes to the words of the speech of that great man against Sir Edward Sawyer. If that is the passage in question, though we allow it is very pregnant, we cannot think it amounts to the power of a perpetual disability, for all that Selden says is 'to maintain the privileges of our house, we can fine as well as the lords. And as they disable lords from sitting there, so we can disable any member of our own house from sitting there.' After all, it is very possible that this writer might have had some other passage of Selden in his view, which has not come to our knowledge." Such a passage is still untraced.

7. Blackstone, *Commentaries*, Book II, ch. 27: "It is held, indeed, that if a man starts any game within his own grounds, and follows it into another's, and kills it there, the property remains in himself. And this is grounded on reason and natural justice: for the property consists in the possession; which possession commences by finding it in his own liberty and is continued by the immediate pursuit."

possess, of regulating their own House, and of inflicting punishment on their own delinquents. They have therefore no other way to enforce the sentence of incapacity, than that of adhering to it. They cannot otherwise punish the candidate so disqualified for offering himself, nor the electors for accepting him. But if he has any competitor, that competitor must prevail, and if he has none, his election will be void; for the right of the House to reject, annihilates with regard to the man so rejected[1] the right of electing.

It has been urged, that the power of the House terminates with their session; since a prisoner committed by the Speaker's warrant cannot be detained during the recess. That power indeed ceases with the session, which must operate by the agency of others, because, when they do not sit, they can employ no agent, having no longer any legal existence; but that which is exercised[m] on themselves revives at their meeting, when the subject of that power still subsists. They can in the next session refuse to readmit him, whom in the former session they expelled.

That expulsion inferred exclusion, in the present case, must be, I think, easily admitted. The expulsion and the writ issued for a new election were in the same session, and since the House is by the rule of Parliament bound for the session by a vote once passed, the expelled member cannot be admitted. He that cannot be admitted, cannot be elected, and the votes given to a man ineligible being given in vain, the highest number for an eligible candidate becomes a majority.

To these conclusions, as to most moral, and to all political positions, many objections may be made. The perpetual subject of political disquisition is not absolute, but comparative good. Of two systems of government, or two laws relating to the same subject, neither will ever be such as theoretical nicety would desire, and therefore neither can easily force its way against prejudice and obstinacy; each will have its

l. rejected *76*] rejected, *70*   m. That power . . . is exercised *76*] Their power indeed ceases with the session, so far as it operates by the agency of others, because, when they do not sit, they can employ no agent, having no longer any legal existence. But the power which operates *70*

excellencies and defects, and every man, with a little help from pride, may think his own the best.

It seems to be the opinion of many, that expulsion is only a dismission of the representative to his constituents, with such a testimony against him as his sentence may comprise; and that if his constituents, notwithstanding the censure of the House, thinking his case hard, his fault trifling, or his excellencies such as overbalance it, should again choose him as still worthy of their trust, the House cannot refuse him, for his punishment has purged his fault, and the right of electors must not be violated.

This is plausible but not cogent. It is a scheme of representation, which would make a specious appearance in a political romance, but cannot be brought into practice among us, who see every day the towering head of speculation bow down unwillingly to grovelling experience.

Governments formed by chance, and gradually improved by such expedients, as the successive discovery of their defects happened to suggest, are never to be tried by a regular theory. They are fabricks of dissimilar materials, raised by different architects, upon different plans. We must be content with them as they are; should we attempt to mend their disproportions, we might easily demolish, and difficultly rebuild them.

Laws are now made, and customs are established; these are our rules, and by them we must be guided.

It is uncontrovertibly certain, that the Commons never intended to leave electors the liberty of returning them an expelled member, for they always require one to be chosen in the room of him that is expelled, and I see not with what propriety a man can be rechosen in his own room.

Expulsion, if this were its whole effect, might very often be desireable. Sedition, or obscenity, might be no greater crimes in the opinion of other electors, than in that of the freeholders of Middlesex; and many a wretch, whom his colleagues should expel, might come back persecuted into fame, and provoke with harder front a second expulsion.

Many of the representatives of the people can hardly be said to have been chosen at all. Some by inheriting a borough inherit a seat; and some sit by the favour of others, whom perhaps they may gratify by the act which provoked the expulsion. Some are safe by their popularity, and some by their alliances. None would dread expulsion, if this doctrine were received, but those who bought their elections, and who would be obliged to buy them again at a higher price.

But as uncertainties are to be determined by things certain, and customs to be explained, where it is possible, by written law, the patriots have triumphed with a quotation from an act of the 4th and 5th of^n Anne, which permits those to be rechosen, whose seats are vacated by the acceptance of a place of profit. This they wisely consider as an expulsion, and from the permission, in this case, of a re-election, infer that every other expulsion^o leaves the delinquent entitled to the same indulgence. This is the paragraph.

"If any person, *being chosen a member* of the House of Commons, shall accept of any office from the crown, *during such time as he shall continue a member*, his election shall be, and is hereby declared to be void, and a new writ shall issue for a new election, as if such person so accepting was naturally dead. *Nevertheless such person shall be capable of being again elected*, as if his place had not become void as aforesaid."[8]

How this favours the doctrine of re-admission by a second choice, I am not able to discover. The statute of 30 Ch. II. had enacted, That "he who should sit in the House of Commons, without taking the oaths and subscribing the test, should be disabled to sit in the House during that Parliament, and a writ should issue for the election of a new member, in place of the member so disabled, as if such member had naturally died."[9]

This last clause is apparently copied in the act of Anne, but with the common fate of imitators. In the act of Charles,

n. of 76] *om. 70*　　o. expulsion 76] expulsion, 70

---

8. 4 & 5 Anne, c.8, Sect. xxvii. SJ omits "of profit" after "office"; and the last sentence begins "Providing nevertheless that such person."
9. 30 Charles II (i.e., 1679), c.2, Sect. viii. SJ's wording is a paraphrase of the provisions of the section,

not a verbatim quotation. The "test" is that provided in the Test Act (1673), whereby holders of public office were required to sign a declaration against transubstantiation and receive communion in the Church of England.

the political death continued during the Parliament, in that of Anne it was hardly worth the while to kill the man whom the next breath was to revive. It is, however, apparent, that in the opinion of the Parliament, the dead-doing[1] lines would have kept him motionless, if he had not been recovered by a kind exception.[p] A seat vacated, could not be regained without express permission of the same statute.

The right of being chosen again to a seat thus vacated, is not enjoyed by any general right, but required a special clause, and solicitous provision.

But what resemblance can imagination conceive between one man vacating his seat, by a mark of favour from the crown, and another driven from it for sedition and obscenity. The acceptance of a place contaminates no character; the crown that gives it, intends to give with it always dignity, sometimes authority. The Commons, it is well known, think not worse of themselves or others for their offices of profit; yet profit implies temptation, and may expose a representative to the suspicion of his constituents; though if they still think him worthy of their confidence, they may again elect him.

Such is the consequence. When a man is dismissed by law to his constituents, with new trust and new dignity, they may, if they think him incorruptible, restore him to his seat; what can follow, therefore, but that when the House drives out a varlet with public infamy, he goes away with the like permission to return.

If infatuation be, as the proverb tells us, the forerunner of destruction,[2] how near must be the ruin of a nation that can be incited against its governors, by sophistry like this. I may be excused if I catch the panick, and join my groans at this alarming crisis, with the general lamentation of weeping patriots.

Another objection is, that the Commons, by pronouncing the sentence of disqualification, make a law, and take upon

p. exception 76] reception 70

---

1. A pseudo-archaic phrase, apparently first used by Spenser. See *OED*.
2. "*Quem Juppiter vult perdere, dementat prius.*" Attributed by *Oxford Dic-* *tionary of Quotations* (2nd ed.) to James Duport (1606–79). See *Life*, IV.181, n.3.

themselves^q the power of the whole legislature. Many quotations are then produced to prove that the House of Commons can make no laws.

Three acts have been cited, disabling members for different terms on different occasions, and it is profoundly remarked, that if the Commons could by their own power^r have made a disqualification, their jealousy of their privileges^s would never have admitted the concurrent sanction of the other powers.

I must forever remind these puny controvertists, that those acts are laws of permanent obligation: that two of them are now in force, and that the other expired only when it had fulfilled its end. Such laws the Commons cannot make; they could, perhaps, have determined for themselves, that^t they would expel all who should not take the test, but they could leave no authority behind them, that should oblige the next Parliament to expel them. They could refuse the South Sea directors,[3] but they could not entail the refusal. They can disqualify by vote, but not by law; they cannot know that the sentence of disqualification pronounced today may not become void to-morrow, by the dissolution of their own House. Yet while the same Parliament sits, the disqualification continues unless the vote be rescinded, and while it so continues, makes the votes, which freeholders may give to the interdicted candidate, useless and dead, since there cannot exist, with respect to the same subject at the same time, an absolute power to chuse and an absolute power to reject.

In 1614, the attorney-general was voted incapable of a seat in the House of Commons,[4] and the nation is triumphantly told, that though the vote never was revoked, the attorney-general is now a member. He certainly may now be a member without revocation of the vote. A law is of perpetual obligation, but a vote is nothing when the voters are gone. A law

q. themselves *76*] themselves, *70*   r. privilege *76*   s. privileges *76*] privileges, *70*   t. that *76*] *om. 70*

3. Several were expelled from the House of Commons at the time of the South Sea Bubble: cf. *Parliamentary History*, VII.708.
   4. *Parliamentary History*, I.1163 (8 Apr 1614). For Wilkite use of this precedent, see *A Vindication of the Right of Election* (Woodfall, 1769), p. 70, and *A Fair Trial of the Important Question* (Almon, 1769), pp. 190–97.

is a compact reciprocally made by the legislative powers, and therefore not to be abrogated but by all the parties. A vote is simply a resolution, which binds only him that is willing to be bound.

I have thus punctiliously and minutely persued this disquisition, because I suspect that these reasoners, whose business is to deceive others, have sometimes deceived themselves, and I am willing to free them from their embarrassment, though I do not expect much gratitude for my kindness.

Other objections are yet remaining, for of political objections there cannot easily be an end. It has been observed,[5] that vice is no proper cause of expulsion, for if the worst man in the House were always to be expelled, in time none would be left. But no man is expelled for being worst, he is expelled for being enormously bad; his conduct is compared, not with that of others, but with the rule of action.

The punishment of expulsion being in its own nature uncertain, may be too great or too little for the fault.

This must be the case of many punishments. Forfeiture of chattels is nothing to him that has no possessions. Exile itself may be accidentally a good; and indeed any punishment less than death is very different to different men.

But if this precedent be admitted and established, no man can hereafter be sure that he shall be represented by him whom he would choose. One half of the House may meet early in the morning, and snatch an opportunity to expel the other, and the greater part of the nation may by this stratagem be without its lawful representatives.

He that sees all this, sees very far. But I can tell him of greater evils yet behind. There is one possibility of wickedness, which, at this alarming crisis, has not yet been mentioned. Every one knows the malice, the subtilty, the industry, the vigilance, and the greediness of the Scots. The Scotch members are about the number sufficient to make a House.[6] I propose it to the consideration of the Supporters of the

---

5. By William Dowdeswell, formerly Chancellor of the Exchequer in the Rockingham administration, in the House of Commons on 17 Feb 1769 (*Parliamentary History*, XVI. 579).

6. I.e., to form a quorum. It is interesting to find SJ, by implication, defending the Scots against Wilkite abuse. For all the legend of SJ's animosity against the Scots, he had as-

Bill of Rights,[7] whether there is not reason to suspect, that these hungry intruders from the North, are now contriving to expel all the English. We may then curse the hour in which it was determined, that expulsion and exclusion are the same. For who can guess what may be done when the Scots have the whole House to themselves?

Thus agreeable to custom and reason, notwithstanding all objections, real or imaginary;[u] thus consistent with the practice of former times, and thus consequential to the original principles of government, is that decision by which so much violence of discontent has been excited, which has been so dolorously bewailed, and so outrageously resented.

Let us however not be seduced to put too much confidence in justice or in truth, they have often been found inactive in their own defence, and give more confidence than help to their friends and their advocates. It may perhaps be prudent to make one momentary concession to falsehood, by supposing the vote in Mr. Lutterel's favour to be wrong.

All wrong ought to be rectified. If Mr. Wilkes is deprived of a lawful seat, both he and his electors have reason to complain; but it will not be easily found, why, among the innumerable wrongs of which a great part of mankind are hourly complaining, the whole care of the public should be transferred to Mr. Wilkes and the freeholders of Middlesex, who might all sink into non-existence, without any other effect, than that there would be room made for a new rabble, and a new retailer of sedition and obscenity. The cause of our country would suffer little; the rabble, whencesoever they come, will be always patriots, and always Supporters of the Bill of Rights.

u. notwithstanding . . . imaginary 76] om. 70

---

sociations in the 1760's with many Scottish politicians (e.g., Bute, Wedderburn, Elibank, George Dempster), supporters of George III, who "rejoiced in the name of Briton"—not merely "Englishman." Wilkes's *North Briton* had, of course, been originally directed against George's Scottish advisers.

7. The Society for the Defence of the Bill of Rights was organized in Feb 1769, under the leadership of Wilkes's friends, John Horne Tooke and Serjeant John Glynn. The implication of the title is that the ministry's action in the Middlesex election was contrary to the Bill of Rights, drawn up at the time of the Revolution of 1688.

The House of Commons decides the disputes arising from elections.[8] Was it ever supposed, that in all cases their decisions were right? Every man whose lawful election is defeated, is equally wronged with Mr. Wilkes, and his constituents feel their disappointment with no less anguish than the freeholders of Middlesex. These decisions have often been apparently partial, and sometimes tyrannically oppressive. A majority has been given to a favourite candidate, by expunging votes which had always been allowed, and which therefore had the authority by which all votes are given, that of custom uninterrupted. When the Commons determine who shall be constituents,[9] they may, with some propriety, be said to make law, because those determinations have hitherto, for the sake of quiet, been adopted by succeeding Parliaments. A vote therefore of the House, when it operates as a law, is to individuals a law only temporary, but to communities perpetual.

Yet though all this has been done, and though at every new Parliament much of this is expected to be done again, it has never produced in any former time such an *alarming crisis*.[1] We have found by experience, that though a squire has given ale and venison in vain, and a borough has been compelled to see its dearest interest in the hands of him whom it did not trust, yet the general state of the nation has continued the same. The sun has risen, and the corn has grown, and whatever talk has been of the danger of property, yet he that ploughed the field commonly reaped it, and he that built a house was master of the door: the vexation excited by injustice suffered, or supposed to be suffered, by any private man, or single community, was local and temporary, it neither spread far, nor lasted long.

The nation looked on with little care, because there did not seem to be much danger. The consequence of small

8. For the scandalously partisan way in which this was done, and its rectification by George Grenville's Controverted Elections Act (introduced in the House of Commons 7 Mar 1770), see, e.g., William Hunt, *The History of England, 1760–1801*, 1905 (Vol. x in *The Political History of England*), pp. 108–09.

9. E.g., when, by a resolution of the House in 1718, the qualifications for voting in the borough of Lichfield were modified (*Politics*, p. 34).

1. See n. 1, p. 317 above.

irregularities was not felt, and we had not yet learned to be terrified by very distant enemies. But quiet and security are now at an end. Our vigilance is quickened, and our comprehension is enlarged. We not only see events in their causes, but before their causes; we hear the thunder while the sky is clear, and see the mine sprung before it is dug. Political wisdom has, by the force of English genius, been improved at last not only to political intuition, but to political prescience.[v]

But it cannot, I am afraid, be said, that as we are grown wise, we are made happy. It is said of those who have the wonderful power called second sight, that they seldom see any thing but evil: political second sight has the same effect; we hear of nothing but of an alarming crisis of violated rights, and expiring liberties. The morning rises upon new wrongs, and the dreamer passes the night in imaginary shackles.

The sphere of anxiety is now enlarged; he that hitherto cared only for himself, now cares for the public; for he has learned that the happiness of individuals is comprised in the prosperity of the whole, and that his country[w] never suffers but he suffers with it, however it happens that he feels no pain.

Fired with this fever of epidemic patriotism,[x] the taylor slips his thimble, the drapier drops his yard, and the black-smith lays down his hammer; they meet at an honest alehouse,[2] consider the state of the nation, read or hear the last petition, lament the miseries of the time, are alarmed at the dreadful crisis, and subscribe to the support of the Bill of Rights.

It sometimes indeed happens, that an intruder of more benevolence than prudence attempts to disperse their cloud of dejection, and ease their hearts by seasonable consolation. He tells them, that though the government cannot be too diligently watched, it may be too hastily accused; and that, though private judgment is every man's right, yet we cannot judge of what we do not know. That we feel at present no

v. not only . . . prescience 76] to political intuition 70   w. country 76] county 70   x. patriotism; 70, 76

2. The Society for the Defence of the Bill of Rights met in the London Tavern. "Honest" (analogous to "pa- triotic") is no doubt intended ironically.

evils which government can alleviate, and that the publick business is committed to men who have as much right to confidence as their adversaries. That the freeholders of Middlesex, if they could not choose Mr. Wilkes, might have chosen any other man, and that "he trusts we have within the realm five hundred as good as he":[3] that even[y] if this which has happened to Middlesex had happened to every other county, that one man should be made incapable of being elected, it could produce no great change in the Parliament, nor much contract the power of election; that what has been done is probably right, and that if it be wrong it is of little consequence, since a like case cannot easily occur; that expulsions are very rare, and if they should, by unbounded insolence of faction, become more frequent, the electors may easily provide a second choice.

All this he may say, but not half of this will be heard; his opponents will stun him and themselves with a confused sound of pension and[4z] places, venality and corruption, oppression and invasion, slavery and ruin.

Outcries like these, uttered by malignity, and ecchoed by folly; general accusations of indeterminate wickedness, and obscure hints of impossible designs, dispersed among those that do not know their meaning, by those that know them to be false, have disposed part of the nation, though but a small part, to pester the court with ridiculous petitions.

The progress of a petition is well known. An ejected placeman goes down to his county or his borough, tells his friends of his inability to serve them, and his constituents of the corruption of the government. His friends readily understand that he who can get nothing, will have nothing to give. They agree to proclaim a meeting, meat and drink are plentifully provided, a crowd is easily brought together, and

y. even 76] om. 70   z. pension and 76] om. 70

---

3. From the ballad *Chevy Chase*, stanza four in the form given by Addison (*Spectator*, No. 70).

4. Many of the replies to *The False Alarm* reflected acidly on SJ's pension; e.g., *The Crisis* (1770), p. 31: "I would

refer him [the author of *The False Alarm*] to Johnson's Dictionary for the idea of a Pensioner." SJ's introducing the word into his revised version is no doubt a riposte to show his contempt.

those who think that they know the reason of their meeting, undertake to tell those who know it not. Ale and clamour unite their powers, the crowd, condensed and heated, begins to ferment with the leven of sedition. All see a thousand evils, though they cannot show them, and grow impatient for a remedy, though they know not what.

A speech is then made by the Cicero of the day, he says much, and suppresses more, and credit is equally given to what he tells, and what he conceals. The petition is read and universally approved. Those who are sober enough to write add their names, and the rest would sign it if they could.

Every man goes home and tells his neighbour of the glories of the day; how he was consulted and what he advised; how he was invited into the great room, where his lordship called him by his name; how he was caressed by Sir Francis, Sir Joseph, or Sir George;[5] how he eat turtle and venison, and drank unanimity to the three brothers.[6]

The poor loiterer, whose shop had confined him, or whose wife had locked him up, hears the tale of luxury with envy, and at last enquires what was their petition. Of the petition nothing is remembered by the narrator, but that it spoke much of fears and apprehensions, and something very alarming, and that[a] he is sure it is against the government; the other is convinced that it must be right, and wishes he had been there, for he loves wine and venison, and is resolved as long as he lives to be against the government.

The petition is then handed from town to town, and from house to house, and wherever it comes the inhabitants flock

a. that 70(2), 76] then 70(1)

---

5. The names are not merely generic: among the noisiest petitioners were Sir Francis Vincent, M.P. for Surrey; Sir Joseph Mawbey, M.P. for Southwark (together with Henry Thrale, but politically opposed to him); and Sir George Savile, M.P. for Yorkshire (Sir George Armytage, though not then M.P., was also prominent in the agitation in Yorkshire). SJ is thought to have been the author of a little squib against Mawbey published in the *Gentleman's Magazine*, Mar 1769, p. 162 (Boswell, *Life*, ed. J. W. Croker, 1831, II.68n.).

6. Richard Grenville, Earl Temple; George Grenville; and their brother-in-law, William Pitt, Earl of Chatham. Temple actively sponsored Wilkes, and the other two were in vigorous opposition to the administration's policy in the affair.

together, that they may see that which must be sent to the
King. Names are easily collected. One man signs because
he hates the papists; another because he has vowed destruction to the turnpikes;[7] one because it will vex the parson;
another because he owes his landlord nothing; one because
he is rich; another because he is poor; one to shew that he is
not afraid, and another to shew that he can write.

The passage, however, is not always smooth. Those who
collect contributions to sedition, sometimes apply to a man of
higher rank and more enlightened mind, who instead of
lending them his name, calmly reproves them for being
seducers of the people.

You who are here, says he, complaining of venality, are
yourselves the agents of those, who having estimated themselves at too high a price, are only angry that they are not
bought. You are appealing from the Parliament to the rabble,
and inviting those, who scarcely, in the most common affairs,
distinguish right from wrong, to judge of a question complicated with law written and unwritten, with the general
principles of government, and the particular customs of the
House of Commons; you are shewing them a grievance, so
distant that they cannot see it, and so light that they cannot
feel it; for how, but by unnecessary intelligence and artificial
provocation, should the farmers and shopkeepers of Yorkshire
and Cumberland know or care how Middlesex is represented.[8]
Instead of wandering thus round the county to exasperate
the rage of party, and darken the suspicions of ignorance,
it is the duty of men like you, who have leisure for enquiry,
to lead back the people to their honest labour; to tell them,

---

7. The construction of turnpikes had
recently been accelerated. Improvements in transportation in eighteenth-
century England gave rise to much
irrational opposition; cf. Tom Tempest in *Idler* 10.

8. The petition from Yorkshire was
one of the largest and most publicized; there seems to have been no
petition specifically from Cumberland.
But cf. Richard Rigby in the House

of Commons, 9 Jan 1770: "If it were
not for the officious diligence of these
incendiaries, how is it possible that
the farmers and weavers in Yorkshire
and Cumberland should know or take
an interest in the Middlesex election
of representatives in Parliament?" (*Parliamentary History*, xiv.698). Rigby's
speech goes on to describe "the progress of a petition" in a way curiously
like SJ's.

that submission is the duty of the ignorant, and content the virtue of the poor;[9] that they have no skill in the art of government, nor any interest in the dissentions of the great; and when you meet with any, as some there are, whose understandings are capable of conviction, it will become you to allay this foaming ebullition, by shewing them that they have as much happiness as the condition of life will easily receive, and that a government, of which an erroneous or unjust representation of Middlesex is the greatest crime that interest can discover, or malice can upbraid, is a government approaching nearer to perfection, than any that experience has known, or history related.

The drudges of sedition wish to change their ground, they hear him with sullen silence, feel conviction without repentance, and are confounded but not abashed; they go forward to another door, and find a kinder reception from a man enraged against the government, because he has just been paying the tax upon his windows.[1]

That a petition for a dissolution of the Parliament will at all times have its favourers, may be easily imagined. The people indeed do not expect that one House of Commons will be much honester or much wiser than another; they do not suppose that the taxes will be lightened; or though they have been so often taught to hope it, that soap and candles will be cheaper; they expect no redress of grievances, for of no grievances but taxes do they complain; they wish not the extension of liberty, for they do not feel any restraint; about the security of privilege or property they are totally careless, for they see no property invaded, nor know, till they are told, that any privilege has suffered violation.

Least of all do they expect, that any future Parliament

---

9. SJ's definition of "the poor" in his *Dictionary* should be noted: "Those who are in the lowest rank of any community; those who cannot subsist but by the charity of others; but it is sometimes used with laxity for any not rich." SJ here is presumably not using the expression with laxity.

1. The window tax was first levied in 1697, "according to the number of windows and openings on houses having more than six windows and worth more than £5 per annum. . . . The tax fell with peculiar hardship on the middle classes" (*Encyclopedia Britannica*, 11th ed., s.v.) It was repealed in 1851.

will lessen its own powers, or communicate to the people that authority which it has once obtained.

Yet a new Parliament is sufficiently desirable. The year of election is a year of jollity; and what is still more delightful, a year of equality. The glutton now eats the delicacies for which he longed when he could not purchase them, and the drunkard has the pleasure of wine without the cost. The drone lives a while without work, and the shopkeeper, in the flow of money, raises his price. The mechanic that trembled at the presence of Sir Joseph, now bids him come again for an answer; and the poacher, whose gun has been seized, now finds an opportunity to reclaim[b] it. Even the honest man is not displeased to see himself important, and willingly resumes in two years that power which he had resigned for seven.[2] Few love their friends so well as not to desire superiority by unexpensive benefaction.

Yet, notwithstanding all these motives to compliance, the promoters of petitions have not been successful. Few could be persuaded to lament evils which they did not suffer, or to solicit for redress which they do not want. The petition has been, in some places, rejected; and perhaps in all but one,[3] signed only by the meanest and grossest of the people.

Since this expedient now invented or revived to distress the government, and equally practicable at all times by all who shall be excluded from power and from profit, has produced so little effect, let us consider the opposition as no longer formidable. The great engine has recoiled upon them. They thought that "the terms they sent were terms of weight," which would have "amazed all and stumbled many"; but the consternation is now over, and their foes "stand upright," as before.[4]

b. reclaim 70(2), 76] retain 70(1)

---

2. The Septennial Act, in force between 1716 and 1912, set the maximum term of a parliament at seven years. Before 1784, Parliament was seldom dissolved much before its full term.

3. Perhaps the Buckinghamshire petition, thought to have been drafted by Burke.

4. The quoted words are adapted from *Paradise Lost*, vi. 621–27—Belial's report to Satan of the effect of the "great engine" discharged at the army of loyal angels.

With great propriety and dignity the king has, in his speech, neglected or forgotten them.[5] He might easily know, that what was presented as the sense of the people, is the sense only of the profligate and dissolute; and that whatever Parliament should be convened, the same petitioners would be ready, for the same reason, to request its dissolution.

As we once had a rebellion of the clowns,[6] we have now an opposition of the pedlars. The quiet of the nation has been for years disturbed by a faction, against which all factions ought to conspire; for its original principle is the desire of levelling; it is only animated under the name of zeal, by the natural malignity of the mean against the great.

When in the confusion which the English invasions produced in France, the vilains, imagining that they had found the golden hour of emancipation, took arms in their hands,[7] the knights of both nations considered the cause as common, and, suspending the general hostility, united to chastise them.

The whole conduct of this despicable faction is distinguished by plebeian grossness, and savage indecency. To misrepresent the actions and the principles of their enemies is common to all parties; but the insolence of invective, and brutality of reproach, which have lately prevailed, are peculiar to this.

An infallible characteristic of meanness is cruelty. This is the only faction that has shouted at the condemnation of a criminal, and that, when his innocence procured his pardon, has clamoured for his blood.[8]

---

5. The Speech from the Throne, the official statement of the ministry's plans at the opening of a session of Parliament, delivered on 9 Jan 1770, greatly offended the Wilkites by its contemptuous omission of any reference to the agitation over the Middlesex election. It began, "My Lords and Gentlemen, It is with much concern that I find myself obliged to open this session of Parliament with acquainting you that the distemper among the horned cattle has lately broke out in the kingdom" (*Parliamentary History*, XIV.642).

6. Either the Peasants' Revolt of 1381, led by Wat Tyler, or the uprising of 1549, led by Robert Kett.

7. The peasant rising of the Jacquerie in 1358, during the Hundred Years' War. "Vilain" (or "villain," the 1776 reading) is a normal eighteenth-century spelling for "villein."

8. At a Middlesex election meeting on 8 Dec 1768, a brawl between gangs of pro- and anti-Wilkite toughs re-

All other parties, however enraged at each other, have agreed to treat the throne with decency; but these low-born railers have attacked not only the authority, but the character of their Sovereign,[9] and have endeavoured, surely without effect, to alienate the affections of the people from the only king, who, for almost a century,[1] has much appeared to desire, or much endeavoured to deserve them. They have insulted him with rudeness and with menaces, which were never excited by the gloomy sullenness of William, even when half the nation denied him their allegiance;[2] nor by the dangerous bigotry of James, unless when he was finally driven from his palace;[3c] and with which scarcely the open hostilities of rebellion ventured to vilify the unhappy Charles, even in the remarks on the cabinet of Naseby.[4]

It is surely not unreasonable to hope, that the nation will consult its dignity, if not its safety, and disdain to be pro-

c. palace; _76_] palace, _70_

sulted in the death of a Wilkite weaver, George Clerke. Two Irish chairmen, Edward McQuirk and Lawrence Balfe, were found guilty of murder, 14 Jan 1769, and sentenced to death. There being some doubt as to their exact part in the affair, they were given the royal pardon 10 Mar 1769. A correspondent in the _Gentleman's Magazine_ (Mar 1769, p. 139) protests against "the inhuman rage with which some persons (and particularly Mr. W——es himself) have demanded the blood of the two Irishmen." Junius wrote violently against the pardon, and the _North Briton_ No. 131 (21 Oct 1769), made the pardon of McQuirk an article of impeachment against Grafton.

9. In the Middlesex and City of London petitions, and, of course, Junius's notorious letter to the King of 19 Dec 1769.

1. I.e., since Charles II. SJ was right: George III was to become perhaps the most widely beloved mon-

arch in English history.

2. In 1689 all persons in public offices were required to swear allegiance to William III and Mary, on pain of deprivation of office. There were many refusals by "non-jurors," but SJ is grossly exaggerating when he says "half the nation."

3. On the rude treatment of James on the Kentish coast after his flight from Whitehall (12 Dec 1688), see Macaulay, _History of England_, Ch. x. The account of this cited by Macaulay (Harl. MS 6852) could conceivably have been encountered by SJ when cataloguing the Harleian library, although it is printed in Tindal's and Ralph's histories.

4. After the battle of Naseby (1645) Charles I's "cabinet" of secret papers was captured by the Parliamentarians, who, to discredit Charles, published a selection from them with pejorative comments. Cf. Clarendon, _History of the Rebellion_, Book IX, Sect. 41.

tected or enslaved by the declaimers or the plotters of a city-tavern. Had Rome fallen by the Catilinarian conspiracy, she might have consoled her fate by the greatness of her destroyers; but what would have alleviated the disgrace of England, had her government been changed by Tiler or by Ket?[5]

One part of the nation has never before contended with the other, but for some weighty and apparent interest. If the means were violent, the end was great. The civil war was fought for what each army called and believed the best religion, and the best government. The struggle in the reign of Anne, was to exclude or restore an exiled king.[6] We are now disputing, with almost equal animosity, whether Middle-sex shall be represented or not by a criminal from a jail.

The only comfort left in such degeneracy is, that a lower state can be no longer possible.

In this contemptuous censure, I mean not to include every single man. In all lead, says the chemist, there is silver; and in all copper there is gold.[7] But mingled masses are justly denominated by the greater quantity, and when the precious particles are not worth extraction, a faction and a pig must be melted down together to the forms and offices that chance allots them.

Fiunt urceoli, pelves, sartago, patellae.[8]

A few weeks will now shew whether the Government can be shaken by empty noise, and whether the faction which

---

5. See n. 6, p. 341.

6. SJ presents the popular interpretation of the political events of the last years of Anne's reign, culminating in the struggle for power between Oxford and Bolingbroke. His expression is somewhat inaccurate: the "exiled king," James II, had died in 1701; the object of Jacobite activity at the time was his son, the Old Pretender, who had been merely Prince of Wales at the time of his "exile."

7. A commonplace of the alchemical theory of transmutation, still accepted to some extent even in SJ's time; for instance, by Hermann Boerhaave ("Alchemy," *Encyclopaedia Britannica*, 11th ed.).

8. Juvenal, x.64. After the fall of Sejanus, his brazen statue was melted down—"Of head and limbs are made / Pans, cans, and pisspots, a whole kitchen trade" (Dryden's translation).

depends upon its influence, has not deceived alike the public
and itself. That it should have continued till now, is sufficiently shameful. None can indeed wonder that it has been
supported by the sectaries,[9] the natural[d] fomenters of sedition,
and confederates[e] of the rabble, of whose religion little now
remains but hatred of establishments, and who are angry
to find separation now only tolerated, which was once rewarded;[1] but every honest man must lament, that it has
been regarded with frigid neutrality by the Tories,[2] who,
being long accustomed to signalize their principles by opposition to the court, do not yet consider that they have at
last a king who knows not the name of party, and who wishes
to be the common father of all his people.

As a man inebriated only by vapours, soon recovers in the
open air; a nation discontented to madness, without any
adequate cause, will return to its wits and its allegiance when

d. natural *76*] constant *70*   e. and confederates *76*] and never-failing confederates *70*

---

9. Some Dissenters were active on
the side of Wilkes, notably Joseph
Priestley, who engaged in a lively controversy with Sir William Blackstone
over it. See, e.g., *London Chronicle*, 10–
12 Oct 1769, p. 356, and *A View of
the Principles and Conduct of the Protestant Dissenters, with Respect to the Civil
and Ecclesiastical Constitution of England*,
published Dec 1769.

1. SJ probably refers to the alleged
patronage of Dissenters by the Walpole and Newcastle regimes, in return
for their support.

2. For instance, in the division in
the House of Commons in 1764 on
the question of the legality of general
warrants (a question arising out of
the earlier contest between supporters
of the administration and those of
Wilkes), Sir Lewis Namier calculated
that the votes of the "country gentlemen," the genuine Tories, were divided

41 on one side and 45 on the other
("Country Gentlemen in Parliament,"
Personalities and Powers, 1955). The mis-
conception so frequent in nineteenth-
century historiography of the period,
that George III's ministries were
largely "Tory," has only recently begun to be corrected, although such a
statement as this of SJ's ought to have
thrown suspicion on it. Cf. Richard
Pares, *King George III and the Politicians* (1953), p. 72: "Though George
III was willing to take loyal tories
into his service, as he told Pitt in
1765, few of them came; some of them
cold-shouldered him, others were useless." SJ correctly describes their traditional attitude as one of "opposition
to the court"—i.e., to whatever
administration was in power at Westminster: the characteristic of eighteenth-century English Toryism was
suspicion of centralized political power.

a little pause has cooled it to reflexion. Nothing, therefore, is necessary, at this *alarming crisis*,[f] but to consider the alarm as false.[3] To make concessions is to encourage encroachment. Let the court despise the faction, and the disappointed people will soon deride it.

FINIS.[g]

f. *No italics 70*   g. *Om. 76*

3. See n. 1, p. 317.

THOUGHTS ON THE LATE TRANSACTIONS RESPECTING FALKLAND'S ISLANDS. 1771.

The Falkland Islands crisis in late 1770 and early 1771 had two aspects, international and domestic.[1] In its international aspect, it was part of the aftermath of the Seven Years' War. Formally allied to France by the Family Compact of 1761, Spain had joined in the war against Britain the next year, to the disgust of Pitt, who had resigned a few months earlier as Secretary of State and chief director of the war because the Cabinet had refused his proposal for a sudden attack on Spain, to relieve pressure on Britain's ally, Frederick the Great of Prussia. In spite of Pitt's absence, however, Britain was able, in the few months before the Peace of Paris was concluded, to inflict humiliating defeats on Spain by capturing Havana and Manila and seizing huge amounts of Spanish treasure.

All this rankled in the minds of Carlos III and his foreign minister Grimaldi. Expecting support from the French minister Choiseul, who was likewise anxious to recoup his country's losses to Britain in the war, the Spanish were looking for an opportunity to take an aggressive line. They found one in the disputed question of the sovereignty of the Falkland Islands. There is no need to recapitulate here the actions of the Spanish from 1769 to 1771 and the British reaction to them. Johnson has provided an account of masterly lucidity—so much so that when, shortly after the Second World War, the Argentine Republic, heir to the Spanish claim to the islands, reopened the dispute, an enterprising publisher reprinted Johnson's *Thoughts* as the clearest exposition available of its complicated history.[2]

As for the implications of the incident in domestic politics, the key is given by Johnson's comment (pp. 378, 379 below) that "Junius knows his own meaning . . . he is an enemy to the ministry, he sees them growing hourly stronger," and "The real crime of the ministry is that they have found the means of avoiding their own ruin." The appointment of the comparatively young and unknown Lord North as First Lord of the Treasury in February 1770, after Newcastle, Bute, Grenville, Rockingham, Chatham, and Grafton had successively held the reins of office and been forced to abandon them, was looked on as the King's last desperate resort, and the older political leaders and their partisans confidently expected that North would quickly ruin himself, and one or more of themselves would triumphantly return to office. The Falkland Islands incident was the first real test of the strength of North's ministry, and his opponents did their best to take advantage of it. The ministry, it was thought, was caught in a dilemma: either it would have to declare war and wage it unsuccessfully,

1. A detailed study of the incident is found in Julius Goebel, Jr., *The Struggle for the Falkland Islands* (1927).
2. Leigh-on-Sea, Essex: Thames Bank Publishing Co., 1948.

since Britain's military strength was at a low ebb; or else it would have to beat an ignominious retreat before Spanish aggression, with consequent loss of national "honour."

But two things took place that the opposition to North had not foreseen. When it came to the ultimate question of war and peace, Louis XV decided for peace, and dismissed Choiseul; without the support from France they had relied on, the Spanish dared not proceed and quickly backed down. And North and his allies handled the situation most astutely, never losing their nerve, never giving the appearance of relinquishing any rightful British claim, and at the same time doing their best to keep from pushing Spain over the brink of war. Two points in North's strategy may be singled out for special notice. One, which Johnson comments on, was the device of formulating the protest about the seizure of the islands as a complaint specifically against the captain-general of Buenos Aires, so as to give the Spanish government the opportunity to save face by disowning his actions (as, in the end, it did). The second, the details of which have only recently been carefully studied,[3] was North's handling of the cabinet crisis in December 1770. The minister responsible for the conduct of the Falkland Islands affair was the Secretary of State for the Southern Department, Lord Weymouth, a member of the "Bedford" group, uneasily allied with North. Weymouth had been active and powerful in the cabinet, and regarded himself as a contender for the prime ministership, if not prime minister already (there were no rules about this completely unofficial post; whoever could attract to himself the main conduct of affairs was "the Minister")[4]. Weymouth was determined on war. North, however, had the majority of the cabinet on his side in striving for peace, if possible, and by a series of delicate negotiations, Weymouth was eased out of office (without alienating the rest of the Bedford group), and replaced by the Earl of Rochford, a less ambitious, more pacific, and generally more responsible individual. North's power was consolidated, and for some five or six years at least, he gave Britain a very stable administration.

The opposition were of course furious to see North snatch victory out of the jaws of defeat, and a large section of Johnson's paper is devoted to scornful rebuttal of "patriotic" clamour at what the opposition tried to present as a diplomatic triumph for Spain. The noisiest were Chatham, with his eternal obsession about Spain[5] (as the chief hindrance to Britain's becoming the dominant imperial and commercial power in the world), and the trading interests of the City of London, represented by such men as

3. L. H. Brown, "The Grafton and North Cabinets" (dissertation, University of Toronto, 1963), pp. 269–92.

4. A letter to the *Public Advertiser*, 2 Apr 1771, comments that the *Thoughts on Falkland's Islands* is "said, upon good ground, to have been written by the learned Dr. Johnson, under the special direction of the Minister-Apparent" (i.e., North).

5. Some of Chatham's remarks at the time are almost incredible. Cf., from his speech to the House of Lords 22 Nov 1770: "My Lords, the English are a candid, an ingenuous people; the Spaniards are as mean and crafty, as they are proud and insolent. The integrity of the English merchant, the generous

William Beckford, Barlow Trecothick (who, as Lord Mayor, while breathing fire against Spain, refused as Lord Mayor to allow impressment for the depleted Navy to take place in London),[6] Wilkes, and John Sawbridge, brother of Johnson's *bête noire*, Mrs. Catharine Macaulay. Johnson's indignant charge that they wanted war in order to profit from it—"These are the men who . . . rejoice when obstinacy or ambition adds another year to slaughter and devastation; and laugh from their desks at bravery and science, while they are adding figure to figure"—is one of his most effective pieces of writing.

For once, Johnson seems to have made his point in a political matter. Of his better-known political writings, *Thoughts on Falkland's Islands* alone appears to have escaped general condemnation, both by his avowed enemies and by his frequently too candid friends.[7] Even so thoroughgoing a practitioner of the Whig interpretation of eighteenth-century political history as William Hunt can sum the incident up thus:

---

spirit of our naval and military officers, would be degraded by a comparison with their merchants or officers. With their Ministers I have often been obliged to negociate, and never met with an instance of candor or dignity in their proceedings; nothing but low cunning, trick, and artifice; after a long experience of their want of candor and good faith, I found myself compelled to talk to them in a peremptory, decisive language. On this principle I submitted my advice to a trembling Council, for an immediate declaration of a war with Spain. Your Lordships well know what were the consequences of not following that advice" (Debrett, *History, Debates, and Proceedings of Parliament* [1743–74], 1792, v. 345).

6. See Debrett, v. 453, and p. 375 below. Trecothick was supposed to be a follower of Rockingham rather than of Chatham, and hence more moderate than his predecessor as mayor, Beckford.

7. "There was no real counter-attack: one 42-page pamphlet, a few essays, letters, and reviews constituted the only major artillery employed against it [the *Thoughts*]": Helen Louise McGuffie, "Samuel Johnson and the Hostile Press" (diss., Columbia Univ., 1961), p. 186 (now included in her *Samuel Johnson in the British Press, 1749–1784: A Chronological Checklist*, 1976). Professor McGuffie lists some 550 items dealing with Johnson published from 1770 to 1775 inclusive, most of them attacks directed against his political writings during this period (though the *Dictionary* and the edition of Shakespeare come in for some fire too).

The *Thoughts*, however, touched Burke to the quick. Two years after Johnson's death, Burke and Boswell dined with Reynolds, and Boswell reports, "He [Burke] was violent against Dr. Johnson's political writings. He said that he ascribed to Opposition an endeavor to involve the nation in a war on account of Falkland's Islands, which he knew to be a false charge. He [Johnson] imputed to them the wickedness of his own opposition to Walpole. He [Burke] was intemperately abusive to a departed Great Man": *Private Papers of James Boswell from Malahide Castle*, ed. Geoffrey Scott and F. A. Pottle (New York, 1928–34), xv.234. Johnson's charge is, of course, directed primarily at Chatham and his City supporters rather than at Burke's faction, the Rockinghamites.

Throughout the whole progress of the affair the opposition attacked the government, alleging that it was careless of the honour of England, had exhibited a lack of promptitude, and had made a secret agreement with Spain to abandon the island; they even insinuated that the minister had truckled to France in order to prevent her from taking part with Spain. Their attacks were factious. The government had no desire to rush needlessly into war, but it acted with vigour and decision, and carried the matter through with a sufficiently high hand. The islands were soon afterwards deserted as unprofitable, but the British right to them was not abandoned.[8]

This is also a summary of the position Johnson takes in the *Thoughts*.

The pamphlet was published (by Cadell) on 16 March 1771 (*London Chronicle*). It was withdrawn a few days later (see Johnson's *Letters* 246, 20 Mar 1771) to cancel a leaf in order for the ministry to make the notorious correction of Johnson's gibe at Grenville (no. 6, p. 383 below), and released perhaps around 27 March. A second edition was published 11 April; this edition was printed from standing type. With the other three pamphlets of the 1770's, the *Thoughts* was reprinted, with some revisions by Johnson, in *Political Tracts*, 1776. The text given here follows that of the first edition, 1771, with authorial corrections from 1776. Spelling variants between the editions of 1771 and 1776 are unimportant and are not recorded—*enquiry / inquiry, authorised / authorized, stile / style, enterprize / enterprise*, and the like. "Falkland Island(s)" (five instances) throughout 1771 becomes "Falkland's Island(s)" throughout 1776, and "Bucarelli" (two instances) becomes "Buccarelli." The caption title reads "Falkland Islands" in *71*, "Falkland's Islands" in *76*. As with *The False Alarm*, I have accepted the punctuation of 1776 rather than 1771 where it is closer to modern practice and obviates difficulty for the reader.

8. *Political History of England, 1760–1801* (1905), p. 114.

Thoughts on the Late Transactions
Respecting Falkland's Islands

To proportion the eagerness of contest to its importance seems too hard a task for human wisdom. The pride of wit has kept ages busy in the discussion of useless questions, and the pride of power has destroyed armies to gain or to keep unprofitable possessions.

Not many years have passed since the cruelties of war were filling the world with terror and with sorrow; rage was at last appeased, or strength exhausted,[a] and to the harassed

a. strength exhausted *76*] strength was exhausted *71*

nations peace was restored,with its pleasures and its benefits.[1] Of this state all felt the happiness, and all implored the continuance; but what continuance of happiness can be expected, when the whole system of European empire can be in danger of a new concussion, by a contention for a few spots of earth, which, in the deserts of the ocean,[b] had almost escaped human notice, and which, if they had not happened to make a sea-mark,[2] had perhaps never had a name.

Fortune often delights to dignify what nature has neglected, and that renown which cannot be claimed by intrinsick excellence or greatness, is sometimes derived from unexpected accidents. The Rubicon was ennobled by the passage of Caesar, and the time is now come when Falkland's Islands demand their historian.

But[c] the writer to whom this employment shall be assigned, will have few opportunities of descriptive splendor, or narrative elegance. Of other countries it is told how often they have changed their government; these islands have hitherto changed only their name. Of heroes to conquer, or legislators to civilize, here has been no appearance; nothing has happened to them but that they have been sometimes seen by wandering navigators, who passed by them in search of better habitations.

When the Spaniards, who, under the conduct of Columbus, discovered America, had taken possession of its most wealthy regions, they surprised and terrified Europe by a sudden and unexampled influx of riches. They were made at once insupportably insolent, and might perhaps have become irresistibly powerful, had not their mountainous treasures been scattered in the air with the ignorant profusion of unaccustomed opulence.

The greater part of the European potentates saw this stream of riches flowing into Spain without attempting to

b. ocean, 76] ocean 71   c. *No new paragraph 71*

---

1. The Peace of Paris, between Britain and France, terminating the Seven Years' War, was signed 10 Feb 1763.

2. "Point or conspicuous place distinguished at sea, and serving to mariners as directions of their course" (*Dictionary*).

dip their own hands in the golden fountain. France had no naval skill or power; Portugal was extending her dominions in the East over regions formed in the gaiety of Nature; the Hanseatick league, being planned only for the security of traffick, had no tendency to discovery or invasion; and the commercial states of Italy growing rich by trading between Asia and Europe, and not lying upon the ocean, did not desire to seek by great hazards, at a distance, what was almost at home to be found with safety.

The English alone were animated by the success of the Spanish navigators, to try if any thing was left that might reward adventure, or incite appropriation. They sent Cabot[3] into the North, but in the North there was no gold or silver to be found. The best regions were pre-occupied, yet they still continued their hopes and their labours. They were the second nation that dared the extent of the Pacifick Ocean, and the second circumnavigators of the globe.

By the war between Elizabeth and Philip, the wealth of America became lawful prize, and those who were less afraid of danger than of poverty, supposed that riches might easily be obtained by plundering the Spaniards. Nothing is difficult when gain and honour unite their influence; the spirit and vigour of these expeditions enlarged our views of the new world, and made us first acquainted with its remoter coasts.

In the fatal voyage of Cavendish (1592) Captain Davis,[4] who, being sent out as his associate, was afterwards parted from him or deserted him, as he was driven by violence of weather about the Straits of Magellan, is supposed to have been the first who saw the lands now called Falkland[d] Islands, but his distress permitted him not to make any observation, and he left them, as he found them, without a name.

d. Falkland's *76* (*and throughout the rest of the essay*)

---

3. See n. 2, p. 147 above. These opening paragraphs are a recapitulation of what Johnson had said in the "Introduction to the Political State of Great-Britain," pp. 130–47 above.

4. John Davys (so spelled in *DNB*). The account is found in *The Last Voyage of Thomas Candish*, in Vol. XI of Hakluyt, *Principal Navigations* (Hakluyt Society, 1904), pp. 359–416.

Not long afterwards (1594) Sir Richard Hawkins, being in the same seas with the same designs, saw these islands again, if they are indeed the same islands, and in honour of his mistress, called them Hawkins's Maiden Land.[5] This voyage was not of renown sufficient to procure a general reception to the new name, for when the Dutch, who had now become strong enough not only to defend themselves, but to attack their masters, sent (1598) Verhagen and Sebald de Wert, into the South Sea, these islands, which were not supposed to have been known before, obtained the denomination of Sebald's Islands, and were from that time placed in the charts; though Frezier[6] tells us, that they were yet considered as of doubtful existence.

Their present English name was probably given them (1689) by Strong,[7] whose journal, yet unprinted, may be found in the Museum. This name was adopted by Halley, and has from that time, I believe, been received into our maps.

The privateers which were put into[e] motion by the wars of William and Anne, saw those islands and mention them; but they were yet not considered as territories worth a contest. Strong affirmed that there was no wood, and Dampier suspected that they had no water.

Frezier describes their appearance with more distinctness, and mentions some ships of St. Maloes, by which they had been visited, and to which he seems willing enough to ascribe the honour of discovering islands which yet he admits to have been seen by Hawkins, and named by Sebald de Wert. He, I suppose, in honour of his countrymen, called them the Malouines, the denomination now used by the Spaniards, who seem not, till very lately, to have thought them important enough to deserve a name.

e. into 76] in 71

---

5. Hawkins's account is in Vol. xvii of *Purchas His Pilgrimes* (Hakluyt Society, 1906), p. 106.

6. Amédée-François Frézier, *Relation du Voyage de la Mer du Sud* (1716); translated as *A Voyage to the South-Sea . . .* [with] *A Postscript by Dr. E. Halley* (1717).

7. Captain John Strong. The journal was later printed in James Burney, *A Chronological History of the Discoveries in the South Seas* (1816). The islands were named after Anthony Cary, 5th Viscount Falkland, one of the Lords Commissioners of the Admiralty and later First Lord.

Since the publication of Anson's voyage,[8] they have very much changed their opinion, finding a settlement in Pepys's[9f] or Falkland's Island recommended by the authour as necessary to the success of our future expeditions against the coast of Chili, and as of such use and importance, that it would produce many advantages in peace, and in war would make us masters of the South Sea.

Scarcely any degree of judgement is sufficient to restrain the imagination from magnifying that on which it is long detained. The relater of Anson's voyage[1] had heated his mind with its various events, had partaken the hope with which it was begun, and the vexation suffered by its various miscarriages, and then thought nothing could be of greater benefit to the nation than that which might promote the success of such another enterprize.

Had the heroes[2] of that history even[g] performed and attained all that when they first spread their sails they ventured to hope, the consequence would yet[h] have produced very little hurt to the Spaniards, and very little benefit to the English. They would have taken a few towns; Anson and his companions would have shared the plunder or the ransom; and the Spaniards, finding their southern territories accessible, would for the future have guarded them better.

That such a settlement may be of use in war, no man that considers its situation will deny. But war is not the whole business of life; it happens but seldom, and every man, either good or wise, wishes that its frequency were still less. That conduct which betrays designs of future hostility,

f. Pepys's 76] Pepy's 71   g. even 76] om. 71   h. yet 76] om. 71

---

8. *A Voyage Round the World in the Years 1740, 1, 2, 3, 4* (1748). An abridgement of this in the *Gentleman's Magazine*, Sept 1749–Mar 1750, has been attributed to SJ (C. L. Carlson, *The First Magazine*, 1938, p. 22).

9. This nonexistent island, named after the diarist and Secretary to the Admiralty, was said by Ambrose Cowley to have been sighted in 1684.

Search for it continued until the nineteenth century.

1. Reverend Richard Walter, Anson's chaplain.

2. The sarcasm is in keeping with SJ's usual attitude toward Anson, an active Whig politician much involved in Lichfield, as well as Westminster, politics. See p. 217 above.

if it does not excite violence, will always generate malignity; it must for ever exclude confidence and friendship, and continue a cold and sluggish rivalry, by a sly reciprocation of indirect injuries, without the bravery of war, or the security of peace.

The advantage of such a settlement in time of peace is, I think, not easily to be proved. For what use can it have but of a station for contraband traders, a nursery of fraud, and a receptacle of theft? Narborough,[3] about a century ago, was of opinion, that no advantage could be obtained in voyages to the South Sea, except by such an armament as, with a sailor's morality, "might trade by force." It is well known that the prohibitions of foreign commerce are, in these countries, to the last degree rigorous, and that no man not authorised by the King of Spain can trade there but by force or stealth. Whatever profit is obtained must be gained by the violence of rapine, or dexterity of fraud.

Government will not perhaps soon arrive at such purity and excellence, but that some connivance at least will be indulged to the triumphant robber and successful cheat. He that brings wealth home is seldom interrogated by what means it was obtained. This, however, is one of those modes of corruption with which mankind ought always to struggle, and which they may in time hope to overcome. There is reason to expect, that as the world is more enlightened, policy and morality will at last be reconciled, and that nations will learn not to do what they would not suffer.

But the silent toleration of suspected guilt is a degree of depravity far below that which openly incites and manifestly protects it. To pardon a pirate may be injurious to mankind; but how much greater is the crime of opening a port in which all pirates shall be safe? The contraband trader is not more worthy of protection: if with Narborough he trades by force, he is a pirate; if he trades secretly, he is only a thief. Those who honestly refuse his traffick he hates as obstructors of his profit; and those with whom he deals he cheats, because

---

3. Admiral Sir John Narborough. His voyage through the Straits of Magellan took place 1669–71. His *Account of Several Late Voyages and Discoveries to the South and North* was published in 1694.

he knows that they dare not complain. He lives with a heart full of that malignity which fear of detection always generates in those who are[i] to defend unjust acquisitions against lawful authority; and when he comes home with riches thus acquired, he brings a mind hardened in evil, too proud for reproof, and too stupid for reflection; he offends the high by his insolence, and corrupts the low by his example.

Whether these truths were forgotten or despised, or whether some better purpose was then in agitation, the representation made in Anson's voyage had such effect upon the statesmen of that time, that (in 1748) some sloops were fitted out for the fuller knowledge of Pepys and Falkland Islands, and for further discoveries in the South Sea. This expedition, though perhaps designed to be secret, was not long concealed from Wall,[4] the Spanish ambassador, who so vehemently opposed it, and so strongly maintained the right of the Spaniards to the exclusive dominion of the South Sea, that the English ministry relinquished part of their original design, and declared that the examination of those two islands was the utmost that their orders should comprise.

This concession was sufficiently liberal or sufficiently submissive; yet the Spanish court was neither gratified by our kindness, nor softened by our humility. Sir Benjamin Keene, who then resided at Madrid,[5] was interrogated by Carvajal[6] concerning the visit intended to Pepys and Falkland Islands in terms of great jealousy and discontent; and the intended expedition was represented, if not as a direct violation of the late peace, yet as an act inconsistent with amicable intentions, and contrary to the professions of mutual kindness which then passed between Spain and England. Keene was directed to protest that nothing more than mere discovery was intended, and that no settlement was to be established. The Spaniard readily replied, that if this was a voyage of wanton curiosity, it might be gratified with less trouble, for he was

---

i. those who are 76] him, who is 71

---

4. Richard Wall (Ricardo Wall y Uzer). An Irishman in the Spanish service.

5. "Resided" in the diplomatic sense—he was resident British minister.

6. José de Carvajal y Lancáster, Spanish statesman.

willing[j] to communicate whatever was known. That to go so far only to come back, was no reasonable act; and it would be a slender sacrifice to peace and friendship to omit a voyage in which nothing was to be gained: That if we left the places as we found them, the voyage was useless; and if we took possession, it was a hostile armament, nor could we expect that the Spaniards would[k] suppose us to visit the southern parts of America only from curiosity, after the scheme proposed by the authour of Anson's *Voyage*.

When once we had disowned all purpose of settling, it is apparent that we could not defend the propriety of our expedition by arguments equivalent to Carvajal's objections. The ministry therefore dismissed the whole design, but no declaration was required by which our right to persue it hereafter might be annulled.

From this time Falkland's Island was forgotten or neglected, till the conduct of naval affairs was entrusted to the Earl of Egmont,[7] a man whose mind was vigorous and ardent, whose knowledge was extensive, and whose designs were magnificent; but who had somewhat vitiated his judgment by too much indulgence of romantick projects and airy speculations.

Lord Egmont's eagerness after something new determined him to make enquiry after Falkland's Island, and he sent out Captain Byron,[8] who, in the beginning of the year 1765, took, he says, a formal possession in the name of his Britannick Majesty.

The possession of this place is, according to Mr. Byron's representation, no despicable acquisition. He conceived the island to be six or seven hundred miles round, and represented it as a region naked indeed of wood, but which, if that defect were supplied, would have all that nature, almost all that luxury could want. The harbour he found capacious and secure, and therefore thought it worthy of the name of

j. willing *76*] ready *71*   k. would *76*] should *71*

---

7. John Perceval, 2nd Earl. First Lord of the Admiralty, 1763–66, in the Grenville and Rockingham administrations.

8. John Byron ("Foul-weather Jack"), later rear-admiral. Grandfather of the poet. His *Voyage Round the World in the Years 1764–1766* was published in 1767.

Egmont. Of water there was no want, and the ground, he described as having all the excellencies of soil, and as covered with antiscorbutick herbs, the restoratives of the sailor. Provision was easily to be had, for they killed almost every day an hundred geese to each ship, by pelting them with stones. Not content with physick and with food, he searched yet deeper for the value of the new dominion. He dug in quest of ore, found iron in abundance, and did not despair of nobler metals.

A country thus fertile and delightful, fortunately found where none would have expected it, about the fiftieth degree of southern latitude, could not without great supineness be neglected. Early in the next year (January 8, 1766) Captain Macbride[9] arrived at Port Egmont, where he erected a small blockhouse, and stationed a garrison. His description was less flattering. He found, what he calls, a mass of islands and broken lands, of which the soil was nothing but a bog, with no better prospect than that of barren mountains, beaten by storms almost perpetual. Yet this, says he, is summer, and if the winds of winter hold their natural proportion, those who lie but two cables length from the shore, must pass weeks without any communication with it. The plenty which regaled Mr. Byron, and which might have supported not only armies, but[1] armies of Patagons,[1] was no longer to be found. The geese were too wise to stay when men violated their haunts, and Mr. Macbride's crew could only now and then kill a goose when the weather would permit. All the quadrupeds which he met there were foxes, supposed by him to have been brought upon the ice; but of useless animals, such as sea lions and penguins, which he calls vermin, the number was incredible. He allows, however, that those who touch at these islands may find geese and snipes, and in the summer months, wild sellery and sorrel.

No token was seen by either, of any settlement ever made upon this island, and Mr. Macbride thought himself so

1. not . . . but 76] *om. 71*

9. John Macbride, later admiral.
1. Byron crossed Patagonia on foot and reported on the Patagonian "giants" in his *Narrative of the Hon. John Byron* (1769). Cf. *Life*, v.387, n. 6.

secure from hostile disturbance, that when he erected his wooden blockhouse he omitted to open the ports and loopholes.

When a garrison was stationed at Port Egmont, it was necessary to try what sustenance the ground could be by culture excited to produce. A garden was prepared, but the plants that sprung up withered away in immaturity. Some fir-seeds were sown; but though this be the native tree of rugged climates, the young firs that rose above the ground died like weaker herbage. The cold continued long, and the ocean seldom was at rest.

Cattle succeeded better than vegetables. Goats, sheep, and hogs, that were carried thither, were found to thrive and increase as in other places.

Nil mortalibus arduum est.[2] There is nothing which human courage will not undertake, and little that human patience will not endure. The garrison lived upon Falkland's Island, shrinking from the blast, and shuddering at the billows.

This was a colony which could never become independant, for it never could be able to maintain itself. The necessary supplies were annually sent from England, at an expence which the Admiralty began to think would not quickly be repaid. But shame of deserting a project, and unwillingness to contend with a projector that meant well, continued the garrison, and supplied it with regular remittances of stores and provisions.

That of which we were almost weary ourselves, we did not expect any one to envy; and therefore supposed that we should be permitted to reside in Falkland's Island, the undisputed lords of tempest-beaten barrenness.

But, on the 28th of November 1769, Captain Hunt,[3] observing a Spanish schooner hovering about the island and surveying it, sent the commander a message, by which he required him to depart. The Spaniard made an appearance

---

2. Horace, *Odes*, I. 3. 37.

3. Anthony Hunt, captain of the frigate *Tamar*. Johnson's account of the events subsequent to this date is based on documents laid before the House of Commons by Lord North on 4 Feb 1771 (Debrett, *Debates*, v.464-504). They are included in *Papers Relative to the Late Negotiation with Spain and the Taking of Falkland's Island from the English* (Almon, 1771).

of obeying, but in two days came back with letters written by the governor of Port Solidad,[4] and brought by the chief officer of a settlement on the east part of Falkland's Island.

In this letter, dated Malouina, November 30, the governor complains, that Captain Hunt, when he ordered the schooner to depart, assumed a power to which he could have no pretensions, by sending an imperious message to the Spaniards in the King of Spain's own dominions.

In another letter sent at the same time, he supposes the English to be in that part only by accident, and to be ready to depart at the first warning. This letter was accompanied by a present, of which, says he, "if it be neither equal to my desire nor to your merit, you must impute the deficiency to the situation of us both."[m]

In return to this hostile civility, Captain Hunt warned them from the island, which he claimed in the name of the King, as belonging to the English by right of the first discovery and the first settlement.

This was an assertion of more confidence than certainty. The right of discovery indeed has already appeared to be probable, but the right which priority of settlement confers I know not whether we yet can establish.

On December 10, the officer[5] sent by the governor of Port Solidad made three protests against Captain Hunt; for threatening to fire upon him; for opposing his entrance into Port Egmont; and for entering himself into Port Solidad. On the 12th the governor of Port Solidad formally warned Captain Hunt to leave Port Egmont, and to forbear the navigation of these seas, without permission from the King of Spain.

To this Captain Hunt replied by repeating his former claim, by declaring that his orders were to keep possession, and by once more warning the Spaniards to depart.

The next month produced more protests and more replies, of which the tenour was nearly the same. The operations of such harmless enmity having produced no effect, were then

m. if it . . . us both 76] *no italics (here double quotation marks)* 71

---

4. Felipe Ruiz Puenta.
5. Mario Plata, Lieutenant of Infantry.

reciprocally discontinued, and the English were left for a time to enjoy the pleasures of Falkland Island without molestation.

This tranquillity, however, did not last long. A few months afterwards (June 4, 1770) the *Industry*, a Spanish frigate,[n] commanded by an officer whose name was Madariaga,[6] anchored in Port Egmont, bound, as was said, for Port Solidad, and reduced, by a passage from Buenos Ayres of fifty-three days, to want of water.

Three days afterwards[o] four other frigates entered the port, and a broad pendant, such as is born by the commander of a naval armament, was displayed from the *Industry*. Captain Farmer of the *Swift* frigate, who commanded the garrison, ordered the crew of the *Swift* to come on shore, and assist in its defence; and directed Captain Maltby to bring the *Favourite* frigate, which he commanded, nearer to the land. The Spaniards easily discovering the purpose of his motion, let him know, that if he weighed his anchor, they would fire upon his ship; but paying no regard to these menaces, he advanced towards the shore. The Spanish fleet followed, and two shots were fired, which fell at a distance from him. He then sent to inquire the reason of such hostility, and was told that the shots were intended only as signals.

Both the English captains wrote the next day to Madariaga the Spanish commodore, warning him from the island, as from a place which the English held by right of discovery.

Madariaga, who seems to have had no desire of unnecessary mischief, invited them (June 9) to send an officer who should take a view of his forces, that they might be convinced of the vanity of resistance, and do that without compulsion which he was upon refusal prepared to enforce.

An officer was sent, who found sixteen hundred men, with a train of twenty-seven cannon, four mortars, and two hundred bombs. The fleet consisted of five frigates from twenty to thirty guns, which were now stationed opposite to the blockhouse.

He then sent them a formal memorial, in which he main-

---

n. frigate, 76] frigate 71   o. afterwards 76] afterwards, 71

6. Juan Ignacio Madariaga.

tained his master's right to the whole Magellanick region, and exhorted the English to retire quietly from the settlement, which they could neither justify by right, nor maintain by power.

He offered them the liberty of carrying away whatever they were desirous to remove, and promised his receipt for what should be left, that no loss might be suffered by them.

His propositions were expressed in terms of great civility; but he concludes with demanding an answer in fifteen minutes.

Having while he was writing received the letters of warning written the day before by the English captains, he told them, that he thought himself able to prove the King of Spain's title to all those countries, but that this was no time for verbal altercations. He persisted in his determination, and allowed only fifteen minutes for an answer.

To this it was replied by Captain Farmer, that though there had been prescribed yet a shorter time, he should still resolutely defend his charge; that this, whether menace or force, would be considered as an insult on the British flag, and that satisfaction would certainly be required.

On the next day (June 10) Madariaga landed his forces, and it may be easily imagined that he had no bloody conquest. The English had only a wooden blockhouse built at Woolwich, and carried in pieces to the island, with a small battery of cannon. To contend with obstinacy had been only to lavish life without use or hope.[p] After the exchange of a very few shots,[q] a capitulation was proposed.

The Spanish commander acted with moderation; he exerted[7] little of the conqueror; what he had offered before the attack,[r] he granted after the victory; the English were allowed to leave the place with every honour, only their departure was delayed by the terms of the capitulation twenty days; and to secure their stay, the rudder of the *Favourite* was taken off. What they desired to carry away they removed without molestation; and of what they left an inventory was

p. or hope *76*] and without hope *71*   q. shots, *76*] shots *71*   r. attack, *76*]
attack *71*

---

7. ". . . to exhibit, reveal" (*OED*, I.b).

drawn, for which the Spanish officer by his receipt promised to be accountable.

Of this petty revolution, so sudden and so distant, the English ministry could not possibly have such notice as might enable them to prevent it. The conquest, if such it may be called, cost but three days; for the Spaniards,[s] either supposing the garrison stronger than it was, or resolving to trust nothing to chance, or considering that as their force was greater, there was less danger of bloodshed, came with a power that made resistance ridiculous, and at once demanded and obtained possession.

The first account of any discontent expressed by the Spaniards was brought by Captain Hunt, who arriving at Plymouth June 3, 1770, informed the Admiralty that the island had been claimed in December by the governor of Port Solidad.

This claim, made by an officer of so little dignity, without any known direction from his superiors, could be considered only as the zeal or officiousness of an individual, unworthy of publick notice or the formality of remonstrance.

In August Mr. Harris,[8] the resident at Madrid, gave notice to Lord Weymouth[9] of an account newly brought to Cadiz, that the English were in possession of Port Cuizada, the same which we call Port Egmont, in the Magellanick sea; that in January they had warned away two Spanish ships; and that an armament was sent out in May from Buenos Ayres to dislodge them.

It was perhaps not yet certain that this account was true; but the information, however faithful, was too late for prevention. It was easily known, that a fleet dispatched in May had before August succeeded or miscarried.

s. Spaniards, 76] Spaniards 71

---

8. James Harris, later 1st Earl of Malmesbury; son of James "Hermes" Harris. Only 24 at the time and *chargé d'affaires* at Madrid during a change of ambassadors, his handling of the Falkland Islands crisis marked the beginning of his brilliant career as a diplomat.

9. Thomas Thynne, 3rd Viscount Weymouth, later 1st Marquess of Bath, Secretary of State for the Southern Department, Oct 1768. Resigned Dec 1770 over the Falkland Islands crisis and was succeeded by the Earl of Rochford. See p. 346f. above.

In October, Captain Maltby came to England, and gave the account which I have now epitomised, of his expulsion from Falkland's Islands. From this moment the whole nation can witness that no time was lost. The navy was surveyed, the ships refitted, and commanders appointed; and a powerful fleet was assembled, well manned and well stored, with expedition after so long a peace perhaps never known before, and with vigour which, after the waste of so long a war, scarcely any other nation had been capable of exerting.

This preparation, so illustrious[1] in the eyes of Europe, and so efficacious in its event, was obstructed by the utmost power of that noisy faction which has too long filled the kingdom, sometimes with the roar of empty menace, and sometimes with the yell of hypocritical lamentation. Every man saw, and every honest man saw with detestation, that they who desired to force their sovereign into war, endeavoured at the same time to disable him from action.

The vigour and spirit of the ministry easily broke through all the machinations of these pygmy rebels, and our armament was quickly such as was likely to make our negotiations effectual.

The Prince of Masseran,[2] in his first conference with the English ministers on this occasion, owned that he had from Madrid received intelligence that the English had been forcibly expelled from Falkland's Island by Buccarelli,[3] the governor of Buenos Ayres, without any particular orders from the King of Spain. But being asked, whether in his master's name he disavowed Buccarelli's violence, he refused to answer without direction.

The scene of negotiation was now removed to Madrid, and in September Mr. Harris was directed to demand from Grimaldi[4] the Spanish minister the restitution of Falkland's Island, and a disavowal of Buccarelli's hostilities.

---

1. The first definition in SJ's *Dictionary* is "conspicuous."

2. Felipe Ferrero y Fresco, Príncipe de Masserano. Ambassador in London from 1763.

3. Francisco Bucarelli, captain-general of Buenos Aires, in whose jurisdiction the Falkland Islands territory lay.

4. Jerónimo Grimaldi, Marqués de Grimaldi. Minister of state.

It was to be expected that Grimaldi would object to us
our own behaviour, who had ordered the Spaniards to depart
from the same island. To this it was replied, That the English
forces were indeed directed to warn other nations away;
but[t] if compliance were refused, to proceed quietly[u] in making
their settlement, and suffer the subjects of whatever power
to remain there without molestation. By possession thus taken,
there was only a disputable claim advanced, which might
be peaceably and regularly decided, without insult and without force; and if the Spaniards had complained at the British
court, their reasons would have been heard, and all injuries
redressed; but that, by presupposing the justice of their own
title, and having recourse to arms, without any previous
notice or remonstrance, they had violated the peace, and
insulted the British government; and therefore it was expected that satisfaction should be made by publick disavowal
and immediate restitution.

The answer of Grimaldi was ambiguous[v] and cold. He did
not allow that any particular orders had been given for
driving the English from their settlement; but made no
scruple of declaring, that such an ejection was nothing more
than the settlers might have expected; and that Buccarelli
had not, in his opinion, incurred any blame, as the general
injunctions to the American governors were, to suffer no
incroachments on the Spanish dominions.

In October the Prince of Masseran proposed a convention
for the accommodation of differences by mutual concessions,
in which the warning given to the Spaniards by Hunt should
be disavowed on one side, and the violence used by Buccarelli
on the other. This offer was considered as little less than a
new insult, and Grimaldi was told, that injury required
reparation; that when either party had suffered evident wrong,
there was not the parity subsisting which is implied in conventions and contracts; that we considered ourselves as openly
insulted, and demanded satisfaction plenary and unconditional.

Grimaldi affected to wonder that we were not yet appeased
by their concessions. They had, he said, granted all that

t. but 76] but, 71   u. quietly 76] om. 71   v. ambiguous 76] indefinite 71

was required; they had offered to restore the island in the state in which they found it; but he thought that they likewise might hope for some regard, and that the warning sent by Hunt would be disavowed.

Mr. Harris, our minister at Madrid, insisted that the injured party had a right to unconditional reparation, and Grimaldi delayed his answer that a council might be called. In a few days orders were dispatched to Prince Masseran, by which he was commissioned to declare the King of Spain's readiness to satisfy the demands of the King of England, in expectation of receiving from him reciprocal satisfaction, by the disavowal, so often required, of Hunt's warning.

Finding the Spaniards disposed to make no other acknowledgements, the English ministry considered a war as not likely to be long avoided. In the latter end of November private notice was given of their[w] danger to the merchants at Cadiz, and the officers absent from Gibraltar were remanded to their[x] posts. Our naval force was every day encreased, and we made no abatement of our original demand.

The obstinacy of the Spanish court still continued, and about the end of the year all hope of reconciliation was so nearly extinguished, that Mr. Harris was directed to withdraw, with the usual forms, from his residence at Madrid.

Moderation is commonly firm, and firmness is commonly successful; having not swelled our first requisition with any superfluous appendages, we had nothing to yield, we therefore only repeated our first proposition, prepared for war, though desirous of peace.

About this time, as is well known, the King of France dismissed Choiseul[5] from his employments. What effect this revolution of the French court had upon the Spanish counsels, I pretend not to be informed. Choiseul had always professed pacifick dispositions, nor is it certain, however it may be suspected, that he talked in different strains to different parties.

It seems to be almost the universal error of historians to

w. their 76] the 71   x. their 76] the 71

5. Étienne-François, Duc de Choi-   Prime Minister of France, 1758–70.
seul. Foreign minister and, in effect,

suppose it politically, as it is physically true, that every effect
has a proportionate cause. In the inanimate action of matter
upon matter, the motion produced can be but equal to the
force of the moving power; but the operations of life, whether
private or publick, admit no such laws. The caprices of
voluntary agents laugh at calculation. It is not always that
there is a strong reason for a great event. Obstinacy and
flexibility, malignity and kindness, give place alternately to
each other, and the reason of these vicissitudes, however
important may be the consequences, often escapes the mind
in which the change is made.

Whether the alteration which began in January to appear
in the Spanish counsels had any other cause than conviction
of the impropriety of their past conduct, and of the danger
of a new war, it is not easy to decide; but they began, whatever
was the reason, to relax their haughtiness, and Mr. Harris's
departure was countermanded.

The demands first made by England were still continued,
and on January 22d, the Prince of Masseran delivered a
declaration, in which the King of Spain "disavows the
violent enterprize" of Bucarelli, and promises "to restore the
port and fort called Egmont, with all the artillery and stores,
according to the inventory."

To this promise of restitution is subjoined that "this
engagement to restore Port Egmont, cannot, nor ought in any
wise to affect the question of the prior right of sovereignty of
the Malouine otherwise called Falkland's Islands."

This concession was accepted by the Earl of Rochford,[6]
who declared on the part of his master, that the Prince of
Masseran being authorised by his Catholick Majesty, "to
offer in his Majesty's name, to the King of Great Britain,
a satisfaction for the injury done him by dispossessing him
of Port Egmont," and having signed a declaration expressing
that his Catholick Majesty "disavows the expedition against
Port Egmont," and engages to restore it in the state in which
it stood before the 10th of June 1770, "his Britannick Majesty
will look upon the said declaration, together with the full

6. William Henry Zuylestein, 4th   mouth as Southern Secretary of State
Earl of Rochford. Succeeded Wey-   Dec 1770.

performance of the engagement on the part of his Catholick Majesty, as a satisfaction for the injury done to the crown of Great Britain."

This is all that was originally demanded. The expedition is disavowed, and the island is restored. An injury is acknowledged by the reception of Lord Rochford's paper, who twice mentions the word "injury" and twice the word "satisfaction."

The Spaniards have stipulated that the grant of possession shall not preclude the question of prior right, a question which we shall probably make no haste to discuss, and a right of which no formal resignation was ever required. This reserve has supplied matter for much clamour, and perhaps the English ministry would have been better pleased had the declaration been without it. But when we have obtained all that was asked, why should we complain that we have not more? When the possession is conceded, where is the evil that the right, which that concession supposes to be merely hypothetical, is referred to the Greek Calends for a future disquisition? Were the Switzers less free or less secure, because after their defection from the house of Austria they had never been declared independent before the treaty of Westphalia? Is the King of France less a sovereign because the King of England partakes his title?[7]

If sovereignty implies undisputed right, scarce any prince is a sovereign through his whole dominions; if sovereignty consists in this, that no superiour is acknowledged, our King reigns at Port Egmont with sovereign authority. Almost every new acquired territory is in some degree controvertible, and till the controversy is decided, a term very difficult to be fixed, all that can be had is real possession and actual dominion.

This surely is a sufficient answer to the feudal gabble of a man[8] who is every day lessening that splendour of character which once illuminated the kingdom, then dazzled, and

---

7. The style of "King of France," assumed by Edward III in token of his claim to the French throne, was not abandoned by English sovereigns until 1801.

8. William Pitt the Elder, Earl of Chatham. Chatham's speeches on the Falkland Islands dispute are full of "patriotic" rant. See n. 5, p. 347.

afterwards inflamed it; and for whom it will be happy if the nation shall at last dismiss him to nameless obscurity with that equipoise of blame and praise which Corneille allows to Richlieu, a man who, I think, had much of his merit, and many of his faults.

> *Chacun parle a son gré de ce grand Cardinal,*
> *Mais pour moi je n'en dirai rien;*
> *Il m'a fait trop de bien pour en dire du mal,*
> *Il m'a fait trop de mal pour en dire du bien.*[9]

To push advantages too far is neither generous nor just. Had we insisted on a concession of antecedent right, it may not misbecome us either as moralists or politicians, to consider what Grimaldi could have answered. We have already, he might say, granted you the whole effect of right, and have not denied you the name. We have not said that the right was ours before this concession, but only that what right we had, is not by this concession vacated. We have now for more than two centuries ruled large tracts of the American continent, by a claim which perhaps is valid only upon this consideration, that no power can produce a better; by the right of discovery and prior settlement. And by such titles almost all the dominions of the earth are holden, except that their original is beyond memory, and greater obscurity gives them greater veneration. Should we allow this plea to be annulled, the whole fabrick of our empire shakes at the foundation. When you suppose yourselves to have first descried the disputed island, you suppose what you can hardly prove. We were at least the general discoverers of the Magellanick region, and have hitherto held it with all its adjacencies. The justice of this tenure the world has hitherto admitted, and yourselves at least tacitly allowed it, when

---

9. Cf. Corneille, *Oeuvres*, ed. Marty-Laveaux (Paris, 1862), x.86. The first two lines of the epigram read "Qu'on parle mal ou bien du fameux car-dinal, / Ma prose ni mes vers ne diront jamais rien." The last two lines are as SJ gives them. Hume's comment on this passage was "I think that Mr. Johnson is a great deal too favourable to Pitt, in comparing him with Car-dinal Richelieu" (*Letters*, ed. J. Y. T. Grieg, 1932, II.242), and he goes on to denounce "our Cutthroat" in terms far more scathing than SJ's.

about twenty years ago you desisted from your purposed expedition, and expressly disowned any design of settling, where you are now not content to settle and to reign, without extorting such a confession of original right, as may invite every other nation to follow you.

To considerations such as these, it is reasonable to impute that anxiety of the Spaniards, from which the importance of this island is inferred by Junius,[1] one of the few writers of his despicable faction whose name does not disgrace the page of an opponent. The value of the thing disputed may be very different to him that gains and him that loses it. The Spaniards, by yielding Falkland's Island, have admitted a precedent of what they think encroachment; have suffered a breach to be made in the outworks of their empire; and notwithstanding the reserve of prior right, have suffered a dangerous exception to the prescriptive tenure of their American territories.

Such is the loss of Spain; let us now compute the profit of Britain. We have, by obtaining a disavowal of Buccarelli's expedition, and a restitution of our settlement, maintained the honour of the crown, and the superiority of our influence. Beyond this what have we acquired? What, but a bleak and gloomy solitude, an island thrown aside from human use, stormy in winter, and barren in summer; an island which not the southern savages have dignified with habitation; where a garrison must be kept in a state that contemplates with envy the exiles of Siberia; of which the expence will be perpetual, and the use only occasional; and which, if fortune smile upon our labours, may become a nest of smugglers in peace, and in war the refuge of future buccaniers. To all this the Government has now given ample attestation, for the island has been since abandoned, and perhaps was kept only to quiet clamours, with an intention, not then wholly concealed, of quitting it in a short time.[y]

This is the country of which we have now possession, and of which a numerous party pretends to wish that we had mur-

y. To all this . . . a short time. 76] om. 71

---

1. See Junius's letter of 30 Jan 1771.

dered thousands for the titular sovereignty. To charge any men with such madness, approaches to an accusation defeated by its own incredibility. As they have been long accumulating falsehoods, it is possible that they are now only adding another to the heap, and that they do not mean all that they profess. But of this faction what evil may not be credited? They have hitherto shewn no virtue, and very little wit, beyond that mischievous cunning for which it is held by Hale that children may be hanged.[2]

As war is the last of remedies, *cuncta prius tentanda*,[3] all lawful expedients must be used to avoid it. As war is the extremity of evil, it is surely the duty of those whose station intrusts them with the care of nations, to avert it from their charge. There are diseases of animal nature which nothing but amputation can remove; so there may, by the depravation of human passions, be sometimes a gangrene in collective life for which fire and the sword are the necessary remedies; but in what can skill or caution be better shewn than preventing such dreadful operations, while there is yet room for gentler methods?

It is wonderful with what coolness and indifference the greater part of mankind see war commenced. Those that hear of it at a distance, or read of it in books, but have never presented its evils to their minds, consider it as little more than a splendid game; a proclamation, an army, a battle, and a triumph. Some indeed must perish in the most successful field, but they die upon the bed of honour, "resign their lives amidst the joys of conquest, and, filled with England's glory, smile in death."[4]

The life of a modern soldier is ill represented by heroick fiction. War has means of destruction more formidable than the cannon and the sword. Of the thousands and ten thousands that perished in our late contests with France and Spain,

---

2. Sir Matthew Hale, *History of the Pleas of the Crown* (1678), Pt. i, Ch. iii: "*Aetas pubertati proxima* [ten to twelve years of age, as Hale explains] is regularly presumed *capax doli*, and so may be guilty of a capital offence."

3. Ovid, *Metamorphoses*, i.190: "*cuncta prius tentata.*"

4. Addison, *The Campaign* (1705), ll. 313–14: "In joys of conquest he resigns his breath, / And, fill'd with England's glory, smiles in death."

a very small part ever felt the stroke of an enemy; the rest languished in tents and ships, amidst damps and putrefaction; pale, torpid, spiritless, and helpless; gasping and groaning,[z] unpitied among men made obdurate by long continuance of hopeless misery; and were at last whelmed[a] in pits, or heaved into the ocean, without notice and without remembrance. By incommodious encampments and unwholesome stations, where courage is useless, and enterprise impracticable, fleets are silently dispeopled, and armies sluggishly melted away. Thus is a people gradually exhausted, for the most part with little effect. The wars of civilized nations make very slow changes in the system of empire. The publick perceives scarcely any alteration but an increase of debt; and the few individuals who are benefited, are not supposed to have the clearest right to their advantages. If he that shared the danger enjoyed the profit, and after bleeding in[b] the battle grew rich by the victory, he might shew his gains without envy. But at the conclusion of a ten years war,[5] how are we recompensed for the death of multitudes and the expence of millions, but by contemplating the sudden glories[6] of paymasters and agents, contractors and commissaries, whose equipages shine like meteors and whose palaces rise like exhalations.[7]

These are the men who, without virtue, labour, or hazard, are growing rich as their country is impoverished; they rejoice when obstinacy or ambition adds another year to slaughter and devastation; and laugh from their desks at bravery and science, while they are adding figure to figure, and cipher to cipher, hoping for a new contract from a new armament, and computing the profits of a siege or tempest.

z. groaning, 76] groaning 71   a. misery . . . whelmed 76] misery, and whelmed 71   b. profit . . . in 76] profit; if he that bled in 71

5. As SJ points out in "Observations on the Present State of Affairs," p. 184 above, hostilities between the French and English had been going on in America—and, he might have added, in India—long before the official commencement of the Seven Years' War.

6. Thomas Fuller, *Gnomologia* (1732),

No. 4282: "Sudden glory soon goes out."

7. *Paradise Lost*, i. 710–11: "A fabrick huge / Rose like an exhalation." Quoted in *Dictionary* under "exhalation." The reference is, wittily, to Pandemonium.

Those who suffer their minds to dwell on these considerations will think it no great crime in the ministry that they
have not snatched with eagerness the first opportunity of
rushing into the field, when they were able to obtain by quiet
negotiation all the real good that victory could have brought
us.

Of victory indeed every nation is confident before the sword
is drawn; and this mutual confidence produces that wanton-
ness of bloodshed that has so often desolated the world.
But it is evident, that of contradictory opinions one must be
wrong, and the history of mankind does not want examples
that may teach caution to the daring, and moderation to
the proud.

Let us not think our laurels blasted by condescending to
inquire, whether we might not possibly grow rather less than
greater by attacking Spain. Whether we should have to
contend with Spain alone, whatever has been promised by our
patriots, may very reasonably be doubted. A war declared
for the empty sound of an ancient title to a Magellanick rock
would raise the indignation of the earth against us. These
encroachers on the waste of nature, says our ally the Russian,
if they succeed in their first effort of usurpation, will make war
upon us for a title to Kamschatscha. These universal settlers,
says our ally the Dane, will in a short time settle upon Green-
land, and a fleet will batter Copenhagen, till we are willing
to confess that it always was their own.

In a quarrel like this, it is not possible that any power should
favour us, and it is very likely that some would oppose us.
The French, we are told, are otherwise employed; the contests between the King of France and his own subjects are
sufficient to withold him from supporting Spain. But who does
not know that a foreign war has often put a stop to civil
discords? It withdraws the attention of the publick from
domestick grievances, and affords opportunities of dismissing
the turbulent and restless to distant employments. The
Spaniards have always an argument of irresistible persuasion.[c]
If France will not support them against England, they will
strengthen England against France.

c. persuasion 76] compulsion 71

But let us indulge a dream of idle speculation, and suppose that we are to engage with Spain, and with Spain alone; it is not even yet very certain that much advantage will be gained. Spain is not easily vulnerable; her kingdom, by the loss or cession of many fragments of dominion, is become solid and compact. The Spaniards have indeed no fleet able to oppose us, but they will not endeavour actual opposition; they will shut themselves up in their own territories, and let us exhaust our seamen in a hopeless siege. They will give commissions to privateers of every nation, who will prey upon our merchants without possibility of reprisal. If they think their plate fleet[8] in danger, they will forbid it to set sail, and live a while upon the credit of treasure which all Europe knows to be safe; and which, if our obstinacy should continue till they can no longer be without it, will be conveyed to them with secrecy and security by our natural enemies the French, or by the Dutch our natural allies.

But the whole continent of Spanish America will lie open to invasion; we shall have nothing to do but march into these wealthy regions, and make their present masters confess that they were always ours by ancient right. We shall throw brass and iron out of our houses, and nothing but silver will be seen among us.

All this is very desirable, but it is not certain that it can be easily attained. Large tracts of America were added by the last war to the British dominions; but, if the faction credit their own Apollo,[9] they were conquered in Germany. They at best are only the barren parts of the continent, the refuse of the earlier adventurers, which the French, who came last, had taken only as better than nothing.

Against the Spanish dominions we have never hitherto been able to do much. A few privateers have grown rich at their expence, but no scheme of conquest has yet been successful. They are defended not by walls mounted with cannons

---

8. The ships conveying silver and other treasures from South America to Spain.

9. Chatham. See [Cobbett's] *Parliamentary History*, xv.1267, speech of

9 Dec 1762, on the Peace of Paris: "He said, with an emphasis, that America had been conquered in Germany."

which by cannons may be battered, but by the storms of the deep and the vapours of the land, by the flames of calenture and blasts of pestilence.

In the reign of Elizabeth, the favourite period of English greatness, no enterprises against America had any other consequence than that of extending English navigation. Here Cavendish perished after all his hazards; and here Drake and Hawkins, great as they were in knowledge and in fame, having promised honour to themselves and dominion to the country, sunk by desperation and misery in dishonourable graves.

During the protectorship of Cromwel, a time of which the patriotick tribes still more ardently desire the return, the Spanish dominions were again attempted; but here, and only here, the fortune of Cromwel made a pause. His forces were driven from Hispaniola, his hopes of possessing the West Indies vanished, and Jamaica was taken, only[d] that the whole expedition might not grow ridiculous.

The attack of Carthagena[1] is yet remembered, where the Spaniards from the[e] ramparts saw their invaders destroyed by the hostility of the elements; poisoned by the air, and crippled by the dews; where every hour swept away battalions; and in the three days that passed between the descent and re-embarkation, half an army perished.

In the last war the Havanna was taken,[2] at what expence is too well remembered. May my country be never cursed with such another conquest![f]

These instances of miscarriage, and these arguments of difficulty, may perhaps abate the military ardour of the publick. Upon the opponents of the government their operation will be different; they wish for war, but not for conquest; victory would defeat their purposes equally with peace, because[g] prosperity would naturally continue trust in those hands which had used it fortunately. The patriots gratified

d. taken, only 76] taken only, 71   e. the 76] their 71   f. conquest! 76] conquest. 71   g. peace, because 76] peace; for 71

1. In what is now Colombia. The siege took place in 1741. The classic description is in Smollett's *Roderick Random*.

2. On 12 Aug 1762, after a long investment. It was said that at one time 5,000 British soldiers and 3,000 seamen were incapacitated by sickness.

themselves with expectations that some sinistrous[3] accident, or erroneous conduct, might diffuse discontent and inflame malignity. Their hope is malevolence, and their good is evil. Of their zeal for their country we have already had a specimen. While they were terrifying the nation with doubts whether it was any longer to exist; while they represented invasive armies as hovering in the clouds, and hostile fleets as emerging from the deeps; they obstructed our levies of seamen, and embarrassed our endeavours of defence.[4] Of such men he thinks with unnecessary candour who does not believe them likely to have promoted the miscarriage which they desired, by intimidating our troops or betraying our counsels.

It is considered as an injury to the publick by those sanguinary statesmen, that though the fleet has been refitted and manned, yet no hostilities have followed; and they who sat wishing for misery and slaughter are disappointed of their pleasure. But as peace is the end of war, it is the end likewise of preparations for war; and he may be justly hunted down as the enemy of mankind, that can chuse to snatch by violence and bloodshed, what gentler means can equally obtain.

The ministry are reproached as not daring to provoke an enemy, lest ill success should discredit and displace them. I hope that they had better reasons; that they paid some regard to equity and humanity; and considered themselves as entrusted[h] with the safety of their fellow-subjects, and as the destroyers of all that should be superfluously slaughtered. But let us suppose that their own safety had some influence on their conduct, they will not, however, sink to a level with their enemies. Though the motive might be selfish, the act was innocent. They who grow rich by administering physick are not to be numbered with them that get money by dispensing poison. If they maintain power by harmlessness and peace, they must for ever be at a great distance from ruffians who would gain it by mischief and confusion. The watch of a city may guard it for hire; but are well employed

h. entrusted 76] charged 71

---

3. "Absurd; perverse; wrong-headed; in French *gauche*" (*Dictionary*). Not the same word as *sinister*.

4. On this, see the House of Commons debates of 7 Dec and 14 Dec 1770.

in protecting it from those who lie in wait to fire the streets and rob the houses amidst the conflagration.

An unsuccessful war would undoubtedly have had the effect which the enemies of the Ministry so earnestly desire; for who could have sustained the disgrace of folly ending in misfortune? But had wanton invasion undeservedly prospered, had Falkland's Island been yielded unconditionally with every right prior and posterior; though the rabble might have shouted, and the windows have blazed, yet those who know the value of life, and the uncertainty of publick credit, would have murmured, perhaps unheard, at the increase of our debt, and the loss of our people.

This thirst of blood, however the visible promoters of sedition may think it convenient to shrink from the accusation, is loudly avowed by Junius, the writer to whom his party owes much of its pride, and some of its popularity. Of Junius it cannot be said, as of Ulysses, that he scatters ambiguous expressions among the vulgar;[5] for he cries *havock* without reserve, and endeavours to let slip the dogs of foreign or of civil war,[6] ignorant whither they are going, and careless what may be their prey.

Junius has sometimes made his satire felt, but let not injudicious admiration mistake the venom of the shaft for the vigour of the bow. He has sometimes sported with lucky malice; but to him that knows his company, it is not hard to be sarcastick in a mask. While he walks like Jack the Giant-killer[7] in a coat of darkness, he may do much mischief with little strength. Novelty captivates the superficial and thoughtless; vehemence delights the discontented and turbulent. He that contradicts acknowledged truth will always have an audience; he that vilifies established authority will always find abettors.

Junius burst into notice with a blaze of impudence which has rarely glared upon the world before, and drew the rabble

5. *Aeneid*, ii.98: "*Spargere voces / In vulgum ambiguas.*" Applied to Junius in Sir William Draper's letter of 26 Jan 1769 in the *Public Advertiser*.

6. Shakespeare, *Julius Caesar*, iii. i. 273: "Cry 'Havoc!' and let slip the dogs of war."

7. Which SJ had been reading in 1768 (*Letters* 197), and ranked higher as children's literature than Mrs. Barbauld and Mrs. Trimmer (*Life*, iv.8, n. 3).

after him as a monster makes a show. When he had once provided for his safety by impenetrable secrecy, he had nothing to combat but truth and justice, enemies whom he knows to be feeble in the dark. Being then at liberty to indulge himself in all the immunities of invisibility; out of the reach of danger, he has been bold; out of the reach of shame, he has been confident. As a rhetorician, he has had the art of persuading when he seconded desire; as a reasoner, he has convinced those who had no doubt before; as a moralist, he has taught that virtue may disgrace; and as a patriot, he has gratified the mean by insults on the high. Finding sedition ascendant, he has been able to advance it; finding the nation combustible, he has been able to inflame it. Let us abstract from his wit the vivacity of insolence, and withdraw from his efficacy the sympathetick favour of plebeian malignity; I do not say that we shall leave him nothing; the cause that I defend scorns the help of falsehood; but if we leave him only his merit, what will be his praise?

It is not by his liveliness of imagery, his pungency of periods, or his fertility of allusion, that he detains the cits of London, and the boors of Middlesex. Of stile and sentiment they take no cognizance. They admire him for virtues like their own, for contempt of order, and violence of outrage, for rage of defamation and audacity of falsehood. The Supporters of the Bill of Rights[8] feel no niceties of composition, nor dexterities of sophistry; their faculties are better proportioned to the bawl of Bellas, or barbarity of Beckford;[9] but they are told that Junius is on their side, and they are therefore sure that Junius is infallible. Those who know not whither he would lead them, resolve to follow him; and those who cannot find his meaning, hope he means rebellion.

Junius is an unusual phaenomenon on which some have gazed with wonder and some with terrour, but wonder and terrour are transitory passions. He will soon be more closely

---

8. See n. 7, p. 333 above.

9. George Bellas, attorney, member of the Common Council of London, one of Wilkes's most active supporters (see George Rudé, *Wilkes and Liberty*, 1962). For William Beckford, Chatham's great supporter in the City, see *DNB*. Beckford had died 21 June 1770, while holding the office of Lord Mayor.

viewed or more attentively examined, and what folly has
taken for a comet that from its flaming hair shook pestilence
and war, enquiry will find to be only a meteor formed by the
vapours of putrefying democracy, and kindled into flame
by the effervescence of interest struggling with conviction;
which after having plunged its followers in a bog, will leave
us enquiring why we regarded it.[1]
Yet though I cannot think the stile of Junius secure from
criticism, though his expressions are often trite, and his
periods feeble, I should never have stationed him where he
has placed himself, had I not rated him by his morals rather
than his faculties. What, says Pope, must be the priest, where
a monkey is the God?[i] What must be the drudge of a party
of which the heads are Wilkes and Crosby, Sawbridge and
Townshend?[2]
Junius knows his own meaning and can therefore tell it.
He is an enemy to the ministry, he sees them growing hourly
stronger. He knows that a war at once unjust and unsuccessful
would have certainly displaced them, and is therefore, in his
zeal for his country, angry that war was not unjustly made,
and unsuccessfully conducted. But there are others whose
thoughts are less clearly expressed, and whose schemes
perhaps are less consequentially digested; who declare that
they do not wish for a rupture, yet condemn the ministry for
not doing that, by which a rupture would naturally have
been made.[j]
If one party resolves to demand what the other resolves
to refuse, the dispute can be determined only by arbitration;
and between powers who have no common superiour, there
is no other arbitrator than the sword.
Whether the ministry might not equitably have demanded
more, is not worth a question. The utmost exertion of right

i. a monkey is the God? *76*] the monkey is a God? *71*   j. that, by . . . been made
76] that which a rupture would naturally have followed *71*

---

1. A remarkable example of what
SJ could do with an extended meta-
phor—indeed, a "conceit."
2. Pope, *Dunciad*, III.207–08: "Oh,
worthy thou of Egypt's wise abodes, /
A decent priest where monkeys were
the Gods!" He is speaking of the
Reverend John ("Orator") Henley.
For Aldermen John Wilkes, Brass
Crosby, and John Sawbridge, see
DNB. For James Townsend, see index
to *Life*, Vol. VI. All held the office of
Lord Mayor of London at some time.

is always invidious, and where claims are not easily determinable is always dangerous. We asked all that was necessary, and persisted in our first claim without mean recession, or wanton aggravation. The Spaniards found us resolute, and complied after a short struggle.

The real crime of the ministry is, that they have found the means of avoiding their own ruin;[3] but the charge against them is multifarious and confused, as will happen, when malice and discontent are ashamed of their complaint. The past and the future are complicated in the[k] censure. We have heard a tumultuous clamour about honour and rights, injuries and insults, the British flag, and the *Favourite's* rudder, Bucarelli's conduct, and Grimaldi's declarations, the Manilla ransom,[4] delays and reparation.

Through the whole argument of the faction runs the general errour, that our settlement on Falkland's Island was not only lawful but unquestionable; that our right was not only certain but acknowledged; and that the equity of our conduct was such, that the Spaniards could not blame or obstruct it without combating their own conviction, and opposing the general opinion of mankind.

If once it be discovered that, in the opinion of the Spaniards, our settlement was usurped, our claim arbitrary, and our conduct insolent, all that has happened will appear to follow by a natural concatenation. Doubts will produce disputes and disquisition, disquisition requires delay, and delay causes inconvenience.

Had the Spanish government immediately yielded unconditionally all that was required, we might have been satisfied; but what would Europe have judged of their submission? That they shrunk before us as a conquered people,

k. the 76] their 71

3. An accurate diagnosis. The Falkland Islands crisis was a test of the strength of Lord North's new administration. See pp. 346f. above.

4. On 25 Sept 1762, a British fleet landed at Manila and took the city by storm. The inhabitants were allowed to ransom their property for the sum of four million pesetas. A substantial part of this payment was in the form of bills on the Spanish treasury, which Madrid later refused to honour. The question of obtaining payment was a subject of political agitation in Britain for many years afterwards.

who having lately yielded to our arms, were now compelled
to sacrifice to our pride. The honour of the publick is indeed
of high importance; but we must remember that we have had
to transact with a mighty king and a powerful nation, who
have unluckily been taught to think that they have honour
to keep or lose as well as ourselves.

When the Admiralty were[1] told in June of the warning
given to Hunt, they were, I suppose, informed that Hunt had
first provoked it by warning away the Spaniards, and naturally
considered one act of insolence as balanced by another,
without expecting that more would be done on either side.
Of representations and remonstrances there would be no end,
if they were to be made whenever small commanders are
uncivil to each other; nor could peace ever be enjoyed, if
upon such transient provocations it be imagined necessary
to prepare for war. We might then, it is said, have encreased
our force with more leisure and less inconvenience; but this is
to judge only by the event. We omitted to disturb the publick,
because we did not suppose that an armament would be
necessary.

Some months afterwards, as has been told, Buccarelli, the
governor of Buenos Ayres, sent against the settlement of Port
Egmont a force which ensured the conquest. The Spanish
commander required the English captains to depart, but they
thinking that resistance necessary which they knew to be
useless, gave the Spaniards the right of prescribing terms of
capitulation. The Spaniards imposed no new condition except
that the sloop should not sail under twenty days; and of this
they secured the performance by taking off the rudder.

To an inhabitant of the land there appears nothing in all
this unreasonable or offensive. If the English intended to keep
their stipulation, how were they injured by the detention of
the[m] rudder? If the rudder be to a ship what his tail is in
fables to a fox, the part in which honour is placed and of
which the violation is never to be endured, I am sorry that the
Favourite suffered an indignity, but cannot yet think it a cause
for which nations should slaughter one another.

When Buccarelli's invasion was known, and the dignity of

l. were 76] was 71   m. the 76] their 71

the crown infringed, we demanded reparation and prepared for war, and we gained equal respect by the moderation of our terms, and the spirit of our exertion. The Spanish minister immediately denied that Buccarelli had received any particular orders to seize Port Egmont, nor pretended that he was justified otherwise than by the general instructions by which the American governors are required to exclude the subjects of other powers.

To have enquired whether our settlement at Port Egmont was any violation of the Spanish rights, had been to enter upon a discussion which the pertinacity of political disputants might have continued without end. We therefore called for restitution, not as a confession of right, but as a reparation of honour, which required that we should be restored to our former state upon the island, and that the King of Spain should disavow the action of his governor.

In return to this demand, the Spaniards expected from us a disavowal of the menaces with which they had been first insulted by Hunt; and if the claim to the island be supposed doubtful, they certainly expected it with equal reason. This, however, was refused, and our superiority of strength gave validity to our arguments.

But we are told that the disavowal of the King of Spain is temporary and fallacious; that Buccarelli's armament had all the appearance of regular forces and a concerted expedition; and that he is not treated at home as a man guilty of piracy, or as disobedient to the orders of his master.

That the expedition was well planned, and the forces properly supplied, affords no proof of communication between the governor and his court. Those who are entrusted with the care of kingdoms in another hemisphere, must always be trusted with power to defend them.

As little can be inferred from his reception at the Spanish court. He is not punished indeed, for what has he done that deserves punishment? He was sent into America to govern and defend the dominions of Spain. He thought the English were encroaching, and drove them away. No Spaniard thinks that he has exceeded his duty, nor does the King of Spain charge him with excess. The boundaries of dominion in that part of the world have not yet been settled; and he mistook, if a mistake there was, like a zealous subject,[n] in his master's favour.

But all this enquiry is superfluous. Considered as a reparation of honour, the disavowal of the King of Spain, made in the sight of all Europe, is of equal value, whether true or false. There is indeed no reason to question its veracity; they, however, who do not believe it, must allow the weight of that influence by which a great prince is reduced to disown his own commission.

But the general orders upon which the governor is acknowledged to have acted, are neither disavowed nor explained. Why the Spaniards should disavow the defence of their own territories, the warmest disputant will find it difficult to tell; and if by an explanation is meant an accurate delineation of their[o] southern empire, and the limitation of their claims beyond the line, it cannot be imputed to any very culpable remissness, that what has been denied for two centuries to the European powers, was not obtained in a hasty wrangle about a petty settlement.

The ministry were too well acquainted with negotiation to fill their heads with such idle expectations. The question of right was inexplicable and endless. They left it as it stood. To be restored to actual possession was easily practicable. This restoration they required and obtained.

But they should, say their opponents, have insisted upon more; they should have exacted not only reparation of our honour, but repayment of our expence. Nor are they all satisfied with the recovery of the costs and damages of the present contest; they are for taking this opportunity of calling in old debts, and reviving our right to the ransom of Manilla.

The Manilla ransom has, I think, been most mentioned by the inferior bellowers of sedition. Those who lead the faction know that it cannot be remembered much to their advantage. The followers of Lord Rockingham remember that his ministry begun and ended without obtaining it; the adherents to Grenville would be told, that he could never be taught to understand our claim. The law of nations[5] made little of his

n. subject, 76] subject 71   o. their 71] the 76

---

5. The modern term is "international law."

knowledge. Let him not, however, be depreciated in his grave. If he was sometimes wrong, he was often right.[6p] Of reimbursement the talk has been more confident, though not more reasonable. The expences of war have been often desired, have been sometimes required, but were never paid; or never, but when resistance was hopeless, and there remained no choice between submission and destruction. Of our late equipments I know not from whom the charge can be very properly expected. The King of Spain disavows the violence which provoked us to arm, and for the mischiefs which he did not do, why should he pay? Buccarelli, though he had learned all the arts of an East-Indian governor,[7] could hardly have collected at Buenos Ayres a sum sufficient to satisfy our demands. If he be honest, he is hardly rich; and if he be disposed to rob, he has the misfortune of being placed where robbers have been before him.

The King of Spain indeed delayed to comply with our proposals, and our armament was made necessary by unsatisfactory answers and dilatory debates. The delay certainly increased our expences, and it is not unlikely that the increase of our expences put an end to the delay.

p. grave ... right. 76] grave; he had powers not universally possessed; if he could have got the money, he could have counted it. 71 (1) *original reading;* grave; he had powers not universally possessed; and if he sometimes erred, he was likewise sometimes right. 71 (1) *reading of cancel leaf,* 71 (2)

---

6. On this famous emendation, see p. 349 above and *Life*, II.135. The ministry's "softening" of the expression made the remark "He had powers not universally possessed" pointless, and SJ removed it in 1776, as well as changing "sometimes right" to "often right": if Grenville was not to be censured, then he might as well be properly complimented. As G. B. Hill points out, the original version was probably also a gibe at Grenville's predecessor as Chancellor of the Exchequer under Bute, Sir Francis Dashwood, who probably could not even have counted the money. Since North depended for support on the followers of both Grenville and Bute, one can perhaps sympathize with him for the embarrassment SJ's outspokenness caused him. North's ministry was able to make changes like this in SJ's text because the printer was William Strahan, M.P., a stalwart supporter of North (who saw to it that Strahan obtained his fair share of government printing contracts).

7. A glance at Robert Clive in particular, whom SJ detested and whose tenure of the Governorship of Bengal resulted in his acquisition of huge sums of money. His enemies charged that he illegally extorted these from the natives.

But this is the inevitable process of human affairs. Negotiation requires time. What is not apparent to intuition must be found by enquiry. Claims that have remained doubtful for ages cannot be settled in a day. Reciprocal complaints are not easily adjusted but by reciprocal compliance. The Spaniards thinking themselves intitled to the island, and injured by Captain Hunt, in their turn demanded satisfaction, which was refused; and where is the wonder if their concessions were delayed![q] They may tell us, that an independent nation is to be influenced not by command, but by persuasion; that if we expect our proposals to be received without deliberation, we assume that sovereignty which they do not grant us; and that if we arm while they are deliberating, we must indulge our martial ardour at our own charge.

The English ministry asked all that was reasonable, and enforced all that they asked. Our national honour is advanced, and our interest, if any interest we have, is sufficiently secured. There can be none amongst us to whom this transaction does not seem happily concluded, but those who having fixed their hopes on publick calamities, sat like vultures waiting for a day of carnage. Having worn out all the arts of domestick sedition, having wearied violence, and exhausted falsehood, they yet flattered themselves with some assistance from the pride or malice of Spain; and when they could no longer make the people complain of grievances which they did not feel, they had the comfort yet of knowing that real evils were possible, and their resolution is well known of charging all evil on their governours.

The reconciliation was therefore considered as the loss of their last anchor; and received not only with the fretfulness of disappointment, but the rage of desperation. When they found that all were happy in spite of their machinations, and the soft effulgence of peace shone out upon the nation, they felt no motion but that of sullen envy; they could not, like Milton's prince of hell,[r] abstract themselves a moment from their evil;[8] as they have not the wit of Satan, they have not his virtue; they tried once again what could be done by sophistry

q. delayed! *76*] delayed? *71* r. not, . . . hell, *76*] not . . . hell *71*

8. *Paradise Lost*, IX.463–64.

without art, and confidence without credit. They represented their Sovereign as dishonoured and their country as betrayed, or, in their fiercer paroxisms of fury, reviled their Sovereign as betraying it.

Their pretences I have here endeavoured to expose by showing that more than has been yielded was not to be expected, that more perhaps was not to be desired, and that if all had been refused, there had scarcely been an adequate reason for a war.

There was perhaps never much danger of war or of refusal, but what danger there was proceeded from the faction. Foreign nations, unacquainted with the insolence of Common Councils,[9] and unaccustomed to the howl of plebeian patriotism, when they heard of rabbles and riots, of petitions and remonstrances, of discontent in Surry, Derbyshire, and Yorkshire,[1] when they saw the chain of subordination broken, and the legislature threatned and defied, naturally imagined that such a government had little leisure for Falkland Island; they supposed that the English when they returned, ejected from Port Egmont, would[s] find Wilkes invested with the protectorate; or see the mayor of London, what the French have formerly seen their mayors of the palace, the commander of the army and tutor of the King; that they would be called to tell their tale before the Common Council; and that the world was to expect war or peace from a vote of the subscribers to the Bill of Rights.

s. returned . . . would 76] returned, would 71

---

9. The Common Council and Livery of the City of London had drawn up a strongly worded "address, remonstrance, and petition," which Lord Mayor Beckford presented to the King on 14 Mar 1770. The King replied to it with a rebuke. Another such remonstrance was presented 23 May. The King replied that his sentiments were unchanged. Beckford then launched into a harangue, to which the King returned no answer. Beckford and his friends then protested about the King's silence. What purports to be Beckford's speech is en-graved on a memorial to him in the Guildhall. As William Hunt says (*Political History of England, 1760–1801*, p. 111), "Beckford tried to entrap the King into entering into a personal altercation and reply without consultation with his constitutional advisers."

1. On the history of the extra-parliamentary "Association" movement in the English counties, see Herbert Butterfield, *George III, Lord North, and the People* (1949), and E. C. Black, *The Association* (1963).

But our enemies have now lost their hopes, and our friends I hope are recovered from their fears. To fancy that our government can be subverted by the rabble, whom its lenity has pampered into impudence, is to fear that a city may be drowned by the overflowing of its kennels.[2] The distemper which cowardice or malice thought either decay of the vitals, or resolution of the nerves, appears at last to have been nothing more than a political *phthiriasis*,[3] a disease too loathsome for a plainer name; but the effect of negligence rather than of weakness, and of which the shame is greater than the danger.

Among the disturbers of our quiet are some animals of greater bulk, whom their power of roaring persuaded us to think formidable, but we now perceive that sound and force do not always go together. The noise of a savage proves nothing but his hunger.

After all our broils, foreign and domestick, we may at last hope to remain awhile in quiet, amused with the view of our own success. We have gained political strength by the increase of our reputation; we have gained real strength by the reparation of our navy; we have shewn Europe that ten years of war have not yet exhausted us; and we have enforced our settlement on an island on which twenty years ago we durst not venture to look.

These are the gratifications only of honest minds; but there[t] is a time in which hope comes to all. From the present happiness of the publick the patriots themselves may derive advantage. To be harmless though by impotence obtains some degree of kindness; no man hates a worm as he hates a viper; they were once dreaded enough to be detested, as serpents that could bite; they have now shewn that they can only hiss, and may therefore quietly slink into holes, and change their slough unmolested and forgotten.

FINIS.[u]

March, 1771.[v]

t. there 76] this 71   u. FINIS 71] *om. 76*   v. March, 1771. 76] *om. 71*

2. "*Kennel.* . . . 4. The water-course   3. Infestation by lice.
of a street" (*Dictionary*).

THE PATRIOT. 1774.

As with *The False Alarm*, the composition of *The Patriot* can be precisely dated. Johnson and the Thrales cut short their leisurely return from their journey to North Wales in the summer of 1774 when they received the news (appropriately, at Burke's house at Beaconsfield) that Parliament had been unexpectedly dissolved and a general election was quickly to take place. They returned to London on Friday, September 30, and the Thrales at once plunged into the campaign to retain Thrale's seat for Southwark. "We lead a wild life," Mrs. Thrale wrote Johnson on Tuesday, October 4 (*Letters* 360a), "but it will be over tomorrow sevennight." Johnson also took an active part in the campaign, writing short political addresses to the electors of Southwark on behalf of his friend,[1] and the pamphlet printed below. Later in the fall, Boswell, disturbed by the delay in the appearance of Johnson's *Journey to the Western Islands of Scotland*, wrote to Johnson to complain that his political writings had interrupted his work on the Scottish book. Johnson replied, denying the charge (*Letters* 363): "The Patriot was called for by my political friends on Friday, was written on Saturday, and I have heard little of it"—meaning, perhaps, that he had not been bothered by ministerial demands for its revision, as with *Thoughts on Falkland's Islands*. According to the advertisement in the *London Chronicle*, the first edition was published Wednesday, 12 October, so that Johnson wrote it either on Saturday, 8 October, or, not impossibly, on Saturday, 1 October, the day after his return from the country.

Clearly the pamphlet could not have had much influence on the election in Southwark, which, if Mrs. Thrale's letter quoted above is right, was over for the Thrales on the date of its publication (Thrale's address of thanks to the electors, probably composed by Johnson, appeared in the newspapers on 14 October.) But of course the issues with which *The Patriot* deals are not local, but very general indeed; it was intended to influence the whole electorate of Britain, as the appearance of a "Second edition" on 5 November indicates (polling dragged on as long as this in some constituencies). Moreover, it was considered to be of more than merely electioneering value, for long after the election was over, on 8 May 1775, Cadell published "the third edition." A Dublin edition also appeared in 1775, and the piece was collected in Johnson's *Political Tracts*, 1776.

The Patriot is one of Johnson's most satisfying shorter pieces of political writing, in its effective blend of general political wisdom and comments on specific political issues of the time. Among the latter, the most impressive is Johnson's contrast between the noise made over the Wilkes

1. Discussed in J. D. Fleeman, "Dr. Johnson and Henry Thrale, M.P.," in *Johnson, Boswell, and Their Circle* (1965).

affair and the quiet adoption of Grenville's Elections Act (1770); looking
back from the perspective of two centuries, it is impossible not to agree
with Johnson that the latter was far more significant in advancing the
cause of "democratic" representation in Parliament. As for the larger
picture, the exploding of the hoary cant about "patriotism" was long
overdue. From the 1730's on, the word had been the "cry" of every disgruntled opposition group, however disparate their composition or their
aims. In a recent monograph on the development of the Opposition in
the eighteenth and early nineteenth centuries (A. S. Foord, *His Majesty's
Opposition, 1714–1830*, 1964), a fourth of the text is devoted to this phenomenon (Chapter 2, "The Spirit of Patriotism, 1725 to 1742," and Chapter
3, "The Operation of the Patriot Coalition"), and the reader soon comes
to respond to the recurrence of the word, as Johnson and his contemporaries
did, with weariness and cynicism. At its best, the term can be defined as
another recent writer has done:

> 'Patriotism': a group of ideas associated in the 1730's with Wyndham,
> with Pitt and the 'boy patriots,' with the *Craftsman, or Countryman*,
> and taken up by radicals in the 1760's and by parliamentary reformers
> in the 1780's. These ideas are inseparably linked with the name of
> Bolingbroke. . . . The patriot programme meant, in practice, place
> bills, short parliaments, free elections, the destruction of the King's
> influence over Parliament.[2]

There was nothing wrong with these "ideas" in themselves, as Johnson
himself would have granted—he too had followed the "patriot" line for
a time in the 1730's. But they were very seldom put into "practice": once
they had served their purpose as the stock Opposition "programme" and
helped an Opposition politician into power, they were forgotten, or, at
best, only a feeble gesture at implementing them was made. The word had
some use, Foord concedes, in helping to crystallize the conception of "the
Opposition," not yet accepted as a fundamental part of the British constitution: but Johnson himself has hardly anything more caustic to say
about it than the modern historian of the Opposition has:

> The first great achievement of 'the spirit of patriotism' was to cast
> the malcontents in an heroic mould. Evoking the shades of Eliot,
> Pym, and Hampden, they made their political expediency a virtue.
> [But] the world of Westminster knew the Opposition for what it was,
> a loose agglomeration of placehunting factions rent by conflicting
> views and principles.

By the time Johnson wrote his pamphlet, the term had become utterly
fly-blown.

> Ever since 1726 malcontents had made a great show of their patriotism.
> In peace they demanded a policy better designed to protect British

2. Betty Kemp, "Frederick, Prince of Wales," in *Silver Renaissance: Essays in
Eighteenth-Century English History*, Alex Natan, ed. (1961), p. 53.

interests. In war they clamoured for more vigorous measures to ensure victory. Now both Chathamites and Rockinghamites espoused the cause of fellow subjects in armed revolt against the King. They rejoiced publicly in the triumphs of Britain's enemies. Military and naval officers with Opposition connexions refused to serve in the war. By the strict letter of the law the malcontents may well have been guilty of treason. In the political contest they laid themselves open to charges of hampering the war effort, seeking to dismember the Empire, and aggrandizing the power of France and Spain. Dr. Johnson was not the only man in these years who thought this form of Patriotism "the last refuge of a scoundrel" (Foord, pp. 154, 323).

It would be very naïve, then, to think, as some apparently have, that the "patriotism" Johnson condemned was any form of political idealism.[3] His own counter-definition of true patriotism still makes excellent sense.

The only textual variants among the first three editions of *The Patriot* (two in 1774, one in 1775) are minor ones of spelling and punctuation. The text below follows the first edition, incorporating and recording the few minor authorial changes that were introduced into the 1776 edition.

3. For instance, Crane Brinton, in an astonishing footnote in his *History of Western Morals* (1959), p. 321: "It is unfortunate that we so often quote Samuel Johnson, 'Patriotism is the last refuge of a scoundrel,' without knowing what he really meant. He meant, of course[!], by 'patriot' the enlightened citizen of the world, not the nationalist patriot. Actually—though many of his admirers would be offended by this statement—I think Johnson himself was an English 'patriot' in our modern sense of the word." It would be interesting to know on what evidence Brinton based this judgement.

The Patriot. Addressed to the Electors of Great Britain

> They bawl for freedom in their senseless mood,
> Yet still revolt when truth would set them free,
> License they mean, when they cry liberty,
> For who loves that must first be wise and good.
> Milton[1]

To improve the golden moment of opportunity, and catch the good that is within our reach, is the great art of life. Many wants are suffered, which might once have been sup-

1. This was anything but a novel epigraph for a political pamphlet in the eighteenth century, but SJ must have derived a good deal of satisfaction from the author's name and the title of the piece from which it is taken—it is Milton's second sonnet "On the Detraction Which Followed upon My Writing Certain Treatises."

plied; and much time is lost in regretting the time which had been lost before.

At the end of every seven years comes the Saturnalian season, when the freemen of Great Britain may please themselves with the choice of their representatives. This happy day has now arrived, somewhat sooner than it could be claimed.[2]

To select and depute those, by whom laws are to be made, and taxes to be granted, is a high dignity and an important trust: and it is the business of every elector to consider, how this dignity may be well sustained, and this trust faithfully discharged.

It ought to be deeply impressed on the minds of all who have voices in this national deliberation, that no man can deserve a seat in Parliament who is not a Patriot. No other man will protect our rights, no other man can merit our confidence.

A *Patriot* is he whose public conduct is regulated by one single motive, the love of his country; who, as an agent in Parliament, has for himself neither hope nor fear, neither kindness nor resentment, but refers every thing to the common interest.

That of five hundred men, such as this degenerate age affords,[3] a majority can be found thus virtuously abstracted, who will affirm? Yet there is no good in despondence: vigilance and activity often effect more than was expected. Let us take a Patriot where we can meet him; and that we may not flatter ourselves by false appearances, distinguish those marks which are certain, from those which may deceive: for a man may have the external appearance of a Patriot, without the constituent qualities; as false coins have often lustre, tho' they want weight.

Some claim a place in the list of Patriots by an acrimonious and unremitting opposition to the Court.

This mark is by no means infallible. Patriotism is not

---

2. The previous general election had taken place in 1768. Under the Septennial Act (1716), the next need not have been held until 1775.

3. Pope, *Dunciad*, II.39–40: "But such a bulk as no twelve bards could raise, /

Twelve starveling bards of these degenerate days." As J. R. Sutherland points out in his note on the passage in the Twickenham Edition, the reference probably goes back to Homer, *Iliad*, v.303.

necessarily included in rebellion. A man may hate his king, yet not love his country. He that has been refused a reasonable or unreasonable request, who thinks his merit under-rated, and sees his influence declining, begins soon to talk of natural equality, the absurdity of "many made for one,"[4] the original compact, the foundation of authority, and the majesty of the people. As his political melancholy increases, he tells, and perhaps dreams of the advances of the prerogative, and the dangers of arbitrary power; yet his design in all his declamation is not to benefit his country, but to gratify his malice.

These, however, are the most honest of the opponents of government; their patriotism is a species of disease; and they feel some part of what they express. But the greater, far the greater number of those who rave and rail, and enquire and accuse, neither suspect, nor fear, nor care for the public; but hope to force their way to riches by virulence and invective, and are vehement and clamorous, only that they may be sooner hired to be silent.

A man sometimes starts up a Patriot, only by disseminating discontent and propagating reports of secret influence, of dangerous counsels, of violated rights and encroaching usurpation.

This practice is no certain note of patriotism. To instigate the populace with rage beyond the provocation, is to suspend public happiness, if[a] not to destroy it. He is no lover of his country, that unnecessarily disturbs its peace. Few errors, and few faults of government can justify an appeal to the rabble; who ought not to judge of what they cannot understand, and whose opinions are not propagated by reason, but caught by contagion.

The fallaciousness of this note of patriotism is particularly apparent, when the clamour continues after the evil is past. They who are still[b] filling our ears with Mr. Wilkes, and the Freeholders of Middlesex, lament a grievance, that[c] is now at an end. Mr. Wilkes may be chosen,[5] if any will choose

a. if 76] om. 74, 75   b. still 76] now 74, 75   c. that 76] which 74, 75

---

4. Pope, *Essay on Man*, III.242.
5. See headnote to *The False Alarm*, p. 314 above.

him, and the precedent of his exclusion makes not any honest, or any decent man, think himself in danger.

It may be doubted whether the name of a Patriot can be fairly given as the reward of secret satire,[6] or open outrage. To fill the news-papers with sly hints of corruption and intrigue, to circulate the *Middlesex Journal* and *London Pacquet*, may indeed be zeal; but it may likewise be interest and malice. To offer a petition, not expected to be granted; to insult a king with a rude remonstrance,[7] only because there is no punishment for legal insolence, is not courage, for there is no danger; nor patriotism, for it tends to the subversion of order, and lets wickedness loose upon the land, by destroying the reverence due to sovereign authority.

It is the quality of patriotism to be jealous and watchful, to observe all secret machinations, and to see public dangers at a distance. The true "Lover of his country" is ready to communicate his fears and to sound the alarm, whenever he perceives the approach of mischief. But he sounds no alarm, when there is no enemy: he never terrifies his countrymen, till he is terrified himself. The patriotism therefore may be justly doubted of him, who professes to be disturbed by incredibilities; who tells, that the last peace was obtained by bribing the Princess of Wales;[8] that the King is grasping at arbitrary power; and that because the French in the new conquests enjoy their own laws,[9] there is a design at court of abolishing in England the trial by juries.

Still less does the true Patriot circulate opinions, which he knows to be false. No man, who loves his country, fills the nation with clamorous complaints, that the Protestant religion is in danger, because "Popery is established in the extensive province of Quebec,"[1] a falsehood so open and shameless, that it can need no confutation among those who

---

6. No doubt a reference to Junius.

7. See n. 9, p. 385 above.

8. Augusta of Saxe-Gotha, Princess Dowager of Wales, mother of George III. Her alleged intrigues with Bute and domination of her son were part of the Opposition myth.

9. By the Quebec Act, 1774, French civil law was continued in Quebec, and certain privileges of the Roman Catholic clergy retained.

1. On the furore aroused in Britain and America by the Quebec Act, see Lecky, *History of England in the XVIIIth Century*, Chs. XI and XII, and *Taxation No Tyranny*, pp. 438f. below.

know[d] that of which it is almost impossible for the most unenlightened zealot to be ignorant,

That Quebec is on the other side of the Atlantic, at too great a distance to do much good or harm to the European world:

That the inhabitants, being French, were always Papists, who are certainly more dangerous as enemies,[e] than as subjects:

That though the province be wide, the people are few, probably not so many as may be found in one of the larger English counties:

That persecution is not more virtuous in a Protestant than a Papist; and that while we blame Lewis the Fourteenth, for his dragoons and his gallies,[2] we ought, when power comes into our hands, to use it with greater equity:

That when Canada with its inhabitants was yielded, the free enjoyment of their religion was stipulated; a condition, of which King William, who was no propagator of Popery, gave an example nearer home, at the surrender of Limerick:[3f]

That in an age, where every mouth is open for "liberty of conscience," it is equitable to shew some regard to the conscience of a Papist, who may be supposed, like other men, to think himself safest in his own religion; and that those at least, who enjoy a toleration,[4] ought not to deny it to our new subjects.

If liberty of conscience be a natural right, we have no power to with-hold it; if it be an indulgence, it may be allowed to Papists, while it is not denied to other sects.

A Patriot is necessarily and invariably a lover of the people. But even this mark may sometimes deceive us.

The people is a very heterogeneous and confused mass of the wealthy and the poor, the wise and the foolish, the good and the bad. Before we confer on a man, who caresses the

---

d. those who know 76] those, who know, 74, 75   e. dangerous as enemies, 76] dangerous, as enemies 74, 75   f. Limerick 76] Limeric 74, 75

---

2. Persecution of French Protestants by "dragonnades" and condemnation to serve as galley slaves after the revocation of the Edict of Nantes in 1685.

3. By the Peace of Paris, 1763. On the siege and Treaty of Limerick, 1690, see Macaulay, *History of England*, Ch. XVII.

4. English Protestant Dissenters, under the Toleration Act, 1689.

people, the title of Patriot, we must examine to what part of the people he directs his notice. It is proverbially said, that he who dissembles his own character, may be known by that of his companions.[5] If the candidate of patriotism endeavours to infuse right opinions into the higher ranks, and by their influence to regulate the lower; if he consorts chiefly with the wise, the temperate, the regular and the virtuous, his love of the people may be rational and honest.[g] But if his first or principal application be to the indigent, who are always inflammable; to the weak, who are naturally suspicious; to the ignorant, who are easily misled;[h] and to the profligate, who have no hope, but from mischief and confusion; let his love of the people be no longer boasted.[i] No man can reasonably be thought a lover of his country, for roasting an ox, or burning a boot,[6] or attending the meeting at Mile-end, or registering his name in the Lumber-troop.[7] He may, among the drunkards, be a "hearty fellow," and among sober handicraftsmen, a "free spoken gentleman"; but he must have some better distinction, before he is a *Patriot*.

A Patriot is always ready to countenance the just claims, and animate the reasonable hopes of the people; he reminds them frequently of their rights, and stimulates them to resent encroachments, and to multiply securities.

But all this may be done in appearance, without real patriotism. He that raises false hopes to serve a present purpose, only makes a way for disappointment and discontent. He who promises to endeavour, what he knows his endeavours unable to effect, means only to delude his followers by an empty clamour of ineffectual zeal.

A true Patriot is no lavish promiser: he undertakes not

g. rational and honest 76] urged in his favour 74, 75   h. misled; 76] misled 74, 75   i. let . . . boasted 76] his love of the people proves little in his favour 74, 75

---

5. There are innumerable traditional versions of "A man is known by the company he keeps."

6. Burning a jack-boot in public was a favourite form of protest against John, Earl of Bute. Frequently a petticoat was added, to signify the Princess of Wales.

7. The Assembly-room at Mile End, just east of the City of London, was a favourite site for meetings of Wilkites during the Middlesex elections. The Lumber Troop was one of a number of Wilkite clubs (see Horace Bleackley, *Life of John Wilkes*, 1917, p. 222).

to shorten parliaments;[8] to repeal laws; or to change the mode of representation, transmitted by our ancestors: he knows that futurity is not in his power, and that all times are not alike favourable to change.

Much less does he make a vague and indefinite promise of obeying the mandates of his constituents.[9] He knows the prejudices of faction, and the inconstancy of the multitude. He would first enquire, how the opinion of his constituents shall be taken. Popular instructions are commonly the work, not of the wise and steady, but the violent and rash; meetings[j] held for directing representatives are seldom attended, but by the idle and the dissolute; and he is not without suspicion, that of his constituents, as of other numbers of men, the smaller part may often be the wiser.

He considers himself as deputed to promote the public good, and to preserve his constituents, with the rest of his countrymen, not only from being hurt by others, but from hurting themselves.

The common marks of patriotism having been examined, and shewn to be such as artifice may counterfeit, or folly misapply, it cannot be improper to consider, whether there are not some characteristical modes of speaking or acting, which may prove a man to be *not a Patriot.*

In this enquiry, perhaps clearer evidence may be discovered, and firmer persuasion attained: for it is commonly easier to know what is wrong than what is right; to find what we should avoid, than what we should pursue.

As war is one of the heaviest of national evils, a calamity, in which every species of misery is involved; as it sets the

j. meetings 76] and meetings 74, 75

---

8. Repeal of the Septennial Act and the holding of annual, or triennial, parliaments were advocated by "reform" groups for many decades. (SJ himself had once done so, in "The State of Affairs in Lilliput" (1738), reprinted in this edition with the *Parliamentary Debates.*)

9. The giving of "instructions" to Members of Parliament by their constituents (or rather, as SJ points out, by a noisy meeting of some of them) was popular during the 1760's and 1770's. The classic reply to the practice is Burke's speech to the electors of Bristol in 1774, given about the same time SJ was writing *The Patriot* (Burke, *Works*, Boston, 1865–76, II. 89–98).

general safety to hazard, suspends commerce, and desolates
the country; as it exposes great numbers to hardships, dangers,
captivity and death; no man, who desires the public prosperity, will inflame general[k] resentment by aggravating minute
injuries, or enforcing disputable rights of little importance.

It may therefore be safely pronounced, that those men
are no Patriots, who when the national honour was vindicated in the sight of Europe, and the Spaniards having
invaded what they call[1] their own, had shrunk to a disavowal
of their attempt and a relaxation[m] of their claim, would
still have instigated us to a war for a bleak and barren spot
in the Magellanic ocean, of which no use could be made,
unless it were a place of exile for the hypocrites of patriotism.[1]

Yet let it not be forgotten, that by the howling violence of
patriotic rage, the nation was for a time exasperated to such
madness, that for a barren rock under a stormy sky, we might
have now been fighting and dying, had not our competitors
been wiser than ourselves; and those who are now courting
the favour of the people by noisy professions of public spirit,
would, while they were counting the profits of their artifice,
have enjoyed the patriotic pleasure of hearing sometimes,
that thousands had been slaughtered in a battle, and sometimes that a navy had been dispeopled by poisoned air and
corrupted food.

He that wishes to see his country robbed of its rights,
cannot be a Patriot.

That man therefore is no Patriot, who justifies the ridiculous claims of American usurpation;[2] who endeavours to
deprive the nation of its natural and lawful authority over
its own colonies: those colonies, which were settled under

k. general *76*] national *74, 75*   l. call *76*] called *74, 75*   m. relaxation *76*]
cession *74, 75*

1. A reference to the Falkland Islands incident, 1771 (see pp. 346–86
above, SJ's *Thoughts on Falkland's Islands*).

2. Agitation about American colo-
nial affairs had been going on since
Grenville's imposition of the Stamp
Act, 1765. In the next few paragraphs,
SJ summarizes views about colonies
he has already expressed in "Obser-
vations on a Letter from a French
Refugee" (1756), pp. 167–76 above,
and will elaborate on in *Taxation No
Tyranny* (1775), pp. 419f. below.

English protection; were constituted by an English charter; and have been defended by English arms.

To suppose, that by sending out a colony, the nation established an independent power; that when, by indulgence and favour, emigrants are become rich, they shall not contribute to their own defence, but at their own pleasure; and that they shall not be included, like millions of their fellow subjects, in the general system of representation; involves such an accumulation of absurdity, as nothing but the shew of patriotism could palliate.

He that accepts protection, stipulates obedience. We have always protected the Americans; we may therefore subject them to government.

The less is included in the greater. That power which can take away life, may seize upon property. The Parliament may enact for America a law of capital punishment; it may therefore establish a mode and proportion of taxation.

But there are some who lament the state of the poor Bostonians,[3] because they cannot all be supposed to have committed acts of rebellion; yet all are involved in the penalty imposed. This, they say, is to violate the first[n] rule of justice, by condemning the innocent to suffer with the guilty.

This deserves some notice, as it seems dictated by equity[o] and humanity, however[p] it may raise contempt, by the ignorance which it betrays of the state of man, and the system of things. That the innocent should be confounded with the guilty, is undoubtedly an evil; but it is an evil which no care or caution can prevent. National crimes require national punishments, of which many must necessarily have their part, who have not incurred them by personal guilt. If rebels should fortify a town, the cannon of lawful authority will endanger equally the harmless burghers and the criminal garrison.

In some cases, those suffer most who are least intended to be hurt. If the French in the late war had taken an English

n. first *76*] just *74, 75*   o. equity *76*] justice *74, 75*   p. however *76*] however, *74, 75*

---

3. After the "Boston Tea Party" in 1773, the government had closed the port of Boston.

city, and permitted the natives to keep their dwellings, how could it have been recovered, but by the slaughter of our friends? A bomb might as well destroy an Englishman as a Frenchman; and by famine we know that the inhabitants would be the first that should perish.

This infliction of promiscuous evil may therefore be lamented, but cannot be blamed. The power of lawful government must be maintained; and the miseries which rebellion produces, can be charged only on the rebels.

That man likewise is *not a Patriot*, who denies his governours their due praise, and who conceals from the people the benefits which they receive. Those therefore can lay no claim to this illustrious appellation, who impute want of public spirit to the late Parliament; an assembly of men, whom, notwithstanding some fluctuation of counsel, and some weakness of agency, the nation must always remember with gratitude, since it is indebted to them for a very ample concession in the resignation of protections,[4] and a wise and honest attempt to improve the constitution, in the new judicature instituted for the trial of elections.[5]

The right of protection, which might be necessary when it was first claimed, and was very consistent with that liberality of immunities in which the feudal constitution delighted, was by its nature liable to abuse, and had in reality been sometimes misapplied, to the evasion of the law, and the defeat of justice. The evil was perhaps not adequate to the clamour; nor is it very certain, that the possible good of this privilege was not more than equal to the possible evil. It is however plain, that whether they gave any thing or not to the public, they at least lost something from themselves. They divested their dignity of a very splendid distinction, and shewed that they were more willing than their predecessors to stand on a level with their fellow-subjects.

---

4. The statute 10 Geo. III, c.50, which limited the immunity from arrest for debt and civil action conferred by membership of Parliament. See Lecky, Ch. x.

5. Grenville's Elections Act, 1770, which removed jurisdiction over contested elections from the scandalous partisanship of trial by the whole House of Commons to a small, impartial committee. See n. 8, p. 334 above. The abuses SJ goes on to describe were familiar to him in connexion with the hotly contested elections at Lichfield (cf. *Politics*, Ch. III).

The new mode of trying elections, if it be found effectual, will diffuse its consequences further than seems yet to be foreseen. It is, I believe, generally considered as advantageous only to those who claim seats in Parliament; but, if to chuse representatives be one of the most valuable rights of Englishmen, every voter must consider that law as adding to his happiness, which makes his suffrage efficacious; since it was vain to chuse, while the election could be controled by any other power.

With what imperious contempt of ancient rights, and what audaciousness of arbitrary authority, former Parliaments have judged the disputes about elections, it is not necessary to relate. The claim of a candidate, and the right of electors are said scarcely to have been, even in appearance, referred to conscience; but to have been decided by party, by passion, by prejudice, or by frolick. To have friends in the borough was of little use to him, who wanted friends in the house; a pretence was easily found to evade a majority, and the seat was at last his, that was chosen not by his electors, but his fellow-senators.[q]

Thus the nation was insulted with a mock election, and the Parliament was filled with spurious representatives; one of the most important claims, that of a right to sit in the supreme council of the kingdom, was debated in jest, and no man could be confident of success from the justice of his cause.

A disputed election is now tried with the same scrupulousness and solemnity, as any other title. The candidate, that has deserved well of his neighbours, may now be certain of enjoying the effect of their approbation; and the elector, who has voted honestly for known merit, may be certain that he has not voted in vain.

Such was the Parliament, which some of those, who are now aspiring to sit in another, have taught the rabble to consider as an unlawful convention of men, worthless, venal, and prostitute, slaves of the court, and tyrants of the people.

That the next House of Commons may act upon the principles of the last, with more constancy and higher spirit, must be the wish of all[r] who wish well to the public; and it is

q. electors . . . fellow-senators 76] electors but his judges 74, 75   r. all 76] all, 74, 75

surely not too much to expect, that the nation will recover
from its delusion, and unite in a general abhorrence of those
who, by deceiving the credulous with fictitious mischiefs,
overbearing the weak by audacity of falsehood, by appealing
to the judgment of ignorance, and flattering the vanity of
meanness, by slandering honesty and insulting dignity, have
gathered round them whatever the kingdom can supply of
base, and gross, and profligate; and "raised by merit to this
bad eminence,"[6] arrogate to themselves the name of *Patriots*.

FINIS.[s]

s. *Om. 76*

---

6. Milton, *Paradise Lost*, II.5–6: "Satan exalted sat, by merit raised / To that
bad eminence."

TAXATION NO TYRANNY. 1775.

While Johnson was composing *The Patriot* in the autumn of 1774, the first session of the American Continental Congress was meeting in Philadelphia (5 September to 26 October). The formation of this body, which was to continue in existence until its replacement in 1789, under the newly adopted Constitution, by the Congress of the United States, was perhaps the most decisive single act in the long series of incidents that led to the breaking away of the Thirteen Colonies from Britain and the establishment of the new republic. Delegates attended from all the thirteen except Georgia. The initiative for convoking the Congress came from the House of Assembly of Massachusetts, which had determined to resist the measures of coercion taken by the British government in the spring of 1774 to enforce the trade and navigation laws in that province. The Congress devoted its first session chiefly to formulating the principles on which the colonies agreed to take their stand in their relations with Britain—principles that, it at once became apparent, were incompatible with those on which the central government proposed to act. These principles it expressed in a forcefully written and well-publicized set of documents: a series of "resolves" (sometimes termed the "Declaration of Rights" or "Bill of Rights," by analogy with those famous instruments of seventeenth-century British history), which asserted, as of right, the colonies' autonomy in matters of fiscal legislation; addresses to the King and the people of Great Britain, declaring their grievances and justifying their actions; and an appeal to the people of the newly formed province of Quebec to join in their cause. All these were couched in impressive rhetoric (the principal writer seems to have been John Dickinson) and were widely reprinted in British newspapers, magazines, and pamphlets during late 1774 and early 1775.

To provide a quasi-official reply to this highly important and influential manifesto, North's ministry called in the services of the most skilled writer among its supporters, Samuel Johnson. The chief intermediary seems to have been Sir Grey Cooper, Secretary to the Treasury; no doubt William Strahan, who printed the work and was a strongly pro-government Member of Parliament, also assisted in conveying the government's wishes to Johnson and in watering down Johnson's bold language to the milder terms the government wished to employ. "How humiliating to the great Johnson!" to have his work revised by Cooper, Boswell wrote originally in the *Life* (but, perhaps since Cooper was still a political force of some potency, thought better of it and struck it out).[1] Whether humiliated or not, Johnson was disgusted, as he wrote Strahan on 1 March (*Letters* 381): "I am sorry

---

1. R. W. Chapman, "Boswell's Revises of the Life of Johnson," in *Johnson and Boswell Revised* (1928), p. 37.

to see that all the alterations proposed are evidence of timidity. You may be sure that I do not wish to publish what those for whom I write do not like to have published," and on 3 March (*Letters* 382), after returning without change the proofs revised "by authority": "I had no great difficulty in persuading myself to admit the alterations, for why should I in defense of the ministry provoke those whom in their own defense they dare not provoke.—But are such men fit to be the governours of kingdoms?" Much of the alteration was to the emphatic conclusion of the pamphlet. Johnson dissented—"It ends well enough as it is"—and asked Strahan to print for him "half a dozen copies in the original state." No such copies have ever been found; Chapman suggests "Strahan might be afraid to print them," although this seems far-fetched. Boswell, however, had a few proof sheets in his possession, which contain stylistic changes in Johnson's hand, and important deletions (recorded in the textual notes below). But the conclusion is missing.

The revisions were ordered because, as Johnson goes on to note in his letter of 3 March, North's policy at the moment was one of somewhat grudging appeasement: he had recently introduced his own "Conciliation" bill in Parliament, which conceded some of the colonists' demands. But it was unavailing; matters had progressed too far for such a proposal to be effective, and the Americans scornfully rejected the overture. Modern historians agree that by 1775 the movement for American autonomy had reached the point where the Congress's resolutions were merely a formulation of matters on which American opinion had long since hardened, not the introduction of novel and still debatable propositions. Johnson, unlike North, seems to have understood this: if *Taxation No Tyranny* was ineffective as propaganda, it was because the time for propaganda, for discussion, for "dialogue" was long past. The Congress's resolutions were a manifesto, a preamble to a declaration of independence, if necessary a declaration of war. *Taxation No Tyranny*, whatever the ministry may have wanted it to be, was a counter-manifesto, a "Declaration of Rights" of the British subject (and taxpayer) as against those of the Americans. The issue had been joined: Johnson was not concerned to persuade the Americans to change their minds but to present an effective statement of the British case "to a candid world," for posterity, if necessary, to judge.

What is that case? It is summed up in the title of the piece: taxation is not, as American patriotic rhetoric seemed to maintain, tyranny, enslavement, chains. Since many of those who deplore *Taxation No Tyranny* seem not to have read it carefully or to be aware that in it Johnson is developing a coherent argument that deserves to be taken seriously, it may be useful to provide an outline of that argument:

> It is self-evident [Johnson begins] that the supreme governing body of any community has the right to levy taxes on its members for the purpose of furthering the public welfare. This universally accepted proposition the American publicists deny. Much has been said about the hardships and (contradictorily) the prosperity and power of the Americans, the difficulty of coercing them, and the loss to our trade caused by our trying to coerce them. But all this is beside the main

point, which is the American contention that British taxation of them is unconstitutional. This point must be examined.

"A tax is a payment exacted by authority from part of the community for the benefit of the whole." The American colonies have not denied that they have benefited from British protection, but maintain that they alone must decide what, if anything, they will contribute to the cost of its maintenance. This raises the question of the nature of a colony. In early times, colonies that went out from the mother country at once became and remained independent nations. But with the more complex political and economic organization of modern society, this has not been the case with modern colonies: the central government of the colonizing nation has retained its omnicompetence, even though powers of local government may be delegated to the more distant and better developed colonies. But these remain delegated powers, and can be resumed by the central government at any time if the actions of the colony seem to threaten the welfare of the whole.

It has been maintained (following Locke) that a government derives its power of taxation only from the consent of those who are taxed; that this consent is given through their representatives in Parliament, and the Americans have no such representatives. But this theory is mistaken: in Britain only a small proportion of taxpayers have any voice in the choice of members, and even of them, in a close election, "almost half must be governed not only without, but against their choice." Government derives its powers not from the myth of representation but from the tacit consent of the governed.

The first Resolution of the Congress, that they have not yielded to any power the right to dispose of their life, liberty, and property, is correct but trivial: so long as they remain in "a state of nature," this is so. But they contradict this in their second Resolution, that their ancestors, on emigration, retained their rights as Englishmen: if they were Englishmen they had not only rights but the condition of subjection to English law—they had become amenable to being deprived *without* their consent of their lives and liberty (by the criminal law) and of their property (by tax legislation). True, they retained their *rights* as Englishmen to elect representatives to Parliament, but by crossing the ocean made it physically impossible to exercise those rights. Much has been said about the rights conferred on them by the various provincial charters; but these rights, derived from the charters, are as revocable as the charters themselves—just as the privileges of a corporation are. The appeal to the analogy of Ireland, with its own Parliament, fails: by statute the British Parliament can make laws for Ireland. It is true that local American assemblies have the power of levying taxes for local purposes; but so does every English parish, whose inhabitants nonetheless remain amenable to taxation by Parliament. The question of providing representation for the Americans in Parliament raises difficult practical problems; but they are not really anxious for such representation: "they mean not to exchange solid money for such airy honour."

With the convocation of the Congress, they have in fact assumed the

posture of an independent nation: they have declared economic warfare against Britain, and, "being now in their own opinion, free states,
they are not only raising armies but forming alliances." Their exhortation to the people of Quebec to join them makes odd reading
in conjunction with their condemnation of Parliament's grant of
toleration of Popery to Quebec. Their complaints about injustice to
the Bostonians are ill-judged: Bostonians deliberately broke the law
and should be punished. The establishment of admiralty courts is
likewise necessary to uphold the laws. Their complaint about the
appointment of inefficient governors and magistrates is justified; but
other parts of the British dominions suffer from such appointments.

It has been argued that the wealth extorted by taxation from the
Americans will be used to enslave the British as well. This is fantasy.
In the past the flow of wealth has been in the other direction, in the
form of British defence expenditure. The writers affect to believe that
the Crown, not Parliament, has the power of levying taxes. But though
they hope to inflame the minds of their hearers by this rigmarole, they
know better than to believe it; their teacher in the art of propaganda
has been the "master of mischief," Franklin. The absurdity of the
Congress's manifesto becomes evident if we imagine an analogous one
drawn up by a Congress in Cornwall. Particularly absurd and pernicious is the loose talk about "slavery," which comes with an especially
bad grace from southern slave-owners.

Since the Americans "consider themselves emancipated from obedience, and as being no longer the subjects of the British crown," the
question is now whether to yield to this claim or resist it by force.
Much pathos has been expended, and much alarm aroused, to dissuade
us from the use of force, and ingenious schemes of conciliation have
been proposed, which, however, leave the basic question of authority
unsettled. It has also been proposed to grant them independence
immediately. Yet it seems hard, having expended so much in order to
keep them from being seized by the French, to let them thus go: it
would have been better to grant them independence before the war
with France (if we are to lose them anyway), or even to restore Canada
to the French and see what happens to their wish for independence.
Parliament, however, seems to have decided on coercion; if so, the
best method will be to send over so large a military force as to cow
them into submission without bloodshed. Those who really deserve
punishment are their British "friends," who incited this mischief. If
we win, let us settle the administration of America on a more secure
basis. If in the end, however, we lose, let us hope that amicable relations of some kind may be restored between the new nation and the
British, even with the British on a footing of inferiority.

Johnson's aim in the first, and longest, section of the pamphlet is to
explode the flimsy legalistic and "patriotic" arguments advanced by the
Congress in justification of the Americans' actions—to show that they
are absurd cant, which their authors themselves do not believe: the real

motives of its inspirers are different, and Johnson hints pretty strongly that they are self-aggrandizement and self-enrichment. Waiving the question of what the real motives of men like Sam Adams and Patrick Henry were— and there was a time when some historians, notably the Beards, would have agreed with Johnson in finding them less than completely idealistic—we may explore the question of the validity of the points made by the Congress. They can be reduced to three. The first two are constitutional: first, did the central government at Westminster, the Parliament of Great Britain, have the constitutional right to enforce fiscal legislation in the outlying parts of the British dominions, and, second, is "taxation without representation" legal and equitable? To both questions the Congress answers no and Johnson yes. The first question was fully debated in the 1920's by two eminent American historians: C. H. McIlwain, in *The American Revolution: A Constitutional Interpretation* (1923), upheld the negative, and R. L. Schuyler, in *Parliament and the British Empire: Some Constitutional Controversies Concerning Imperial Legislative Jurisdiction* (1929), vigorously affirmed the proposition— "The jurisdiction of Parliament was never confined to the realm of England. From the earliest times parliaments were imperial in the scope of their authority" (p. 33). A more recent historian, Richard Pares, has adjudicated between them (*George III and the Politicians*, 1953, p. 32, n. 2), concluding, "I can only say that, in my opinion, Professor Schuyler had the better of the argument," and no one so far seems to have taken up Pares's challenge. As for "taxation without representation," it is so familiar and accepted a feature of the individual's life in the twentieth century (as in all previous centuries)—even in Massachusetts, where the doctrine was so loudly protested[2]—that even the emotional overtones of the phrase have largely disappeared: its serious use by a modern politician would evoke only smiles. The late L. H. Gipson, one of the most respected historians of the period, passed judgement on these two basic questions in the concluding paragraphs of the book in which he distilled his immense learning about the events that led up to the American Revolution (*The Coming of the Revolution, 1763–1775*, 1954, pp. 233–34):

> In our own day the fundamental positions taken by Great Britain and America in the year 1775 are reversed. For Great Britain in the twentieth century repudiated its earlier position that sovereignty was

---

2. Besides those mentioned by Gipson in the following passage, American residents regularly taxed without representation include minors, aliens, residents of one state employed in another, and residents of one community shopping in another which levies a purchase tax (until 1917, they included the large category of women). In the 1950's the Commonwealth of Massachusetts vigorously repudiated appeals to the "no taxation without representation" principle made by residents of New Hampshire who were employed in Massachusetts and assessed for Massachusetts state income tax, but who had no right to vote there. It went so far as to throw into prison for an indefinite period (until he agreed to pay the tax) a recalcitrant New Hampshireman who took his American history too literally.

indivisible within the Empire. . . . The United States, on its part, as a
result of the outcome of the Civil War, has just as fully repudiated
the Revolutionary War idea that each state is a sovereign entity
within the federal system, in favor of the unitary concept of sovereignty as resting in the whole American nation. . . . Finally, on the
issue of taxation without representation, the earlier American position
has likewise been disregarded. With the erection of the District of
Columbia, the establishment of territories, and the acquisition of
overseas possessions, the federal government, sustained in its powers
by the Supreme Court in the Insular Cases, assumes the right to tax
people who are not and may never be represented in Congress.

In short, on the two main issues discussed in *Taxation No Tyranny*, Americans
have, in practice, come around to Johnson's view.

The third issue, the Congress's contention that the policies pursued by
the ministries of George III were bound to lead to "enslavement" of
the British people as well as the Americans, strikes Johnson as the height
of fantastic cant: there is no evidence of any such tendency; as he says
drily, "The present generation [of British, who are paying the cost of the
Seven Years' War] seems to think itself in more danger of wanting money
than of losing liberty." Historians have long exploded the myth of George
III's conspiracy to exalt his own powers into those of an absolute despot;
and the British who in 1780 perpetrated the Gordon Riots give the modern
reader the impression of having been in need of rather less than more
liberty of individual action.

It is difficult, then, to see how Johnson can be faulted on any of the three
positions he maintains in the earlier part of the pamphlet. What of the
concluding section, where he talks about what now should be done about
the American situation? He discusses the various alternatives. That of
"conciliation,"[3] of compromise, must be rejected, because there can be no
compromise on the basic issue—either Parliament is to have the final
authority over America, or it is not. If it is, then force must be used, as
Lincoln was to use it in an analogous situation.[4] Parliament has in effect

3. SJ's account of the arguments of the "conciliators" reads remarkably
like parts of Burke's famous speech on conciliation. This was not delivered,
however, until a fortnight after the publication of SJ's pamphlet, and presumably
such arguments were general in the vast pamphlet and periodical literature of
the time.

4. "When may coercion be applied by a state to restrain subordinate units
or groups within it? Was President Lincoln justified in calling upon Congress to
permit him to save the Federal Union by the use of force against the southern
secessionists who insisted that the Union was only a conditional pact between
fully sovereign states? Were the King and Lord North justified under existing
circumstances in asking Parliament to take drastic action to curb the insub-
ordination of the radical elements in Massachusetts Bay in order to save the old
British Empire from disintegration? In each instance subordinate units defied
the central government, demanding that the latter must accept their own
interpretation of what was constitutional on the one hand and unconstitutional

already determined on this, and therefore Johnson supports it, with the recommendation that so large a force be used as to overawe the Americans and cause them to submit without bloodshed. If it is not, then America's existence as a separate nation must be recognized. Although Johnson goes through the motions of rejecting this solution (which had been urged by, among others, Dean Tucker), his line of reasoning at this point is not very convincing; he merely says that it seems hard to have to give up all this territory after spending so many millions during the Seven Years' War to save it from the French; it would be, in short, a blow to British national pride and, perhaps, the British pocketbook (though Tucker denies the latter). Yet when, in his short account of the history of colonization, Johnson notes that in more primitive times colonies automatically became independent communities at the time of their establishment, he by no means reprobates that practice; on the contrary, it is the history of later colonization, the "imperialistic" kind of the fifteenth and sixteenth centuries, when the colonies remained extensions of the mother country, that he condemns, uttering a heartfelt wish that Columbus had stayed at home. The uneasily jocular tone of the latter part of the essay may make us wonder whether, although officially committed here to support the ministerial policy of coercion, what would have given him most pleasure at this point was, as he puts it, to "whistle them down the wind"; and it may be significant (though, with the ending of the piece botched by ministerial revision, we cannot be sure) that in fact he concludes it by contemplating American independence with no particular symptoms of alarm. Johnson had, indeed, with considerable prescience, discussed the possibility twenty years earlier, in the midst of the Seven Years' War, when it was foreseen that the French settlements to the north and west of the Atlantic colonies might no longer be French. "We shall then have," wrote Johnson, in his neglected review in the *Literary Magazine*, 1756, of Lewis Evans's *Geographical* . . . *Essays*,[5] "an addition of land greater than a fourth part of Europe." But he is well aware how complex the subject of imperial expansion is, and he makes the remarkably astute observation: "This great country, for which we are so warmly incited to contend, will not be honestly our own though we keep it from the French." It can perhaps be made so, in a sense, by emigration from the British Isles, but "since the end of all human actions is happiness, why should any number of our inhabitants be banished from their trades and their homes to a trackless desert? . . . What advantage . . . can arise equivalent to the exile of the first planters?" These questions are more difficult than naïve imperialists like the Pittites seem to think. But, given the happiness of the individual as the ultimate criterion of the desirability of political action, he has to conclude:

on the other. In each instance subordinate units set themselves up as ultimate judges of the constitutionality of particular measures, and in each case their stand challenged the concept of national unity. In the face of this challenge George III and North, whether wisely or not, did not hesitate to act—any more than did Lincoln": L. H. Gipson, *The Coming of the Revolution*, p. 223.

5. Pp. 197–212 above.

The fear that the American colonies will break off their dependence on England, I have always thought, with this writer, chimerical and vain. Yet though he endeavours for his present purpose to show the absurdity of such suspicions, he does not omit to hint at something that is to be feared if they are not well used. Every man and every society is entitled to all the happiness that can be enjoyed with the security of the whole community. From this general claim the Americans ought not to be excluded—

although at present the question of independence does not arise, because of the threat from the French.

For all Johnson's alleged "detestation of the Americans"—which is rather, on the evidence of *Taxation No Tyranny*, a detestation of the cant used by some of their publicists, British as well as Americans—there is no reason to think that in 1775 he seriously denied their right to seek happiness in the way that seemed best to them any more than he did in 1756. It was not clear to him, however, that in the long run their happiness would be best served by fostering the political and historical mythology incorporated in the declarations of the Continental Congress (which was to reappear in more extravagant form two years later in the Declaration of Independence); and those American historians[6] who have been investigating the same matters discussed in *Taxation No Tyranny* seem to agree that, even today, Americans would be none the worse and possibly the better for abandoning such mythology, however hallowed by tradition, when it conflicts with the evidence of history.

The pamphlet appeared on 8 March 1775, and went into four editions within a month. It was reprinted, along with Johnson's three other political tracts of the 1770's, in *Political Tracts*, 1776, after considerable revision by Johnson. Johnson's name was immediately attached to it, for example, in the notice of it in the *Gentleman's Magazine*. Johnson's reward for the effort *may* have been his honorary D.C.L. from Oxford, which was conferred on 30 March, three weeks after the publication: the award was initiated by the Chancellor of the University, who, perhaps by no coincidence, was Lord North. The reception of the work was explosively hostile: within a very few weeks a flood of attacking pamphlets appeared, *An Answer to a Pamphlet Entitled Taxation No Tyranny*, *Tyranny Unmasked*, *The Pamphlet Entitled Taxation No Tyranny Candidly Considered*, even one entitled *Taxation Tyranny*! The most curious riposte, perhaps, was the reprinting of Johnson's thirty-five-year-old *Marmor Norfolciense*, with a sarcastic preface by "Tribunus." Some of these replies are listed in W. P. Courtney's bibliography of Johnson, 1915, and a more complete list is given in Helen Louise McGuffie's *Samuel Johnson in the British Press, 1749–1784: A Chronological Checklist* (1976). Boswell's position on the American question (as on the Wilkes affair) was the opposite of Johnson's, and he gives a consistently disparaging account

6. As well as the works by Gipson and Schuyler mentioned above, Clinton Rossiter, *Seedtime of the Republic* (1953), and Bernard Bailyn, ed., *Pamphlets of the American Revolution* (1965), Vol. I, General Introduction, pp. 3–202, are particularly helpful in following the ideological arguments of the time.

of the pamphlet in the *Life*. But from this chorus of dispraise, there have been at least two dissentients whose opinions are worth noting. One was Sir John Hawkins, an experienced lawyer and magistrate:

> *Taxation No Tyranny* has not only never received an answer, but the converse of the proposition has never yet been so proved, by arguments founded on legal principles, as to make a vindication of Johnson's reasoning necessary, for any other purpose than that of preventing the ignorant from being misled (*Life of Johnson*, ed. B. H. Davis, 1961, p. 222).

The other was a great critic of literature and politics, who dropped some of the most scathing comments on Johnson ever uttered, and generally regarded him as the symbol of everything he had revolted against. But Coleridge made one exception (*Table Talk*, 16 Aug 1833):

> I like Dr. Johnson's political pamphlets better than any other parts of his works—particularly his *Taxation No Tyranny* is very clever and spirited. . . .

Coleridge goes on to dilute this by adding "though he sees only half of his subject, and that not in a very philosophical manner"; but, from Coleridge, it is astounding praise. Coleridge then delivers a short dissertation on the subject himself, though it is hard to see in what way his own conclusion— "As to the right to tax being only commensurate with direct representation, it is a fable, falsely and treacherously brought forward by those who know its hollowness well enough"—is more philosophically expressed than Johnson's own remarks to the same effect.

The text of *Taxation No Tyranny* presents some interesting problems, which have been discussed by William B. Todd, "Concealed Editions of Samuel Johnson," *The Book Collector*, II, 1953, and D. J. Greene, "*The False Alarm* and *Taxation No Tyranny*: Some Further Observations," *Studies in Bibliography*, XIII, 1960. In the latter article, I attempt to show, by a study of the many variants in the four 1775 editions of the work, that Johnson introduced a number of significant changes into the third edition of that year, some of them purely stylistic, others material to the purport of the work; that these were inadvertently dropped in the fourth edition, which in large part used the second edition for its copy text; and that when Johnson, in 1776, revised the work for inclusion in his collected *Political Tracts*, he followed the fourth edition and thus failed to recapture his more mature intentions as represented by the third edition. Following this reasoning, I have retained the stylistic changes of the third edition in the text below, since there seems to be no justification for reintroducing a clearly inferior choice of phraseology merely because Johnson happened to use an inferior copy text for his last revised edition. Inconsistently, perhaps, I have not ventured to handle the third edition's changes of substantive argument so boldly: it *may* be only through similar inadvertence that Johnson in 1776 failed to call the Continental Congress "a seditious meeting punishable by law," as he had done in the third edition of 1775; but on the other hand he *may* have remembered it and decided it was too strong, whereas he could *not* possibly have changed "floods" back to "streams" and so recreated the repetition of the word "streams" that the use of "floods" in the third edition was intended to rectify.[7] The text given below, then, preserves the accidentals of the first edition, 1775, together with the substantive revisions made in the 1776 edition, and *some* of the revisions (stylistic, but not material) found in the third edition of 1775. In the textual notes, 75 (*1*), 75(*2*), etc., mean the first, second, etc., editions of 1775, and 75 alone means the consensus of the four editions of that year.

The five proof pages of the work preserved by Boswell[8] give still more evidence of Johnson's habit of painstaking revision—and, of course, of the revision requested by the administration. Boswell, in a MS note on the back of proof page 82, tells the story of how he acquired them: "Part of the Proof Copy of Dr. Johnson's *Taxation no Tyranny* [*sic*] which I found lying as waste paper at Mr. Thrale's at Streatham in May 1778. I preserve it on account of several small variations but chiefly on account of a paragraph on William Earl of Chatham (pages 95 & 96) which has been struck out before publication. The paragraph I take it, also glances at Lord Camden as a Chancellor." The variant readings in the proofs have been incorporated in the textual notes below (deletions are enclosed by pointed brackets, ⟨ ⟩, and marginal and interlinear insertions in Johnson's hand by carets, ∧ ∧). It may be noted that the transcription given by Boswell in the *Life* II.313–15) contains some small inaccuracies. The five pages preserved are 82, 89, 90, 95, 96. The last page of the first edition, which is page 91 and contains only three lines, corresponds to the middle of page 95 of the proof copy; that is, a total of more than four pages has been deleted from the text up to that point. In addition, the last half of the page 95 and all of page 96 of the proof copy were omitted from the published text; and the proof copy continued beyond page 96, for the last word on the page ("whiggism") is a catch word. As well as the omissions noted by Boswell in the *Life*, the proof pages show numerous stylistic revisions by Johnson, which were incorporated in the first edition. Also, interestingly, there are two readings in the proofs, not shown there as corrected, which vary from those of the first edition: "every other act," which appears in the edition as "every act," and "miseries," which becomes "sufferings" in the edition (p. 449, notes d, g). The first of these might have been a compositorial slip, but the second seems to be an authorial change, made to avoid the repetition of "miseries" two paragraphs before. Moreover, not all of the two paragraphs following the ending of the published pamphlet are marked by Johnson for deletion, as Boswell's account seems to indicate—only the part of the first of these paragraphs following its first sentence (from "If a new monarchy" to "may want a Chancellor") is so marked. Presumably, then, the proofs preserved by Boswell could not have been the final set, returned

7. See note 2, p. 438, and note k, p. 442 below.
8. Now in the possession of Mrs. Donald F. Hyde, to whom I am grateful for permission to use them. See illustration facing p. 455.

George Grenville as Chancellor of the Exchequer, by Sir Joshua Reynolds. Collection
Columbia University; gift of Mr. and Mrs. John Bass.

by Johnson to Strahan on 1 or 2 March, but represent an earlier stage of revision. Johnson points out to Strahan that he had earlier toned down his conclusion: "The last paragraph was indeed rather contemptuous, there was once more of it which I put out myself" (*Letters* 381). Boswell records Johnson's repeating another passage deleted "by those in power" (*Life*, II. 313).

Taxation No Tyranny; an Answer to the Resolutions and Address . of the American Congress

In all the parts of human knowledge, whether terminating in science merely speculative, or operating upon life private or civil, are admitted some fundamental principles, or common axioms, which being generally received are little doubted, and being little doubted have been rarely proved.

Of these gratuitous[1] and acknowledged truths it is often the fate to become less evident by endeavours to explain them, however necessary such endeavours may be made by the misapprehensions of absurdity, or the sophistries of interest. It is difficult to prove the principles of science, because notions cannot always be found more intelligible than those which are questioned. It is difficult to prove the principles of practice, because they have for the most part not been discovered by investigation, but obtruded by experience, and the demonstrator will find, after an operose deduction, that he has been trying to make that seen which can be only felt.

Of this kind is the position, that "the supreme power of every community has the right of requiring from all its subjects such contributions as are necessary to the public safety or public prosperity,"[2] which was considered by all mankind as comprising the primary and essential condition

1. Probably in the sense of the second definition in SJ's *Dictionary*, "asserted without proof."

2. If this is a quotation, its source has not been traced. But it may be SJ's own formulation (of a position common enough in earlier works on government), the italics (here double quotation marks) emphasizing its importance as the basis for the following argument. The *Monthly Review* (Mar 1775, p. 253), which devotes considerable space to examining the proposition, seems to treat the phraseology as SJ's own; so does Sir John Hawkins (*Life*, ed. B. H. Davis, 1961, p. 218).

of all political society, till it became disputed by those zealots of anarchy, who have denied to the Parliament of Britain the right of taxing the American colonies.

In favour of this exemption of the Americans from the authority of their lawful sovereign,[3] and the dominion of their mother-country, very loud clamours have been raised, and many wild assertions advanced, which by such as borrow their opinions from the reigning fashion have been admitted as arguments; and what is strange, though their tendency is to lessen English honour, and English power, have been heard by English-men with a wish to find them true. Passion has in its first violence controlled interest, as the eddy for a while runs against the stream.

To be prejudiced is always to be weak; yet there are prejudices so near to laudable, that they have been often praised, and are always pardoned. To love their country has been considered as virtue in men, whose love could not be otherwise than blind, because their preference was made without a comparison; but it never has[a] been my fortune to find, either in ancient or modern writers, any honourable mention of those, who have with equal blindness hated their country.

These antipatriotic prejudices are the abortions of Folly impregnated by Faction, which being produced against the standing order of Nature, have not strength sufficient for long life. They are born only to scream and perish, and leave those to contempt or detestation, whose kindness was employed to nurse them into mischief.

To perplex the opinion of the publick many artifices have been used, which, as usually happens when falsehood is to be maintained by fraud, lose their force by counteracting one another.

a. never has *75 (1, 3)*] has never *75 (2, 4), 76*

---

3. Serious misunderstanding of SJ's position can be caused by taking this to mean simply "King George III." As used by Jean Bodin and most subsequent writers on government, "sovereign" means the final, omni- competent authority in any state, the *suprema potestas*, Locke's "Legislative." In Britain this was and is Parliament, consisting of the King, Lords, and Commons.

The nation is sometimes to be mollified by a tender tale of men, who fled from tyranny to rocks and desarts,[b] and is persuaded to lose all claims of justice, and all sense of dignity, in compassion for a harmless people, who having worked hard for bread in a wild country, and obtained by the slow progression of manual industry the accommodations of life, are now invaded by unprecedented oppression, and plundered of their properties by the harpies of taxation.

We are told how their industry is obstructed by unnatural restraints, and their trade confined by rigorous prohibitions; how they are forbidden to enjoy the products of their own soil, to manufacture the materials which Nature spreads before them, or to carry their own goods to the nearest market: and surely the generosity of English virtue will never heap new weight upon those that are already over-laden, will never delight in that dominion, which cannot be exercised but by cruelty and outrage.

But while we are melting in silent sorrow, and in the transports of delirious[c] pity, dropping both the sword[4] and balance from our hands, another friend of the Americans thinks it better to awaken another passion, and tries to alarm our interest, or excite our veneration, by accounts of their greatness and their opulence, of the fertility of their land, and the splendour of their towns. We then begin to consider the question with more evenness of mind, are ready to conclude that those restrictions are not very oppressive which have been found consistent with this speedy growth of prosperity, and begin to think it reasonable that they, who thus flourish under the protection of our government, should contribute something towards its expence.

But we are soon[d] told that the Americans, however wealthy, cannot be taxed; that they are the descendants of men who left all for liberty, and that they have constantly preserved the principles and stubbornness of their progenitors; that they are too obstinate for persuasion, and too powerful for

b. desarts 75(1)] deserts 75(2–4), 76   c. delirious 76] delicious 75   d. soon 76] then 75

4. Cf. *London*, l. 251 (Yale *Works*, vi. 60): "Held high the steady scale, but drop'd the sword."

constraint; that they will laugh at argument, and defeat violence; that the continent of North America contains three millions, not of men merely, but of Whigs,[5] of Whigs fierce for liberty, and disdainful of dominion; that they multiply with the fecundity of their own rattle-snakes, so that every quarter of a century doubles their numbers.[6]

Men accustomed to think themselves masters do not love to be threatened. This talk is, I hope, commonly thrown away, or raises passions different from those which it was[e] intended to excite. Instead of terrifying the English hearer to tame acquiescence, it disposes him to hasten the experiment of bending obstinacy before it is become yet more obdurate, and convinces him that it is necessary to attack a nation thus prolific while we may yet hope to prevail. When he is told through what extent of territory we must travel to subdue them, he recollects how far, a few years ago, we travelled in their defence.[7] When it is urged that they will shoot up like the Hydra, he naturally considers how the Hydra was destroyed.[8]

Nothing dejects a trader like the interruption of his profits. A commercial people, however magnanimous, shrinks at the thought of declining traffick, and an unfavourable balance.[9] The effect of this terrour has been tried. We have been

e. was 76] om. 75

---

5. "This glorious spirit of Whiggism animates three millions in America": the Earl of Chatham speaking in the House of Lords 20 Jan 1775 (*Parliamentary History*, xviii, 154).

6. "There are supposed to be now upwards of one million English souls in North America. . . . This million doubling, suppose but once in 25 years, will in another century be more than the people of England": Benjamin Franklin, *Observations Concerning the Increase of Mankind and the Peopling of Countries*, 1751 (*Papers of Benjamin Franklin*, 1961, iv.233). The rattlesnake as a symbol of American radicalism was familiarized by the "Don't Tread on Me" flag.

7. I.e., during the Seven Years' War.

8. SJ's emphasis would perhaps be better captured if we read "that" for "how."

9. For a survey of the various views expressed by SJ on commerce, see John H. Middendorf, "Johnson on Wealth and Commerce," in *Johnson, Boswell, and Their Circle: Essays Presented to L. F. Powell* (1965), pp. 47–64. In this paragraph, SJ is alluding mainly to a group of petitions from traders of London and other cities calling for conciliation of the colonies and debated in Parliament in Jan 1775 (*Parliamentary History*, xviii.167–82).

stunned with the importance of our American commerce, and heard of merchants with warehouses that are never to be emptied, and of manufacturers starving for want of work. That our commerce with America is profitable, however less than ostentatious or deceitful estimates have made it,[1] and that it is our interest to preserve it, has never been denied; but surely it will most effectually be preserved, by being kept always in our own power. Concessions may promote it for a moment, but superiority only can ensure its continuance. There will always be a part, and always a very large part of every community that have no care but for themselves, and whose care for themselves reaches little farther than impatience of immediate pain, and eagerness for the nearest good. The blind are said to feel with peculiar nicety. They who look but little into futurity, have perhaps the quickest sensation of the present. A merchant's desire is not of glory, but of gain; not of publick wealth, but of private emolument; he is therefore rarely to be consulted about war and peace, or any designs of wide extent and distant consequence.

Yet this, like other general characters, will sometimes fail. The traders of *Birmingham* have rescued themselves from all imputation of narrow selfishness by a manly recommendation to Parliament of the rights and dignity of their native country.[2]

To these men I do not intend to ascribe an absurd and enthusiastick contempt of interest, but to give them the rational and just praise of distinguishing real from seeming good, of being able to see through the cloud of interposing difficulties, to the lasting and solid happiness of victory and settlement.

Lest all these topicks of persuasion should fail, the great

---

1. According to a communication in the *Public Advertiser*, 17 Jan 1769 (perhaps by Benjamin Franklin), the loss to British business as a result of American nonimportation and nonconsumption agreements then amounted to £7,250,000 (L. H. Gipson, *The Coming of the Revolution, 1763–1775*, 1954, p. 193).

2. In opposition to the petitions mentioned in n. 9 above, a group of Birmingham traders presented one to the effect that "your petitioners are apprehensive that any relaxation in the execution of the laws respecting the colonies of Great Britain will ultimately tend to the injury of the commerce of this town and neighbourhood" (*London Chronicle*, 31 Jan–6 Feb 1775).

actor of patriotism[3] has tried another, in which terrour and pity are happily combined, not without a proper super-addition of that admiration which latter[f] ages have brought into the drama. The heroes of Boston, he tells us, if the Stamp Act had not been repealed, would have left their town, their port, and their trade, have resigned the splendour of opulence, and quitted the delights of neighbourhood, to disperse themselves over the country, where they would till the ground, and fish in the rivers, and range the mountains, *and be free.*

These surely are brave words. If the mere sound of freedom can operate thus powerfully, let no man hereafter doubt the story of the Pied Piper. "The removal of the people of Boston into the country" seems even to the Congress not only "difficult in its execution," but "important in its consequences."[4] The difficulty of execution is best known to the Bostonians themselves; the consequence, alas! will only be, that they will leave good houses to wiser men.

Yet before they quit the comforts of a warm home for the sounding something which they think better, he cannot be thought their enemy who advises them to consider well whether they shall find it. By turning fishermen or hunters, woodmen or shepherds, they may become wild, but it is not so easy to conceive them free; for who can be more a slave than he that is driven by force from the comforts of life, is compelled to leave his house to a casual comer, and whatever he does, or wherever he wanders, finds every moment some

---

f. latter 76] later 75

---

3. Chatham. SJ goes on to paraphrase his speech of 20 Jan (n. 5 above). "Terrour and pity" (from Aristotle's *Poetics*) carry on the figure of "the great actor."

4. SJ now begins an extensive series of quotations from the reports of the proceedings of the Continental Congress. They were widely printed in the London newspapers and magazines at the time. References are given here to *Extracts from the*

Votes and Proceedings of the American Continental Congress Held at Philadelphia on the Fifth of September, 1774. . . . Containing the Bill of Rights, a List of Grievances, Occasional Resolves, the Association, an Address to the People of Great-Britain, and a Memorial to the Inhabitants of the British American Colonies. Published by Order of the Congress. Philadelphia Printed. London Reprinted for F. Almon. . . . 1774. The present sentence is on p. 9.

new testimony of his own subjection? If choice of evil be[g] freedom, the felon in the gallies has his option of labour or of stripes.[5] The Bostonian may quit his house to starve in the fields; his dog may refuse to set, and smart under the lash, and they may then congratulate each other upon the smiles of liberty, "profuse of[h] bliss, and pregnant with delight."[6]

To treat such designs as serious, would be to think too contemptuously of Bostonian understandings. The artifice indeed is not new: the blusterer who threatened in vain to destroy his opponent, has sometimes obtained his end, by making it believed that he would hang himself.

But terrours and pity are not the only means by which the taxation of the Americans is opposed. There are those who profess to use them only as auxiliaries to reason and justice, who tell us that to tax the colonies is usurpation and oppression, an invasion of natural and legal rights, and a violation of those principles which support the constitution of English government.

This question is of great importance. That the Americans are able to bear taxation is indubitable; that their refusal may be over-ruled is highly probable: but power is no sufficient evidence of truth.[7] Let us examine our own claim, and the objections of the recusants, with caution proportioned to the event of the decision, which must convict one part of robbery, or the other of rebellion.

A tax is a payment exacted by authority from part of the community for the benefit of the whole. From whom, and in what proportion such payment shall be required, and to what uses it shall be applied, those only are to judge to whom government is intrusted. In the British dominion taxes are

g. choice . . . be 76] the choice of evil is 75   h. of 76] with 75

5. Cf. "The Bravery of the English Common Soldiers" (p. 283 above): "Liberty is, to the lowest rank of every nation, little more than the choice of working or starving."
6. Addison, *A Letter from Italy to . . . Lord Halifax* (1701), ll. 119–120: "O Liberty, thou goddess heavenly bright, / Profuse of bliss, and pregnant with delight!"
7. "Milton," *Lives*, 1.108 (par. 58): "If nothing may be published but what civil authority shall have previously approved, power must always be the standard of truth."

apportioned, levied, and appropriated by the states assembled in parliament.

Of every empire all the subordinate communities are liable to taxation, because they all share the benefits of government, and therefore ought all to furnish their proportion of the expence.

This the Americans have never openly denied. That it is their duty to pay the cost of their own safety they seem to admit; nor do they refuse their contribution to the exigencies, whatever they may be, of the British empire; but they make this participation of the public burden a duty of very uncertain extent, and imperfect obligation, a duty temporary, occasional and elective, of which they reserve to themselves the right of settling the degree, the time, and the duration, of judging when it may be required, and when it has been performed.

They allow to the supreme power nothing more than the liberty of notifying to them its demands or its necessities. Of this notification they profess to think for themselves, how far it shall influence their counsels, and of the necessities alleged, how far they shall endeavour to relieve them. They assume the exclusive power of settling not only the mode, but the quantity of this payment. They are ready to co-operate with all the other dominions of the King; but they will co-operate by no means which they do not like, and at no greater charge than they are willing to bear.

This claim, wild as it may seem, this claim, which supposes dominion without authority, and subjects without subordination, has found among the libertines of policy many clamorous and hardy vindicators. The laws of Nature,[8] the rights of humanity, the faith of charters, the danger of liberty, the encroachments of usurpation, have been thundered in our ears, sometimes by interested faction, and sometimes by honest stupidity.

It is said by Fontenelle, that if twenty philosophers shall resolutely deny that the presence of the sun makes the day, he will not despair but whole nations may adopt the opinion.[9]

---

8. Cf. "Observations on a Letter from a French Refugee" (p. 174 above): "His cant about nature and Providence would prove that no human legislature has a right to make any prudential laws."

9. Not traced.

So many political dogmatists[1] have denied to the mother country the power of taxing the colonies, and have enforced their denial with so much violence of outcry, that their sect is already very numerous, and the publick voice suspends its decision.

In moral and political questions the contest between interest and justice has been often tedious and often fierce, but perhaps it never happened before that justice found much opposition with interest on her side.[2]

For the satisfaction of this inquiry, it is necessary to consider how a colony is constituted, what are the terms of migration as dictated by Nature, or settled by compact, and what social or political rights the man loses, or acquires, that leaves his country to establish himself in a distant plantation.

Of two modes of migration the history of mankind informs us, and so far as I can yet discover, of two only.

In countries where life was yet unadjusted, and policy[3] unformed, it sometimes happened that by the dissensions of heads of families, by the ambition of daring adventurers, by some accidental pressure of distress, or by the mere discontent of idleness, one part of the community broke off from the rest, and numbers, greater or smaller, forsook their habitations, put themselves under the command of some favourite of fortune, and with or without the consent of their countrymen or governours, went out to see what better regions they could occupy, and in what place, by conquest or by treaty, they could gain a habitation.

Sons of enterprise like these, who committed to their own swords their hopes and their lives, when they left their country, became another nation, with designs, and prospects, and interests, of their own. They looked back no more to their former home; they expected no help from those whom they had left behind: if they conquered, they conquered for themselves; if they were destroyed, they were not by any other power either lamented or revenged.

---

1. *"Dogmatist* . . . A magisterial teacher; a positive asserter; a bold advancer of principles" (*Dictionary*).

2. SJ means that British supporters of the American claims are opposing both justice and their own interests.

3. *"Policy* . . . 1. The art of government, chiefly with respect to foreign powers" (*Dictionary*).

Of this kind seem to have been all the migrations of the early[i] world, whether historical or fabulous, and of this kind were the eruptions of those nations which from the North invaded the Roman Empire, and filled Europe with new sovereignties.

But when, by the gradual admission of wiser laws and gentler manners, society became more compacted and better regulated, it was found that the power of every people consisted in union, produced by one common interest, and operating in joint efforts and consistent counsels.[j]

From this time independence perceptibly wasted away. No part of the nation was permitted to act for itself. All now had the same enemies and the same friends; the government protected individuals, and individuals were required to refer their designs to the prosperity of the government.

By this principle it is, that states are formed and consolidated. Every man is taught to consider his own happiness as combined with the publick prosperity, and to think himself great and powerful, in proportion to the greatness and power of his governors.

Had the western continent been discovered between the fourth and tenth century, when all the northern world was in motion; and had navigation been at that time sufficiently advanced to make so long a passage easily practicable, there is little reason for doubting but the intumescence of nations would have found its vent, like all other expansive violence, where there was least resistance; and that Huns and Vandals, instead of fighting their way to the south of Europe, would have gone by thousands and by myriads under their several chiefs to take possession of regions smiling with pleasure and waving with fertility, from which the naked inhabitants were unable to repel them.

Every expedition would in those days of laxity have produced a distinct and independent state. The Scandinavian heroes might have divided the country among them, and have spread the feudal subdivision of regality from Hudson's Bay to the Pacifick Ocean.

But Columbus came five or six hundred years too late for

i. early 76] old 75   j. counsels 75(1-3)] councils 75(4), 76

the candidates of sovereignty. When he formed his project of discovery, the fluctuations of military turbulence had subsided, and Europe began to regain a settled form, by established government and regular subordination. No man could any longer erect himself into a chieftain, and lead out his fellow-subjects by his own authority to plunder or to war. He that committed any act of hostility by land or sea, without the commission of some acknowledged sovereign, was considered by all mankind as a robber or a pirate, names which were now of little credit, and of which therefore no man was ambitious.

Columbus in a remoter time would have found his way to some discontented lord, or some younger brother of a petty sovereign, who would have taken fire at his proposal, and have quickly kindled with equal heat a troop of followers; they would have built ships, or have seized them, and have wandered with him at all adventures[4] as far as they could keep hope in their company. But the age being now past of vagrant excursion and fortuitous hostility, he was under the necessity of travelling from court to court, scorned and repulsed as a wild projector, an idle promiser of kingdoms in the clouds: nor has any part of the world yet had reason to rejoice that he found at last reception and employment.[5]

In the same year,[6] in a year hitherto disastrous to mankind, by the Portuguese was discovered the passage of the Indies, and by the Spaniards the coast of America. The

---

4. "*At all adventures* [*à l'aventure,* Fr.]. By chance; without any rational scheme" (*Dictionary,* s.v. "adventure").

5. Like some of his contemporaries (Voltaire, for instance), SJ often censures the European explorations of the fifteenth and sixteenth centuries. Cf. his introduction to *The World Displayed* (1759)(on Prince Henry the Navigator): "What mankind has lost and gained by the genius and designs of this prince, it would be long to compare and very difficult to estimate. Much knowledge has been acquired, and much cruelty been committed; the belief of religion has been very little propagated, and its laws have been outrageously and enormously violated. The Europeans have scarcely visited any coast but to gratify avarice, and extend corruption; to arrogate dominion without right, and practise cruelty without incentive. Happy had it then been for the oppressed, if the designs of Henry had slept in his bosom, and surely more happy for the oppressors."

6. 1498, when Vasco da Gama reached India, and Columbus (on his third voyage) the coast of Venezuela.

nations of Europe were fired with boundless expectation, and the discoverers pursuing their enterprise, made conquests in both hemispheres of wide extent. But the adventurers were contented with plunder; though they took gold and silver to themselves, they seized islands and kingdoms in the name of their sovereigns. When a new region was gained, a governour was appointed by that power which had given the commission to the conqueror; nor have I met with any European but Stukeley of London,[7] that formed a design of exalting himself in the newly found countries to independent dominion.

To secure a conquest, it was always necessary to plant a colony, and territories thus occupied and settled were rightly considered as mere extensions or processes of empire; as ramifications which by[k] the circulation of one publick interest communicated with the original source of dominion, and which were kept flourishing and spreading by the radical vigour of the mother-country.

The colonies of England differ no otherwise from those of other nations, than as the English constitution differs from theirs. All government is ultimately and essentially absolute,[8]

k. which by 76] through which 75

7. Thomas Stukeley, or Stucly. Cf. Thomas Fuller, *The Worthies of England* (ed. John Freeman, 1952, p. 130): when planning a settlement in Florida, "he blushed not to tell Queen Elizabeth that 'he preferred rather to be sovereign of a molehill than the highest subject to the greatest prince in Christendom,' adding moreover that 'he was assured he should be a prince before his death.' "

8. This remark is often cited as though it were SJ's manifesto of a personal political creed, and evidence of his extreme "Toryism" or absolutism. But he is merely expounding an accepted definition of the word, a universal commonplace of the time, as the continuation of the sentence (usually ignored) clearly indicates. Cf. *Dictionary:* "*Government* . . . 1. Form of a community with respect to the disposition of the supreme authority. . . . 2. An establishment of legal authority." Under the second definition, SJ cites that staunchest of Whigs, Addison, "Everyone knows who has considered the nature of government that there must be in each particular form of it an absolute unlimited power." This is from *Freeholder* No. 16, and is preceded there by Addison's statement that he is discussing "the first principles of government which . . . are of no party but assented to by every reasonable man." Cf. Blackstone, *Commentaries,* 1.49: "There is and must be a supreme, irresistible, uncontrolled authority in which the *jura summi imperii*, or the rights of sovereignty reside."

but subordinate societies may have more immunities, or individuals greater liberty, as the operations of government are differently conducted. An Englishman in the common course of life and action feels no restraint. An English colony has very liberal powers of regulating its own manners and adjusting its own affairs. But an English individual may by the supreme authority be deprived of liberty, and a colony divested of its powers, for reasons of which that authority is the only judge.

In sovereignty there are no gradations. There may be limited royalty, there may be limited consulship; but there can be no limited government. There must in every society be some power or other from which there is no appeal, which admits no restrictions, which pervades the whole mass of the community, regulates and adjusts all subordination, enacts laws or repeals them, erects or annuls judicatures, extends or contracts privileges, exempt itself from question or control, and bounded only by physical necessity.

By this power, wherever it subsists, all legislation and jurisdiction is animated and maintained. From this all legal rights are emanations, which, whether equitably or not, may be legally recalled.[9] It is not infallible, for it may do wrong; but it is irresistible, for it can be resisted only by rebellion, by an act which makes it questionable what shall be thenceforward the supreme power.

An English colony is a number of persons, to whom the King grants a charter permitting them to settle in some distant country, and enabling them to constitute a corporation, enjoying such powers as the charter grants, to be administered in such forms as the charter prescribes. As a corporation

---

9. In his contributions to Sir Robert Chambers's Vinerian law lectures, SJ makes much of the traditional distinction in English jurisprudence between "law" and "equity": e.g., "The decisions of equity as contra-distinguished from those of law are not *contra legem* but *preter legem*, they do nothing which the law forbids, they do only what the law desires but cannot perform" (E. L. McAdam, Jr., *Dr. Johnson and the English Law*, 1951, p. 119). His use of the terms "equitably" and "legally" here is important to the interpretation of SJ's intention in writing the pamphlet: Congress has stated its claim in terms of a case in law, rather than in equity, and SJ rebuts it in law, without prejudice to its possible merits if it were presented as a claim in equity.

they make laws for themselves, but as a corporation subsisting by a grant from higher authority, to the controll of that authority they continue subject.

As men are placed at a greater distance from the Supreme Council[1] of the kingdom, they must be entrusted with ampler liberty of regulating their conduct by their own wisdom. As they are more secluded from easy recourse to national judicature, they must be more extensively commissioned to pass judgment on each other.

For this reason our more important and opulent colonies see the appearance and feel the effect of a regular legislature, which in some places has acted so long with unquestioned authority, that it has been[21] forgotten whence that authority was originally derived.

To their charters the colonies owe, like other corporations, their political existence. The solemnities of legislation, the administration of justice, the security of property, are all bestowed upon them by the royal grant. Without their charter there would be no power among them, by which any law could be made, or duties enjoined, any debt recovered, or criminal punished.

A charter is a grant of certain powers or privileges given to a part of the community for the advantage of the whole, and is therefore liable by its nature to change or to revocation. Every act of government aims at publick good. A charter, which experience has shewn to be detrimental to the nation, is to be repealed; because general prosperity must always be preferred to particular interest. If a charter be used to evil purposes, it is forfeited, as the weapon is taken away which is injuriously employed.

The charter therefore by which provincial governments are

1. om. 76

1. Parliament. SJ's use of this unusual phrase may be designed, consciously or unconsciously, to blind the reader to a defect in his argument at this point. The "authority" under which a colony, like a corporation, was said in the previous sentence to subsist was the King, who was the sole signatory of the colonial charters, not Parliament. The distinction became a very important one in the American case.

2. It seems more likely that "been" was dropped from the 1776 text by accident than as a result of deliberate revision by SJ.

constituted, may be always legally, and where it is either inconvenient in its nature, or misapplied in its use, may be equitably repealed; by[m] such repeal the whole fabrick of subordination is immediately destroyed, and[n] the constitution sunk at once into a chaos: the society is dissolved into a tumult of individuals, without authority to command, or obligation to obey; without any punishment of wrongs but by personal resentment, or any protection of right but by the hand of the possessor.

A colony is to the mother-country as a member to the body,[3] deriving its action and its strength from the general principle of vitality; receiving from the body, and communicating to it, all the benefits and evils of health and disease; liable in dangerous maladies to sharp applications,[4] of which the body however must partake the pain; and exposed, if incurably tainted, to amputation, by which the body likewise will be mutilated.

The mother-country always considers the colonies thus connected, as parts of itself; the prosperity or unhappiness of either is the prosperity or unhappiness of both; not perhaps of both in the same degree, for the body may subsist, though less commodiously, without a limb, but the limb must perish if it be parted from the body.

Our colonies therefore, however distant, have been hitherto treated as constituent parts of the British Empire. The inhabitants incorporated by English charters, are intitled to all the rights of Englishmen. They are governed by English laws, entitled to English dignities, regulated by English counsels, and protected by English arms; and it seems to follow by consequence not easily avoided, that they are subject to English government, and chargeable by English taxation.

To him that considers the nature, the original, the progress, and the constitution of the colonies, who remembers that the first discoverers had commissions from the crown, that the

m. repealed; by 76] repealed, and by 75   n. and 76] om. 75

---

3. SJ alludes to the fable of "The Body and the Members" in Aesop. The same figure is used in his "Observations on a Letter from a French Refugee" (p. 176 above).

4. SJ thinks of this word primarily in a medical sense. Cf. *Dictionary*, defs. 1 and 2.

first settlers owe to a charter their civil forms and regular magistracy, and that all personal immunities and legal⁰ securities, by which the condition of the subject has been from time to time improved, have been extended to the Colonists, it will not be doubted but the Parliament of England has a right to bind them by statutes, and "to bind them in all cases whatsoever,"⁵ and has therefore a natural^p and constitutional power of laying upon them any tax or impost, whether external or internal, upon the product of land, or the manufactures of industry, in the exigencies of war, or in the time of profound peace, for the defence of America, "for the purpose of raising a revenue,"⁶ or for any other end beneficial to the empire.

There are some, and those not inconsiderable for number, nor contemptible for knowledge, who except the power of taxation from the general dominion of Parliament, and hold that whatever degrees of obedience may be exacted, or whatever authority may be exercised in other acts of government, there is still reverence to be paid to money, and that legislation passes its limits when it violates the purse.

Of this exception, which by a head not fully impregnated with politicks is not easily comprehended, it is alleged as an unanswerable reason, that the colonies send no representatives to the House of Commons.

It is, say the American advocates, the natural distinction of a freeman, and the legal privilege of an Englishman, that he is able to call his possessions his own, that he can sit secure in the enjoyment of inheritance or acquisition, that his house is fortified by the law, and that nothing can be taken from him but by his own consent. This consent is given for every man by his representative in Parliament. The Americans unrepresented cannot consent to English taxations, as a corporation, and they will not consent as individuals.

Of this argument, it has been observed by more than one,

---

o. legal 76] personal 75   p. natural 76] legal 75

5. *Votes and Proceedings*, p. 48, quoting from the Declaratory Act, 1766, annexed to the act repealing the Stamp Act.
6. *Votes and Proceedings*, p. 48, quoting from the Revenue Act, 1767 (Townshend's Act), imposing taxes on American glass, paper, and tea.

that its force extends equally to all other laws, for^q a freeman is not to be exposed to punishment, or be called to any onerous service but by his own consent. The Congress has extracted a position from the fanciful Montesquieu, that "in a free state every man being a free agent ought to be concerned in his own government."[7] Whatever is true of taxation is true of every other law, that he who is bound by it, without his consent, is not free, for he is not concerned in his own government.

He that denies the English Parliament the right of taxation, denies it likewise the right of making any other laws civil or criminal, yet this power over the colonies was never yet disputed by themselves. They have always admitted statutes for the punishment of offences, and for the redress or prevention of inconveniencies; and the reception of any law draws after it by a chain which cannot be broken, the unwelcome necessity of submitting to taxation.

That a free man is governed by himself, or by laws to which he has consented, is a position of mighty sound; but every man that utters it, with whatever confidence, and every man that hears it, with whatever acquiescence, if consent be supposed to imply the power of refusal, feels it to be false. We virtually and implicitly allow the institutions of any government of which we enjoy the benefit, and solicit the protection. In wide extended dominions, though power has been diffused with the most even hand, yet a very small part of the people are either primarily or secondarily consulted in legislation. The business of the publick must be done by delegation. The choice of delegates is made by a select number, and those who are not electors stand idle and helpless spectators of the commonweal, "wholly unconcerned in^r the government of themselves."

q. for 76] that 75   r. in 76] with 75

---

7. In its Address to the Inhabitants of Quebec (*Votes and Proceedings*, pp. 74–75) the Congress gives this as one of the "maxims . . . sanctified by the authority of a name which all Europe reveres." The source is Montesquieu, *Esprit des Lois* (1748), Book xi, Ch. 6: "Dans un état libre, tout homme qui est censé avoir une âme libre doit être gouverné par lui-même." SJ gives a more exact translation, "governed by himself," in the second paragraph following.

Of electors the hap is but little better. They are often far
from unanimity in their choice, and where the numbers
approach to equality, almost half must be governed not only
without, but against their choice.

How any man can have consented to institutions established
in distant ages, it will be difficult to explain. In the most
favourite residence of liberty, the consent of individuals is
merely passive, a tacit admission in every community of the
terms which that community grants and requires. As all are
born the subjects of some state or other, we may be said to have
been all born consenting to some system of government.
Other consent than this, the condition of civil life does not
allow. It is the unmeaning clamour of the pedants of policy,[8]
the delirious dream of republican fanaticism.

But hear, ye sons and daughters of liberty, the sounds
which the winds are wafting from the western continent.
The Americans are telling one another, what, if we may judge
from their noisy triumph, they have but lately discovered,
and what yet is a very important truth. "That they are entitled
to life, liberty, and property, and that they have never ceded
to any sovereign power whatever a right to dispose of either
without their consent."[9]

While this resolution stands alone, the Americans are free
from singularity of opinion; their wit has not yet betrayed
them to heresy. While they speak as the naked sons of Nature,
they claim but what is claimed by other men, and have with-
held nothing but what all with-hold. They are here upon firm
ground, behind entrenchments which never can be forced.

---

8. See n. 3, p. 419 above.

9. Resolution 1, *Votes and Proceedings*, p. 4. "Life, Liberty, and
Property" had long been a catchword
in British politics (cf. Locke, *On Civil
Government*, Sect. 131: "Men . . . enter
into society . . . with an intention in
every one the better to preserve
himself, his liberty, and property").
" 'Liberty and Property' was the
pithy slogan under which the first
whig generation fought its way to

power from 1689 to the accession of
the House of Hanover": John Cars-
well, *The Old Cause* (1958), p. 6. By
1713 it was so hackneyed that an
opposing cry had developed, "No
Liberty and Property Men!" (Cars-
well, p. 120). In the American Declaration of Independence, of course,
Jefferson modified it to "Life, Liberty,
and the Pursuit of Happiness." See
p. 212 above.

Humanity is very uniform. The Americans have this resemblance to Europeans, that they do not always know when they are well. They soon quit the fortress that could neither have been mined by sophistry, nor battered by declamation. Their next resolution declares, that "their ancestors, who first settled the colonies, were, at the time of their emigration from the mother-country, entitled to all the rights, liberties, and immunities of free and natural-born subjects within the realm of England."[1]

This likewise is true; but when this is granted, their boast of original rights is at an end; they are no longer in a state of nature. These lords of themselves, these kings of *Me*, these demigods of independence, sink down to colonists, governed by a charter. If their ancestors were subjects, they acknowledged a sovereign; if they had a right to English privileges, they were accountable to English laws, and what must grieve the lover of liberty to discover, had ceded to the King and Parliament, whether the right or not, at least the power, of disposing, "without their consent, of their lives, liberties, and properties." It therefore is required of them to prove, that the Parliament ever ceded to them a dispensation from that obedience, which they owe as natural-born subjects, or any degree of independence or immunity not enjoyed by other Englishmen.

They say, that by such emigration they by no means forfeited, surrendered, or lost any of those rights; but that "they were, and their descendents now are, entitled to the exercise and enjoyment of all such of them as their local and other circumstances enable them to exercise and enjoy."[2]

That they who form a settlement by a lawful charter, having committed no crime, forfeit no privileges, will be readily confessed; but what they do not forfeit by any judicial sentence, they may lose by natural effects. As man can be but in one place at once, he cannot have the advantages of multiplied residence. He that will enjoy the brightness of sunshine, must quit the coolness of the shade. He who goes voluntarily to America, cannot complain of losing what he leaves in Europe.

1. Resolution 2, *Votes and Proceedings*, p. 4.

2. Resolution 3, *Votes and Proceedings*, p. 4.

He perhaps had a right to vote for a knight or burgess:[3] by crossing the Atlantick he has not nullified his right; but[s] he has made its exertion no longer possible*. By his own choice he has left a country where he had a vote and little property, for another, where he has great property, but no vote. But as this preference was deliberate and unconstrained, he is still "concerned in the government of himself"; he has reduced himself from a voter to one of the innumerable multitude that have no vote. He has truly "ceded his right," but he is still governed by his own consent; because he has consented to throw his atom of interest into the general mass of the community. Of the consequences of his own act he has no cause to complain; he has chosen, or intended to chuse, the greater good; he is represented, as himself desired, in the general representation.

But the privileges of an American scorn the limits of place; they are part of himself, and cannot be lost by departure from his country; they float in the air, or glide under the ocean.

Doris amara suam non intermisceat undam.[5]

A planter, wherever he settles, is not only a freeman, but a legislator, *"ubi imperator, ibi Roma.* As the English Colonists are not represented in the British Parliament, they are entitled to a free and exclusive power of legislation in their several legislatures, in all cases of taxation and internal polity, subject only to the negative of the sovereign, in such manner as has been heretofore used and accustomed. We cheerfully consent to the operation of such acts of the British Parliament as are

*Of this reasoning, I owe part to a conversation with Sir John Hawkins.[4]

s. but 76] for 75

---

3. A "knight" ("of the shire") is a member of the House of Commons representing a county; a "burgess" one representing a borough.

4. The asterisk and footnote were added in *1776*. Hawkins was as deeply committed as SJ to the government side in the American controversy. On 7 Oct 1774 he had presided over a noisy meeting of Middlesex freeholders in Westminster Guildhall,

intended to provide support for the government, but was voted out of the chair and replaced by Alderman Sawbridge.

5. Virgil, *Eclogues*, x.5: "Let salt Doris not mingle her wave with thine." (The context is a description of the river Arethusa, which runs beneath the sea undefiled. Doris is the consort of the sea-god, Nereus.)

bona fide restrained to the regulation of our external commerce
—excluding every idea of taxation, internal or external, for
raising a revenue on the subjects of America without their
consent."[6]

Their reason for this claim is, "that the foundation of
English liberty, and of all government,[7] is a right in the people
to participate in their legislative council."

They inherit, they say, "from their ancestors, the right
which their ancestors possessed,[t] of enjoying all the privileges
of Englishmen."[8] That they inherit the right of their ancestors
is allowed; but they can inherit no more. Their ancestors
left a country where the representatives of the people were
elected by men particularly qualified, and where those who
wanted qualifications, or who did not use them, were bound
by the decisions of men whom they had not deputed.

The colonists are the descendants of men, who either had
no votes[u] in elections, or who voluntarily resigned them for
something, in their opinion, of more estimation: they have
therefore exactly what their ancestors left them, not a vote
in making laws, or in constituting legislators, but the happiness
of being protected by law, and the duty of obeying it.

What their ancestors did not carry with them, neither
they nor their descendants have since acquired. They have
not, by abandoning their part in one legislature, obtained
the power of constituting another, exclusive and independent,
any more than the multitudes, who are now debarred from
voting, have a right to erect a separate parliament for themselves.

Men are wrong for want of sense, but they are wrong by
halves for want of spirit. Since the Americans have discovered that they can make a parliament, whence comes it
that they do not think themselves equally empowered to
make a king? If they are subjects, whose government is
constituted by a charter, they can form no body of independent
legislature. If their rights are inherent and underived, they

t. possessed *75(3,4), 76, Resolutions*] professed *75(1,2)*   u. vote *76*

---

6. Resolution 4, *Votes and Pro-*
ceedings, pp. 4–5 (somewhat abbreviated).

7. Resolution 4 reads "all free

government."

8. A rephrasing of Resolution 2
above.

may by their own suffrages encircle with a diadem the
brows of Mr. Cushing.[9]

It is farther declared by the Congress of Philadelphia,
"that his Majesty's colonies are entitled to all the privileges
and immunities granted and confirmed to them by royal
charters, or secured to them by their several codes of provincial laws."[1]

The first clause of this resolution is easily understood,
and will be readily admitted. To all the privileges which a
charter can convey, they are by a royal charter evidently
entitled. The second clause is of greater difficulty; for how
can a provincial law secure privileges or immunities to a
province? Provincial laws may grant to certain individuals
of the province the enjoyment of gainful, or an immunity
from onerous offices; they may operate upon the people to
whom they relate; but no province can confer provincial
privileges on itself. They may have a right to all which the
King has given them; but it is a conceit of the other hemisphere, that men have a right to all which they have given
to themselves.

A corporation is considered in law as an individual, and
can no more extend its own immunities, than a man can by
his own choice assume dignities or titles.

The legislature of a colony, let not the comparison be too
much disdained, is only the vestry of a larger parish, which
may lay a cess[2] on the inhabitants, and enforce the payment;
but can extend no influence beyond its own district, must
modify its particular regulations by the general law, and
whatever may be its internal expences, is still liable to taxes
laid by superior authority.

The charters given to different provinces are different, and
no general right can be extracted from them. The charter
of Pensylvania,[v] where this congress of anarchy has been
impudently held,[w] contains a clause admitting in express

v. Pennsylvania 76   w. held, 75(2–4), 76] held 75(1)

---

9. Thomas Cushing, Speaker of
the General Court of Massachusetts.

1. Resolution 7, *Votes and Proceedings*, pp. 5–6. The original reads
"immunities and privileges."

2. "A levy made upon the inhabitants of a place, rated according
to their property" (*Dictionary*, def.
1).

terms taxation by the Parliament. If in the other charters no such reserve is made, it must have been omitted as not necessary, because it is implied in the nature of subordinate government. They who are subject to laws, are liable to taxes. If any such immunity had been granted, it is still revocable by the legislature, and ought to be revoked as contrary to the publick good, which is in every charter ultimately intended.

Suppose it true that any such exemption is contained in the charter of Maryland, it can be pleaded only by the Marylanders. It is of no use for any other province, and with regard even to them, must have been considered as one of the grants in which the King has been deceived, and annulled as mischievous to the publick, by sacrificing to one little settlement the general interest of the empire; as infringing the system of dominion, and violating the compact of government. But Dr. Tucker has shewn that even this charter promises no exemption from parliamentary taxes.[3]

In the controversy agitated about the beginning of this century, whether the English laws could bind Ireland, Davenant, who defended against Molyneux[4] the claims of England, considered it as necessary to prove nothing more, than that the present Irish must[x] be deemed a colony.

The necessary connexion of representatives with taxes, seems to have sunk deep into many of those minds, that admit sounds without their meaning.

Our nation is represented in Parliament by an assembly

x. must 76] might 75

---

3. Josiah Tucker, Dean of Gloucester, "Tract III. A Letter from a Merchant in London to His Nephew in America Concerning the Late and Present Disturbances in the Colonies," in *Four Tracts . . . on Political and Commercial Subjects* (1774), p. 97, n.

4. William Molyneux, *The Case of Ireland's Being Bound by Acts of Parliament Stated* (1698). Charles Davenant, *An Essay on the Probable Methods of Making a People Gainers in the Balance of Trade* (1699): "That the greatest part of the present inhabitants of Ireland, chiefly those who claim the land property, are a colony from England, has been here sufficiently made out. . . . And if they are a colony, it would be a strange defect in our constitution, if we wanted any of the powers requisite to pursue the ends of government" (*The Political and Commercial Works of Charles D'Avenant*, ed. Sir Charles Whitworth, 1771, II.250).

as numerous as can well consist with order and dispatch, chosen by persons so differently qualified in different places, that the mode of choice seems to be, for the most part, formed by chance, and settled by custom. Of individuals far the greater part have no vote, and of the voters few have any personal knowledge of him to whom they entrust their liberty and fortune.

Yet this representation has the whole effect expected or desired; that of spreading so wide the care of general interest, and the participation of publick counsels, that the advantage[y] or corruption of particular men can seldom operate with much injury to the publick.

For this reason many populous and opulent towns[5] neither enjoy nor desire particular representatives: they are included in the general scheme of publick administration, and cannot suffer but with the rest of the empire.

It is urged that the Americans have not the same security, and that a British legislature[z] may wanton with their property; yet if it be true, that their wealth is our wealth, and that their ruin will be our ruin, the Parliament has the same interest in attending to them, as to any other part of the nation. The reason why we place any confidence in our representatives is, that they must share in the good or evil which their counsels shall produce. Their share is indeed commonly consequential and remote; but it is not often possible that any immediate advantage can be extended to such numbers as may prevail against it. We are therefore as secure against intentional depravations of government as human wisdom can make us, and upon this security the Americans may venture to repose.

It is said by the Old Member[6] who has written an *Appeal* against the tax, that "as[a] the produce of American labour is

y. advantage 76] interest 75   z. legislature 75 (1, 3)] legislator 75(2,4), 76
a. as 76] om. 75

5. Notably Birmingham and Manchester, which were not enfranchised until the Reform Act of 1832. As SJ says, there was no particular agitation at this time for their representation.
6. In *An Appeal to the Justice and Interests of the People of Great Britain*, in the Present Dispute with America. By an old member of Parliament, 4th ed. (Almon, 1774), pp. 32–33. The work is generally attributed to Arthur Lee; cf. *Life*, iii.68, when SJ met him and Wilkes at Dilly's. But Lee was never a Member of Parliament, and the attribution is sometimes given with a

spent in British manufactures, the balance of trade is greatly against them; whatever you take directly in taxes, is in effect taken from your own commerce. If the minister seizes the money with which the American should pay his debts and come to market, the merchant cannot expect him as a customer, nor can the debts already contracted be paid.— Suppose we obtain from America a million instead of one hundred thousand pounds, it would be supplying our present[7b] exigence by the future ruin of our commerce."

Part of[c] this is true; but the Old Member seems not to perceive, that if his brethren of the legislature know this as well as himself, the Americans are in no danger of oppression, since by men commonly provident they must be so taxed, as that we may not lose one way what we gain another.

The same Old Member has discovered, that the judges formerly thought it illegal to tax Ireland, and declares that no cases can be more alike than those of Ireland and America; yet the judges whom he quotes have mentioned a difference. Ireland, they say, "hath a Parliament of its own." When any colony has an independent parliament, acknowledged by the Parliament of Britain, the cases will differ less. Yet by the 6 Geo. I. chap. 5[8] the acts of the British Parliament bind Ireland.

It is urged that when Wales, Durham, and Chester were divested of their particular privileges or ancient government, and reduced to the state of English counties, they had representatives assigned them.

To those from whom something had been taken, something in return might properly be given. To the Americans their charters are left as they were, nor have they lost any thing[d] except that of which their sedition has deprived them. If

---

b. our present *Appeal*] one personal, *75, 76*   c. Part of *76*] All *75*   d. nor . . . thing *76*] *om. 75*

---

question mark, e.g., in the British Museum catalogue.

7. "One personal," which makes little or no sense, is clearly a misreading of SJ's hand by the original compositor. The *Appeal* also reads "exigences" instead of "exigence"; but the latter may have been SJ's

reading.

8. "An Act for the better securing the dependency of the kingdom of Ireland on the crown of Great Britain." In it, the Parliament of Great Britain is specifically empowered to make laws to which Ireland is subject.

they were to be represented in Parliament, something would be granted, though nothing is withdrawn.

The inhabitants of Chester, Durham, and Wales, were invited to exchange their peculiar institutions for the power of voting, which they wanted before. The Americans have voluntarily resigned the power of voting to live in distant and separate governments, and what they have voluntarily quitted, they have no right to claim.

It must always be remembered that they are represented by the same virtual representation as the greater part of Englishmen; and that if by change of place they have less share in the legislature than is proportionate[e] to their opulence, they by their removal gained that opulence, and had originally and have now their choice of a vote at home, or riches at a distance.

We are told, what appears to the Old Member and to others a position that must drive us into inextricable absurdity, that we have either no right, or the sole right of taxing the colonies. The meaning is, that if we can tax them, they cannot tax themselves; and that if they can tax themselves, we cannot tax them. We answer with very little hesitation, that for the general use of the empire we have the sole right of taxing them. If they have contributed any thing in their own assemblies, what they contributed was not paid, but given; it was not a tax or tribute, but a present. Yet they have the natural and legal power of levying money on themselves for provincial purposes, of providing for their own expence, at their own discretion. Let not this be thought new or strange; it is the state of every parish in the kingdom.

The friends of the Americans are of different opinions. Some think that being unrepresented they ought to tax themselves, and others that they ought to have representatives in the British Parliament.

If they are to tax themselves, what power is to remain in the supreme legislature? That they must settle their own mode of levying their money is supposed. May the British Parliament tell them how much they shall contribute? If the sum may be prescribed, they will return few thanks for the power of raising it; if they are at liberty to grant or to deny, they are no longer subjects.

e. proportionate 76] proportioned 75

If they are to be represented, what number of these western orators are to be admitted. This I suppose the Parliament must settle; yet if men have a natural and unalienable right to be represented, who shall determine the number of their delegates? Let us however suppose them to send twenty-three, half as many as the kingdom of Scotland, what will this representation avail them? To pay taxes will be still a grievance. The love of money will not be lessened, nor the power of getting it increased.

Whither will this necessity of representation drive us? Is every petty settlement to be out of the reach of government, till it has sent a senator to Parliament; or may two of them[f] or a greater number be forced to unite in a single deputation? What at last is the difference[g] between him that is taxed by compulsion without representation, and him that is represented by compulsion in order to be taxed?

For many reigns the House of Commons was in a state of fluctuation: new burgesses were added from time to time, without any reason now to be discovered; but the number has been fixed for more than a century and a half, and the king's power of increasing it has been questioned. It will hardly be thought fit to new model[9] the constitution in favour of the planters, who, as they grow rich, may buy estates in England, and without any innovation, effectually represent their native colonies.

The friends of the Americans indeed ask for them what they do not ask for themselves. This inestimable right of representation they have never solicited. They mean not to exchange solid money for such airy honour. They say, and say willingly, that they cannot conveniently be represented; because their inference is, that they cannot be taxed. They are too remote to share the general government, and therefore claim the privilege of governing themselves.

Of the principles contained in the resolutions of the Congress, however wild, indefinite, and obscure, such has been the influence upon American understanding, that from New-

f. of them 76] *om.* 75   g. difference 76] difference, 75, 76 (*catchword*)

---

9. Possibly a tendentious allusion to Cromwell's "New Model" army of the 1640's. See p. 152 above.

England to South-Carolina there is formed a general combination of all the provinces against their mother-country. The madness of independence[1] has spread from colony to colony, till order is lost and government despised, and all is filled with misrule, uproar, violence, and confusion. To be quiet is disaffection, to be loyal is treason.

The Congress of Philadelphia, an assembly convened by its own authority, has[2] promulgated a declaration, in compliance with which the communication between Britain and the greatest part of North America is now suspended. They ceased to admit the importation of English goods in December 1774, and determine to permit the exportation of their own no longer than to November 1775.[3]

This might seem enough, but they have done more. They have declared, that they shall treat all as enemies who do not concur with them in disaffection and perverseness, and that they will trade with none that shall trade with Britain.

They threaten to stigmatize in their Gazette those who shall consume the products or merchandise of their mother-country, and are now searching suspected houses for prohibited goods.[4]

These hostile declarations they profess themselves ready to maintain by force. They have armed the militia of their provinces and seized the publick stores of ammunition. They are therefore no longer subjects, since they refuse the laws of their sovereign, and in defence of that refusal are making open preparations for war.

Being now in their own opinion free states, they are not only raising armies, but forming alliances, not only hastening to rebel themselves, but seducing their neighbours to rebellion. They have published an address to the inhabitants of Quebec,[5] in which discontent and resistance are openly incited, and

1. Not merely in the sense of administrative separation from Great Britain but also with the connotation of anarchy, of alienation from any system of social obligations.

2. This is the reading of *1775(2,4)* and *1776*. *1775(1)* reads "authority, and as a seditious conventicle punishable by law, has" and *1775(3)* changes "conventicle" to "meeting." On the deletion of the first edition reading, see D. J. Greene, *Studies in Bibliography* (1960).

3. Actually, to "the tenth day of September, 1775" (*Votes and Proceedings*, p. 17, and p. 447 below).

4. *Votes and Proceedings*, pp. 20–21.

5. *Votes and Proceedings*, pp. 66–82.

with very respectful mention of "the sagacity of Frenchmen,"[6] invite them to send deputies to the Congress of Philadelphia, to that seat of virtue and veracity, whence the people of England are told, that to establish Popery, "a religion fraught with sanguinary and impious tenets,"[7] even in Quebec, a country of which the inhabitants are papists, is so contrary to the constitution, that it cannot be lawfully done by the legislature itself, where it is made one of the articles of their association, to deprive the conquered French of their religious establishment; and whence the French of Quebec are, at the same time, flattered into sedition, by professions of expecting "from the liberality of sentiment, distinguishing" their "nation," that "difference of religion will not prejudice them against a hearty amity," because "the transcendent nature of freedom elevates all who unite in the cause above such low-minded infirmities."[8]

Quebec, however, is at a great distance. They have aimed a stroke from which they may hope for greater and more speedy mischief. They have tried to infect the people of England with the contagion of disloyalty. Their credit is happily not such as gives them influence proportionate to their malice. When they talk of their pretended immunities "guarrantied by the plighted faith of government, and the most solemn compacts with English Sovereigns,"[9] we think ourselves at liberty to inquire when the faith was plighted and the compact made; and when we can only find that King James and King Charles the First promised the settlers in Massachuset's Bay, now famous by the appellation of Bostonians, exemption from taxes for seven years, we infer with Mr. Mauduit[1] that by this "solemn compact," they were, after the[2h] expiration of the stipulated term, liable to taxation.

h. the 75] om. 76

---

6. *Votes and Proceedings*, p. 76.

7. *Votes and Proceedings*, p. 28. ("To the People of Great-Britain").

8. *Votes and Proceedings*, p. 79.

9. *Votes and Proceedings*, p. 27. "Guarrantied" and "guarantied" (ed. 3) were accepted spellings of the time. The spelling here was not changed to the modern "guaranteed"

until the 1823 ed. of SJ's *Works*.

1. Israel Mauduit, *A Short View of the History of the Colony of Massachusetts Bay, with Respect to Their Charters and Constitution*, 3rd ed. (1774).

2. It seems more likely that the omission of "the" in *1776* was accidental than deliberate. See n. 2, p. 424 above.

When they apply to our compassion, by telling us, that they are to be carried from their own country to be tried for certain offences, we are not so ready to pity them, as to advise them not to offend. While they are innocent they are safe.

When they tell of laws made expressly for their punishment, we answer, that tumults and sedition were always punishable, and that the new law prescribes only the mode of execution.

When it is said that the whole town of Boston is distressed for a misdemeanour of a few, we wonder at their shamelessness;[i] for we know that the town of Boston, and all the associated provinces, are now in rebellion to defend or justify the criminals.

If frauds in the imposts of Boston are tried by commission without a jury, they are tried here in the same mode; and why should the Bostonians expect from us more tenderness for them than for ourselves?

If they are condemned unheard, it is because there is no need of a trial. The crime is manifest and notorious. All trial is the investigation of something doubtful. An Italian philosopher observes, that no man desires to hear what he has already seen.[3]

If their assemblies have been suddenly dissolved, what was the reason? Their deliberations were indecent, and their intentions seditious. The power of dissolution is granted and reserved for such times of turbulence. Their best friends have been lately soliciting the King to dissolve his Parliament, to do what they so loudly complain of suffering.

That the same vengeance involves the innocent and guilty is an evil to be lamented, but human caution cannot prevent it, nor human power always redress it. To bring misery on those who have not deserved it, is part of the aggregated guilt of rebellion.

That governours have been sometimes given them only that a great man might get ease from importunity, and that they have had judges not always of the deepest learning,

i. shamelessness 75] shamefulness 76

---

3. Not traced. There are proverbs in many languages about the superiority of sight over hearing.

or the purest integrity, we have no great reason to doubt, because such misfortunes happen to ourselves.[4] Whoever is governed will sometimes be governed ill, even when he is most "concerned in his own government."[j]

That improper officers or magistrates are sent, is the crime or folly of those that sent them. When incapacity is discovered, it ought to be removed; if corruption is detected, it ought to be punished. No government could subsist for a day, if single errors could justify defection.

One of their complaints is not such as can claim much commiseration from the softest bosom. They tell us, that we have changed our conduct, and that a tax is now laid by Parliament on those which were never taxed by Parliament before. To this we think it may be easily answered, that the longer they have been spared, the better they can pay.

It is certainly not much their interest to represent innovation as criminal or invidious; for they have introduced into the history of mankind a new mode of disaffection, and have given, I believe, the first example of a proscription published by a colony against the mother-country.

To what is urged of new powers granted to the Courts of Admiralty, or the extension of authority conferred on the judges,[5] it may be answered in a few words, that they have themselves made such regulations necessary; that they are established for the prevention of greater evils; at the same time, it must be observed, that these powers have not been extended since the rebellion in America.

One mode of persuasion their ingenuity has suggested, which it may perhaps be less easy to resist. That we may

j. concerned . . . government *italic (here double quotation marks) 76]* roman 75

---

4. SJ puts it more strongly in "An Introduction to the Political State of Great Britain," p. 150 above: "They [the French Canadians] are said to be supplied from France with better governors than our colonies have the fate to obtain from England. . . . To be a bankrupt at home, or to be so infamously vicious that he cannot be decently protected in his own country, seldom recommends any man to the government of a French colony."

5. In 1768, Vice-Admiralty courts, whose judges had enlarged powers, were ordered to be set up at Halifax, Boston, Philadelphia, and Charleston, to aid in the enforcement of navigation and trade laws.

not look with indifference on the American contest, or imagine that the struggle is for a claim, which, however decided, is of small importance and remote consequence, the Philadelphian Congress has taken care to inform us, that they are resisting the demands of Parliament, as well for our sakes as their own.

Their keenness of perspicacity has enabled them to pursue consequences to a great distance; to see through clouds impervious to the dimness of European sight; and to find, I know not how, that when they are taxed, we shall be enslaved.

That slavery is a miserable state we have been often told, and doubtless many a Briton will tremble to find it so near as in America; but how it will be brought hither, the Congress must inform us. The question might distress a common understanding; but the statesmen of the other hemisphere can easily resolve it. Our ministers, they say, are our enemies, and "if they should carry the point of taxation, may with the same army enslave us. It may be said, we will not pay them; but remember," say the western sages, "the taxes from America, and we may add the men, and particularly the Roman Catholics of this vast continent will then be in the power of your enemies. Nor have you any reason to expect, that after making slaves of us, many of us will refuse to assist in reducing you to the same abject state."[6]

Thus formidable are their menaces;[7] but suspecting that they have not much the sound of probability, the Congress proceeds: "Do not treat this as chimerical. Know that in less than half a century the quit-rents reserved to the crown from the numberless grants of this vast continent will pour large streams of wealth into the royal coffers. If to this be added the power of taxing America at pleasure, the crown will possess more treasure than may be necessary to purchase *the remains* of liberty in your island."

All this is very dreadful; but amidst the terror that shakes my frame, I cannot forbear to wish that some sluice were opened for these floods[k] of treasure. I should gladly see America return half of what England has expended in her

k. floods 75(*3*)] streams 75(*1,2,4*), 76

---

6. *Votes and Proceedings*, pp. 39–40.
7. This is the reading of *1775*(*3*); all other editions read "These are dreadful menaces." On the text here and in the next two paragraphs, see headnote, p. 409 above.

defence; and of the "stream"[1] that will "flow so largely in less than half a century," I hope a small rill at least may be found to quench the thirst of the present generation, which seems to think itself in more danger of wanting money than of losing liberty.

It is difficult to judge with what intention such airy bursts of malevolence are vented: if such writers hope to deceive, let us rather repel them with scorn, than refute them by disputation.[m]

In this last terrifick paragraph are two positions that, if our fears do not overpower our reflection, may enable us to support life a little longer. We are told by these croakers of calamity, not only that our present ministers design to enslave us, but that the same malignity of purpose is to descend through all their successors, and that the wealth to be poured into England by the Pactolus[8] of America will, whenever it comes, be employed to purchase "the remains of liberty."[9]

Of those who now conduct the national affairs we may, without much arrogance, presume to know more than themselves, and of those who shall succeed them, whether minister or king, not to know less.

The other position is, that the Crown, if this laudable opposition should not be successful, "will have the power of taxing America at pleasure." Surely they think rather too meanly of our apprehensions, when they suppose us not to know what they well know themselves, that they are taxed, like all other British subjects, by Parliament; and that the Crown has not by the new imposts, whether right or wrong, obtained any additional power over their possessions.

It were a curious, but an idle speculation to inquire, what effect these dictators of sedition expect from the dispersion of their letter among us. If they believe their own complaints of hardship, and really dread the danger which they describe,

l. stream *italic (here in double quotation marks)* 75(*3*)] roman 75(*1,2,4*), 76   m. *par. om.* 75(*3*)

---

8. The river in which Midas bathed, and which thus became gold-bearing. Franklin's *Observations* (1751) (see n. 6, p. 414 above) has much to say about America's probable future wealth.

9. Quoted from *Votes and Proceedings*, p. 40. Italics (here double quotation marks) in *1776* only.

they will naturally hope to communicate the same[1] perceptions to their fellow-subjects. But probably in America, as in other places, the chiefs are incendiaries, that hope to rob in the tumults of a conflagration, and toss brands among a rabble passively combustible. Those who wrote the Address, though they have shown no great extent or profundity of mind, are yet probably wiser than to believe it: but they have been taught by some master of mischief,[2] how to put in motion the engine of political electricity; to attract by the sounds of liberty and property, to repel by those of Popery and slavery; and to give the great stroke by the name of Boston.

When subordinate communities oppose the decrees of the general legislature with defiance thus audacious, and malignity thus acrimonious, nothing remains but to conquer or to yield; to allow their claim of independence, or to reduce them by force to submission and allegiance.

It might be hoped, that no Englishman could be found, whom the menaces of our own colonists, just rescued from the French, would not move to indignation, like that of the Scythians, who, returning from war, found themselves excluded from their own houses by their slaves.[3]

That corporations constituted by favour, and existing by sufferance, should dare to prohibit commerce with their native country, and threaten individuals by infamy, and societies with at least suspension of amity, for daring to be more obedient to government than themselves, is a degree of insolence, which not only deserves to be punished, but of which the punishment is loudly demanded by the order of life, and the peace of nations.

Yet there have risen up, in the face of the publick, men who, by whatever corruptions or whatever infatuation, have undertaken to defend the Americans, endeavour to shelter

---

1. All editions of *1775* read "their own" for "the same." This was changed in *1776* to avoid the repetition of "their own" at the beginning of the sentence.

2. An amusing glance at Franklin, whose work on electricity SJ mentions (with admiration) in his reviews of scientific works and of Lewis Evans's

Geographical . . . Essays (1756). See p. 201. The "conceit" is continued with the words "engine," "attract," "repel," and "give the great stroke." Franklin was, however, still in England at the time of the meeting of the Continental Congress.

3. See Herodotus, IV.1.

them from resentment, and propose reconciliation[4] without submission.

As political diseases are naturally contagious, let it be supposed for a moment that Cornwal,[n] seized with the Philadelphian frenzy, may resolve to separate itself from the general system of the English constitution, and judge of its own rights in its own parliament. A congress might then meet at Truro, and address the other counties in a style not unlike the language of the American patriots.

"Friends and Fellow-subjects,

"We the delegates of the several towns and parishes of Cornwal,[n] assembled to deliberate upon our own state and that of our constituents, having, after serious debate and calm consideration, settled the scheme of our future conduct, hold it necessary to declare the[o] resolutions which we think ourselves entitled to form by the unalienable[p] rights of reasonable beings, and into which we have been compelled[q] by grievances and oppressions, long endured by us in patient silence, not because we did not feel, or could not remove them, but because we were unwilling to give disturbance to a settled government, and hoped that others would in time find like ourselves their true interest and their original powers, and all co-operate to universal happiness.

"But since having long indulged the pleasing expectation, we find general discontent not likely to increase, or not likely to end in general defection, we resolve to erect alone the standard of liberty.

"*Know then*, that you are no longer to consider Cornwal as an English county, visited by English judges, receiving law from an English Parliament, or included in any general taxation of the kingdom; but as a state distinct, and independent, governed by its own institutions, administered by its

n. Cornwal 75(*1,2*)] Cornwall 75(*3,4*), 76   o. declare the 76] declare in this publick manner, the 75   p. the unalienable 76] the immutable laws of Nature, and the unalienable 75   q. been compelled 76] been at last compelled 75

---

4. Burke's famous speech on "Conciliation" was not delivered until 22 Mar, two weeks after the publication of *Taxation No Tyranny*. But the word had been much used during the debate on the petition from the London merchants in Jan (see n. 9, p. 414 above).

own magistrates, and exempt from any tax or tribute but such as we shall impose upon ourselves.

"We are the acknowledged descendants of the earliest inhabitants of Britain, of men, who, before the time of history, took possession of the island desolate and waste, and therefore open to the first occupants. Of this descent, our language is a sufficient proof, which, not quite a century ago, was different from yours.

"Such are the Cornishmen; but who are you? who but the unauthorised and lawless children of intruders, invaders, and oppressors? who but the transmitters of wrong, the inheritors of robbery? In claiming independence we claim but little. We might require you to depart from a land which you possess by usurpation, and to restore all that you have taken from us.

"Independence is the gift of Nature. No[r] man is born the master of another. Every Cornishman is a freeman, for we have never resigned the rights of humanity; and he only can be thought free, who is not governed but by his own consent.

"You may urge that the present system of government has descended through many ages, and that we have a larger part in the representation of the kingdom, than any other county.

"All this is true, but it is neither cogent nor persuasive. We look to the original of things. Our union with the English counties was either compelled by force, or settled by compact.

"That which was made by violence, may by violence be broken. If we were treated as a conquered people, our rights might be obscured, but could never be extinguished. The sword can give nothing but power, which a sharper sword can take away.

"If our union was by compact, whom could the compact bind but those that concurred in the stipulations? We gave our ancestors no commission to settle the terms of future existence. They might be cowards that were frighted, or blockheads that were cheated; but whatever they were, they could contract only for themselves. What they could establish, we can annul.

"Against our present form of government it shall stand in

r. Nature. No. 76] Nature, bestowed impartially on all her sons; no 75

the place of all argument, that we do not like it. While we are governed as we do not like, where is our liberty? We do not like taxes, we will therefore not be taxed; we do not like your laws, and will not obey them.

"The taxes laid by our representatives are laid, you tell us, by our own consent: but we will no longer consent to be represented. Our number of legislators was originally a burthen, and[s] ought to[t] have been refused: it is now considered as a disproportionate advantage; who then will complain[5] we resign it?[u]

"We shall form[v] a senate of our own, under a president whom the King shall nominate, but whose authority we will limit, by adjusting his salary to his merit. We will not withhold a proper[w] share of contribution to the necessary expence of lawful government, but we will decide for ourselves what share is proper,[x] what expence is necessary, and what government is lawful.

"Till our council is[y] proclaimed independent and unaccountable we will, after the tenth day of September,[6] keep our tin in our own hands: you can be supplied from no other place, and must therefore comply or[z] be poisoned with the copper of your own kitchens.

"If any Cornishman shall refuse his name to this just and laudable association, he shall be tumbled from St. Michael's Mount, or buried alive in a tin-mine; and if any emissary shall be found seducing Cornishmen to their former state, he shall be smeared with tar, and rolled in feathers,[7] and chased with dogs out of our dominions.

"From the Cornish Congress at Truro."

s. burthen, and] burthen imposed upon us by English tyranny, and *75(1-3)*; burden imposed upon us by English tyranny, and *75(4)*; burden, and *76*
t. ought to *76*] ought then to *75*   u. it is now . . . complain we resign it? *76*] if it be now considered as a disproportionate advantage, there can be no reason for complaining that we resign it. *75*   v. shall form *76*] shall therefore form *75*
w. a proper *75(3,4)*, *76*] our *75(1,2)*   x. is proper *75(3,4)*, *76*] we shall pay *75(1,2)*
y. our council is] the authority of our council is acknowledged, and we are *75(1)*; the authority of our counsel is acknowledged, and we are *75(2-4)*; our counsel is *76*   z. comply or *76*] comply at last, or *75*

5. "if" was inserted after "complain" in editions of SJ's *Works* from 1801 onward. A better conjecture might be "that."

6. See n. 3, p. 438 above.
7. Tarring and feathering was frequently threatened (and sometimes

Of this memorial what could be said but that it was written in jest, or written by a madman? Yet I know not whether the warmest admirers of Pennsylvanian eloquence can find any argument in the Addresses of the Congress, that is not with greater strength urged by the Cornishman.

The argument of the irregular troops of controversy, stripped of its colours, and turned out naked to the view, is no more than this. Liberty is the birthright of man, and where obedience is compelled, there is no liberty. The answer is equally simple. Government is necessary to man, and where obedience is not compelled, there is no government.

If the subject refuses to obey, it is the duty of authority to use compulsion. Society cannot subsist but by the power,[a] first of making laws, and then of enforcing them.

To one of the threats hissed out by the Congress, I have put nothing similar into the Cornish proclamation; because it is too wild for folly and too foolish[b] for madness. If we do not withhold our King and his Parliament from taxing them, they will cross the Atlantick and enslave us.

How they will come they have not told us: perhaps they will take wing, and light upon our coasts. When the cranes thus begin to flutter, it is time for pygmies to keep their eyes about them.[8] The Great Orator[9] observes, that they will be very fit, after they have been taxed, to impose chains upon us. If they are so fit as their friend describes them, and so willing as they describe themselves, let us increase our army, and double our militia.

It has been of late a very general practice to talk of slavery

a. the power, 76] some power; 75   b. too wild . . . too foolish 76] too foolish for buffoonery, and too wild 75

carried out) for British sympathizers and customs officials attempting to enforce the trade acts in America. See an engraving illustrating the process, reproduced in L. H. Gipson, *The Coming of the Revolution* (1954), Plate 24. Gipson records many other forms of mob violence.

8. An allusion to the Greek myth of the war between the cranes and the pygmies. As a boy, SJ made a charming rendering into English verse of Addison's Latin poem on the subject (Yale *Works*, VI.21–27).

9. Chatham, who had made several impassioned speeches on the question of America early in 1775.

among those who are setting at defiance every power that keeps the world in order. If the learned author of the *Reflections on Learning* has rightly observed, that no man ever could give law to language,[1] it will be vain to prohibit the use of the word "slavery"; but I could wish it more discreetly uttered; it is driven at one time too hard into our ears by the loud hurricane of Pennsylvanian eloquence, and at another glides too cold into our hearts by the soft conveyance of a female patriot bewailing the miseries of her "friends and fellow-citizens."[2]

Such has been the progress of sedition, that those who a few years ago disputed only our[c] right of laying taxes, now question the validity of every act[d] of legislation.[e] They consider themselves as emancipated from obedience, and as being no longer the subjects of the British Crown. They leave us no choice but of yielding or conquering, of resigning our dominion, or maintaining it by[f] force.

From force many endeavours have been used, either to dissuade, or to deter us. Sometimes the merit of the Americans is exalted, and sometimes their sufferings[g] are aggravated. We are told of their contributions to the last war, a war incited by their outcries, and continued for their protection, a war by which none but themselves were gainers. All that they can boast is, that they did something for themselves, and did not wholly stand inactive, while the sons of Britain were fighting in their cause.

If we cannot admire, we are called to pity them; to pity those that shew no regard to their mother country; have

c. ⟨the⟩ ∧ our ∧ *Proofs*   d. every act] every other act *Proofs*   e. Legislature changed to legislation *Proofs*   f. ⟨our⟩ it by *Proofs*   g. miseries *Proofs*

---

1. Thomas Baker, *Reflections upon Learning* (1699): "Words, like other things, are subject to the common fate of vicissitude and change. . . . No prince ever gave laws to these. Caesar, who gave laws to Rome, could give none to its language" (7th ed., 1734, p. 13).
2. Catharine Sawbridge Macaulay,

An Address to the People of England, Scotland and Ireland, on the Present Important Crisis of Affairs (1775), p. 5: "It can be no secret to you, my friends and fellow-citizens. . . ." She continues to use the phrase *ad nauseam.* Mrs. Macaulay's pamphlet was in part a direct attack on SJ's *The Patriot.*

obeyed no law which they could violate; have imparted no good which they could withold; have entered into associations of fraud to rob their creditors; and into combinations to distress all who depended on their commerce. We are reproached with the cruelty of shutting one port, where every port is shut against us. We are censured as tyrannical for hindering those from fishing, who have condemned our merchants to bankruptcy and our manufacturers to hunger.

Others persuade us to give them more liberty, to take off restraints, and relax authority; and tell us what happy consequences will arise from forbearance: How their affections will be conciliated, and into what diffusions of beneficence their gratitude will luxuriate. They will love their friends, they[h] will reverence their protectors. They will throw themselves into our arms, and lay their property at our feet. They will buy from no other what we can sell them; they will sell to no other what we wish to buy.

That any obligations should overpower their attention to profit, we have known them long enough not to expect. It is not to be expected from a more liberal people. With what kindness they repay benefits, they are now shewing us, who, as soon as we have delivered them from France, are defying and proscribing us.

But if we will permit them to tax themselves, they will give us more than we require. If we proclaim them independent, they will during pleasure pay us a subsidy. The contest is not now for money, but for power. The question is not how much we shall collect, but by what authority the collection shall be made.

Those who find that the Americans cannot be shewn in any form that may raise love or pity, dress them in habiliments of terrour, and try to make us think them formidable. The Bostonians can call into the field ninety thousand[3] men.

h. friends, they 75] friends. They 76

3. John Wilkes, speech to the House of Commons, Feb 1775: "The single province of the Massachuset's Bay has at this moment about 30,000 men, well-trained and disciplined, and can bring near 90,000 into the field" (*Public Advertiser*, 10 Feb 1775). The rest of SJ's paragraph substantially paraphrases Wilkes's speech.

While we conquer all before us, new enemies will rise up behind, and our work will be always to begin. If we take possession of the towns, the colonists will retire into the inland regions, and the gain of victory will be only empty houses and a wide extent of waste and desolation. If we subdue them for the present, they will universally revolt in the next war, and resign us without pity to subjection and destruction.

To all this it may be answered, that between losing America and resigning it, there is no great difference; that it is not very reasonable to jump into the sea, because the ship is leaky. All those evils may befal us, but we need not hasten them.

The Dean of Gloucester has proposed, and seems to propose it seriously, that we should at once release our claims, declare them masters of themselves, and whistle them down the wind.[4] His opinion is, that our gain from them will be the same, and our expence less. What they can have most cheaply from Britain, they will still buy, what they can sell to us at the highest price they will still sell.

It is, however, a little hard, that having so lately fought and conquered for their safety, we should govern them no longer. By letting them loose before the war, how many millions might have been saved. One wild[i] proposal is best answered by another. Let us restore to the French what we have taken from them. We shall see our colonists at our feet, when they have an enemy so near them. Let us give the Indians arms, and teach them discipline, and encourage them now and then to plunder a plantation.[5] Security and leisure are the parents of sedition.

While these different opinions are agitated, it seems to be determined by the legislature, that force shall be tried.[6] Men of the pen have seldom any great skill in conquering kingdoms, but they have strong inclination to give advice. I cannot

---

i. wild 76] ridiculous 75

---

4. Josiah Tucker, "Tract IV. The True Interest of Great-Britain Set Forth in Regard to the Colonies," in *Four Tracts* (1774), pp. 195 ff. SJ misquotes *Othello*, III.3. 266–7: "I'd whistle her off, and let her down the wind / To prey at fortune."

5. The reader should not fail to note that SJ presents this ironically, as a "wild proposal."

6. See n.7 below.

forbear to wish, that this commotion may end without bloodshed, and that the rebels may be subdued by terrour rather than by violence; and therefore recommend such a force as may take away, not only the power, but the hope of resistance, and by conquering without a battle, save many from the sword.

If their obstinacy continues without actual hostilities, it may perhaps be mollified by turning out the soldiers to free quarters, forbidding any personal cruelty or hurt. It has been proposed, that the slaves should be set free, an act which surely the lovers of liberty cannot but commend. If they are furnished with fire arms for defence, and utensils for husbandry, and settled in some simple form of government within the country, they may be more grateful and honest than their masters.

Far be it from any Englishman to thirst for the blood of his fellow-subjects. Those who most deserve our resentment are unhappily at less distance. The Americans, when the Stamp Act was first proposed, undoubtedly disliked it, as every nation dislikes an impost; but they had no thought of resisting it, till they were encouraged and incited by European intelligence from men whom they thought their friends, but who were friends only to themselves.[j]

On the original contrivers of mischief let[k] an insulted nation pour out its vengeance. With whatever design they have inflamed this pernicious contest, they are themselves equally detestable. If they wish success to the colonies, they are traitors to this country; if[l] they wish their defeat, they are traitors at once to America and England. To them and them only must be imputed the interruption of commerce, and the miseries of war, the sorrow of those that shall be ruined, and the blood of those that shall fall.[m]

j. themselves, ⟨and made by their selfishness the enemies of their country.⟩ *Proofs* k. mischief ⟨rather than on those whom they have deluded,⟩ let *Proofs* l. country; if 75] country. If *Proofs*; country, if 76 m. *Proofs have further paragraph:* ⟨Unhappy is that country in which men can hope for advancement by favouring its enemies. The tranquillity of stable government is not always easily preserved against the machinations of single innovators; but what can be the hope of quiet, when factions hostile to the legislature can be openly formed and openly avowed?⟩

Since the Americans have made it necessary to subdue them, may they be subdued with the least injury possible to their persons and their possessions. When they are reduced to obedience, may that obedience be secured by stricter laws and stronger obligations.

Nothing can be more noxious to society than that erroneous clemency, which, when a rebellion is suppressed, exacts no forfeiture and establishes no securities, but leaves the rebels in their former state. Who would not try the experiment which promises advantage without expence? If rebels once obtain a victory, their wishes are accomplished; if they are defeated, they suffer little, perhaps less than their conquerors; however often they play the game, the chance is always in their favour. In the mean time, they are growing rich by victualing the troops that we have sent against them, and perhaps gain more by the residence of the army than they lose by the obstruction of their port.[7]

Their charters being now, I suppose, legally forfeited, may be modelled as shall appear most commodious to the mother-country. Thus the privileges, which are found by experience liable to misuse, will be taken away, and those who now bellow as patriots, bluster as soldiers, and domineer as legislators, will sink into sober merchants and silent planters, peaceably diligent, and securely rich.

But there is one writer, and perhaps many who do not write, to whom the contraction of these pernicious privileges appears very dangerous, and who startle at the thoughts of "England free and America in chains."[8] Children fly from their own shadow, and rhetoricians are frighted by their own voices. "Chains" is undoubtedly a dreadful word; but

---

7. In May 1774 General Gage, the new Governor of Massachusetts, arrived in Boston with four regiments, to enforce the Boston Port Act.

8. Perhaps a reference to the opening of the Continental Congress's Address to the People of Great Britain (in *Votes and Proceedings*): "When a nation, led to greatness by the hand of Liberty, and possessed by all the glory that heroism, munificence, and humanity can bestow, descends to the ungrateful task of forging chains for her Friends and Children, and instead of giving support to Freedom, turns advocate for Slavery and Oppression. . . ." The author may have been John Jay (cf. Edmund Cody Burnett, *The Continental Congress*, 1941, p. 52).

perhaps the masters of civil wisdom may discover some gradations between chains and anarchy. Chains need not be put upon those who will be restrained without them. This contest may end in the softer phrase of English superiority and American obedience.

We are told, that the subjection of Americans may tend to the diminution of our own liberties: an event, which none but very perspicacious politicians are able to foresee. If slavery be thus fatally contagious, how is it that we hear the loudest yelps for liberty among the drivers of negroes?[9]

But let us interrupt a while this dream of conquest, settlement, and supremacy. Let us remember that being to contend, according to one orator, with three millions of Whigs, and according to another, with ninety thousand patriots of Massachusets Bay, we may possibly be checked in our career of reduction. We may be reduced to peace upon equal terms, or driven from the western continent, and forbidden to violate a second time the happy borders of the land of liberty. The time is now perhaps at hand, which Sir Thomas Brown predicted between jest and earnest,

> When America shall no more send out her treasure,
> But spend it at home in American pleasure.[1]

If we are allowed upon our defeat to stipulate conditions, I hope the treaty of Boston will permit us to import into the confederated cantons such products as they do not raise, and such manufactures as they do not make, and cannot buy cheaper from other nations, paying like others[n] the appointed customs; that if an English ship salutes a fort with four guns, it[o] shall be answered at least with two;[p] and

n. ⟨them⟩ ∧ others ∧ *Proofs*   o. ⟨he⟩ ∧ its ∧ *Proofs*   p. two ⟨,⟩ ∧ ;∧ *Proofs*

---

9. Southern slave-owners, notably Patrick Henry and Thomas Jefferson, were among the most voluble propagandists for American "freedom." It may be to this memorable comment that SJ referred four years later in his "Life of Milton": "It has been observed that they who most loudly clamour for liberty do not most liberally grant it" (*Lives*, 1.157, par. 170).

1. "A Prophecy Concerning Several Nations," in *Certain Miscellany Tracts:* "When America shall cease to send forth its treasure / But employ it at home in American pleasure."

them the appointed cuſtoms; that if an Engliſh ſhip ſalutes a fort with four guns, he ſhall be anſwered at leaſt with two, and that if an Engliſhman be inclined to take a plantation, he ſhall only take an oath of allegiance to the reigning powers, and be ſuffered, while he lives inoffenſively, to hold his own opinion of Engliſh rights, unmoleſted in his conſcience by an oath of abjuration.

If by the fortune of war they drive us utterly away, what they will do next can only be conjectured. If a new monarchy is erected, they will want a king. He who firſt takes into his hand the ſcepter of America ſhould have a name of good omen. William has been known both as conqueror and deliverer, and perhaps England, however contemned, might yet ſupply them with another William. Whigs indeed are not willing to be governed, and it is poſſible, that King William may be ſtrongly

A page from the proof sheets of *Taxation No Tyranny*, with corrections in Johnson's hand. By kind permission of Mrs. Donald F. Hyde.

that if an Englishman be inclined to hold^q a plantation, he
shall only take an oath of allegiance to the reigning powers,
and be suffered, while he lives inoffensively, to retain^r his
own opinion of English rights, unmolested in his conscience
by an oath of abjuration.^{2s}

FINIS.^{t}

q. ⟨take⟩ ∧ hold ∧ *Proofs*   r. ⟨hold⟩ ⟨retain⟩ ∧ retain ∧ *Proofs*
s. *Proofs have two further paragraphs:*
If by the fortune of war they drive us utterly away, what they will do next can
only be conjectured. ⟨If a new monarchy is erected, they will want a king. He
who first takes into his hand the scepter of America should have a name of good
omen. William has been known both as conqueror and deliverer, and perhaps
England, however contemned, might yet supply them with another William
[i.e., William Pitt. King William the "deliverer" was William III]. Whigs
indeed are not willing to be governed, and it is possible, that King William may
be strongly inclined to guide their measures; but Whigs have been cheated,
like other mortals, and suffered their leader to become their tyrant, under the
name of their Protector [i.e., Oliver Cromwell's title]. What more they will
condescend to receive from England no man can tell. In their rudiments of
empire they may want a Chancellor [Charles Pratt, Lord Camden, Pitt's
ex-Lord Chancellor].⟩
Their numbers are at present not quite sufficient for the greatness which, in
some form of government or other, is to rival the ancient monarchies; but by
Dr. Franklin's rule of progression, they will in a century and a quarter be more
than equal to the inhabitants of Europe. When the Whigs of America are thus
multiplied, let the princes of the earth tremble in their palaces. If they should
⟨then⟩ continue to double and to double, their own hemisphere will not long
contain them. But let not our boldest oppugners of authority look forward with
delight to this futurity of [whiggism.—*catchword*]
t. FINIS. *75*] THE END. *76*

2. Such as office-holders (including   abjuring allegiance to James II and
SJ's father) were required to swear,   the Pretender.

INDEX

The Chronological Table (pp. xxxix–xliv) has not been indexed.

457